Guide to Global Compensation and Benefits

EXECUTIVE
COMPENSATION
ADVISORY
SERVICES

2000 Guide to Global Compensation and Benefits

Edited by
Calvin Reynolds

Harcourt
Professional Publishing

SAN DIEGO NEW YORK CHICAGO WASHINGTON, D.C. LONDON

Printed in the United States of America

ISBN: 0-15-606855-9

00 01 02 02 EBA 5 4 3

Preface

The field of global compensation and benefits is complex and its scope is huge. No one in the world is an expert on every aspect of the subject, which includes such diverse topics as stock options in Sweden, salary plans in Russia, compensation strategies for Japanese expatriates, acquired rights of employees in Mexico, and pension plans in Botswana. Recognizing the challenges and limitations, *Guide to Global Compensation and Benefits* has brought together more than 20 of the world's leading experts to cover the specific subjects that each knows best.

The primary objectives of this Guide are to:

- Describe and analyze how companies worldwide compensate and provide benefits to locally hired and internationally mobile employees.
- Consider cultural and governmental supports and constraints for different compensation and benefits programs throughout the world.
- Suggest compensation and benefits strategies for global operating executives and human resources managers that support specific corporate goals and objectives.
- Offer counsel on coping with the compensation and benefits challenges associated with mergers and acquisitions.
- Provide advice to international compensation and benefits administrators and consultants about how to design and manage effective programs and where to find additional help.
- Identify the best practices in compensation and benefits throughout the world and guide readers to other sources of useful information.

Today's mantra of "think globally, act locally," while descriptive, is not sufficient to guide the international compensation and benefits professional. It is not enough to design local programs based on local practice. Often the two are in conflict. Compensation and benefits programs must be integrated for overall effectiveness yet differentiated to effectively motivate and meet the specific needs of the various categories of employees.

No universal program satisfies the needs of every company. Corporate objectives differ. In some companies, global consistency and integration predominate. In others, market differentiation and adaptation are considered essential. Staffing patterns vary. In some organizations—many major commercial banks, among others—there are relatively high percentages of global careerists of many nationalities working side-by-side with local employees, who are often limited to support roles. As another example, locally recruited employees are the dominant players in many manufacturing companies, and expatriates fill short-term roles during startup, hold key leadership positions, transfer technology, and return home as soon as they are able to accomplish their objectives. Operating a nickel mine in Indonesia has significantly different human resources challenges than managing a bank branch in London. Given these variations, the belief that there are a limited number of compensation and benefits "silver bullets" to satisfy every company's needs is optimistic at best, frequently self-defeating, and certainly naïve. But the search is important and will continue.

More realistically, compensation and benefits professionals should seek to maximize corporate competitiveness by designing programs that motivate local employees in each country and internationally mobile employees of all nationalities. Exporting what works well in the headquarters country without adaptation is rarely the best answer, if for no other reason than that very few people appreciate having someone else's solution imposed on their challenge. Yet, there are situations in which corporate programs do motivate employees worldwide and are appropriate. The trick is to find the most effective balance between corporate objectives on the one hand and the compensation and benefits programs that are most effective to motivate different groups of employees in each country to realize those objectives on the other. This clearly requires input from around the world.

The primary goal of *Guide to Global Compensation and Benefits* is to provide practitioners with the tools needed to design and manage global compensation and benefits programs and to provide advice on how to use those tools within the context of sound corporate strategies. The Guide is divided into five sections and three appendixes. Section 1, an overview of the field of global compensation and benefits, introduces the reader to the evolving remuneration challenges faced by corporate practitioners as their companies grow from purely domestic organizations to global corporations.

Section 2 examines expatriate compensation strategies and practices. Because of the inherent complexity of the subject and the small numbers of employees involved (less than 2% of the overseas workforces of North

American and European corporations), there has been a tradition of surveying the practices of other companies and adopting a majority position with the hope that this represents best practice. Indeed, this section includes the results of several surveys and suggests other similar sources of information. The intent of this section, however, is to describe the many options that have been developed for compensating expatriates and to guide readers to the approach or combination that best meets their objectives, demographics, dynamics, and needs. It includes extensive "how to" material and a thorough discussion of expatriate taxation.

Section 3 covers government social security programs and corporate employee benefit programs worldwide. A well-known consultant and a leading corporate benefits executive describe significant differences in government programs around the world and recommend approaches to satisfy the complex legal and financial reporting requirements of both headquarters and foreign governments and other agencies. They describe how to design corporate benefits programs to meet the varying requirements of different countries.

Section 4 divides the world into nine major regions and countries. Specialists summarize compensation and benefits practices within each area, highlight major differences in practices within the area and compared with other regions, and provide guidance on additional sources of information and assistance.

Section 5 analyzes specific compensation challenges for motivating professionals in sales and research and development as their corporations globalize. A leading consultant assesses the impact of technology on the field. Finally, based largely on the foundation of the earlier chapters, a speculation about where the field is headed is provided.

The appendixes include lists of contributors and specialists, a bibliography, and other useful information for global compensation practitioners and consultants.

The editor, contributors, and publisher wish you the best of good fortune as you work through the complexities of the many subjects covered and become experts in this rapidly evolving field. We would particularly welcome your comments and recommendations for improving future editions of *Guide to Global Compensation and Benefits*. Send your comments by fax to 619-699-6593 or by e-mail to propub@harcourt.com; please type "Global Compensation Editor" in the subject box.

Contents

CD-ROM Contents

SECTION 5. OTHER GLOBAL STRATEGY ISSUES

SECTION 6. CHECKLISTS AND RESOURCES

About the Electronic Workpapers

The CD-ROM provided with 2000 *Guide to Global Compensation and Benefits* contains checklists, questionnaires, sample documents, and other practice aids found throughout the book.

Subject to the conditions in the license agreement and the limited warranty, which is displayed on screen when the CD-ROM is installed and is reproduced at the end of the book, you may duplicate the files on this CD-ROM, modify them as necessary, and create your own customized versions. Installing the CD-ROM contents and/or using the CD-ROM in any way indicates that you accept the terms of the license agreement.

The CD-ROM is intended to be used in conjunction with your word processing software. There are versions of each document in WordPerfect® 6.0 and Microsoft Word® 6.0, both for Windows™. If you do not own either of these programs, your word processing package may be able to convert the documents into a usable format. Check your owner's manual for information on the conversion of documents.

Installing the Templates

To install the files on the CD-ROM using Windows 95 or above, select the Control Panel from the Start menu. Then choose Add/Remove Programs and select Install. If you are using Windows 3.1, choose File, Run from the Windows Program Manager and type D:/INSTALL in the command line or type D:/INSTALL at the DOS prompt. You will be asked a series of questions. Read each question carefully and answer as indicated.

First, the installation program will ask you to specify which drive you want to install to. You will then be instructed to specify the complete path where you would like the files installed. The installation program will suggest a directory for you, but you can name the directory anything you like. If the directory does not exist, the program will create it for you.

You can choose to install the entire system (both Word and WordPerfect files) or just the files for one application. The program will automatically install the files in Word and/or WordPerfect subdirectories.

Opening the Files

Open your word processing program. If you are using Microsoft Word or WordPerfect 6.0, choose Open from the File menu. Select the subdirectory that contains the loaded files to list the names of the files. Highlight the name of the file you want to open and click OK or press ENTER. You can also open a document in the Windows Explorer (in Windows 95 or above) or from the File Manager (in Windows 3.1) by highlighting the name of the file you want to use and double-clicking your left mouse button.

Refer to the CD-ROM Contents section of the book to find the file name of the document you want to use. The CD-ROM Contents is also available on your CD-ROM in a file called "Contents." You can open this file and view it on your screen or print a hard copy to use for reference.

Word Processing Tips

Wherever possible, the text of the documents has been formatted as tables so that you can modify the text without altering the format of the documents. To maneuver within a table, press TAB to move to the next cell, and SHIFT + TAB to move backward one cell. If you want to move to a tab stop within a cell, press CTRL + TAB. For additional tips on working within tables, consult your word processor's manual. It might be helpful to turn on the invisible table lines in Microsoft Word while modifying the document by selecting Gridlines from the Table menu. In WordPerfect, select Reveal Codes from the View menu to reveal all formatting codes at the bottom of the screen; this will help you to determine the shape of the table.

Microsoft Word and WordPerfect are equipped with search capabilities to help you locate specific words or phrases within a document. The Find option listed under the Edit menu performs a search in both Microsoft Word and in WordPerfect 6.0.

Important: When you are finished using a file you will be asked to save it. If you have modified the file, you may want to save the modified file under a different name rather than the name of the original file. (Your word processing program will prompt you for a file name.) This will enable you to reuse the original file without your modifications. If you want to replace the original file with your modified file, save but do not change the name of the file.

Print Troubleshooting

If you are having difficulty printing your document, the following suggestions may correct the problem:

Microsoft Word

- Select Print from the Microsoft Word File menu. Then choose the Printer function.
- Ensure that the correct printer is selected.
- From this window, choose Options.
- In the media box, make sure that the paper size is correct and that the proper paper tray is selected.
- Check your network connections if applicable.
- If you still have trouble printing successfully, it may be because your printer does not recognize the font Times New Roman. At this point, you should change the font of the document to your default font by selecting the document (CTRL + A) and then choosing Font from the Format menu and highlighting the name of the font you normally use. Changing the font of the document may require additional adjustments to the document format, such as margins, tab stops, and table cell height and width. Select Page Layout from the View menu to view the appearance of the pages before you try to print again.

WordPerfect

- Select Print from the WordPerfect 6.0 File menu. Then choose Select.
- Make sure the correct printer is selected.
- From this menu, press Setup.
- Ensure the correct paper size and paper source are selected.
- You may be having difficulty because your printer does not recognize the selected font. You can correct this problem by changing the base font of the document to your default font. From the Edit menu choose Select All (or press CTRL+A). The entire text of the document should be highlighted. Then choose Font from the Layout menu

and highlight the font you normally use. Changing the font of the document may require additional adjustments to the document format, such as margins, tab stops, and table cell height and width. Select Two Page from the View menu to view the appearance of the pages before you try to print again.

About the Editor

Calvin Reynolds is a senior counselor of Organization Resources Counselors, Inc. (ORC) and an advisor to global organizations on international human resources strategies and issues. He is on the faculty of the American Compensation Association and teaches courses in Global Total Remuneration and Expatriate Compensation. He is on the Editorial Review Board and is a contributing author of AlignMark *Compensation Guide*.

Reynolds was a Senior Vice President of ORC responsible for its international consulting, data services, publications, and meeting groups. He has managed and participated in consulting projects for the United Nations, the governments of Canada, France, and Australia, and global organizations in Europe, the Americas, Africa, the Middle East, and several countries on the Pacific Rim. He was on the Board and Chairman of the International Council of the American Compensation Association. He was an adjunct associate professor of international management at New York University's Graduate School of Business Administration, a senior fellow at Wharton, and has lectured at various other universities. He spent several years as an expatriate executive for a Fortune 100 multinational where his latest role was as Director of European Operating Services in Geneva, Switzerland.

Reynolds has written dozens of articles on international human resources and compensation that have been published in several publications including *Journal of World Business, Human Resource Planning, ACA Journal, California Management Review, Business Horizons,* and *Benefits and Compensation International.* He wrote chapters on international compensation for McGraw Hill's *Handbook of Human Resources Administration* (Second Edition) and *The Executive Handbook of Compensation* published by The Free Press (forthcoming). He is the author of two booklets on international compensation for the American Compensation Association's Building Block Series. He was the creator and first publisher of *Innovations in International Compensation*, now ORC's *Innovations in International Human Resources.*

For biographies of contributors, see Appendix A.

Acknowledgments

2000 *Guide to Global Compensation and Benefits* could not have been compiled without the help and support of many experts who have given unselfishly of their time and expertise. In addition to the authors, I want to express my appreciation to those who reviewed and recommended improvements to various chapters, particularly Geoffrey Latta, Executive Vice President and Roger Herod, Vice President, both of Organization Resources Counselors (ORC), and Professor Randall Schuler of the Rutgers School of Management and Labor Relations. Sam Bernstein of Hewitt Associates, Carol Kaplan of Donnelly Corporation, and John de Leon of ORC, all authors, reviewed chapters other than those they wrote. Bernadette Steele, Vice President and her staff at ORC provided invaluable editorial assistance and advice. And Lori Woehrle, Senior Acquisitions Editor at Harcourt Professional Publishing kept me on track when the challenges seemed somewhat overwhelming.

The authors of Chapter 20, "Australia and New Zealand" wish to acknowledge the valuable assistance and research provided by their colleagues Leslie Breackell, Mark Iob, and Keith McCoy.

Ms. Morgan, the author of Chapter 10, "Immigration," acknowledges the editing assistance of Jennifer Solon, a law clerk currently studying at the Kent College of Law in Chicago, Illinois, who works with Ms. Morgan at Baker & McKenzie's offices in Chicago.

Guide to Global Compensation and Benefits

SECTION ONE

INTRODUCTION TO GLOBAL COMPENSATION AND BENEFITS

CHAPTER 1

COMPENSATION AND BENEFITS IN A GLOBAL CONTEXT

CALVIN REYNOLDS

As we approach the new millennium, the field of international human resources is in a period of rapid transformation. Thirty years ago, international personnel professionals in U.S.-based multinationals devoted more than 80% of their time to the management of expatriate assignments—nearly all of it (more than 70%) spent on expatriate compensation.[1] In the early '90s, expatriate compensation still consumed more than half of the time of corporate international human resources (HR) staffs,[2] and it currently remains a primary international HR activity. But the allocation of corporate staff time and emphasis is changing significantly. Expatriate compensation now competes with strategic issues such as the integration of compensation, global staffing, and business strategies and with local-national remuneration, selection, management development, employee benefits, and a wide variety of other important international HR challenges. As a result of intense pressures on head count, global corporations are limiting staff in functions not considered strategic, and many primarily administrative activities formerly handled by corporate international HR staffs are now outsourced. HR executives are fighting for seats at the management table with varying degrees of success.

The primary objective of this chapter is to examine several of the critical forces affecting international HR today, with particular emphasis on global compensation and benefits. It will serve as an overview and introduction to global remuneration practices discussed in greater detail in the chapters that follow.

In light of the increasing interest in and emphasis on local-national compensation and benefits strategies and practices, four of the five sections in this guide cover these subjects and related topics. But expatriate compensation does not get short shrift: The eight chapters of Section 2 focus on expatriate issues.

Before summarizing and highlighting the key points covered in later chapters, it is important to put a few major concepts in context and define several frequently used words.

- *Local nationals* are employees recruited and employed in local operating companies (usually in *foreign* or *nonheadquarters* countries in the context of this guide). Typically, local nationals receive compensation and benefits packages consistent with practices specific to their country. But increasingly in global companies, some elements of pay are being standardized on a worldwide basis. It is not unusual for some employees who are not nationals of a country to be compensated as local nationals, particularly if they are recruited there or their assignments in that country are considered permanent or very long term.
- *Expatriates* are employees who are transferred on temporary assignments (usually for two to five years) from headquarters or from their home country to another country. Many professionals eschew the term *expatriate* as demeaning or old-fashioned and substitute terms such as *foreign service employee* (FSE), *international assignee* (IA), and *global staff* (GS). Professor Nancy Adler has contributed *transpatriate* (TP perhaps) and *galactipat* to the lexicon. Our use of *expatriate* interchangeably with other terms in this guide does not reflect a lack of sensitivity on the issue but recognizes that *expatriate* is still the most common term in use, and most people understand what the word means even if they prefer other terminology. Right or wrong, we have chosen clarity over current jargon correctness.
- *Foreign* is also an emotionally charged word, but probably less so than others such as *overseas* or *abroad,* used to refer to assignments or activities in countries other than one's own.

In later chapters, other vocabulary issues will be addressed. All of the authors who have contributed to this guide are seasoned international professionals who have made a substantial effort to be sensitive to the connotation of the terms they have used. But some readers will undoubtedly react negatively to certain words and phrases. I readily admit that I have been criticized by some for occasionally employing ethnocentric expressions despite the fact that I have spent my entire career in international business, have lived and worked in other countries for a third of my adult life, and have always prided myself on being able to work effectively in other cultures. While English is the first language of a majority of the contributors, approximately half learned the language in the United States and the remainder learned it in other countries. Therefore, unanimity and even consensus on vocabulary is difficult to attain. Indeed, several of the contributing authors from Australia, Canada, Great Britain, and other predominantly English-speaking countries are understandably cringing as they read the Americanization of their prose in this guide. On behalf of us all, I apologize to any readers (or contributors) who may be offended by any of our expressions.

Overview of Section 1: Introduction to Global Compensation and Benefits

In Chapter 2, Alan Ritchie, vice president of compensation, employee benefits, and health services, and Steven Seltz, international compensation and benefits vice president, of Lucent Technologies describe the challenges they face in globalizing compensation and benefits programs in a huge and rapidly expanding company that has only recently entered the international arena. Both Alan and Steven joined Lucent after it was spun off by AT&T in 1996.

Eric Marquardt of Towers Perrin and Ron Reynolds of Compensation Resource Group point out in Chapter 3 that "75% of all cross-border mergers are disappointments or outright failures" and that cultural differences are often the primary problem. They describe the strategic and operational roles that compensation and benefits practitioners can and should play to improve the chances of success.

Overview of Section 2: Expatriate Strategies and Practices

In Chapter 4, I suggest some basic approaches to expatriate compensation appropriate for companies just entering the international arena and for compensation and benefits practitioners new to the field. Chapter 5 provides additional tools for more experienced practitioners as their companies mature internationally and become organizationally more complex. Both chapters emphasize and describe how to design expatriate practices that support corporate business and global staffing strategies.

In Chapter 6, John de Leon of Organization Resources Counselors, Inc. (ORC), reports on the increasing number of employees transferred from other countries to the headquarters country, with an emphasis on assignments to the United States. He comments on the various ways global companies compensate and provide benefits to these employees and on the link between assignment rationale and remuneration approach.

In Chapter 7, Julian Pollard, who formerly coordinated research on expatriate policies and practices for ORC, reports on the expatriate practices of global companies worldwide.

Expatriate taxation is the subject of Chapter 8, prepared by Sam Russo and Dan Orchant, both partners of KPMG Peat Marwick. They outline several expatriate tax strategies and caution practitioners about the many pitfalls of administering expatriate taxes.

Susan Schenkel-Savitt, partner, and Emily Giffin, associate, with Winston and Strawn in New York describe in Chapter 9 the challenges that U.S. employment law presents to U.S. companies with foreign operations and to foreign companies with operations in the United States. They point out that U.S.-based companies must comply not only with the employment laws of every country in which they have operations (and which possess very little consistency worldwide) but also with many U.S. employment laws as well.

In Chapter 10, Betsy Stelle Morgan of Baker and McKenzie in Chicago summarizes some of the immigration requirements of several countries. She provides some useful hints for practitioners about how to avoid passport, visa, work permit, and similar problems when employees are assigned or traveling to foreign countries.

Jonathan Zamet, assistant vice president of Equitable Life, presents a corporate expatriate administrator's perspective on managing expatriate compensation and benefits in Chapter 11.

Overview of Section 3: Local-National Compensation and Benefits

John Maxwell, formerly managing director of the Global Remuneration Organization (GRO) and now Managing Director of Sidstar, summarizes in Chapter 12 some of the major theories of motivation that have been developed. He also describes the importance of motivation theory in designing compensation and benefits programs around the world.

Neil Coleman, vice president of global compensation with ORC, covers local-national compensation practices in depth in Chapter 13. He describes some of the major differences in pay levels and remuneration architecture around the world and suggests approaches for managing compensation and benefits within this complex environment.

Sam Bernstein of Hewitt Associates and Carol Kaplan of Donnelly Corporation prepared the two very comprehensive Chapters 14 and 15 on global benefits. Chapter 14 includes an overview of corporate global benefit strategies, a description of government social security programs around the world, and suggestions to companies for supplementing government retirement plans to provide their employees with appropriate pensions. Chapter 15 covers all other forms of benefits, including medical care, death and disability, and several types of insurance. The authors discuss government programs, typical local practice, and suitable corporate supplements to benefit programs in many countries worldwide. They provide an overview of time off with pay, including holidays, vacations, sabbatical leaves, and maternity. They also discuss a host of other benefits-related issues such as multinational insurance pooling and acquired rights and suggest sound procedures for conducting due diligence reviews.

Overview of Section 4: Regional/Country Characteristics of Local Remuneration Practices

James Delaney, principal, and Ruthanne Huising, consultant, with William M. Mercer Limited in Toronto describe in Chapter 16 some of the important similarities and differences in compensation and benefits practices between Canada and its giant neighbor to the south. They focus on the influence of Canada's government policies and strong labor unions on compensation and benefits practices.

In Chapter 17, John de Leon, director of consulting services for ORC, and Margaret Coolbaugh, an independent consultant, discuss compensation and benefits practices in several Latin American countries and how they have been influenced by culture and economics. They illustrate how the importance of family has led to the proliferation of family-related perquisites and how hyperinflation has affected retirement systems and termination policies.

Pete Burgess, general editor of *European Management Guides* for Incomes Data Services in London, covers Western Europe in Chapter 18. He describes the traditional European emphasis on social policy and its reflection in compensation and benefits practices. He comments on how these practices are evolving under the influence of globalization, the strengthening of the European Union, and the creation of the European Monetary Union.

In Chapter 19, Giles Tulk, senior consultant, and David Atkins of Monks Partnership in Great Britain cover in depth senior executive remuneration in major British companies. They illustrate the similarities and differences in approach in Britain compared with Continental Europe and with North America.

Compensation and benefits practices in Australia and New Zealand are described in Chapter 20 by three senior consultants of the Hay Group. Graham O'Neill and Kim Neuhold are in the Melbourne office, and Andrew Mackmurdie is in Auckland. They discuss how high marginal tax rates in both countries have affected compensation and benefits practices and have led to assessing total employment cost (TEC).

Heather Bowker, president of Bowker Consulting in Mill Valley, California, covers Asia (except for China and Japan) in Chapter 21. She describes the heterogeneity of the region and the wide variety of compensation and benefits practices in effect. She comments on the impact of the Asian economic crisis, which began in Thailand in 1997, on remuneration practices.

In Chapter 22, Willis Shen of Watson Wyatt, Shanghai, reports on the evolution in the People's Republic of China from the "iron rice bowl," with its guaranteed lifetime employment and cradle-to-grave benefits, to the current "socialist market economy." He evaluates the impact of this evolution on Chinese human resources and compensation and benefits practices.

Toshio Nirei, president, and Junko Kudo, consultant, with Yokogawa ORC in Tokyo report in Chapter 23 on the upheaval in traditional Japanese human resources practices brought on by the economic downturn, globalization, and shifting workforce demographics. They describe specific changes in compensation and benefits policies as well as recruiting and staffing practices.

In Chapter 24, Sam Bernstein of Hewitt Associates describes human resources practices in the emerging economies of Africa, the Middle East, and Eastern/Central Europe. He comments on the wide variety of compensation and benefits practices found in these countries, discusses how they have evolved, and provides guidance to practitioners who are faced with analyzing and possibly influencing them.

Overview of Section 5: Other Global Strategy Issues

In Chapter 25, Bill O'Connell, Sibson and Company's national practice leader, sales and marketing effectiveness, recommends compensation approaches to optimize the effectiveness of global marketing programs and teams. Jerry Bratkovich, chief operating officer of The Columbus Group, and Ronald Schaeffer of ORC provide comparable advice on research and development in Chapter 26.

As we move further into the information age, technology has become critical to the success of virtually all corporate activities, not the least of which are compensation and benefits. In Chapter 27, Gary Parker, Aon Consulting's international practice leader, assesses the current state of global compensation and benefits technology and provides a road map for the future.

Finally, in Chapter 28, I build on the foundation of the earlier chapters and project and speculate about how the field of global compensation and benefits will evolve over the next several years—and what can be done to influence that evolution.

The Evolution of Global Compensation and Benefits

Not long ago, a significant majority of companies that did business internationally prided themselves on being multinational corporations. Each foreign subsidiary competed in its local market with local companies and with other multinationals. While most companies staffed several key management positions with expatriates, it was the responsibility of those expatriates and other local management to staff their operations as they saw fit, consistent with agreed-to growth and profit targets. Compensation and benefits were clearly the responsibility of local management. In most countries, compensation levels were much lower than in the United States, and law generally regulated benefits programs. Overall, compensation budgets often required corporate approval, as did salary increases for senior local executives and the introduction of major new benefits plans, but rarely did anyone from headquarters try to second-guess local decision makers about the structure or details of local-national compensation and benefits plans. Indeed, few at headquarters had either the experience or the knowledge to do so.

Local-National Compensation and Globalization

As corporations have globalized, most notably during the last decade, the focus of global compensation and benefits practitioners has shifted. Management salaries, particularly in the industrialized world, are converging.

Except for the very highest executive levels, salaries in several countries—Germany, Japan, and Switzerland, for example—are now higher than in the United States. And the gap in many others, Argentina for example, is narrowing. In most industries, local nationals constitute more than 98% of the workforce in the foreign operations of North American and Western European multinationals. Local-national compensation and benefits costs, to a much greater extent than those of expatriates, affect profitability. Major cost components attract management attention.

In addition to the issue of costs, corporations, particularly those with headquarters in the United States, have concentrated their attention on motivating employees worldwide to support company objectives and improve corporate competitiveness. Global vision statements abound. Many have exported compensation programs that have proved to be effective in motivating domestic employees to their overseas operations with the expectation (some say "hope") that employees worldwide will be equally motivated.

In a recent survey of the global compensation practices of leading U.S., Western European, and Latin American corporations,[3] ORC found that more than 80% of the companies (regardless of headquarters location) set the base salaries of key local executives in line with local competitive conditions. In contrast, more than 60% of U.S.-based companies include key local executives in their headquarters' (as opposed to local or regional) incentive plans, compared with only one-third of the non-U.S. companies. Typically, the U.S. incentive plans represent a higher percentage of total compensation than do those of other corporations with a stock-based long-term component rather than cash, which is more common in non-U.S. companies.

Broad-based global stock option programs are becoming progressively more popular with U.S.-based companies. Since PepsiCo introduced Share Power, which granted stock options to virtually all of its 250,000 employees worldwide, in 1989, others, including Bristol-Myers Squibb, DuPont, and Merck, have introduced similar programs. Some of these programs have made employees very wealthy. For example, in the decade following Share Power's introduction, PepsiCo employees in the original program have been enriched by $2.5 billion; their options, on average, are now worth 1.5 times annual compensation. When Lucent was spun off from AT&T in 1996, it granted options for 100 shares to all 130,000 employees. In the following three years, the stock split twice, and the original grant increased in market value to $24,000 as of July 1999 for each employee. In some countries, employees gained more money in three years through stock price appreciation than they would earn over several years in salary. The challenge now is to retain a workforce that has become comparatively wealthy overnight.

Because U.S. tax laws favor stock options to a greater extent than the tax laws of other countries do, other companies have questioned the wisdom of this approach and concluded that such programs are unlikely to be as effective overseas as they are in the United States. Some companies that question the effectiveness of broad-based global stock option programs have still recognized the motivational value of employee stock ownership and have made stock grants or introduced various subsidy programs to facilitate stock purchases by their overseas employees. Others have questioned whether stock ownership programs have sufficient line of sight for employees in nonheadquarters countries to be motivational; instead, they have introduced compensation programs that focus greater employee attention on local or regional objectives.

The Importance of National and Corporate Cultures

Since the pioneering research of Geert Hofstede for IBM in the 1960s,[4] many have recognized the importance of culture and its impact on human resources and compensation programs. North American compensation practices encourage individualism and high performance; continental European programs emphasize social responsibility; the traditional Japanese approach considers age and company service as primary determinants of compensation. Fons Trompenaars extended Hofstede's research and added many valuable insights about culture and its impact on business worldwide.[5]

Some experts take issue with the importance of national cultures in establishing compensation programs around the world. George Milkovich and Matt Bloom,[6] for example, argue that national culture is relatively unimportant. They support their argument by pointing out that, with the pressures of globalization, such practices as lifetime employment in Japan and industry-wide bargaining in Germany are breaking down. They suggest that basing compensation on national culture leads to "blatant stereotyping." They recommend instead "strategic flexibility," with which companies can achieve competitive advantage by "customizing multiple compensation and reward systems, [thus offering] managers the opportunity to tailor the total compensation system to fit the context in which they compete within a framework of corporate principles."

It is clear that there are strong opinions on both sides of this argument. Milkovich and Bloom have serious reservations about the theses of Hofstede and Trompenaars. Charles Hampden-Turner, who coauthored *The Seven Cultures of Capitalism* with Fons Trompenaars, has taken an equally strong position on the other side. In a *Harvard Business Review* article,[7] he observed, "The distinguishing characteristic of the American cultural paradigm is 'universalism'—the conviction that principles of general validity can be discovered that apply to all people everywhere. . . . [There is] an ingrained inability on the part of American managers to learn from other cultures."

My own opinion is that the soundest approach lies somewhere between these two extremes. There is little doubt that culture does influence national practices. Remuneration systems are different around the world, and many of these differences result from cultural mind-sets and historical influences. This is a far cry, however, from stating that people around the world are locked into specific sets of practices or will refuse to consider alternatives because of cultural imperatives. Several Japanese companies, Sony for example, have introduced such "radical foreign practices" as employee stock options. Similarly, many U.S.-based companies have adopted equally radical foreign approaches such as profit sharing and team-based pay, although they often believed (erroneously) that these were purely homegrown innovations. No one country has a monopoly on best practices, and those who believe they do are putting themselves at a serious competitive disadvantage.

Inherent in these observations is the recognition that people from virtually all cultures are convinced that their way is best or at least as good as proposed alternatives. They will continue in those beliefs until convinced that some other way is better or that there are valid reasons for change.

Introducing New Programs

Introducing a policy or practice in another country simply because "it works well at home" is unlikely to be successful. Many who have worked abroad with other nationalities have become familiar with a reaction appropriately identified as "malicious compliance," the tendency of many nationals in foreign subsidiaries to say "Yes, if you say so" to every edict from headquarters—and then make the process fail. Local employees may recognize and even respect the fact that headquarters has the authority to impose its will. But unless they are convinced that a new approach makes sense within their environment, they are likely to drag their feet or undermine implementation—or both. There is a big difference between the Japanese management at Sony concluding that stock options make sense for Sony, even if they are uncommon among its Japanese competitors, and a staff representative from a U.S. headquarters telling the managers in a Japanese subsidiary that performance-based pay is the only way to go. The essential issue here is the importance of local buy-in. Many headquarters representatives with excellent ideas have failed to implement them because they have not understood the importance of listening to and appreciating local culture and viewpoints as well as supporting the headquarters' party line. On the other hand, others fail because they believe that practices are so different in other countries that new practices are impossible to introduce. Both approaches are ineffective. Time spent ensuring local understanding and commitment is well worth it.

It is easy (and often very expensive) for corporate representatives who have been stymied in the past to be thrilled by the positive reaction of employees in overseas subsidiaries to some new compensation program introduced by headquarters. Very often, these new programs mean additional compensation for local employees and, not incidentally, higher cost for the company. It is hardly surprising that most people, no matter what their cultural heritage, welcome additional compensation. If, for example, base compensation in a local market is competitive with the total compensation of local employees in other companies, new programs that provide additional income with little or no downside risk are likely to engender enthusiasm. But at what cost?

There is no guarantee that additional compensation will ensure additional output. Some have found that additional pay in some countries has resulted in employees' working less. As soon as employees have earned enough to satisfy their needs, time spent with family or in other noncompany activities is perceived as more valuable than additional cash. The real challenge is to introduce compensation programs that improve motivation, increase productivity, and limit costs, which may or may not be those that have been developed at headquarters.

As you examine local remuneration programs around the world, it will quickly become apparent that there are major differences from country to country in salary levels, compensation architecture, and benefit programs. One of the major differences between practices in North America and those elsewhere is the prevalence of perquisites. Although perquisites are certainly not unheard of in North America, they are far less common than in other regions of the world. Many cite as an example the case of company automobiles in Great Britain and several of its former colonies. Despite the fact that company cars are no longer as tax-effective a way of delivering compensation in Great Britain as they were in the past, company cars are still very common at much lower levels of management in Britain than they are elsewhere.

Once introduced, perquisites are very difficult to eliminate. In parts of Asia, housing, servants, transportation (including chauffeurs), and other perquisites are frequently provided. The list of perquisites offered in much of Latin America, many of them related to family participation in company activities, can be mind-boggling. In countries where income tax rates are very high, Scandinavia for example, salary increases are often less valued than more tax-effective perquisites. Perquisites are often common in countries in which salary and wage levels are notoriously low. In assessing compensation levels around the world, be careful to include perquisites as well as cash and other forms of remuneration. Above all, avoid providing additional cash as a substitute while continuing a perquisite the cash is designed to replace. Several later chapters will cover these issues in greater depth.

Integration and Differentiation

As markets and companies globalize, there is frequently an attitude that all or at least all "important" policies and practices should be globalized as well. This is, of course, inconsistent with the popular mantra of think globally, act locally, but nonetheless many have a mind-set of "if it's not globalized, it's not strategic." And for many, "globalized" means standardized on headquarters practices.

Before standardizing any compensation and benefits program around the world, it is always useful to ask "why?" For example, many companies provide supplemental benefits coverage that duplicates existing local plans; this topic is covered in greater depth in Section 3. Others have introduced point-factor evaluation systems for all levels of employees in all of their overseas subsidiaries. More often than not, these programs duplicate evaluation systems already in place and are systematically ignored by local management. They may be useful for international comparisons of senior employees at levels likely to be transferred to other countries, but beyond that, they simply add to costs. This is particularly true if headquarters insists on periodic reports on the status of the new programs. Does this mean that point-factor systems have no place in the international compensation practitioner's toolkit? Of course not. But it does suggest that introducing new programs without being sure that the old ones they replace are eliminated and that they really add value is counterproductive. There may very well be significant competitive advantages for introducing new systems, but far too many excessively costly programs have been installed overseas with no more justification than global consistency.

Donald Hastings, the former CEO of Lincoln Electric, recently described a striking example of the dangers of exporting a successful domestic compensation program to other countries.[8] The lack of acceptance overseas of Lincoln's U.S. plan was a major factor in nearly destroying the financial viability of the company. After hiring several internationally experienced and competent executives, Lincoln wisely backed off its approach and avoided disaster. But it also found that its U.S. compensation approaches could work in some countries if introduced progressively after establishing local buy-in.

Many years ago, Paul Lawrence and Jay Lorsch[9] recognized the importance of balancing integration and differentiation. Recently, there has been a tendency to emphasize integration and lose sight of the value of differentiation.

The Challenges of International Compensation and Benefits

One of the major challenges of international compensation and benefits results from the broader base of comparisons that must be considered to assure fair and equitable treatment:

- Local nationals in each country of operation versus local nationals in all other countries of operation
- Local nationals versus expatriates
- Expatriates from headquarters versus expatriates of every other country of origin

Compensation and benefits practitioners instinctively try to find a system that motivates and can be applied to all employees. Many rebel against discrimination unless it is based on position, merit, and performance. And some have trouble with position and merit unless they are performance driven. In considering the relationships just enumerated, it is clearly unlikely that any one compensation system will provide equality for every employee group relative to every other category.

A frequent argument for providing the same compensation advantages to all employees, particularly those in the same location, is that those who are not included in a particular program will feel discriminated against. For example, there is the presumption that local nationals will resent that expatriates are better compensated than they are. Dianne Cyr, in her study of international joint ventures (JV), found that "contrary to . . . predictions, multiple compensation arrangements did not seem problematic for JV staff. . . . What seemed to be more important to employees in judging the fairness of their compensation systems was whether reward systems were consistently applied within the group."[10] My own experience supports this finding. What I have also found is that local nationals resent comparatively highly paid expatriates only when the assignees with whom they work are incompetent, do not bring skills that are scarce in the local market, or remain in expatriate status for excessively long periods without training local replacements. This argues for better expatriate selection procedures and more effective career planning, not for avoiding differentiated compensation programs.

As you read further, it will become more and more evident that the field of international compensation and benefits is very complex and challenges some cherished convictions. But it is also fascinating and provides practitioners, whether corporate staff, third-party providers, or professional consultants, with unlimited opportunities to be innovative and to make a significant impact on the success of global companies.

Notes

1. Calvin Reynolds, "Expatriate Compensation in Historical Perspective," *Journal of World Business* 32, no. 2 (1997).
2. Calvin Reynolds, "Are You Ready to Make IHR a Global Function?" *SHRM-HR News* (February 1992).
3. Organization Resources Counselors, Inc., *Survey of Global Compensation Practices* (September 1998).
4. Geert Hofstede, *Culture's Consequences* (1980); updated and revised as *Cultures and Organizations* (New York: McGraw-Hill, 1991).

5. Fons Trompenaars, *Riding the Waves of Culture* (Burr Ridge, IL: Irwin, 1993/1994).
6. George T. Milkovich and Matt Bloom, "Rethinking International Compensation," *Compensation & Benefits Review* (January/February 1998).
7. Charles Hampden-Turner, "The Boundaries of Business: The Cross-Cultural Quagmire," *Harvard Business Review* (September/October 1991).
8. Donald F. Hastings, "Lincoln Electric's Harsh Lessons from International Expansion," *Harvard Business Review* (May/June 1999).
9. Paul R. Lawrence and Jay W. Lorsch, *Organization and Environment* (Boston, MA: Harvard University Press, 1967).
10. Dianne J. Cyr, *The Human Resource Challenge of International Joint Ventures* (Westport, CT: Quorum Books, 1995).

CHAPTER 2

GLOBALIZATION OF THE COMPENSATION AND BENEFITS FUNCTION

ALAN J. RITCHIE AND STEVEN P. SELTZ

There is a rich business tradition of large, monolithic U.S. companies operating on multiple continents, typically employing thousands of employees representing an array of cultures, languages, and traditions. The history of many of these large, successful multinationals—such as Exxon, Ford, Coca-Cola, IBM, and Citicorp—is well documented. During the past two decades, we have witnessed more companies, of all sizes and shapes, embarking on the globalization of their operations. Indeed, "going global" has become an increasingly common—and essential—element of many companies' business strategies, making the world a much smaller and dynamic place.

Although it may be a smaller world, it is no less complex. As organizations break through the literal and figurative boundaries of single-country operations and begin to function across borders, they face a multitude of difficult strategic and tactical challenges. How should they structure the operations? Who should manage the business? Should they centralize or decentralize operations? Where should they locate? How should they deploy support-function resources? How should they manage human resources? The approach a company takes to its human resource (HR) programs must support the organization's chosen path of globalization and must link to the organization's business plan or strategy. When it does, it can provide answers to many of these questions.

Indeed, a critical step in the evolution of any emerging global business is the development of HR policies, practices, and procedures that aid the organization in integrating strategy, technology, operations, and resources (human and otherwise) while at the same time demonstrating sensitivity to cultural differences and realities. For every organization, HR strategy and tactics can be instrumental in communicating, instilling, and operationalizing the mission, vision, and values of the organization and its leadership. No set of HR programs is more visible or has greater impact than compensation and benefits.

This chapter provides an overview of some of the key human resource challenges and opportunities—and their relationship to compensation and benefits (C&B)—that face companies as they take steps toward globalizing. We will discuss some of the constraints, risks, misconceptions, and sensitivities that almost invariably confront an "indigenous" company transforming itself into a truly global organization. These learnings, we hope, will provide a road map for other organizations to follow—and will help them to avoid customary errors in thinking and in practice.

What Is "Global"? Why Globalize?

One of the first questions organizations contemplating the global expansion of their business need to answer is "What exactly does *global* mean?" The fact is that operating globally means very different things to different people, and the programs and policies developed to support global activities can be as varied as the definition.

For some, going global suggests *exporting* corporate programs abroad. For others, it can mean *adapting* the corporate approach to local norms. For still others, it implies loosely coordinated but *locally unique* programs. Any of these approaches may be appropriate depending on the business needs and resources available to support the global business strategy.

Another critical question to answer before seeking to globalize compensation and benefits programs is "why?" Among the responses that organizations typically provide to this question are:

- A desire to better influence or exercise control over and ensure compliance with corporate objectives and mandates;
- An attempt to facilitate the management of a cadre of senior executives with a global mind-set;
- An effort to reinforce desired messages (e.g., vision, mission, values, etc.) through C&B programs;
- A wish to facilitate employee movement between and across geographical boundaries;
- A plan to create and exploit economies of scale in C&B; and/or
- An effort to transfer technology and build "local" technical C&B competence.

These are worthy objectives, and the transfer and communication of corporate standard, U.S.-based compensation and benefit programs can certainly contribute to the realization of each. However, the "value added" of implementing such an approach must be considered in the broader context of both the local interpretation of the message it sends and the practical complexities of implementation.

One of the problems that often arises when organizations try to install headquarters/corporate C&B policies and programs overseas is that they quickly realize few programs and issues are truly global. Quite literally, these programs tend to lose something in translation. In fact, even regionally uniform programs are few and far between; that is, *almost all* are local. Cultural, legal, social, and attitudinal differences among countries cause "one size fits all" programs to consistently fall short of addressing "local" employee needs and motivating the desired employee behaviors.

Compensation and Benefits Challenges

Background

Over the past 20 years, many of the C&B principles and practices thoroughly embedded in U.S. organizations have been exported to the rest of the world and tested against local norms, customary practices, cultures, and employee attitudes. Such concepts as pay-for-performance, economic value added (EVA), variable pay, executive and broad-based employee stock ownership programs, and flexible benefits are now becoming more common outside the United States. It is not at all unusual, in fact, for the first step in a U.S.-based organization's globalization to be the imposition of familiar home-country practices on overseas operations.

Challenges arise, however, when these practices conflict—as they often do—with local realities. Commonly, strict market customs; regulatory, tax, and legal requirements; incompatible employee attitudes and values; and organizational culture all must be taken into account when establishing C&B programs abroad. The ever-changing and fluid nature of these external considerations is a fact of life. Two common themes arise when considering the hurdles to success: "one size does *not* fit all" and "different strokes for different folks."

The importance of these themes may be further highlighted by the way globalization is achieved, because the process creates a host of additional

C&B challenges, whether organically driven or achieved through mergers and/or acquisition. Entering a new market for the first time often requires C&B professionals to operate very differently from how they would in countries where the business is established and the company brand is well recognized. Mergers and acquisitions create their own set of C&B challenges, such as securing talent, assimilating cultures and value systems, and fostering a "one-firm" atmosphere.

Rewards

In any case, a fundamental decision that needs to be made is whether the focus of compensation for employees outside the United States should be driven by corporate objectives or by local "line of sight" objectives. Corporate philosophy that guides U.S.-based compensation programs is often difficult to capture and communicate to U.S. employees. It is far more complex when different countries and people are brought into the picture. Furthermore, the business objectives and challenges in various countries are unique and often vary enough from those of the corporate headquarters that the strategy to support pay and benefits programs in the United States does not support local needs. That, in turn, may also vary by the employee's organizational levels. It may be, for instance, that senior employees outside the United States should participate in corporate programs, while compensation for lower-grade employees is locally driven.

Employee relations structures and legal structures within countries can be "real" barriers to the implementation of corporate programs. Indeed, what is possible in the United States may or may not be acceptable practice and/or permitted outside the United States, or it may be possible but only with great difficulty. For example, the implementation of some compensation and benefits programs within Germany is complicated by the need to agree or negotiate with works councils. The implementation of stock plans in the emerging markets of Eastern Europe is hindered by the lack of precedent and legislation that has only recently begun to develop.

Custom and tradition should also be taken into account. The local organizations need to motivate and reward employees through compensation and benefits programs that recognize and reflect the culture and tradition of their country. For example, pay-for-performance, one of the more common elements—indeed, one of the building blocks—of contemporary U.S. C&B programs, is generally considered an alien concept in more "egalitarian" countries such as Japan or Korea, where the principle of tenure- and age-based reward and recognition, rather than meritocracy, has been historically embraced and culturally reinforced.

Another common U.S. practice—the growing trend to introduce "variable" pay into the total compensation equation—must be introduced slowly (if at all) in the many countries where fixed pay is the norm. In several European countries, the need for pay and position security, coupled with the influence of organized labor, makes any pay-at-risk program problematic. Even programs as attractive to U.S. employees as stock options may not be embraced in countries where employees struggle to maintain a moderate standard of living, such as in the Philippines, or where they are influenced by historical and culturally embedded reasons, such as in Germany.

In short, the effort to introduce C&B practices potentially alien to local custom must be carefully considered and, if attempted, be accompanied by a sincere and focused effort to *communicate* the tenets and intents of these activities if they are to be successful.

Pay Management

It also needs to be acknowledged that "pay management" tools are not globally developed. Fortunately, many U.S. firms are already migrating toward a greater reliance on market pricing as the foundation of their rewards programs, so the concept of abandoning rigid and formulaic job descriptions is reasonable. What is not reasonable, though, is an assumption that market data to support a market pricing strategy are available around the world. In fact, there is a scarcity of quality market data in many parts of the world—especially in developing countries such as China—and the obstacles are many. Furthermore, the science of job matching is unknown in many countries, and the idea of benchmarking or comparing positions using title is difficult because of the cultural norms that influence how positions are leveled and titled.

An additional impediment to market pricing in many countries is the unwillingness of many organizations to participate in the surveys that are necessary to establish market trends. In Russia, for example, the idea of divulging details about employees, their pay, and position is offensive. In other places, such as Mexico, the public release of this kind of information may even be legally prohibited. Furthermore, in some developing nations, such as the Ukraine, there may be so few professionals nationwide in a given field that to release pay and position data would be compromising to the incumbents. As the world moves toward market-based C&B programs, this lack of reliable data becomes a critical deficiency in the effort to support global career development and promotion programs.

Advancement and Development

It is critical in the C&B planning process to recognize that programs should not just focus on monetary rewards. The opportunity for personal growth and challenging work are highly valued in many cultures, and C&B programs—in fact, any human resources initiative—must support these values. For example, the idea of upward mobility is universal in most developed countries, not just upward mobility marked by enhanced compensation opportunities and rewards but also upward movement in the organization's hierarchy.

The concept of promotion, too, is almost universally common in developed markets. Employees in most countries around the world need to perceive that they have the opportunity for upward advancement and future career opportunities. Of course, in the flatter organizations more common today, the relative scarcity of upward mobility opportunities may be a problem, and a focus on development without a traditional promotion up the corporate hierarchy often needs to be considered.

Conversely, it is important to note that, in some developing countries, giving employees additional salary and/or rewards has actually proven to decrease output, because after the employees have made "enough" money to survive, they have little constructive incentive to do more until they are "in need" again. From the perspective of the typical multinational organization—particularly those that are grounded in a Western conception and philosophy of work—this can be an unusually difficult concept to grasp. Thus, the design and installation of global C&B programs need to be sensitive to this reality.

Another challenge many U.S.-based multinational firms face in supporting promotion and career-development opportunities abroad is the often common belief that an assignment at corporate headquarters in the United States is a requirement for true career advancement within the organization. Although this may be the case for some positions, not all long-term career growth should be tied to U.S. assignments. Career-development programs must be robust enough to support advancement globally.

Moreover, most promotion and career-development programs in the United States are typically built and administered around well-documented position matrices and job ladders that detail job requirements, levels of proficiency, scope of responsibility, and other common job factors. These tools are less common outside the United States, however. To support career growth internationally, there must be less emphasis on rigid job descriptions and complicated point-factor systems and an increasing reliance on market data. The conundrum, of course—as noted above—is that reliable and valid market data are difficult, if not impossible, to come by in many locations and/or for many jobs.

Organizational Considerations

Another significant challenge facing global C&B professionals is navigating the structure of the organization. To manage the wide-reaching operations of global firms, companies are typically organized into business units or divisions. Sometimes these units are organized according to the type of business or the product; sometimes the structure is driven by geography; and sometimes it is a combination of the two. Further complicating matters is that it is not at all uncommon within large multinationals to find more than one business in the same country.

In some companies, in fact, there may be numerous distinct business units all operating in a single country. Although these operating units may share a common corporate direction, they each confront unique business challenges. And although the units may coexist within a common country, they may also have unique organizational cultures, driven by business history and tradition, and their own particular competitive environment and employee population. This is further complicated by the need to provide service for customers who operate globally, often requiring the organization to flexibly build and disband teams from across business units and geographic borders.

In designing C&B programs, resolving the conflict between the requirements established by the country or region and those driven by the business can be cumbersome and contentious. Which factor is most critical: the organization's business strategy, the organization's country and customs, the organization's region (geographic or corporate), or the company's C&B philosophy? The answer is all of them, and depending on the program, one may take precedence over the others at any given point.

It is imperative to understand, however, that in addition to solid business reasons, the organizational structure adopted by the corporation is often influenced by legal or financial reasons. The structure represents an artificial framework that shifts and adapts according to business products, customer requirements, or the whim and convenience of senior management.

To work through this maze of potentially conflicting—and frequently vacillating—organizational structures, an understanding of the common characteristics that extend across business units or divisions, as well as the unique needs within each of the operations, is critical. When establishing C&B programs in countries or regions where multiple businesses—often replete with various and conflicting needs and desires—are evident, the experience of the authors suggests that the most effective approach is one that emphasizes "country first" and "business unit second." Though the opposite may be true for a particular operating structure, in any case, both the needs of the business and the demands of the country must be balanced for C&B programs to be effective and truly global.

Responding to the Challenges

A Global Mind-Set

One key to managing the plethora of challenges facing an international C&B function is to think globally, act locally, and balance the strategy of the corporation with that of the local business organization. This is no small task, however, given the degree of social, public (institutional), and organizational change taking place today, as well as changing worker attitudes and work patterns, demographic trends, and so on.

Buy-In and Implementation Awareness

As with any human resource initiative, global C&B programs must be designed to support the business strategy, have the endorsement of senior management, and align with other human resources strategies and programs. Effective C&B programs often serve as the catalyst to clearly define and understand local business strategy and financial metrics. "Buy-in" to the corporate philosophy is often easy to obtain. However, translating that philosophy into financial and behavioral metrics on which profit can be converted into reward—which, in theory, then motivates employees to further improve profits—may be another matter entirely. In addition, some fundamental compensation-philosophy questions must be answered, such as the following: What is the organization's target market position and why? Who is the competition and what is their compensation and benefit approach? What is the organization's ability to pay? What employee needs is the organization intending to meet?

Centralization-Decentralization Balance

Successful global C&B programs include a high degree of decentralization, affording each local organization the freedom to adapt programs based on local needs, but at the same time are built on a foundation of a well-defined corporate culture and guiding principles. The expectation is that C&B programs and philosophies will reflect the flavor of the home country of the company (i.e., the United States) but be tailored to support unique local legislative, cultural, and business requirements. If these local requirements can be captured in the plan design, employees are more likely to be supportive of the programs, thereby making them more effective motivational tools.

Communicate Appropriately

Of course, communication is key in any business relation, but an even greater commitment to effective communication is required when supporting global operations. It is important that compensation and benefits-related communication initiatives be as localized as possible—written and presented in local languages—since communication gaps and disconnects can be exacerbated when language differences are introduced. It is also critical to ensure that idiomatic business vocabulary is used in translated documents to ensure that "pure" translations accurately reflect native sensitivities and sensibilities.

Adaptation of home-country *subject matter* to ensure appropriateness for local cultures is crucial as well, as is consideration of the presentation *methodology* itself. For example, in some locations, communication via intranet and electronic bulletin board announcements is effective, while in other cultures, group meetings are well received. In other places, personal, one-on-one communication methods might be most effective. Sometimes, only printed materials will do. In fact, some cultures are better able to publicly discuss matters of pay, position, and performance than are others.

The one consistent fact is that some form of communication is critical if C&B programs are to be effective. After all, even though reward programs rarely drive organizational strategy, they are certainly key to supporting and reinforcing this strategy, and the effective communication of these programs is routinely the prerequisite to understanding, acceptance, and "buy-in."

Building a Global C&B Function

To build an effective international C&B function, developing a global mindset and "thinking global" are again key. Resources with experience in and understanding of local business customs must be partnered with C&B experts from the United States in order to build an organization that identifies the appropriate balance between corporate and local cultures. Many multinational firms will *export* excellent C&B talent but fail to take advantage of—or to develop—local expertise. While U.S. experts can certainly develop and become proficient, they require a steep learning curve before they are truly effective in capturing and understanding the many nuances and indigenous considerations that must be supported by the C&B programs.

There is a tremendous opportunity to build diverse C&B functions by partnering talent from around the globe. This "cross-fertilization" of the function enables global C&B organizations to build on the best practices from many cultures. In fact, one mark of a truly effective global firm is one in which the transfer of excellence in any discipline is two-way—"in" and "out"—building on the best that each organization and each country has to offer. For U.S. companies, it is important to remember that while exporting policies, programs, and practices is imperative, it is equally valuable to import the best of these from international organizations.

Indeed, developing this cross-cultural and cross-functional sharing of skills, processes, and best practices is a crucial element in the evolution of a global C&B function. For instance, certain countries and cultures may have a deeper and/or broader expertise than corporate headquarters in such areas or concepts as team pay, change management, mergers and acquisitions, or retrenchment practices. It is critical that the organization recognize and take advantage of such expertise—regardless of its geographic origins.

In building a global C&B team, it is also necessary to have the tools in place to minimize the impact of working across scattered time zones. Unique team-building techniques need to be introduced, and technology to enable effective communication between team members is vital. Indeed, development of a "networking culture" is the end objective—and one of the fundamental building blocks of success.

To this end, C&B professionals must develop a keen sense of cultural awareness and international sensitivity. This is true for all C&B professionals, not just those from the United States. Short-term developmental assignments (U.S. and non-U.S.), mentoring programs, cross-country/cross-cultural project teams, common global tools, common programs, and training are all elements that may be effective in building a competent global C&B function.

The key is to build common compensation skills across a diverse compensation and benefits function. To do this, training is critical. Effective training, of course, enables the building of technical skills in C&B design and development and teaches strategies and methods for effectively implementing compensation programs in an organization. One particularly effective idea is to combine within the training *both* the theory and the application of compensation techniques and technologies. Training programs may use existing offerings such as those provided through professional associations such as the Global Remuneration Organisation (GRO) or the American Compensation Association (ACA), or they may be developed internally.

Training programs that bring together C&B professionals from around the world provide a superb opportunity to reinforce the universal mission, vision, and values of the organization, the corporation, and human resources. The cultural exchange that is fostered through training can also help to build a deeper awareness of and appreciation for the corporation's cultural diversity. Furthermore, such sessions provide invaluable opportunities for relationship building so that the C&B function represents a strong global network of professionals.

The successful, fully proficient global C&B professional must not only master the technical theory and practical application of C&B but also demonstrate interpersonal and consulting competencies. While these are certainly more difficult to teach, many can be incorporated into training programs; others may be developed through on-the-job experiences (short-term international assignments, for example) and through mentoring.

Some of the core competencies often identified as crucial elements of behavior for success within the global C&B function include the ability to be adaptable and flexible, consensus- and team-building skills, strong interpersonal and intercultural sensitivity, business and financial awareness, and organizational astuteness. Skills in communication and facilitation are also necessary.

For many human resources organizations, the challenge in building a global team of C&B professionals possessing such competencies will be in finding opportunities to develop these attributes. Because an effective global C&B function is critical, some multinational firms provide incentives to encourage and reward the building and demonstration of these competencies among the C&B team.

Summary

Globalizing compensation and benefits is essential to support the business needs of a global organization. The definition of *global*, however, will vary from company to company and must be aligned to the nature and strategy of the business. Global C&B programs, regardless of where they are implemented around the world, reflect the local organization's political, social, cultural, and economic business environment while rewarding and supporting the behaviors necessary for organizational and corporate success.

Creating effective global C&B programs requires recognizing and addressing a host of considerations, particularly concerning how global C&B programs should be applied; how they can best "fit" within local environments; what the implementation constraints are; and the more practical issues of communication, implementation, and administration. These considerations should not deter organizations from globalizing C&B programs, however, or overshadow the reasons for and benefits derived from globalization.

The development of an effective global C&B function is one necessary key to success for a truly global organization. It can only truly be achieved, however, by cultivating local expertise empowered with the training, tools, and structures to enable effective work outputs.

CHAPTER 3

MANAGING COMPENSATION PLANS IN CROSS-BORDER MERGERS AND ACQUISITIONS

ERIC P. MARQUARDT AND RONALD N. REYNOLDS

Global merger and acquisition activity totaled $2.4 trillion in 1998, with a growing percentage of the total coming from Europe and Asia. The total number of global mergers and acquisitions is twice what it was only five years earlier, and all indications are that this frenzied pace of cross-border merger and acquisition activity will continue and even grow.[1]

However, 75% of all cross-border mergers are disappointments or outright failures.[2] Management has frequently been unable to successfully accomplish the arduous task of combining two separate companies into one. Cultural differences, predominant in cross-border mergers, are frequently cited as the major reason for failed merger negotiations, as well as failed mergers themselves. These cultural issues, along with other operational and human resource issues, must be solved if investors are to see the potential added value created in the merged company.

Cross-border mergers typically share a common set of strategic issues with domestic mergers. These will be detailed later in this chapter. However, company culture, operating practices, and human resources practices in an international merger are different enough from those in a domestic merger to require different approaches to solving these issues.

Often, the acquiring company will see its operating and human resources practices as superior to those of the acquired company. This is particularly true if cross-border cultural differences color the evaluation. The *Wall Street Journal,* reporting on the Daimler-Chrysler megamerger, indicated that Daimler executives had hoped that Chrysler's freewheeling and informal culture would lead to improved engineering and design practices in the new company.[3] However, the more bureaucratic German approach appears to be prevailing and is cited as the major cause of the departure of three key Chrysler manufacturing and engineering executives to Ford Motor Company in the initial months after the announcement of the merger.

One of the biggest human resource issues to solve in a newly merged company is the discrepancies in compensation philosophy, design, and practice that each company brings to the table. Imagine the challenge of linking the pay plans of Upjohn, a U.S.-based pharmaceutical company with a heavy emphasis on stock compensation, and its European partner, Pharmacia AB, whose Swedish tax and securities laws make stock compensation rare and difficult. Compensation practitioners play an important role in solving or at least improving these compensation discrepancies.

This chapter is organized around the two roles for the compensation practitioner in a cross-border merger or acquisition: the strategic and the operational role. By the end of the chapter, the reader will have insight into how pay and benefits programs can be implemented consistently and successfully in cross-border transactions.

Roles of the Compensation Practitioner

Regardless of whether a merger is on domestic or foreign soil, the compensation professional's role is twofold throughout the merger process. The compensation professional has both an *operational role* and a *strategic role*. The operational role focuses on tactical issues. These tactical issues often arise during the early stages of the merger and must be resolved before a pay strategy is put in place. An example of an early-stage tactical issue is how to convert existing equity plans of one or both partners into the equity of the new company. The strategic role for the compensation professional is directional and focuses on developing principles that will shape future pay and benefits decisions. An example of a directional issue is how to determine and set competitive pay levels in different labor markets around the world following a cross-border merger. Both roles are integral to the short- and long-term success of the newly formed company.

Operational Role

During the initial stages of the merger, the compensation practitioner will play a key role in the resolution of four broad issues. These issues are generally addressed in sequential order and are discussed in more detail immediately below.

1. *Due diligence.* Identify compensation and benefits liabilities and issues affecting integration.
2. *Assimilation.* Determine whether or not to merge or eliminate pay plans.
3. *Compliance.* Ensure that pay and benefit programs and decisions meet multicountry legal and regulatory standards.
4. *Communications.* Decide how, when, and in what form pay information will be given to employees.

In addition, one very basic operational task that is easily overlooked is ensuring that payrolls are met and that employees get timely paychecks. When operations are being closed, consolidated, or simply changed following a merger, it can be disastrous to overlook the necessary steps to ensure that employees continue to be paid. Although no recognition will likely be granted for succeeding at this operational task, much unwanted recognition will be received for failure. Failure will increase employee anxieties about the merger and can reduce confidence in the new employer.

Due Diligence

Many of the issues involved in due diligence spill over into the integration process. Issues such as how jobs are valued or how the competitive position is pegged in the marketplace tell a lot about how people work together, what they value, or how challenging the "fit" in the new organization will be. However, in the operational role we are discussing here, due diligence is focused on quantifying the differences in pay and benefits programs and understanding how modifying the programs will affect staff retention and labor costs, and ensuring that compensation plans can or will deal effectively with transitional pay issues. It is not easy to quantify with precision all financial costs in acquiring a business. In a global setting with limits on ease of information exchange, it is even more difficult. However, the discipline of attempting to do so is valuable in itself. Even broad estimates of costs and liabilities can be useful in measuring potential business success.

A key role for the compensation practitioner in the due diligence process is the preparation of a due diligence checklist. The checklist allows both parties to the transaction to accurately size the financial implications of the human resources issues and, if necessary, offer a consensus on value for negotiating purposes. The following table shows a listing of categories that should be covered in the due diligence checklist.[4]

Exhibit 3-1. Due Diligence Checklist Categories

Employment Terms	Compensation and Benefits	Other Elements of Pay	Other HR Issues	Systems and HRIS
Work Contracts	Salary and Bonus	Family Policies	Recruitment	Payrolls
Collective Bargaining Agreements	Pay Management	Perquisites	Communication Policy	Benefits Processing
Employment Law	Retirement Practices	Equity Compensation	Termination Benefits	HRIS Data Availability and Accuracy
Notice Periods	Supplemental Medical			
Termination Procedures	Social Security Systems			
HR Policies				

Termination Benefits

The compensation practitioner may or may not play a direct role in the actual collection of the data. Particularly in cross-border transactions, a senior member of the acquisition team may actually approve this due diligence checklist, authorize data gathering, and interface with management in the acquired company.

The due diligence issues in a global merger are many and varied, with differences resulting simply from the differences in countries in which the two parties do business. Within the categories listed in the table are common issues to be addressed in a due diligence process in a cross-border merger. Three key issues follow.

1. *How do liabilities for reductions in force differ in the various countries in which the two partners do business?* When consolidation and overhead reduction is a critical strategic element of a merger or acquisition, this assessment is critical. In the merger of Pharmacia and Upjohn, a decision to locate the new company's corporate headquarters in London, rather than in the United States or Sweden, significantly reduced and slowed the anticipated cost reductions anticipated in the merger. Employees of Pharmacia's Swedish headquarters had to receive a lengthy notice if their job was moved to the United Kingdom. For many U.S.-based Upjohn executives, the move was a constructive termination following a change of control triggering substantial payments of two-plus years under existing employment and termination agreements.
2. *How do the benefit plans differ within each country in which the two companies do business, and what are the cost implications of elimi-*

nating these differences? This assessment provides critical background for subsequent decisions on whether to terminate plans, merge plans, or simply maintain separate plans. Assume one of two merger partners both doing business in the United Kingdom maintains a private executive retirement plan while the other offers only the statutory pension scheme. Before a strategy can be developed in the new company, a due diligence review must address certain questions. Is the private plan properly funded? Are there any past compliance issues? Can a portion of the plan be pulled out and sold with a portion of the business? What liabilities would a plan termination generate?

3. *How do overall pay levels and pay mixes differ in the countries where the new partners do business?* This assessment provides a framework for developing a pay philosophy for the new company and the costs of change. In a global merger, this is complicated by the fact that pay levels and the mix of the pay elements differ by country. In Europe, most companies do not make use of the full range of pay vehicles used in the U.S. companies and may have considerably greater use of benefits and perquisites than their U.S. partner.[5] The challenge can be seen in Exhibit 3-2 in a comparison of a country merger for a $1 billion business in the United States, Germany, and the United Kingdom.

Assimilation or Integration of Compensation Programs

Once due diligence is completed and the terms of the merger are approved, the two partners can take one of two paths to becoming one company: assimilation or integration. Bill Paul, a partner at Deltech Consulting, describes *assimilation* as one of the merging or acquiring companies making the other company just like itself. Paul goes on to describe *integration* as either the creation of a completely new third company or two partners maintaining separate identities while sharing common strengths.

It was not uncommon a decade or so ago for U.S. companies to approach integration and/or assimilation by attempting to "Americanize" the programs of their foreign merger partners. In other words, they were force-fitting U.S. programs into the global merger partner's organization. Since then, compensation practitioners have found that country-specific programs can be locally oriented and still have a global focus on corporate strategies and objectives. This is especially true with international executive compensation programs in which various financial strategies, such as

Exhibit 3-2. Breakdown of Pretax Pay

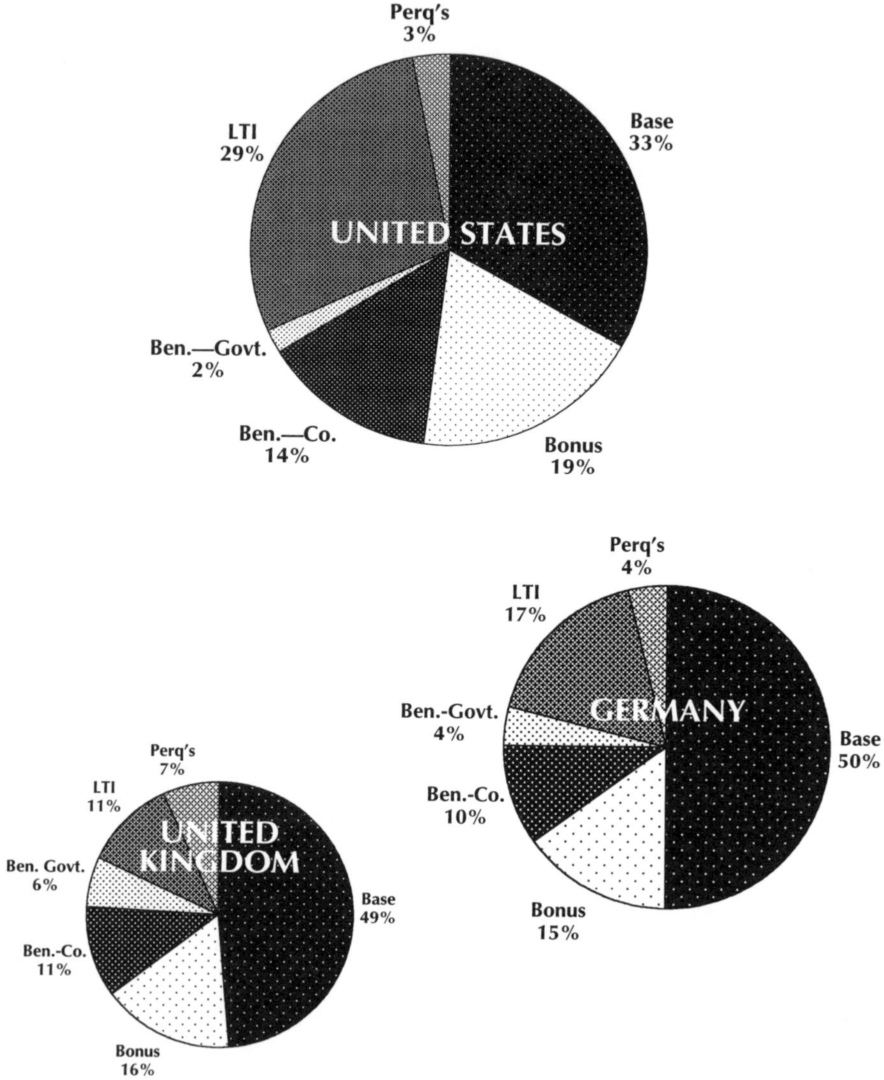

Relative Size of Pies:
United States=100%; Germany=79%; United Kingdom=69%

earnings per share growth, can be translated through incentive objectives to the next level of management in foreign locations.

In the early 1990s, Quaker Oats acquired an Italian grocer, Chianti & Fiori (C&F). Quaker intended to assimilate C&F and enhance its European distribution network. Quaker's incentive system was based on quantitative performance factors, whereas C&F used informal incentives based on qualitative results. Today, C&F participates in Quaker's worldwide management incentive plan. Funds available for incentives are based 60% on quantitative measures of C&F growth and value-added performance and 40% on overall Quaker value-added results. However, C&F management retains discretion in allocating the available pool of funds to individuals, deviating from the formula typically by +/–20%.

The choice between assimilation and integration of compensation programs should depend in large part on whether the merger itself will assimilate one company into the other or whether the companies will integrate to create a new company. Assimilation of one company into another is more likely to occur when both companies are in the same industry, such as banking. A global example of assimilation is the 1999 merger between Deutsche Bank and Bankers Trust. Another example of assimilation is the combination of Scott and Kimberly Clark. This combination created the largest towel and tissue producer in the world. Scott provided Kimberly Clark with a great deal of needed paper-converting capacity. However, the Scott organization disappeared into Kimberly Clark. Compensation programs at the new Kimberly Clark remained virtually unchanged from those plans in place prior to assimilating Scott Paper. Scott's plans were either terminated or changed to fit into Kimberly Clark's pay programs.

Integration is more common when the two merging companies are from different industries or different segments of the same industry. Two global examples of integrating companies representing different segments of the same industry are the 1999 acquisition of Volvo's automotive division by Ford Motor Company and the merger of Daimler Benz and Chrysler. Juergen Schremmp, chairman and CEO of the new Daimler-Chrysler, speaking in February 1999 at the Economic Club of Chicago, indicated that the fundamentals and culture of Chrysler would be utilized to enhance the success of the combined businesses. At the time of this writing, it remains to be seen whether this goal will be accomplished.

The compensation practitioner will need to identify or create program changes consistent with the overall strategy to assimilate or integrate.

Simply, if company "A" will assimilate into company "B," it is likely that very few, if any, of company A's compensation programs will be used in the newly merged company. Conversely, if company "A" and company "B" are going to unite as a new company, then the compensation practitioner will likely be called on to find the right combination of existing plans from both companies.

Compliance

The list of potential compliance issues that can arise in a cross-border merger or acquisition is extremely long. The list below is included primarily to raise awareness of the general issues. Specific issues will vary depending on the countries in which the two merger partners are doing business.

- *Work Contracts/Collective Agreements* What contracts are in force, and are they in compliance with all legal requirements, especially regarding mergers or acquisitions?
- *Employment Law* What specific restrictions and requirements apply to merger situations? What reporting and information requirements are there?
- *Notice Periods* What notice is required for change in employment terms and for which employee groups? Is a merger a change of employment? What changes in current policy are required to achieve compliance?
- *Termination Periods* What are the mandated termination procedures and financial obligations? Do the current severance policies comply?
- *Social Security and Compulsory Benefits* Is the company in compliance with reporting and contribution requirements? Do mandatory benefits duplicate company benefits?
- *Stock Plans* Does the current company-sponsored plan comply with local tax and securities laws? What is needed to achieve compliance?
- *HRIS* Does the system comply with all local restrictions on data transfer and employee connection?

Practitioners should get involved with these regulatory and legal discussions as soon as possible so that they are aware of these hurdles as they proceed with combining and redesigning compensation programs.

Compliance must also take into account one other prime consideration. Compensation programs can affect the financial structure of the merger or acquisition deal itself. Any global merger involving a company with registered securities in the United States will have to account for the merger using one of two methods, a pooling of interests or purchase accounting. Pooling, which involves a combination of two companies through an exchange of equity, is most desirable because it does not dilute reported earnings. To comply with the requirements of pooling-of-interests accounting, the rights of stock compensation plan participants should be preserved intact after the merger. The following are examples of common changes to equity plans that could preclude compliance with pooling-of-interests accounting: acceleration of vesting; changes to voting rights; changes to option terms; repricings; or conversion from one type of equity vehicle, such as premium-priced options, to another, such as a stock appreciation right.

In global mergers, securing pooling of interests can face added challenges. Prior to the merger between James River Corporation and Fort Howard Corporation that, when completed, formed the global company Fort James Corporation, the second largest towel and tissue producer in the world, employees around the world held options in one or the other of the new partners. The company wanted to comply with the requirements of APB-16 to avoid losing the desired pooling-of-interest accounting methodology for the merger. At the same time, if unchanged, many stock options would have resulted in a taxable event for participants in multiple countries and may not have complied with existing labor agreements. In some European locations, for example, any change in stock option benefits could be deemed a constructive termination and trigger government-mandated severance benefits. In the end, a slightly different methodology was used in each country involved, but all options were dealt with under principles that maintained pooling-of-interest accounting.

Communications

In the early stages of a merger or acquisition, a simple rule of human nature that crosses geographic borders must be adhered to: *The average employee hates a vacuum.* Although a company may make decisions following an announced merger with the style and exquisite logic of a chess master, its employees will not wait patiently in limbo while decisions are pondered. Employees will interpret inaction and take action of their own.

Employees on both sides of any merger are uneasy about their job security or their compensation and benefit packages or both. In a global setting, local law may affect the information needs and desires of the average worker. In the United States, job security is most often the first concern. U.S. employment-at-will statutes provide reason for concern and lead companies to communicate aggressively about job security. In Europe, job security is regulated and sometimes guaranteed by governmental mandate. Job actions by companies are subject to oversight review by works councils. Thus, communications there may need to focus much more on severance benefits.

Deciding on a communication strategy during and after a merger requires defining how information is shared, what audiences will be targeted for communications, and the level of information each will receive. In a cross-border merger, a company must also consider cultural differences that affect the flow of information.

Consider a hypothetical merger between a public U.S. company with clear and objective policies and procedures, a centralized infrastructure, and a culture of open decision making and a Latin American family-run business that operates on loyalty and trust in a paternalistic and decentralized infrastructure. The U.S. human resources executive proposes the publication of a weekly newsletter for all staff providing up-to-date information about the progress of the merger, employee benefits, and new pay systems. The publication also encourages employees to speak to management about issues and concerns. Following much discussion and some compromise, the Latin American company agrees to adopt the U.S. company's communication strategy, but in a slightly altered form. In addition to the newsletter, the Latin American company will sponsor open forums and meetings to answer employee questions. Human resources, not management, will answer employee questions and concerns generated by the newsletter and forums. The changes in communications allow the Latin American company to avoid being "too open" while at the same time address the U.S. company's desire to have some form of feedback during the merger as well as an outlet for concerned employees.

One other caution regarding compensation communications across borders should be noted. It is important to avoid jargon and to translate key themes and messages into words and phrases that give the desired meaning in the local countries. Chevrolet's fiasco in the 1970s trying to sell a car in Mexico called the Nova, which in Spanish translates to "no go," is an example of the problems faced in communicating a message across borders.

Strategic Role

The second role of the compensation practitioner requires solving strategic concerns. This role usually begins soon after the merger is consummated and, it is hoped, continues as the business reshapes itself to meet market demands. The strategic role involves the following:

1. Identifying new or revised business strategies and objectives
2. Redefining compensation philosophies and strategies
3. Developing new short- and long-term programs that are aligned to those philosophies and strategies
4. Communicating compensation philosophies and programs

Over the long term, the strategic role takes precedence over the operational role. After resolving the tactical issues needed to get the deal done, strategic planning and design assists in creating the road map for future pay and benefit decisions.

Identifying New Business Strategy and Objectives

The focus here is much different from the operational role. The questions for the compensation practitioner are no longer *how* but rather *why.* Compensation decisions may need to support a new longer-term business strategy. The $2.9 billion acquisition of the Sterling Drug chain from Eastman Kodak by SmithKline (United Kingdom) was a key step in a renewed short- and longer-term growth strategy. It provided the company with access to new markets and increased control of the traditional distribution channels. The merger of Pharmacia AB (Sweden) and Upjohn in 1995 was a move to improve short-term profitability. The *Wall Street Journal* reported in August of that year that the merger would result in a loss of 4,000 jobs and annual cost savings of more than $500 million. The differences in business strategy and objectives should and did lead to different pay philosophies and strategies.

The following example demonstrates the review and development of new programs in light of a revised business strategy following a global merger. The case is based on a real situation, but the name of the company has been withheld.

Redefining Pay Philosophies and Strategies

Following the completion of a cross-border merger, the compensation professional faces the task of potentially updating or changing the new company's pay philosophy and programs. He or she must create a business plan for the compensation program, answering key questions such as with whom do we now compete for talent, how competitive do we want to be, and how will we measure success? In our example case, this unfolded as described below:

Following the completion of a merger to form a global consumer products company, senior management identified a heightened short-term operating focus on earnings per share (EPS) growth. EPS was also seen as the key driver of long-term total shareholder return (TSR). Both parties to the merger had solid growth histories for EPS and TSR. However, on the basis of the price paid for the acquisition, the new company faced significantly higher investor expectations of EPS and TSR than the combined results of the two companies prior to the merger.

The merger was an assimilation of one company into the other. The combined company added several products to its own list of products that were well positioned throughout the world and that led in market share. The newly formed company had added global capacity and increased profit potential from the efficiencies of the new production capacity.

Within a month after the consummation of the merger, the new management team developed several critical short-term (18 months or less) strategies for improving EPS and TSR results. They were as follows:

1. Capture "X" millions of dollars in cost savings by realizing operating synergies.
2. Develop three new products that take advantage of the enhanced distribution channels and improved market strength.
3. Increase marketing efforts to penetrate existing customers with a more profitable product mix.

Consequently, the following groups of employees were given the responsibility for executing the key strategies:

- Top executives and general management were responsible for oversight of all strategies and delivering EPS and TSR goals.
- Divisional operating executives around the world were responsible for realizing the benefits of operating synergies and delivering improved operating income.

- Sales and marketing management was responsible for improved customer results and successful introduction of new products.

This information represented the backbone for development of a global compensation strategy.

The head of compensation for this company decided that a strategy to pay competitive base salaries and provide high short- and long-term opportunities was consistent with the business strategy. Top executives would be paid competitive U.S. base salaries regardless of work location or country of origin. These executives were viewed as mobile and treated as a "corporate asset" rather than as local-country employees. All other employees would be paid at market salaries based on work-country pay levels for leading consumer products companies.

In addition, the following compensation principles for program design were developed:

- Sixty to eighty percent of total pay at the management and executive levels will be tied to global short- and long-term performance results.
- As employees are promoted to higher management levels, a greater portion of their incentive compensation will be tied to creating shareholder wealth.
- All employees will share in the profits of the company when profit hurdles are achieved.
- Methods of allocating incentives to individuals may differ in different countries, but the size of the overall payouts must be tied to a combination of the business unit results and the overall company performance.
- Employee ownership will be promoted at all levels, except where severely limited by local-country tax or securities laws.

Developing New Short- and Long-Term Programs Aligned to Those Philosophies and Strategies

The following are examples of selected plan-design decisions made to implement the compensation strategies and programs globally.

1. All managers and above participated in a short-term incentive plan that was based on line-of-sight parameters that rolled up in to EPS calculations. Country management had 50% of its short-term in-

centive tied to its local operating income, 20% to cost maintenance, and 30% to global EPS.

2. All non-incentive-eligible employees participated in a worldwide cash profit-sharing plan that triggered payments based on a combination of 60% global profits and 40% local income from operations. Profit-sharing payments would be approximately 10% of pay at budgeted profit attainment.
3. Management and executives received performance-accelerated stock options whose vesting could be accelerated when/if certain performance hurdles were achieved. The benchmark was compared against other multinationals in their company peer group.
4. Following the merger, all U.S. employees below the management level received an initial stock option grant that vested over a specified length of time in equal installments. Ownership was highly encouraged and rewarded by additional grants if the initial options were bought and held. U.S. employees also received a considerable company match into their 401(k) account in the stock fund.

The company did not initially roll out the same programs outside the United States because of its concerns with both potential dilution of reported EPS and its ability to administer the stock options in the many countries in which it was doing business. However, at the time of this writing, a onetime worldwide stock option grant was under consideration, pushed along by rapid growth in the company's market capitalization and by the success of other consumer products companies in administering worldwide stock option programs.

Communicating Compensation Philosophies and Programs

The company decided that communications were key to the success of a global company and a global pay program. As a result, every employee receives an annual summary of his or her compensation program, with a description of how each component works. Each employee also participates in an annual 360-degree performance appraisal. On a monthly basis, each employee receives an update of company financial successes. Management is expected to communicate with all employees, provide feedback on individual progress toward objectives, and discuss how these successes translate to compensation. Communications are common and frequent in all types of media. Global satellite communications are used extensively to keep employees apprised of company results. All written materials are translated into the approximately 32 local languages in which the company does business.

Summary

According to Harvard professor Jeffrey Pfeffer, it is the willingness of employees to execute the merger or acquisition plan more than the underlying strategy or complementary nature of products, technology, or markets involved in the merger that will determine the success of the merger or acquisition.[6] Compensation and benefits programs can be and often are remarkably effective tools for managers to use in maintaining and enhancing the willingness of employees to contribute to the success of the merger or acquisition.

When a company decides to expand beyond its geographic borders, the tendency is to place strategy in a position of overriding importance. Cultural and legal constraints in a local market become secondary. However, 60% of the cross-border mergers in the past five years did not generate sufficient cash flow to pay for themselves. Mishandling of human assets has been mentioned as a key cause of 80% of the failures.[7]

Compensation and benefits professionals involved in a cross-border merger must contribute both short-term tactical support and strategic support for the merger or acquisition to be successful. He or she must avoid the temptation to "Americanize" the acquired company. Rather, the successful company will take advantage of the best elements of each company's culture. And they will communicate—translating key themes and messages into words and phrases that give the desired meaning to employees in each country and engender the potential prosperity from facing and responding to the challenges of global competition.

Notes

1. "Mergers and Acquisitions," *Dealmakers Journal*, April 1998.
2. Atkins, F. Roger, "Developing a Global HR Strategy," in E. P. Marquardt (ed.), *Out of the Vortex: Finding Order in Merger and Acquisition Chaos, A Guide for Compensation and Benefits Professionals,* pp. 113–121. Scottsdale, AZ: American Compensation Association, 1999.

3. Warner, Fara and White, Gregory L., "Two Top Daimler-Chrysler Executives Leave Company to Join Ford," *Wall Street Journal,* March 2, 1999, p. B11.

4. Craggs, Andy, "Supporting Global Pay Programs Across Company Cultures," in E. P. Marquardt (ed.), *Out of the Vortex: Finding Order in Merger and Acquisition Chaos, A Guide for Compensation and Benefits Professionals,* pp. 122–138. Scottsdale, AZ: American Compensation Association, 1999.

5. Romanchek, R. A., "Executive Compensation in a Global Merger," *American Compensation Journal,* vol. 8, no. 1, 1st Quarter 1999.

6. Pfeffer, Jeffrey, *Competitive Advantage Through People: Unleashing the Power of the Workforce.* Cambridge, MA: Harvard Business School Press, 1994.

7. Ibid., p. 1.

SECTION TWO

EXPATRIATE STRATEGIES AND PRACTICES

CHAPTER 4

EXPATRIATE COMPENSATION: THE BASICS

CALVIN REYNOLDS

If you are the head of HR or the director of compensation and benefits and the CEO announces that she has just signed an agreement to open your company's first overseas operation in Great Britain, be prepared for one of her first questions: "How soon can we get Jack Burns and Sally Mercer to move to London for two or three years, and how much will we have to pay them?" The primary objectives of this chapter are to suggest a few effective responses to the CEO's questions and to provide a basic tool kit for those responsible for compensating expatriates. Chapter 5 will describe other methodologies and how to determine which approach or combination of approaches will be most effective to support various business and staffing strategies.

The first obvious response to the question of how soon can we get Sally and Jack to move to London is "Are either or both of them willing to move, and if they are, do they really want to go?" Because of the high percentage and increasing number of dual-career couples, the number of turndowns of overseas assignments has become a significant obstacle to international expansion. And, if either of the prime candidates (or both) does not want to expatriate because of spousal careers or for any other reason, it is wise to consider other options. Are there other qualified candidates who are anxious to move? Can we structure a series of shorter assignments without moving families that can accomplish the same objectives? Can we find candidates either here or in other countries who have the basic skills to handle the challenges and supplement whatever background they lack with business trips by skilled professionals—very possibly Jack and Sally themselves? Avoid, if at all possible, "forcing" with excessive compensation or other incentives—positive or negative—employees who do not want to move to accept foreign assignments. The percentage of unwilling candidates who have failed as international assignees after finally saying "yes" following progressively and absurdly more generous financial offers is scary.

Assuming, however, that both Jack and Sally are reasonably enthusiastic about moving to London for a couple of years, there are a few options, some better than others, for compensating them. Some companies new to international business start with *pure negotiation:* "How much will it take to get you to move?" Others try *localization:* "We'll give you a salary comparable to what your local peers in London are getting plus fifteen percent to sweeten the pot." And still others begin with *home-country plus:* "Since standards of living and salaries are higher in the U.S. than in England, we'll continue to pay you your U.S. salary and you should be fine. But to be sure, we'll give you an additional ten percent." The companies with the greatest chance of success, however, are the ones that base their approach on an analysis of "best practices," which they can either purchase or research themselves. And they will either develop in-house expatriate compensation expertise or outsource this activity to a competent service provider. We will return to the uses and abuses as well as the strengths and weaknesses of these various approaches later, but first I will describe the methodology that is used by a significant majority of successful global companies worldwide.

The Balance Sheet Approach

In its "1997–98 North American Survey of International Assignment Policies and Practices," Organization Resources Counselors (ORC) reported that more than 85% of North American corporations have an expatriate compensation philosophy designed "to provide equivalent purchasing power abroad to help maintain home lifestyle"—often called the *balance sheet approach* in North America and *home-country buildup* in Europe. ORC's "Worldwide Survey," which included responses from more than 600 companies, about half of which have headquarters outside of North America, reported that more than 70% of the non–North American companies employ the balance sheet approach as well. These surveys and others are reported more fully in Chapter 7, "Expatriate Practices." The fact that such a high percentage of companies worldwide employ the balance sheet approach does not suggest that it is the ideal approach for compensating all expatriates in all companies. But it is a good place to start. And there are many variations of the basic methodology that will be described in this and the next chapter. Whether you decide to develop a system internally or outsource the work to an outside provider, consider the balance sheet as a viable—and probably the most viable—option as you enter the complex field of expatriate compensation. Later, as your company develops global experience, it is important to revisit this decision and consider other options. This we will do in the next chapter.

Exhibit 4-1. Balance Sheet

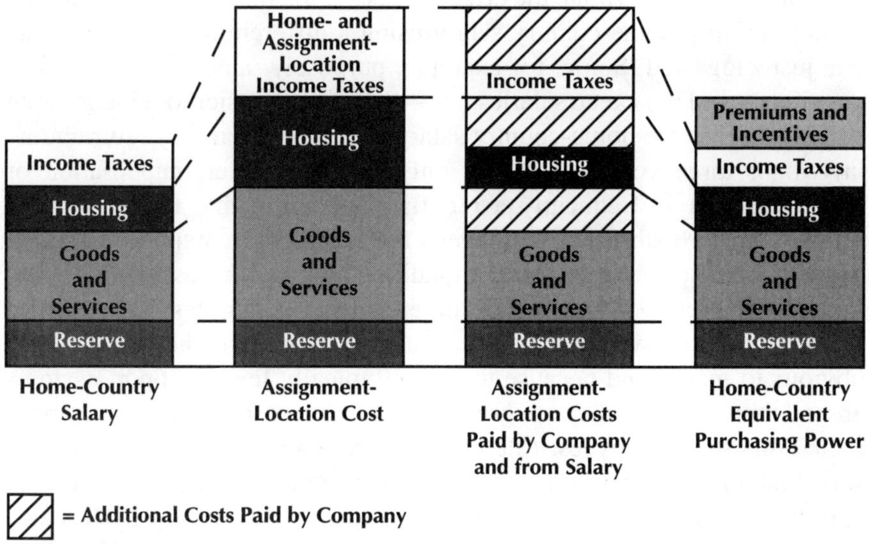

The balance sheet approach is shown graphically in Exhibit 4-1. The primary objective of the balance sheet approach is to provide expatriates (defined as employees transferred *temporarily*—typically two to five years— from one country, "home," to another country, "host" or "assignment") with a standard of living roughly equivalent to that of their home-country peers.

Home-Country Salary

The first column in Exhibit 4-1, "home-country salary," is the salary that would typically be paid in the home country for a position evaluated at the same level as that of the expatriate. Home-country salary is expressed in home-country currency. For example, if your company is headquartered in the United States (the "home" country) and you are contemplating sending a U.S. expatriate to England (the "host" or "assignment" country), the position should be evaluated within the U.S. job-evaluation system, the salary slotted in the U.S. salary structure, and the pay denominated in U.S. dollars. For purposes of this analysis, we will consider the home country to be the United

States, but it is important to recognize that the "home" country could be any country in the world. We will return to this subject in the next chapter.

Some companies vitiate the effectiveness of the balance sheet approach by determining home-country salary using a different approach than the one just suggested. Some, for example, purposely undervalue expatriate positions—and thus keep salaries low—to "make it easier to reincorporate employees into the home-country salary structure when they return home in two or three years." This not only leads to undercompensation of expatriates but is frequently a red flag indicating that the expatriates selected are probably not employees for whom the company has great expectations. Selecting marginally qualified international assignees is dangerous and expensive. As will become evident, expatriates, regardless of the compensation system selected, are always expensive; their weaknesses obvious to many; and because there are typically fewer support systems abroad than at home, they are greater risks to the corporation than comparable domestic employees. And underevaluation is by no means the only way that initial expatriate salaries are distorted. The determination of appropriate base salaries is not only significant in the salary itself; since most, if not all, allowances and incentives (as well as benefit plans) are related to base salary, base salary has an important multiplier effect on all components of the compensation package.

It is also important to keep expatriate base salaries in line with domestic base salaries as time goes on. If your company's base salaries increase on average by 4% domestically, expatriate salaries should (assuming comparable performance) increase by 4% as well. If outstanding domestic employees receive 8% raises, so too should outstanding foreign service employees. And this is not to suggest that base pay is the only element of compensation that should be considered: Comparability should cover the entire compensation and benefits package. Many companies have a problem with this. Since an expatriate's primary evaluators are usually in the expatriate's assignment location, there is a tendency to give typical assignment location, rather than home-country, increases to expatriates. In addition, if raises for local employees in an expatriate's assignment location are generally greater than in the home country, because of high inflation for example, expatriates will also argue that their raises should be in line with their assignment-country peers. But, as you will see, the difference between assignment- and home-country inflation is taken care of in the allowances described below. It is essential to keep expatriate salaries in line with home-country peers, not with those of their assignment-country colleagues.

Notice that the first column of Exhibit 4-1 is divided into four categories: income taxes, housing, goods and services, and reserve. Salary is divided in this way because each of the expenditure categories behaves quite differently as family size and income increase. In the United States, as in most countries, income taxes are progressive; that is, taxes increase both in amount and as a percentage of income as income increases. Social Security and other taxes based on income are included in the income tax category in the exhibit, but non-income-related taxes (e.g., real estate and sales) are not. Housing is a large, relatively stable month-to-month expenditure that increases in amount but decreases as a percentage of income as income increases. At a given income level, families typically spend more on housing than do single people, but at least in the United States (so government research tells us), expenditures for housing do not increase significantly as children are added. Goods and services are the myriad expenditures we make every day for food, clothing, transportation, medical care, entertainment, and so on. Like housing, these expenditures also increase in amount but decrease as a percentage of income as income increases. But unlike housing, each increase in family size typically leads to a significant increase in goods and services expenditures. The reserve, or remainder, is the amount that is left over after taxes, housing, and goods and services expenditures. It includes savings, investments, home-country benefits, mortgage amortization (but not interest, which is included in housing), university education, and alimony. The reserve, like income taxes, increases in amount and as a percentage of income as income goes up. Exhibit 4-2 is a 1999 breakdown of expenditures for a typical U.S. family of three based on research by the Bureau of Labor Statistics of the U.S. Department of Labor and adapted by Organization Resources Counselors, Inc.

Host-Country Costs

The second column of Exhibit 4-1 represents the costs in an assignment location of replicating the expenditures in the first column. If, for example, you are considering a U.S. expatriate family of three assigned to London, the first column reflects how that family at a given income level would spend its income in the United States. The second column shows how much it would cost in London to obtain "appropriate comparable" housing, to purchase "similar" goods and services, and the taxes that would have to be paid to both the assignment- and home-country taxing authorities. Notice that the reserve block is the same size in both columns; this is

Exhibit 4-2. Disposition of Income for a U.S. Family of Three 1999 (Percentage of Base Pay)

Annual Base Pay	Income Taxes*	Social Security	Housing	Goods and Services	Reserve
$25,000	$1,856 (7.4%)	$1,951 (7.8%)	$6,706 (26.8%)	$14,315 (57.3%)	$172 (0.7%)
75,000	11,891 (15.9%)	5,596 (7.5%)	14,369 (19.1%)	32,787 (43.7%)	10,357 (13.8%)
125,000	27,076 (21.7%)	6,321 (5.1%)	20,702 (16.5%)	48,768 (39.0%)	22,133 (17.7%)
175,000	43,389 (24.8%)	7,046 (4.0%)	25,927 (14.8%)	62,293 (35.6%)	36,345 (20.8%)
225,000	62,153 (27.6%)	7,771 (3.5%)	31,124 (13.8%)	75,981 (33.8%)	47,971 (21.3%)

* Federal tax, with federal variable deduction rate and average state and local tax deduction included, plus average state and local taxes.

Source: *Bureau of Labor Statistics, U.S. Department of Labor, adapted by Organization Resources Counselors, Inc.*

because these expenditures will normally be made by expatriates at "home" in home-country currency and therefore there will not be any differences in cost for an expatriate and a domestic employee remaining at home.

"Appropriate comparable" housing is an elusive concept. Housing varies dramatically around the world, and it is very difficult, if not impossible, to find a house or apartment "just like the one we had at home." Most companies are reasonably liberal about where expatriates can live—for example, they take into consideration such things as proximity to international schools and transportation—but they typically discourage expatriate home ownership and place limits on how much rent an expatriate can pay. Despite these limitations, rental housing suitable for expatriates is very expensive in almost every country of the world. It is usually the single largest marginal cost of expatriation.

Goods and services expenditures are also usually higher for expatriates than for domestic employees, even in so-called low-cost countries. It takes a while to get used to different currencies, measurement systems, brands, and even products. "What does F20 for 100 grams really mean? And the brands are so different!" is a typical reaction. Identical spending patterns in two countries are essentially impossible. Some international assignees work very hard to localize their consumption habits as rapidly as possible. But many try to avoid "going native," at least in the short term. To the extent that assignees retain their home-country spending habits, they usually incur very high costs. Although these problems decline or disappear with experience, they do pose significant challenges in the early months of expatriate assignments.

The primary reason that expatriate income taxes are so high is that not only are salaries and incentives taxable but most of the supplements paid to expatriates for housing, goods and services, and for other allowances are taxable as well. And, as discussed in Chapter 8 on expatriate taxation, the United States is a relatively "low-tax" country.

Equalizing Expatriate Purchasing Power

The third column of Exhibit 4-1 shows that, under the balance sheet approach, an expatriate is financially responsible for the same costs and expenses as a home-country counterpart is (the solid blocks). The company pays any additional costs and expenses related to income taxes, housing, and goods and services that result from expatriation (the crosshatched blocks). We will discuss below how this cost sharing can be accomplished.

The fourth column of Exhibit 4-1 demonstrates the primary objective of the balance sheet approach—the equalization of purchasing power of expatriates compared with employees who remain at home—and introduces another category, "premiums and incentives," which may be necessary to induce employees to accept expatriate assignments. All of the categories—income taxes, housing, goods and services, the reserve, and premiums and incentives—will be discussed in greater depth in the sections that follow.

Income Taxes

Recall in Exhibit 4-1, column 3, that the balance sheet approach postulates that the employer will offset any differences in costs between the assignment- and home-country categories of expenditures. When the balance sheet approach was developed shortly after World War II, this meant, as far as income taxes were concerned, that if taxes were higher for an expatriate than they would have been at home, the expatriate could substantiate that difference and receive a reimbursement from the company for excess taxes. If taxes were lower, the expatriate kept the windfall. This approach is called *tax protection*.

In the 1960s, companies began to note that tax protection had three major weaknesses:

1. Limited international mobility (expatriates would either resist leaving countries in which they profited from tax windfalls or negotiate for higher pay on their next assignments);
2. High company costs (expatriates could win in low-tax countries, but not lose elsewhere); and
3. Tax evasion (expatriates would sometimes "forget" to declare all of their income to the local authorities, particularly if only part of their compensation was paid in the assignment country and/or tax evasion was a national sport in the host location; several countries meted out severe penalties to both expatriates and their employers).

To overcome these weaknesses, companies developed and began to introduce *tax equalization.* Instead of paying supplements when expatriates report excess taxes, companies deduct from expatriate salaries a hypothetical tax equivalent to what expatriates would have had to pay in tax on compensation at home and agree to pay all income taxes directly or indirectly on behalf of employees. Tax equalization eliminates tax windfalls in low- and no-tax assignment countries and puts assignees in a tax situation comparable to that of home-country counterparts. When first introduced, corporate international personnel departments usually administered tax equalization. Expatriates were required to have their tax returns prepared by "approved professionals" who assured that all income was reported. In the late 1970s, several major accounting firms developed expatriate tax practices, and companies started to outsource their tax return preparation to them. As the accounting firms have become more and more involved, they have introduced better financial controls and sophisticated tax-planning methodologies.

According to ORC's latest "Survey(s) of International Policies and Practices," 91% of North American, 69% of European, and 63% of Asian companies tax equalize their expatriates. Tax protection is used by 6% of North American, 12% of European, and 4% of Asian companies. While 23% of Asian and 8% of European companies pay all of their expatriates' income taxes (expatriates live tax-free), this level of generosity is rare in North America. The remaining companies (3% of North American, 11% of European, and 10% of Asian) generally permit their expatriates to handle their own tax situations.

There are several other important tax policy issues that must be addressed, such as whether or not to consider state and local as well as federal or provincial taxes and how to handle noncompany source income. These subjects are covered in depth in Chapter 8 on expatriate taxation.

Housing

As with income taxes, in the early days of the balance sheet approach, many companies "protected" expatriates by paying them the difference between foreign and home-country housing costs as an allowance. If an expatriate had to pay more for housing overseas than a typical domestic employee at the same income level and family size at home would, the company would pay a housing allowance in home-country currency to make up the difference.

Note that the comparison here is to housing of a typical comparable domestic employee rather than to what the expatriate was actually paying for housing before expatriation. The balance sheet approach is based on home-country norms rather than on individual preassignment actual expenditures to ensure that expatriates at comparable levels receive comparable compensation. A housing illustration will help explain why. Assume that two domestic employees, George and Alice, are employed by you and have similar jobs and identical salaries. Both are married and have two children. They live next door to each other and have essentially identical homes. The only significant difference is that George inherited his home 20 years ago and has no mortgage; Alice purchased hers last year and pays $1,500 per month in interest plus amortization. They both pay $500 per month in taxes. You decide to send both employees to the same overseas location and they again live side by side in houses for which each pays $4,000 per month. Each of them rented out their houses back home for $3,000 per month. A data provider's housing table indicated a home-country monthly housing norm of $2,000. This fact pattern is shown in Exhibit 4-3.

The housing allowance is determined by subtracting the home-country norm from the actual assignment-country rent; this is the amount by which the company subsidizes expatriate housing. Note that if the company uses home-country norms, both expatriates are fully financially protected for high overseas housing costs. George has a higher net income from housing than Alice does, but that is no different from the situation they had before

Exhibit 4-3. Expatriate Housing Allowances Illustrated

	George	Alice
Home-Country Rental Income	$3,000	$3,000
Home-Country Costs (taxes and interest)	500	2,000
Home-Country Net Income	$2,500	$1,000
Home-Country Housing Norm per Consultant	$2,000	$2,000
Assignment-Country Rent	$4,000	$4,000
Allowance Based on Actual Home-Country Costs	$3,500	$2,000
Allowance Based on Housing Norm	$2,000	$2,000
Employee Income and Allowance Based on Actual Home Costs	$6,000	$3,000
Employee Income and Allowance Based on Home-Country Norm	$4,500	$3,000

expatriation. If actual home-country costs are used as the home-country deduction, George's financial advantage is doubled.

Although many companies continue to protect expatriates for high overseas housing costs using the traditional methodology just described, a majority have shifted to an approach similar to tax equalization: The company deducts a home-country housing norm from salary and pays total overseas housing costs either by paying the expatriate local currency or by actually providing a house. In many countries, Japan and several other Asian countries for example, there are very significant tax advantages when the company buys or rents a house in its name and provides it to the expatriate, as opposed to giving the employee the equivalent cash. There are two primary reasons why companies have moved away from paying housing allowances in home-country currency:

- As just mentioned, it is often more tax and cost effective for a company to provide a house rather than to pay an expatriate cash to rent a home. In this case, the easiest way for the expatriate to pay his or her share is to have the norm deducted from salary.

- An allowance in home-country currency must be converted into local currency to pay the rent. And this is not all—the employee's share must be converted into local currency as well. Therefore, each time there is any change in exchange rate between the home- and host-country currencies, the allowance and the amount contributed by the expatriate must change. This combination of factors invariably leads to unnecessary administration and confusion. It is far more straightforward to deduct a home-country norm from home-country salary in home-country currency and provide the expatriate a house or local currency to pay the total rent. Using this approach, exchange-rate variation will have no effect on compensation.

Many other issues related to expatriate housing are discussed in Chapter 7 on expatriate practices and in Chapter 11 on expatriate administration.

Goods and Services

Although protecting international assignees' purchasing power for goods and services cost differences is usually less costly for a company than protecting for either income taxes or housing differences, it is typically far more provocative. Most administrators and expatriates can clearly identify the amounts associated with taxes and housing, but with goods and services, they cannot. Tax equalization is a matter of tax codes, corporate policy, and complex administration, while housing is a few clearly identifiable numbers. Expatriates may have problems with corporate tax and housing policy, but once understood, it is usually difficult to dispute the amounts. Goods and services, on the other hand, represent thousands of relatively small purchases, and therefore it is impossible to simply refer to anything comparable to a tax code or a lease agreement to demonstrate how much people spend on them. The problem is further complicated because, though most goods and services expenditures are usually, but not always, made in an assignment location, others are often made at home, and still others are made in third countries. Assignees will often try to demonstrate that they are unique and that standardized data do not fit their particular situations.

Despite these challenges, it is difficult to imagine equalizing goods and services expenditures without using standardized data; virtually every organization does so. The alternative is individual negotiation. When

U.S.-headquartered companies first introduced the balance sheet approach in the 1950s, the most popular source of such data was the U.S. Department of State. Today, a significant majority of companies obtain their data from one or more of a handful of specialized providers who tailor the data to meet the particular needs of their many clients and often for specific groups of expatriates within their client organizations.

Most expatriate goods and services data collection starts with a home-country expenditure-pattern survey that identifies a few hundred frequently purchased items grouped into 10 or more categories such as food at home, recreation, clothing, transportation, restaurant meals, and the like. Trained pricing specialists collect prices for each item in a variety of stores. For an unadorned expatriate pricing, prices of the same items (or as close to the same as possible) priced in the home country are collected by pricing specialists in most countries in the world and matched against the home-country prices. Price ratios comparing expatriate prices to home-country prices are developed for all items. Weightings, based on typical buying patterns, are applied. Tables (or diskettes or other delivery vehicles) are prepared showing how much more it will cost in each assignment location for expatriates of various family sizes and a wide range of income levels to live as closely to the way they did at home as possible.

Three different types of goods and services tables are often available:

- One showing typical home-country expenditures in home-country currency by income level and family size,
- A second reporting comparable host-country costs in local currency, and
- A third showing the differences between the first two tables after converting the second table to home-country currency—often called a "goods and services differential" or "cost-of-living allowance" table.

Tables calculated as just described produce goods and services differentials that are among the most generous to expatriates available. The calculations are based on the presumption that assignees will maintain their home-country consumption habits and make no attempt to adapt to less costly locally available goods and services. Recognizing that this methodology produces very generous subsidies, many companies (and a growing number) pay their expatriates allowances with what are sometimes called "efficient purchaser indexes" (EPI) data. EPIs are based on home-country spending patterns, but prices are collected abroad on high-quality local brands pur-

Exhibit 4-4. Goods and Services Differentials for a U.S. Expatriate Assigned to London—Salary: $8,000 per Month; Family Size: 3

Type of Table	Monthly G&S Differential	Difference Compared to Expatriate Standard (%)
Expatriate Standard	$2,308	
Efficient Purchaser	$1,748	$560 (24%)
EPI—No Private Transportation	$1,526	$782 (34%)

Source: *Organization Resources Counselors, Inc.*

chased in good local outlets instead of on home-country brands available in specialty stores catering primarily to expatriates.

In many countries, some or all employees benefit from certain perquisites that are not often available in other countries. For example, employees in Great Britain are generally provided company cars at much more junior levels than in the United States. This practice was started in Britain when it was much more tax effective to provide cars than the equivalent cash. Although this is much less true today than in the past, the practice has continued. It is always difficult to take away a perquisite once granted, even when the reason for it is no longer valid. Because of this, many U.S.-headquartered companies will provide their lower-level U.S. expatriates in Great Britain with company cars even though these employees would not be entitled to them if they were in the United States. It is rare indeed for these companies to offset this benefit by, for example, requiring their American employees to reimburse the company for the costs. In fact, this generosity is often compounded by giving unadjusted goods and services allowances that include additional compensation for the cars the company provides. The cost of this generosity for an American expatriate assigned to London who has a family size of three and a salary of $8,000 per month is illustrated in Exhibit 4-4. The savings using EPI data are $560 per month; eliminating the company car from the allowance, the savings are $782.

Actually, since the company would normally pay these allowances net of tax, the savings potential is even much higher. The objective here is not to be "unfair" to expatriates, as some claim, but to equalize expatriate purchasing power and be fair to both the company and expatriates.

Companies employ two different methodologies for protecting expatriates' goods and services purchasing power. Some pay cost-of-living allowances in home-country currency, as described above. This approach is consistent with the methodology that a majority of companies formerly used for protecting income taxes and housing. And it suffers from some of the same weaknesses: primarily, that any change in exchange rates precipitates, or should precipitate, a change in allowance. Those changes often prove challenging for administrators to explain—many don't even try.

Exhibit 4-5 illustrates the sequence that is followed in developing goods and services differentials (often called "cost-of-living allowances") and the impact of foreign exchange (FX) rates on those differentials. Note that

Exhibit 4-5. Goods and Services Differentials

	U.S. Dollars	Alphas
Home-Country Costs	(1) $10,000	
Differential	(4) 2,000	
Host-Country Costs	(3) $12,000	(2) A60,000

Steps to Calculate Differential (shown in parentheses in tables)

1. Determine cost of market basket in home country (US$)
2. Determine cost of same market basket in host country (Alphas)
3. Convert foreign cost to US$ (US$1 = A5) – A60,000/5 = $12,000
4. Host-Country Cost – Home-Country Cost = Differential = $2,000

Note: In practice, the differential is usually calculated by developing an index by dividing host-country by home-country costs (12,000/10,000 = 1.20, generally expressed as 120) and multiplying the index minus 100 over 100 times home-country costs (.20 x 10,000 = 2,000). But the result is the same.

Exchange Rate Changes from US$1 = A5 to US$1 = A4

Home-Country Costs	$10,000	
Differential	(2) 5,000	
Host-Country Costs	(1) $15,000	A60,000

1. Convert foreign cost to US$ at new FX rate – A60,000/4 = $15,000
2. New differential = $5,000 ($15,000 – 10,000 = $5,000)

Exchange Rate Changes to US$1 = A6

Home-Country Costs	$10,000	
Differential	(2) -0-	
Host-Country Costs	(1) $10,000	A60,000

1. Convert foreign cost to US$ at new FX rate – A60,000/6 = $10,000
2. New differential = 0 ($10,000 – $10,000)

as the FX rate moves from US$1 = A5 to US$1 = A4, a 20% strengthening of the fictitious Alpha relative to the US dollar, the differential increases from $2,000 to $5,000, a 150% increase. Under these conditions, assignees who do not understand the math are usually thrilled. If, however, the Alpha weakens to US$1 = A6, the differential completely disappears. When this happens, be prepared for some hostile e-mail. The reason for these apparent anomalies is that a change in exchange rate affects not only the differential but also the employees' contribution to goods and services (which is included in salary). To explain the impact of exchange-rate variation, some administrators send expatriates an explanation of the change using before-and-after tables similar to those in Exhibit 4-5. Absent such explanations, assignees cannot be expected to understand changes in their compensation, and they will consistently react negatively.

Other companies (and an increasing number) follow basically the same approach for goods and services equalization as they do for income taxes and housing: They deduct a home-country norm from salary and pay the amounts required for goods and services in the currency (sometimes *currencies)* with which expatriates will make purchases. Referring to Exhibit 4-5, this means deducting the $10,000 from salary and paying the A60,000 to the expatriate. Notice that neither of these numbers is affected by exchange-rate variation. This is often called the "split-pay approach." While this approach is generally easier for expatriates to understand and usually requires less administration, it is by no means trouble free, particularly for expatriates in countries with very volatile or rapidly depreciating currencies. And there may be other valid reasons for paying in one currency or another as discussed in Chapter 7 on expatriate practices. Despite these problems, the advantages of the split-pay approach generally outweigh the disadvantages, and we will use it to illustrate balance sheet administration below.

The Reserve

As previously described, the *reserve* is the amount left after taxes and expenditures for housing and goods and services. It includes a variety of expenditures that assignees would normally make in home-country currency such as tuition for university education of their children, savings, and investments. It is important to note that it also includes amounts for corporate benefit plans and any home-country taxes (Social Security, for example, if not part of the tax equalization calculation) that may be payable. The company typically pays the reserve into a home-country bank after deductions for such amounts as home-country benefits. Unlike taxes, housing, and goods and services, the reserve is not affected by different financial conditions in a host country. Following the split-pay approach described in the previous paragraph, it would be the only amount discussed so far that would be paid at home. Premiums and similar incentives, the subject of the next section, would also typically be paid into a home-country bank account.

Premiums and Incentives

The discussion of the balance sheet approach up to this point has focused on equalizing the purchasing power of expatriates to home-country levels. If these techniques are applied as described, expatriates should be about as well off financially as their home-country counterparts, at least during the early period of expatriation. As assignees gain experience and learn how to live more cost effectively, there is little doubt that they can live more graciously than they could at the same salary level at home. This is certainly true if companies use standard expatriate goods and services data, and it is even likely if less generous approaches, such as efficient purchaser data described above, are used.

But equalization of purchasing power is often not financially attractive enough to induce an employee to accept an overseas assignment. Accordingly, approximately three-fourths of North American corporations and even higher percentages of European and Asian companies offer additional financial incentives to expatriate. Historically, a higher percentage of North American companies paid expatriate premiums and more generous ones than at present. Some (and an increasing number) have recently taken the position that, in this period of globalization, employees should be pleased to work in other countries and that therefore financial incentives are not really necessary.

However, many of the companies that reject paying expatriate premiums end up compensating expatriates more generously than those that do pay them. Not necessarily and not always, but often these are the companies that continue to pay the most generous cost-of-living allowances and are liberal when approving expatriate housing. Not only are these "hidden" incentives very costly, but they are rarely appreciated by expatriates, who will ignore "excessive allowances" and point out that they are treated badly because they don't receive premiums as their counterparts employed by competitors do. The advantage of financial premiums is that they are clearly recognized for what they are: incentives to transfer and to work abroad.

Companies often pay other types of incentives to international assignees who work in difficult and/or dangerous places. It usually takes a greater incentive to induce an employee to move to Siberia than to Paris, to a war zone than to London, or to an oil platform in the North Sea than to Rome. These and many other issues related to expatriate incentives are discussed in greater depth in Chapter 7.

As previously mentioned, expatriate premiums and other incentives designed to encourage employees to move to a particular location (as opposed to performance bonuses, for example) are usually paid into an assignee's home-country bank account.

Balance Sheet Administration

To summarize this discussion of the balance sheet approach and to provide guidance to administrators, Exhibit 4-6 is provided as an example of a simple expatriate compensation worksheet. It covers a U.S. expatriate assigned to London, Jack Burns, married with one child and with a salary of $8,000 per month. Exhibit 4-7 is an extract from various compensation tables used to prepare Exhibit 4-6.

Note that, even using relatively restrictive data (EPI/no private transportation instead of standard expatriate; state and local taxes as well as federal; no monthly foreign service premium), this expatriate's *net* compensation in London is 65% higher than his *gross* U.S. salary. Using unadjusted standard data and comparing gross compensation figures, Jack Burns will cost the company significantly more than twice as much as a domestic counterpart. And this does not include any incentives, the cost of moving, any subsidies for his child's education, home leave, or the myriad other costs associated with expatriation. Note particularly the cost of housing in London, five times the U.S. norm; this is not at all unusual for limited-term rentals in major cities around the world.

Other Approaches

At the beginning of this chapter, several other approaches often used by companies entering the international arena were mentioned. All of these have serious drawbacks.

Exhibit 4-6. Expatriate Comparison Worksheet

Name:	Jack Burns	Date of Assignment:	February 1, 1999
Assigned to:	London	Salary:	$8,000/month
Family Size:	3		

Pay into U.S. Bank Account	
Salary:	$8,000.00
Hypothetical Tax Deduction (Federal)	(1,126.00)
Hypothetical Tax Deduction (State)	(379.00)
Social Security	(492.00)
Housing Norm	(1,412.00)
Goods and Services Norm	(3,112.00)
Reserve	$1479.00
Pay to Employee Overseas	
Housing	£4,334.00
Goods and Services	2,827.00
Total	£7,161.00
Total in U.S. Dollars (US$1 = £0.61):	$11,739.44
Reserve (from above):	1,479.00
Total Net Pay in US$:	$13,218.44
Mobility Premium (at time of transfer):	$16,000.00

Exhibit 4-7. Expatriate Compensation Worksheet

Monthly Salary	Federal Taxes by Family Size			Average State Taxes by Family Size			Social Security
	2	3	4	2	3	4	
$7,900–7,999	$1,207	$1,102	$998	$379	$373	$368	$490
$8,000–8,099	$1,230	$1,126	$1,022	$384	$379	$373	$492
$8,100–8,199	$1,254	$1,150	$1,046	$390	$384	$379	$493

Family Housing Data

Monthly Salary	U.S. Housing Norm	London Housing (£/$@0.61)
$7,500–$7,799	$1,375	£4,244/$6,957
$7,800–$8,099	$1,412	£4,334/$7,105
$8,100–$8,399	$1,449	£4,423/$7,251

Goods and Services Data—EPI/No Private Transportation (Family of Three)

Monthly Salary	U.S. G&S Norm	London G&S Costs (£/$@0.61)
$7,500–$7,799	$3,022	£2,746/$4,502
$7,800–$8,099	$3,112	£2,827/$4,634
$8,100–$8,399	$3,201	£2,909/$4,769

Source: *Organization Resources Counselors, Inc., January 1999*

A primary problem with *pure negotiation* is that the compensation of each expatriate will depend almost entirely on the negotiating skills of the negotiators. Consider Jack Burns, for example: He's married, with a daughter in high school and a wife who has a successful law practice in the United States. He convinces the company that, since his wife will not be able to practice law in England, the company should pay half her salary during their overseas assignment. Jack negotiates further, and the company agrees to pay his daughter's tuition in a private American school so that she will be able to advance to the next higher grade when she returns home. Now consider the company's negotiation position with Sally, who is single and has no children but supports her mother, with whom she lives. Sally can effectively argue that she should not be discriminated against and should receive payments equivalent to Jack's subsidies for his wife's salary and his daughter's education. After all, "The company doesn't care whether Jack's wife works in the United States and certainly would not subsidize private schools for his daughter. Why do so in England? They speak English, have excellent schools, and need good lawyers. So let's talk about the company supporting my mother." And so it goes. Often these additional payments, if agreed to, can be very difficult to eliminate when they are no longer appropriate. And they are very expensive. As a practical matter, Jack's and Sally's requests would at least be considered by most companies, but most would refuse to pay half of Jack's wife's salary and resist subsidizing Sally's mother. And if these are the only subsidies that they received, Jack and Sally would both be in serious financial trouble. The important point here is don't start to negotiate with potential expatriates unless you have a clearly defined policy or, at the very least, a clearly understood set of parameters within which to bargain.

Localization—that is, paying expatriates on a scale similar to locally hired employees in the country of assignment—can work well with some employees. But imagine Jack Burn's dilemma when he tries to rent a house or apartment in London and finds out what they cost. A 15% sweetener would not go very far. Localization is appropriate for employees who ask to be transferred and expect to spend several years, or even the rest of their careers, in the new country. Localization has been used successfully by companies for paying inexperienced employees who want to get their international cards punched before they get locked into family and professional relationships that will limit their mobility. And there is a small but increasing number of very senior global executives who are compensated on "local" scales but very generously, taking into consideration the taxability of various perquisites and compensation delivery vehicles in the assignment country.

But for more typical expatriates, such as Jack and Sally, who are assigned to another country for two to five years, then repatriated or transferred to another country, localization has severe limitations. In almost all cases, it involves paying additional "temporary" allowances for housing, for transportation, and often for education, taxes, and other expenses. The theory is that these allowances will be phased out over time, but, in practice, these phaseouts are frequently deferred or waived. A common expatriation model is for a company to offer an employee a three-year assignment that is to be followed by repatriation. Various allowances are paid during the three years, after which they are planned to be phased out. At the end of the three years, however, the company decides that it would like the expatriate to remain and approaches him or her with the following proposition: "We know that we agreed that you would be here for three years, but we want you to stay. You have done such a great job that the subsidiary has grown much more rapidly than we anticipated. And if you agree to stay, your allowances will be phased out and your compensation reduced." Tough sell.

Outsourcing versus Do-It-Yourself

As we move into the twenty-first century, many companies are restricting their internal staffing to "core competencies" and outsourcing other functions to specialized providers. A host of specialized organizations, many of them well qualified, provides companies with services for expatriates. There is little doubt that it makes sense to get help from specialized firms for issues such as expatriate tax planning and tax return preparation; immigration; physically moving expatriates to other countries; cultural briefing; benefits plan design; and a variety of other specialized activities. How much of the expatriate selection and compensation and benefits functions should be outsourced, however, is a subject of considerable debate.

If a company is new to the international arena, it is important to get experienced professional help in developing a basic expatriate strategy and designing a comprehensive set of international policies. But the ownership of that strategy and policy should clearly remain with the company. It is discomforting the number of times that we hear, "We didn't have anyone on the staff who understands expatriate compensation, so we outsourced it." This is a disaster waiting to happen.

In my opinion, responsibility for expatriate strategy and policy should never be outsourced. The important issue is to decide how much of the implementation of established policy should be handled by noncompany personnel.

Arguments in favor of keeping at least some expatriate administration within the firm include the following:

- Some hands-on administration is useful experience for policy designers.
- The person(s) responsible for coordinating relationships with outside providers should have a firm grasp of the providers' services and be able to assess their effectiveness.

- While some companies have outsourced all or most of their expatriate functions to a "full service" provider and have been very satisfied, others have found that they can get better service by being the "general contractor" themselves and coordinating the services of several more specialized providers.
- Expatriates should have a company human resources contact to whom they can turn when inevitable compensation and benefits questions arise. It is unreasonable for noncompany employees to respond.
- A company human resources representative should periodically visit overseas locations to field questions and interact with expatriates and local-national employees with the objectives of better understanding local conditions and improving company policies and support systems.
- Some expatriate compensation experience is useful in preparing employees for further responsibilities.
- It is unreasonable to outsource such important compensation decisions as salary determination, incentives, and package design.

Does this mean that all of the transactional details of expatriate compensation should be retained in-house? Not at all. But some companies do prefer to handle a significant portion of their expatriate compensation themselves rather than outsource it. Some have found that it is very difficult to find an outside provider with a sufficient understanding of the company's dynamics to be able to handle this important and complex activity effectively. In the next chapter, we will discuss the increasing complexity of these issues as companies expand to become major global organizations.

Review of Key Issues

This chapter has described some basic approaches to compensating expatriates. It has concentrated on issues of particular interest to companies first entering the world of global operations. The descriptive material on the balance sheet approach should be particularly useful for emerging corporate practitioners but also of interest to the growing number of administrators employed by specialized service providers. Throughout, the focus has been on employees expatriated from a headquarters country, with particular emphasis on the United States. In the next chapter, we revert to some of the subjects covered here but concentrate on options that companies should consider as they increase the size of their expatriate workforces and employ international assignees of several nationalities.

Further Reading

Reynolds, Calvin. *Compensation Basics for North American Expatriates.* Scottsdale, AZ: American Compensation Association, 1994.

CHAPTER 5

EXPATRIATE COMPENSATION STRATEGIES

CALVIN REYNOLDS

When a company first decides to "go global" and initiates its first operations abroad, it typically has two types of employees overseas:

- *Local nationals,* who are hired in each country where it has businesses, and
- *International assignees,* who are sent from headquarters to transfer technology and fill the managerial and technical gaps that cannot be filled adequately or that management, for a variety of reasons, may not want to fill with available local nationals.

Methodologies for compensating local nationals are described in Chapter 13 and in Section 4. How to compensate expatriates during an international start-up is the primary subject of Chapter 4. This chapter builds on the previous one and proposes several strategies for managing expatriate compensation as a company matures internationally from a single foreign operation to a fully integrated transnational corporation. It introduces additional methodologies and illustrates how to adapt some of the systems already considered to evolving business and staffing requirements.

As companies mature globally, they typically add several categories of employees to their international workforces:

- *Third-country nationals* (TCNs): Locally hired employees in one country transferred temporarily to a company location in another country other than the headquarters. For example, a French engineer employed by a subsidiary of a Canadian-headquartered company in France transferred temporarily to the Côte d'Ivoire to help set up a new operation.
- *Regionalists* (a subcategory of "third-country nationals"): Employees transferred temporarily to another country within the same geographic region. An example would be a Chilean salesman transferred to Argentina as sales manager. Often there is an issue of whether such

assignments are "temporary" or "permanent"; the compensation issues associated with this distinction will be discussed later.

- *Headquarters assignees:* Foreign nationals assigned to the headquarters country. Again there is a question about whether such assignments are "temporary" or "permanent." These employees and how to compensate them are discussed in Chapter 6.
- *Short-term assignees:* Employees sent abroad for periods shorter than the designated minimum length of an expatriate assignment, often one year, and usually without family.
- *Permanent transferees:* Employees transferred permanently or for extended open-ended assignments to another country.

A few additional observations on terminology may be useful. Just as many professionals, as I mentioned in Chapter 1, shun the term *expatriate* as demeaning and outdated (some have been known to spell it *expatriot*, terminology that certainly *is* demeaning), even more resist such designations as *third-country national* and *regionalist* for the same reasons. Indeed, I have avoided using *inpatriate* or *impatriate* in this guide, terms often used in place of *headquarters assignee*. A major problem with these vocabulary debates is that they often obscure the differentiation by categories that companies frequently use in paying employees. For example, "third-country nationals," "regionalists," and "inpatriates," and in deference, their employers, often resist these terms because they imply that these employees are different (and probably less well paid) than "international assignees" from headquarters. In most cases, they are right. Even if all of these employees are included in an overarching euphemistic category such as "globalist," the fact of the matter is that many of them probably are paid differently—and in most cases, the euphemism *differently* does mean *less*. For this discussion of compensation, it may be helpful to try to suspend your particular terminology preferences, justified though they may be, and focus on the concepts.

The entire field of expatriate compensation suggests the classification of employees and the identification of peer groups. As such, it is inherently discriminatory, particularly from the perspective of any group that is compensated less well than its perceived peers. This bothers many professionals around the world. It is understandable that there are many debates on the subject, with some pushing for equality, others emphasizing global mobility, and still others cost effectiveness. Consider, from a compensation perspective, a few possibilities:

- Who are the peers of a U.S. employee sent to Tokyo for three years? Her Japanese colleagues working at the same level in Japan or those who have comparable positions "back home"?
- Who are the peers of a German from Frankfurt employed by a corporation with headquarters in the United States assigned to Islamabad, Pakistan? His Pakistani colleagues at the same level in Islamabad? An American expatriate at the same level from headquarters? An assignee from London? Or his peers who are still working in Frankfurt?
- Who are the peers of a U.S. citizen employed by the subsidiary of a company with headquarters in the United States who has been living and working in São Paulo for 15 years and is married to a Brazilian executive? Brazilian nationals employed in similar positions? Other U.S. citizens living in Brazil for similar periods? Or U.S. citizens assigned to São Paulo for two years?

From a compensation perspective, any one of these answers could be defended. And often each of them is. But it is not very helpful for a compensation administrator to be faced with considering all of the possible options each time a person is selected for international transfer. The alternative to negotiation, anarchy, and chaos is a basic system, or at most a very limited number of systems, for paying employees who are transferred from one country to another. Some have announced that they have developed the "perfect" system, but experience to date suggests the Holy Grail of expatriate compensation has not yet been found—or is it likely to be. Too many depend on surveys and follow the majority or, with selectivity, believe that they have found the one "best practice." Or they simply "outsource the whole mess to a specialist who understands this stuff." It is more effective, however, to understand several systems that have been or could be developed, appreciate their strengths and weaknesses, and tailor a system or systems to the unique business and staffing needs of your company. The remainder of this chapter will describe some additional expatriate methodologies and provide analysis techniques to help you determine which approaches are most suited to your own corporate dynamics.

Third-Country Nationals

Assuming that you have an expatriate compensation system with which you are satisfied, one that is administered either in-house or by a specialist provider, you will arrive at a key decision point when you decide to transfer your first third-country national. Consider the case of a German transferred to London by a company headquartered in the United States. Will you compensate him or her the same way that you would compensate a British employee because, after all, this is a move within the European Union and "that's what we would do if we moved someone from Boston to San Francisco—and that's much farther"? Or will you compensate the German transferee the same way you would compensate an expatriate from the U.S. headquarters (as an American with a U.S. dollar salary and allowances such as the balance sheet approach described in Chapter 4, for example) on the basis that expatriates of all nationalities should be paid alike and you already know how to do that? Or would you tie his or her compensation to Germany and pay allowances following the same basic methodology as you would for an American but with a different base—"we don't know how to do that yet, but we can certainly find out"? Or would you consider one of the many other optional methodologies available? Note that each of these responses makes a different assumption about peer relationships:

- Local British compensation seeks equity with local peers.
- Paying the German assignee as an American emphasizes equity among expatriates of all nationalities.
- Using a German home-country balance sheet stresses the importance of maintaining home-country ties.

But none of these approaches satisfies the desire to ensure equity with all (or even more than one) of the several relevant peer groups. As a result, some practitioners devise hybrid methodologies that attempt to arrive at a viable compromise.

"Localization" and the "Higher of Home or Host"

To help appreciate some of the implications of these differences, consider some actual compensation numbers. A recent international compensation survey reported that a local manager in London (let's call her Melissa Blair-Jones) with a position comparable to Jack Burns (the American who earns $8,000 per month in the United States described in Chapter 4) would be paid £4,200 a month. A similar manager in Frankfurt (Hans Klein) might earn DM17,000 a month. Using the January 1999 exchange rate of £1 = DM2.81, the German manager earning DM17,000 currently receives the equivalent of £6,050, or 44% more than the typical British manager in a comparable position in London. This difference results from several factors: the relative costs of living in the two countries, the exchange rate, and the values that the two markets place on the job. A change in any one of these factors would influence the compensation comparison. All other things being equal, which they seldom are, Hans Klein might readily accept a transfer to London at his current German salary, but he would certainly resist being localized (i.e., paid a typical British salary). Melissa Blair-Jones, on the other hand, would reject out-of-hand an offer to work in Frankfurt at her British salary and, justifiably, would expect at least DM17,000, the fair market value of the position in Germany.

This discussion about Blair-Jones and Klein suggests a common approach to expatriate compensation on such transfers: the "higher of home or host." Employees transferred to lower salary countries retain their home-country salaries; employees transferred to higher salary countries are localized. Klein keeps his DM17,000 or, more accurately, he will receive £6,050. In both cases, however, and particularly on transfers to higher salary countries, additional allowances for housing, and possibly other expenses as well, are common and appropriate.

There are several advantages to the "higher of home or host" approach:

- It is relatively simple to administer. Once compensation is set, there is little ongoing administration. The transferee's compensation is typically managed by the location in which the employee is working.
- It establishes compensation equity with assignment-location peers, at least for employees transferred to higher cost countries.
- It works particularly well if a transferee remains in a host country indefinitcly or for many years.
- It is relatively low cost, assuming that a relevant proportion of employees are transferred to higher cost countries and are localized.

There are, however, several disadvantages:

- This approach usually requires maintaining a "home-country shadow salary," particularly for any retirement and other home-country benefit programs maintained, and a salary base for repatriation.
- Assignees resist returning home to lower salary structures.

- Every country offers a different standard of living. The financial attractiveness of each country is different, and assignees resist moving to countries with lower standards of living.
- The methodology may, but usually does not, take into consideration the impact of exchange-rate fluctuations on assignees' home-country obligations.
- If any allowances, housing for example, are paid, they should normally be phased out. As discussed elsewhere, phasing out allowances is almost always a challenge.
- Assignees on a series of international assignments without a designated "home" tend to accumulate the advantages of each country in which they work. A German, for example, throughout his international career, would try to maintain his high German salary and very generous vacations; if he moved to London, he would "acquire the permanent right" to a company car; after an assignment in Saudi Arabia, he would no longer expect to pay income taxes; and so on. Because there is no ongoing identified "home," each new country of assignment represents an opportunity to expand the entitlement base.
- Although it is more effective than some other approaches (most balance sheet formulations, for example) in establishing equity with assignment-country peers, it is less effective in equalizing purchasing power with other internationally mobile employees.

"Net-to-Net" and Other Refinements to Home/Host Compensation

"Net-to-net" is a common variant of "higher of home or host." Instead of gross, net-pay-after-tax-compensation comparisons are made between a home and host country. The advantage of this refinement is that it eliminates an important element of distortion. As shown in Chapter 8, income tax rates vary significantly around the world, and factoring out these taxes improves compensation comparability. Since tax rates in Germany and Great Britain are similar, however, this would not have a significant bearing on our options for Hans Klein and Melissa Blair-Jones. Even at the net-income-after-tax level, Klein earns over 40% more than Blair-Jones. But if we were considering a transfer from Saudi Arabia (with no income taxes) to Sweden (with income taxes exceeding 50%), taxes would be an essential part of the discussion.

Some companies introduce comparative purchasing power into the analysis. They adjust after-tax income for any differences in purchasing power between the two countries under consideration. This approach is often described as establishing "purchasing power parity," or PPP. The *Economist* periodically publishes a "Big Mac Index" that reports the cost of a Big Mac in several countries and thus offers the potential for establishing purchasing power parity among them. More seriously, several government agencies, consulting firms, and private research organizations provide broad-based data that make such comparisons meaningful.

Some advocates of this approach, most notably several major European companies, go through a full balance sheet calculation (as described in Chapter 4 and more fully below) to develop a host-country net pay. They then compare the net thus derived with the net pay of a comparable local national and "gross up" that net to arrive at an appropriate "local salary."

These refinements certainly improve the effectiveness of "higher of home or host compensation" approaches, but they still suffer from several, but not all, of the disadvantages described above. For example, these approaches obviate, or at least reduce, the problem of different standards of living. But they leave intact such troubling issues as the need to maintain shadow salaries, allowance phaseout, ongoing equity with home-country peers, the gain or loss on foreign exchange needed for home-country obligations, and entitlement accumulation. Some companies are very imaginative and have developed methodologies for mitigating the impact of some of these apparent disadvantages.

In cases in which it is expected that such transfers will be permanent or extended beyond five years, these home or host approaches have several clear advantages over a home-country-based system such as the balance sheet. They avoid most ongoing administration; their focus is on equity with local peers; and they are usually less costly. Over many years, most of the disadvantages cited above decrease in importance. There is significant evidence to suggest that, particularly during the early phases of internationalization, most companies pay very little attention to the repatriation of third-country nationals (even less than for expatriates from headquarters, and that certainly is not much) and therefore these compensation approaches may be desirable options. Balance sheet approaches are usually more effective for companies that have well-defined global staffing strategies, but such strategies are by no means universal. For companies that want to integrate business, staffing, and expatriate compensation, the several balance sheet methodologies described next should be considered.

Headquarters-Based Balance Sheet Approach

Chapter 4 described in considerable detail the application of the balance sheet approach to employees expatriated from headquarters. It introduced Jack Burns, an American with a wife and teenage daughter and a salary of $8,000 per month, assigned to London. In the preceding section of this chapter, we met Hans Klein, a German with a comparable position and a monthly salary of DM17,000; he too is married and has a 15-year-old son. And consider Eleanor McKenzie, a Canadian who is married, has a 14-year-old daughter, a position at the same level as Jack and Hans, and a salary of C$8,100 a month, competitive within the Canadian salary structure. All three will be assigned to London and will hold similar positions at the same level. And don't forget Melissa Blair-Jones, the English member of the same team whose salary is £4,200 a month.

Assume that you are the compensation manager responsible for developing the expatriate compensation packages of all three employees who are moving from other countries to London. You have sought the guidance of the vice president of international, who said, "Pay 'em all the same way." Since you have already figured out how to pay Jack Burns (see Chapter 4), you have interpreted "the same way" to mean "just like Jack Burns." Hans and Eleanor are both going to get salaries of US$8,000 per month (or at least in the same range) and about the same allowances as Jack.

If you follow through with this approach, ponder some of the challenges and reactions you will likely face as you proceed. Eleanor first objected to getting a lower salary than she already had ($8,000 instead of $8,100), but she quickly accepted that she would be much better off financially with the proposed package when you made it clear that you were talking about U.S. and not Canadian dollars—US$8,000 versus C$8,100. At January 1999 exchange rates (US$1 = C$1.52), US$8,000 = C$12,160. Eleanor will be getting a 50% increase in salary, and all of her allowances will be calculated on that higher base. The primary advantages of this approach are that two employees, both North Americans, working side by side at the same level in the same location will be "compensated equitably," and the data requirements and administration will be minimal. The disadvantages are that it is probably not necessary to increase Eleanor's salary by 50% to induce her to move, thus a very costly approach, and it will be difficult to reintegrate her into the lower Canadian salary structure when her assignment is completed. This assumes, of course, that the spread between

Canadian and U.S. salaries will persist throughout the period of her assignment—not necessarily a valid assumption. As a practical matter, most companies would not grant the full increase immediately but phase it in over time, contingent on performance and other factors. But note that this does not completely eliminate the problems of cost and reintegration.

You have a quite different problem with Hans Klein. Hans's monthly salary of DM17,000, at January 1999 exchange rates (US$1 = DM1.71), translates to US$9,942, or 24% more than you would expect to pay a U.S. counterpart. Considering that U.S.–based allowances will be added to salary, is it necessary or appropriate to pay this much for an intraregional transfer? Companies that use the headquarters-based balance sheet would address this dilemma in different ways:

- Some would "red circle" salary and phase in to a "more realistic" base over time.
- Others would conclude that the difference is not material.
- Some would factor out some or all of the difference by using less generous allowances and/or incentives on the basis that the transfer is intraregional.
- A few would look for another candidate.

The facts in these illustrations are not at all unusual. Even with the "simplicity" of the headquarters-based balance sheet approach in which expatriates of all nationalities are "paid the same way" and data requirements are minimal, there are several options to consider and frequent decisions to make.

The headquarters-based balance sheet, while not the most common approach, is often used by companies in the consumer products industries, usually in conjunction with other approaches discussed below, and by some major commercial banks. It works particularly well when there are expatriates of several nationalities on series of overseas assignments working side by side in multiple locations. Consider, for example, a case in which all of the employees we have introduced in this and the preceding chapter are working in Tokyo, they are all on their fifth international assignments, and none has worked "at home" for 15 years. You could expect some very serious objections from Eleanor and Melissa if their compensation was still not in line with that of expatriates from higher salary countries. After five overseas assignments and 15 years, "home" country loses significance—at least in terms of compensation. The headquarters-based balance sheet approach is expensive—it standardizes most elements of compensation at a high level—and it is difficult to convince expatriates who have it, particularly those from low salary countries, to give it up, repatriate, and return to their home-country salary structure. It clearly establishes that, from a compensation perspective, the relevant peer relationships are with internationally mobile employees of all nationalities—not with assignment-country colleagues (the *net* pay of the three assignees is nearly twice the *gross* pay of their local colleague, Melissa Blair-Jones) or with home-country employees.

Home-Country-Based Balance Sheet

Because of the disadvantages of the headquarters-based balance sheet cited above, most notably cost and resistance by expatriates from low salary countries to repatriate, many companies have adopted the home-country-based balance sheet. Indeed, it is currently the most popular of all expatriate compensation methodologies. The calculations are essentially the same as with the headquarters-based approach except that, instead of linking the compensation of all expatriates to the headquarters pay structure, all international assignees are linked to their respective home countries. Each expatriate has a home-country salary denominated in home-country currency and allowances to equalize purchasing power to that of their home-country peers.

Consider the employees already introduced in this and the previous chapter and their assignments to London. You will recall that their monthly salaries were as follows: Jack Burns—US$8,000; Eleanor McKenzie—C$8,100; and Hans Klein—DM17,000. Using the same methodology and the same type of expatriate compensation data that we used for Jack Burns in Chapter 4, their compensation will be as shown in Exhibit 5-1.

Note that, among the figures for the three expatriates, there are proportionately smaller differences in the net-pay figures than in gross compensation. There are three primary reasons for this:

1. The cost-of-living (goods and services) data reflect differences in the standards of living in the four countries (Great Britain and the three expatriates' home countries). Since the three expatriates are all foreigners living in London, you should expect these results.
2. The income tax rates are lower in the United States than in either Canada or Germany.

Exhibit 5-1. Three Expatriates in London
Home Country Balance Sheet Approach—Split Pay

	From U.S.A.	From Canada	From Germany
Pay into Home Country Bank Account			
Salary	US$8,000	C$8,100	DM17,000
Hypothetical Tax Deduction (Federal)	(1,126)	(1,711)	(4,772)
Hypothetical Tax Deduction (State/Province)	(379)	(815)	
Social Security	(492)	(173)	(1,631)
Home Housing Norm	(1,412)	(1,079)	(2,387)
Goods and Services Norm	(3,112)	(3,221)	(6,421)
Reserve	US$1,479	C$1,101	DM1,789
Pay to Employee in London			
Housing	£4,334	£4,334	£4,334
Goods and Services	2,887	2,169	3,062
Total Host Payment (£ Sterling)	£7,221	£6,503	£7,396
Total Host Payment (Home Currency)	US$11,739	C$16,152	DM20,539
Total Net Pay in Home Currency	US$13,218	C$17,253	DM22,328
Total Net Pay in US Dollars	US$13,218	US$11,351	US$13,057
Net Pay as Percent of U.S. Expatriate	100.0%	85.9%	98.8%

Source: *Organization Resources Counselors, Inc., January, 1999 data*

3. I used the same London housing figures for all three expatriates. In practice, most companies would pay actual rent and utilities, subject to limitations, in London. While there will be some actual differences, companies would rarely force expatriates of different nationalities at the same level in the organization to live in different kinds of housing (in terms of cost).

Advantages of the home-country balance sheet approach include the following:

- It allows for the maintenance of home-country salaries. It facilitates compensation comparisons with home-country peers and provides a base for pensions and other home-country benefits. It also obviates the need for "shadow salaries."
- It facilitates repatriation and reintegration into home-country salary structures at the completion of overseas assignments.
- It is less costly than the headquarters-based approach.

- Since it is the most popular methodology, it is often perceived as competitive and a "best practice."

On the other hand, some of its disadvantages include the following:

- It requires much more data and is more complex to administer than other systems are.
- It discriminates by nationality. Although this may be an advantage when employees are sent overseas on relatively short assignments followed by repatriation, it can raise serious issues by international assignees from low salary countries who have been on a series of international assignments over many years. This is the other side of one of the arguments in support of the headquarters approach.

The home-country-based balance sheet approach recognizes that, from a compensation perspective, the relevant peer group of all expatriates is their home-country peers, not expatriates of other nationalities or local-national colleagues.

Modified Home-Country Approach

Some companies, most notably in the petroleum industry, have recognized the advantages and disadvantages of both the headquarters and home-country balance sheet approaches and have developed hybrid methodologies.

One common model is often referred to as the "modified home-country approach." In most respects, the calculations are the same as the "pure" home-country approach just described. The one major difference is that, instead of using host-country goods and services data differentiated by nationality, one or an average of several nationalities is used as the standard. One option is to use headquarters data. A schedule of peer equivalents is prepared, and a table of allowances related to those peer relationships is developed. In essence, we have already done that by establishing that Jack Burns, Eleanor McKenzie, and Hans Klein are peers. If we use the United States as the base for calculations, Exhibit 1 will remain unchanged except for the host-country goods and services line and the totals in which host-country goods and services are included. These modifications are shown in Exhibit 5-2. All differences, compared to the pure home-country approach, are shown in italics.

Exhibit 5-2. Three Expatriates in London Modified Home Country Balance Sheet

	From USA	From Canada	From Germany
Reserve (home currency - from Exhibit 1)	US$1,479	C$1,101	DM1,789
Pay to Employee in London			
Housing	£4,334	£4,334	£4,334
Goods and Services	*2,887*	*2,887*	*2,887*
Total Host Payment (£ Sterling)	*£7,221*	*£7,221*	*£7,221*
Total Host Payment (US dollars)	*US$11,739*	*US$11,739*	*US$11,739*
Reserve (US dollars)	US$1,479	US$724	US$1,046
Total Net Pay in US Dollars	*US$13,218*	*US$12,463*	*US$12,785*
Net Pay as Percent of US Expatriate	*100.0%*	*94.3%*	*96.7%*

Source: *Organization Resources Counselors, Inc., January, 1999 data*

Following this methodology, the only compensation-element difference among the three nationalities, compared to the pure home-country approach, is the amount of reserve. Even though differences in base salary remain, the amounts paid in the assignment location are not differentiated by nationality. As a compromise between two other balance sheet methodologies, this approach has some clear advantages:

- As with the "pure" home-country approach, it preserves home-country salary.
- As with the headquarters approach, it equalizes compensation among the various nationalities, at least in the assignment location.
- Since it uses data for only one nationality, it is easier to administer and requires less information support than the "pure" home-country approach.
- Compensation costs are lower than they are under the headquarters-based system.

However,

- Compensation costs will usually be higher than with a pure home-country methodology. But note that, in this case, the German would receive less than he would under the pure approach.
- Repatriation will be a challenge because it means reducing the pay or grandfathering the compensation of assignees from lower salary

countries. This is less of a problem than under the headquarters approach, but often a challenge nonetheless.

- As a compromise between two systems, it is somewhat more difficult to explain to expatriates.

Some companies that have experimented with it have found that a lack of clarity in objectives has led to negotiation with expatriates, and they have reverted to a more pure system. But for others, the modified home-country approach works well, particularly for large project teams with many nationalities.

Lump-Sum, "Flexpat," and "Cafeteria" Systems

Two criticisms that have been leveled at the balance sheet approaches are that they are not as tax effective as they could be or as flexible:

- If less money is paid to expatriates on an ongoing basis, it is possible to legitimately avoid some foreign income taxes.
- Expatriates should have more freedom to spend their compensation as they see fit rather than have allowances for specifically identified categories, such as housing or education, that are lost if not expended for the identified purposes. Alternatively, or in addition, they should be able to choose from a list of optional perquisites or benefits rather than have them specified.

In the early 1970s, companies started paying "mobility premiums" as incentives to transfer to other countries.[1] These are lump-sum payments to expatriates before they start and after they complete overseas assignments. Mobility premiums are often used to replace traditional premiums, percentages of salary paid every month during assignments, which tend to be perceived as part of salary. The primary objective of mobility premiums, as the name suggests, is to encourage international mobility. But an additional benefit is that they are not paid during an assignment and hence do not ordinarily attract foreign taxes. This innovation has worked well, and today approximately one-third of North American companies, and more than a quarter of global corporations worldwide, pay their international assignees mobility premiums. This subject is discussed more fully in Chapter 7.

More recently, some companies have followed the same reasoning for other elements of over–base expatriate compensation such as goods and services and other allowances. For example, instead of deducting a goods and services norm from salary and paying an amount in local currency that will provide comparable purchasing power (as described above relative to the balance sheet approach), a company will pay a lump sum, usually in home-country currency, before the assignment to cover the higher costs of goods and services overseas. Generally, this does reduce taxes. It also provides expatriates with considerable expenditure flexibility and may reduce administration. It may also be embraced enthusiastically by expatriates in countries with currencies that weaken relative to their home countries'. They may be much better off than either they or the company expected. On the other hand, the lump sums may be insufficient to cover the higher costs overseas; this will be inevitable if home-country currency weakens. Essentially, this approach transfers foreign exchange risk from the company to the employee. A lump sum paid at the time of a transfer as a mobility premium works well because it is designed as an incentive to move. In contrast, allowances are paid to protect the purchasing power of an expatriate throughout an assignment. Since it is impossible to predict what economic conditions will be in the future, prepaid lump sums as allowances are sure to be either excessive or inadequate. Predictably, expatriates are pleased when the system works in their favor but rebel when it works against them. If it works against them, they often negotiate to recoup their losses. Some companies that have tried this approach have moved away from it when they found it was more expensive and more complex to administer than the system it replaced.

Another approach that has been tried is to combine all allowances and incentives, and sometimes taxes, into one overall lump sum paid on an ongoing basis, before the assignment as just described, or periodically (e.g., quarterly). The objective is to give expatriates the flexibility to spend their compensation as they see fit and avoid micromanaging expatriate finances. Theoretically, this should also reduce administration. It more closely reflects the way a company would handle compensation on a domestic transfer. There are, however, a few problems with this approach:

- As pointed out in Chapter 4, it is often more tax effective for a company to buy or rent housing in its name and provide the housing to an expatriate than it is to give the expatriate the equivalent cash. In countries in which this is true, Japan for instance, it is very costly not to factor housing out of the allowance. This leads to different policies for different countries.

- If differences in income taxes are netted out in the allowance, the problems associated with tax protection, described in Chapter 4, apply.
- If a change in allowance for any category of expenditure is justified by changes in economic conditions, that category will have to be separated from the overall allowance in order to explain the change.

This may not be an issue if the assignment-country currency strengthens and you increase the allowance proportionately. But, if you do not increase the allowance under these conditions, you will certainly be deluged with newspaper articles and economic statistics pointing out why you should. On the other hand, if economic conditions suggest a decrease in the allowance, you will either have to ignore the decrease, a probably costly decision, or be prepared to explain it by separating out the category affected. If you separate out the category to explain it, your "black box" is open. Some companies that follow this approach increase but never decrease allowances and thus preserve their black boxes. If all international assignments are very short and consistently followed by repatriation, this may be an acceptable trade-off. If not, this can be, and often has proved to be, a very expensive approach. Most companies that have tried these approaches have dropped them because of high costs and unanticipated problems such as those illustrated above.

Some companies, most notably in business services, follow a "cafeteria" approach to expatriate compensation. Instead of allowances for various categories of expenditures such as housing, country club memberships, company cars, and children's education, they provide a list of options from which expatriates can choose, subject to certain limitations. Several of these options in many countries are more tax and cost effective than cash. Some firms that have introduced this approach have been very pleased with it, particularly for very highly paid executives. Others, particularly those with significant numbers of middle management and lower level expatriates, have found it very difficult to develop meaningful lists of options. For example, consider how expatriates with different family situations would address the question of choosing two of the following three options: education for children in an international school, a company car, or a country club membership. For a senior executive, particularly one with no children, these choices are attractive. For a junior accountant with two children, the choice is often more difficult. Although very few companies have introduced cafeteria expatriate compensation programs to date, it is an approach that should be considered, particularly for senior executives.

Regional and Multiple Systems

Mature multinationals, particularly those that have significant numbers of third-country nationals on headquarters-based balance sheet systems, often find that their approach to expatriate compensation is dysfunctional. Why should we pay a German a U.S. salary and allowances to move to France? Or a Mexican a U.S. package for an assignment in Argentina? Some companies convert to a home-country-based system, but this conversion is not an easy one—a significant majority of current third-country nationals will either have to take a reduction in compensation, difficult at best and sometimes illegal, or be grandfathered with their present compensation. They often conclude that new transferees will be paid under a new system; current assignees will be phased in to it over time. This transition also illustrates why it is important to develop a sound international staffing strategy and a compensation system to support it before you have many third-country nationals.

Other companies have preferred to maintain their traditional systems and introduce additional methodologies for certain groups of employees with unique assignment patterns or other common characteristics. The questionable compensation packages of the German in France and the Mexican in Argentina, mentioned above for example, suggest one option: regionalization. Companies have introduced cost-effective systems for Europeans of one nationality working in other countries in Europe, for Asians working in other countries in Asia, and so on. These regional systems need not be uniform but reflect the unique needs of each region. For example, the Asian system may recognize the importance of subsidized housing, Latin America may offer hard currencies, and Europe may provide generous vacation policies. Europe may have a headquarters-based balance sheet system with the European headquarters as the base, whereas Latin America may use a net-to-net approach. In almost all cases, the regional systems will be less generous than the corporate headquarters-based balance sheet system, which may be retained for intercontinental transfers. Indeed, cost saving is usually one of the major reasons why such systems are introduced. Regional approaches make the most sense when there are regional management organizations to administer them. But before introducing regional systems, consider the following issues:

- Maintaining two expatriate compensation systems, particularly when there are expatriates working side by side under the two systems, is always problematic. Consider, for example, the situation in which the general manager in Belgium, a French woman, is paid less than a Canadian subordinate simply because she is European and the Canadian is from another continent and therefore compensated under the more generous headquarters plan. Negotiation is inevitable.
- Maintaining two plans is more costly than maintaining only one.
- Unless the number of intraregional transfers is significant and the number of regionalists large enough to represent a critical mass, it is difficult to justify an additional system.
- When there are two or more systems, it is extremely important to clearly define the criteria for being compensated under each plan. Exceptions will very quickly vitiate the effectiveness of the program.
- When two systems are managed by different organization units (for example, the interregional program by a headquarters group and the intraregional systems by regional management), they can easily move away from their original objectives. There are cases in which regional programs have become more generous than corporate programs as regional executives manipulated the systems they control for their own benefit.

Despite these challenges, some companies, particularly in the consumer products industries, have found regional programs effective, and significant savings have been realized.

In recent years, there has been the development of a group of senior global executives whose ties to particular countries are tenuous. Compensation systems, which link them to a home country, such as the home-country-based balance sheet, or to the headquarters, are not particularly relevant or cost-effective. Some companies have found that a more effective approach is to design a compensation package for each one that takes into consideration the tax laws of the assignment country and the unique financial needs of each executive. Some follow a "cafeteria" approach and offer a list of incentives and perquisites, subject to limitations, that may appeal to this group of executives. Such an approach is not usually practical for all expatriates within an organization and therefore is most easily justified as an additional compensation program for a limited number of very senior executives. Some of the same caveats that were identified for regional systems are relevant.

Historically, most multinationals have avoided sending young, inexperienced employees overseas as expatriates. They have limited expatriation to those who could "hit the ground running" and perform vital company functions. One of the major perceived barriers to expatriating junior and less experienced employees has been the high cost of expatriate compensation. Some companies have approached this challenge differently and have designed less generous compensation packages specifically for this group. Many aspiring globalists, before they are locked into professional and personal commitments at home, are willing to go abroad with "bare bones" or local compensation packages with the understanding that this is an important first step in a global management career. As with cafeteria compensation for senior executives, localization for entry-level and junior expatriates is a viable additional compensation methodology that has been and can be used in addition to a primary approach reserved for the majority of management, professional, and technical international assignees.

The key questions to consider before introducing any expatriate compensation system in addition to a primary methodology are as follows:

- Can you clearly identify a significant group of employees whose compensation requirements are unique and for whom your primary expatriate compensation system is inappropriate? It may be inappropriate for senior executives because it is insufficiently tax effective or inflexible; a cafeteria plan may work better. It may be too generous for inexperienced employees and cannot be cost justified; consider localization or other bare-bones approaches.
- Do the potential advantages or savings justify the inevitable costs and hassle of managing multiple systems?
- Do you have a critical mass of employees in the category for which you envision a separate compensation system?
- Have you anticipated the conflict and potential adverse effect on motivation that are likely to follow compensating one group of employees differently (particularly less well) than others?

Other Overseas Assignments

We have defined expatriate assignments as typically lasting from two to five years in one location, followed by repatriation or transfer to another country. These are the assignments for which the compensation policies we have been analyzing have been designed. But it is important to consider assignments that extend beyond the defined maximum or are shorter than the minimum.

Many companies extend their definition of *temporary international assignment* well beyond five years. Recently, I asked a group of international human resources managers for their definitions of *temporary,* and one replied, "For us, it's sixteen years." When questioned about how his company had arrived at such an unusual number, he observed that "We have a superstar who has been in Hong Kong for fifteen years and a turkey who has been there for seventeen." What this manager was recognizing was that, while his company had a policy that states that various expatriate incentives and allowances will be phased out after a stated number of years, they often waive the phaseout for outstanding performers but enforce their policy for less effective assignees. There is no doubt that it is often necessary to face such realities, but this type of reality is difficult to maintain over time and will become costly. Once exceptions start, they quickly become a habit. Since most expatriate allowances are predicated on assignments of limited duration, extending their length leads to expatriate windfalls and higher-than-planned costs. What are the options?

- Try to enforce assignment duration.
- Consistently enforce incentive and allowance phaseouts and minimize exceptions.
- If possible, anticipate which assignments are likely to be more than five years and design an enforceable separate compensation policy to cover those assignments.
- Recognize that the beneficiaries of these exceptions will become progressively less willing to give up their windfalls, less mobile, and ultimately very expensive to move to another location.
- Accept that some policy exceptions are inevitable and anticipate the high costs of these exceptions.
- Recognize that policy is rarely enforced and change it.

If it is possible to identify before an assignment starts that it will be permanent or very long term, it is desirable to localize the employee's compensation from the start. This is often possible when an employee asks for a transfer or understands beforehand that it is a permanent move. Under these circumstances, it is often appropriate to provide some onetime or short-term allowances to facilitate integration into a new country. But an expatriate compensation package such as those described above will become overly generous in three to five years. On this subject, it is important to point out a trap that some companies have fallen into: Do not assume that because someone is enthusiastic about working overseas they should be paid less than those who have to be "bribed" into going. This only discourages your best potential candidates from identifying themselves.

Assignments of up to six or nine months are usually treated as extended business trips, and expenses are reimbursed accordingly. Longer assignments that do not meet the minimum for expatriation are often treated as "short-term assignments," and a separate compensation policy is developed to cover them. Typical short-term policies provide either per diems or allowances that recognize that assignees will be living in furnished accommodations in assignment countries while still maintaining their homes in their home countries. Some consulting firms provide appropriate data for these assignments.

Outsourcing Versus Do-It-Yourself Revisited

In Chapter 4, I suggested that the outsourcing of many expatriate administrative responsibilities has advantages, particularly for companies new to international operations. Surveys have shown that the most common reason that companies outsource international human resources functions is that they lack in-house expertise. Given a lack of international experience and the great number of specialized functions, coupled with the typically small numbers of international assignees, outsourcing is very appealing. Early on, it would be virtually impossible for an emerging multinational to attract and fully employ all or even most of the necessary expertise in-house.

But as companies mature internationally, the dynamics change. It should be evident from the analysis above that expatriate compensation for companies with significant numbers of expatriates is certainly not a straightforward activity for which all the rules can be readily spelled out. It is not unusual for a single decision about the compensation of one expatriate to cost tens, if not hundreds, of thousands of dollars. While it is important to have as clear and comprehensive an expatriate policy as possible, a policy that supports your business and staffing strategies, a significant number of policy exceptions that require management attention is inevitable. It is vital to have open communication between expatriates and responsible decision makers about the reward systems that seriously affect motivation and performance. Delegating important expatriate compensation decisions to third parties can be counterproductive and costly. If there are many exceptions to policy and these exceptions are referred back to the company for resolution (which they should be), the provider simply becomes another step in the process, slows down communications and decisions, and adds to cost.

What these observations suggest is that, as companies globalize, they should develop significant in-house expatriate compensation expertise as soon as possible. They should develop clear policies that support their business and staffing strategies, even if they get professional help in the development of those policies. Transactional activities that can be standardized may be either outsourced or processed using one of the available computer programs, but the extent to which standardization is possible or desirable should not be exaggerated. (The strengths and limitations of technology are discussed more fully in Chapter 27.) Companies should maintain clear and open communications with expatriates about their compensation and avoid delegating policy development and exception management to third parties. One approach that some companies determined to minimize head count through outsourcing have employed successfully is to insist that their providers locate their employees on the company's premises. Where the line is drawn between managing expatriate compensation in-house and contracting it out to third parties is obviously a decision reflecting corporate culture and priorities. But expecting others to manage complex policies that a company neither understands nor supports is unlikely to be a successful approach.

Deciding Which Expatriate Compensation Policy or Policies Are for You

Expatriate compensation design often requires the delineation of peer groups and the analysis of career patterns. There is no one methodology that is "best" for all types of overseas assignments. Most companies try to standardize one approach to simplify administration. But, as they mature globally, many companies find that their methodology does not fit all of their needs. They either switch to an approach that more nearly does or

Exhibit 5-3. Expatriate Compensation System Criteria

Evaluation Criteria		Headquarters Based	Home Based	Modified Home Based	Host Based	Net-to-Net (for TCNs)	Cafeteria	Multiple Systems
Nationality of Expatriates								
HQ	**TCN**							
>95%	<5%	5	3	4	X	4	X	1
75	25	4	4	4	X	4	X	2
50	50	3	4	4	X	4	X	3
25	75	3	5	5	X	4	X	4
<10	>90	3	5	5	X	4	X	5
Number of Expatriates								
<10		5	2	3	2	5	X	1
10 – 49		5	3	3	2	4	X	1
50 – 100		4	4	4	2	3	X	3
>100		4	5	4	2	2	X	4
Organization Level								
Senior Executives		4	3	2	4	3	5	4
Management, Professional		5	5	5	1	3	3	X
Entry level, Trainees		1	2	2	5	4	1	4
Assignment Patterns								
One-time out and back home		2	5	3	1	3	3	3
Multiple overseas assignments		5	2	4	1	3	4	4
Facilitates Repatriation								
Assignees from HQ		5	5	4	1	2	2	X
TCNs		1	5	3	1	2	2	X
Permanent Transfers		1	2	2	5	3	4	X
Compensation Costs		2	4	3	5	4	4	4
Administration		4	2	3	4	4	3	2

Key: 5 = most effective; 1 = least effective; X = other factors more important introduce multiple methodologies. Exhibit 5-3 lists a number of criteria for evaluating expatriate compensation systems.

Note that different mixes of nationalities, numbers of international assignees, types of assignment patterns, and levels of responsibility all suggest different compensation methodologies. And each approach implies significantly different costs. Some professionals may disagree about the details of these evaluation criteria, but the important point here is that there is no one approach that will satisfy every company's needs or probably even satisfy all the requirements of a single company with large numbers of expatriates.

Note

1. Calvin Reynolds, "International Mobility and the Overseas Premium," Benefits International (London, April 1972), and "International Mobility Premiums: Three Years Later," Benefits International (June 1975).

Further Reading

Reynolds, Calvin. *Compensating Globally Mobile Employees.* Scottsdale, AZ: American Compensation Association, 1995.

CHAPTER 6

INTERNATIONAL ASSIGNMENTS TO U.S. HEADQUARTERS

JOHN DE LEON

Introduction

As organizations' dependence on cross-border commerce and global business relationships grows, the practice of attracting a broader spectrum of talented people with specialized skills and abilities to the headquarters country also increases and gains importance. Companies of all sizes search for and recruit foreign nationals residing abroad. Organizations with existing international operations take advantage of their diverse pools of talent by transferring employees from branches and subsidiaries to the headquarters country, on either a temporary or a permanent basis. This is becoming an important human resources tactic in the realization of a truly global business strategy, one that provides the advantages of blending cultures; expanding the breadth of managerial, language, and cultural skills in the workforce; and creating a work environment that draws on worldwide expertise and approaches.

Assignments to the headquarters country are not a new practice. But the number of such assignments has increased in recent years. For U.S.-based companies, a greater diversity and mix of nationalities addresses many objectives, including heightened sensitivity and awareness about things not uniquely "American."

This chapter will focus on the important steps a U.S.-based company should take to effectively manage these transfers to the United States, from assignment initiation to repatriation, including development of an appropriate compensation package linked to the objectives of the assignment. The issues are similar to those associated with moves to almost any headquarters country, but the appropriate solutions may vary greatly with the country of assignment.

Linking Compensation Strategy to the Purpose of the Assignment

According to the *1999 Survey of Expatriate Assignments to the United States*, conducted by Organization Resources Counselors, Inc. (ORC), about two-thirds of U.S. multinationals with 50 or more expatriates assigned to the United States (22 companies) have a formal policy for dealing with such assignments. About half of the other 142 U.S. companies, however, have no formal policy and, for the most part, administer such assignments on an ad hoc basis. We have also observed that many of these assignment packages are structured and administered without the involvement of corporate international compensation staff, which has the potential for inconsistencies and inequities.

When there is retrospective criticism of the pay and benefits package for an assignee to the headquarters country, it is often recognized that the purpose of the transfer was not fully understood and the subsequent assignment or potential for repatriation was not adequately predicted. The rationale for the assignment should largely determine the rationale that shapes the assignment package. Thus, it is important to articulate why the move to the United States is taking place and what the probability is that the assignee will return home at the end of the assignment or depart the United States for a destination other than the home location.

Typical Assignment Scenarios

Of the many possible reasons that an expatriate would be assigned to the United States or any other headquarters country, the five following scenarios are probably the most prevalent. Each has a "most likely" outcome, which in turn suggests a particular compensation strategy.

Scenario 1: Transfer International Business Culture and Know-How. Not many years ago, only very large multinational organizations sought international business skills offshore. Now, even relatively small companies may transfer seasoned foreign branch and subsidiary employees to the headquarters location in order to leverage their international business acumen for competitive advantage and sustained growth. The continuing emergence of free-trade zones and the disappearance of tariffs are resulting in global sourcing strategies that increase the interdependence of all company units, wherever the location. International transferees help accelerate this operational integration and other positive changes. By design, these assignments tend to be temporary.

Scenario 2: Acquire Critical Skills. The scarcity of specialized skills and abilities in the U.S. labor market has resulted in a large number of foreign-born hires and intercompany transfers. The best example of this can be found in the Silicon Valley corridor between San Francisco and San Jose, where a facility tour quickly reveals the strong dependence of the software industry on imported skills. Such transfers have a high potential for becoming long-term or permanent assignments.

Scenario 3: Career Development and Succession Planning. Succession planning in a global context requires casting a broad net to identify the strongest people needed to play major roles in a company's future. One of the success factors of very strong international organizations has been the attention given to facilitating multicountry work and living experiences. Bringing fast-track managers to the headquarters country enhances their ability to function more effectively because of direct and constant contact with the company culture. It is usually the intention to repatriate these individuals, who have gained enhanced networking capability, improved language fluency, and communications and presentation skills that are so critical to selling ideas and programs internally and externally.

Scenario 4: Short-Term Assignments. The objectives of Scenario 1, the transfer of business culture and know-how, and Scenario 3, career development and succession planning, can at times be accomplished with a short-term assignment. The usual duration of a short-term assignment is 3 to 12 months. Visits up to 3 months' duration are generally categorized as extended business trips. The many advantages of a short-term assignment include the possibility of a more clearly defined repatriation plan, a less costly compensation package, and a less complicated relocation process. The incidence of short-term assignments has grown steadily over past years.

Scenario 5: One-Way Move at the Employee's Request. At times, a branch or subsidiary employee will make a request to line management to be relocated to the headquarters country. More often than not, the line manager will ask the human resources function to define the terms and conditions of the transfer as though it were a company-requested transfer.

The expectations of the line manager and the employee must be carefully managed in such cases. Since the transfer is considered to be permanent, the terms and conditions of the transfer, with the exception of the visa requirements, should be no more complicated than those for a domestic relocation.

With respect to the expatriate's career plan, repatriation to the home country or other non-U.S. location is a more likely outcome of Scenarios 1, 3, and 4. Scenarios 2 and 5 have a higher probability for a long-term or permanent U.S. assignment.

Approaches to Designing Pay and Benefits

According to the previously cited ORC survey of expatriate assignments to the United States, most U.S. multinationals use a single approach to compensating these expatriates: 51% integrated them into U.S. programs (also known as localization), and 44% used the home-country balance sheet approach.[1] Only 5% used both approaches. Although the survey did not investigate the relationship between individual assignment rationale and compensation approach, it is reasonable to assume that companies that transfer several expatriates to the United States do so for a variety of reasons. Hence, a uniform approach for all headquarters assignments may not adequately accommodate the various scenarios described above.

Since most U.S. multinationals use the home-country balance sheet approach for their expatriates assigned to other countries,[2] it would appear that the companies that localize their U.S.-assigned expatriates compensate them differently from the rest of their expatriates. This could be a potentially inequitable approach unless the rationale for the U.S. assignments clearly necessitates a different arrangement.

As with assignments to other parts of the world, it is generally the case that a permanent assignment to the United States, or one that has a high probability of eventually becoming permanent, is best accommodated by localizing the expatriate to U.S. pay structures and programs. At the other end of the spectrum, a temporary assignment, in which the expatriate can expect either repatriation to the home country or an eventual transfer to another location, is best managed under the home-country balance sheet approach. Other scenarios can be effectively managed with modifications to one of these approaches.

Localization

A complete localization program entails full integration of the transferee into the U.S. base pay structure and into incentive, benefits, and pension plans. Partial localization programs can retain participation in home-country benefits plans, especially social security and pension, with the addition of selected expatriate benefits.

Complete Localization

Complete localization is the appropriate pay and benefits option when there is no relocation or repatriation plan for the employee, as in a permanent transfer or a one-way move at the request of the employee. The potential for errors in pay and benefits administration are minimal, since the employee's terms and conditions of employment fit the established U.S. pattern. Thus, the localization terms are internally equitable, and the employee is paid competitively in the U.S. labor market. Compensation package costs under complete localization are no higher than the costs of a U.S. employee, with the exception of transition payments and relocation costs. Exhibit 6-1 summarizes the recommended treatment of individual compensation elements in a complete localization package.

Complete localization should require the termination of the assignee's employment in the home country, with the employee submitting a voluntary resignation. The employee is then hired in the United States. This step serves to avoid ongoing employment status in the home country that would subject the subsidiary to continuing termination indemnity accruals and other employment-related liabilities. It also has the following potential consequences, from the employee's point of view, which require clear communication.

State and Company Pension Schemes. In the case of home countries with defined-benefit pension plans, the transferee may not be entitled to a vested benefit. If vested at the time of transfer, the probability is remote that the employee will receive a full pension from the home-country social system and subsidiary-company pension plan at normal retirement age.

For transferees not very close to retirement age, employers generally assume that the transferee will accumulate sufficient quarters of contribution in the assignment-country social security plan to qualify for either a full or reduced benefit. Companies with defined-benefit pension plans will

Exhibit 6-1. Complete Localization

Component	Suggested Approach	Advantages	Disadvantages
Base Pay	For transferred employees, consider setting base pay at a comp-ratio similar to the home-country pay range position; for new hires, fix pay at usual new-hire pay position.	Compensation is equitable when compared with peers. Employee fits nicely into ongoing salary-planning process.	Employees from countries with high salary levels may feel disadvantaged. People from very low-paying countries may be perceived by management as receiving a windfall.
Bonuses and Long-Term Incentives	Adopt same measures, targets, and payout opportunities as headquarters-country peers.	Establishes internal equity with headquarters peers.	Employees from countries with minimal pay at risk may try to negotiate a guaranteed bonus regardless of individual and business performance.
Taxes	Employee is subject to all applicable local, state, and federal taxes.	Company and employee are in compliance with tax laws.	People from low- or no-tax jurisdictions may object to lower net pay.
Social Security	Withhold all social taxes.	Employer is in compliance with applicable legislation, and employee earns entitlement to future benefits.	Employees from highly socialized countries may be dismayed by social security pensions lower than those anticipated from the home country.
Health, Welfare, and Savings Plans	Make employee immediately eligible for all plans, contingent on plan document limitations.	Employee is usually positively motivated with coverage in the new location.	Plan document language may require an eligibility waiting period.
Pensions	Enroll employee in headquarters-country pension plan.	Employee begins to accrue service toward future retirement in headquarters country.	Plan document may not allow credit for prior service with subsidiaries.
Vacations	Apply headquarters-country policy.	Establishes internal equity with headquarters-country peers.	Home-country entitlement could be much more generous.

give transferred employees credit for continuous service when the retirement plan rules and regulations allow this practice. In the case of defined contribution plans, benefit funding begins when the employer is placed on the U.S. payroll or at the next enrollment eligibility date.

Termination Indemnities. Some countries, particularly in Latin America, have legislated severance payments in cases in which a company terminates the employment. In some cases, a reduced payment is made even if the employee resigns. Customary practice is to request that the transferee resign from employment in the home-country legal entity and then pay severance only if legally required to do so. Even in the case of an employee-initiated resignation, some companies pay the leaving service indemnity when there is no company-provided home-country pension plan in place. This payment is viewed as equivalent to providing a vested pension payment. These payments are made prior to arrival in the United States to legally avoid unnecessary income tax consequences.

Provident Funds. A few countries, such as Singapore and Malaysia, use a defined contribution approach to fund state retirement pensions. Permanent transferees resign from the home company and are entitled to a deferred and vested provident fund payment at normal retirement age. An employee who requests continuation in a provident fund may not have been clearly informed that the company considers the transfer to be a one-way move.

Future Expatriations. Some permanent transferees to the United States subsequently become valued members of an international cadre and are reassigned to another country as expatriates. For U.S.-based companies, the usual practice is to treat these assignees as U.S. expatriates with the rationale that they are permanent U.S. employees and therefore entitled to the same treatment as U.S. nationals.

Transfers to Country of Origin. Some one-way transfers do not remain permanent and assignees return home. When home-country levels of pay and benefits are similar to U.S. levels, the customary practice is to transfer the employee back home as a local national. In the case of moves to lower-paying home countries, it is not unheard of, though not completely logical, to assign very senior people, such as regional and country managing directors, back to their home country with some U.S. remuneration components. An employee may attempt to negotiate a move back with a full

U.S. expatriate package of pay and benefits. While this may appear to be an expedient solution to demands for high levels of pay and benefits, the practice eventually creates internal inequities in the home country that the employer would not desire to maintain long term.

Modified Localization

The modified localization alternative may be the best choice for transfers that are intended to bring critical skills to the headquarters country and include no plan to repatriate the employee and in cases in which management believes there is some possibility that the U.S. assignment will become permanent. The objective of a modified localization program is to pay the assignee similar to U.S. peers and to provide benefits to help with real or anticipated economic challenges resulting from relocation. It usually includes some or all of the following elements:

- Base salary that replicates in the U.S. pay range the employee's current position in the home-country pay range
- Continued participation in home-country benefits plans
- A housing allowance (typically with no housing norm deduction—although such deductions are made for U.S. nationals expatriated to other countries—and with no reimbursement for costs associated with home-country home retention)
- Automobile assistance (typically reimbursement of part or all of a car lease payment)
- Reimbursement for the preparation of home-country and U.S. tax returns (tax protection is more appropriate than tax equalization in these cases)
- Annual home leave for the employee and dependents accompanying him or her on the assignment

Potential Issues with Localization Programs

Relocations from Countries with Low Levels of Compensation. Line management can be reluctant to approve a level of pay that is perceived as substantially higher in common currency terms. An increase to the higher rate of pay can be justified on the basis that the transferee and family should be able to live comfortably with a level of pay and purchasing power equivalent to U.S. peers.

Moves from Countries with Higher Compensation Practices. Some high-paying countries have expensive social and income tax structures, so it is advisable to compare both gross and net pay levels before presuming the transferee will be financially disadvantaged. It may be that, while gross pay is higher at home, net pay after home-country taxes is more in line with U.S. levels of compensation.

When net pay is adversely affected, the solution could be as simple as paying the transferee higher in the U.S. range. But when the home-country pay, converted to U.S. dollars, exceeds the maximum of the U.S. pay range, merely compensating at the higher pay level produces internal inequities most companies are not willing to live with. Some companies set pay at headquarters' levels and adopt a take-it-or-leave-it attitude. Others set pay at internally equitable levels and then pay a lump-sum relocation bonus to partially offset the difference. The timing and place of such a payment should be planned to maximize the tax effectiveness of the payment. A variation of the lump-sum payment is a position allowance payment equivalent to the difference between the higher home-country pay and the lower host-country compensation.

Home-Country Balance Sheet Approach

The home-country-linked program makes the most sense when the term of the assignment is identified (i.e., a temporary assignment) and there is a commitment to repatriate the transferee back home or to another international assignment, such as in Scenarios 1, 3, and 4. Employment status continues in the home country and the employee is also hired in the United States.

The home-country balance sheet approach has the following objectives:

- Provide a linkage of pay and benefits to the home-country company plans
- Confirm to the employee that there is an intention to repatriate in the future
- Facilitate subsequent international moves
- Provide continuity in accrual of benefits and entitlements in home-country social schemes
- Contribute to equitable treatment of all assignees from the same home country regardless of host-country location

Home-Country Balance Sheet Design

When a home-country balance sheet approach is used, the assignee remains in the home-country pay structure, which is the basis for determining salary and bonus potential. If the home-country pay structure is lower than the U.S. pay structure, additional compensation is provided in the form of either a cost-of-living allowance or a temporary adjustment to base pay to permit the assignee and family to maintain a reasonable standard of living. A "net-to-net" calculation (see Chapter 13 for an illustration) is a useful mathematical exercise for determining what level of adjusted pay would be required to allow the expatriate to maintain an equivalent standard of living while in the headquarters country (the United States or otherwise). The net-to-net calculation assesses the impact on gross pay of payroll and income taxes, housing costs, health insurance, and the goods and services differential.

Exhibit 6-2 summarizes the recommended treatment of individual compensation elements in a home-country balance sheet package. The home-country balance sheet option for assignment pay and benefits is usually structured to address the potential for financial hardship and to avoid the possibility of a monetary windfall. As long as the rationale of the policy is effectively communicated, employees view the results of this remuneration philosophy positively since they are generally well compensated with a home-country-based assignment package. When there are protracted negotiations with assignees, the issue is usually not the overall approach to pay but, rather, concerns about selective components of the package, such as the quality of subsidized housing or the value of an auto allowance.

Other Issues

When the transferee returns home as planned, the assignment is usually regarded as a successful one. The employee has developed closer ties with U.S. staff and operations and can more effectively network, all to the benefit of the company. There is also a better understanding of corporate culture, which is helpful in the accomplishment of business objectives. The repatriated employee, it is hoped, becomes a positive proponent of the corporate point of view. As a result of such an experience, many managing directors have enhanced their competitive position with respect to peers who remained home.

Exhibit 6-2. Home Country Balance Sheet Approach

Component	Suggested Approach	Advantages	Disadvantages
Base Pay	Link base pay to home-country salary structure.	Maintains equity with home-country peers and eases repatriation.	From a low-pay to a high-pay country, an equalizing cash allowance may have to be paid.
Bonuses and Long-Term Incentives	Treat similarly to home-country peers, although some bonus measures might be linked to headquarters country.	Approach supports and emphasizes links to home country.	May be perceived as unfair when headquarters-country peers receive richer bonuses or long-term incentives.
Taxes	Either tax protect or equalize to home country.	Preserves integrity of home-country net pay.	Tax policies are very expensive in terms of both service delivery and tax reimbursement costs.
Social Security	Use totalization agreements when available. Otherwise continue home-country contributions and reimburse duplicate employee social taxes.	Maintains continuity in home-country schemes, with no interruption of accrued entitlements.	When totalization is not an option, the reimbursement of social taxes can be costly.
Health, Welfare, and Savings Plans	Maintain participation in home-country plans. Enroll in headquarters medical plan to cover emergency and nonelective surgical events.	When medical situations require emergency care, employee and eligible family members are covered.	Potential exists for company-paid duplicate medical plan premiums.
Pensions	Maintain participation in home-country pension plans and either split pay to provide for employee contributions or establish a notional salary at home.	Employee experiences no interruption in pension accruals and receives a full home-country career pension at retirement.	In the case of contributory pension plans, employee may be required to remit funds on a timely basis to home-country plan administrators.
Vacations	Provide the higher of home- or headquarters-country vacation entitlement.	The employee is treated fairly when compared to home-country practice.	The assignee may enjoy a much greater vacation entitlement than peers in the headquarters country.

Component	Suggested Approach	Advantages	Disadvantages
Automobile	Provide auto allowance, especially when car is provided as a home-country perquisite.	Maintains consistency with home-country benefits package.	Headquarters peers may view practice as inequitable.
Dependent Education	Encourage use of public schools when they are acceptable for headquarters-country peers; otherwise reimburse private school costs.	Interruption of dependent children's education is minimized.	Some nationalities will react negatively to educating children in public schools because of language, home-country certification issues, or concern about personal security.
Cost of Living	Pay an ongoing goods and services allowance when costs are higher in the headquarters location.	The employee and family are protected from the effects of higher costs.	Possibility for frequent changes in goods and services allowances increases payroll administration tasks.

Unfortunately, career-path planning and design is at best an art, rather than a science, with a high probability of modification as time goes on. Frequently, a highly promotable employee is transferred to headquarters for a defined period of time, and, rather than repatriation, a series of new assignments materializes at corporate. The employee usually obtains permanent resident immigration status; the spouse, also now a permanent resident, embarks on a new career; and the children settle in and resist returning home. Meanwhile, the employee expects to continue to enjoy the benefits of a very expensive expatriate package and actively resists the inevitable elimination of expatriate pay and benefit components.

If the U.S. assignment becomes permanent, pay and benefits should be converted—sooner rather than later—from the home-country balance sheet approach to complete localization. This conversion is best accomplished by offering the employee only two choices: returning home or remaining in the United States on local-national status. Discussions of other options that involve elimination of some, but not all, pay and benefits components are almost always painful and protracted, usually requiring more time to design than the original expatriate package.

The best approach for avoiding such complications is to dedicate the time at the beginning of the initial relocation process to determine the probability of repatriation at the scheduled end of the assignment. If it appears that a scheduled repatriation is not probable, immediate localization at the time of the initial assignment is the recommended approach.

Relocation and Settling In

There is a general tendency to underestimate the personal requirements of employees and family members transferred on international assignment, which can result in unnecessary stress and obstacles to a smooth settling-in process. The assistance of outside vendors can be helpful in anticipating and finding solutions to the challenges faced by the transferred employee and family. (See list of vendors in Appendix B.) The availability of answers and clear communication to the employee will help to facilitate a smooth transition.

Visas and Work Permits—Immigration Strategies

Relocations to the United States will almost always require the approval of a visa that permits the employee to work and accompanying family members to reside temporarily in the United States. There are specific requirements for approval of work visas, most of which address the match between the job's specifications and the employee's educational background and prior work experience.

Most U.S. companies retain outside legal counsel to manage the visa application process. U.S. immigration law is neither complicated nor difficult to understand. The challenges are dealing with the bureaucracy and the high potential for delays and miscommunications if one is unfamiliar with the process. Professionals who are well versed in the visa application process and have up-to-date information on Immigration and Naturalization Service (INS) issues can usually obtain the necessary approvals in an efficient manner.

Usually, the visa conveys approval for only the employee to work in the United States. It is very rare for an accompanying spouse to qualify for a work visa. The proliferation of dual-career families and the barrier the visa poses to the spouse's working legally has resulted in an increasing number of rejections of offers to expatriate. This information is important to communicate to the family—during the familiarization trip at the very latest—so that the members can consider and evaluate the full impact of the assignment on the family.

Line management customarily expects the transferred employee to report to work immediately. However, the visa application and approval process can take weeks or even months. To require the employee to report for work while the visa application is in process may, in some instances, jeopardize the approval of the authorization to work.

To initiate the visa application process, it is necessary to compile all the information required for the INS application form. The prospective transferee should be advised about what documents and information to bring along on the familiarization trip to the United States so that the INS application can be completed without delay.

> [Note: Since most U.S. headquarters assignments are filled by managers and professionals, the following brief summary of immigration options is limited to these scenarios.[3]]

The immigration visas most widely used by U.S. corporations are the L-1A, L-1B, and H-1B nonimmigrant visa categories. Both L-1 and H-1 visa applications require at least a one-paragraph description of the specialized knowledge requirements associated with the job duties. Line management should provide sufficient information on the job content of the new position to sustain the argument that a non-U.S. national is needed to fill the vacancy.

L-1A Visa Category. The L-1A nonimmigrant visa facilitates the transfer of overseas branch or subsidiary employees to the United States to be legally employed on a temporary basis in executive or managerial assignments. Petitioners must have at least one continuous year of service with the company during the prior three years. Employees approved for entry into the country on an L-1A visa are allowed to work for up to three years, with the possibility of an extension to a maximum of seven years. When all requirements are satisfied, approval of an L-1A visa can be obtained in as little as 30 days. L-2 visas are issued to the accompanying spouse and dependent children, who are entitled to the same length of stay as the employee although not authorized to work.

L-1B Visa Category. This category has the same characteristics as the L-1A visa category except that it applies to an incumbent with job content involving specialized knowledge rather than content of a managerial or executive capacity. This visa is usually renewable up to five years.

H-1B Visa Category. This category allows prospective employees to enter the United States to perform a "specialty occupation" that generally requires at least the equivalent of a U.S. university bachelor's degree. A determination must be made that the wage offered to the prospective employee is equal to the prevailing wage or the actual wage paid to other workers similarly employed by the company, whichever is higher. Initial approval to work in the United States is for up to three years and may be extended to a total of six years.

Other visa categories are available for unique situations. When consulting an attorney specializing in U.S. immigration and naturalization matters, it is useful to provide very complete information on the nature of the assignment. On the basis of the facts and circumstances of the transfer, a nontraditional visa category may be recommended.

Assistance with Moving and Settling In

Professionals dedicated to assisting families in transition can satisfy most common relocation needs. Household goods movers in the country of origin have alliances with U.S. organizations that deliver and unpack furniture and personal effects. There is an extensive network of destination services people trained in orienting newly arrived families to the community, including finding suitable housing, schools, and medical facilities.

Tax Counseling. The employer should consider retaining an international personal income tax consultant to meet with the assignee during the familiarization trip. If the employee is considering the execution of personal financial transactions before or after the relocation, expert tax advice can help to legally avoid the unnecessary payment of taxes on personal income.

Because most countries' income tax reporting requirements are so complex, reimbursement of tax return preparation services for all assignment years is advised. For permanent moves, if only one benefit is to be provided for localized employees, preparation of income tax returns for the year of the move should be that benefit.

Language Lessons. Oddly enough, U.S. employers tend not to arrange and subsidize special English-language training for expatriates newly assigned to headquarters. It is assumed that the employee has a level of proficiency necessary to perform the tasks in the new job. Presumably, the children will become proficient in English at school. The spouse's degree of fluency is generally not considered. Enlightened employers evaluate with the transferred employee the need for special tutoring for the children and language lessons to help the spouse settle in more smoothly.

Business-Culture Orientation. Transferees from most countries will benefit from an orientation to U.S. work culture, interpersonal relationships in the workplace, and legislation addressing conduct between the sexes. What assignees consider normal and courteous behavior in the home country may be deemed inappropriate in the U.S. office environment. For example, people from Latin cultures should learn that physical contact between coworkers is less acceptable than it is at home. They should also understand that getting down to business immediately is neither rude nor indicative of a lack of interest in the personal aspects of business relationships—it is simply the way business gets transacted in the United States.

Home Purchase. When the employment commitment to the transferee and the nature of the visa are temporary, it is usually a mistake to support the employee's goal of purchasing a residence. If the visa is not renewed, leaving the employee with no option but to depart the United States, a forced-sale scenario will occur. An employee who purchased at the top of the market and is forced to sell at a time of declining prices will look to the company for financial assistance. A home sale may result in a profit but the U.S. dollar may have devalued in relation to the home-country currency, resulting in an overall net loss that the transferee may request the company to cover. In either case, these amounts can be significant.

Home Rental. Leasing living accommodations is the preferable solution to obtaining housing, but unfortunately many landlords view "foreigners" as suspect and unworthy credit risks. Prior to the familiarization trip, it is helpful for the employer's relocation coordinator to visit local rental agents to identify any barriers the assignee may encounter when leasing a residence. Because suitable housing options for incoming managers are limited in many rental markets, the renter is usually at a disadvantage. The involvement of corporate legal staff can be helpful in determining if the company can co-sign a lease. A few preparations such as these will assure that when the family finds the perfect rental property, all hurdles will have been cleared.

Expatriates promised a housing allowance might communicate a strong preference for housing in the most upscale neighborhoods. The employer may wish to identify the neighborhoods where the expatriate's U.S. peers live, then advise the destination services coordinator or real estate rental agent of the approved neighborhoods and price ranges.

Schooling for Dependents. When transferees lease homes in neighborhoods where their new coworkers live, the chances are that they will find the public school district acceptable. But any special schooling needs should be identified during the familiarization trip. Non-English-speaking children may be challenged in the early months of relocation, and classes on English as a second language (ESL) can be very helpful. Some parents may need financial assistance to contract for special tutoring during the first or second semesters, until the child's fluency in English improves. French assignees are more likely to ask about private schooling in their children's native language. It is best to determine the need to fund private schooling before finalizing the pay and benefits package with the employee.

Establishing Credit. Assignees to the United States often describe their status as "nonpersons" when dealing with a consumer environment that depends so heavily on credit references. Even if there is a credit bureau in the home country of the transferee, the information provided by the home country will not necessarily be useful in establishing an acceptable credit history. Even many of the large U.S.-owned international banks do not recognize and evaluate credit history from most of the countries where they issue local credit cards.

The usual solution to the credit dilemma is effective networking between the company's treasury function and a local bank. A company credit union, if one exists, might extend credit to the employee. At times, some credit card companies will relax credit standards when the company provides a letter explaining the circumstances of the relocation.

A short-term solution to the credit card dilemma is to authorize the employee to use the corporate credit card for personal purchases. However, the finance department is usually reluctant to approve this option because the company is exposed to greater risk. Also, this is not a solution for the credit-related needs of the spouse.

Automobiles and Insurance Coverage. Since the acquisition of automobiles is one of the first transactions transferees make, resolution of the creditworthiness issue is very important. Companies with experience managing transfers to the United States work with providers of fleet automobiles and car dealerships to facilitate the process. Many U.S. automobile insurance companies will place newly arrived assignees in the highest risk category, with correspondingly high premiums. However, some insurance companies have been known to reclassify the risk based on a certificate of insurability—including a record of any prior accidents—provided by the assignee's home-country insurance company.

Bank Accounts. To open a bank account, the transferee will typically need to provide a U.S. bank with identification in the form of a Social Security card or a W8 form (Certificate of Foreign Status) obtainable from the local office of the Internal Revenue Service.

U.S. Social Security Cards. U.S. payroll departments need Social Security numbers to properly report earnings and to remit payroll taxes to federal and local governments. Upon arrival, the assignee should visit the local Social Security Administration office to request a Social Security identification number. A copy of the document authorizing employment in the United States is required, together with evidence of date of birth and legal identity. The Social Security card is sent within two weeks, but the interviewer can provide the number by phone in 24 hours if the assignee requests this at the time of the initial visit.

Driver's Licenses. Many states now accept a passport and the entry visa as acceptable identification to request a driver's license. Only a few states still require a Social Security card as a piece of personal identification. There can be as many bureaucratic requirements as there are states and Department of Motor Vehicle offices. Experienced international relocation coordinators will visit the local licensing facility prior to the transfer to determine what documentation is required to establish identification. Some states still do not recognize the validity of a non-U.S. driver's license and may require that the assignee apply for a learning permit as a first step.

Conclusion

The problems that arise with moves to the U.S. headquarters can often be attributed to an oversight of human resources professionals and line managers in two important areas. Both are linked to the assignment-planning phase prior to the employee's arrival.

The first area entails the identification of the main reasons for the move—particularly the predictability of a permanent stay versus repatriation—and the choice of a compensation strategy best suited to that case. The two principal approaches to compensation and benefits, home-country balance sheet and localization, can be modified in many ways to fit the needs of the company and the assignee. A high chance of repatriation usually bodes for some form of home-country balance sheet compensation package. If there is no clear plan for return back to the home country, the best approach is immediate localization, in some cases with special one-time payments to offset any potential financial hardship that results from the relocation.

Either alternative or a variation of it can be the right solution as long as the resulting pay and benefits package supports the purpose of the transfer to the headquarters country and the career plan for the assignee. The best approach is to use common sense, make the solution fit the present assignment and future reassignment, and seek a balance between company requirements and the needs of the employee and family. The compensation package should be easy to administer and, above all, understandable and easily communicated to the assignee and line management.

The second area that is often overlooked is detailed planning for the move, with a concentration on visa and work-permit requirements, the identification of appropriate housing and schools, and a strategy for dealing with the almost inevitable problem that transferees encounter in establishing credit. Anticipation of the barriers to a successful relocation is the prevailing formula used by experienced human resources professionals.

Notes

1. See Chapters 4 and 5 for a detailed discussion of both approaches.
2. *1998 North American Survey of International Assignment Policies and Practices* (New York: Organization Resources Counselors, Inc., 1999).
3. The author wishes to thank the law firm of Ronald S. Shapiro, Northbrook, Illinois, which provided the information on visas and work permits.

CHAPTER 7

EXPATRIATE PRACTICES

JULIAN POLLARD

Introduction

This chapter presents an overview of current international assignment policies and practices. It provides a snapshot of how companies handle expatriate compensation issues in practice and how and why those practices have changed over time. The analysis focuses primarily on North American corporate practice but also includes European and Asian practices that differ significantly because of legal, cultural, or other factors.

The information contained in this chapter is based primarily on survey data published by Organization Resources Counselors, Inc. (ORC) and Employment Conditions Abroad, Ltd. (ECA). In particular, it draws from ORC's *1997–98 Worldwide Survey of International Assignment Policies and Practices* and ECA's *1997/98 Expatriate Salary Management Survey.* The ORC survey includes the responses of 649 North American, Asian, and European firms with a total expatriate population of more than 70,000. ORC has been conducting surveys on international compensation policies for more than 40 years. The ECA survey is based on 269 responses from a wide cross-section of international companies and organizations worldwide. Where data from other sources are reported, the source is indicated.

Expatriate Usage

Various factors contribute to the number of expatriates a company may have on assignment at a given time. Increased foreign investment by companies typically results in higher expatriate usage, as has been seen in the emerging economies of Eastern Europe and Asia. The need for expatriates to staff any particular operation depends primarily on the maturity of the particular foreign operation and the availability of a local skilled workforce. As overseas operations become firmly established and as they mature, the number of expatriates used to staff the business typically declines (as local-national employees replace expatriates). Expatriate usage typically remains

Exhibit 7-1. Nationality of Expatriates

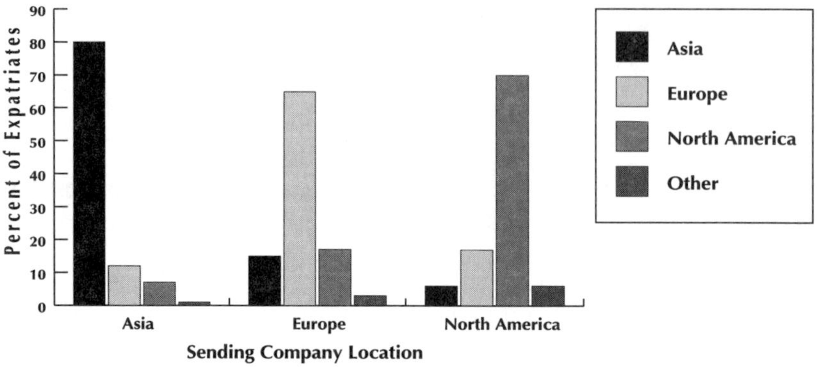

Source: *ORC 1997–98 Worldwide Survey of International Assignment Policies and Practices*

high in developing countries (where business skills tend to be lower) and in new operations in developed countries. The effort to localize a foreign operation may in fact result in a short-term increase in expatriation since local employees may be sent as expatriates to the headquarters location for training. The use of technology for better communications may in some cases reduce the need for expatriates in the future.

Survey data continue to show increasing use of expatriates. ECA's *Expatriate Salary Management Survey* reports that 66% of companies

Exhibit 7-2. Assignment Duration

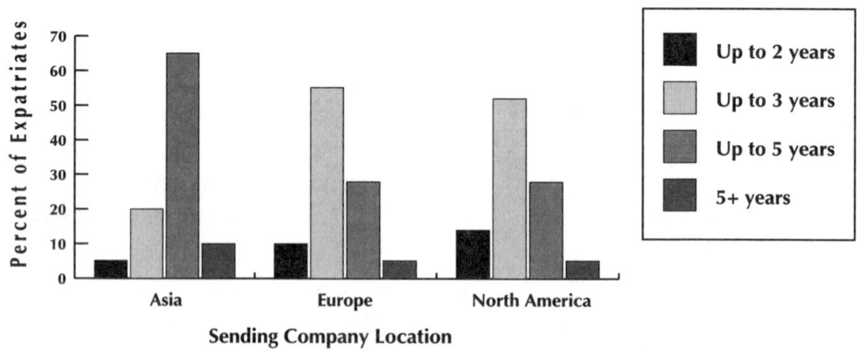

Source: *ORC 1997–98 Worldwide Survey of International Assignment Policies and Practices*

expect the numbers of expatriates to increase over the next three years. These figures include expatriates from the headquarters country and elsewhere. Of the ECA companies surveyed, 73% reported using expatriates of different nationalities. ORC's *Worldwide Survey* found that approximately 44% of North American firms expected to send more Europeans and North Americans on assignment, and 55% expected to send more Asians on assignment (see Exhibit 7-1).

The changes in expatriate demographics identified above pose issues of cultural and legal diversity, and companies may choose to treat expatriates differently on the basis of home country or to introduce a common approach or policy.

Assignment Categories

According to ORC's *1997–98 Worldwide Survey*, the majority of companies send employees abroad on a onetime basis with a planned repatriation. Seventy percent of North American, 61% of European, and 58% of Asian companies report that this best describes the nature of their expatriates' foreign assignments. Expatriates in this situation are typically sent abroad to fulfill a specific role, such as technology transfer, the establishment of a new office in the host location, and so on. Once the objectives have been met, the employee is usually repatriated.

European and North American firms prefer sending employees abroad on shorter assignments than Asian firms do (see Exhibit 7-2). This difference appears to be mainly the result of cultural and historical reasons. Asian expatriates have become more accustomed to being sent on long-term assignments (often single status—leaving the family behind).

Many companies distinguish three types of assignments on the basis of assignment duration.

Short-Term Assignment

ORC survey data show that there has been an increase in the use of short-term assignments over recent years. The ORC survey found that virtually all North American and European companies and the vast majority of Asian companies have a specific definition of *short-term assignment*. Most commonly, any assignment less than 12 months (but longer than an extended business trip) is considered short term. The ORC *Worldwide*

Survey found that 84% of North American companies, 58% of European, and 53% of Asian firms set an anticipated assignment length of 12 months as the cutoff between short-term and regular assignments.

Short-term assignments are often seen as a quick and relatively inexpensive way of getting an objective met. In addition, with the increase in dual-career couples (see below), short-term assignments in which the employee leaves the family at home are seen as an alternative to a long-term assignment. The ORC survey found that, by and large, families do not accompany employees on short-term assignments. More North American and European organizations than Asian ones have expatriates on short-term assignments (typically defined as one year or less). The percentages of expatriates on short-term assignment range from 9% in Asian companies to 16% in North American and 19% in European companies, according to ORC.

More than 80% of European and North American respondents have terms and conditions for short-term assignments that are different from those for business trips or expatriate assignments. Asian firms provide fewer incentives and trips home for short-term assignments than do their European and North American counterparts.

Standard Assignment

The most common length of standard expatriate assignment is three to five years. This seems to be generally considered the longest amount of time that an employee can or should be sent on assignment if the intention is to maintain the employee's ties to the home country. According to ORC's *Worldwide Survey*, 53% of North American companies and 55% of European companies typically have assignments of up to three years. As noted, Asian companies tend to send employees on longer assignments. Sixty-five percent of Asian companies report that their typical assignment length is up to five years. In the ORC survey, 17% of companies in North America reported a trend toward shorter assignments.

Indefinite/Long-Term Assignment

Some companies have an additional assignment category for indefinite-term assignments. In many cases, employees on such assignments may be treated as permanent transfers or be subject to localization procedures. According to ECA's *Expatriate Salary Management Survey*, 48% of companies have a policy to phase out expatriate terms and conditions if the expatriate assignment exceeds the planned length. In some cases, the ECA survey found, the transfer to indefinite status is determined from the outset of the assignment. In many cases, however, the employee starts off as a regular expatriate employee and, after many years in the assignment location, is converted to different assignment terms, either gradually or in one fell swoop.

Some companies further differentiate expatriate assignments based on the type of employee. This is founded on the assumption that different incentives are required to attract different types of employees. The organization may need to be more generous to attract an established senior executive for an assignment than it would to attract a young hire whose future career growth may well depend on international experience. Although no formal survey data are currently available on multitier policies, such policies typically differentiate among two or three different types of assignee categories, often senior executives, managers and experienced professionals, and entry-level and technical employees.

Conditions of Employment

Policy Communication

Expatriate policies are rarely static. In the ORC *Worldwide Survey*, fully 55% of companies said their policies were under review, had recently been reviewed, or would be reviewed in the near future. Although formal survey data about the main reasons for review do not exist, policy changes may be needed to make the organization more cost-effective, to deal with employee equity issues, to be competitive with market practices, to implement new technology, and so on.

There are various ways that companies communicate policy to employees. It seems that North American companies are typically wary of creating binding legal relationships, feeling that these could restrict the company's flexibility to change assignment terms and conditions and, where necessary, terminate employees. North American companies are most likely to express assignment terms in a letter of understanding (used by 79% of companies in the ORC survey). In many cases, the letter of understanding will explicitly retain the employer's right to amend policy at any time. Although North American firms wish to clearly communicate

Exhibit 7-3. Communication of Expatriate Terms

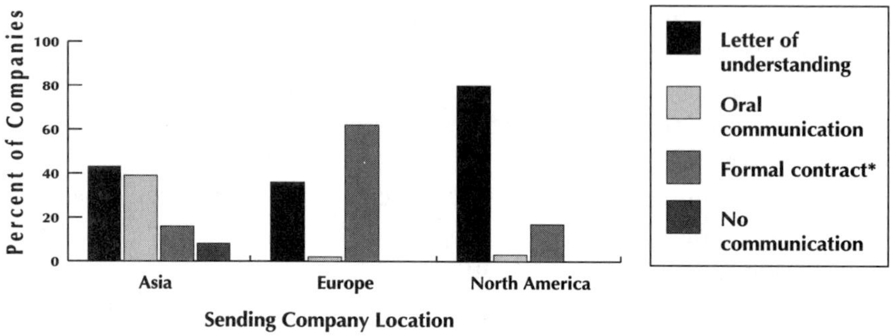

*or variation of existing contract

***Source:** ORC 1997–98 Worldwide Survey of International Assignment Policies and Practices*

policy, they generally do not want to create a potentially binding agreement with their employees. In contrast, corporations based in Europe (where employment contracts are generally provided to employees and considered to be legally binding) tend to list specifications for expatriates in formal contracts. Expatriate contracts in Europe can therefore be viewed as extensions of the domestic contract. Asian firms in the ORC survey are split fairly evenly between orally communicating expatriation terms and conditions to their employees and using a letter of understanding to do so (see Exhibit 7-3).

Expatriate Selection

Anecdotal sources suggest that HR involvement in expatriate selection is certainly a goal of most corporate human resources departments but that HR managers generally have little input in candidate selection. Not surprisingly, most companies in ORC's *Worldwide Survey* report that employees are selected for expatriation overwhelmingly on the basis of skills or competencies and job performance. Other indicators of the likelihood of assignment success, such as prior international living experience, language abilities, and familiarity with the assignment country, are typically a distant secondary consideration (see Exhibit 7-4).

Some HR departments, however, have become involved in the selection process. Psychometric and preassignment testing is used at least occasionally by 10% of North American companies, according to ORC's *Worldwide Survey*. Of the North American companies that use such screening,

Exhibit 7-4. Factors Used Worldwide to Select Expatriates

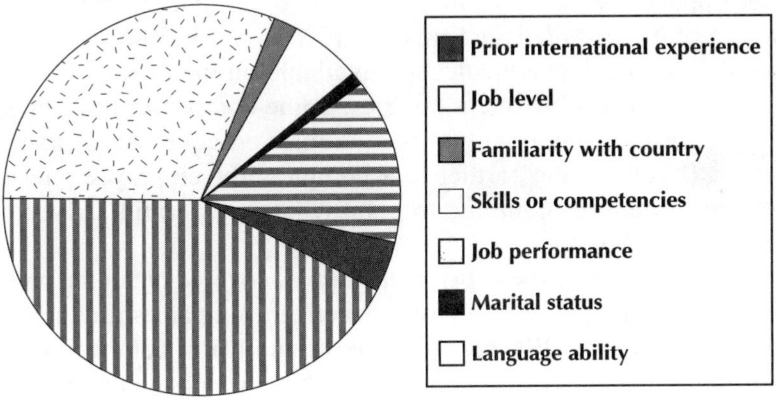

Source: *ORC 1997–98 Worldwide Survey of International Assignment Policies and Practices*

50% also extend it to include the expatriate's family. ECA's *Expatriate Salary Management Survey* (which has a higher proportion of European companies than the ORC survey) found that 34% of companies conduct preassignment tests to help select expatriates. According to ECA, psychometric tests are used in 69% of cases and competency-based testing is used in 58% of cases.

Although no formal survey data are available, a number of companies have instituted "candidate self-selection" programs that allow employees to formally express an interest in taking an expatriate assignment. Some HR departments have made a concerted effort to educate line management on the expatriation process, assignment costs, and candidate selection tools and to communicate the expatriation process to current employees.

Definition of Family

When developing an expatriate policy for the first time, companies may not give full consideration to defining the terms that they are using. It is particularly important to define terms to avoid ambiguity. The majority of companies specifically define the terms *spouse* and *family*. In North America and Asia, the majority of companies (approximately 64%, according to ORC's *Worldwide Survey)* follow a strict legal definition of *spouse* to include only a lawful wife or husband. European companies are much more likely to include a long-term partner of the opposite sex than are North American companies. Fifty-one percent of European companies include opposite-sex partners in their definition of *spouse*, compared with only 13% of North American firms and 19% of Asian firms.

No widespread data are currently available on the inclusion of same-sex partners under assignment policies. Some companies have included same-sex partners, although (as with unmarried couples) in practice it may be difficult for the partner to accompany the employee on assignment. Most countries continue to grant residency permits only to legal spouses and children.

Some companies define *dependent children* covered under the policy as children under age 18 (18% of North American companies use this definition, according to the ORC survey). A large number of companies expand the definition to include dependent children at school or attending a recognized college or university at the undergraduate level (46% of North American companies). Approximately 15% of North American companies extend policy coverage to other persons living with and supported by the expatriate. This compares with 7% of European companies and 39% of Asian companies. The broad definition of *family* by Asian companies is indicative of the traditional Asian respect for the extended family.

Cultural Orientation and Language Training

Cultural orientation programs are primarily intended to enhance expatriation success by improving an expatriate's understanding of and comfort with the differences in culture, living conditions, and business environment that he or she will encounter in the foreign location. Orientation training also provides an opportunity for employees to withdraw themselves from consideration for an expatriate assignment if they feel they will experience problems adapting to the host location.

Approximately 43% of companies worldwide provide formal cultural orientation training to their employees, according to ECA's *Expatriate Salary Management Survey*. ORC's *Worldwide Survey* shows that the percentage of North American companies, at 63%, is somewhat higher than what the ECA survey showed for worldwide usage, indicating a higher degree of acceptance of such programs in North America.

In many cases, training is conducted internally using company personnel who have experience with the host location. Written materials such as *Craighead's Country Reports*, videos, and other guides are also often used. According to ORC's survey, in approximately 42% of cases, external consultants conduct orientations for North American companies. The ORC survey found that European and Asian companies are less likely to use formal programs. A significant proportion of assignment failures is attributed to family adjustment problems, and most North American HR managers include the entire family in any program that is offered, according to the ORC survey. European and Asian companies typically include the spouse or domestic partner but are more likely to exclude children. Some organizations exclude young children who may not benefit from such programs but do include teenage children.

ORC's *1992 Survey on Clients' Use of Cultural Orientation Programs*, which had 220 North American participants, found that expatriates and their companies considered cultural orientation highly successful in improving assignment satisfaction and success levels. The major obstacle to increased usage of orientations was found to be the cost or the small size of some companies' expatriate population. Many companies in the survey reported that the decision about who receives orientation often ultimately depends on how different the assignment country is from the home country. For example, North American employees being sent to Western European locations (particularly the United Kingdom) are less likely to be offered an orientation than are employees sent to Asia because the cultural difference is often considered to be less extreme.

Most programs are comprehensive in the topics they cover, according to the survey. Exhibit 7-5 shows topics in order of their inclusion in respondents' programs.

Exhibit 7-5. Topics Covered in Orientation Programs

Social etiquette, custom	100%
Economy, history, politics	93%
Business protocol	90%
Domestic topics	89%
Practical information (e.g., banking, shopping)	85%
Coping with stress	85%
Medical issues	82%
Education system	82%
Dress codes	77%
Women's roles	75%
Food and diet	67%

Source: *ORC 1992 Survey on Clients' Use of Cultural Orientation Programs*

Practical areas are generally considered most useful. This includes such things as shopping, opening a bank account, social customs, and etiquette. These are seen as the kinds of things that allow the employee to "hit the ground running." Orientation topics considered of least importance are the historical, political, and economic backgrounds of the host country. Although they may be considered of interest, these topics do not teach the skills that employees can use in those difficult first few months in the assignment location.

ORC survey data show that most companies provide language training to employees when deemed necessary. This may be done in the home location prior to departure, in the host location, or both. Training is typically limited regarding total cost or number of hours of formal education. Again, North American companies are most likely to provide language lessons to the entire family. ORC's *Worldwide Survey* found that 84% of the 91% of North American companies that offer such lessons include the whole family. Asian and European companies are more likely to exclude family members; however, the majority still do provide such training to the entire family.

Medical Examinations

Health issues are an important concern for most employers and expatriates. In many locations, medical care may be inadequate by Western standards. Should a problem arise, the cost of medical evacuation can be very high. Most companies would prefer to identify health problems before the commencement of the assignment rather than risk a medical emergency or incur the costs of replacing an expatriate who falls ill while on assignment. Approximately 42% of North American companies always require medical examinations for the expatriate prior to an international assignment, according to ORC's *Worldwide Survey;* in most cases, this requirement is extended to include family members. Eighty-five percent of Asian companies require such examinations. Many of the companies that do not require medical examinations strongly recommend and pay for them.

Dual-Career Issues and Other Barriers to Employee Mobility

Resistance to relocation often arises when employees give domestic circumstances and family life precedence over the career opportunities arising from the assignment. Barriers to employee mobility include things such as elderly parents (a problem that will become more common as the population ages), disruption to children's education, undesirability of the assignment location, inadequate compensation, and so on.

A 1996 joint ORC/Confederation of British Industry (CBI) worldwide survey, *Dual Careers and International Assignments*, showed that the expatriate world is still very male dominated. A significant number of organizations reported that more than 90% of their expatriate population is male. This means that, in general, expatriate spouses are still women. Recent decades have witnessed the increasing participation of women in the workforce, the dependence of couples on two incomes to maintain their standard of living, and an increasing number of female professionals. Consequently, issues such as disruption to a spouse's career and loss of income are being raised with increasing frequency when employees are asked to go on assignment.

Disruption of a spouse's career is clearly an issue even in the case of domestic employee relocations. Issues such as the availability of work permits for spouses and cultural isolation make this even more of a problem for international transfers. Almost 70% of companies in the ORC/CBI survey said that issues of working spouses or partners are being raised more frequently as barriers to international assignments. More than 46% of companies stated that these concerns were resulting in more employees refusing an international assignment. Even so, only 38% of companies have a written spouse/partner assistance policy included in their assignment policy. Forty-two percent of companies take a more informal or ad hoc approach. North American companies are less likely than their European or Asian counterparts to address these issues either formally or informally. The most popular assistance options among North American companies are shown in Exhibit 7-6.

Not one company in the survey offered total financial compensation for loss of a spouse's or partner's income. The potential expense to the company of providing reimbursement could be immense. For this reason, as well as equity between married and unmarried expatriates, companies shy away from providing such assistance. Only a very small percentage of companies offered partial financial compensation, and the maximum that was offered (by one North American company) was four months' salary.

Very few companies keep records on employees' reasons for rejecting international assignments or on why they fail. The ORC survey found that only 20% of companies keep records on rejection and 23% keep records on failure. Knowing why employees are reluctant to take assignments or

Exhibit 7-6. Provision of Spousal Assistance

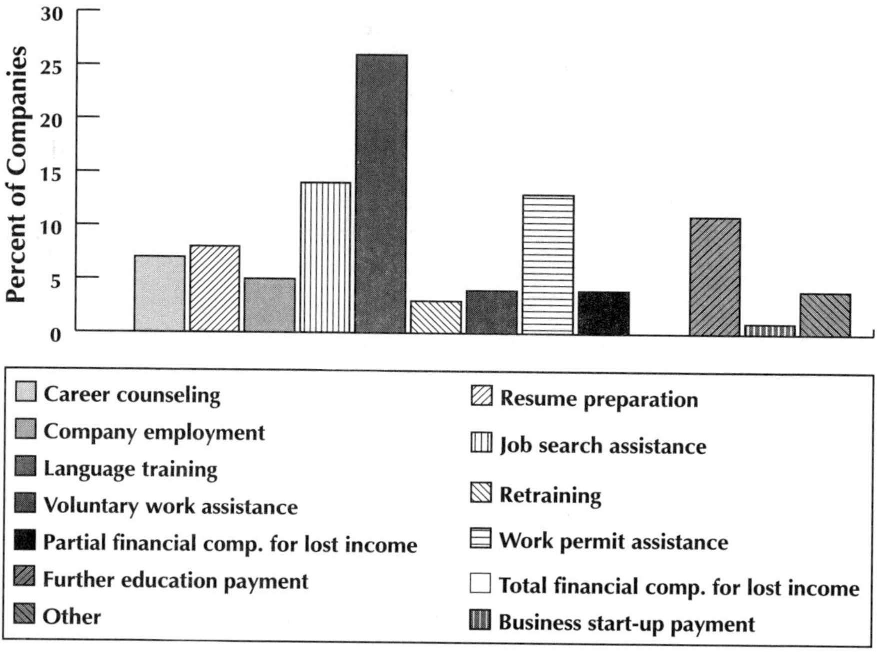

Source: ORC/CBI Dual Careers and International Assignments

why they fail while on assignment is an important first step in developing an effective policy to address barriers to employee mobility.

Remuneration

One of the most important steps in the development of any expatriation policy is the determination of the organization's compensation philosophy, which is discussed in Chapter 5.

Localization/Host Pay

Localization (or host pay) involves paying expatriate employees at a compensation level equivalent to that of a local national in the same or similar position. Although there has been some discussion of the merits of a host-pay approach to expatriate compensation, survey data show that very few companies have implemented this concept, except for permanently transferred employees or employees on extremely extended duration assignments. A small number of companies also use this approach for compensating some entry-level expatriates on developmental assignments. ECA's *Expatriate Salary Management Survey* found that those companies using a localization approach cited a goal of achieving consistency/equity with the expatriate or local market rate. Some companies also cited the need to control costs.

Less than 6% of North American companies and only 1% of Asian companies have adopted a host-pay approach, according to ORC's *Worldwide Survey.* The approach is somewhat more widespread within Europe; approximately 11% of European companies said that their approach for transferring Europeans within Europe is to fit expatriates into the assignment-location salary structure. According to ECA's Expatriate Salary Management Survey, approximately 7% of companies worldwide use a host-pay approach.

Home-Buildup or Balance Sheet System

The home-buildup or balance sheet system remains by far the most common approach to expatriate compensation (see Exhibit 7-7). It is used by the overwhelming majority of North American companies (between 80 and 90%, according to the ECA and ORC surveys) and is used by more than 70% of Asian and 60 to 70% of European companies. The home-

Exhibit 7-7. North American Expatriate Pay Policy

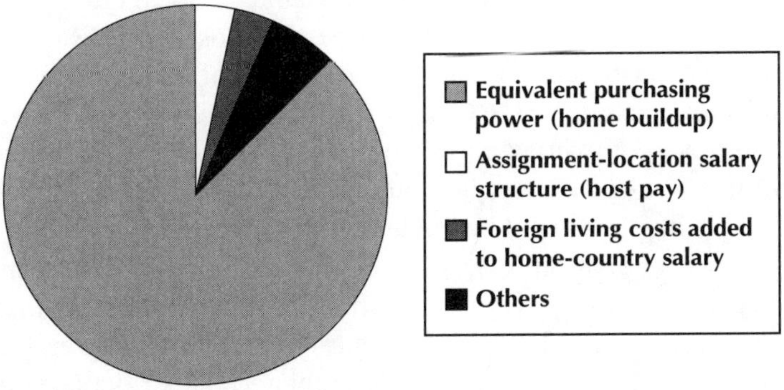

Source: *ORC 1997–98 Worldwide Survey of International Assignment Policies and Practices*

buildup approach allows for the maintenance of a home-country base salary during the course of the assignment and ensures that, during time abroad, the employee neither gains nor loses financially compared with his or her home-country peers. In ECA's survey, two-thirds of respondents who use home buildup cite this as a major reason for its selection.

Companies sometimes choose to use more than one approach. European companies in particular compare compensation packages under both a localization system and home-buildup system and then pay the higher of the two. This approach is used by approximately 12% of European companies for at least some of their expatriates, according to ORC. ECA, which surveyed primarily European companies, found that this approach applied to approximately 25% of companies and reported that this figure has increased in recent years.

A home-buildup approach can take a number of forms. According to ECA, 22.4% of companies use headquarters-based or one-country-based balance sheets and 16.8% of companies use a modified home-country-based balance sheet.

Compensation Delivery

Once companies have determined how to calculate expatriate compensation, they must then decide how to deliver that compensation. Survey data show that the most common approach is to pay a portion of total compensation in home-country currency and a portion in host currency. Many companies refer to this method as a "split-pay" approach. However, technically, *split pay* refers to the practice of deducting home-country norms for taxes, housing, and goods and services from salary and paying housing and goods and services host-location spendables in local currency.

North American companies tend to be the most flexible in allowing employees to determine the nature of the portion of compensation paid in home and local currency. ORC's *Worldwide Survey* found that 58% of North American companies allow compensation to be split according to the expatriate's wishes. European and Asian companies tend to be less flexible, requiring that a split be made in accordance with company policy.

As indicated in Exhibit 7-8, the second most common compensation-delivery approach is to pay compensation entirely in home-country currency. This may be perceived as being administratively simpler, but it can in fact create increased complexity as exchange rates fluctuate. A small percentage of companies pay entirely in host-country currency; this cre-

Exhibit 7-8. Remuneration Delivery

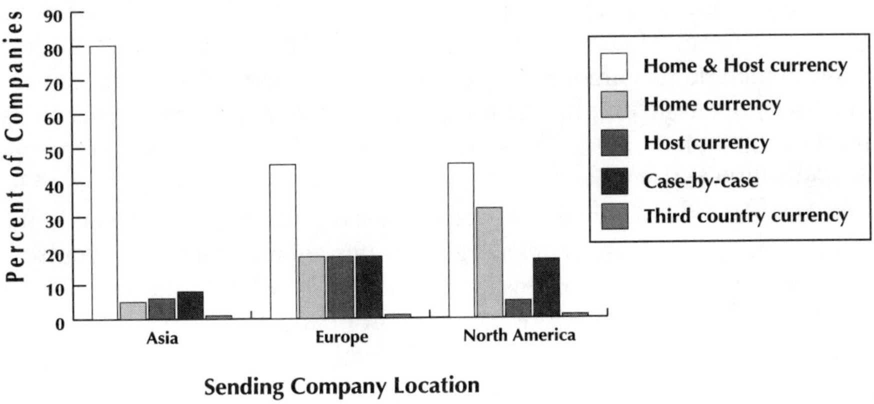

Source: *ORC 1997–98 Worldwide Survey of International Assignment Policies and Practices*

ates similar exchange-rate problems if the employee needs to convert a portion of compensation into home-country currency to meet ongoing financial obligations at home. A significant number of companies address delivery of compensation on a case-by-case basis.

Goods and Services Allowance/COLA

Survey data indicate that very few companies attempt to undertake the complex and time-consuming task of developing cost-of-living allowance (COLA) data in-house; rather, they typically use data provided by an external consultant. Increasingly, ORC surveys have shown attempts by companies to be as cost-effective as possible. Companies have reduced allowances in developed locations on the premise that it may be easier for employees to become accustomed to the local market and live more cheaply. ECA reports that more than 50% of companies expressed concerns over cost containment and that, over the last three years, 51% of companies have modified one or more elements of their compensation packages. In 21% of cases, this change was in the type of cost-of-living index used. Of those companies that modified COLA, 35% changed to cost-effective indexes and 10% reduced the items covered in the index. ORC's *Worldwide Survey* reports that 46% of companies use their efficient purchaser index (EPI) where available.

A further 38% of companies modify the index in some way, according to ORC. Indexes are typically modified to exclude certain items that the company is reimbursing for separately. For example, if the company pays for car expenses, domestic service, or a furnished apartment, it may not want to include this amount in COLA. In some cases, companies choose not to compensate for the additional cost of certain "sin" items (e.g., tobacco and alcohol) or items deemed luxuries or unnecessary (e.g., domestic service).

When the cost of living is lower in the assignment country than in the home country, North American organizations are reluctant to deduct from an allowance or total compensation, whereas 40% of Asian and 37% of European organizations make some form of deduction. Japanese companies in particular are likely to make a deduction from an employee's pay. Since Japan is such a high cost-of-living location, many Japanese nationals find it cheaper to live when sent on assignment. If the company deducts this saving from compensation, the employee does not receive a windfall. Making the deduction is in keeping with the home-buildup/balance sheet approach, since it ensures that the employee is kept on a par with home-country peers. Most North American companies, however, find it difficult to explain to management and employees that they will receive reduced compensation, so they simply let the employee receive the windfall.

The vast majority of companies do not set a maximum (cap) on the goods and services allowance; 89% of Asian, 82% of European, and 79% of North American firms have no maximum, according to the ORC survey. Companies that do cap typically either choose a maximum reference base salary (e.g., $150,000) or set a maximum on the allowance itself. Maximum allowance levels seem to be typically imposed as a cost-containment measure; however, some companies apparently justify the policy on the basis that COLA is intended to cover day-to-day expenses and not to subsidize a luxurious lifestyle.

Because the cost of living in any particular location changes over time as a result of currency fluctuations (this is an issue only for those who do not use a "pure" split-pay approach), inflation, changes in consumption patterns, and so on, the majority of companies in the ORC survey update allowances during the course of the assignment. European companies distinguish themselves as being the least likely to update allowances during the course of the assignment. This is partly because allowances are sometimes set in the expatriate contract.

Exhibit 7-9 indicates how North American companies handle COLAs.

Exhibit 7-9. Update of COLA—North American Companies

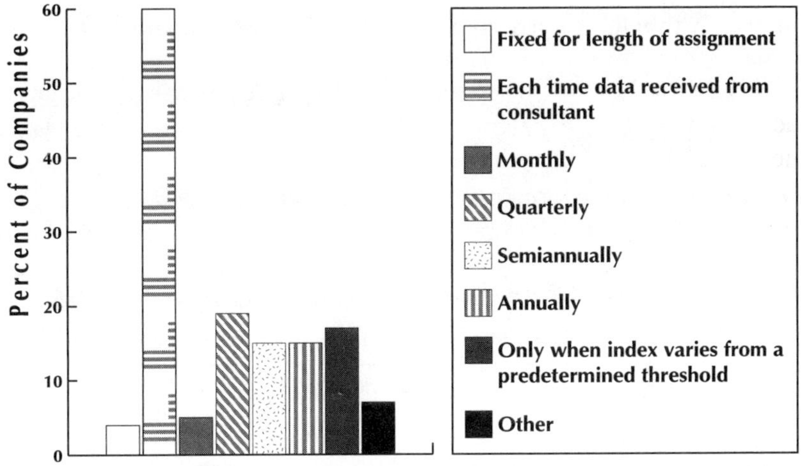

Source: *ORC 1997–98 Worldwide Survey of International Assignment Policies and Practices*

Premiums and Incentives

The practice of paying expatriation premiums has received increasing scrutiny in recent years. The majority of companies, however, continue to pay such premiums. Typically, premiums are paid as a separately identified element of compensation on an ongoing basis during the course of the assignment.

For moves within the same continent, 58% of North American firms pay a premium, as do 73% of European companies and 84% of Asian firms, according to ORC. Not surprisingly, the percentage of companies providing premiums for moves from one continent or region to another is higher still. Seventy-three percent of North American firms, 79% of European companies, and 87% of Asian firms pay a premium. (See Exhibit 7-10.)

There has been a small trend toward decreasing premiums in recent years. Companies are questioning the need for premiums in certain developed locations, for certain regional transfers, and in cases in which an international assignment will significantly improve the employee's future career prospects with the company. ORC's surveys show that, in the last two years, 8% of North American firms have generally decreased the

Exhibit 7-10. Typical Premium Amounts as a Percentage of Base Pay

For moves within the same continent (by company nationality):

Asia	Europe	North America	Total
22%	17%	13%	17%

For moves from one continent or region to another (by company nationality):

Asia	Europe	North America	Total
22%	22%	16%	19%

Source: *ORC 1997–98 Worldwide Survey of International Assignment Policies and Practices*

premium, while only 4% reported an increase in the premium. The trend is even more apparent among European companies: 14% reported a general reduction in premiums, while only 1% reported an increase.

There has also been a trend away from the ongoing foreign service premium and toward the payment of lump-sum premiums (often referred to as mobility premiums). ORC's survey shows that 7% of North American and 8% of European firms have initiated a lump-sum payment in the last two years. Typically, payments are made at both the outset and completion of the assignment. The lump-sum mobility premium is viewed as a way to reward expatriates for having met certain assignment criteria (in some cases payment may be tied to specific performance goals) and to encourage them to undertake additional assignments. In addition, mobility premiums are often more tax efficient than the typical ongoing foreign service premium. Exhibit 7-11 shows the percentage of companies using various premium approaches for interregional transfers.

Exhibit 7-12 shows the average percentages of base pay used to calculate lump-sum mobility premiums for transfers within the same continent and to another continent.

Hardship Allowance

Evaluating the hardship that an expatriate will experience in any particular location is extremely subjective and difficult to do. Most organizations

Exhibit 7-11. Percentage of North American Companies Using Various Premium Approaches for Interregional Transfers

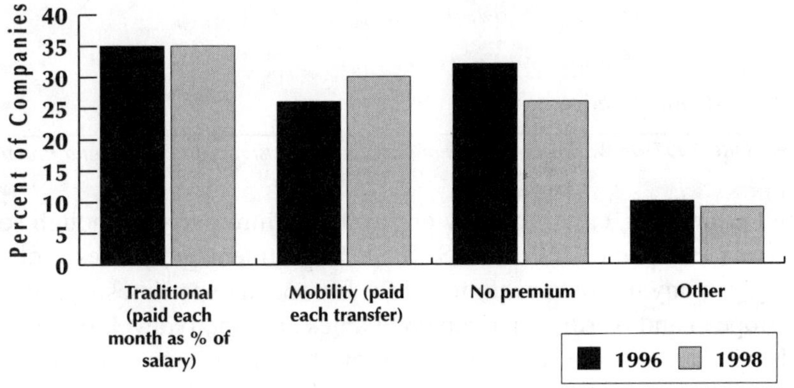

***Source:** ORC 1997–98 Worldwide Survey of International Assignment Policies and Practices*

want a reliable, simple, and consistent system for doing this. For this reason, many companies look to external organizations to provide advice. Approximately 70% of European and 80% of North American firms use external resources and/or consultants to evaluate hardship locations, according to ORC. Most North American firms use data provided by the U.S.

Exhibit 7-12. Percentages of Base Pay to Calculate Lump-Sum Premiums

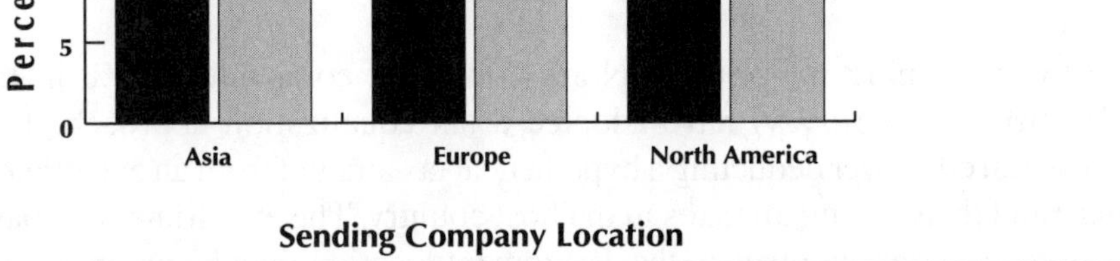

***Source:** ORC 1997–98 Worldwide Survey of International Assignment Policies and Practices*

Exhibit 7-13. Percentage of Companies Capping Hardship (by Company Nationality)

Asia	52%
Europe	40%
North America	37%

Source: *ORC 1997–98 Worldwide Survey of International Assignment Policies and Practices*

State Department, either directly or through a third party. Although some European companies follow U.S. State Department guidelines, not surprisingly, many use data customized for European expatriates. A minority of European and North American companies attempt to develop their own hardship data. This is actually the most common approach for Asian companies; fully 55% of Asian companies in the ORC survey report that management determination is the basis for hardship levels.

Hardship (for countries that warrant it) is typically calculated as a percentage of base pay, and survey data show that most organizations pay the same percentage for hardship in a particular host location regardless of the employee's nationality. A small minority (17% of North American firms, according to ORC) use separate hardship schedules for each nationality or group of nationalities with similar characteristics. This would allow a company to distinguish, for example, between expatriates assigned to China from Hong Kong and from the United States. This methodology assumes that it will represent a greater hardship for the U.S. national. A minority of companies place a limit on the amount that can be paid as a hardship allowance. (See Exhibit 7-13.)

Income Taxes

Tax Policy

The overwhelming majority of North American companies (91% in the ORC *Worldwide Survey)* have adopted a tax equalization approach. This involves an employer deducting a hypothetical tax amount from an expatriate's salary and then paying all taxes in the host country. The expatriate then pays no more or no less in taxes in the assignment location than he or she would have paid in the home country. Approximately 6% of North American firms

Exhibit 7-14. Expatriate Income Tax Policies

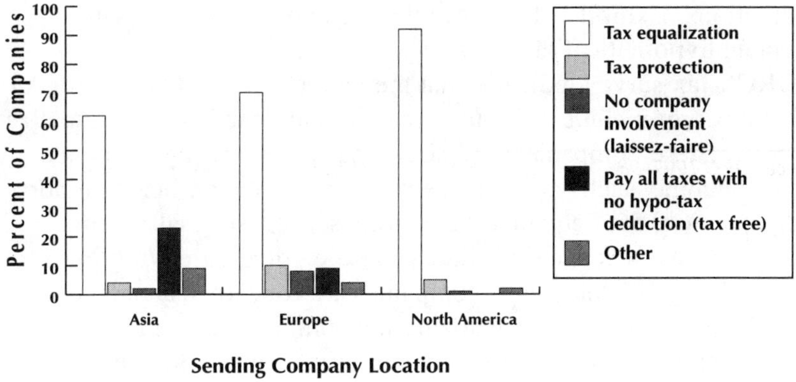

Source: *ORC 1997–98 Worldwide Survey of International Assignment Policies and Practices*

adopt a tax protection approach under which the employee pays no more than he or she would have paid in the home country but may pay less in certain situations. This approach is slightly more common in Europe, where tax equalization is only just becoming the norm. ECA's survey reports that, generally, 75% of companies apply tax equalization and that, over recent years, there has been a trend toward more companies using tax equalization. A very small percentage of North American firms has no involvement at all in expatriate tax affairs. (See Exhibit 7-14.)

Hypothetical Tax

Survey data show that, when determining the home-country hypothetical tax (the amount of tax the employee would have paid if he or she had stayed in the home location), most companies subject the entire compensation package to hypothetical tax. Since companies typically pay foreign taxes on these amounts, it is considered only fair that the employee pay home-country hypothetical taxes on these amounts.

Companies are becoming increasingly sophisticated in their calculation of hypothetical taxes. They are moving away from normative or average approaches and toward calculations specifically tailored to the circumstances of the individual employee. Among North American companies, the use of accounting firms to calculate hypothetical taxes rose sharply in 1998 to 50.7% of companies, from 39.2% in 1995, according to ORC's *1998 Survey of Tax Policies for U.S. Expatriates* (163 participants). Most companies use a "Big 5" accounting firm to do these calculations. Exhibit 7-15 shows the elements of compensation used to calculate hypothetical tax.

ORC's tax survey indicates that the majority (62.7%) of North American companies include noncompany source income in the tax equalization process. These companies pay additional taxes arising on noncompany source income such as investment income. A significant minority of companies (40.5%) equalize taxes imposed on spousal income. This is seen as yet another way of addressing the "dual-career/trailing spouse" issue. Having said that, many companies are concerned about the potential financial exposure of tax equalizing noncompany source income (an employee could have significant personal investments, and the tax on those investments could be substantial). Just over 24% of companies indicate that they place a formal limit on the amount of outside investment income they equalize or protect.

Not surprisingly, the ORC tax survey found that most assignment-related supplemental compensation (such as foreign service premiums, hardship allowance, housing, COLA, relocation, etc.) is delivered tax-free to the expatriate.

Exhibit 7-15. Elements of Compensation Used to Calculate Hypothetical Tax

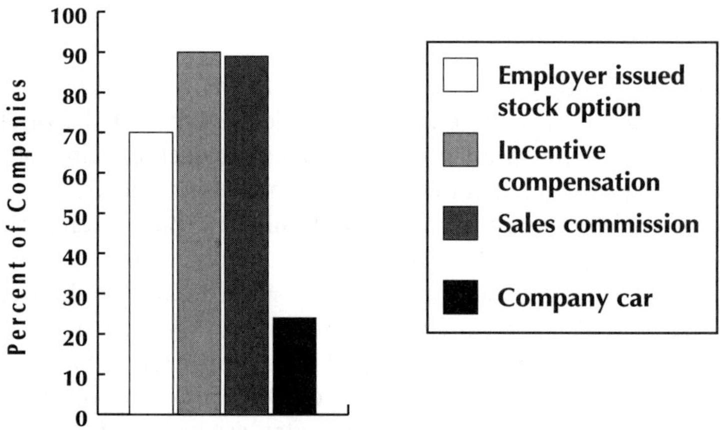

Source: *ORC 1998 Survey of Tax Policies for US Expatriates*

Housing

Host-Location Housing

ORC's survey shows that almost 100% of companies provide some form of housing assistance in the assignment location. In most cases, the company will pay for foreign housing costs (either by taking the lease out in the company name directly or reimbursing the employee for the ongoing cost) and expect the employee to make some contribution toward the total cost. Determination of housing allowances and/or the location and type of appropriate housing can be a difficult process requiring a greater degree of judgment than many other areas of expatriate compensation. Most companies set predetermined limitations on the type and cost of host housing they are willing to pay for. ORC's survey shows that almost half of North American companies rely on consultant data, at least in part, when determining the appropriateness of foreign housing. Most organizations will also seek local management input.

The decision to provide a housing allowance to the employee, to take out a lease in the company's name, or to purchase housing in the host location is often driven by taxes. In some locations, for example, it may be more tax advantageous for the company to take out the lease on the property directly.

Most companies discourage home ownership by employees in foreign locations. Home ownership can be a barrier to employee mobility and can have financial consequences for the company and the employee if, for example, the employee is forced to sell at a loss upon repatriation or reassignment. In ORC's survey, 81% of North American companies report that they discourage expatriates from purchasing homes in the assignment location regardless of assignment length.

Deduction of Home Housing Norm

Between 80 and 90% of North American corporations, according to ORC and ECA, expect the employee to make some form of contribution toward the cost of housing in the assignment location. This is generally accomplished through the imposition of a home housing offset (often known as a home housing norm). European companies are much less likely to deduct a housing norm. Free housing has traditionally been considered an expatriate

Exhibit 7-16. Foreign Housing Policies

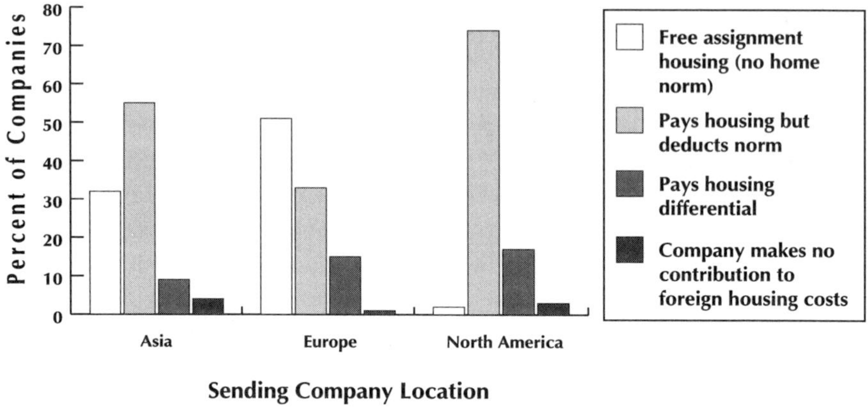

Source: *ORC 1997–98 Worldwide Survey of International Assignment Policies and Practices*

perquisite in Europe. ECA's survey indicates that there is a continuing but small trend toward companies generally either expecting some contribution from the employee toward host-country accommodation or imposing greater control of costs.

When taken, the home housing norm is generally representative of the cost the employee would typically incur on housing had he or she remained in the home location. There are various ways to determine this amount. According to ORC, 73% of North American companies use consultant data (compared with 23% of Asian firms and 43% of European ones), 11% use the employee's actual home-country cost, and 8% assume that home-country housing cost is a fixed percentage of base salary. A small minority (about 3% of companies) calculate a home housing offset internally. In most cases, the offset is tied to the employee's base salary or base salary plus bonus. Exhibit 7-16 presents an overview of foreign housing policies.

Provision of Home-Country Property Management and Sale Assistance

The majority of North American companies provide assistance to the employee who retains his or her home while on assignment; ORC reports that approximately 75% of companies pay property management fees for the entire length of the assignment or manage the rental of the employee's house. Substantially fewer European companies (23%) and Asian compa-

Exhibit 7-17. Specific Home-Sale Assistance as a Percentage of Companies Offering Assistance

Closing Costs	92%
Brokerage Fees	90%
Appraisal Costs	83%
Inspection Costs	74%
Advertising Costs	49%
Taxes	31%

Source: *ORC 1997–98 Worldwide Survey of International Assignment Policies and Practices*

nies (39%) provide such assistance. This is primarily because European and Asian companies do not impose a home housing offset as frequently and therefore do not feel the need to further subsidize housing expenses. North American firms expect the assignee to be able to cover the expense of the home housing offset while on assignment by renting out the property in the home country.

Most companies around the world neither encourage nor discourage the sale of the expatriate's home-country house prior to transfer. Nevertheless, 67% of North American companies will reimburse all or some of the costs related to the sale of the home-country house, according to ORC. European and Asian companies are much less likely to provide such assistance. Exhibit 7-17 shows common expenses for which North American companies provide assistance.

In addition, it is common for North American companies to protect employees going on foreign assignment against a monetary loss on sale of their homes. ORC's survey found that more than 70% of companies provide some form of assistance, most commonly by offering to buy the house at the appraised market value or covering the loss in the event that the sale price is below original purchase price (the value of improvements to the property are frequently included).

Benefits Plans

Health Care

According to ORC's survey, there are significant differences among the regions of the world in terms of how companies provide health care to

Exhibit 7-18. Health Care Coverage

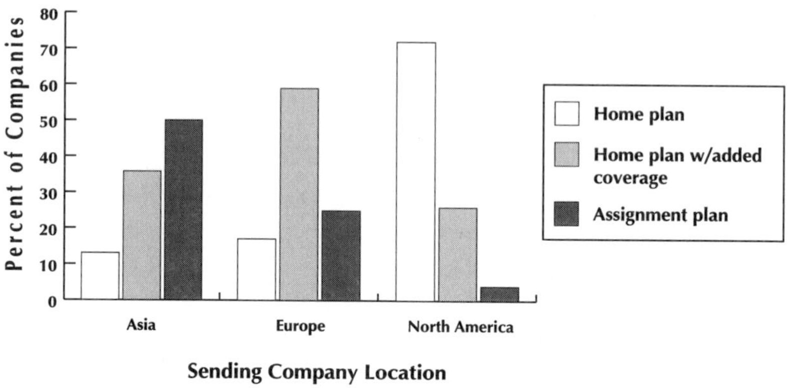

Source: *ORC 1997–98 Worldwide Survey of International Assignment Policies and Practices*

expatriates. North American firms generally keep their expatriates in the home-country medical program and do not provide any additional benefits. North American firms are more likely to have health care plans in the first place, and their coverage can normally be readily extended to cover expatriates. Half of all Asian companies enroll their expatriates in the assignment-location plan, whereas most European companies allow expatriates to stay in the home-country medical program and provide additional coverage. This practice for European companies probably reflects the prevalence of free or governmentally subsidized medical care within European countries and the consequent need to provide additional assistance in certain circumstances once the employee leaves the home country (see Exhibit 7-18).

Most companies have provisions for emergency repatriation for medical reasons. Approximately 70% of European and North American firms have a formalized program with an established emergency evacuation service, according to ORC's survey.

Pension/401(k)

Virtually all organizations (96% in North America, according to ORC's survey) around the world keep expatriates in the home-country pension plan. Similarly, coverage for items such as life insurance, profit sharing, and stock options is based on the same criteria that are used for home-country employees. The ORC survey indicates that the earnings base for expatriates' participation in home-country benefit plans typically does not include any expatriation allowances or premiums. These policies follow the home-buildup or balance sheet approach, which calls for employees to be kept on the same basis as their home-country counterparts for base salary, pension, and so on.

Other Expatriate Policies

Car Policies. Companies rarely ship expatriates' automobiles to the assignment locations (71% of North American firms will never ship an employee's car, according to ORC's survey). Most companies would rather not get involved in the legal complexities and costs of importing a car. Many organizations, however, do provide automobiles in the host location, with certain restrictions. Almost half of North American companies always offer a car or car allowance to middle management and above, while 38% of their European counterparts and 33% of Asian organizations do so. Companies from all regions do not so readily offer a car or car allowance to lower-level employees. When they do, it is with the condition that the job requires a car, that it is local practice, or that the expatriate had a company car in the home country. Most companies will consider the local market and host-country's corporate practice when determining appropriate cars.

For North American companies, there has been a continuing trend to require the expatriate to share in the capital or lease costs of the automobile. ORC found that more than 60% of firms require such a contribution for management-level and other expatriates.

A small number of companies in the ORC survey provide assistance to the employee to purchase or lease a car if one is not directly provided. Such assistance may include low- or no-interest loans, an ongoing allowance, or a lump-sum payment.

For those companies that directly reimburse the running expenses of an automobile in the assignment location, it is relatively common (as mentioned earlier in this chapter) to remove all or some of private transport from goods and services allowances/COLA. This ensures that the employee is not compensated twice for transportation costs—once directly by the company and once again through the COLA.

A majority of North American firms (70%, according to ORC) protect employees against loss on the sale of personal cars prior to transfer.

Typically, this is based on the difference between the sale price and market value (frequently with a set maximum limit). Protection against loss on sale is less common among European companies and significantly less common among Asian firms.

Travel. ORC survey data indicate that, when traveling either on business or between the assignment location and the home country, senior management flies via business class more often than other expatriates do. This holds true for home-leave trips, the first visit to the assignment location, and the final trip back to the home country for repatriation. Asian companies are most likely to differentiate between senior management expatriates and other expatriates.

Home Leave. Approximately 77% of European and 86% of North American companies typically provide annual home leave for expatriates, according to ORC. If the expatriate is married and unaccompanied, European firms grant additional home leave at a greater rate than those in other regions do. On the whole, Asian companies offer home leave less frequently than do their counterparts in Europe or North America. Most companies worldwide (more than 60%) do not require the employee to spend home leave in the home country.

Exhibit 7-19 shows the frequency with which North American companies reimburse or provide certain items during home leave:

Vacation Entitlement. The majority of North American companies retain their expatriates on a home-country level of vacation entitlement. Approximately 18% of North American firms provide home-country entitlement plus additional time, according to ORC. A minority provides vacation

Exhibit 7-19. Home-Leave Expense Reimbursement as a Percentage of Companies Offering Reimbursement

Airfare	85%
Car Rental	31%
Cost of Living	25%
Accommodation	21%
Other Expenses	16%

Source: *ORC 1997–98 Worldwide Survey of International Assignment Policies and Practices*

according to assignment-location entitlement (for U.S. expatriates, this invariably results in increased vacation because of the relatively low vacation entitlement in the United States). Approximately 14% of companies provide the higher of home- or assignment-location entitlement.

Rest and Recreation (R&R). ORC's *Worldwide Survey* found that most companies will provide R&R leave only in locations that they classify as hardship locations. Some companies will extend R&R to other locations that are perceived as being difficult locations to live in (e.g., because of isolation, crime, or pollution) but that do not qualify for hardship. Typical R&R entitlement is twice a year in addition to home leave. In some cases, three R&R leaves are provided. Companies have various options in deciding where R&R time should be spent. Cost considerations are often important. Exhibit 7-20 shows typical practices of North American firms in selecting R&R locations.

Companies typically pay all actual expenses during rest and recreation leave (35% of North American companies) or provide a per diem allowance (24% of companies, according to ORC). The remainder only pay for travel or travel plus accommodation/meals.

Security Programs. ORC's survey found that very few companies have a personal security policy in place for expatriates. Many Asian firms (35%) do provide expatriates limited assistance in personal security matters, far more than European (12%) and North American (7%) companies do. Approximately 29% of North American firms have an established program for evacuation in the event of a political or natural disaster in the assignment country. A further 24% of companies have an informal evacuation program. Additional security provisions may include the provision of

Exhibit 7-20. Choice of R&R Locations as a Percentage of Companies Providing R&R

Expatriate has free choice	28%
Company chooses	27%
Specified radius from assignment location	25%
Nearest nonhardship location	19%
Home country	1%

Source: *ORC 1997–98 Worldwide Survey of International Assignment Policies and Practices*

secure housing (e.g., housing with an alarm system or in a building with a doorman, a compound, or guarded property), the provision of a car and driver, and, in some cases, a bodyguard.

A recent ORC study of security measures for more than 4,000 individuals in 50 countries showed that tight security measures were most common in Argentina, Brazil, Chile, China, Hong Kong, Indonesia, Korea, Malaysia, Mexico, Peru, Philippines, Puerto Rico, Saudi Arabia, Singapore, Taiwan, and Thailand. This list is by no means exhaustive.

Education Allowances. Surveys show that virtually all European and North American organizations pay the educational expenses for primary and secondary school children of expatriates. Companies are, however, conscious of the high cost of education. In most locations, a private international school is the only option because of language barriers, the need for a particular curriculum, or the quality of education in the host location. However, companies are increasingly scrutinizing the local school systems. ORC found that 59% of North American firms would pay for education costs only if no suitable free education was available. It should be noted, however, that, because of the reasons outlined above, suitable free education is not available in the vast majority of locations.

Only a small minority of North American companies (5%, according to ORC's survey) pay for the cost of university-level education. This practice is probably more common among Canadian than U.S. firms. Some companies will pay for any additional costs incurred for college education as a result of the assignment (e.g., the loss of free or subsidized education as a result of nonresidency in the state or country).

For children attending school in the home country, the norm for North American companies (40%, according to ORC) is to pay for the full cost of two round-trips a year to visit parents in the assignment location. Twenty-nine percent of companies pay the cost of only one round-trip a year.

Shipping and Storage Policies. Virtually all companies provide some allowance for the shipment of an expatriate's household furnishings between the home and assignment locations. The majority of North American companies (60%, according to ORC) limit the amount of total weight and/or volume that may be shipped. A further 34% of companies will pay all "reasonable" shipping costs. Reasonable would typically exclude boats, cars, expensive antiques, and so on.

Exhibit 7-21. Payment of Social Club Membership Fees among North American Companies

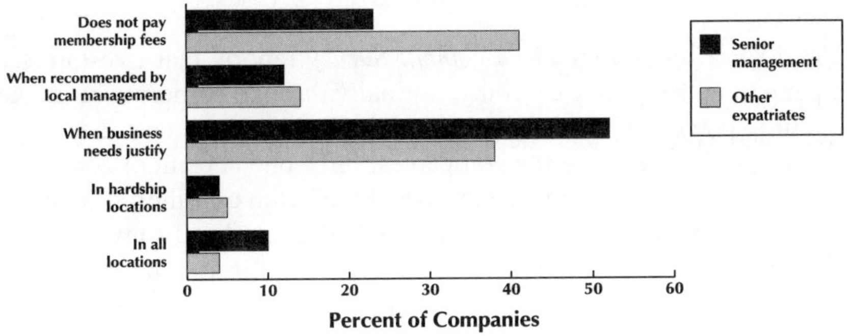

Source: *ORC 1997–98 Worldwide Survey of International Assignment Policies and Practices*

The majority of companies (55% in North America) pay for the storage of household furnishings not taken abroad. In more than half the cases, there is no restriction on the total cost of storage.

Relocation Allowance. Most companies (88% of North American firms in ORC's survey) recognize that there are costs associated with starting up a household in a foreign location and provide a miscellaneous relocation allowance for this reason. Most companies (76%) either pay a flat amount or an allowance based on a company-determined formula—often one to three months' base salary or a percentage of base salary.

Club Membership. Club membership used to be a relatively common expatriate perquisite. Nowadays, survey data show that companies are becoming more cost conscious and are reviewing their policy in this area, particularly for less senior employees. (See Exhibit 7-21.)

Pets. Company treatment of employees' pets is one of the most emotionally charged areas of expatriation. The majority of companies around the world (89% in Asia, 65% in Europe, and 61% in North America, according to ORC) provide no assistance for transportation and quarantine costs for domestic animals taken to or from the assignment location. The costs of extended quarantine in locations that require it can be very high.

Expatriate Administration

Policy Control and Administration

ECA's *Expatriate Salary Management Survey* reports that two-thirds of companies control policy centrally, normally through corporate headquarters. Thirty percent of companies allow joint control between either corporate headquarters or operating companies. Fifty-one percent of companies administer their policies on a centralized basis, with a further 35% having joint control and only 10% using completely decentralized administration.

Companies in ECA's survey that have decentralized policies cite several benefits:

- Increased local management accountability (mentioned by 36% of companies with decentralized administration but only 21% of those with a "decentralized" policy function)
- Improvement of understanding at the divisional or local level
- Moving authority to business units with financial responsibility
- Increasing autonomy and flexibility

Exhibit 7-22 shows gains cited by companies that have decentralized policy and/or administration of expatriates.

Exhibit 7-22. Gains Cited by Companies That Have Decentralized Policy and/or Administration of Expatriates

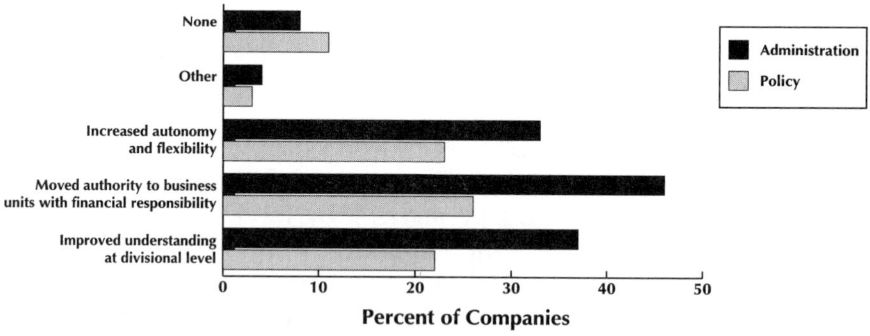

***Source:** ECA 1997/98 Expatriate Salary Management Survey*

Exhibit 7-23. Gains Cited by Companies That Have Centralized Policy and/or Administration of Expatriates

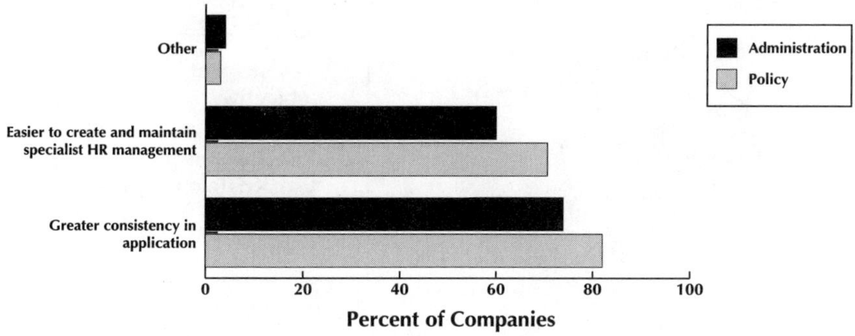

***Source:** ECA 1997/98 Expatriate Salary Management Survey*

Companies in ECA's survey that are more centralized cite such benefits as consistency of policy and administration (more than 70% of companies) and ease of creation of a specialized human resources management. (See Exhibit 7-23.)

Repatriation

Planning in advance for the repatriation of employees does not seem to be a top priority for most multinational companies. ORC found that most companies around the world do not guarantee the job level to which an expatriate will return. The majority of organizations place repatriated employees in whichever positions are available. European and North American firms are more likely to repatriate employees to their preassignment or assignment-location positions than are Asian firms.

Contrary to general perception, relatively few expatriate assignments end prematurely. ORC's survey found that the percentage of expatriates who request that their assignments be ended ranges from 2 to 3% across all regions, and relatively few assignments are terminated by the company. An interesting fact is that most repatriated employees are with their same employers one year after completing their overseas assignments. One year after repatriation, 84% of Asian, 81% of European, and 79% of North American repatriated employees are still with their companies.

According to ECA's *Expatriate Salary Management Survey,* 64% of companies apply a formal system to measure the performance of an expatriate. The systems used are shown in Exhibit 7-24.

Exhibit 7-24. Expatriate Performance Measurement Systems

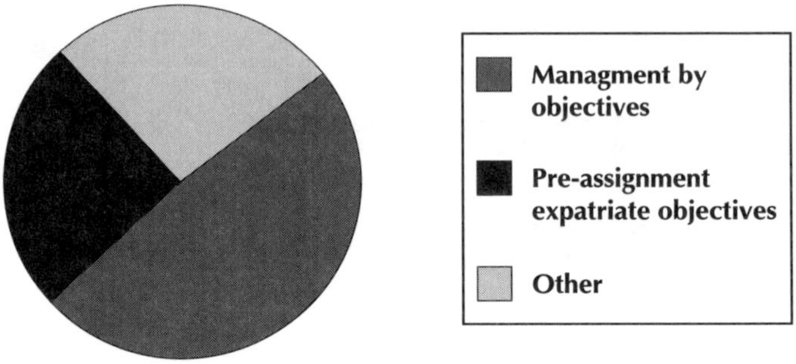

Source: *ECA 1997/98 Expatriate Salary Management Survey*

Outsourcing

ORC's survey found that, on the whole, Asian and North American companies are more likely to outsource expatriate administration and support functions than are European companies. In North America in particular, this reflects the relative maturity of outsourcers as well as shifts in corporate attitude toward outsourcing. While relocation is outsourced by 82% of the Asian respondents to ORC's survey, only 50% of North American and 44% of European participants outsource relocation. Asian organizations also outsource international compensation (20%) at twice the rate of their North American and European counterparts, according to ORC.

North American firms outsource tax administration (79%, according to ORC) far more than Asian and European companies do. This is partly because of the fact that more North American firms tax equalize—a process that normally involves the services of an accounting firm. Similarly, 60% of North American firms outsource home-sale programs, compared with 26% of Asian firms and 29% of European companies. This is probably because North American firms are more likely to be involved in the home housing area generally. This is done, for example, through the imposition of a home housing norm and the provision of property management assistance. ORC reports, however, that outsourcing is gaining ground in Europe; outsourcing of home sale/management has increased by 14% between 1996 and 1998, for example.

Exhibit 7-25. Outsourcing of Expatriate Program Elements among North American Companies

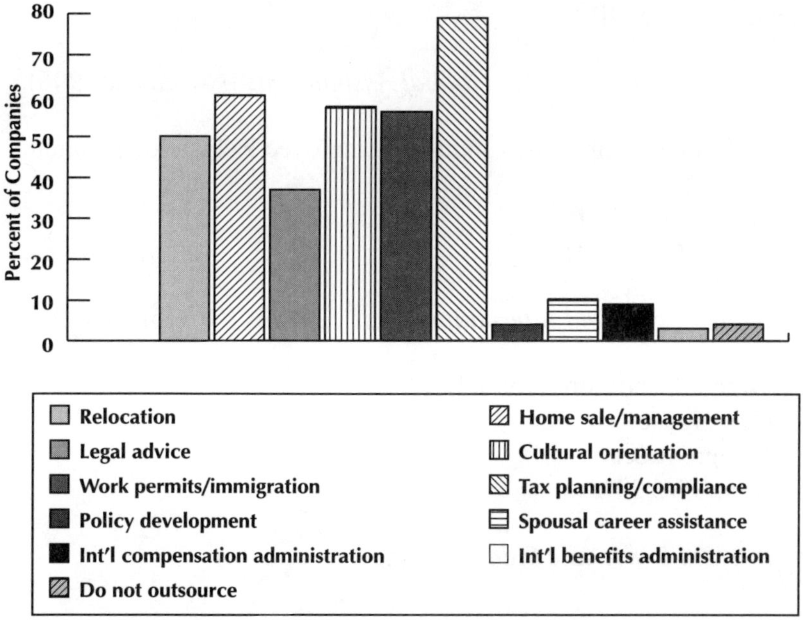

Source: *ORC 1997/98 Worldwide Survey of International Assignment Policies and Practices*

Exhibit 7-25 shows the prevalence of outsourcing among North American firms.

Further Reading

Organization Resources Counselors, Inc.
1211 Avenue of the Americas
New York, NY 10036

- *1997–98 Worldwide Survey of International Assignment Policies and Practices*
- *1998 Survey of Tax Policies for U.S. Expatriates*
- *Survey of Companies' Use of Cultural Orientation Programs* (1992)

Organization Resources Counselors, Inc.
Liscartan House
127/131 Sloane Street
London SW1X 9BA

- *Dual Careers and International Assignments* (November 1996)

The Confederation of British Industry Employee Relocation Council
Centre Point
103 New Oxford Street
London WC1A 1DU

- *Dual Careers and International Assignments* (November 1996)

Employment Conditions Abroad Ltd.
Anchor House
15 Britten Street
London SW3 3TY

- *1997/98 Expatriate Salary Management Survey*

CHAPTER 8

EXPATRIATE TAXATION

SAMUEL M. RUSSO AND DAN ORCHANT

This chapter will focus on the tax issues that international program managers face as they transfer employees on global assignments.

From a tax perspective, most human resources professionals find transfers to and from the United States more complex than other employee transfers. Since the United States taxes its citizens on worldwide income, and may tax temporary inbound assignees in a similar manner, the tax implications can be significant, and traps exist for those not well versed in how the U.S. tax system operates. For this reason, this chapter explores the U.S. tax issues in some detail.

We also provide general guidelines on tax rates in various countries, review some of the tax-planning techniques that can minimize those assignment costs, provide some checklists that may help you as you administer your program, and advise on how to best use outside consultants for tax-planning advice and compliance services.

U.S. Taxation of Its Citizens and Permanent Residents ("Green Card" Holders) Working Abroad

Unlike most countries in the world, the United States taxes its citizens and residents on their worldwide income while residing outside the United States. However, the United States does provide for the foreign-earned income exclusion and foreign tax credits to mitigate the U.S. tax liability on foreign-earned income.

Foreign-Earned Income Exclusion

Qualifying U.S. citizens and residents working outside the United States are permitted to elect to exclude a portion of their foreign-earned income under Internal Revenue Code (IRC) section 911. This section provides a general exclusion limited to a specified amount; another exclusion measured by foreign housing costs; and, for self-employed persons, a foreign housing cost deduction. The general exclusion of foreign-earned income has been $70,000 since 1987. Beginning in 1998 under current law, the maximum income exclusion will be increased in $2,000 increments each year (for 1998, $72,000) until 2002, when the annual exclusion reaches $80,000. The exclusion will be indexed for inflation beginning in 2008.

Qualifying for the Exclusions

To qualify for the foreign-earned income and housing-cost exclusions, an individual must have foreign-earned income; his or her tax home must be in a foreign country; and he or she must meet either of two tests:

- The bona fide residence test, which requires the individual to be a bona fide resident of a foreign country (or countries) for an uninterrupted period that includes a full tax year, or
- The physical presence test, which requires the individual to be present in a foreign country (or countries) at least 330 full days during a period of 12 consecutive months.

A U.S. citizen may qualify under either the bona fide residence or physical presence test. A U.S. resident alien working abroad can qualify under the physical presence test, and, in certain limited cases, tax treaty nondiscrimination rules may permit qualification under the bona fide residence rule.

Bona Fide Residence Test

Bona fide residence is determined based on a subjective review of individual facts and circumstances, including the nature of the assignment and the length of stay in the foreign country. Foreign residence may be established even though the expatriate will return to the United States when the work assignment is over. Bona fide residence is not the same as domicile, which is normally the individual's permanent home to which he or she eventually plans to return.

Generally, it is not difficult to establish that an expatriate is a bona fide resident of a foreign country if the move includes the expatriate's family and if they intend to make the foreign country their home. The test of bona fide residence is primarily a factual one, requiring an analysis of all relevant facts and circumstances. Factors that might indicate that an expatriate is a bona fide resident include the following:

- Acquisition of a home or long-term lease in the foreign country
- Intent to become involved in the social life and culture of the foreign country
- The nature of any conditions or limitations concerning the employment agreement, as well as the type and term of the visa or residence permit

Once residence is established, to meet the requirements of this test, the individual must be a bona fide resident of a foreign country (or countries) for an uninterrupted period that includes an entire U.S. taxable year (normally the calendar year). An individual may move from one foreign country to another or make temporary visits to the United States or elsewhere without interfering with this test period, as long as he or she does not interrupt the qualifying period with an interval of U.S. residence.

Physical Presence Test

This test requires that an expatriate be physically present in a foreign country (or countries) for 330 full days during any consecutive 12-month period and that the expatriate's tax home be in a foreign country (or countries) throughout the 330 full days of presence. This test is purely objective and requires only counting the qualifying days. No intention regarding residence or any other factors need be considered.

Any period of 12 consecutive months may be used to determine eligibility under the physical presence test. The months do not have to be full calendar months, as long as they are consecutive. Two or more overlapping 12-month periods may be used in a single tax year to gain additional exclusion. For purposes of determining the number of eligible days, a full day is a 24-hour period commencing at midnight; thus, if a taxpayer is in the United States for part of a day, it will not qualify. Travel over international waters does not constitute presence in a foreign country for purposes of the test. However, if the travel is between two foreign points, the period of foreign physical presence is not interrupted if the travel over international waters or in the United States is for less than 24 hours.

Foreign Tax Credit

All or a portion of an expatriate's income may be subject to tax in a foreign jurisdiction as a result of either the individual's residence or his or her presence in the foreign country. Since U.S. citizens and residents are subject to U.S. tax on their worldwide income, the expatriate may be subject to tax in both the foreign country and the United States. The foreign tax credit provisions of the Internal Revenue Code are designed to eliminate the double taxation of foreign-source income by allowing a credit against U.S. tax for qualifying foreign taxes. This credit is generally limited to the U.S. tax on the individual's foreign-source income, and it cannot exceed the actual foreign tax paid or accrued.

Disallowance of Credit Allocable to Exempt Income

Allowable foreign taxes paid or accrued can be used as credits, except to the extent that the foreign income tax was imposed on foreign-source earned income excluded from gross income under IRC section 911. The theory of this statutorily imposed denial of double benefits rule is that an individual should not be able to exclude earned income from taxation *and* claim credit for foreign tax imposed on such income.

Limitation on Credit

The portion of the foreign taxes that is not disallowed can be claimed as a credit, subject to limitations. The amount of credit allowable in a taxable year is limited to the lesser of the actual foreign taxes paid or accrued (after disallowance) or the amount of U.S. tax on foreign-source taxable income for the year.

Carryback and Carryover of Unused Credits

Foreign tax credits that exceed the limitation may be carried back two taxable years and forward five taxable years. The excess credit must first be carried back to the earliest taxable year and then forward to each succeeding taxable year.

Under most corporate-sponsored international assignment plans, the host-country tax is paid by the company. Therefore, it is important that the employee understand that if he or she uses such excess foreign tax credits in future years when no longer on assignment, such tax benefit should be returned to the company. Many companies establish tracking mechanisms so that in future years they recoup such benefits from employees who have returned from an international assignment.

Foreign Income Tax Rates

Most foreign countries have effective income tax rates that are higher than the United States. Some countries like the Philippines and Eritrea have a nominal tax on their citizens working abroad. Other countries like Australia and Canada have an exit tax but do not tax their citizens during their nonresidency period. (See Exhibit 8-1.)

Tax-Planning Techniques

Timing of Assignments

Various techniques can be used to reduce the tax costs of an international assignment. In cases in which an individual is not subject to home-country tax while on assignment, the reduction of host-country taxes can bring dramatic savings to the sponsoring company or the individual.

Proper timing of assignments can produce significant tax savings in the arrival or departure year. Some countries impose lower tax rates for individuals who may be deemed nonresidents under local law. Also, most countries allow the benefit of the lower graduated rates in an arrival or a departure year.

Income tax treaties provide relief from double taxation. Individuals who incur tax in a country with which the United States, or another country, has entered into a tax treaty should consider the relevant treaty provisions. Typically, under the "Dependent Personal Services" article of most treaties, an individual would qualify to be taxed only in the home country if:

1. The individual is present in the host country for less than 183 days;
2. The remuneration is paid by, or on behalf of, a foreign employer; and
3. The remuneration is not borne by a permanent establishment or fixed base in the host country.

Exhibit 8-1. Foreign Income Tax Rates

Annual Salary: $150,000
Married Filing Joint
Tax Year 1998

Country	Total Tax Liability (U.S. Dollars)	Effective Tax Rate
High-Tax Countries		
United Kingdom	48,810	34.13%
Germany	53,844	35.35%
South Africa	64,061	42.71%
Australia	66,287	44.19%
Japan	47,908	45.00%
Netherlands	69,304	46.20%
Sweden	79,076	54.02%
Low-Tax Countries		
Hong Kong	22,500	15.00%
Singapore	27,136	18.56%
Argentina	32,093	19.39%
Similar to the United States		
United States	34,051	24.76%
Brazil	37,209	24.96%
Thailand	43,094	29.32%
Mexico	48,954	32.66%
France	46,815	32.00%

One must carefully consider the total tax cost of invoking the treaty. Even if an individual qualifies for the treaty, it may be more advantageous not to invoke the treaty. A tax adviser should be consulted to determine the applicability and the tax benefit of invoking any treaty.

Delivery of Compensation

The delivery of compensation can significantly affect total tax reimbursement costs. One of the most common planning strategies is to deliver compensation in a form that enjoys some preferential tax treatment in the host country. Typically, benefits-in-kind like foreign housing, company car, children's education, home leave, and so on, may not be taxable or are

Exhibit 8-2. Treaty Countries with the United States

Australia	Malta
Austria	Mexico
Barbados	Morocco
Belgium	Netherlands
Canada	Netherlands Antilles
Cyprus	New Zealand
Czech Republic	Norway
Egypt	Philippines
Finland	Poland
France	Portugal
Germany	Romania
Hungary	Slovak Republic
Iceland	South Africa
India	Spain
Indonesia	Sweden
Ireland	Switzerland
Israel	Thailand
Italy	Tunisia
Jamaica	Turkey
Korea	United Kingdom

taxed at preferential rates by the host country. Accordingly, providing these benefits in lieu of taxable cash compensation reduces the overall assignment cost.

Lump-sum pre-/postassignment bonuses are often used to avoid or reduce the foreign tax cost on that payment. By paying a bonus in a period before or after the foreign-country residency period, the payment may escape foreign taxation or be taxed at favorable nonresident tax rates.

Deferred compensation arrangements can often be used to award performance bonuses during the assignment period. By attaching a future contingency (e.g., covenant not to compete), the payment generally does not become taxable until the contingency has been satisfied. Again, this strategy may escape foreign taxation entirely or be taxed at favorable nonresident tax rates.

With these strategies, it is also important to consider the corporate tax implications. It may cause concern if a deferred compensation payment is not taxed in the host country but the company charges the expense to that country.

Many foreign countries tax income on a remittance basis. Dual contracts are typically used for employees with regional responsibilities.

These contracts specify how much compensation is allocated for services provided to each of the regional countries. This strategy generally allows the individual to take advantage of those countries' lower graduated rates or favorable nonresident tax rates.

Tax Reimbursement Methods

There are four generally used tax reimbursement methods. Each approach differs principally in how the reimbursement is reported for tax purposes. The four methods are current-year gross-up, current-year reimbursement, one-year rollover, and loan bonus. Of course, some companies do not have a tax reimbursement policy and the employee is responsible for his or her own home- and host-country taxes. This approach is most commonly used for nonexpatriates employed as local hires.

Example

Salary	$50
Less: Hypothetical tax	(20)
Plus: Housing	30
Net salary desired	$60
Tax rate	40%

When using the current-year gross-up method, an employer reimburses the entire tax liability any time compensation is paid. When providing the tax reimbursement, the employer pays it on a grossed-up basis to cover all taxes due, including the additional tax on the tax reimbursement ("tax on tax"). For example, an employer delivers a net salary payment of $60. At first glance, it would appear that a tax reimbursement of $24 is needed (60 X 40%). However, the $24 tax reimbursement is also subject to tax. Therefore, on a grossed-up basis, the employer must actually pay the individual $100 ($40 tax reimbursement and $60 net salary) to keep the employee whole. This approach works in every country; however, it is also the most expensive from a tax reimbursement cost perspective. Furthermore, there are some countries where this is the only allowable approach under the tax law. For example, in the United Kingdom, pay-as-you-earn (PAYE) rules mandate this method.

When using the current-year reimbursement method, an employer reimburses taxes at the time compensation is paid. However, only the minimum required withholding is reimbursed. For example, an employer wants to provide an employee with a net salary payment of $60, and, while the tax rate is 40%, only 30% withholding is required. Therefore, the employer must actually pay the individual $85.7 (85.7 x 30% = 25.7 withholding tax due, and a $60 net payment is achieved). The remaining tax liability of 10% (40% – 30%) is due when the individual files his or her return, and it is included in the annual tax settlement. That reimbursement is included in income in year 2. Since a portion of the tax reimbursement is not included in income until the following year, this method is slightly cheaper than current-year gross-up. (Time value of money, slower tax gross-up spiral, and a lower tax rate may apply in the year after repatriation when the final settlement is reported.) However, not all countries allow this method.

When using the one-year rollover method, an employer advances or loans the employee an amount equivalent to the requisite taxes due on the compensation paid. At the time the returns are filed in the following year, an accounting determines what the actual obligation for taxes is for both the employee and the employer. Any difference between the employer liability and the amount advanced is settled at that time, resulting in a "net" loan outstanding. The "net" loan for taxes is then forgiven, and the amount of the forgiven loan is included in income. For example, an employer wants to provide an employee with a net salary payment of $60 and the tax rate is 40%. Therefore, the employer pays the individual $60 and advances $24 toward the tax obligation. Because the $24 is a loan, it is not reported as compensation until the following year. In year 2, assuming that no additional settlement is needed, the $24 loan is forgiven, and that amount is included in income. Since the tax reimbursement is not included in income until the following year, this method is cheaper than the previous two methods. (Time value of money, slower tax gross-up spiral, and a lower tax rate may apply in the year after repatriation when the final settlement is reported.) However, not all countries allow this method.

When using the loan bonus method, an employer has the employee approach a third-party bank that will extend an unsecured loan in a series of payments that approximate the actual tax liabilities on compensation plus interest due on the loan. At the end of the assignment, after the individual is no longer resident in the host country, a bonus is paid to the individual that is equivalent to the outstanding loan. Therefore, no tax reimbursements are reported in income during the assignment. Furthermore, no written agreement to guarantee the loan is given to the bank or to the employee by the employer. (Presently, there are several U.S. banks that have such a service.) This method usually carries a high degree of risk and is not allowed in most countries. Since tax laws are constantly changing, companies should consult with their tax advisers to determine the appropriate tax reimbursement method in each country of presence.

Employer Tax Reimbursement Policies

Most U.S. multinational employers have expatriate compensation policies designed to ensure that American employees on overseas assignments receive total compensation that is comparable to that which they would have earned if living in the United States, taking into account additional costs of living overseas, including income taxes. Income and social security taxes in many foreign countries are higher than in the United States, particularly when it is considered that most countries tax the various allowances provided to expatriates to offset extra costs. Generally, the policy is designed to ensure that the individual will not suffer combined taxes on income (U.S. and foreign income and social security taxes) in excess of what the individual would have paid if he or she were living in the United States. The method of accomplishing this objective may be either tax protection or tax equalization. A brief explanation of the two types of tax reimbursement plans is provided below.

Tax Protection

The concept of tax protection is that the individual will be reimbursed to the extent that his or her combined total income and social security taxes (home and host countries) exceed the amount that he or she would have paid if living in the home country. If combined actual taxes are lower because of the foreign assignment (because foreign taxes are low or nonexistent and home-country tax is reduced or eliminated), then the individual realizes a tax benefit from being overseas, and he or she is entitled to personally retain the benefit.

A disadvantage of tax protection is that it may restrict employee mobility. An expatriate employee may be unwilling to move from a low-tax foreign country to a high-tax country because of the lost "tax benefit" that would result, even though the individual would pay no more tax in the new country than he or she would if living in the home country. Similarly, if foreign tax laws change to increase taxation during an expatriate's assignment, the loss of the former "benefit" may cause economic difficulties for expatriate employees and create morale problems, even though, in theory, they are no worse off than in the home country.

Tax protection is most often used by employers that have a small workforce of expatriates who go to a foreign country for a limited period of time and do not move from one foreign country to another. Effectively, the possibility of a tax benefit is considered an additional inducement for the foreign assignment.

Tax Equalization

Tax equalization plans are designed to make taxes a neutral factor in an expatriate's compensation package. The theory is that all expatriates should continue to incur a tax burden equal to that incurred if they were living in the home country. This holds true regardless of actual tax liabilities under local conditions. From a personnel administration standpoint, this permits other elements of compensation (cost-of-living and hardship allowances, education reimbursements, etc.) to be determined without regard to taxes. Under this method, any tax benefit resulting from low-tax jurisdictions would be to the employer's advantage.

Administration of a tax equalization plan may be more complex than for a tax protection plan. For example, a calculation will always be required to determine the benefit or detriment realized by each expatriate employee. On the other hand, overall tax savings may be realized from such a plan because savings from individuals in low-tax countries will offset extra costs incurred by individuals in high-tax countries. Furthermore, taxes in high-tax jurisdictions may be reduced by charging the expatriate, as a reduction in monthly salary, the tax that he or she would pay if he or she were living in the home country. This saves current taxes because the payment is treated as a reduction of taxable salary. Furthermore, it ensures the individual expatriate a more manageable cash flow because his or her personal taxes are satisfied by the regular payment of "hypothetical taxes" (tax as if living in the home country, see discussion below).

Hypothetical Taxes

A key element in any tax equalization plan is the determination of the tax that the expatriate would have paid if he or she had stayed in the home country. This is generally referred to as the hypothetical tax. For example, when only one or a small number of expatriates is involved, the amount may be determined relative to the individual expatriate's circumstances, taking account of deductions in tax returns for periods prior to moving overseas. Because of the complexities and subjectivity involved in administering such a plan, the hypothetical tax is sometimes computed on base salary and normal incentive compensation, using a formula that provides a standard allowance for deductions to be used in calculating the hypothetical tax. This allowance for deductions is intended to cover all types of normal deductions (home mortgage interest, state and local taxes, charities, etc.), and no reference is made to actual deductions incurred.

Net Pay Arrangements

Because most non-U.S. citizens sent on overseas assignment do not continue to pay a home-country tax, many companies establish a guaranteed net pay for the international assignee. For example, if a Dutch citizen is sent on assignment to London, the company will establish a guaranteed net pay based on U.K. tax rates and deliver that amount of pay to the employee. This method also is easy to administer, and usually no tax equalization settlement is required since the employee receives the guaranteed pay; either the employee or employer pays any tax on personal income. Such agreements are typically addressed in the letter of understanding that explains the terms of the assignment.

Administration of Tax Equalization and Tax Protection Plans

Numerous tax calculations are required to properly administer tax reimbursement policies for expatriate employees. Hypothetical taxes must be calculated; actual home- and host-country tax returns need to be completed; and company income and personal income must be verified. Exchange rates for conversion into dollars may vary when foreign taxes are finally paid, and foreign tax assessments may be incorrect and require protest to prevent overpayment. A sample summary report is shown as Exhibit 8-3.

To determine that taxes are not overpaid and to preserve the confidentiality of employees' personal tax returns, most employers use independent tax accountants to prepare tax returns and calculate tax equalization settlements.

Exhibit 8-3. Summary Report

Summary Report for Joe Smith
Assignment from the United States to France
Prepared on October 12, 1998

	1995	1996	1997	1998	1999	2000	Total
Base Compensation:							
Salary	100,000	100,000	100,000	100,000	274	0	400,274
Bonuses	0	20,000	20,000	20,000	20,000	55	80,055
Stock Options	0	0	0	0	0	0	0
Miscellaneous Salary Adjustment	0	0	0	0	0	0	0
Employer Pension Contribution	0	0	0	0	0	0	0
Total Compensation	100,000	120,000	120,000	120,000	20,274	55	480,329
Allowances:							
Cost-of-Living Allowance	35,000	35,000	35,000	35,000	96	0	140,096
Net Housing Allowance	35,000	35,000	35,000	35,000	96	0	140,096
Automobile	4,500	4,500	4,500	4,500	12	0	18,012
Moving Expense Reimbursement	0	0	0	0	0	0	0
Home Leave	15,000	15,000	15,000	15,000	15,000	0	75,000
Education Allowance	25,000	25,000	25,000	25,000	68	0	100,068
Expatriate Premium	12,000	12,000	12,000	12,000	33	0	48,033
Hardship Premium	0	0	0	0	0	0	0
Home Management/Maintenance	0	0	0	0	0	0	0
Club Membership/Fees	5,000	5,000	5,000	5,000	14	0	20,014
Tax Services Provided	0	0	0	0	0	0	0
Other Allowances	0	0	0	0	0	0	0
Mobility Premium	0	0	0	0	0	0	0
Relocation Allowance—First Year Only	0	0	0	0	0	0	0
Other Earned Income	0	0	0	0	0	0	0
Loan Bonus Interest	0	0	0	0	0	0	0
Nontaxable Assignment Costs	0	0	0	0	0	0	0
Other Adj. to Salary/Allowance Detail	0	0	0	0	0	0	0
Total Allowances	131,500	131,500	131,500	131,500	15,319	0	541,319
Tax Costs:							
Actual Tax Liabilities:							
U.S. Federal	5,562	3,713	5,200	6,063	31,014	64,092	115,644
U.S. FICA	6,922	8,034	8,842	9,415	8,499	7,679	49,391
New Jersey	1,331	552	657	715	3,668	10,694	17,617
France Income	55,741	101,150	125,304	145,480	57,551	0	485,226
France Social Insurance	0	0	0	0	0	0	0
Total Actual Tax	69,556	113,449	140,003	161,673	100,732	82,465	667,878
Less Hypothetical Tax:							
U.S. Federal	(23,165)	(22,834)	(22,434)	(22,173)	(22,173)	(22,173)	(134,952)
U.S. FICA	(5,487)	(5,580)	(5,748)	(5,934)	(5,934)	(5,934)	(34,617)
New Jersey	(3,907)	(3,374)	(3,362)	(3,349)	(3,349)	(3,349)	(20,690)
Total Hypothetical Tax	(32,559)	(31,788)	(31,544)	(31,456)	(31,456)	(31,456)	(190,259)
Employer's Soc. Ins.—United States	5,392	8,034	8,842	9,415	7,100	1,746	40,529
Employer's Soc. Ins.—France	0	0	0	0	0	0	0
Other Corporate Tax	0	0	0	0	0	0	0
Tax Cost to Company	42,389	89,695	117,301	139,632	76,376	52,755	518,148
TOTAL COSTS	273,889	341,195	368,801	391,132	111,969	52,810	1,539,796

Assignment Period: 1/1/95 through 1/1/99 Report Denominated In: U.S. Dollars

Timing of Tax Reimbursements

Companies should carefully consider the timing of tax reimbursements, because proper planning can significantly reduce the overall tax reimbursement costs in some cases. The options are to make tax reimbursements currently (by grossing up the expatriate's current compensation), to make tax reimbursements in a subsequent year, or to defer tax reimbursements until after the expatriate has returned to the home country.

If not properly designed, communicated, and administered, employer tax reimbursement policies can be the single most important and unsettling element of an expatriate compensation package. A well-designed plan can reduce the employer's tax reimbursement outlays and administrative expenses. Each plan must necessarily be adapted specifically for each employer.

Corporate Tax Ramifications of Individual Income Tax Planning Ideas

Planning for international assignments usually focuses on human resource issues and individual income tax planning. However, international assignments can have a significant impact on the home- and host-country tax liabilities of an employer. It is important that both individual and corporate tax issues are considered when adopting a tax strategy, because saving individual tax may result in a corporate tax increase.

Totalization Agreements

U.S. citizens and residents transferred overseas and foreign nationals on assignment in the United States may be subject to both home- and host-country social security taxes. Because of this, the United States has entered into international social security agreements (totalization agreements) that provide relief from double taxation and integrated coverage. Similar agreements exist within Europe as well. Totalization agreements by the United States are currently in force with the following countries:

- Austria
- Belgium
- Canada
- Finland
- France
- Germany
- Greece
- Ireland
- Italy
- Luxembourg
- Netherlands
- Norway
- Portugal
- Spain
- Sweden
- Switzerland
- United Kingdom

Totalization agreements for each country and pamphlets summarizing the agreements are available upon request from the Social Security Administration. They can also be obtained electronically at the following Web site address: www.ssa.gov/international/inter_intro.html.

Detached Worker Exception

Totalization agreements ensure that social security taxes are paid to only one country and that dual benefit coverage is eliminated. The standard rule is territorial, providing that an employee is subject to social security tax only in the country where services are performed. There is an exception, allowing the assignee to retain home-country coverage, when the employee is deemed a "detached worker." A *detached worker* is defined as an employee who is *temporarily* transferred to work for the *same employer* in another country. The employment must be expected to last *five years or less,* and the employee must remain in the host country as an employee of the *sending* employer.

Certificates of Coverage

To properly document the exemption from U.S. or foreign social security tax, a "certificate of coverage" for the transferred worker must be obtained from the country that will continue to cover the employee. Generally, employers are required to request certificates on behalf of employees they have transferred abroad. If required, a copy of the certificate should be presented to the foreign authorities as proof of entitlement to the foreign exemption.

An extension of the transfer period may be requested by an employer. The extension request should be made in writing before expiration of the assignment, should fully explain the reason for the request, and should specify length of the extension. Approval by both countries is required if the extension extends the transfer period beyond five years.

U.S. Taxation of Foreign Nationals

The United States taxes aliens differently depending on whether they are considered "resident aliens" or "nonresident aliens." Therefore, for federal tax purposes, it is important to determine if an individual is a resident alien or a nonresident alien. Residency must be determined for each member of the family. This affects marital filing status, exemptions, elections, and so on.

Exhibit 8-4. Sample Certificate of Coverage

Date: ______________

Original Application: ______________

Extension Application: ______________

GENERAL INFORMATION

Name: ____
Last First Middle

Social Security Number: ______________ Marital Status: ______________

Date of Birth: __________ Place of Birth: ______________________________
City State Country

Citizenship: ______________ If Not a U.S. Citizen, U.S. Visa Type: ______________

Country of Permanent Residence: ______________________________

HOME-COUNTRY EMPLOYMENT INFORMATION

Date of Hire with [Company Name]: ______________ Place of Hire with [Company Name]: ______________

U.S. Employer's Name: ______________________________

Address: ______________________________

HOST-COUNTRY EMPLOYMENT INFORMATION

Country Subsidiary Name: ______________________________

Address: ______________________________

Nature of Assignment: ______________________________

Assignment Begin Date: ______________ Assignment End Date: ______________

Resident Aliens

The United States generally taxes resident aliens on their worldwide income in much the same manner that it taxes a U.S. citizen. When computing taxable income, a resident alien is generally entitled to claim the same deductions and personal exemptions available to a U.S. citizen. A foreign national who meets either of two tests—the lawful permanent resident test or the substantial presence test—will generally be treated as a U.S. resident. An alien who is a lawful permanent resident (green-card holder) under the immigration laws is considered a resident for U.S. income tax purposes.

Unlike the lawful permanent resident test, the substantial presence test focuses on physical presence in the United States. Under the substantial presence test, an alien will be considered a U.S. resident for tax purposes if:

- The alien is present in the United States for 183 days or more in the current year, or
- The alien is present in the United States on at least 31 days during the current calendar year, and
- The sum of the number of days of U.S. presence during the current calendar year, plus one-third of the U.S. days during the first preceding calendar year, plus one-sixth of the U.S. days during the second preceding calendar year equals or exceeds 183 days.

The substantial presence test requires both actual 31 days in the current year and 183 or more equivalent days considering current-year days as well as U.S. days for the prior two years. Therefore, an alien who meets the 183-day threshold but is in the United States for fewer than 31 days in the current year will be nonresident under the substantial presence test.

Example

J, a Japanese executive employed by a U.S. company, is present in the United States for 130 days during 1997, 120 days during 1996, and 120 days during 1995. He is not a green-card holder. J is considered a resident alien for 1997 since he is present in the United States on at least 31 days in 1997 and on more than 183 equivalent days during the applicable three-year period, computed as follows:

Year	Actual Days	Equivalent Days
1997	130 x 1	130
1996	120 x 1/3	40
1995	120 x 1/6	20
		190

Nonresident Aliens

Nonresident aliens generally are taxed only on their income from U.S. sources and certain foreign-source income connected with a U.S. trade or business. As a result of limited exposure to U.S. tax, deductions and exemptions available to nonresident aliens are limited. Moreover, different tax rates and deductions are available depending on residency status.

Exceptions

Days of presence in the United States will not count as days of U.S. presence for exempt individuals, certain individuals with a medical condition, individuals who are in transit, or commuters. In addition, a facts and circumstances exception known as the "closer connection test" with the home country may allow an alien to maintain nonresident status for U.S. tax purposes in arrival and departure years.

An alien will not be treated as being present in the United States on any day in which the alien is considered an exempt individual. Except as noted below, an exempt individual is anyone temporarily present in the United States as a foreign government-related individual; a teacher or trainee who holds a "J" visa; a student holding either an "F," "J," or "M" visa; or a professional athlete temporarily in the United States to compete in a charitable sports event.

Days of presence in the United States will be excluded for individuals who were unable to leave the United States because of medical conditions that arose while the individuals were present in the United States.

Working with an Outside Consultant

Outside consultants who have a global network of tax, international human resources, and technology professionals can provide important support to an organization with global employees. To most effectively use these consultants, the company must involve them as early as possible in the assignment process. The best opportunities to achieve tax savings occur during the predeparture period when the company can consider when to start the assignment and when to implement certain compensation delivery strategies, such as using preassignment bonuses, deferred compensation, and benefits-in-kind.

It is also important to have your tax consultant meet with the transferring employee so that he or she gains an understanding of the tax process, the timing of compliance events in the home and host countries, and how the tax adviser will support the transferee during the assignment. Examples of preassignment checklists are shown as Exhibit 8-5. Your international adviser can also help you develop and benchmark your assignment compensation and tax equalization policies and calculate tax and compensation costs with software products.

By involving an outside consultant early in the assignment process, and then before an assignment is concluded, tax savings can be achieved through proactive planning. Also, the transferee gains a better sense of the assignment tax process and how the outside adviser supports both the assignee and the sponsoring employer.

Exhibit 8-5. Foreign Nationals in the United States—Preassignment Consultation

Client Name ____________	Social Security No. ____________
Spouse's Name ____________	Phone Number ____________
Anticipated Assignment Length _____	Fax Number ____________
Home Country ____________	E-Mail ____________
Date of Consultation ____________	Assignment Location ____________
Visa Status ____________	Transfer Date ____________

Items Discussed with Client: **Check If Discussed**

1. Filing Status

A. U.S. taxation on worldwide income .... ❐
B. Resident versus nonresident .... ❐
C. Dual-status filing .... ❐
D. Section 6013/7701(b) elections .... ❐

2. Overview of U.S. Taxation

A. Review of Form 1040 .... ❐
B. Explanation of taxable income .... ❐

Items Discussed with Client: **Check If Discussed**

C. Temporary versus long-term business assignment .... ❐
D. Rental income, expense, depreciation (if applicable) .... ❐
E. Itemized deductions .... ❐
F. Calculation of tax .... ❐
G. Foreign tax credit/foreign-earned income exclusion (if applicable) ❐

3. Tax Reimbursement

A. Intent of tax reimbursement policy .... ❐
B. Completion of forms .... ❐
C. Gross-up of tax reimbursement (if applicable) .... ❐
D. Confidentiality of all personal tax data .... ❐
E. Authorization to release certain summary information to company solely for the purpose of determining tax reimbursement calculations (if applicable) .... ❐

4. Record-Keeping Requirements

A. U.S./foreign workdays .... ❐
B. Foreign income and foreign tax receipts .... ❐
C. Other-itemized deductions, rental expenses .... ❐
D. Temporary business expenses .... ❐

5. Foreign Residence

A. Sale of foreign residence... ❐
B. Capital gain/exchange-rate gain .... ❐

6. Responsibilities

A. U.S. office contact (name and phone number) .... ❐
B. Preparation of U.S. tax return based on questionnaire completed by assignee .... ❐
C. Preparation of tax settlement forms .... ❐
D. Respond to notices and inquiries from the IRS and other taxing authorities .... ❐

Items Discussed with Client: **Check If Discussed**

7. Assignee's Responsibilities

A. Immediate contact of U.S. office upon arrival ❐

B. Complete the questionnaire clearly and accurately ❐

C. Review and complete the tax settlement forms prepared by Company ❐

D. Notify Company immediately upon the receipt of any notification from taxing authorities ❐

8. Publications Provided

A. U.S. taxation of foreign citizens ❐

B. Company contact sheet ❐

C. Service evaluation and return envelope ❐

D. Form W-4 ❐

E. Social Security application ❐

U.S. EXPATRIATE-PREASSIGNMENT CONSULTATION

Client Name ____________

Spouse's Name ____________

U.S. Home Address ____________

Anticipated Assignment Length ______

Home State ____________

Date of Consultation ____________

Social Security No. ____________

Home Phone Number ______

Work Phone Number ______

Fax Number ____________

E-Mail ____________

Assignment Location ______

Transfer Date ____________

Items Discussed with Client: **Check If Discussed**

1. Filing Status

A. U.S. taxation on worldwide income ❐

B. Foreign-country tax liability ❐

Items Discussed with Client: **Check If Discussed**

2. Tax Equalization

A. Intent of tax equalization .... ❐

B. Explanation of theoretical tax and year-end equalization .... ❐

C. Confidentiality of all personal tax data .... ❐

D. Authorization to release certain information to company solely for the purpose of determining tax reimbursement calculations (if applicable) .... ❐

3. U.S. Tax Return Matters

A. Location for return preparation .... ❐

B. Foreign-earned income and housing exclusions .... ❐

C. Physical presence/bona fide resident tests.................................... ❐

D. New Forms: 2555, 1116, 6251, Sch. E, 8582 .... ❐

E. Long extension period-federal and state....................................... ❐

F. Estimated tax payments/withholding .... ❐

4. Record-Keeping Requirements

A. U.S./foreign workdays .... ❐

B. Foreign tax receipts .... ❐

C. Foreign housing expenses .... ❐

D. Other-itemized deductions, rental expenses .... ❐

E. Three years' prior returns (please bring copies with you overseas) .... ❐

5. Personal Residence and State Return

A. Domicile issue.. ❐

B. Alternative for residence-See Attachment 2 .... ❐

- Keep vacant .... ❐
- Rental .... ❐
- Sale .... ❐

6. Responsibilities

A. Foreign office contact (name and phone number) .... ❐

B. Preparation of foreign and U.S. tax returns based on questionnaire completed by assignee .... ❐

Items Discussed with Client:	**Check If Discussed**
C. Preparation of tax equalization forms	❐
D. Respond to notices and inquiries from the IRS and other taxing authorities	❐
7. Assignee's Responsibilities	
A. Immediate contact of foreign office upon arrival	❐
B. Complete the questionnaire clearly and accurately	❐
C. Review and complete the tax settlement forms prepared by Company; return balances due to the Company (if applicable)	❐
D. Notify Company immediately upon the receipt of any notification from taxing authorities	❐
8. Publications Provided	
A. U.S. taxation of Americans abroad	❐
B. Company contact sheet	❐
C. Service evaluation and return envelope	❐
D. Form 673 (Bona fide residence stmt.)	❐

APPLYING U.S. EMPLOYMENT LAWS TO U.S. EMPLOYEES OF FOREIGN EMPLOYERS AND EMPLOYEES OF U.S. EMPLOYERS ABROAD

SUSAN SCHENKEL-SAVITT, ESQ.
EMILY F. GIFFIN, ESQ.

Introduction

With the ever-increasing globalization of business, it is important for employers with multinational operations to understand U.S. laws against employment discrimination, because they apply to all aspects of the human resources operations both in the United States and abroad. No longer can an organization assume that its foreign status automatically will protect it or that simple adherence to the laws of the location of incorporation or residence will provide a safe harbor. Instead, foreign or domestic multinational companies with operations outside the United States that are controlled by a U.S. employer and that recruit and employ American citizens to work abroad must adhere to certain U.S. employment laws that have extraterritorial effect (i.e., the impact of the law expands beyond the U.S. borders). Likewise, a non-U.S. company that has affiliates or subsidiaries in the United States must be aware of the requirements of U.S. employment law applied domestically.

Because coverage is often predicated on such things as the citizenship of employees abroad, the nationality of a corporation, and whether such corporation is controlled by a U.S. company, multinational employers should become familiar with the parameters of domestic and foreign employment law, as well as with the possible application and protection of certain friendship, commerce, and navigation treaties. This chapter explains basic U.S. federal employment laws and provides practical tips and considerations for multinational employers interested in minimizing liability and creating respect within the workplace, both abroad and in the United States. The chapter will first examine issues relating to U.S.-based companies with overseas operations and then discuss foreign companies operating in the United States.

U.S.-Owned or -Controlled Companies with Overseas Operations

American citizens working abroad for a U.S.-owned or -controlled company retain the right to sue in the United States for alleged violations of certain federal employment laws.[1] When U.S. citizens are involved, a U.S.-based company operating abroad cannot escape the teeth of U.S. employment laws simply because it is located on foreign soil. Three of the most significant laws with extraterritorial application are discussed below.

U.S. Employment Laws That Apply Extraterritorially

Title VII and the Americans with Disabilities Act. Title VII of the Civil Rights Act of 1964, 42 U.S.C. §2000e–2000e-17 ("Title VII"), states that it is unlawful for an employer to discriminate against any applicant or employee in regard to recruiting, hiring, firing, compensation, promotion, and/or all other terms, conditions, or privileges of employment on the basis of race, color, religion, sex, or national origin. Title VII prohibits covered employers from limiting, segregating, or classifying employees in any way that would tend to deprive individuals of employment opportunities or adversely affect their employment status. Sexual harassment and pregnancy discrimination are also prohibited by Title VII.

The Americans with Disabilities Act (ADA), 42 U.S.C. §12101 et seq., prohibits employers from discriminating against "qualified individuals with disabilities"—that is, individuals with a disability who, with or without reasonable accommodation, can perform the essential functions of the job that the individual either holds or desires. Both Title VII and the ADA cover all private employers with 15 or more employees. A company's employees worldwide may be counted in the aggregate to determine if the employer employs the requisite 15 employees. This means that even if a foreign employer employs fewer than 15 employees in the United States but has more than 15 employees worldwide, the employer's U.S. operation may be covered.

Section 109 of the Civil Rights Act of 1991 amended Title VII and the ADA and clarified the extraterritorial application of these laws, holding that:

1. The definition of *employee* includes *citizens* of the United States working in a foreign country;
2. Discrimination against U.S. citizens abroad will be covered if *engaged in by an American employer or by a foreign corporation controlled by an American employer;* and
3. Neither Title VII nor the ADA will apply to a foreign company not controlled by an American employer.

To date, foreign nationals working abroad are not protected by Title VII or the ADA, even if they work for American employers. However, these rules are being challenged.[2]

Case Study #1

Issue: Can an employer in the United States refuse to send a female corporate officer abroad because of the belief that foreign customers would feel uncomfortable dealing with a woman?

Answer: No. Stereotyped gender or racial preferences or customs do not justify sexually discriminatory practices.[3] If challenged, human resource professionals must be able to justify employment decisions on the basis of job-related criteria, capable of validation.

Case Study #2

Issue: An American subsidiary in France advertises for a receptionist. An American citizen suffering from multiple sclerosis moves abroad with her husband, an expatriate of another company, and applies for the position. The American subsidiary rejects her for fear that she does not "look right" for the job. Can she sue the subsidiary in the United States?

Answer: Yes. The ADA protects American citizens abroad. Although the applicant must prove she can do the job, with or without "reasonable" accommodation, the subsidiary will be vulnerable to suit under U.S. labor law.

Case Study #3

Issue: A wholly owned subsidiary of a U.S. corporation is recruiting for an administrative assistant to work for a foreign national overseas. The human resource manager in the foreign subsidiary, believing herself to be aware of the manager's preferences, places an ad for "women only." The husband of a woman expatriate employee, who is a U.S. citizen, applies for the position and is rejected. Can he file a Title VII charge in the United States against the subsidiary?

Answer: Yes. Title VII covers U.S. citizens abroad in all areas of employment, including recruiting, training, assignments, promotions, termination, compensation, and sexual harassment. As discussed in this chapter's "Conflict with Foreign Law" section, both Title VII and the ADEA will control an employment relationship with a U.S. citizen even where local customs indicate that a practice is acceptable. If the expatriate's husband applies for the advertised position and is rejected, a Title VII claim may be filed. If a male foreign national or "green card holder" in the same circumstances is rejected, he will not have a Title VII claim. Human resource professionals concerned about U.S. employment law should consider placing their ads in both the "men's" and "women's" columns, despite local custom, and choose a candidate based on legitimate, job-related criteria, not customer preference.

Case Study #4

Issue: A U.S. citizen working for a subsidiary of a U.S. company in Paris claims that he was sexually harassed by his male supervisor who is French. Is the U.S. parent vulnerable?

Answer: Yes, if the employee can show that the parent controls the foreign subsidiary. Same-sex harassment is covered by Title VII if it can be shown that the harassment is "gender related." A sexual harassment policy and complaint procedure should be promulgated and regularly distributed to all employees. Periodic training in this area is extremely important for supervisory as well as all other employees.

The ADEA

The Age Discrimination in Employment Act of 1967 (ADEA) prohibits covered employers[4] from discriminating against any individual 40 years of age and above on the basis of age. The statute also prohibits discrimination because of age against one person in the protected age group (40 and above) in favor of another younger person also within that same age group. Like Title VII, the ADEA applies to all terms and conditions of employment, such as recruiting, termination, promotion, employment advertising, preemployment inquiries, hiring, compensation and benefits, and all human resource policies and procedures.[5] The Older Americans Act Amendments of 1984 (OAAA) amended the ADEA and *expanded coverage of the act to American citizens working abroad for U.S.-owned or -controlled companies.*[6]

Case Study #1

Issue: An American citizen works for a subsidiary of a U.S. company abroad and is about to be transferred from the subsidiary. The employee, who is 55, will be replaced by a local worker who is 48 years old. Can the U.S. citizen sue his employer even though he resides outside of the United States?

Answer: Yes. The protections of the ADEA followed this employee overseas. Because he is over 40 and is being replaced by a younger individual, he may claim and must prove that the economic reason given for replacing him was merely a "pretext" and not a "legitimate business reason." A jury will generally decide whether the employee will prevail. Care should be taken to clearly articulate and/or document the legitimate business reasons for the decision. Human resource directors may also want to use disclaimer language in assignment letters to avoid breach-of-contract claims if an assignment must be changed. The disclaimer should state that the assignment letter is not a contract, express or implied, and does not guarantee the employment or assignment for any specific duration and that the employee can be transferred or terminated at any time at the employer's discretion, for any reason, with or without cause. If possible, the assignment letter should also not express salary in "annual" terms, because some courts have held that a salary expressed as "$50,000 *per year*" creates a one-year contract. Instead, compensation should, when possible, be expressed in terms of the normal payroll cycle, such as "base salary will be calculated on the basis of $2,000 per semi-monthly pay period (equivalent to $48,000 on an annualized basis)."

How to Determine If U.S. Employment Law Applies Extraterritorially

Is the Corporation an American Employer? To determine the nationality of a corporation, the place of incorporation is often controlling. Thus, if a company is incorporated in the United States, it is presumed to be a U.S. employer "because an entity that chooses to enjoy the legal and other benefits of being incorporated here must also take on concomitant obligations."[7]

If a corporation is not incorporated in the United States, it may still be considered a covered employer if it has sufficient contacts with a U.S. company. In making such a determination, the Equal Employment Opportunity Commission (EEOC), the administrative body charged with the implementation of Title VII, the ADEA, and the ADA, will examine the totality of circumstances, including several key factors:

1. The company's principal place of business;
2. The nationality of dominant shareholders and/or those holding voting control; and
3. The nationality and location of management.

These same factors are applied in determining coverage for nonincorporated entities such as partnerships.

Even if a company has a foreign nationality, an "American" corporation can still be liable for discrimination if it *controls* the foreign subsidiary. To determine control, the EEOC often uses the "integrated enterprise" concept, which examines the following:

1. The interrelation of operations;
2. The common management;
3. The centralized control of labor relations; and
4. The common ownership or financial control of the employer and the corporation.

Case Study #1

Issue: An American employee working domestically for a U.S. subsidiary controlled by a British corporation was denied an overseas job by the British parent company. Alleging age discrimination, the employee argued that the ADEA applied because the British parent was "highly integrated" with the American subsidiary. Was the employee covered by the ADEA?

Answer: No. The British parent was not controlled by its American subsidiary. Rather, the parent controlled the subsidiary. Thus, the ADEA did not apply to the British parent.[8]

Case Study #2

Issue: A U.S. company gives an employee a package of benefits applicable only to expatriates; the employee's "trailing" spouse applies for a position with the same company once abroad. Is that spouse, a U.S. citizen, entitled to "equal treatment" with his or her spouse under U.S. employment law?

Answer: The "trailing spouse," a U.S. citizen, is covered by Title VII's protection and can sue. Whether he or she will have a successful lawsuit will depend on factual, job-related issues such as policies, reasons for denial of benefits, consistency of application, impact on the protected class, and the like.

Conflict with Foreign Law

At times, compliance with U.S. employment law may cause an employer to violate the *law* of the foreign country in which a workplace is located. In these rare situations, corporations may violate U.S. labor law, claiming reliance on the "foreign law defense." According to the EEOC, a company can only do so if it shows that (1) the action was taken in a workplace in a foreign country (U.S. territories excluded) where (2) compliance with the U.S. employment laws would cause the company to violate the *law* of the foreign country (3) in which the workplace is located. In other words, an employer must show that it is impossible to comply with both U.S. employment law and foreign law. For example, conversion to the Muslim religion was found to be a legal requirement for helicopter pilots who were to work in Saudi Arabia because pilots were required to fly into Mecca and Saudi Arabian law provided that non-Muslims entering Mecca would be beheaded.[9] However, an employer's actions must violate the *law*, not mere *custom,* of a country. Thus, a Saudi Arabian hospital that refused to accept Jewish applicants was found to be following custom, rather than law, and was not excused under the foreign law defense.[10]

An employer must show "a current, authoritative, and factual basis" and "cannot rely upon mere conjecture about the policies of a foreign country."[11] Such requirements may be difficult to show in countries such as Japan and certain Islamic states, "where the distinction between law and social custom is not as sharply defined as it is in the United States."[12] In addition, an employer must be prepared to show that it took all possible steps to obtain an *exemption* from the foreign-country law before it followed such law.[13]

Case Study #1

Issue: A U.S. corporation fired three U.S. citizen employees working in Germany under a German collective bargaining agreement that set a mandatory retirement age of 65. The American employees filed an ADEA claiming that, although the corporation was contractually bound to dismiss the employees, no German law prohibited employment of the Americans. Did they successfully show that U.S. labor law applied?

Answer: No. The court held that the collective bargaining agreement, supported by the German law of contracts, was a "conflicting" law that the corporation would be violating if it retained the Americans. Therefore, the ADEA was not applied to the claims.[14] If the agreement had been grounded in custom, not law, the result may not have been the same.

Application to Non-U.S. Citizens Abroad

As opposed to U.S. citizens, a foreign national may not invoke the protection of U.S. antidiscrimination laws if he or she is employed by a U.S. company and is based *outside the United States*. (For example, a federal district court in New York held that a Lebanese surgeon employed by an American organization in Lebanon lacked standing to sue his employer for religious discrimination under Title VII. The court explained that, because the plaintiff is a citizen of Lebanon, rather than the United States, he is not an "employee" under Title VII.[15]) Such rulings have recently been challenged by non-U.S. citizens working overseas for an American-owned or -controlled company. For instance, a Canadian citizen working as a reporter in Hong Kong for CNN has attempted to bring an action under the ADEA by filing a charge with the EEOC in Atlanta, Georgia, claiming that she lost her job on the basis of age discrimination. Whether this challenge will be successful remains to be seen. What is clear is that attempts to seek expanded protection of U.S. antidiscrimination laws have begun. The outcome of such challenges should be watched closely by all human resource personnel.

Case Study #1

Issue: An American airline acquired another airline and hired many of its flight attendants. Ten foreign-national flight attendants were not hired. They brought suit in the United States under Title VII and the ADEA. Were the plaintiffs employed outside the United States, and did U.S. employment law cover them?

Answer: No. If the flight attendants had been hired, the employees would have been based in London, but their work would have involved a number of flights to and from the United States. Since most of the plaintiffs' work time would have been spent in international airspace and only about 20% of their work time would have been in the United States, for purposes of the ADEA and Title VII, the employment was extraterritorial. Since the plaintiffs were foreign nationals, their claims were dismissed.[16]

Miscellaneous Human Resource Issues Applying to American Companies Abroad

While all aspects of employment are vulnerable to scrutiny under federal employment law, recruiting, hiring, and termination create much of an employer's liability. The precepts described below apply equally to all aspects of employment and should be adhered to internationally.

Recruiting and Hiring. If U.S. employment law applies, U.S.-owned or -controlled employers cannot intentionally discriminate on the basis of protected classifications such as race, sex, age, religion, color, national origin, or disability in making recruiting and hiring decisions. They also cannot employ selection procedures that appear neutral but have an adverse impact on certain groups. Screening mechanisms such as scored tests, education requirements, height and weight requirements, and interviews have all been challenged for their disparate impact on certain groups and may be vulnerable to challenge even if applied outside of the continental United States.

Employers can avoid liability by conducting the recruitment process in a nondiscriminatory manner and limiting their information inquiries, job qualifications, and job advertisements to qualifications that are *strictly job-related.* Questions concerning an applicant's race, color, religion, national origin, ancestry, sex (including pregnancy), age, disability, marital status, or veteran's status must be avoided. Interviewers and recruitment and hiring tools must also avoid questions that indirectly solicit the same information. For example, asking a candidate about his or her native language or maiden name is unlawful because it is interpreted as being an indirect way of gaining knowledge about one's national origin. Once challenged, whether in France or the United States, the employer may have the burden of proving the job-relatedness of its recruitment tools.

Interviewers must also be concerned with statements made during the course of the interview and comments written on application forms or other human resource documents. For example, statements such as "We are looking to create a young, aggressive workforce" could leave unsuccessful candidates for job openings with the impression that the interviewer is actively seeking younger people. Likewise, ads under "men only" columns in foreign newspapers may indicate an unacceptable gender bias. (See Appendix 9-1 at the end of this chapter for a useful checklist of recruiting "dos" and "don'ts.")

The following are examples of lawful (under U.S. labor laws), job-related reasons for rejecting candidates for employment abroad or in the continental United States:

- The applicant has insufficient job-related experience, knowledge, or education.
- The applicant submitted a vague, sloppy, incomplete, or inaccurate job application or résumé.
- The applicant has changed jobs frequently, without satisfactory explanation.
- The applicant has an unprofessional business demeanor.
- The applicant did not show up for an interview or arrived late.

- The applicant is incapable of expressing him- or herself clearly and concisely or has poor grammar. (Note: This reason is sufficient only if good verbal communication skills are a job-related requirement.)

Termination. Race, color, religion, sex, national origin, disability, age, marital status, or retaliation cannot be the motivating factor for the decision to discharge an employee working for an American-owned or -controlled company abroad. The key inquiry is, Would the employee still have been discharged if the decision-making process had been discrimination-free? Because lawsuits frequently center on the reason for an employee's termination, an employer should carefully document the nondiscriminatory circumstances surrounding the termination.

Generally, employers cannot justify their decision to fire an employee by using evidence discovered after the plaintiff filed suit for discrimination, although in certain jurisdictions "after-acquired evidence" may limit damages. For example, an employee, after being fired, filed suit under the ADEA. During her deposition, she admitted to copying confidential documents. The employer claimed that if it had been aware of this activity, the plaintiff would have been terminated anyway. The court explained that the ADEA was still violated because the only factor that had motivated the decision was age, and a legitimate business reason had not been properly articulated.[17] If the employer, however, could show that, had it known of the activity, the employee would have immediately been terminated, damages may stop accruing as of the date the organization discovered the improper activity.

When terminating a citizen abroad, a U.S.-owned or -controlled company must ask itself the following questions:

1. Is there a foreign law that controls? Did you get an exemption or have you taken steps to try to get an exemption? If you were denied, what reasons were given for the denial?
2. Is there a written employment agreement? If so, what terms govern termination?
3. Are there company policies, letters, or handbooks that promise continued employment unless specific termination procedures are followed? If so, what has been done to fulfill these requirements?
4. Have oral representations regarding terms of employment been made?
5. Does the employee belong to a protected class, including age, sex, religion, color, race, disability status, or national origin?

6. Was sexual harassment, retaliation, or pregnancy involved?
7. Is the decision based on legitimate business reasons or subjective judgments?
8. How will compensation be affected?
9. What is the distribution of your workforce (age, race, sex, etc.)?
10. What do you know about the decision maker?
11. Has anyone similarly situated been treated differently?
12. Who will be replacing the employee?
13. Do you want/need a separation agreement or waiver and release?

The above are a limited number of questions designed to alert a company to potential litigation triggers applicable to citizens abroad. If any of these triggers exist, you should seek guidance. As discussed above, U.S. citizens may carry their protection against discrimination abroad.

Practical Pointers. Human resource directors of American-owned or -controlled companies abroad should be aware of the following issues and questions when making all employment-related decisions:

1. All hiring, recruiting, promotion, assignment, transfer, and termination practices are subject to the scrutiny of antidiscrimination laws. Antidiscrimination laws cover sexual harassment, same-sex harassment, and pregnancy.
2. Determine the nationality of the organization.
3. Determine if the individual belongs to a protected class, including:
   - Age (over 40 years)
   - Race or color
   - National origin or ancestry
   - Sex, including pregnancy
   - Religion
   - Perceptible mental or physical disability unrelated to the ability to do the job with reasonable accommodation
4. Is the employee an American citizen?
5. By whom is the person employed (e.g., parent, subsidiary, foreign corporation, wholly owned subsidiary)? Check, at a minimum, to see what corporate name appears on offer letters, transfer and assignment letters, payroll checks, and benefit booklets.

6. By whom is the worker controlled (i.e., is he or she an employee or independent contractor)?
7. Are there local laws abroad that control, or are practices merely governed by custom? If there are local laws, how does an organization apply for an exemption? Have you done so?
8. Have local managerial employees been trained regarding Title VII, the ADEA, and the ADA? Is there a sexual harassment policy and complaint procedure? Have all employees received training?
9. Is an employee being retaliated against for attempting to assert his or her rights under Title VII, ADEA, or the ADA?
10. Are there company policies, and have they been followed? Has the employment decision been reviewed?
11. Were there any contracts of employment? Did disclaimer language appear on human resource documents?

Human resource directors and other personnel should consider such issues before litigation arises and, when necessary, seek guidance from experts knowledgeable in the field.

Foreign Companies Operating in the United States

In addition to the growth of U.S. companies abroad, many foreign companies are bringing their operations to the United States—setting up subsidiaries and acquiring U.S. companies. This expansion raises a host of unique legal concerns addressed briefly in this section. First, these employers must be aware of the enforceability of U.S. civil rights laws. Second, foreign employers should understand that, although certain treaties may afford them latitude in preferring their own citizens in hiring decisions, this freedom is not unlimited. Finally, this section will provide practical advice regarding dual compensation systems, under which expatriate employees assigned to jobs in the United States are compensated in accordance with compensation policies set in the home country.

Major U.S. Employment Laws

In addition to the "big three" laws highlighted in the first section—Title VII, the ADA, and the ADEA—foreign employers with U.S. subsidiaries must adhere to other federal employment laws or risk liability. These laws are outlined below.

Civil Rights Act of 1866, as amended, 42 U.S.C. §1981 et seq. Section 1981 prohibits racial discrimination in the making of public or private contracts. The courts have construed it to cover virtually all private contractual arrangements (whether written or not), including employment. The U.S. Supreme Court has held that the statute reaches claims of race, ancestry, and alienage discrimination; however, citizenship is generally not covered.

Coverage: Section 1981 contains no statutory minimum number of employees.

Equal Pay Act of 1963, as amended, 29 U.S.C. §206 et seq. The Equal Pay Act (EPA), which is an amendment to the Fair Labor Standards Act, 29 U.S.C. §201 et seq., requires that men and women receive equal pay for equal work. The act makes it illegal for an employer to discriminate by paying employees of one sex lower wages than those paid to employees of the opposite sex employed in the same establishment for work requiring substantially equal skill, effort, and responsibility and performed under similar working conditions. The statute protects men and women.

Coverage: The EPA applies to employees engaged in commerce or in the production of goods for commerce and to all individuals employed in an enterprise engaged in commerce or in the production of goods for commerce.

Rehabilitation Act of 1973, as amended, 29 U.S.C. §701 et seq. The Rehabilitation Act of 1973 is designed to promote the employment of handicapped individuals and to prevent discrimination against them. It also requires covered employers to develop written affirmative action plans with respect to handicapped individuals.

Coverage: The act applies to the federal government, federally funded programs, and federal contractors and subcontractors.

Executive Order 11246. Executive Order 11246 prohibits discrimination and requires affirmative action on the basis of race, national origin, sex, and religion.

Coverage: Executive Order 11246 applies to all contractors entering into contracts or subcontracts with the U.S. government for more than $10,000 for the provision of goods and/or services. Employers with government contracts or subcontracts in excess of $50,000 and with more than 50 employees are required to develop written affirmative action plans.

Vietnam Era Veterans' Readjustment Assistance Act of 1974, as amended, 38 U.S.C. §4212 et seq. The Vietnam Era Veterans' Readjustment Assistance Act requires covered employers to undertake affirmative action to employ and advance in employment qualified disabled veterans generally and Vietnam era veterans whether disabled or not.

Coverage: This act applies to all employers who enter into government contracts or subcontracts for goods or services of $10,000 or more. Employers with government contracts or subcontracts in excess of $50,000 and with 50 or more employees are required to develop written affirmative action plans.

The Family and Medical Leave Act of 1993, 29 U.S.C. §2611 et seq. The Family and Medical Leave Act (FMLA) provides that employees who have worked for the same employer for at least one year and at least 1,250 hours in the previous 12 months are entitled to take up to 12 weeks of unpaid leave during any 12-month period for any of the following reasons:

- The birth of a child of the employee;
- The placement of a child with the employee for purposes of adoption or foster care;
- To care for a seriously ill child, spouse, or parent; or
- The employee's own serious health condition makes the employee unable to perform the functions of his or her position.

Employees taking leave will be entitled to reinstatement to the same or an equivalent position, with the continuation of preexisting health insurance during the leave period.

Coverage: The FMLA covers all employers engaged in commerce or in any industry affecting commerce that employ 50 or more employees for at least 20 weeks per year, and all public employers without regard to the number of employees employed.

FCN Treaties

A Brief Background. Antidiscrimination laws generally apply to any foreign employer doing business within the United States. That being said, many foreign corporations operating in the United States prefer to hire the citizens of its parent company's country of origin. Such a preference may be protected by "employer choice" provisions of various friendship, commerce, and navigation (FCN) treaties, which represent a narrow exception to Title VII and which historically have led to complex litigation. One such FCN treaty, between the United States and Japan, states, "Nationals and companies of either Party shall be permitted to engage, within the territories of the other Party, accountants and other technical experts, executive personnel, lawyers, agents and other specialists of their choice." This treaty represents a narrow exception to antidiscrimination laws and arguably allows foreign employers, under specific situations, to hire certain citizens of their own nation.

By the terms of the treaties, most courts have allowed companies to prefer their own citizens for a small number of executive, management, and other identified positions.[18] The FCN treaties do not allow those same employers to discriminate between U.S. citizens or in favor of persons of a particular national origin who do not fit into the narrowly read exception. For example, a Japanese company reorganized its U.S. operations, causing its American subsidiary to dismiss certain American executives yet spare similarly situated Japanese employees. The court dismissed the claims of national origin discrimination, citing the FCN treaty, but at the same time allowed claims of age discrimination to remain.[19] An FCN treaty may protect the right of covered companies to prefer citizens of their own countries *but only because of their citizenship*. Thus, courts draw a careful distinction between permissible citizenship discrimination under an FCN treaty and impermissible national origin discrimination under Title VII.[20]

Case Study #1

Issue: A Japanese advertising company purchases an American agency to help with business in the United States. During a layoff period, the company fires American executives but retains Japanese expatriates and other American executives of Japanese ancestry. In addition, Japanese-American executives are given greater opportunities for business travel and advancement. Is the Japanese-owned American agency liable?

Answer: Yes. The company is liable for national origin discrimination because the company, instead of simply favoring its own nationals, favored U.S. citizens of the same ancestry.[21]

American courts continue to disagree over what motivating factors are acceptable when a company hires its own nationals. Although some courts allow wide prerogative, finding almost any reason based on citizenship acceptable, the Second Circuit (a U.S. appeals court covering New York, Connecticut, Vermont, and the Virgin Islands) applies a tougher standard: whether foreign citizenship is "reasonably necessary for successful operations." In other words, foreign citizenship will be allowed as a preferred requirement only if there is a business necessity for (1) linguistic and cultural skills; (2) knowledge of foreign products, markets, customs, and business practices; or (3) familiarity with the parent enterprise. Simply preferring a foreign national for reasons of loyalty or general comfort is not acceptable in this court's view. An employer also cannot link staffing decisions with foreign customer preferences, such as preferring a male to a female.[22] Thus, to avoid costly litigation, a corporation must ensure that it has legitimate reasons for employing a citizenship requirement.

Who May Raise the Defense. According to a unanimous U.S. Supreme Court decision, a wholly owned *subsidiary* of a foreign corporation that is incorporated in the United States may not assert an FCN treaty defense against a claim of Title VII discrimination.[23] The Court distinguished between foreign-owned companies that are incorporated in the United States, and are therefore American companies under the terms of the FCN treaty, and those entities that are unincorporated branch or representative offices of companies incorporated abroad. The Supreme Court expressly declined to decide whether an American-incorporated subsidiary of a foreign company could *derivatively* (i.e., indirectly) claim the FCN treaty rights of its Japanese parent corporation, as differentiated from claiming *its own* FCN treaty rights. It appears, however, that an American-incorporated subsidiary could, under certain circumstances, assert its parent corporation's FCN treaty rights.[24]

However, a consequence of this derivative extension of an FCN treaty's protection is the expansion of the jurisdiction of the U.S. courts. Thus, when a subsidiary invokes its parent's FCN treaty rights, the parent becomes exposed, as a party defendant, to discrimination lawsuits brought by local staff employees of the subsidiary.[25] This exposure, however, may be limited. To begin with, expatriates who remain employees of the parent should be insulated from directly making decisions regarding hiring, promoting, transferring, and/or terminating local staff, as well as other day-to-day involvement in local staff personnel matters.[26] At most, expatriate employees should be given only "veto" power with respect to local staff decisions. In addition, care should be taken to ensure that personnel practices applicable to employees not covered by the treaty meet all U.S. and local employment laws and are administered fairly and consistently.

Local Staff Management

As foreign organizations doing business in the United States grow in size and influence, the qualifications and compensation of the staff needed to manage these American business operations change significantly. Companies needing employees with sophisticated experience may find themselves having to recruit for management-level positions in the competitive marketplace, as opposed to promoting long-service employees from within. Some of the more significant legal ramifications of such external recruiting may be allegations of unlawful employment discrimination—often age discrimination, since older, long-service employees are being denied promotional opportunities, overlooked, or replaced by younger recruits. In addition, the companies may have exposure to sex and race discrimination if, by chance, the composition of the long-service employees includes more women or minorities, in comparison with the new hires, or if women and/or minorities are not being competitively compensated.

To avoid claims of unlawful employment discrimination, it is critical for all employers to focus on the job-related qualifications required for all positions, but especially for the more senior-level positions that could be filled by local staff. In this connection, companies must develop and implement American-style job descriptions for all management positions (and especially for those senior positions occupied by expatriate staff), setting forth in detail the necessary qualifications required for such positions. Thus, if several years of experience working for large multinational corporations and/or sophisticated education is a quantifiable job-related requirement, then detailing this in writing (and marshaling the objective back-up data in support in advance) can be advantageous for many reasons: (1) It will serve to provide proof that the long-service employee or other candidate does not have the requisite qualifications necessary for such positions; and (2) it will provide job-related documentation to defend against possible claims of unlawful employment discrimination.

It is also advisable to review performance appraisal and compensation systems to ensure that all employees, including long-service employees, are receiving accurate performance evaluations and compensation and that written evaluations are not overly generous or vague with respect to comments. Indeed, properly utilized and professionally validated performance appraisal and compensation systems can assist the company in defending employment decisions, including, among other things, the denial of promotions or salary increases to long-service employees. Common mistakes made by employers and their supervisory staff include the following:

- Letting one outstanding quality of the employee unduly influence the rating of all factors; each factor in the performance appraisal or compensation system should be considered separately
- Being too generous with the employee's rating or being reluctant to rate an employee unfavorably
- Having a tendency to put all employees into an average range
- Allowing personal likes and dislikes to influence the rating process These flaws in the performance appraisal or compensation system procedures have the effect of unduly inflating an employee's rating and thus making it difficult to deny that employee a position or salary increase.

It is also important for an employer to ensure that any changes to the performance appraisal or compensation systems be "validated" by experts in the field and that the new system be applied uniformly to all employees. In sum, it should not appear as though certain employees or classifications of employees are being targeted favorably or otherwise. Instead, companies should rely on job-related, nondiscriminatory qualifications for promotions and increases, valid job performance evaluations, and a validated compensation system. These practices should limit exposure to employment discrimination suits.

Expatriate Compensation

Generally. As foreign corporations continue to expand into the United States, the issue of compensation of expatriate employees becomes critical. Because of expenses related to relocation, as well as inherent differences in pay standards in the home country, the parent corporation often seeks to implement dual compensation systems for expatriate and local staff employees. Such a system recognizes that expatriates remain employees of the parent company, and therefore the home country's law, practice, and customs should govern their compensation. Compensating expatriates according to home-country standards ensures that they do not fall behind or move ahead of domestic peers.

Antidiscrimination Statutes. Dual compensation systems are generally not a problem under Title VII and other antidiscrimination statutes provided that they are *consistently* applied to *all* of a company's expatriate employees (including U.S. citizens sent abroad) regardless of their place of origin, nationality, and/or sex, race, age, disability, religion, or marital status. Moreover, additional monetary allowances (i.e., payments other than base salary) must be based on actual costs and expenses incurred in relocating abroad or, alternatively, be related to a previously established formula for determining such allowances. If these conditions are met, the EEOC has generally indicated that it will not find the use of expatriate compensation systems in and of themselves to violate Title VII.[27]

At least one U.S. court has accepted an employer's explanation that nondiscriminatory reasons explained differences in relocation expenses paid to U.S. and Japanese employees working in the United States.[28] Similarly, if consistent with the facts, an employer could also argue that only expatriate foreign employees receive additional compensation and not local staff of foreign-national origin. This fact, which has been critical to the outcome of at least two court cases, would tend to disprove that impermissible national origin and/or race discrimination was the employer's intention.[29]

Because expatriate pay systems based on home-country standards are a worldwide practice, such systems arguably can be considered the result of global market forces. In this regard, market considerations have been found by U.S. courts to be legitimate, nondiscriminatory reasons for pay differentials between particular classes of employees.[30] Given the longstanding practice of U.S. and European multinational companies determining base pay according to home-country standards, and the realities of the international marketplace, U.S. courts would be unlikely to require the dismantling of an explainable (not black box) dual compensation system because it has home-country base pay as a component. As a practical matter, it is a good idea for employers to explain to their employees the dual compensation and expatriate compensation systems and the rationale underlying such pay systems. Such candor tends to eliminate suspicion among coworkers and reduce the number of lawsuits initiated.

Conclusion

In the world of multinational organizations, it is crucial for employers to understand U.S. federal employment laws and their coverage requirements. Many laws, including Title VII, the ADA, and the ADEA, apply to employers with operations outside of the United States that are owned or controlled by U.S. companies and to non-U.S. companies that have affiliates or subsidiaries in the United States. However, coverage is not always straightforward; rather, it can turn on technicalities, such as employer-employee status, the nationality of a corporation, and whether the corporation is "controlled" by a U.S. corporation. Employers must become familiar with these tests and with possible defenses such as the foreign law defense and FCN treaties. Finally, even when a multinational employer might be able to assert a defense, it is prudent for all employers to follow certain policy considerations in attempts to reconcile antidiscrimination laws with such issues as hiring practices, local staff management, and compensation systems.

Appendix 9-1

RECRUITING AND INTERVIEWING DOS AND DON'TS

1. When recruiting, carefully phrase any advertisements seeking applicants for particular positions that the company may place in magazines or newspapers. It is unlawful for a company to advertise any job opening in a manner indicating any preference, limitation, specification, or discrimination based on sex, age, race, color, or national origin, except in the extremely limited circumstance when the restriction is a bona fide occupational qualification.
   - Avoid terms like *recent graduates* or *youthful appearance* because they may imply age discrimination.
   - Do not use words like *attractive* or *single* because they may imply sex discrimination.
   - Use terminology like *this company is an equal opportunity employer* or, if applicable, *an affirmative action employer.*
   - Do not rely on word-of-mouth employee recommendations, especially if the internal workforce is statistically skewed; reach out to all "qualified" population groups.

2. It is unlawful for a company to place a discriminatory job order with an employment agency specifying race, color, sex, religion, national origin, age, or disability.
   - Employment agencies are subject to the same employment laws as companies.
   - Employment agencies that receive job orders containing unlawful specifications will share liability with the employer.

3. Interviewers should limit inquiries to those that are strictly related to the position being sought by the applicant. Preemployment inquiries should not address an applicant's race, color, religion, national origin, ancestry, sex (including pregnancy), marital status, sexual orientation, disability, and veteran's status.

4. The following are examples of impermissible interview questions:[31]
   - Maiden name
   - "Do you own or rent your home?"

- Birth date
- Citizenship
- Dates of attendance or completion of elementary or high school
- Names and ages of children, if any
- Provisions for child care
- Future childbearing plans
- "Does your religion prevent you from working weekends and holidays?"
- Color of skin, eyes, or hair
- Height or weight
- Request that applicant submit a photograph
- Applicant's or applicant's parents' birthplace
- Clubs, societies, and organizations to which applicant belongs
- Medical condition, state of health, or illnesses
- Receipt of workers' compensation
- "Do you have AIDS?/Do you have asthma?"
- "Do you have a disability that would interfere with your ability to perform the job?"
- How much alcohol is consumed weekly or whether applicant has been treated for alcohol problems
- How many days an applicant was sick last year

5. It is acceptable to inquire about the following:
    - Name and use of another name
    - Place and length of residence
    - "Are you 18 years of age or older?"
    - Names of applicant's relatives working for the employer
    - "By whom were you referred for a position here?"
    - Relevant skills acquired through past work experience
    - Work experience
    - "Are you capable of performing in a reasonable and safe manner the duties and responsibilities of the position for which you have applied?"
    - "Can you perform the functions of this job with or without reasonable accommodation?"

- "Are you legally able to work in the United States?"
- Military service, including whether applicant received a dishonorable discharge, but dishonorable discharge may not be an absolute bar to employment
- Whether applicant can meet the attendance requirements of the job
- "How many days did you take leave last year?"
- Whether applicant currently uses illegal drugs

6. It is acceptable for the interviewer to make the following statements:
   - Company policy regarding work assignment of employees who are related
   - Regular days, hours, or shifts to be worked
   - A photograph and other personal types of information may be required after hiring, for benefit and security purposes
   - An interview, written test, or job demonstration may be included in the hiring process

7. An interviewer cannot ask about a previous arrest; however, it is permissible to ask about conviction, but a conviction record without more cannot be the basis for denying an individual a job. This is because denying an individual employment based solely on a conviction record may have a disparate impact on racial or ethnic groups.
   - Employment decisions must be made on a case-by-case basis, examining a variety of factors to determine whether the conviction affects the applicant's ability to safely and efficiently perform the job.
   - Some of the factors that may be considered include nature and brevity of the offense; amount of time that has passed since the offense; age at the time of the offense; relationship between the offense and fitness for position sought; and rehabilitation efforts.

8. An interviewer should avoid not only direct questions about protected characteristics and personal traits but also indirect questions soliciting this information. For example,
   - An interviewer may ask if the applicant is fluent in a foreign language, if job related, but may not ask how the applicant acquired language fluency.

- Do not ask "Of what country are you a citizen?" or "Are you a citizen of the United States?" Instead, ask "Are you able to legally work in the United States for all employers?"
- Avoid statements and questions with a discriminatory tone, such as "We are looking to create a young, aggressive workforce" or "How long do you plan to work before you retire (or have a family)?"

Notes

1. Currently, foreign nationals working abroad are not protected under these laws whether they do or do not hold a "green card."
2. Title VII does, however, cover foreign nationals working inside the U.S. domestic borders. See, e.g., *Espinoza v. Farah Mfg. Co., Inc.*, 414 U.S. 86 (1973). Although the ADA does not contain a specific coverage provision regarding aliens, the Equal Employment Opportunity Commission has interpreted the language of Section 109 to mean that the standards for aliens are the same under both statutes.
3. See, e.g., *Fernandez v. Wynn Oil Co.*, 653 F.2d 1273 (9th Cir. 1981).
4. The ADEA applies to employers engaged in interstate commerce with 20 or more employees.
5. The Older Workers Benefit Protection Act (OWBPA) amended the ADEA by extending its coverage to all employee benefits, whether provided pursuant to an employee benefit plan or not. In addition, it codifies the "equal benefit or equal cost principle," which holds that the only justification for age discrimination in employee benefits is the increased cost to the employer in providing the benefits. Finally, it prohibits all waivers of ADEA rights, unless the waiver is knowing and voluntary, by establishing minimum standards for the waiver of any ADEA rights by employees.
6. See *Sumitomo Shoji Am., Inc. v. Avagliano*, 457 U.S. 176, 188–89 (1982).
7. See EEOC notice "Extraterritorial Enforcement: Title VII/ADA," N:2406.
8. *Denty v. Smithkline Beecham Corp.*, 907 F. Supp. 879, aff'd, 109 F.3d 147 (3d Cir. 1997), cert. denied, 118 S. Ct. 74 (1997).

9. *Kern v. Dynalectron Corp.,* 577 F. Supp. 1196 (N.D. Tex 1983), aff'd mem., 746 F.2d 810 (5th Cir. 1984).
10. *Abrams v. Baylor College,* 581 F. Supp. 1570, 1577 (S.D. Tex. 1984).
11. *EEOC Decision No. 85-10,* Empl. Prac. Guide (CCH) Par. 6851, at 7054–55 (1985).
12. Michael Starr, *Who's the Boss? The Globalization of United States Employment Law,* 51 Bus. Law 635, 640 (1996).
13. EEOC notice "Extraterritorial Enforcement: Title VII/ADA," at N:2313–27.
14. *Mahoney v. RFE/RL, Inc.,* 818 F. S upp. 1 (D.C.C. 1992), rev'd, 47 F.3d 447 (D.C. Cir. 1994), cert. denied, 116 S. Ct. 181 (1995). Note, however, that according to the EEOC's more restrictive view, the conduct would have violated the ADEA because the labor contract is not equivalent to a binding statute.
15. See *Ghandour v. Am. Univ. of Beirut,* 1998 WL 856114 (S.D.N.Y. 1998).
16. *Gantchar v. United Airlines, Inc.,* 1995 WL 137053 (N.D. Ill. 1995).
17. *McKennon v. Nashville Banner Publishing Co.,* 115 S. Ct. 879 (1995).
18. See, e.g., *Fortino v. Quasar Co.,* 950 F.2d 389 (7th Cir. 1991), rev'd on other grounds, 950 F.2d 389 (7th Cir. 1991).
19. Id., at 394.
20. See, e.g., *Goyette v. DCA Advertising, Inc.,* 828 F. Supp. 227 (S.D.N.Y. 1993). It should be noted that the Immigration Reform and Control Act of 1986, unlike Title VII, specifically contains a provision purporting to prohibit discrimination on the basis of citizenship. As of this writing, it remains unclear what effect, if any, this might have on the invocation of the treaty.
21. See *Goyette,* 828 F. Supp., at 240.
22. See, e.g., *Fernandez v. Wynn Oil Co.,* 653 F.2d 1273 (9th Cir. 1981).
23. *Sumitomo Shoji Am., Inc. v. Avagliano,* 457 U.S. 176 (1982).
24. See, e.g., *Fortino v. Quasar Co.,* 950 F.2d 389, 393 (7th Cir. 1991).
25. See, e.g., *Goyette v. DCA Advertising Inc.,* 828 F. Supp. 227 (S.D.N.Y. 1993).
26. *Linskey v. Heidelberg Eastern, Inc.,* 470 F. Supp. 1181 (E.D.N.Y. 1979). In this case, the Danish parent and the U.S. subsidiary were both subject

to the jurisdiction of the American courts in connection with a claim of unlawful employment discrimination because the activities between the management of the parent and the subsidiary were so closely related that they constituted an integrated enterprise or caused the subsidiary to be merely the agent or instrumentality of the parent.

27. See EEOC opinion letter dated February 23, 1984. Although, in a more recent, rather lengthy and convoluted, opinion letter, the EEOC did indicate that it would carefully scrutinize any expatriate compensation system, it has continued to take the same position it had taken in the past.
28. See *Walsh v. Eagle Wings Industries,* 55 Fair Empl. Prac. Cas. (BNA) 570 (C.D. Ill. 1991) (differences in relocation expenses or in length of time employer would pay for storage of household goods of American and Japanese employees explained by fact that American was new hire and Japanese employees were on temporary assignment and came long distance).
29. See, e.g., *Fortino v. Quasar Co.,* 950 F.2d 389 at 393.
30. See, e.g., *AFSCME v. Washington,* 770 F.2d 1401 (9th Cir. 1985) (stating that law is not violated by "payment of wages according to prevailing rates" and "neither law nor logic deems the free market system a suspect enterprise"); *Horner v. Mary Institute,* 613 F.2d 706 (8th Cir. 1980) (holding that employer may consider "market place value" of skills of individual when determining his or her salary); *Christensen v. State of Iowa,* 563 F.2d 353, 356 (8th Cir. 1977) (stating that Title VII does not require employer to ignore market in setting wage rates for genuinely different work classifications).
31. The examples listed in the remainder of the appendix are based on what is set forth in the *Uniform Guidelines on Employee Selection Procedures* promulgated by the EEOC. See 29 C.F.R. §1607 et seq.

Further Reading

Berkowitz, Philip M. *Avoiding Perils of Overseas Employment Practices,* 1057 Practicing Law Institute /Corp. 1213 (1998).

Isenberg, Beth Ann. *The Evolving Conflict Between Employment Discrimination Laws and Immunity Under Title VII of the Civil Rights Act and*

Article VII of the Treaty Between the United States and Japan: The Papaila Case, 60 Albany: Law Review 1441 (1997).

Kiesling, Donald F., Jr. *Title VII and the Temporary Employment Relationship,* 32 Valparaiso University Law Review 1 (1997).

Nobile, Robert J. *Affirmative Action Compliance Manual for Banks.* Washington, D.C.: American Bankers' Association, 1992.

Nobile, Robert J. *Essential Facts of Employment.* Boston, MA: Warren, Gorham & Lamont, 1998.

Nobile, Robert J. *Guide to Corporate HR Policies and Procedures Manuals.* Boston, MA: Warren, Gorham & Lamont, 1997.

Nobile, Robert J. *Guide to Employee Handbooks.* Boston, MA: Warren, Gorham & Lamont, 1998.

Nobile, Robert J. *Human Resources Guide.* Boston, MA: Warren, Gorham & Lamont, 1997.

Outten, Wayne N., & Raisner, Jack A. *Multinational Employment: U.S. Employees of Foreign Employers and Employees of U.S. Employers Abroad,* 586 Practicing Law Institute/Lit. 577 (1998).

Perkins, William P. *Guide to Employee Recruitment and Hiring.* Boston, MA: Warren, Gorham & Lamont, 1996.

Starr, Michael. *Who's the Boss? The Globalization of United States Employment Law,* 51 Business Law 635 (1996).

Wilson, David T. *Foreign Owned Subsidiaries and National Origin Discrimination: Can Federal Employment Discrimination Law and Employer Choice Provisions Be Reconciled?* 10 Arizona Journal of International & Comparative Law 507 (1993).

CHAPTER 10

IMMIGRATION

BETSY STELLE MORGAN

Introduction

At some point, most international human resource professionals will be faced with the task of obtaining employment authorization for an individual who is being transferred by his or her employer to a country of which he or she is not a citizen. This task often falls to the bottom of the list of things to do when preparing an employee for an international assignment. Unfortunately, if an individual does not have appropriate authorization to work in a country, it is unlikely that the individual will be able to enter that country to commence his or her assignment, and all of the complex tax, compensation, and benefit planning will be for naught. The purpose of this chapter is to expose international human resource professionals to the processes commonly involved in obtaining work authorization in a foreign jurisdiction. Obviously, it is impossible to cover the legal idiosyncrasies of every country in a single chapter, and the following information is not meant to be a comprehensive guide to immigration planning. Rather, this chapter is designed to assist international human resource professionals in identifying the immigration-related tasks that should be placed at the top of the "to do" list when orchestrating an international transfer. The information contained in this chapter is drawn from the author's experiences working with employers and law offices around the world in transferring executives and professionals to foreign countries.

What Visa Requirement?

Consider the following scenario. An executive employee has been asked to assist with the start-up of a branch office in a foreign country. The assignment is expected to last two years. After months of planning, the expatriate agreement has been signed; the compensation plan has been finalized; the household goods have been packed and are en route to the foreign destination; and the plane tickets have been purchased for the executive and her family. The executive arrives in the foreign country with spouse and children in tow, tired from the long trip overseas. Suddenly, she finds herself asking a stern-faced immigration officer, "What visa requirement?"

The failure to obtain appropriate employment authorization can have many unpleasant consequences. The employee and her family may be detained at the airport or sent back home on the next return flight. If the employee is allowed to enter the country, it is unlikely that she will be able to retrieve her household goods from customs. It is also possible that the goods will not be accepted by customs in the receiving country. Most certainly, the employee will not be able to work legally in the foreign country. If the local employer allows the employee to work without authorization, both the local employer and the parent company may be exposed to financial or criminal sanctions. The family of the employee may also suffer hardships. In England, for example, the children may not be allowed to attend school. In Holland, the family may be denied access to electricity and telephone services.

Consequences such as these may be easily avoided by anticipating the visa requirement. As soon as an international transfer is proposed, the following questions should be asked:

- What type of visa is required?
- How long will it take to process the visa application?

The type of work authorization appropriate for an international transfer usually depends on the employee's education, experience, and position. In addition, in most countries, processing for employment authorization will take approximately two to three months to complete. Thus, the above questions will help to determine (1) if the individual possesses the credentials or holds the type of position necessary to support a particular type of employment authorization and (2) when the employee can reasonably be expected to commence the foreign assignment.

Maximizing Time to Meet Corporate Demands

International human resource professionals are not always afforded the luxury of two or three months to plan the international transfer of an employee. Although it is difficult, if not impossible, to control government processing times, there are ways to maximize the time spent preparing an application for employment authorization. An easy way to facilitate the process is to anticipate documentation requirements. Although the requirements of each country will vary, the following documents and/or information are commonly required from the individual, as well as from the sending and receiving companies, in order to begin the process of pursuing employment authorization.

From the Employee

- A complete copy of the employee's passport
- A copy of the employee's résumé (with detailed job descriptions)
- Copies of diplomas and transcripts for university and advanced degrees
- Copies of certificates, professional licenses, awards, etc.
- A copy of the employee's birth certificate (the original may also be required)
- A copy of the employee's marriage certificate, if applicable (the original may also be required)
- If family members will accompany the employee,
  - full names of spouse and children
  - dates of birth
  - countries of birth
  - complete copies of all passports
  - birth certificates (originals may be required)

From the Employer

- A copy of the domestic and/or foreign company's most recent annual report
- A copy of the domestic and/or foreign company's product brochure or catalogue
- A copy of the domestic and/or foreign company's personnel chart
- A detailed description of the employee's current and proposed job duties

- A listing of *all* work sites in the foreign country where the employee will perform services on behalf of the foreign employer
- A summary of the *salary* and *benefits* that will be afforded to the employee while in the foreign country (this can usually be satisfied with a copy of an offer letter)

This list is by no means exhaustive. But it is a good starting point. This type of list should be distributed to the human resource professional handling the transfer, the potential candidates for the transfer, and the appropriate managers as soon as the topic of an international assignment is raised. Not only will this information help to determine which employees are qualified for an international assignment from an immigration perspective, but it will also simplify the completion of a visa application.

While management is deciding which employee will be sent abroad, the counsel in the local jurisdiction can determine what additional documentation is needed. The local counsel may also be able to commence visa processing for one or more candidates based on the initial information provided. This will increase the possibility that a visa will be ready for the selected employee by the time the final decision is made.

Are All Countries Alike?

Immigration laws are peculiar to each country. However, many countries' immigration laws are similar in terms of the underlying policy, the types of visas offered, and the requirements for specific visa categories.

Like the United States, many countries have structured their immigration laws in a manner that encourages foreign investment yet protects jobs for local workers. As a result, most countries have more types of visas available to foreign workers with unique or specialized skills. The developed nations tend to have the widest range of employment-based visas in order to accommodate the specific industries and businesses existing or being established in those countries.

As a general rule, the visa application process is simpler for individuals who are being transferred within an international organization, particularly if those individuals have worked for that organization for at least one year prior to the transfer. In contrast, individuals who have not previously worked with the organization to which they are being transferred often face a more complex application process. For example, the individual might have to prove that he or she has at least a bachelor's degree and that such degree is the minimum qualification for individuals in his or her position within the particular industry. In addition, the foreign company might have to test the local labor market to ensure that there are no workers who are qualified and available for the position being offered to the foreign worker. Most countries make it difficult or impossible for laborers and minimally skilled workers to obtain employment authorization.

The Application Process

Most countries require all foreign workers to be sponsored by a local employer.[1] The sponsoring company must submit a formal request for employment authorization on behalf of the worker. The application form is generally accompanied by an explanation of the foreign worker's proposed responsibilities with the sponsoring company as well as evidence of the foreign worker's professional and educational credentials. Some countries require detailed and personal information regarding the employee. For example, many countries require that individuals present a certificate confirming that they have never been arrested or have never filed for bankruptcy in their home jurisdiction. Other countries require individuals to present information from a doctor regarding inoculations. Some countries require individuals to be examined by a designated physician for such communicable diseases as tuberculosis and HIV.

In some instances, the application requires a single submission to one government agency in the foreign country. In other scenarios, the application process involves a series of submissions to several government agencies, including the Departments of Immigration, Labor, and Health. The complexity of the application process often depends on the type of work authorization requested. An application for a short-term business visitor's visa may be very simple, whereas an application for permanent work authorization may require a lot of detailed information.

Isn't There a Faster Way?

Most countries do not offer expedited processing of visa applications simply to accommodate an employer's needs. As businesses have become increasingly global, the immigration systems of many countries have become flooded with requests for work authorization. Most immigration systems are understaffed and simply cannot handle special processing requests. Often, the best way to facilitate processing is to prepare a thorough application and to follow the prescribed application procedures carefully. This minimizes the effort required by the immigration officer to review and adjudicate the visa application.

As a matter of policy, some countries do assign a higher priority to certain categories of employment authorization. For example, a company or individual that will be making a substantial investment in the foreign country and will be creating jobs for local workers may receive preferential treatment regarding the processing of visas for its foreign workers. Commonly, a country will offer a more streamlined application procedure in such situations (i.e., reduce the number of submissions required) rather than provide expedited processing.

Sanctions for Sending Employees to a Foreign Country before Employment Authorization Is Granted

When sending an employee to a country where he or she is not a citizen, it is tempting to use the visitor's visa as a mechanism for the initial transfer. A visitor's visa is relatively simple to obtain and can get the employee "on the ground" in the foreign country usually within a few days. Unfortunately, in most countries, a visitor's visa does not authorize an employee to work for a foreign company, even on a short-term basis. Rather, such visas generally allow an employee to conduct limited business activities on behalf of the domestic employer. In many countries, including the United States, the concept of "employment authorization" is separate from and contradictory to "visitor's status." Thus, entering a foreign country on a visitor's visa with the intent to work is commonly viewed as fraud. In countries such as Singapore and Malaysia, immigration fraud is punishable by caning; less draconian penalties may include detention and deportation.

As mentioned above, individuals who do not have proper authorization often will not be able to (1) retrieve furniture and other goods from customs, (2) hook up electricity and water in an apartment, (3) sign a lease or buy a home, or (4) enroll their children in school. In addition, an unauthorized employee may expose the host employer to greater scrutiny by the local Immigration Labor and Tax authorities.

How Will My Dependents Be Treated?

In most countries, the *family unit* is defined as the spouse of the primary worker and their children who are under 21 years old. Only those dependents falling within each country's definition of *dependent* will be authorized to reside in a foreign country with the primary worker. Generally, dependent status will not be given to (1) the parents of the worker or of the worker's spouse; (2) housekeepers, nannies, and other household workers; and (3) common-law spouses or same-sex spouses. It is important to note that dependent status does not confer employment authorization. Thus, family members who desire to work in the foreign country will have to be separately sponsored for work authorization.

Some countries have special rules regarding the treatment of the primary worker's dependents. In Singapore, the female spouse of a male worker may accompany her husband on his foreign assignment as a nonworking dependent. However, the male spouse of a female professional will not be able to obtain a dependent visa of any type because the Singapore government does not recognize that a man may be a dependent of a woman.

In the United Kingdom, a law was recently passed allowing dependent status to be conferred on the common-law spouse or same-sex spouse of a primary worker. In many instances, the United Kingdom will also grant employment authorization to the spouse of a dependent worker. The United Kingdom is unlike most countries in this respect.

Conclusion: Avoiding the Pitfalls

- Make the application for employment authorization a top priority when planning the international transfer of an employee.
- Start gathering documentation as soon as the international transfer is proposed, and begin the application process before the international assignment is made definite.
- Consult with local counsel regarding specific documentation requirements and application procedures.
- Pursue work visas for the top candidates while a final decision is being made about the employee who will be sent to the international location. Often, the final determination is made after many months of deliberation. If the processes are begun when the field is narrowed to

two or three applicants, an application can be submitted and approved for each of them and will be ready when the final determination is made.

- Avoid sending an employee to an international assignment without proper employment authorization to avoid both individual and corporate sanctions for such a violation.
- Remember, each country has its own immigration system and will make the sponsoring company in the host country justify the hire of a foreign worker instead of a local worker.

Note

1. This requirement may cause problems for companies that would like to set up a foreign office but do not currently have a presence in a foreign country. Sometimes, it is possible to obtain sponsorship through a customer, distributor, or joint venture partner in the foreign country. However, it may be necessary to establish a corporate presence in the foreign country prior to applying for work authorization on behalf of an employee. This may be a cumbersome and expensive process.

CHAPTER 11

THE ADMINISTRATION OF EXPATRIATE ASSIGNMENTS

JONATHAN M. ZAMET

Introduction

This chapter will approach expatriate administration from the perspective of a small but developing program and of a manager who is relatively inexperienced in the field. It will be a short chapter in relation to the business of managing expatriates, focusing on critical points. What are the elements of an expatriate program that really need to be understood? How can they be managed? What resources exist to support the management of expatriates?

The focus will be on an assignment of two to five years followed by repatriation to the country of origin. This is the typical assignment length and that for which the core balance sheet idea is essentially designed. There are, of course, all manner of other patterns: shorter, longer, repetitive, and so on. But the onetime assignment for a medium-term period has some important characteristics that make it a suitable focus. It is long enough to expect that the entire family will vacate its home-country residence and relocate; if the term is much less than two years, the full relocation is increasingly compromised, with varying consequences for compensation and other aspects of assignment design. At the other end, once five years passes, the pattern begins to change in other ways. Some of the tax benefits of shorter assignments, such as social security totalization agreements, are lost. And the longer the assignment goes, the more the issue of localization raises its head, especially as the connection to the home-country corporate environment becomes increasingly tenuous.

There are many multinational companies that have hundreds, even thousands, of expatriates. They have been in the business of managing expatriates for many years. This chapter will scarcely teach them anything they do not already know. If it provokes any new thought in these quarters about old problems, it will have served a useful purpose.

Expatriate Assignments

Three adjectives that come immediately to mind in relation to expatriate assignments are expensive, complex, and stressful.

- ***Expensive.*** A rough rule of thumb says that an assignment will likely cost at least double the home-country cost of the same employee. Often it will be three times or more, even though a reasonably cost-efficient approach is used.
- ***Complex.*** One measure of the complexity of expatriate assignments is the number of businesses that support their management. The list includes shippers, immigration lawyers, tax accountants, cultural advisers, providers of comparative cost-of-living data, emergency medical services, property managers, selection assessment services, international schools, temporary accommodation services, and outsourced administrative services, to name but the most obvious. Many are listed in Appendix B.
- ***Stressful.*** It is easy to imagine that an assignment from a major industrial nation to a third-world location presents difficulties. It is relatively easy to understand the difficulty facing an expatriate assigned to a distant country that is linguistically and culturally different, such as an American going to Japan. It is less obvious, but no less true, that the same American's expatriation to favorite tourist destinations, such as London or Paris, can be equally challenging. Often, indeed, the latter give more trouble because less thought and preparation are given to them.

In a nutshell, any expatriate assignment requires that the employee adapt to different ways of doing business. The expatriate family must adapt to a new environment that lacks the familiar web of support of the home country. It is a bit like going to college or leaving home for the first time except that the pressure of responsibilities on the expatriate and spouse is considerably greater.

Objectives of Expatriate Administration

If cost, complexity, and stress are the preeminent problems of expatriate assignments, then cost efficiency, simplicity, and stress reduction are the objectives of their administration. In achieving these objectives, the expatriate administrator must also balance the needs of the various constituencies he or she serves: expatriate, company, and, sometimes, the business unit or units that are sponsoring the assignment.

Cost

Cost has been a focal concern of expatriate management since at least the mid-1980s. This has had a general source in the broad drive to cut costs in the corporate world. For American companies, it has also been the consequence of a weaker dollar and lowered U.S. tax rates that drove up the cost of overseas allowances.

It is, of course, important to spend wisely. However, those who design expatriate programs should be careful not to cut too far. A company sponsors an expatriate assignment presumably because it believes it is going to profit directly or indirectly. The expatriate is entitled to profit in some way too. One way that an expatriate can benefit is from the enhancement of career prospects or other personal goals. But, absent such benefits—and they are often absent—there needs to be some quid pro quo, and, in this respect, financial rewards count. A program that is lean in career prospects and lean in cash will, eventually, be lean in volunteers.

Complexity

As illustrated above, an employee must cope with a wide variety of issues when taking a position abroad: visas and work permits; the disposition of home-country residence(s); foreign- and (at least in the United States) home-country taxes; shipping and/or storage of personal belongings; education for children; foreign bank accounts; exchange rates; foreign housing; and so on.

It is not in the company's interest to leave the employee and his or her spouse and family all alone to resolve such issues. The first concern in a foreign assignment is to get the employee up and running in the job. Leaving the employee to his or her own devices to solve these problems will seriously detract from job performance. Moreover, most employees do not have the skills needed to bring all the issues to an efficient closure.

For example, most assignees rent homes in the foreign location. Few are equipped to deal with the local real estate market or to negotiate the details of leases. Providing assistance gets the job done faster and better and avoids costly mistakes.

The complexity is compounded by the fact that every assignment brings individual problems that require attention. Because of this, expatriate administration tends to be time-consuming and labor intensive. It is not unusual for an expatriate program to have one administrator for as few as every 15 expatriates.

Not surprisingly, companies have looked for ways to simplify the administrative burdens. Outsourcing has been one approach, which we shall return to below. Another approach to simplification began by laying the blame on the balance sheet system—the most commonly used methodology for managing expatriate assignments in the United States and, increasingly, worldwide. Pure balance sheet approaches tend to look at each element of an expatriation separately and deal with the economic consequences through a series of specific payments or allowances. Some companies have tried to develop bundled packages in which the expatriate is given either a lump sum or a periodic payment designed to cover a range of eventualities. The assignee is then left to manage alone. Ostensibly, this avoids much of the record keeping and constant adjustments that the balance sheet system can generate. Lump summing can also be used to mask cost-reduction measures.

As with cost control, simplification can be taken too far. The disadvantages of bundled packages can include a loss of flexibility, increased cost, and lower expatriate satisfaction because the basis for the bundle is opaque. I was recently involved in resolving some compensation issues for an expatriate technology team in New York. Some were compensated on a traditional balance sheet system, and some were given a host-country salary with a partial allowance for housing. The latter were vociferous in their disbelief when informed that they were better paid than they would have been under a balance sheet approach. And yet it was true, simpler but true.

Stress

A major objective of expatriate administration is to relieve the expatriate of as many concerns as possible that can eat up time, energy, and enthusiasm, thereby promoting the success of the assignment.

Perhaps the most obvious example, particularly for American expatriates or assignees to the United States, is assistance with tax reporting obligations. Preparing and filing expatriate tax returns can be extremely complex and beyond the capabilities of many expatriates. But, above and beyond return preparation, the program of tax equalization (see Chapter 8) almost entirely eliminates concerns about tax obligations. Rental management of the home-country residence is another area in which company assistance can alleviate expatriate concerns and worries. Likewise, companies can help expatriates by providing pay delivery processes (see below) that neutralize the impact of currency fluctuations. In these and other ways, expatriates are freed from incidental concerns that have no bearing on the jobs they were sent to do.

The focus, however, is not entirely on the employee. The success or failure of an expatriate assignment often depends on how well the accompanying family adapts.

An area of particular concern in recent years has been the dual-career couple. Occasionally, dual assignments can be arranged because both partners work for the same company or the trailing spouse works for another company that can provide an expatriate assignment. In many cases, however, the trailing spouse's career must be put on hold or the assignment has to be turned down (commuter expatriation is rarely a viable alternative). Replacing the lost income is not usually an economically feasible choice for a company because assignments are already extremely expensive. However, a number of companies have begun to experiment with support programs that may include job search and work permit assistance in the new location. Another recent innovation has been to provide the trailing spouse with an allowance that can be spent on educational courses during the assignment or can be used to develop a hobby or even to support retraining and job search at the end of the assignment. Provisions such as these are relatively inexpensive in the context of the overall cost of an assignment, and they can contribute significantly to its success—to achieving a return on the investment.

The Phases of an Assignment

An expatriate assignment is a cycle of events. It begins with the identification of a job opportunity and the determination that it should be filled by an expatriate. The next phase is recruitment and selection. Once a candidate has been identified, the terms and conditions of the assignment are developed. When the terms have been agreed on, the relocation process, which may have already started, gets into full swing. After the expatriate is safely ensconced in the new environment, the phase of ongoing administration commences. The administration phase is primarily concerned with the everyday issues of compensation delivery and various benefits and allowances provided under the expatriate policy or individual contract. In this phase, it is easy to neglect issues of career development and ultimate repatriation. However, these issues are better thought about early and often. While the expatriate is on assignment, connections with the home office should be maintained. After the expatriate has returned, it is often too late to solve the problem of reintegration. The assignment ends with the repatriation and successful reassignment of the employee.

Policy

Before going any further, the value of a policy and a letter of understanding cannot be overemphasized. It may seem that, if a company has only one or two expatriates, it is simple enough to negotiate individual agreements. It can appear an onerous and unrewarding task to put together a policy in such circumstances. However, the effort is well worthwhile if there is any possibility that expatriate assignments will proliferate or continue for the foreseeable future. A policy has a number of uses:

- It is a basic tool for communicating to a potential expatriate.
- It forms the basis for the expatriate contract.
- It allows for consistency over time and between expatriates.
- It helps control expenses.
- It provides a format for developing budgets.
- It fosters working relationships with internal departments such as expense accounting and payroll.
- It provides a standard for managing the work of outside vendors.

If expatriate administration is to be completely outsourced, a policy is an almost essential prerequisite. This may seem like a tall order, especially for human resources professionals who have been dropped in at the deep end without prior experience. Fortunately, there is help at hand. A number of consulting organizations will assist with policy development. Some, such as Organization Resources Counselors, have pro forma policies with options and explanations. These can be used to develop a serviceable policy in a short period of time that is basic yet tailored to the needs of the company. Otherwise, at all costs, beg or borrow a prepackaged policy one way or another.

In addition to a policy, it is very useful to have a standard letter of understanding that specifies the terms and conditions of an individual assignment. In many cases, such a document merely summarizes the policy as it applies to the individual, but it represents more than just policy:

- It constitutes the final sign-off by the company and the employee.
- It is a personal document.
- Any special circumstances or exception to the policy—and few assignments lack such deviations—can be documented.
- The letter can specify, and is often signed by, the official who is going to be responsible for the expatriate's career during the assignment.

Selection

The failure of expatriate assignments has been much debated. It is a serious issue because the cost is enormous. A failed assignment often means substantial direct economic cost to the company as well as, in many cases, damaged business relationships and botched projects. For the expatriate, there may be a damaged career and considerable personal and family psychological trauma.

It is not surprising then that many experienced multinational companies pay considerable attention to expatriate selection as a critical first step toward assignment success. A number of commercially available profiling or testing processes have been developed to help screen potential expatriates and, importantly, their families. A few companies have also resorted to psychologist interviews to identify personal problems, such as alcoholism or marital stress, that are likely to be exacerbated rather than resolved by expatriation.

When all is said and done, the two most common criteria for selection as an expatriate are skills and availability. In a small program, there may not be an adequate pool of candidates to make a more sophisticated choice. Still, there are some that simply should not be sent.

Success in the home country does not guarantee success abroad. A candidate should have some cultural flexibility. In addition, the candidate's family should support the assignment; unhappy spouses and children are the primary cause of failure. But there is no universal prescription. One reason for this is that each host country is different, and culture can vary by industry and company as well. Some of the most apparently unlikely expatriates succeed quite well because of who they are and how they are perceived as much as for what they bring. One company found that older men from the South and Midwest who had never been abroad before were successful in Latin American countries. Their age was respected, and they fell easily into a role of mentor that was welcomed. On the other hand, I have seen a young couple return from a European capital after less than a year because the trailing spouse was terribly unhappy—they had lived there before, spoke the language, were enthusiastic about going, and both had jobs, but it just did not work out.

Preparation

There are a number of steps that can be taken in between selecting an assignee and the actual expatriation that can help smooth the transition and help ensure that the assignment gets off to a good start.

Cultural Orientation. Cultural orientation exists at several levels. There are plenty of basic guides to almost every country and major city that provide information on all aspects of everyday life. There are many other sources as well, from America Online to the State Department, from chambers of commerce to local expatriate societies.

There is another level that is particularly valuable for those who have to manage employees or other business relationships. A number of firms offer intensive training on how to do business in different cultures. I believe the approach to culture differences and value systems proposed by Fons Trompenaars[1] is particularly valuable. Its strength is that it helps expatriates understand where they are coming from as well as where they are going.

Preassignment Visits. Many companies will offer the potential expatriate and, usually, his or her spouse the opportunity for a preassignment visit. One week, if well planned, is generally adequate. The preassignment visit performs several useful functions. It is an opportunity to meet one's new colleagues. It offers the chance to evaluate the assignment location as a place to live. On either or both counts, it is an opportunity to back away from commitment at an early stage. However, if all is well, it is also a first step in the relocation process—a time to research housing and schools and otherwise pave the way for the final move.

Program Orientation. It is important, from the outset, to allow the expatriate to begin to think through the practical implications of an assignment.

Providing a potential expatriate with a copy of the company policy up front is a very good way to start this. It is also useful to provide pro-forma compensation packages and a draft letter of understanding as early as possible.

As the expatriation process gathers pace, the expatriate administrator should take the time to go over the features of the program and discuss any issue the expatriate may have. Where appropriate, the expatriate should be referred to outside consultants to provide expert advice and counsel in their specialized areas. Tax issues are the most common of the latter, but financial and legal planning (especially estate matters) and medical issues are among other areas that should not be neglected.

All of this helps to build a solid foundation of trust between the administrator and the expatriate that will serve both well as the assignment proceeds.

Housing. The choice of housing at the foreign location is an important element in a successful expatriation. It also tends to be one of the most significant incremental expenses and is thus an issue of double concern.

Expatriate housing tends to be expensive for a number of reasons. First, the expatriate is a latecomer to the market and is not around long enough to enjoy the advantages that often accrue to sitting tenants or stay-put owners. Second, the decision is often made hastily by someone unfamiliar with the local market. Third, expatriates tend to congregate in specific areas, often near the center of the city or in suburbs near the international schools their children attend. Such areas are often very expensive.

Flexibility in housing location could substantially cut foreign assignment costs. However, in practice, this is more difficult than it seems. Expatriates with school-age children often have limited choice. Others tend to simply be inflexible. Some companies have adopted plans that enable an expatriate to participate in the savings or suffer the expense on either side of a target cost range. In most major cities around the world, there are services that can assist with finding housing to budget.

In the end, however, and within reason, the most important thing is for the expatriate family to find appropriate housing. Three things should be taken into account aside from cost:

1. The nature of housing at the location
2. The needs of the expatriate family
3. The kind of housing enjoyed by host-company peers

If one is moving to Tokyo or Riyadh or Beijing or London, what is available varies, and "accommodations" must be made. On the other hand, it is a mistake to assume that the expatriate family can make do with "much less" because it is only for a short period of time. This may work in a cosmopolitan environment in which the opportunities for activities outside the home are extensive. It may be much less satisfactory when the family must spend much more time at home. Finally, there needs to be a balance with the host-country peers. Other things being equal, too much difference in housing arouses "ugly foreigner" sentiments.

The Letter of Understanding. The final stage in preparing for an assignment is to put together a letter of understanding. This document makes explicit the policy as it applies to the individual assignee. It also records any special or exceptional terms and conditions. A sample letter is shown as Exhibit 11-1.

A senior official of the company should sign the letter of understanding, and the expatriate should return a signed copy to indicate acceptance. Often, the official who signs for the company is also assigned as a mentor to the assignee. This is an important role and should be filled by a line manager rather than a human resources functionary. The mentor is responsible for ensuring that the expatriate's career continues to develop and that salary increases keep pace with home-country peers. Finally, the mentor plays a significant role in helping the assignee to reintegrate into the company upon repatriation.

Relocation

Relocation means closing up a home in one place and starting one in another. It involves determining what to do with the home-country residence, furnishings, and other belongings. There is a lot of emotion tied into these blandly obvious decisions.

Visas. It is wise not to take any irrevocable steps before all the requisite visas, health permits, and any other necessary paperwork have been obtained. If you relocate someone without the visa in place, you run a very significant risk. For the most part, visa applications, if professionally handled, proceed surely, but often slowly, to a successful conclusion. Remember that you are dealing with a bureaucratic arm of a sovereign foreign power. They do not take to being rushed or bullied by corporate executives.

Exhibit 11-1. Letter of Understanding for Expatriate Assignment

Dear Fred:

This confirms our mutual understanding of the terms and conditions applying to your transfer to ABC Company, in Paris, France, for a period anticipated not exceeding [x] years. You are expected to commence your assignment on or about August 1, 2000. This assignment, and all terms and conditions attached to it, are contingent upon your obtaining all necessary papers, including visas, work permits, and health certificates. The terms and conditions described in this agreement will be in effect only for the period of this assignment.

Assignment Status

For the purpose of establishing any applicable allowances and reimbursements, your assignment status is as follows:

* Point of origin—[e.g., New York City]
* Family status—[e.g., Married with children]

Employment Status

You will continue to be employed and paid by USA Company. During your assignment, [an officer] of USA Company will be responsible for monitoring your career and performance and, in consultation with ABC, will determine any salary actions.

Host-Company Practices

You will be required to conform to the work practices and schedules of ABC, including vacation and holidays.

Host-Country Laws

You are required to obey all the laws and regulations of France, including tax laws. Failure to uphold these standards may constitute cause for repatriation and termination.

COMPENSATION

Base Salary

During your assignment, your annual basic salary will be $ 100,000. Your base salary will continue to be paid on the usual biweekly basis.

Incentive Compensation

Your annual short-term, incentive compensation target will be $30,000. Payments will continue to be administered according to USA Company's domestic incentive compensation program.

At the discretion of ABC Company, you may be eligible for long-term incentive compensation.

Method of Payment: Compensation, except as otherwise determined, will be paid in U.S. dollars.

Salary Adjustments: Your biweekly paycheck will be adjusted, as set forth in the attached compensation worksheet. These adjustments will be reviewed annually based on data and methodology supplied by an independent consulting firm. These adjustments may vary from time to time and may decrease as well as increase.

Foreign Housing Assistance/Employee's Contribution: USA Company will, consistent with its expatriate policy (copy attached), assist you with the rent and ancillary approved expenses of appropriate housing in Paris. Determination of appropriate housing, rents, and other expenses is made in consultation with ABC and an outside consultant. At this time, USA anticipates that your rent will be in the range of FF 20–25,000 per month. You may choose to exceed the approved expenditure amount at your own expense. USA will deduct a contribution toward your housing in Paris. The amount of this contribution will be based on data from an outside consultant.

USA will not support or assist you with the purchase of a home while you are abroad.

Goods and Services Differential: If the cost of goods and services in Paris is greater than their cost at home, USA will pay an allowance to cover the difference.

Income Taxes: Subject to its tax equalization policy, USA will pay or reimburse all French and U.S. income taxes that exceed what you would have paid had you remained in the United States. USA will provide you with expert assistance to prepare both your foreign and domestic tax returns.

Benefits

You will continue to be covered under USA's benefit plans and will be guaranteed the same benefits available to its domestic employees or the equivalent. Only your base salary and short-term incentive compensation will be used to compute benefits. U.S. Social Security will continue to be deducted from your pay.

Relocation

Shipping and Storage: USA will pay for the shipment of your personal belongings needed in Paris and for storage of the remainder, if required, subject to the limitations described in its expatriate policy.

Travel Expenses: You will be reimbursed reasonable travel costs to the assignment location in accordance with USA policy.

Temporary Living Expenses: If appropriate housing is not available to you as soon as you arrive or if you must vacate your housing prior to departure, USA will meet temporary living costs in accordance with its policy.

Lump-Sum Relocation Allowance: You will be paid a lump-sum mobility allowance of $10,000 net of taxes. This allowance is intended to meet the numerous minor costs of relocation.

Appliance and Furnishing Allowance: USA will provide an allowance up to $15,000 for the purchase of major appliances and furnishings for your apartment in Paris. Any items so purchased will be the property of USA. A proposed list of purchases should be submitted to USA for approval once you have found an apartment.

Home Leave

USA will provide you and your family with one annual round-trip to the United States in accordance with its home leave policy.

Repatriation and Reassignment

USA reserves the right to repatriate you, at its discretion, at any time. In this event, USA will meet all the costs of repatriation in accordance with its expatriate policy.

If the assignment is terminated at your request, USA's responsibilities for the cost of your repatriation will be limited in accordance with its expatriate policy.

Upon completion of your assignment, USA will repatriate you to your new assignment in accordance with its expatriate relocation policy.

In any matter not specifically mentioned above, your assignment will be administered in accordance with USA's expatriate policy.

If these terms and conditions are acceptable to you, please so indicate by signing and returning a copy of this memorandum to me.

Yours Sincerely,

John James Johnson
Senior Vice President

I accept this assignment on the terms and conditions outlined in this letter of understanding:

Name: ______________________________

Date: ______________________________

There are a number of law firms around the world that specialize in this area (see Appendix B). The good ones are not cheap, but their services are well worthwhile, especially if they also provide an ongoing compliance function. Working visas are usually for finite periods of time and often specific to a particular position. As time passes and roles change, a visa can become invalid. Keeping on top of these issues can avoid serious embarrassment, to say the least.

Home-Country Housing. Nowadays, most corporate policies make it clear that the disposition of home-country housing is the sole decision of the expatriate. In recent years, renting has been preferred over sale because the rising housing prices of the late '70s to mid-'80s burned too many expatriates who had sold. Thus, many companies will pay for professional rental management services or meet some of the costs of sale to make the choice open for the expatriate.

It is usually not wise, or practical from an insurance perspective, to leave a house empty. In some cases, circumstances will dictate a sale. If so, the company may be asked to provide the same kind of guaranteed sale programs that are common in domestic relocations. These can be very expensive. What makes sense for a permanent relocation may not make sense for a two- to three-year tour of duty. Thus, all other avenues should be explored before a guaranteed sale program is entered into, and it should be used as an exception rather than a policy option.

There are occasions when renting out is impossible (e.g., in certain co-op and condo situations) and times when sale is difficult (one thinks of the housing market in Houston in the early 1980s). Such situations can often be decided only on an ad hoc basis. A useful rule of thumb is that, if the house is being rented, the rent (not the "rental income" from a tax perspective) should at least cover the contribution the expatriate is asked to make to the foreign housing cost.

Shipping and Storage. Unless the expatriate rents furnished quarters in the foreign location, it is normal (for assignments above two years) to ship most of the furniture and other items that will be needed to furnish the host-country household. The remainder is generally put in to professional storage. This decision, however, is not easy to make (especially with regard to larger pieces of furniture) if foreign housing has not been located or, at least, likely options viewed. From this perspective, the preassignment visit can be very beneficial.

For shorter assignments, furnished homes or furniture rentals can be cheaper than shipping (but beware of the tax implications). Some stores, such as Ikea, also sell complete "home packages" that may be a practical alternative in some instances.

Most companies put some written limit on how much they will ship but are reasonably flexible in practice. Moving companies and other expatriate service providers can advise. In addition to limits on how much can be shipped, companies often proscribe the shipment of large, valuable, or unusual items or items that may not be legally possessed in the host country, such as guns. Many a piano has had to be hoisted by crane through an apartment window because it would not go up the stairs. And what won't go up usually won't come down; either way, the cost is always outrageous.

There should also be some reasonable limits on what expatriates can accumulate overseas and expect the company to ship back. It is better to have a restrictive policy that forces an expatriate to seek an exception than to be burned by poor decisions. Also, make sure that your shipping companies have a copy of your policy and that they understand that you may hold them responsible if they ship anything that is not covered under it.

In all of this shipping and storage, you should only use reputable companies that have substantial experience in international moves and the appropriate network of international correspondents.

Air Shipments. It is often useful to ship some of the family's belongings by airfreight, and most companies make allowance for such shipments. Expatriates often have to spend several weeks in temporary living quarters until permanent quarters are ready for occupation. The usual airline baggage allowance is inadequate to cover the needs of this period. Moreover, especially if temporary furnished housing can be found in lieu of a hotel, the air shipment helps the expatriate family create a pleasant homelike environment early on, and this can mitigate the stress of the move.

Travel. In these cost-conscious days, business, and certainly first-class, travel is being expunged from more and more corporate policies. Still, relocation travel is an area in which a little extra expense may be worthwhile. Expatriate relocation is a tiring and emotional process. A little TLC can pay large dividends.

Assignment-Location Services. It is not always easy to set up a family operation in a new country. Opening a bank account, switching on utilities, finding stores, and so on can consume a great deal of time and energy. There are services in many locations that gather up the arriving family and guide them through the labyrinth. Such services are generally not cheap, but they may be valuable. If your budget won't stretch that far, there are published guides available (see Appendix C) that can substitute. If you have a group of expatriates in a location, it is always helpful if they can play a part in easing in the newcomers, and many are very glad to do so.

Checklists. It is useful to make a checklist of all the things that have to be done in a move. (See Exhibit 11-2 for an example.) The expatriate administrator should also gather a list of key personal information (e.g., passport numbers and next of kin) that can be important if unexpected difficulties arise.

Exhibit 11-2. International Relocation Checklist

Personal details

Name: ______________________ Address: ______________________

Home telephone #: ______________ Social Security #: ______________

FAMILY DATA

Family status

Single/Married: ______________ Number of dependents: __________

Name(s) of dependents: ______________________________________

____

Number of dependents who willaccompany you on assignment: ______________

In case of emergency, who should be contacted in the home country? __________

____

Name(s): ______________________ Address: ______________________

Home telephone #: ______________ Business telephone #: ______________

Next of kin: ______________

Name: ______________________ Address: ______________________

Home telephone #: ______________ ______________________

RELOCATION

Home-country housing

Do you currently **Rent/Own**? __________

While on assignment, will you **Rent/Sell** your primary residence? ______________

Monthly **Rent/Mortgage** payment: $ ______________ Taxes: $ ______________

Maintenance expense (if applicable): $ __________ Common charges/fees: $ ________

Host-country housing

What kind of housing will you be looking for in the foreign location? ______________

____

Home/Apartment? ______________ Number of bedrooms? ______________

Any special requirements? ______________

Shipment

Do you plan to **Store** items in the home country? **Yes/No**

Do you plan to **Ship** items to the host country? **Yes/No**

TAX COMPLIANCE

Do you have copies of the last three years of tax returns, both federal and state? **Yes/No**

Have you been granted stock options? ______________________________

Note: Prior to your assignment commencing, you must meet with a representative of the accounting firm we use to prepare expatriate tax returns.

BANKING

If you would like certain expense reimbursements deposited to a bank other tan the EXPAT Bank Overseas account, please supply the following information:

Bank Name: ____________________ Address: ____________________

Account #: ____________________ ____________________

DOCUMENTATION

Do you have

A current passport? **Yes/No**

If yes, please supply a the name and passport number for each individual who will accompany you to the assigned location: ____________________

____

A certified/embossed birth certificate for all family members? **Yes/No**

A copy of your marriage certificate? **Yes/No**

Does each family member accompanying you on assignment have a Social Security card? **Yes/No**

INSURANCE

Please review all of your insurance coverage and remember tat you are responsible for any coverage needed at the assignment location unless specifically provided otherwise.

AUTOMOBILES

Make: ____________________ Make: ____________________

Model: ____________________ Model: ____________________

Year: ____________________ Year: ____________________

EDUCATION

Number of children attending school in the host country: ____________________

Name: ____________________ Age: ______ Grade: __________

Name: ____________________ Age: ______ Grade: __________

MEDICAL

What medical plan are you enrolled in?

___ ABC HMO
___ ABC POS plan
___ XYZ plan
___ Traditional indemnity plan

Dental

___ Company plan
___ HMO plan

WILLS

Do you have a current will? **Yes/No**

Balance Sheet Administration

The principles and techniques of the balance sheet methodology are described in Chapter 4. Readers who are not familiar with the balance sheet system should review that chapter first. Here the focus will be on a few key areas of implementation and administration.

Exchange Rates and the Split-Payroll Concept

Most expatriates have obligations and needs in two currencies. Foreign housing and day-to-day living expenses require host-country currency. Home-country benefits, savings, mortgage payments, college fees, and other payments and "reserve" items require home-country currency.

Expatriate compensation packages are often delivered from a single payroll and, consequently, in a single currency, typically that of the home country. Exchange rates fluctuate, often significantly. Thus, the amount of home-country currency required to supply foreign needs will vary from one paycheck to another. It is impractical to change payroll amounts constantly, and, in any event, as long as the pay precedes the exchange, the exact amount can never be known. On the other hand, expatriates who receive their pay in a single currency can be whipsawed by exchange-rate fluctuations.

The pure "split-payroll" solution is to divide the pay package into home- and host-country portions, each denominated in its own currency. These two amounts are then delivered off separate payrolls, one in the home country, one in the host.

Often, however, this pure approach is impractical either because the company does not have the requisite facilities or because tax or other considerations preclude it. For example, in one country, payments made onshore must have income tax withheld, but offshore payments are exempt from withholding. In the first case, pay must be delivered with an immediate tax gross-up. In the latter, more beneficial approaches to tax reimbursement can be adopted. (See also Chapter 8 on tax equalization.)

Many companies will adjust packages if the underlying exchange rates sustain a move that exceeds certain parameters for a period of time (e.g., 5% for six weeks). This is reasonable if swings and roundabouts are taken into account, but it leads to a lot of nagging when expatriates are on the short side of the equation.

An alternative, which generally keeps expatriates quiet, is to track exchange-rate fluctuations and settle them periodically. One way to do this is to establish accounts for the expatriates with one of the banks that has special programs to handle overseas executives. These banks will often contract to handle the foreign-currency-requirement delivery for the company. You can also do it yourself on a simple Lotus or Excel spreadsheet using exchange rates from the newspapers (with an allowance for transaction expenses). (See Exhibit 11-3.) The amount of currency due for each paycheck is compared to the amount actually or theoretically delivered, and a running total is kept.

Exhibit 11-3. Foreign Currency Requirement Spreadsheet

Date: 12/27/95

To: Paris Expatriate

Subject: Biweekly Statement

Current Base Rate for Cola: FR 4.9 US: $1.00

Pay Period Ending	$ HLSI	F HLSI	Taxes $Paid	French Taxes	Misc. $ Pymts.	Misc. FR Expense	Total FR Due	FX Rate	Total FR Sent	+/(-)	+/(-) YTD
YRND 1994											(1,434)
01/06/95	1,850.00	9,805	0	0	0	0	9,805	5.28	9,762	(43)	(1,477)
01/20/95	1,850.00	9,805	0	0	0	0	9,805	5.12	9,475	(330)	(1,807)
02/07/94 (1)	1,850.00	9,805	0	0	0	0	9,805	5.18	9,584	(221)	(2,028)
02/17/94	1,850.00	9,805	0	0	0	0	9,805	5.07	9,380	(426)	(2,454)
03/03/95 (2)	1,850.00	9,805	0	0	0	0	9,805	4.97	9,195	(611)	(3,064)
03/17/95	2,863.30	14,030	0	0	0	0	14,030	4.87	13,950	(80)	(3,144)
03/31/95	2,863.30	14,030	0	0	0	0	14,030	4.74	13,572	(458)	(3,602)
04/18/95	2,863.30	14,030	0	0	0	0	14,030	4.72	13,515	(515)	(4,118)
04/28/95	2,863.30	14,030	0	0	0	0	14,030	4.86	13,928	(102)	(4,220)
05/12/95	2,863.30	14,030	0	0	0	0	14,030	4.98	14,268	238	(3,982)
05/26/95 (1)	2,863.30	14,030	0	0	0	0	14,030	4.78	13,690	(340)	(4,322)
06/09/95 (3)	2,863.30	14,030	0	0	1,000	0	14,030	4.86	13,916	(115)	(4,437)
06/23/95	2,863.30	14,030	0	0	0	0	14,030	4.78	18,467	4,436	0
07/07/95	2,863.30	14,030	0	0	0	0	14,030	4.78	13,687	(344)	(344)
07/21/95	2,863.30	14,030	0	0	0	0	14,030	4.75	13,603	(427)	(771)
08/02/95	2,863.30	14,030	0	0	0	0	14,030	4.74	13,559	(471)	(1,242)
08/21/95	2,863.30	14,030	0	0	0	0	14,030	4.97	14,231	200	(1,042)
09/01/95	2,863.30	14,030	0	0	0	0	14,030	4.97	14,231	200	(841)
09/15/95	2,863.30	14,030	0	0	0	0	14,030	5.04	14,431	401	(440)
10/02/95	2,863.30	14,030	0	0	0	0	14,030	4.86	13,906	(124)	(564)
10/13/95	2,863.30	14,030	0	0	0	0	14,030	4.89	13,988	(42)	(606)
10/27/95	2,863.30	14,030	0	0	0	0	14,030	4.82	13,796	(234)	(841)
11/09/95	2,863.30	14,030	0	0	0	0	14,030	4.78	13,693	(337)	(1,178)
11/25/95	2,863.30	14,030	0	0	300	0	14,030	4.08	15,186	1,156	(22)
12/09/95	2,863.30	14,030	0	0	0	0	14,030	4.91	14,052	21	(1)
12/23/95	2,863.30	14,030	0	0	0	0	14,030	4.87	13,945	(85)	(86)
							0		0		

(1) Actual wire not sent. Exchange rate provided by Citibank PBOE.

(2) Revised compensation package. Change in base FX from FF5.3 to FF4.9: $

(3) Miscellaneous payment to adjust remittance shortfall

Record Keeping and Reporting

It is tiresome but essential to keep detailed records. Expatriate compensation, with all the basic balance sheet components, allowances, and reimbursements, can quickly run out of control if good records are not kept. Moreover, the use of bundling techniques only partly alleviates the problem.

There are three primary objectives of an expatriate record-keeping system. The first is communication to the expatriate. Accurate records help keep the expatriate confident that the entire process is being properly and fairly administered. The second objective is to provide the information necessary to manage the tax equalization process, including the status of any tax advances and tax-planning strategies. Such records are essential to tax compliance, the filing of W-2s, or any other tax reporting, including the preparation and filing of tax returns. The third and final objective is to facilitate the development and tracking of expatriate budgets.

In a small program, it is possible to keep adequate records in a series of spreadsheets. For a single expatriate, one sheet that details all payments on a pay period basis plus additional sheets to track currency remittances and tax advances will generally suffice in conjunction with overall budget reports. For a larger program, certainly for one that gets much beyond 15 or 20 expatriates, a more sophisticated approach is desirable. There are a variety of alternatives, from the homegrown variety using a standard database package to software purchased from an outside vendor. Of the latter variety, the offerings of the big accounting firms are the primary contenders, but some HRIS programs such as PeopleSoft have expatriate modules that are worth investigating if your company is already a user. For more on technology, see Chapter 27.

Policy as the Basis for Budgeting and Account Mapping

One of the most significant arguments in favor of a policy is that it is the best foundation from which to build a record-keeping and budgeting system. The main headings of the policy essentially set forth the main elements of expense that are likely to arise. These elements, from base pay to hypothetical taxes to club dues, should be mapped out to the company's budget lines and account codes (and new ones established if necessary). This mapping establishes a framework for budgeting, paying, and tracking expenses and, indeed, for tax planning—each category of expense can be tied into tax-planning strategies for each location. Finally, and in a practical sense very importantly, the mapping facilitates relationships with the budget and expense accounting areas whose support is critical to the smooth functioning of expatriate administration.

Payroll

It is ideal if the primary components of the balance sheet system can be given separate payroll codes that enable them to be separately identified and tracked on the paycheck. Those components that go into the regular paycheck include ongoing premiums, goods and services allowance, housing norm, foreign housing allowance, and hypothetical tax. Besides these, it is useful to have additional lines for tax advances (and be sure that they do not flow into the current W-2); current-year tax payments and settlements; and a miscellaneous code that can handle such things as taxable home-leave reimbursements, education, and other payments.

Tax Process

A great deal of time and effort can be wasted in expatriate assignments if good accurate records and breakdowns cannot be provided to inform the preparation of tax returns and equalizations. From the U.S. perspective, the W-2 statement is important—even if no tax liability ultimately results. In many cases, payments to expatriates come from sources other than the home-country or other primary payroll. Often, if the basic payroll remains at home, payments and imputed payments will arise through the provision of housing, cars, home leave, and other emoluments abroad. All these payments need to be consolidated for tax purposes, for planning, filing returns, and performing equalizations.

Cost Projection

An orderly budgeting and record-keeping process is also a good start for making cost projections, whether using advanced software or just plain rule-of-thumb methods. It is quite possible to develop reasonable budget projections using past experience as a guide. The most difficult element is estimating tax costs, but even this can be done with a little common sense and a modicum of spreadsheet expertise. However, most of the large accounting firms offer sophisticated software packages that will make accurate projections of assignment costs, including detailed tax calculations (see Chapter 8). These packages are not cheap. They also require more than a little expertise to use well. On the other hand, they permit the user to test the impact of a single variable in an assignment package. The impact of slight changes in timing or income characterization can be huge, and a great deal of money can be saved.

I once asked someone I was training to do a projection for a three-year assignment to a European country for a highly paid employee. He returned with a projection that showed a cost far higher than that I had been expecting. I looked at the projection and asked him why he had begun it on January 1 and ended it on December 31. He said I had asked him to look at a three-year assignment, and he had given me three calendar years. I told him to change the end date to the January 1 of the fourth year—only one day later. He returned after a few minutes, shaking his head. The cost of the assignment had been reduced by more than a hundred thousand dollars. The important point here is not the tax saving but, rather, that making use of these terrific tools is scarcely possible if you do not have a good policy and budgeting process to begin with.

Balance Sheet Issues (Cherry-Picking)

It would be impossible to calculate the exact impact of expatriation on each individual. The balance sheet methodology is a generalized approach that looks at norms and averages and makes adjustments accordingly. Nonetheless, it is important to apply the methodology flexibly and intelligently. In this regard, it is worth spending a little time looking at a couple of issues that regularly crop up.

Home/Host Split. The classic payroll split will simply not work for many expatriates because their personal financial needs are structured differently. Also, expenditures do not always occur with payroll regularity. Even aside from necessities, the simple use of home-country-based credit and debit cards for many purchases will upset the theoretical split. It is normal to provide some flexibility in how much of the foreign currency portion of pay is delivered to the host location. For the purposes of currency tracking, however, the full split should be used because this ensures that the expatriate does not experience a windfall gain or loss from favorable or unfavorable exchange rates.

Housing Norms. In many cases, housing norms will prove to be no more, and sometimes less, than the housing expense that the assignee experienced before being transferred abroad. But it will not always be the case. For example, a well-paid expatriate whose package I drew up objected strenuously to the standard housing norm. As a result of a personal choice of where to live and how to allocate her income, her actual housing cost was way below the norm. She complained that the norm was "taking away my play money." She won the argument on appeal to a senior executive. You can try to turn this argument around. In this case, you could argue: "Your foreign housing subsidy, therefore, will be limited to that normally paid to an employee earning half your salary." Well, you can try.

Double Dipping. One of the ways expatriate costs get out of hand is that the company ends up paying twice for the same thing. One of the major components of goods and services differentials for U.S. expatriates is private transportation: insurance, maintenance, and, especially, gasoline. When automobiles are provided to expatriates and these expenses are picked up, the differential should be adjusted accordingly. Furthermore, it is a common mistake to think that because the provision of an automobile is standard practice in the host country, the expatriate should therefore benefit from this practice. This is really a double dip if such benefits are not available to home-country peers. The expatriate, like his home-country peers, is already being paid to provide his own automobile through his normal paycheck. It is another matter if auto purchase is unusually expensive in the host country and some assistance is given as a result.

Career Issues

The idea of the balance sheet system is to keep an expatriate's compensation in line with that of home-country peers. The intent is twofold. First, it ensures that the expatriate continues to be paid a comparable salary for comparable work. If this does not happen, the whole point of the balance sheet is lost whether the actual pay is higher or lower. Second, because pay is kept in line, it facilitates repatriation, although, from this perspective, lower pay is less likely to cause problems than higher pay.

Of course, for pay to keep pace with that of home-country peers, it requires a certain amount of effort and, in particular, the continuation of home-country performance appraisal, performance management, and salary administration programs. All of this is easier said than done. Even the best of companies do not always get it right for their domestic employees, so it is hardly surprising that it should be more difficult for expatriates. In fact, it is one of the essential risks of taking an overseas assignment.

It is pointless for the expatriate administrator to try and lay down any rules in this area or to do more than try to alert company management to the issue. In many respects, circumstances and corporate environment play a very large role in determining how career issues are managed.

There are companies and occupations that are essentially international in nature. Outside the corporate sphere, the diplomatic service is the obvious paradigm. Within the corporate sphere, a number of industries and occupations have a naturally international bent. Geologists in oil companies and engineers in major construction companies are just two career paths that are international by nature. Companies that have extensive international operations—many consumer products, pharmaceutical, and technology companies, for example—have a real need for employees with international experience, and such experience is commonly a component of a fast-track career development program. In all these circumstances, the expatriate assignment is an integral part of the overall business plan. Often, though not always, this fosters an environment in which career issues for the expatriate are handled thoughtfully and effectively in all aspects of an assignment, from selection, through administration, to repatriation.

It becomes far more difficult in a smaller program in which there are only a handful of expatriates. The very nature of this game suggests that there is an imbalance between the expatriate, or international, activity and the domestic operation. This can be worse still when the home country is the subsidiary of a foreign entity and the foreign owners are obtaining needed skills abroad from what are essentially domestic operations with little or no interest in international activities.

In the latter circumstances, it is very tempting to make the classic mistakes of expatriation: selecting assignees because they are not wanted back rather than because they are and then forgetting about them once they are gone. The real difficulty here lies in finding common interest between the domestic and international activities, and, unless this can be done, the probability of a successful outcome is not encouraging.

Sometimes it is better to accept the reality that an expatriate assignment is not necessarily a great career move within the domestic context. However, even if this is the case, there can still be individuals for whom such moves make sense. Often, this is for personal reasons, such as a desire to work abroad, or for family reasons, wanting to work in a country with which a family has ties. Or it may be a desire to give children the opportunity to learn a foreign culture and language. It may fit into a personal career plan. It may be a final preretirement assignment for an employee whose children are grown and out of college. Or it may just be the financial reward that can come from a generous package or a more responsible position.

The End of the Cycle

In the end, the assignment may not be completed successfully if the expatriate is not reeled back in and assimilated into the home-country workforce. Interestingly, this is the part of the package at which corporations are generally said to be least effective. It is less often pointed out that expatriates are often equally ineffective in their contribution to this transition. Both employer and employee have a role to play in this process, just as career development is not a one-sided issue in the purely domestic arena.

Reintegration is often not easy. But the difficulty is compounded if the process begins only after the expatriate has returned home. The place to begin is the selection process. All too often, employees selected for assignments are those whose careers are stalled or who are simply not wanted back in the first place. And during the assignment, the principle, on both sides, is often "out of sight, out of mind." Instead, there needs to be a home-country mentor of sufficient stature who monitors the assignee's career development and is accountable for the successful return. In addition, the expatriate needs to maintain the home-country network. In this regard, visits to the home offices play an important role, if efficiently accomplished. This is one reason for insisting that home-leave funds are actually spent on home leave and that home leave includes a visit to the home office.

The formal reassignment process should begin, ideally, at least four to six months before the planned return. It is helpful to provide a visit for interviews and job discussions, and, in some instances, a family visit for house hunting and other relocation purposes may be justified.

Finally, a job is not the whole story of reintegration. Surprisingly, the effect of culture shock is often stronger on the return than on the outward leg. The employee often has to adjust to being a small fish in a big pond. And the entire family has to reestablish its web of connections in both human and cultural terms. The world left behind has not remained in a time warp any more than the expatriate family has. Friends and relations have gotten on with their lives, and the employee cannot always resume exactly where he or she left off.

Note

1. Fons Trompenaars, *Riding the Waves of Culture* (Burr Ridge, IL: Irwin, 1994); Charles Hampden-Turner and Fons Trompenaars, *The Seven Cultures of Capitalism:* Currency Book, Doubleday (New York, NY: Doubleday, 1993).

SECTION THREE

LOCAL-NATIONAL COMPENSATION AND BENEFITS

CHAPTER 12

THE INFLUENCE OF CULTURE ON MOTIVATION

JOHN S. MAXWELL

Perhaps the greatest variable we are faced with is the effect of culture on the manner in which various people are motivated. A great deal of scientific study has been done, and much has been learned. Much of this will be considered during the course of this chapter. Perhaps the most important lesson to be learned for human resource professionals, indeed for everyone, is that cultural differences are just differences; they are never right or wrong, good or bad, they are merely different. They do provide a wonderful education opportunity, and, in our field, they provide an opportunity of discovering that an approach tried and tested in one culture may or may not be transferable to another culture.

We know from Carley H. Dodd, in his work *Dynamics of Intercultural Communication,* that culture may be defined as "the holistic interrelationship of a group's identity, beliefs, values, activities, rules, customs, communication patterns and institutions. . . . Many cultural imprints are subtle and elusive, if not beyond conscious recognition at times. Culture is so basic to human behavior that we can not ignore its pervasive influence."[1]

Our professional roles are usually more directed toward those activities that will, in some measure, influence coworkers to behave in appropriate and predictable ways. Through the application of organizational development and reward management tools, we expect to influence behavior that matches the perceived needs of our organizations. However, the manner in which those desired behaviors are achieved is dependent on knowing the proper motivation and influencing tactics to use based on the culture of the workforce one is attempting to motivate.

Before one can set about creating motivating programs that wil. influence the intended, or desired, professional behaviors, one must comprehend the true basics of motivation, influence, and ambition.

Recognition Is Desired around the World

Everyone, regardless of their culture, seeks recognition for the things they achieve. The manner in which they expect that recognition to be bestowed upon them (or their group) depends on their cultural background. For example, an old proverb in Japan speaks of the nail that sticks up being hammered down. This shows the obvious desire of the Japanese to earn recognition from the entire group or company and shows their lack of need for personal recognition. The Japanese have long been known for their complete devotion to working long hours and overachieving, all for the good of the company (and in a sense the country). By way of comparison, the entrepreneurial culture of the United States commonly influences individuals to exert themselves for their own recognition and success, for power, status, and wealth. The vast number of entrepreneurs in the United States pushing themselves to succeed in their own start-up companies indicates the great focus on individuality and self-promotion in this country.

Regardless of what type of recognition a worker seeks, companies must realize the importance of this recognition in motivating employees to achieve established goals, whether for the good of the company, a particular department or group, or the employees themselves.

In addition to seeking recognition, in one of many forms, all workers also have ambition. And, similar to their search for recognition on a job well done, all workers have different ambitions in their careers. Workers in nations with more focus on the ambition of providing for one's family and being the "breadwinner" may be striving to make sure their work is complete to avoid long hours away from home. In the fast-paced workday of U.S. executives, the issue of family and family lifestyle may take a back seat to achieving status, power, and greater pay. Just as cultures dictate various habits and rituals people live by and follow, they also influence, if not dictate, what ambitions a worker strives for to make his or her position fulfilling.

All workers have some vision, goal, or achievement for which they are striving. That end result is the force behind motivating employees, because the employees have to believe that they can attain those visions and goals if they continue to be productive in their positions. If management desires continued effort and productivity, it must learn what steps it needs to take to make this fact known to workers. This challenge becomes even more difficult when dealing with workers from a different nationality, who have different belief systems and cultural viewpoints on motivation and success. Their ambitions are most likely going to be different from the manager who comes from another country and culture. In trying to motivate the workforce, managers not only need to learn proper techniques; they have to learn the cultural environment in which they are working so that they are able to select appropriate types of rewards or goals that will achieve greater motivation of the employees. The important point that needs understanding is that "difference" is just that: "different." It is not right or wrong, it is just different.

As an example, a worker from Brazil, whose culture views family as the most important institution, may be more ambitious if he or she was offered compensatory time off at the conclusion of a significant project, rather than, say, a membership to a local country club. The employee's American counterpart on the same project may indeed see the country club membership as something he or she would enjoy much more than a day at home with the family, where housecleaning, laundry, and other chores might await. Compensation professionals need to recognize and learn these cultural differences in order to design the proper reward and compensation packages that will motivate their employees.

Motivation

For centuries, psychologists and philosophers have theorized on and debated about what motivates people. Motivation has been viewed as instinctual, hedonistic, and varying combinations of the two, but no one theory has yet to have universal acceptance. This fact alone makes it impossible for a business to establish an all-embracing incentive strategy that will serve to motivate all employees. If you then add differing cultural views to your business by becoming an international organization, the challenge facing the business becomes increasingly complex. It can become almost exponential with the addition of other countries in which you wish to operate—and thus a greater number of different cultures across which you have employees.

The only aspects of motivation that all psychologists can agree on are that it is goal directed and that there are some base motivations that are involuntary, biological actions, such as hunger, thirst, fatigue, and so on. This was the theory expounded by Maslow. But, beyond this, there are no uniform motivators between any two people, let alone a community, nation, region, or culture. Businesses, therefore, have to determine not only what best motivates the larger number of their workforce but also why those people are motivated by certain goals. For example, is the majority of your workforce more motivated by large salaries for menial, tedious work, such as assembly line workers? Or is your workforce more motivated by the opportunity for advancement and achieving more power within the organization, such as lawyers or corporate executives?

Whatever the case may be, if a company does not match its incentive and reward programs with what its workers are motivated to strive for, the desired result is not going to be achieved.

Again, cultural ideals and norms will come into play in these motivating factors. Offering Egyptian workers their own corner office away from the rest of the workforce in order to motivate them to work extra hours on Fridays so that they can do business at the end of the week with the corporate office in the United States will probably not work. The Egyptians are strictly religious people, with a majority observing their holy day on Friday, and they are also very public people who gravitate toward groups. Therefore, an isolated corner office may not appeal to these workers. However, an up-and-coming junior executive in a U.S. Fortune 500 company would probably offer to work Friday nights, Saturday, and Sunday in exchange for the status of having a corner office and more pay.

The foregoing highlights the difficulty that organizations have in the application of the motivational condition that "success must be rewarded commensurate with its size." The difficulty organizations have in practice is coming to terms with the dichotomy of having a central policy but allowing wide freedom for it to be locally applied. Fons Trompenaars, in his work *Riding the Waves of Culture,* states, "In a truly international or transnational corporation every nation would be charged with finding its optimal mix between personal and group rewards."[2] This translates to the well-known catchphrase "think globally, but act locally."

Another form of motivation comes in humans' intrinsic need for stimulation or activity. D. C. McClelland stated that people have a "desire to perform in terms of a standard of excellence or to be successful in competitive situations." According to this view, people are normally seeking some form of challenge, whether it is the athlete doing her best to achieve a record-breaking performance or the mathematician challenging his mind to solve the unsolvable equation. Conversely, this may also apply to those, such as assembly line workers, who perform repetitive tasks all day. Doing the same "mindless" act for eight to ten hours per day may not offer the proper challenge for some workers. This may lead employees to take more breaks to break up the monotony of the day or to simply seek out a new position that will provide them with the proper challenge or competition. Companies need to keep this philosophy in mind when creating job functions or they may find themselves in a situation in which workers are motivated only to seek employment elsewhere.

Rewards and Incentives

Seizing on the principles of motivation, companies in recent years have begun to realize that societies are changing their view on work and pay. Going to work to earn a salary to meet simple needs is no longer enough motivation for today's generation of workers. Indeed, it is becoming increasingly recognized that there are four elements to rewarding employees: (1) base pay and incentives, (2) benefits, (3) personal development, and (4) work environment. The combination in which these elements are offered or sought varies widely across cultures and age groups. There must be the appropriate incentive to motivate workers to exert their full effort for their employers in today's business world. Reward and incentive packages, especially for executives, have become more elaborate and contain a growing variation in the ways to earn pay and so-called fringe benefits.

Successful incentives, however, will not work to motivate employees unless the worker believes the rewards are attainable. A reward will not motivate an employee if the standard for achieving that reward is set too high. In fact, unattainable rewards may perform in just the opposite manner and cause the employee to feel unappreciated, thus causing disdain or malaise in his or her position. According to Edward E. Lawler III in his book *Motivation in Work Organizations*,[3] most studies have shown that tying pay to performance does increase motivation, as long as the rewards are seen as attainable by the employee.

In addition to motivating employees to work harder and achieve more for a company, incentives and rewards can also be used as a way to attract and retain top employees for the company, specifically when certain desirable rewards are allocated only to specified occupations. "When the positively valued rewards are seen to be attainable by choosing a given occupation, the more desirable membership in that occupation will be," according to Lawler. A young worker with a new family is not likely to seek out a job that requires him to travel for more than half the year; to spend ample time with his family, that worker will more likely desire a job with standard hours in a convenient location. On the other hand, a young, single worker looking to discover the world, and prepared to put at risk how much money she may earn, may be very motivated to undertake a traveling sales position with a compensation package that may have a low salary but the potential for high commission earnings.

Again, when you mix in the variable of culture, the planning of reward and incentive packages takes on another dimension. The various component parts of so-called salary packages will be directly influenced by local custom and practice, which flows from culture. One significant manner in which this is manifested is through the application of taxation, both for the business and for the individual. Though it may be true that the proposed "package" is flexible and it appears to offer appropriate motivation, the impact of individual taxation may totally nullify the proposed benefits of the package to the individual and may not be cost effective for the business. That is, they may not receive appropriate taxation relief for some package component parts.

Incentive packages have now evolved into intricate contracts that can include a number of compensation or benefit items that an employee can achieve. There has been a proliferation of profit-sharing packages, which have moved from being offered only to CEOs and the top executive officers to being available further down the supervisory ranks and indeed possibly throughout the company. The high-tech revolution has been a principal cause of this trend of offering employee ownership down the entire chain of employment. This is usually because, in start-up business environments, businesses are more often cash poor but potentially rich. They therefore seek to motivate their employees with the promise of substantial rewards that would flow to a part owner should the business become successful. There are many examples of this being a very successful plan, especially in the United States. Naturally, those employees who belong to a business that does not achieve its potential feel disadvantaged and will seek other employment opportunities at the earliest moment.

In addition to offering employees shares in the company, the number of which can and often do increase based on the employee's level of employment, many companies are also offering employees the option to purchase company shares at a reduced, fixed rate. Many employees see this as the company's showing dedication to them, and they strive to make the company successful so that their shares are in turn worth more money. This is one form of motivation in which the employees do not necessarily have a direct impact on the amount of their reward, but they realize that the more successful the company becomes, the greater the value of their shares. The converse may also be true, and employees may be demotivated through a falling or flat share price over which they had little influence.

Although this is a reward found mostly in American organizations, many companies are offering their share plan to their international workers, and more and more non-U.S. companies are also designing employee-ownership packages. Some companies are finding out, however, that the idea of owning a piece of the company may not be much of an incentive to workers in some countries. For example, workers in China, or other communist-based cultures, already view the company as theirs, based on the communist ideal that they live in a "people's republic." Under this way of thinking, everything in the country is already owned by the people, so why would they choose to purchase, or want to be rewarded with, shares in a company they already own? It is important to consider, however, that not everyone thinks alike, and there are a number of success stories of share plans working in China. On the other hand, workers in many European nations are accepting the idea of employee ownership with open arms. However, we also find that not all governments support the view that share plans have value, and they often impose severe restrictions on the ownership of shares, through either regulation or individual taxation. This also includes the taxation treatment of share option plans, which may not be beneficial to the employee to participate in because taxation may be levied at issue of option and not on exercise of the option at some future time.

Cultural Values

It can be assumed that each individual is going to have his or her own set of values and principles that drive him or her in everyday life. A great deal of those values are a part of the individual because of the mental programs that are imprinted as the individual is raised within his or her culture. These cultural influences can range from the language people communicate with and the way they respect (or do not respect) their elders to the physical distance they keep from other people and the way they view regular human activities such as eating or sleeping. The majority of these "values" are ingrained into humans at a very young age, when most learning takes place.

The initial work of Geert Hofstede[4] identified four sets of opposing values, the combination of which could be applied to broadly define a "national culture." These cultural dimensions he identified as follows:

- Power distance
- Uncertainty avoidance

- Individualism/collectivism
- Masculinity/femininity

These value sets give us the opportunity of identifying the most appropriate reward for the society in question. For example, in those societies in which power distance is small—that is, societies that are quite egalitarian—you will find that employees will embrace performance-based rewards in a broadband structure.

In societies in which uncertainty is an acceptable value, there often will be less structured activities, more generalist positions are found, and managers will need to be more interpersonal and flexible in their management style. Also, discretionary incentives will be acceptable.

The collective value is best demonstrated through the Japanese consensus-building approach to challenges. The team is the dominant working unit, and individuals are rewarded for their contribution to the team.

When one lives to work rather than works to live, the masculine value is dominant. In this masculine-value culture, of which the United States is an example, time off would not be valued but highly geared incentives would prove attractive.

Within societies, these cultural values can be broken into two types: the desired and the desirable. This is where the notion of culture comes into play and where a person's absorption of the views of his or her culture is evidenced. Desired values are those that an individual personally desires. But desirable values are those that should be desired, which is where the influence of culture comes into play. What should be seen as desirable is obviously based on the community and society in which a person was raised. Consequently, individuals are going to tailor their actions and thought processes to these "acceptable" values so that they are not ostracized from their society.

For example, a Dutch worker seeking to work for an American company in Belgium may have all the qualifications needed and be the best candidate for the job, but the American interviewing the potential candidates may never uncover this fact. In the Dutch culture, the worker has learned that, in seeking a job, it is not desirable to be a braggart on your résumé, the expectation being that the interviewer will seek out the details of qualifications and experience in the interview. However, an American interviewer, accustomed to interviewing U.S. candidates, is expecting the résumé to explicitly list the worker's accomplishments (if not a few embellishments). The interviewer may also be expecting the worker to be assertive and forward in the interview, additionally seeking to impress the interviewer with qualifications and accomplishments. The Dutch worker is accustomed to attending interviews in which the interviewer will ask the worker about his or her qualifications and accomplishments. This is a fine example of cultural values clashing in the business world. While it is not desirable to be a braggart in Dutch culture, it is almost expected in American business culture.

Similarly, in a culture such as Japan, as was previously mentioned, it is almost required that all business decisions be made by a consensus. And a business deal may be undertaken completely through a representative of the CEO. A CEO from a more individualistic nation, such as Australia, may expect that he or she and the CEO of the Japanese company will handle a business deal. To the Australian CEO's surprise, a representative of the Japanese CEO may show up and relay the details of the negotiations back to his or her superior, which then may be referred to a management committee or board of directors before any further negotiations will occur.

These cultural values play a significant role in how individuals carry themselves on a daily basis, in both their personal and professional lives. Therefore, a company seeking to establish incentive and reward programs to motivate workers throughout the world must learn these cultural values or consult with someone from the culture to assist them.

To add to this mix of the different cultures of each nation, each of those nations can have several subcultures within them. For instance, one visiting China will most likely come across the differing subcultures of the Cantonese and Mandarin people. In addition, there is also the very distinct difference (at least to the people of China) among the People's Republic of China (mainland China), the Special Administrative Region, Hong Kong, and the Republic of China (Taiwan). To the Chinese, the difference between the two subcultures is significant, whereas a visitor from the West may not even notice a difference in the languages. It is usual for those from Hong Kong to speak Cantonese and those from Beijing and Taiwan to speak Mandarin. There are also a large number of other different dialects spoken throughout the various parts of China, just as a visitor to Great Britain would indeed find a wide variety of accents and structural composition to the English that is being spoken. The same is true of the United States. As Sir Winston Churchill, the leader of Great Britain during the Second World War, said in regard to Great Britain and the United States, "Two great countries, separated by a common language."

Subcultures play an even larger role in the values a person holds because the subculture is the more close-knit group of people an individual grows up around. The son of a farmer in Iowa, for example, is going to grow up with a very different set of values than that of the son of a Wall Street investor living in Manhattan. This also indicates that surroundings play a large part in the cultural values of a person. This particular theory was proposed by the American psychologist Carl Rodgers. Thus, a business seeking to establish an office in Canada had better know if it is locating in a French-speaking province and had also better know the values held by those who reside in the province.

Hofstede[5] defines *culture* as "the collective programming of the mind which distinguishes the members of one human group from another." Based on that definition, the values derived from that "programming" will be a direct result of the distinguishing characteristics of that culture. A Latin culture such as in Argentina, where business is conducted only between two people who are socially comfortable with one another, will expect business deals to take some time as the two counterparts in the deal get to know each other. In a country such as Australia, where they appreciate honesty and directness, the CEO of the Australian company would most likely expect a direct, to-the-point presentation with as quick and direct a resolution as possible. It is rare for successful international business ventures to be achieved without the establishment of sound personal relations between the parties to the arrangement. Many cultures preclude the possibility of doing business with strangers and thus will want to meet face-to-face and not conduct negotiations by fax or e-mail. Successful U.S. businesspeople are usually those who have understood and acted on this premise.

Conclusion

Cultural "programming" is as unavoidable as hunger and thirst. And cultural predisposition is going to influence the way any person does business and expects business to be done. But how well individuals or companies do business internationally will depend heavily on their representative's understanding of the difference in cultures, their efforts in bridging those differences, and the acceptance that differences can be leveraged to the advantage of all. An open mind, an essential element in international dealings, will allow the possibility of learning from one another to achieve a mutual advantage. The "not invented here" position will almost assuredly result in misunderstandings and communication breakdowns.

Reward professionals must understand the cultural differences in those countries in which they are working if their aim is to create reward and incentive systems that will motivate the workers to improve both quality and productivity.

There is ample evidence from studies that the proper reward system presented to an employee will indeed improve productivity. Thus, the key to positively motivating an international workforce is to discover what it is that drives them.

Often, for larger companies located in several countries, this will mean that they may have to create a unique reward and incentive system for each country in which they operate. And if the subcultures in those countries are extremely variant, they may have to create different incentive programs within a country. Again, "think globally, but act locally."

Understanding the concept of motivation and drives simply is no longer enough. Reward professionals have the opportunity to become strategic architects of the immediate future, and with more and more companies becoming worldwide entities, the need for the recognition of cultural differences and the acceptance of them as positive opportunities is becoming essential. Disneyland sums it up best through the lines of a song: "It's a small world after all."

Notes

1. Carley H. Dodd, *Dynamics of Intercultural Communication,* 5th ed. (New York, NY: McGraw Hill, 1998).
2. Fons Trompenaars, *Riding the Waves of Culture* (Burr Ridge, IL: Irwin, 1993/1994).
3. Edward E. Lawler III, *Motivation in Work Organizations* (Pacific Grove, CA: Brooks/Cole, 1973).
4. Geert Hofstede, *Culture's Consequences: International Differences in Work-Related Values* (Beverly Hills, CA: Sage, 1984).
5. Hofstede, op. cit.

CHAPTER 13

LOCAL-NATIONAL EMPLOYEE COMPENSATION PRACTICES

NEIL K. COLEMAN

Traditionally, U.S. multinationals have left the pay and working conditions of their local employees outside the United States to local management. Now, however, globalization of the workforce has forced corporate, regional, and global product-line management to focus on local practices to a much greater degree. Driven by both economic issues and the desire for improved productivity, corporate human resources are taking a closer look at the compensation of local nationals.

Diversity of Local-National Compensation Issues

In addressing issues concerning the compensation of local nationals, a word of caution is needed at the outset. It is easy to fall into the trap of assuming that each country has a consistent overall practice that relates to the values and historical development of pay policies. This assumption is reinforced in numerous published articles and reference materials that describe particular local pay practices. As companies seek to recruit in the local market, they rely on consultants and others to help design a competitive hiring package, and they assume a consistency that is often unrealistic.

As experienced practitioners know, in a dynamic and changing competitive marketplace, there are a variety of local practices. Even in the most stable and extensively surveyed markets, such as the United States, there is not a simple answer to the question, What is local practice? The realistic answer is that it depends on the industry, the size and scope of the employer, the level of the employee position, the company's stage in the business growth cycle, and the geographic location—as well as other unique marketplace factors such as simple supply and demand. Perhaps the most important factor is management's willingness to be creative and adopt policies and practices that may differ from those in the marketplace but give the company a competitive edge.

Likewise, many U.S.-based companies might assume, mistakenly, that there is a common underlying pay system that exists globally, based on market competitiveness and even meritocracy. Although the market and competition are very important in determining pay levels, they are not the only factors. In some local markets, age, gender, and seniority are equally important. The traditional pay system of Japan is the most notable example of this, and in France, the widely used Pratt survey *(Le Guide des Salaires, Edition Pratt)* displays compensation by age of the incumbent. In a marketplace that is highly dynamic—say, China or Eastern Europe—the diversity of local pay practices is even more pronounced. Perhaps it is best to describe local practices in terms of "a central tendency" but in which there are variations.

Not only is there diversity in pay practices, but there is diversity in the local-national market. Essentially, there are two markets in which these employees work. Local companies that operate primarily within the local economy create one market. Larger companies in some regions (Western Europe, for example) typically participate in "club surveys" with data shared only with participants, but smaller firms generally do not engage in such activities. In many parts of the world, there is no tradition of formal surveys and sharing of information among such companies.

The second local market—the focus of this chapter—is the one created by multinational companies. This market is well known, the subject of compensation-related surveys, and the focal point of groups of like companies that meet to discuss common issues and concerns. Japan offers a good example of the difference between the two markets. Local companies in Japan have historically tied pay and benefits to age, seniority, and an overall concept of loyalty. On the other hand, the large Japanese multinationals are starting to shift to concepts of variable pay, pay related to productivity, and pay systems that, like those used by Western multinationals, focus on jobs rather than seniority or loyalty.

Elements of Local-National Compensation

The following sections address three broad areas: cash compensation, incentives, and conditions of employment. In each area, the discussion compares traditional approaches with emerging practices and, when possible, comments on how practices are likely to evolve over the next few years.

Cash Compensation

There is no question that average compensation paid to local nationals throughout the world falls into a hierarchy. Switzerland, Germany, and the United States are among the countries with the highest levels of pay; India is among the lowest. Exhibit 1 compares the pay levels for a single job on a given date (all local compensation is converted to U.S. dollars for comparison purposes). Granted, the content of the job may not be absolutely consistent in all locations, but the comparison does provide some idea of the variation in pay levels.

Although global compensation managers might prefer to provide equivalent compensation for the same job on a global scale, the reality is that global pay equity is complicated by a variety of factors. Often, jobs are defined differently in different local markets. For example, in many industries in Asia, a job in sales has almost no decision-making responsibility, unlike the same job in North America and Europe. In the same vein, administrative jobs are more highly valued in the United Kingdom than they are in North America. Job comparisons need to consider reporting relationships, decision-making responsibilities, and other factors. Regretfully, most published surveys do not provide sufficient detail to allow for careful job matching.

Exhibit 13-1. Job-Pricing Comparison, Controller

(Company with $100 Million in Revenue)

COUNTRY	U.S. EQUIVALENT, OCTOBER 1, 1998		
	Base Salary	**Total Compensation**	**Percent Incentive**
Switzerland	$122,000	$138,400	13.1%
Germany	99,400	111,500	12.2
United States	90,100	103,800	15.2
United Kingdom	81,300	90,200	11.0
Japan	67,200	75,800	12.8
Canada	60,800	69,900	15.0
Mexico	58,100	64,500	11.2
South Korea	34,400	37,100	7.9
India	18,000	21,600	20.0

Source: *Organization Resources Counselors, Inc.*

Moreover, the process of converting compensation from various locations to a single currency for purposes of comparison is not as useful as it might appear. Since the currency exchange-rate relationships are dynamic, the compensation comparisons also change. For Europe, the emergence of the euro should make comparisons easier among those countries that use it, but the problem will remain in converting other currencies.

In recent years, there has been an interest in using the concept of purchasing power parity (PPP), which compares relative purchasing power between countries. Although such indexes are constructed from disaggregated consumer price data, they are considered an improvement over using unadjusted exchange rates. The International Monetary Fund's *World Economic Outlook* had traditionally converted each country's economic data into U.S. dollars for comparison, but in the mid-1990s, it started using the PPP indexes, which studies had shown to be more realistic for intercountry remuneration comparisons.

Another complication is the wide disparity in how the various elements of total cash compensation are defined. One would think, for example, that a simple comparison of salaries would be clear. However, what is included in salary is different in different locations, as the following examples illustrate:

- *Many countries in Europe, Asia, and Latin America*
  - — Basic salary is defined as monthly salary, expressed on an annualized basis.
  - — Basic guaranteed salary is defined as the basic salary and one or more additional months of salary, typically paid at year-end or in two payments—midyear and year-end.
- *Japan*
  - — Basic salary is monthly salary, expressed on an annualized basis.
  - — Total salary is basic salary plus the extra months' payments made in June and December, which may range from two to six months' salary.
- *Mexico*
  - — Basic salary is monthly salary, expressed on an annualized basis.
  - — Guaranteed salary includes the Christmas bonus, vacation premium, savings fund contributions from the employer, and such allowances as transportation, food, clothing, and housing, but not variable pay, such as performance-related incentives and profit sharing.

It is obvious that one needs to ask what is included in salary and the guaranteed salary when making comparisons. The term *guaranteed salary* covers different elements in different countries. A working definition would include all statutory payments and local practices that are commonly found by the great majority of companies in the marketplace. Some multinational comparisons simply incorporate the extra months' salary into a single "guaranteed" salary when the data are reported in a survey.

Note that the above comparisons are based on relative competitive *market data.* An alternative way of comparing locations, which companies frequently use when they relocate employees, is "net-to-net" comparisons. If a company wishes to relocate an employee and ensure that there is neither a loss nor gain in purchasing power and lifestyle for the employee, this analysis can be helpful. Exhibit 13-2 shows what a U.K. executive relocating to the United States would need to be kept whole.

This net-to-net approach is based on the concept of ensuring a degree of internal equity. This is most important in relocation but much less important when comparing local nationals in one country location with local nationals in another location.

Exhibit 13-2. Net-to-Net Compensation Analysis

Executive Transfer: United Kingdom to Urban United States

Net-to-Net Comparison

United Kingdom Compensation	£	**Equivalent Urban U.S. Compensation**	US$
Base Salary	£70,000	**Proposed Base Salary**	$109,000
Taxes:		Taxes:	
National	(21,401)	Federal	(16,787)
Social Security	(1,905)	State	(5,205)
		Social Security	(6,089)
Housing (including utilities)	(9,919)	Housing (including utilities)	(18,278)
Net Income at Home	£36,775	**Proposed Net Income**	$62,641
Cost-of-Living Adjustment	1,747		
Total Net Income at Host	£38,449	exchange rate: £: $1.6292 →	$62,641

Source: *Organization Resources Counselors, Inc.*

Incentives

Various incentives provide a second element of local-national compensation. Not only do the payouts for these incentives vary widely in the marketplace, but the eligibility to receive them varies as well—by country, size of company, industry, and the compensation philosophy of the company. Various issues arise with both short-term/annual incentives and long-term plans.

Short-Term Incentives. The problematic issue here is the performance criteria on which the annual incentive is based. Typically, two practices are found. Combination plans have goals tied to a mix of local, regional, global, and/or corporate results; the mix would vary based on the level of the executive. The other practice uses corporate or business-line criteria only. These plans focus on issues of internal equity at the expense of a focus on "line of sight" performance issues. A survey of large multinational companies conducted by Organization Resources Counselors, Inc. (ORC), showed that, for senior local-national executives, incentives were frequently *not tied* to the local business unit but, rather, to corporate results or those of larger business units. According to ORC, smaller companies and those in high-growth markets are more likely to use local business results as the basis for the annual incentive.

Long-Term Incentives. More local-national employees at senior levels are receiving stock options. There is also evidence that several U.S.-based multinational companies are extending stock options and stock purchase plans to lower-level local nationals in all country locations where it is permitted. Although these grants, generally of a fixed amount, are modest by U.S. standards, they may appear quite generous by local standards. They serve more as a form of recognition and team building than as an essential compensation element.

In the United States, stock options are the preferred—and almost exclusive—vehicle for long-term incentives. Share option schemes are widely used in the United Kingdom and are gaining popularity throughout Europe. As a trend, stock options are drawing considerable interest worldwide, and local laws are being changed to accommodate their usage. In Asia, where long-term incentives are not yet in wide use, Japan and China have lifted restrictions on them during the past two years. In Europe, multinational companies also use long-term cash bonus plans. (Local tax laws and currency controls in some countries make stock options unattractive.)

Except for the most senior executives in multinational corporations, there does not appear to be an identifiable central tendency in terms of a local long-term incentive plan. Multinational companies typically have a global plan that is frequently adapted to the local market on the basis of perceived global equity.

Emerging Practices. In regard to emerging practices and trends in cash compensation, the driving force is not only economic (increasing productivity) but based on the tendency of multinational companies to expand innovative practices beyond their domestic operations. In many cases, these large firms are challenging the rigidity (and the entitlement mentality) associated with many traditional local pay practices and are seeking ways to increase productivity. The local market is being affected by the adoption of pay delivery vehicles that are considered "best practices." An example would be Japan. As recently as the early 1990s, there were almost no variable pay plans (that is, plans in which an individual's compensation varied based on the company performance) in the local market, but at the end of the decade, such plans are emerging. Likewise, there were no stock option plans in Japanese companies until legislation permitted companies to hold treasury stock.

Another example is Petroleos de Venezuela, which—although it is government controlled—began implementing a pay-for-performance plan for all its Venezuelan employees in 1998. The plan differs substantially from traditional pay systems in Venezuela. Team incentive plans are emerging in various locations around the world as well, as demonstrated by Nortel's plans in North America and in Europe.

Conditions of Employment

Employment conditions of local nationals are typically covered by statute, by labor contracts organized within industries, or by individual company employment contracts. Compared with the United States, there are typically greater levels of employee protection found in the global marketplace. In the United States, the implied lifetime employment contracts formerly found at such companies as General Electric, DuPont, IBM, and Motorola no longer exist, because these companies have determined that flexibility in employment is essential to remaining competitive in the global marketplace. That trend is not yet found to a large degree outside the United States, and U.S. multinationals are finding substantial resistance to changes in employment security in locations around the world.

Emerging Practices. However, resistance to change in employment security does not seem to carry over to how work is organized in local environments. Work concepts that have been developed in many different countries are being implemented more easily than compensation systems. The use of teams, matrix organizations, total quality management (TQM), just-in-time inventory management, empowerment, and reengineering is being accepted by many local employees on the belief that these practices will increase productivity and ensure job security. Companies such as Motorola have established organizational units to ensure the technological transfer of practices designed to improve productivity and to share their best practices with business units in country locations. Can compensation be far behind?

It is not expected that a single global standard for working conditions will emerge in the short term. However, the influence of multinational companies and their drive to increase productivity will have an impact, and the range of local competitive employment will narrow. If the European Union is a model, there is no mistaking that forces are at work to harmonize employment conditions. Changes in retirement plans in regard to age and gender status and the concept of employee participation are largely realities throughout the European Union, albeit with differences in plan design.

Summary

The growing interest in local-national compensation and working conditions has uncovered a very complex and varied set of practices—one for which there is no single or unified database. The evolving situation is complicated by the competitive economic environment, which is causing changes in laws, creating opportunities for creative approaches, and putting pressure on traditional pay systems to modernize. There appear to be no simple answers, and caution must be exercised to ensure that companies understand the consequences of taking new approaches in environments that are strongly influenced by statutory requirements and local practices.

When analyzing local compensation practices, the key is to know what pay and benefit elements are included in any comparative data. Because local surveys are based on very thin data in many locations, multiple data sources provide the most comprehensive view of the market. Major sources of local-national compensation data include local chambers of commerce, government bureaus, surveys by U.S. and U.K. embassies, and the Internet. Many of the major global consultants can provide multiple-country data; the most widely known include MCS (Hewitt), Towers Perrin, Watson/Wyatt Worldwide, Mercer (CRG), Kienbaum, and ORC. Club surveys are conducted by industry but are typically not available to nonparticipants.

Finally, to ensure reasonableness in compensation decisions, it makes sense to obtain anecdotal information from a source within the local market as a check against published information. For global compensation managers, overseas visits are indispensable in ensuring that data are reasonable and accurate.

The growing need for multinational companies to understand local markets will likely result in better data sources. In Eastern Europe, little, if any, compensation and benefits data existed in 1990, but by the late 1990s, the burgeoning need for data has created several sources that improve in quality and scope each year. As more data become available, the impact on the emerging market will assist in stabilizing compensation practices. The global marketplace is constantly changing, and this offers a substantial challenge to human resources professionals to keep informed and remain flexible in designing global pay systems.

CHAPTER 14

BENEFITS: INTRODUCTION AND RETIREMENT PROGRAMS

Z. SAMUEL BERNSTEIN AND
CAROL Y. KAPLAN

Introduction

Many multinational companies have developed a philosophy regarding benefits—what will be provided, how they will be designed, and how they will be administered. For example, such companies take a position on retirement benefits—on the levels they perceive to be adequate, the proportion paid by the company, and similar decisions. Some companies offer no company-paid retirement plans but may offer a savings plan with no company match. There are companies that provide broad-based stock plans, intending these to be their retirement vehicles. Some companies require employees to contribute to their defined benefit plans, while others do not. There are often supplemental plans designed as "top hat" provisions for higher-paid employees.

Whatever the configuration, the company makes a decision based on its size, age, industry, and competitive environment, as well as the financial impact that any form of long-term benefit might have on the financial health of the organization and its business needs in recruitment or retention.

Companies also make conscious decisions concerning health care plans, which are intended to provide employees a desired level of protection against catastrophic illness. These plans are quite varied in the United States, where company-sponsored health care plans are prevalent, often provided through flexible benefit plans that give employees "credits" with which they can buy from a menu of health care and other benefits. Most companies require employees to share in the cost of these plans. Some offer a graduated cost structure depending on the dollar value of the plan, and others offer fully paid plans.

Life insurance and disability plans also take many forms. Life insurance is inexpensive but highly valued by employees, and most companies offer life insurance to employees. Again, there can be much iteration and many choices. Some companies offer all employees a flat-dollar amount. Others offer multiples of salary, such as one or two times annual salary. Often, the employee can purchase additional coverage at the preferred group purchasing rate and might buy additional insurance for a spouse and dependent children. Disability plans, both long and short term, can vary in the amount of salary replacement, whether they are contributory, and what type of employee is covered.

For this discussion of benefits, we're reminded of the old adage that "nothing is as simple as it seems." It is important to note that a parent company cannot simply export its home country's ideas and values. In different parts of the world, the emphasis placed on health care, retirement, disability, life (or death) coverage, and workers' compensation will take on different priorities based on a combination of law, culture, custom, and the competitive environment. Even the terms we use may have a different meaning in different countries.

In the United States, companies have been overwhelmed by the complexity, escalating cost, and delivery of adequate health care. From a company perspective, this issue of health care and wellness consumes benefit resources, both human and financial. In Chapter 15, you will note that health care takes on a very different level of importance to the company depending on which part of the world we are viewing. In many countries, there is socialized medicine, although some locations may require supplemental plans. In some locations, there is only an in-hospital benefit, and the company reimburses employees' out-of-hospital costs from petty cash.

Retirement plans are paramount in some parts of the world. Government plans are much more substantial than U.S. social security in many parts of Europe and are nonexistent in many parts of Asia. Generally, defined benefit plans are more prevalent, with few countries allowing defined contribution plans as we know them. The United Kingdom is a leader in individual defined contribution plans with the personal pension plan (PPP).

Companies need to develop a global benefit philosophy that encompasses the core values of the parent and also recognizes the diversity in law and custom of each of the countries in which they operate. This is an application of the now cliché expression "Think globally, act locally." For example, because profit-sharing plans have become ingrained in a company's culture, it might seem natural to export the same concept. However, some countries—France and Mexico, for example—already have mandatory profit-sharing plans. Be aware that by exporting parent-company plans, companies could find themselves with duplicate coverage and a high cost of benefits with little perceived value to employees, potentially leading to labor strife, adverse publicity, higher costs, and legal actions in a labor court.

This discussion will center on the more traditional forms of benefits such as health and welfare, short- and long-term disability, life/death, and retirement, with some comments on stock options and time off with pay.

What Makes Things Different?

From a certain perspective, all human beings, regardless of their location of employment, are faced with the same basic needs: the need for medical care in times of illness and the desire to retire from employment with some financial stability. Why, then, is it inappropriate to take a home-country approach when implementing benefits outside the home country? Basically, because differences arise from country to country based on different tax treatment, different statutory or social security programs, different cultural perspectives, and different competitive environments.

Tax Treatment

Each country imposes income tax and grants favorable tax treatment under its own rules. The U.S. government wants to encourage companies to have employer-sponsored medical plans and thus grants tax concessions (the company can take a deduction for the expense, and the benefit is not taxable to the employee). The U.K. government does not want to encourage companies to have employer-sponsored medical plans, so company-paid premiums for health insurance in the United Kingdom are taxable income to the employees.

The United States, through the Employee Retirement Income Security Act (ERISA) and other rules, imposes a number of regulatory requirements on plans to achieve "qualified" status for favorable tax treatment. Other taxing jurisdictions impose different requirements. Such tax rules can affect plan design on a wide range of issues, such as vesting, eligibility, benefit formulas, indexation, and payment forms, and can affect funding methods and administration. As a simple example, under German tax law, company contributions to a funded retirement plan generally create current tax for employees. Companies are thus encouraged to use unfunded book reserve plans, exactly the opposite of the U.S. approach, which requires retirement plans to be funded.

Integration with Local Statutory Plans

Statutory plans can include social security, national collective agreements, and various other required benefits. If social security provides most employees with 80% of pay replaced at retirement (as in Italy), what is the need for additional benefits from the company? If the national medical system is already comprehensive (as in Germany), what more would a company do? If employees get 70% of pay, tax-free, from social security upon disability (as in the Netherlands), would a company need to provide more?

Statutory plans will be discussed in more detail later in this chapter.

Cultural Perspectives

Cultural issues are a complex topic. We wish to stress only a few points, demonstrating how different national cultures have an impact on benefits.

- The United States has a culture that encourages individualism, choices, and flexible benefits, and each employee selects the mix that is best for him or her. In most other countries, employees are not used to having such choices or such responsibilities; they believe it is the employer's responsibility to take care of the employees. The typical U.S. employee is willing to take more investment risks with his or her savings plan than is a typical Japanese or German employee.
- The U.S. government is very concerned about tax-favored plans not discriminating in favor of the higher paid. The U.K. government has no such concern; it is anticipated and expected that the higher paid will enjoy more benefits as a reward for having achieved a certain position within the company.
- In Asia, Central America, and South America, where the extended family is still prevalent, the employee needs are very different from those in Europe or the United States, where the nuclear family prevails.

These issues can strike deep emotional chords arising from generations-old traditions, family values, religion and politics, economics and history, climate, and sociology. Two good references on this subject are Geert Hofstede's *Cultures and Organizations* and Fons Trompenaar's *Riding the Waves of Culture: Understanding Diversity in Global Business.*

Competitive Environment and Customary Practice

The competitive environment is very different from country to country and region to region. A U.S.-style life insurance policy of perhaps one times annual salary would not be competitive in the United Kingdom, where company-provided life insurance is more frequently three or four times annual salary.

On the other hand, a U.S.-style retirement benefit in Italy would be providing income after retirement at a level far in excess of what the employee had earned while working.

We are reminded of a German parent company that did not understand the need for its U.S. subsidiary to provide a medical plan—after all, the parent company didn't have one for its executives in Germany. The parent company was amazed to learn that the United States did not have a national health care system and that a private plan for employees was a necessity for all employees in the U.S. subsidiary.

Acquired Rights and Diminution of Benefits

The concept of acquired rights in the laws of many countries is that once you have provided employees a benefit on a regular and repeated basis, there is a contractual agreement: You have agreed to continue to provide that benefit. Taking it away can lead to a labor dispute or to what a court would rule as a "constructive unfair dismissal," triggering large severance payments and potentially requiring reinstatement of the program.

A related term is diminution of benefits. This occurs when a company attempts to change or take away a benefit and the employee perceives that he or she is losing something of value, perhaps even if it is replaced with another benefit of equal or greater value. Again, the aggrieved employee, or group of employees, can file a claim against the company in a labor court. Under European Union directives, for example, reduction of benefits is generally prohibited upon acquisition.

Conclusion

Benefit practices can differ greatly by country. In addition to the factors mentioned above, history, geography, religion, and tradition all can play a role in molding different outlooks on company-provided benefits.

Retirement Benefits: Fundamentals

The underlying basic human need is the same around the world: At some point, an individual ceases to be actively employed, retires, and needs some source of income. We generally think of a retirement plan as a financial provision made today to provide future benefits to current employees when they retire.

This can often be done in a cost-efficient way by setting aside money regularly in some sound investment vehicle. The mathematical miracle of compound interest accumulating during the employee's active career ensures that money will be available to pay benefits at retirement.

In most countries, this can also be done in a tax-effective way. Governments around the world want to relieve some of the stress on already overburdened social security systems and commonly allow favorable tax treatment to encourage companies to sponsor private retirement plans.

Approaches to Design: Defined Benefit or Defined Contribution

Classifications of retirement plans are not pure—there are hybrids and mixtures that may be hard to classify. Nevertheless, the traditional classifications provide a framework for understanding common terminology used by human resource managers around the world.

The two basic concepts of design are defined benefit (DB) and defined contribution (DC), although there is a great deal of variation in different countries.

Defined Benefit (DB)	Defined Contribution (DC)
Step 1 Define the benefit to the employee.	Define the contribution paid by the company.
Step 2 Estimate the future experience (investment return, future salary growth, etc.).	Record the current experience (investment return).
Step 3 Make a company contribution each year to meet the promised benefit.	State the employee's account balance each year.

There is considerable debate on the advantages and disadvantages of each approach. Currently, U.S. parent companies have a strong inclination toward defined contribution plans, which have experienced high market returns over the last few years. Japanese parent companies, on the other hand, are strongly inclined toward defined benefit plans, which provide more predictable benefits for employees.

There are various hybrid approaches that combine elements of defined benefit and defined contribution: cash balance plans, pension equity plans, and the like. For example, the Swiss government requires companies to provide a retirement plan (called BVG) with a defined contribution minimum basis but with a specified rate of investment return. This raises a question: If the rate of investment return is fixed, so the employees bear no risk, is this a defined benefit or a defined contribution plan?

In different countries, different approaches are taken, either by social security or by company plans. Many major U.S. companies, for example, tend to have both a defined benefit plan ("pension") and a defined contribution plan, such as a 401(k). Chilean social security is very much a defined contribution plan, whereas Dutch social security is a defined benefit plan. Most company plans in Hong Kong are defined contribution, whereas most company plans in Germany are defined benefit.

Social Security and Similar Government-Provided Retirement Benefits

The first layer of benefit programs that needs to be considered is social security or similar government-provided programs.

Most developed countries have a social security system in place (probably since the early 1900s) providing not only retirement benefits but benefits payable upon the death or disability of the employee. Most systems also provide some sort of medical insurance or national health services. As one might expect, the types of benefits, the form of benefits, the conditions for payments, the amounts of benefits, and the costs of social security programs are greatly different from country to country.

Terminology, too, differs from country to country. The ceiling on covered earnings is called the wage base in the United States, the upper earnings limit in the United Kingdom, tranches ("slices") in France, and the INPS ceiling in Italy. For this chapter, we will stick to standard (and fairly universal) nomenclature, but note that terminology in one country (even in English) may not translate well to another country.

Our focus here is on social security systems in developed countries. Generally, social security systems were established on a "pay-as-you-go" structure. That is, the contributions charged to employers and active employees are used to pay for current retirees. (This is discussed in more detail in the section on funding retirement benefits.)

Such a financing structure works well as long as the balance between current actives (who are paying contributions) and current retirees (who are receiving benefits) remains fairly stable. However, the financial stability of social security in most developed countries has been eroding in the last decade or so. Because of healthier lifestyles and improved medical treatments, employees are retiring earlier and living longer. Add to that a decreasing or stable birthrate and fewer and fewer active employees are paying for more and more retirees, creating a financial strain on social security systems throughout the developed world.

Social security is almost always focused on the mass of employees. Executives or high-paid salaried employees are typically paid more than the social security ceiling in their country. Because benefits are commonly subject to a maximum, the higher one's salary, the lower the social security benefit as a percentage of pay.

Furthermore, when a government feels a need to cut social security, it is often done at the higher levels of pay, among those who can "afford" it. Since this has the greatest effect on upper management, some form of supplemental retirement income may be important at these levels. However, just because an individual is highly compensated doesn't mean that his or her social security benefit is small. In some countries, such as Spain or Italy, the level of benefit may be substantial, even for very well paid individuals.

When Are Old-Age Benefits Paid?

Exhibit 14-1 shows the ages at which full social security benefits are available in a sampling of countries and any earlier age at which reduced benefits might be paid. While age 65 is quite common, the usual retirement ages in most developing countries are normally earlier, as early as age 50. In Scandinavia, retirement age tends to be somewhat later, such as age 67.

Generally speaking, most company-sponsored retirement plans use the retirement ages from social security as a "trigger" to allow retirement with full benefits under the company plan. Nothing is static in the world of international benefits, and even something as basic as the age at which social security benefits commence has been changing. Since the financial

Exhibit 14-1. Retirement Ages for Receiving Benefits from Social Security

Country	Retirement Age (Full Benefits from Social Security)	Early Retirement Age (Reduced Social Security Benefits Available); Conditions May Apply
France	60	58
Germany	65	63 (males); 60 (females)
Italy	64 (males); 59 (females)[1]	52[2]
Netherlands	65	N/A
United Kingdom	65 (males); 60 (females)[3]	N/A
Australia	65 (males); 61 (females)[4]	N/A
Hong Kong	65	N/A
India	58	[service requirement]
Japan	60 (males); 59 (females)	N/A
Singapore	60[5]	55
Brazil	65 (males); 60 (females)	[service requirement]
Canada	65	60
Chile	65 (males); 60 (females)	55
Mexico	65	60
United States	65[6]	62

1. Increasing to 65 (males) and 60 (females) in 2000.
2. Increasing gradually to 57 in 2006 with 35 years of contributions (any age with sufficient number of contributions).
3. Increasing to 65 between 2010 and 2020.
4. Gradually increasing to 65 by 2013.
5. Gradually increasing to 67 by 2003.
6. Gradually increasing to 67 from 2004 to 2027.

drain on social security is partly from individuals' retiring earlier and living longer, deferring payments (that is, having later retirement age) might encourage people to work longer before retiring.

In seeking solutions to the financial squeeze on social security, developed countries often look toward changes that will not adversely affect those close to retirement. Thus, even delaying retirement ages is usually phased in over a several-year period. In Exhibit 14-1, you can see that several countries are delaying retirement age, usually over many years, even as many as 10 or 20 years.

In some countries, there is a difference in retirement ages for males and females. The logic behind the treatment differing according to gender was the model of the "typical family" on which social security programs were built. It was assumed that the working husband was a few years older than his wife and that the spouse would probably want to retire at the same time, so there was some logic in allowing the female to retire at an earlier age than the male. As the demographics of the "typical family" have been changing, the historic gender distinctions are being eliminated.

However, there is considerable difficulty in equalizing the retirement age for males and females. Lowering the age for males to match that for females will have an enormous cost for an already strained social security system. But raising the age for females to match the age for males will annoy a very large number of female voters. The political arena is a sticky one.

What Benefits Are Payable at Retirement?

It is difficult to summarize the wide variety of benefit formulas and calculations for social security. There are defined contribution plans (such as in Singapore) called provident funds. There are indexed career-average plans (such as in the United States). There are flat amounts, not pay related, in the Netherlands. There are formulas involving different percentages at different levels of earnings (such as in the United States and Switzerland). There are high levels of benefits (such as 80% in Italy and more than 90% in Spain), and there are low levels of benefits (such as in the Philippines and Hong Kong). There are means-tested benefits, which are reduced based on total income and assets available during retirement (such as in Australia).

One can detect patterns, however, that are applicable to many countries. Generally, social security benefits are higher (as a percentage of pay) for the lower paid. And, generally, there is some maximum benefit beyond which the percentage of pay decreases as pay increases.

Exhibit 14-2 shows social security as a rough percentage of pay replaced at retirement for an employee retiring on January 1, 1999, whose earnings are near the social security ceiling in each country.

Exhibit 14-2. Approximate Benefits from Social Security (1999)

Country	Old-Age Pension (employee at ceiling)	Widow/Widower's Pension (as percent of old-age pension)	Orphans' Pension (as percent of old-age pension)
France	50% of covered earnings	54% continued	N/A
Germany	40% to 45% of final covered earnings	100% continued for first three months; 60% thereafter	10% per dependent child; 20% per orphan
Italy[1]	55% to 80% of earnings	60% continued	20% per dependent child; 40% per orphan
Netherlands	Flat-rate benefit based on minimum wage	Flat-rate pension based on minimum wage	Flat-rate pension based on minimum wage
United Kingdom	Flat-rate benefit plus 25% of covered earnings	100% continued	Flat-rate benefit
Australia	Flat-rate benefit	Flat-rate benefit	Flat-rate benefit
Hong Kong	Flat-rate allowance	N/A	N/A
India	60% of covered earnings	50% continued	25% per dependent child (maximum 2)
Japan	75% of covered earnings	75% continued; 100% if there are dependent children	Flat-rate benefit per dependent child
Singapore	Lump-sum account balance (accrued contributions plus interest)	Account balance	Account balance
Brazil	70% to 100% of covered earnings	100% continued	100% continued
Canada[2]	25% of covered earnings	37.5% continued plus flat-rate benefit	Flat-rate benefit
Chile	Account balance	60% continued if annuity purchased	60% if annuity purchased
Mexico	72% of covered earnings	90% continued	20% per dependent child (30% for orphans)
United States	20% of covered earnings	100% of single person's benefit continued	75% of single person's benefit per dependent child

1. Assumes a 40-year career under the prior system, recently revised.
2. Canada pension plan only.

The following questions may be asked: What level of pay replacement is needed at retirement? How do we judge adequacy? How do we integrate our own concepts with the customary practices in other countries?

Most U.S. and U.K. studies seem to indicate that a replacement ratio of 70% to 80% of pay is adequate to keep the retiree from facing a severe reduction of lifestyle at retirement. Of course, not all of that income need come from the company-sponsored plan; some is provided from social security and some from the employee's own savings.

The question most benefits managers face is how to determine a reasonable level of benefits to be provided by the company's retirement plan. We will discuss this in more detail later (in the section devoted to company-sponsored benefits), but the main point here is not to take social security for granted or ignore its impact on the company's overall benefit plan design.

Several years ago, a CEO was visiting his company's plant in Spain. The general manager of the plant did not feel he would get an adequate retirement benefit from social security, but he knew that the CEO would never approve a special executive benefit just for him. So instead of asking for an individual deferred compensation agreement, the general manager mentioned to the CEO that there was no retirement plan in the Spanish operation and that employees had to rely entirely on social security. The CEO was outraged, not realizing what the general manager had omitted to say: Spanish social security was, at that time, providing most employees about 95% of their pay at retirement. In his speech to the Spanish employees the next day, the CEO promised the entire workforce that they would have a company-sponsored retirement plan by the next fiscal year. The general manager was jubilant; he got his pension plan, but most employees would earn more in retirement than they had while working for the company.

Although Spain has very high levels of social benefits, there are some countries (such as Australia and South Africa) where social security is means-tested. That is, an employee with other income (such as from a company-sponsored retirement plan) has his or her benefit reduced according to some formula so that only poverty-level individuals receive social security benefits.

The focus here has been on social security benefits in developed countries. In under- or undeveloped countries, special issues arise that will be discussed later. The essential question in these locations is whether there is a promised benefit, and, if so, what is the stability—or even the political reality—of the social security system? Can you reasonably assume that the promised benefit will materialize?

To summarize, before introducing company-sponsored plans in any country, it is important to understand the levels of social benefits provided and to be sure that any private plans are necessary, that they provide the appropriate level of benefit, and that they are consistent with market practice.

How Are Benefits Paid? What Is the Normal Form of Benefit?

Retirement benefits from social security are generally paid in the form of a lifetime annuity (that is, regular installment payments made over the future lifetime) to the employee. The payment may be monthly (as in the United States), fortnightly (as in Australia), weekly (as in New Zealand), or quarterly (as in France). In Spain, 14 payments are made each year (monthly plus an additional month's amount in July and December). Often, the payment form is a joint-and-survivor annuity, with a certain percentage (commonly 50% or 60%) continued to the spouse upon the death of the employee. In some cases, the benefit is increased for "family," such as in the United States, where a nonworking spouse is entitled to 50% of the benefit due the retiring worker.

What Payments Are Made in Case of Death or Disability While Active?

Most social security systems provide some payment to the spouse of an employee who dies (or becomes disabled) before retirement. The benefit is usually, but not always, tied to either:

- The accrued retirement benefit (that is, the retirement benefit earned as of the date of death or disability, based on service and salary at that time) or
- The projected benefit (that is, the retirement benefit that would have been earned if the employee had worked to normal retirement age, at the salary level as of the date of death or disability).

There are exceptions, such as the benefit based on service projected to early retirement age rather than to full normal retirement age. Sometimes the death or disability benefit is based on an altogether different formula.

Exhibit 14-3. Tax Treatment of Social Security Retirement Benefits

Country	Company Contributions	Employee Contributions	Retirement Benefits
France	Deductible to company	Deductible to employee[1]	Taxable to employee when paid
Germany	Deductible to company	Deductible to employee	Annuities taxable when paid, on excess of pension over capital value
Italy	Deductible to company	Deductible to employee	Taxable to employee when paid
Netherlands	[No company contribution]	Deductible to employee	Pensions taxable when paid; lump sums tax-free
United Kingdom	Deductible to company	Not deductible to employee	Generally taxable when paid
Australia	[No company contribution]	[No employee contribution]	Taxable to employee when paid
Hong Kong	[No company contribution]	[No employee contribution]	N/A
India	Deductible up to 12% of salary	Deductible to employee to limits	Generally not taxable when paid (some restrictions)
Japan	Deductible to company	Deductible to employee	Taxable to employee when paid
Singapore	Deductible to company	Deductible to employee	Tax-free
Brazil	Deductible to company	Deductible to employee to limit	Taxable to employee when paid
Canada	Deductible to company	Tax credit of 17% of contributions to limit	Taxable to employee when paid

Chile	[No company contribution]	Deductible to employee to limit	Taxable to employee when paid
Mexico	Deductible to company	Not deductible to employee	Tax-free
United States	Deductible to company	Not deductible to employee	Generally not taxable when paid[2]

1. A portion (2.4%) of the 7.5% *contribution social généralisée* (CSG) tax is not deductible. The tax is levied on 95% of total salary.
2. Some tax if total income is above threshold.

Tax Treatment of Social Security Payments

The tax treatment of social security programs obviously varies somewhat by country, as shown in Exhibit 14-3. However, there are some common trends that are found in many countries:

- Employee contributions are usually deductible for income tax purposes. (This is not true in the United States or the United Kingdom.)
- Employer contributions are deductible to the company (almost always true).
- Benefits from social security are usually taxed when paid, although perhaps taxed at favorable rates. (This is true in the United States if the income level is high enough.)

Other Social Security Systems

The Free-Enterprise System

The social security model that we have described so far fits many countries, including the United States and the United Kingdom, but it is not the only one. In 1981, Chile introduced a different form based on the free-enterprise model devised by University of Chicago specialists following the Milton Friedman school of economics. However, the funds are private, for-profit companies highly regulated.

The first break was from the traditional notion of current contributions being used to pay current benefits to current retirees. Why not set the social security system up as a savings account, with each employee paying for his or her own benefits? The second break was from the traditional notion of a single monolithic social security system, a monopoly. Why not set up a number of social security funds that compete with each other? And so emerged what has become known as the Chilean model.

The Chilean government licensed 13 funds; most of these were established as joint ventures between a bank and an insurance company. The government imposed certain (fairly stringent) conditions on viability, assets, and so on. Each of these funds is a licensed "social security fund" (called an AFP in Chile) offering a savings fund for investment as well as several insured benefits. However, the funds are private, for-profit, highly regulated companies.

Every employee in Chile must make contributions of 13% of pay, up to a ceiling, to one of the funds; there is no employer contribution. The employee may select which fund receives his or her contributions, and the funds compete for business—through advertising and offering enticements. The employee's own money goes into an individual bank account under his or her social security number, and it is invested by the fund, with earnings accumulating until retirement. If the employee wishes to change funds, he or she may do so up to three times a year.

At retirement, the employee may take his or her money in various forms through annuities offered by the insurance company partner in the AFP. Other options are available, including leaving the money in the AFP and taking gradual scheduled withdrawals.

And thus was born the free-market social security system.

The system has been quite successful over the last 15 years and has recently been used as a model for a few other countries, including Poland, Argentina, Bolivia, Mexico, Peru, and Colombia. Plans will shortly be implemented in Venezuela and Hungary. There has even been talk in the United States of allowing some portion of social security to accumulate in a savings plan. The details of the plans, including contribution rates and forms of benefits payments, are different in different countries, but the basic structure is much like the Chilean system.

The following are a few caveats about this system:

- The transition to a Chilean model is difficult. There are significant problems with grandfathering. What does one do with an older employee who has only a few years of active employment left? The defined contribution or savings plan will not be able to accumulate enough for him or her. And how does the system pay current retirees? Chile imposed the system under a military dictatorship, with the government making up the loss for employees over age 45, but not every country can take that approach. In Argentina and Poland, for example, at the time of transition, employees in certain age brackets may have the choice of remaining in the prior system or joining the new system.

- There is elation when the markets are bull, but markets must also someday go bear. Is the system strong enough to weather a recession in which people see their social security retirement fund decline in value? What are the political ramifications when the entire population, already in recession, also loses faith in their social security savings?

Nonetheless, the experiment is an interesting one and is viewed as having much promise for former communist countries or other countries whose prior social security system is bankrupt or nonexistent, making the transition issues easier to handle.

Other Mandatory Systems

There are other mandatory programs for retirement that are not part of social security. These are usually provided through national collective bargaining or some similar approach.

We cite a few examples here, which are discussed in more detail in the chapters on individual countries.

France. France has a national multiemployer system called *répartition* that supplements social security with two main branches (AGIRC and ARRCO). The system, which is run through a number of funds (*caisses*) that manage investments, is intensely regulated, so there is no longer any difference among the funds in investment performance. The system had allowed different companies to contribute at different rates, but effective January 1, 1999, all companies contribute at the same rate.

The system is complex, with contributions used to purchase "points" each year; at retirement, these points are converted into a quarterly annuity payment.

Sweden. Sweden has a national multiple-employer system. All firms contribute to large national funds, such as ITP for salaried employees, at fixed contribution rates, providing fixed benefits. There are also mandatory savings plans, called ITPK for salaried employees. The system is currently undergoing transition.

Italy. Social security is actually a series of independent, interlocking systems. Participation depends on the employee's (or the company's) affiliation with a national collective agreement. Thus, for example, executives covered by the national collective agreement for industry contribute to INPDAI and PREVINDAI funds, while executives covered by the national collective agreement for commerce contribute to INPS and FPDAC funds. There are other funds for wage earners and salaried employees.

Costs of the Social Security Systems

Exhibit 14-4 shows the current contribution rates for both employer and employee in a select list of countries. It is usually an eye-opener to Americans, who complain about their 7.65% contribution, to see how expensive other systems can be.

There is some distortion in comparing the contribution rates. Some countries, such as Canada and Australia, consider social security to be a government service paid largely from general income tax revenues, without the need for a special employment tax. Canada is slowly assessing a higher contribution rate for social security, but the majority of funds for the system still come from general revenues.

Other systems include the cost (or part of the cost) of national health care in the social security contributions, leading to very high contribution rates. A more complete discussion of this issue can be found in Chapter 15.

Stresses on Social Security Systems

There are some strains on social security systems, and it would be unfair to leave this topic without mentioning some of the problems.

Financial Stress of Changing Demographics. There is not a social security system in the world that does not face the financial impact of an aging population. Japan faces this perhaps more severely than any other country, with about 15% of the population currently over age 65 and growing rapidly;

Exhibit 14-4. Social Security Contribution Rates (as of April 1999)

Country	By Employer		By Employee	
	Percent	Ceiling	Percent	Ceiling
France	8.2%	FRF 173,640	6.55%	FRF 173,640
Germany	9.75% 7.0%	DEM 102,000 DEM 75,600	9.75% 7.0%	DEM 102,000 DEM 75,600
Italy	23.81%	No ceiling	8.89% 9.89%	ITL 65,216,059 Excess[1]
Netherlands	N/A	N/A	29.55%	NLG 48,175
United Kingdom	10% plus 12.2% on earnings above GBP 4,316	No ceiling	10% GBP 43.38 per week	GBP 25,220 Excess
Australia	None	N/A	None	N/A
Hong Kong	None	N/A	None	N/A
India	12%	INR 60,000	12%	INR 60,000
Japan	8.675% 4.25%	JPY 590,000 JPY 980,000	8.675% 4.25%	JPY 590,000 JPY 980,000
Singapore	Under age 55: 10%[2] Age 55 through 60: 4%[2] Over age 60: 2%[2]	SGD 72,000	Under age 55: 20% Age 55 through 60: 12.5% Age 60 through 65: 7.5% Over age 65: 5%	SGD 72,000
Brazil	20%	No ceiling	Graded by pay, from 7.82% on pay under BRL 360 to 11% on pay from BRL 600 to 1,200	No ceiling
Canada	3.5%[3]	CAD 37,400	3.5%[3]	CAD 37,400
Chile	None	N/A	12.78%	60 UF
Mexico	4.9%	MXN 213,762	1.75%	MXN 213,762
United States	6.2% Medicare: 1.45%	USD 72,600 No ceiling	6.2% Medicare: 1.45%	USD 72,600 No ceiling

1. Capped for those entering the system on or after January 1, 1996.
2. Reduced rate for 1999 and 2000.
3. Increasing to 4.9% over the next five years.

within the next 20 years, more than a quarter of the population is expected to be over age 65. Although this is the extreme case, the situation is similar in other countries, with the ratio of active to retired becoming smaller and smaller. The pressure on all social security systems is enormous.

Overpromised Benefits and Administrative Delays. Politicians sometimes promise more than they can deliver, especially in developing or underdeveloped nations. Benefits were promised but are no longer affordable (or perhaps never were).

In some underdeveloped nations, there may be a social security system on paper, but not in reality. The contributions are spent on the infrastructure, or, worse, they are *not* spent on the infrastructure. The masses of employees know that there may be no benefits for them from this system or that they may face inordinate red-tape delays in receiving benefits.

Company-Sponsored Retirement Plans: Design

The decision to implement a company-sponsored retirement plan takes careful thought and analysis. Research should include consideration of a country's social security benefits local tax regulations, competitive practice, and the company's benefits philosophy and business strategy. The cost of implementing a plan increases exponentially with a wrong decision or bad plan design. The concept of acquired, or contractual, rights applies here—you gave it to me, it's mine. Once a plan is implemented, it may be very difficult (or effectively impossible) to amend, revise, or terminate.

Before determining the structure and design of any retirement plan, it is essential to research legal requirements in addition to reviewing plans from other companies that are competitors for employment in the local labor market. An international consultant with solid representation in the relevant location is usually the best resource for information and assistance with plan design.

The process for designing and implementing a plan would ideally include the following data:

- Levels and eligibility for social security and other government-provided benefits
- Any mandates on the company (e.g., the requirements in Switzerland or Hong Kong to maintain a plan that meets certain minimum standards, or the requirements in Italy or Colombia for heavy termination indemnities payable upon retirement)

- Any limitations or restrictions that might be imposed to obtain tax-favorable results
- Competitive practice. There can be differences based on industry, geographic region, or size, and there may be published surveys. Be wary of any surveys with an underlying bias (e.g., a survey published by a firm that sells deferred annuity contracts may have a distorted database). Note too that competitors for employment in the local labor market may be different from competitors for products or services.
- Union or work council directives
- Costs and business needs—a step that should not be overlooked

Following data collection, decisions on plan design need to be taken.

Defined Benefit or Defined Contribution?

We have discussed this topic earlier. However, it is the first design decision to make, since all other design decisions may depend on the overall approach.

Although there are exceptions in those countries that have had a British influence, most company-sponsored retirement plans in Europe, Central America, and Asia take the form of a defined benefit plan. In those countries with a British influence, it is more likely that there will be an opportunity to provide retirement programs with at least a portion of the benefit on a defined contribution basis, including the opportunity for employee contribution. There are many variations and combinations, of course. This can cause a dilemma for many U.S.-based companies. With the emphasis in the United States on defined contribution plans, the continued prevalence of defined benefit could be viewed as a dichotomy of values.

When Are Old-Age Benefits Paid?

In most countries in which there is a social security system, retirement benefits are usually paid from the company-sponsored plan beginning at the same time as social security payments. This coordination allows a retiring employee to receive both company benefits and government benefits at the same time. However, this is not always the case; in certain countries, social security is available to males and females at different ages, but the company either wants or is required to treat males and females equally (in the United Kingdom and Belgium, for example).

Companies also may want to encourage early retirement by paying unreduced benefits at an early age or want to discourage this by having heavy reductions for early retirement. The business decision is whether you want to retain valued employees as long as possible or want to make it comfortable for older employees to retire early for business reasons.

Again, remember that once a benefit is given to employees, it may be difficult to remove it at a later date. A generous early retirement provision may prove costly later.

Vesting is the term used to refer to an employee's right to receive a benefit, even if he or she leaves the company prior to retirement. Vesting requirements differ greatly by country, from the very rapid (such as two years of service in Canada or immediate in Switzerland) to the very slow (more than 10 years in Germany). In some developing countries, there may be no vesting requirement at all.

What Benefits Are Paid at Retirement?

The range of formulas is endless. Decisions need to be made on such diverse issues as the following:

- Whether to integrate with social security (and if so, how)
- Whether to integrate with local severance payments (and if so, how)
- Whether the focus should be on retention (long-term employees) or portability (short-term employees)
- What the targeted pay replacement should be at retirement
- Whether any special provisions should be made for midcareer hires
- How much company support is available for administration and communication
- Whether benefits should be tied to service or to performance (such as a profit-sharing plan)
- If there is a need for equitable treatment by location, by age at hire, by service, or by salary
- If there is a need for inflation protection

There may be other questions in different countries; this is another area that you probably want to discuss with the input and advice of experts.

How Are Benefits Paid? What Is the Normal Form of Benefit?

Benefits can be paid out in the form of a lump sum or as lifetime annuity payments made monthly (or more often); sometimes there is a spousal pension payable upon the death of the retiree. Generally, there is a preferred form of benefit payment in a country, such as a lifetime annuity. Employees who desire a different form of benefit, such as a joint-and-survivor benefit, pay for the actuarial difference so that the form of benefit is cost-neutral to the company.

For any individual, of course, there is no cost neutrality. The benefit reduction is based on actuarial tables and therefore operates like insurance. The employee who elected a joint-and-survivor annuity and then lived for 30 years beyond retirement spent a great deal of money for an insurance that never paid off. The employee who did not elect a joint-and-survivor annuity and died within a year or two of retirement saved the company a fair amount of money. The idea behind the reduction is not its appropriateness for any individual but that, for a large group of employees, the company expects to come out cost-neutral, regardless of which benefit form the employees elect.

In most of Europe, the normal form of benefit is often a joint-and-survivor annuity, with 50% or 60% of the benefit continuing to the spouse for his or her lifetime after the death of the employee. The cost of that benefit is borne by the company (or by the pension trust); there is no reduction for the employee. This tends to add about 20% to the cost of a plan.

In many countries, lump-sum payments are the norm. In some countries (such as Australia, the United Kingdom, and Belgium), a lump-sum retirement payment, for all or part of the benefit, receives more favorable tax treatment than an annuity. Similarly, in countries where there is no social security, as in many countries in Asia, the payout is usually a lump sum.

What Payments Are Made from the Retirement Plan in Case of Death or Disability While Active?

Many plans have provisions in the event of death or disability while the employee is still actively employed. European plans usually have a benefit paid to the spouse and/or dependent children upon the death of the employee. The benefit is often based on current salary, with service projected to the employee's normal retirement date. The cost of such benefits may be borne by the pension plan (i.e., by the company), such as in the United Kingdom or in Germany. In the United States, the employee pays the cost through a reduced benefit.

Often, retirement plans also have a provision that allows for payment of benefits if an employee becomes totally and permanently disabled during the course of employment. In the United States, benefits tend to be separate: Life insurance is one package, disability another, and retirement benefits yet another. In Europe, benefits tend to be bundled: Life insurance and disability protection may come from the retirement plan. Insurance may be purchased to cover the death and disability benefits.

It is important to coordinate payments from the retirement plan with any separate life or disability insurance so that individuals are not overinsured.

Need for Communication

Because there are so many complexities in plan design in each country—some resulting from legalities and government regulations, others from collective agreements, and still others from custom and common practice—good communication is essential. Having a retirement plan can provide comfort, security, and peace of mind to the employees, as well as provide an income after the end of the working career. But it does those things only if the employees are aware of the plan. Active communication with employees is a key feature in the success of a plan.

Some countries may require regular reporting or actuarial examination of the plan. As changes are made, legal documentation and plan registration is essential. Furthermore, employees will need written verification of any changes. Whatever the case, plan features and expectations should be clearly explained to employees.

Implementation

Once the plan is designed, it needs to be implemented. In addition to communication, there is the ongoing need for record keeping, tax reporting, legal filings, benefit payments, and the like. The company needs to determine how much resource can be dedicated to administration, legal compliance and documentation, and so on, and whether to administer internally or to outsource.

Pension or Termination Payment: Redundancy

In the United States, severance benefits, paid in case of certain types of dismissal such as layoff, may be fairly small amounts. In Europe, the term is often *redundancy* rather than *layoff*, and payments may be quite high compared with U.S. standards. For example, in Italy, there is a legally mandated formula used to calculate payments, roughly one month's pay times years of service; these are payable upon any termination, regardless of cause of termination.

Termination payments are often based on a specific benefit per year of service (such as one week's—or one month's—pay per year of service), payable in a lump sum. Under a termination plan or severance indemnity, an employee will also receive a benefit upon voluntarily leaving prior to retirement age or upon involuntary termination. In some cases, there is a vesting schedule and benefits are not payable until vesting is achieved. Italy, Taiwan, Korea, and Venezuela are a few examples of countries that use this form of severance benefit, which also is paid upon retirement.

In Japan, a similar system is used, with final pay included in the formula for calculating the actual benefit. In addition, the traditional Japanese plan has separate schedules for "voluntary" and "involuntary" leavers, with the voluntary schedule paying somewhat less than the involuntary schedule. *Involuntary termination* is defined as having reached normal retirement age, being dismissed, or being terminated as a result of disability or redundancy or for economic reasons.

In Mexico, the statutory severance benefit is paid upon involuntary dismissal but not upon retirement, leading to a potentially awkward situation in terms of employee relations.

Company-Sponsored Retirement Plans: Funding

Financing retirement plans is complex, involving accountants, actuaries, and investment managers; trusts and outside financing entities; fiduciary responsibilities; and legal constraints. When someone asks, "What does the retirement plan cost?" there are potentially several different answers: the actual cash flow cost to the company ("contribution"), the tax deduction that the company can take, and the accounting numbers that appear on the company's books. We will discuss each of these separately, but it is probably best to begin with the funding or cash flow cost.

Financing Retirement Plans: Pay Now or Pay Later?

For defined contribution plans, financing involves making wise choices among investment funds. The amount the company contributes to the plan is established by the plan rules. The employee bears the risk. If investment return is good, the employee reaps the gain; if investment returns are poor, the employee gets less than anticipated.

In the United States, most defined contribution plans allow for employee choice in investments. The belief is that the employee develops more interest in and appreciation for the plan by watching investment performance of his or her fund choices. In addition, since investment risk is borne by the employee, there is some softening of the risk by allowing the employee to select among investments. The element of employee choice is prevalent in the United States but rare outside the United States, although there is a growing trend in this direction, especially in the United Kingdom.

For defined benefit plans, the ultimate cost of the plan will really never be known until the last retiree draws the last benefit payment. However, it is possible to estimate the ultimate cost in advance, using mathematical and statistical techniques called "actuarial science," and thus to spread the costs over the active career of the employees.

For a simple example, let us suppose that we have promised an executive a lump-sump payment of $100,000 in 15 years' time if he is still with the company. There are a number of ways we could meet that payment. For now, let's just think about the cash payment and leave accounting (and tax treatment) to the side. In reality, governments may not permit favorable tax treatment for some of these approaches.

Pay All Now

We could find a guaranteed investment fund that earns, say, 5% each year. We could put $48,102 into that fund today. We would never have to pay any more. The fund would grow at 5% a year, and after 15 years, there would be exactly $100,000 available to pay the executive. We would meet the liability of $100,000 owed in 15 years by having reduced it to $48,102 in present dollars (thanks to future investment return) and paid it off today. There is a certain simplicity to this approach and also a fairly high current cost. We are taking on all the burden of the cost today and leaving future management with no cost at all.

This approach is often called "fully funded" since full payment is made long before the employee reaches retirement age.

Pay All Later

We could wait. We would make no payment now and simply wait for 15 years. At that time, we would pay the executive the $100,000 and hope this doesn't cause a serious drain on cash flow that year. There is simplicity to this approach as well and the lure of a deceptively low current cost. By taking on no cost today, we are deferring all the cost for 15 years' time, leaving future management to pay the price.

This approach is often called "unfunded" or "pay as you go" because no payment is made until the time the employee retires. Most social security systems are financed on this basis, with current contributions being paid to current retirees.

Spread the Cost

A third approach is to spread the cost over the 15 years, investing the money in some investment vehicle and enjoying lower cost because of the investment yield. If we use the same example as above, a fixed fund that earns 5% each year, we need to set aside only $4,414 each year. At 5% interest per year, this amount will accumulate to $100,000 after 15 years.

This approach is usually called "funded" because payments are spread over the employee's active career.

In this example, we have spread the costs evenly as a dollar amount, like a fixed mortgage in the United States. We could have spread costs evenly as a percentage of payroll or paid more (or all) in the first 10 years or in the last 10 years. There are many ways of spreading costs. A company need not attempt to be level each year; for example, it might base the annual payment on profitability, paying more in the good years and less in the lean years.

Most companies prefer to fund the plan by spreading the costs, for the obvious reason that it produces a more fair allocation between current management and future management. In addition, in most countries, there is a tax advantage or an accounting requirement to spread costs over active years of employment, although the actual formulas for doing so vary significantly from country to country.

Accounting versus Fundings

For various reasons, there may be a difference between the cash contribution made each year to a fund and the numbers used in the books for accounting purposes. Some of these reasons include legal requirements or accounting standards, which may be different for different purposes. For instance, the allowable tax deduction might be less than the amount of cash actually being paid.

The term *contribution* usually refers to the cash actually set aside in some sort of investment vehicle. The term *expense* refers to the amount reflected in the books, the accounting numbers.

Trust versus Other

In many countries, there are strict regulations about what can be done with pension assets. The money cannot simply be set aside. Since the government is granting a tax deduction for the cash contribution (within limits), the government requires that the money be protected from fraud, embezzlement, foolish investment, and so forth. In some countries, such as the United States, the cash is set aside in a separate entity called a "trust fund," overseen by a board of trustees.

The notion of trust fund comes from Anglo-Saxon law and is found in the United States, the United Kingdom, Australia, Canada, South Africa, India, New Zealand, and other regions that were subject to British influence. On most of the European continent, there is no notion of trust fund; sometimes the money is set aside in a "foundation" (similar to a charitable institution) and sometimes the money is set aside through an insurance program.

Funding requirements differ greatly by country. Here are two examples:

- In Germany, the money is "booked," so it occurs as an accounting charge but is not funded. Reinsurance is commonly purchased to guarantee that the employee will receive a benefit from the pension, but this is not a separate secured asset. If the company goes bankrupt, the employee has no fund for security (although the employees do become the first creditors in line).
- In Taiwan, the government requires companies to fund within a range (say 3% to 8%) and to invest that money in a limited number of funds approved by the government, usually Taiwan banks.

Tax Treatment of Company-Sponsored Retirement Plans

Once the company has decided to have a retirement plan, and decided how to pay for it, the tax treatment comes into play. For most parent companies, there are two levels of tax to worry about: local tax and the parent company's home-country tax.

Local Tax

Each country sets forth its own regulations and requirements for retirement plans. Generally speaking, the tax authorities in the country are willing to forgo current tax to provide retirement benefits to individuals. However, tax authorities usually impose restrictions on what the company's retirement plan can do, and requirements on what the plan must do, to achieve favorable tax treatment.

There are potentially three tax-paying entities: the company (or plan sponsor), the employee (plan participant), and the plan itself (or the trust). The ideal situation is that the plan, or trust, is not a tax-paying entity.

Not every tax jurisdiction allows this favorable treatment. For example, employee contributions to a defined benefit plan in the United States are not treated as deductible for the employee.

It is generally easy for the company to take a tax deduction for payments to the employee. The advantage of the retirement plan is that those payments are *not* immediately treated as taxable income to the employee. Instead, the tax is deferred (until the employee takes the money in the form of benefit payments).

Furthermore, if the funds are held in some sort of trust or similar investment vehicle, it is desirable that the plan (or trust) itself not be subject to tax. The requirements for tax-exempt status differ vastly from country to country. If a plan meets the requirements, assets can be invested without being subject to local tax. In the United States, a trust is called "qualified" if it meets the requirements to be tax-exempt. In the United Kingdom, the plan is "approved," and in Canada, it is "registered."

Parent-Company Taxes

While the tax rules in the local country determine whether the local subsidiary can obtain the best tax treatment for the retirement plan in that country, the corporate parent may be affected by taxes in its jurisdiction.

Exhibit 14-5. Optimal Tax Treatment

	Company Contribution	Employee Contribution	Investment Return on Assets	Benefit Payments to Retiree (at time of payment)
Tax Treatment to Local Company	Deductible	[not relevant]	Not treated as income (no tax)	[no impact; deduction was taken earlier]
Tax Treatment to Employee	Not treated as income (no tax)	Deductible	Not treated as income (no tax)	Taxable, perhaps at favorable rates
Tax Treatment of Retirement Plan or Trust	Not treated as income (no tax)	Not treated as income (no tax)	Not treated as income (no tax)	Deduction or tax neutrality

The subsidiary reports earnings or dividends back to the corporate parent; those earnings presumably include a deduction for the local company's contributions to the retirement plan. The question is, What earnings or dividends are considered taxable to the corporate parent?

Arguably, the most complicated example is the U.S. multinational parent.

U.S. Taxes. For a U.S. corporate parent, the subsidiary operation in, for example, the United Kingdom must report its income less deductible expenses, called earnings and profits (E&P). The U.S. company then pays taxes on its worldwide corporate income. In calculating the E&P, the IRS requires that all income be reported and then that allowable deductions (technically, reductions) be subtracted.

The question is, What are "allowable" reductions in earnings and profits? Generally speaking, reductions in earnings and profits are very similar to what costs would be deductible for a U.S. company if it were sited in the United States. The mere fact of the expense being spent in a foreign country should not, according to the IRS, have an impact on its deductibility.

Generally, this is not a problem for the U.S. company. But it can be a problem when it comes to retirement plans because the IRS will allow a deduction only for a contribution to a qualified retirement plan, without corresponding taxable income to the employees. And yet many foreign plans (e.g., the Brazilian retirement plan for Brazilian employees) may be very far from meeting the requirements for a U.S. qualified plan.

Generally speaking, for non-U.S. plans that are funded through a trust (or some mechanism that is very much like a trust), there has not been an issue. The IRS has allowed deductions for contributions to such plans without trying to treat those contributions as taxable income for the employees.

However, for some countries, such as Germany and Japan, the foreign retirement plan may not be funded. This has caused considerable difficulty. Would the IRS allow a reduction in earnings and profits for an unfunded foreign plan? Certainly there would be no equivalent deduction for an unfunded U.S. plan, so why should the foreign plan be treated differently?

The situation has been ambiguous for some time. Specific legislation, called 404A after the section of Internal Revenue Code, passed in 1980 allowed the deduction under certain circumstances. Proposed regulations clarifying those circumstances were first offered in 1985, but they were extremely complicated; there was much opposition, and the regulations were never finalized. A different set of regulations proposed in 1993 was more strict than the earlier proposed regulations and, arguably, more strict than even the original legislation. As of the date of this writing, regulations have still not been finalized.

Accounting Standards

The "cost" of a retirement plan can be measured as the amount of cash paid each year. However, the cost of the plan for accounting purposes could be different from the cash flow contribution or the tax deduction. A contribution made just after the end of the calendar year might count for cash flow in one year but for tax deduction in the year just ended. In funding, we described an "unfairness" between current management and future management. For accounting purposes, the unfairness is to current investors and shareholders of the company, compared with future shareholders.

Ultimately, when the last retiree receives the last benefit payment, all of these different "costs" can be reconciled. However, from year to year, they can be quite different.

At the moment of writing, there are several different standards for accounting for retirement plans. The U.S. standard is called Financial Accounting Standard (FAS) 87, promulgated by the Financial Accounting Standards Board (FASB) in line with generally accepted accounting principles (GAAP). The Canadian standard is called CICA Section 3460; the

British standard is Statement of Standard Accounting Practice (SSAP) 24, issued by the British Accounting Standards Committee (ASC) that has jurisdiction in the United Kingdom. The German standard is BiRiLiG, and the Australian standards are AAS 25 and 28. Effective January 1, 1999, there is now an international standard, called International Accounting Standard 19 (IAS 19), promulgated by the International Accounting Standards Committee (IASC). The goal of the IASC is that its standards will form the basis of standardized global financial reporting and be accepted by the International Organization of Securities Commissions (IOSCO) as appropriate for all global markets. The FASB and the IASC have technical differences over points in each other's standards.

The overview is that all these standards are different, and a financial statement in compliance with SSAP 24 is not necessarily in compliance with IAS 19 or with FAS 87. Some of the differences may be minor (hence, "not material"), so a U.K. plan could conceivably use the SSAP 24 accounting to comply with FAS 87. However, this cannot be taken for granted.

Each standard reflects a method of assigning cost (called "expense") to each year, reflecting what the auditors and investors would consider a fair share of the ultimate retirement costs. For defined contribution plans, the expense is usually the annual contribution. For defined benefit plans, the expense is more complicated to calculate.

In the United States, in addition to FAS 87, there is also FAS 88, which deals with settlements and curtailments of defined benefit retirement plans—plan terminations, spin-offs, lump-sum payouts, and similar events that materially alter the employer's liability or obligation.

U.S. retirement plans sponsored by a U.S. company must meet U.S. accounting standards. However, the U.S. standard requires all non-U.S. retirement plans that ultimately are part of the U.S. parent company's operations to also report according to U.S. standards. Thus, the largest foreign retirement plans of U.S. companies must keep two sets of books, one reflecting local requirements and one reflecting U.S. requirements.

CHAPTER 15

OTHER BENEFITS

CAROL Y. KAPLAN AND
Z. SAMUEL BERNSTEIN

Medical Care

Although the corporate benefits practitioner has little control over any social health system, he or she should understand the general provisions of these programs to determine the desirability of or need for a supplemental company-sponsored health plan. It would be impossible to categorize or describe all forms of government-provided medical care, but we can make some generalizations. Government-provided health care, or "social" medicine, may be:

- Provided nationally, as in the United Kingdom and the Netherlands.
- Provided at state or provincial level, as in Canada and Switzerland.
- Provided through various nonprofit regulated agencies, as in Belgium and Germany.
- Provided through industry groups, as in Japan and Korea.

The focus here is on health care provided to local-national employees within their home country. Medical care for people involved in international travel or located away from their home country is addressed separately (see Chapter 7).

A country's health care system is devised around its perceptions and cultural norms, which differ from country to country. Nationalized or socialized medical systems, such as those in Europe, tend to be financed through taxes—income taxes, social security taxes, or special health care taxes. Thus, all taxpayers support the system and receive benefits from it. The United States is almost the only developed country without a national health care program for all: Medicare is just for the aged, and Medicaid is for those who do not have the income for access to care through insurance. Health care in the United States is thus largely tied to employment; in the rest of the developed world, health care is based on citizenship or residency.

The perfect health care system is one that is personalized and enables every person to have immediate access to the highest quality care and the most advanced technology—at no cost. Such a system cannot exist, of course. The question becomes one of allocation of resources, and different countries choose different methods of allocating health care resources. Because health care is a concern for every individual, the cultural perspective toward health care tends to be sacred and extremely subjective.

Typically, Americans are skeptical of European socialized health care systems, tending to believe that the care is minimal and less advanced than in the United States. In contrast, Europeans believe that the American health care system is too expensive and impractical, with service reserved for those who can afford to pay for it.

It is also important to distinguish between medical care in developed countries and in under- or undeveloped countries. For example, Brazil boasts a national health care system, but it has not proven to be responsive to the needs of the population. As a result, most employers in Brazil offer private care.

Stresses on the National Systems

Almost every national health care system is undergoing the same stresses and strains that U.S. health care has endured over the last decade or so. Escalating costs, new technology, and longer lives after retirement have all put strains on the systems needed to pay for health care, whether the payments come from governments, employers, or individuals.

The term *managed care* has received very unfavorable publicity outside the United States and is often perceived as a euphemism for inadequate treatment in the name of cost savings. *Managing costs* has become acceptable terminology, but *managing care* is a phrase loaded with emotional overtones.

Ultimately, even a socialized medical system must ration health care. Health care is a limited resource, and the question is how to allocate that resource. Most countries with socialized medicine allocate the resource based on standards related to need, usually set by a government-regulated medical board. The resource allocation is generally based on the severity of the condition so that emergency care is handled first. This prioritization means that some situations receive very low priority or perhaps are not covered at all. Thus, even though there is a socialized medical system in a country, there may still be need for a company-provided supplement.

Judging the Need for Company-Provided Plans

Supplemental plans are usually provided to fill gaps in the socialized coverage or to allow for private care. We generally can categorize the gaps as limits on access, and limits on services or facilities, and limits on payment or reimbursement.

Competitive practice varies among countries, even for those with socialized medical systems. We have chosen a few countries to make each point below.

- In Brazil and India, companies tend to provide some private arrangement to bypass the national system completely. That is, the company plan is *in lieu of* the national system.
- In France and Canada, companies tend to provide some private arrangement to supplement gaps in the social system. That is, the company plan is *in addition to* the national system.
- In Germany and Australia, individuals may buy their own supplemental coverage. Companies rarely provide coverage, except in cases in which there may be industry-wide collective agreements.

Limited Access or Facilities

The first problem faced by an employee/patient may be getting to medical help. Access may be limited by absence of facilities or by lack of adequate staffing, especially in underdeveloped countries. In some countries, such as India or Indonesia, there may not be government facilities in remote locations away from the major metropolitan areas. The questions for the employer to determine are as follows:

- Where is the company's operation located?
- Where are people employed, and where are they living?
- Are there public or private facilities nearby?
- What are other companies doing to fill any gap?

Oil companies, for example, often have very large operations in remote areas and may establish their own clinics. Likewise, groups of multinational companies may get together to support or establish a clinic in a remote region. In some countries, the company provides an insured plan or establishes its own clinics to bypass the social system.

International transfers are a special consideration dealt with in Chapter 7.

Oversubscribed or Understaffed Government Facilities

In some countries, the social system simply doesn't have enough staff to meet the needs of the population. This results in long waits, especially for conditions that involve elective procedures and are not life threatening. In the United Kingdom, for instance, while emergency treatment is quickly available, the wait to see an ophthalmologist for cataract treatment could easily be six months.

In an environment where an employee will be out of work for an excessive period of time because of the wait to see a doctor, the company may want to provide access to more immediate medical care. For example, in Brazil, the understaffing is so severe that waits for even critical treatments can be intolerable. As a result, most companies provide access through clinics (or HMOs or similar arrangements) and bypass the social system altogether.

Limited Services

Government-provided facilities, especially in underdeveloped nations or in the former Communist bloc, may not have sufficient equipment or up-to-date technology. In Russia, for example, hospitals are sometimes reportedly forced to use the same hypodermic multiple times.

Companies have more difficult decisions to make in such countries because private practice might not be any better equipped than the government system. Sometimes, evacuation to a nearby country is the only remedy; alternatively, as already noted, a company (or group of companies) may set up and equip its own clinic.

Deliberate Omission of Select Coverage

In some situations, the government-sponsored program deliberately does not cover certain procedures. Omitted coverage varies by country, of course, but can include maternity, dental, prescription drugs, AIDS treatment, psychiatric care, or outpatient care. A few examples are as follows:

- The Canadian provincial health care system does not cover prescription drugs for people under age 65, nor does it cover routine dental care.
- The Danish health care system does not cover vision care for adults (over age 16).

- Taiwan's system excludes dental, vision, hearing, and ambulance services; substance abuse and cosmetic surgery are also excluded.

Companies will often provide a supplemental medical plan that focuses on the treatments not covered by the social health system. Thus, a company-sponsored plan in Canada will usually have a very low deductible (CAD 25 is not uncommon) because the plan is intended to cover only the small range of treatment excluded from provincial health.

Limited Reimbursement or Payment

Typically, in countries with social health care systems, there have been little or no payments expected of employees. However, many countries are now facing the stress of escalating cost and have reacted by limiting the amount of reimbursement (or direct payment) for certain treatment. In France, for example, about 80% of costs are covered by the government plan, leaving the other 20% (roughly) for the patients to pay. Most large French companies therefore have private medical plans aimed at covering the difference between the actual cost of treatment and the reimbursable amount from the national health care system.

"Status"

U.S. companies have eliminated or greatly reduced the kinds of programs available to employees based on position in the company. But in many other countries, status-based programs are still an important, emotional, and tax-effective means for compensating management employees. Status is the mark of how well one is doing; in the United States, this may be measured simply by compensation—I am paid well, so I am doing well. In other countries, however, the indicators of how well one is doing are more public and more varied.

In the United Kingdom, for example, national health insurance provides fully paid medical care for all, at taxpayers' expense. Hospitalization is usually in a ward with six to eight beds. It is a mark of status to have a private plan (company paid) that provides access to a private-care service, fairly rapid access to a private physician, and a private or semiprivate room in the hospital. Of course, such private coverage also has positive effects for the business, by reducing lost work time for employees waiting to see a doctor.

In Mexico, too, the national health system is part of social security (IMSS), providing high-level care. However, most executives prefer a private plan from the company, with a private or semiprivate room, access to a private physician, and so forth. Interestingly, if a Mexican executive requires some high-tech treatment (such as chemotherapy or radiation therapy), the national health hospitals have the best equipment and most up-to-date technology, and the executive will often go back to IMSS rather than use the private care. Private care is mainly a matter of status, and a company may find it difficult to hire a Mexican executive if it does not offer a private health care plan.

Access to U.S. health care is another status-driven issue for executives in Central and South American countries. Generally speaking, these requests for treatment in the U.S. have little merit in terms of need and have a significant impact in terms of cost. Companies are usually wise not to comply with such requests or to examine them very carefully on an individual basis (by country).

Determining Competitive Practice and Establishing a Plan

Once you have decided that there is some gap in medical coverage in a country, the question becomes whether the company should provide some plan to fill that gap. As noted, it is impossible to generalize. An approach taken in one country may be inappropriate in another.

The following is one process that might be used:

- Check with local sources for competitive practice. Good sources are trade councils, industry collectives, surveys, and either local or international consultants. Be wary of any survey that may have a built-in bias. For example, a survey produced by an insurance company based on its clients will show an obvious preference for insured plans, which might not be reflective of a broader sample. You might want to compare information from an insurer with information from some noninsurance source. Headhunters also have a vested interest in getting candidates higher salaries and greater benefits, so their surveys might be skewed.
- Carefully read any policy the local broker or consultant suggests.
- Pay attention to what is and is not covered. For example, private care in the United Kingdom, Asian countries, and Australasia commonly excludes certain diseases such as AIDS. In Hong Kong, Korea, and

some other Asian countries, it might be appropriate to cover such things as herbal medicines, acupuncture, and other locally accepted medical practices. In Indonesia and many areas of Africa, most employees will consult the local witch doctor before seeking more "scientific" medicines; failure to cover the costs of this alternative medicine may mean that your employees will not seek medical care.

- Carefully consider the definition of *dependents* and *family,* if coverage is to be extended. The question of "domestic partner" is of growing interest; in the Netherlands, for instance, a domestic partner must be considered on the same footing as a spouse. In a country where polygamy is practiced, the company might want to consider providing coverage only to the principal wife.
- Talk with colleagues at other U.S. companies that have similar locations to see what benefits they are providing.
- Work with your local management to design a plan that is consistent with company philosophy and culture and is sensitive to local competitive market and business needs.
- Meet with benefit insurance providers (discussed more fully in the section on benefit pooling) to discuss viability of a pool and to confirm plan design.
- Be sure that you have eliminated any duplication in coverage. For example, a global business-travel accident policy plus a locally administered 24-hour accident policy may be unnecessary duplication.
- Be aware of gaps in coverage. For example, Israeli medical plans do not include out-of-country coverage; travel insurance or some other insured vehicle would be required if an Israeli employee were traveling out of country. In addition, check whether designed plans will address international transfers and short-term business travelers.
- Prepare an RFP (request for proposal). The suggested avenue for preparing the RFP is to work with a consultant who has experience in multinational insurance pooling. These professionals can sort out what should be asked in the bidding process.
- In reviewing bids, be on the lookout for more than just the lowest price. You should be asking yourself questions such as the following:
- Do the competing providers all have equivalent service? You should be aware of the service differences and determine which bid best suits your needs.

- Are all insurers bidding on exactly the same scenario? For example, did personnel data include married/single status, or were the insurers free to make their own assumptions?
- Is this a bid that should be handled on a local basis, or is there some economy of scale (such as multinational pooling) that adds a cost-saving layer at the global level?

Working with an experienced consultant, you can then analyze the bids to determine which one will provide quality and service at the most competitive cost.

Death and Disability

Death and disability programs often do not get as much attention as other benefits. There are several valid reasons for this:

- Premiums for death and disability benefits are comparatively low and can usually be adjusted annually; in contrast, the costs of medical care and retirement benefits are comparatively high. Furthermore, retirement benefits represent a long-term commitment. Companies have therefore been more concerned with medical plans and retirement benefits than with death and disability benefits.
- Death and disability represent "risk" benefits—the onset is usually unexpected, and claims costs may be unpredictable. Most companies pass this risk over to insurance companies. On the other hand, there is very little risk of an "unexpected" retirement. Although there is an element of risk in medical programs, it is almost certain that there will be continual usage of the programs by a large number of the employee population, so costs are reasonably predictable.
- In many countries, insurers "bundle" death and disability plans, including them within the retirement plan. In addition, many life and disability programs are linked to retirement; benefits are maintained or reduced once retirement age is reached. In large U.S. companies, an unbundled approach is more common.
- U.S. accounting standards require reporting of retirement plans on consolidated books under a complex set of calculations; there is no such standard for death and disability, in which the insurance premium is taken as the annual expense.

This does not mean that death and disability benefits are unimportant or can be ignored. These plans can certainly affect company cost and employee relations.

Death Benefits

Certainly, the single risk faced by every human being, regardless of location or national culture, is mortality. The death of an employee deprives that employee's family of the flow of future income, and companies in almost every country feel obligated to assist the family financially to compensate, at least in part, for that income loss.

Interestingly enough, there is remarkably little variation by country in the form or amount of benefit provision. Life insurance benefits generally take only two forms: lump-sum payment or installment/annuity.

Lump-Sum Payments

Generally, the employee names a beneficiary. The beneficiary is most often the spouse, but the choice is usually the employee's. A lump-sum payment is then made to the beneficiary upon the death of the employee. Ideally, this payment is not taxed (or is taxed at favorable rates). In general, if the payment is from an insurance company licensed in the country where the beneficiary is tax-resident, the payment usually escapes taxation or receives favorable tax treatment. The company's obligations are discharged by the single payment.

The formula is usually related to annual (or monthly) salary; 24 months' pay or one year's pay are common formulas, although higher amounts are common in some countries (such as the United Kingdom).

Benefits may be doubled if the cause of death is accidental. This accidental-death clause is an addition to life insurance benefits, is valued by employees, has a relatively small cost, and is used almost universally.

Cultural differences and tradition may influence how these benefits are designed and paid. In some countries (e.g., France and Belgium), the benefit may vary based on family size. In some countries, the individual's personal circumstances are very important in determining appropriate benefit levels. For example, a married male employee who dies leaving a dependent female spouse and dependent children may receive a higher benefit than an unmarried female employee with no dependents. Other countries take the U.S. perspective that the benefit should be unrelated to the individual employee's personal circumstances. In the firm antidiscrimination culture of the United States, benefits, like any compensation, must depend on the position, not the individual holding that position.

Annuity or Survivor Income

In some plans (in many countries), the employee may name a beneficiary for survivor income benefits. In other countries, the beneficiary is automatically the spouse, and the benefit might not be provided for a nonspouse. Some countries allow a wider definition with the issue of "dependent domestic partner" on the rise; in the Netherlands, for example, a registered domestic partner has the same legal status as a spouse.

Survivor benefits are typically in the form of regular installment payments (e.g., monthly or quarterly) for the duration of the beneficiary's life. There are a number of variations of this approach:

- Additional benefits, commonly called "orphan's benefits," may be provided for dependent children. (An *orphan* is a dependent child who has lost one parent; a *full orphan* is a dependent child who has lost two parents.)
- After the death of the spouse, benefits may be continued to dependent children until they reach some age of maturity.
- Benefits may be discontinued, or greatly reduced, if the spouse remarries or if the age differential between the employee and spouse is greater than some arbitrary number of years (e.g., 10 years).
- In countries that permit polygamy, survivor benefits should be restricted to the principal wife.

Determining the Company-Provided Amount

Generally speaking, there are three factors that should be taken into consideration in determining the amount of life insurance to be provided by the company: statutory sources of benefits, such as social security or workers' compensation; competitive practice; and individual company practices.

Social Security and Other Statutory Sources. In general, social security life insurance is a fairly small benefit. The lump sum is often aimed at defraying funeral expenses and may be quite minimal. However, there is enough variation from country to country that one should not take this for granted. Benefit levels in Italy are very high, for example, and companies should not set up a situation in which the employee is overinsured.

The requirements of collective agreements may be fairly generous, and companies should look carefully before agreeing to supplement them. In addition, workers' compensation may be required, with benefits provided upon occupational death.

Competitive Practice. As with other benefits, it is reasonable to determine competitive market practice based on location, industry, and conditions of collective agreements.

Lump-sum benefits are usually based on salary and can range from one year's pay to four years' pay depending on the country. Benefits exceeding four years' pay are unusual, although accidental death benefits of five or six times annual pay are required in Italy.

Details of plan design would include the definition of *pay,* whether there is an additional benefit upon accidental death, the definition of *spouse,* acceptable nonspouse named beneficiaries, optional employee additional amounts, and the like. In some situations, lump-sum death benefits are fixed amounts (e.g., DM 50,000 in Germany regardless of salary); in these cases, the situation of executives should be examined separately, since the lump-sum death benefit may be inadequate financial protection.

Survivor income benefits are usually expressed in terms of salary (such as 40% of salary continued to the surviving spouse) or as a percentage of the retirement benefit from a defined benefit plan (such as 60% of the projected normal retirement benefit or 50% of the accrued retirement benefit).

Usually, the lump-sum account balance in any defined contribution retirement plan is paid out, perhaps in installments. Any employee contributions to a retirement plan would almost always be paid out to the beneficiary, with all accrued earnings.

Some countries permit variation in benefits on the basis of family status, providing higher benefits upon the death of married employees or employees with dependent children. Some countries permit variation based on level within the company, with separate formulas for hourly paid, salaried, and executive levels.

Other Circumstances. Companies may provide death benefits different from competitive practice because of their own individual circumstances. For example, companies in high-risk industries, such as mining or explosives, may choose to provide higher levels of benefits, reflecting the more perilous environment.

Basically, there is much potential complexity within the general framework we have outlined, and provision of benefits in each country must be considered separately.

Financing Death Benefits

For a small group of employees, the number of deaths (and amount of payments) is unpredictable, so the cash flow needed to pay out benefits cannot be budgeted. Because most companies dislike significant unpredictable fluctuations in their profit/loss from year to year, they tend to use a life insurance product to provide death benefits to their employees. The company pays a predetermined premium so that costs can be predictable and budgeted; the insurance company bears the risk of unexpected claims.

In some cases, the company will be the holder of the insurance policy. In some countries, like the United Kingdom, the pension trust will hold the policy and pay the premium.

Normally, a local life insurance company should be used in each country. Benefits from a locally licensed insurance company are called *admitted* and usually receive favorable tax treatment. Benefits from an insurance company that is not licensed in the country are called *nonadmitted* and could be subject to full taxation (see the section "Benefit Pooling: Paying for Benefits" for a more thorough description).

Disability Benefits

Terminology for disability benefits can be different from country to country. *Long-term disability, invalidity,* and *permanent ill health* are commonly used terms. There are many similarities in the provision of disability and death benefits, so some of the material here is a deliberate repetition of similar information in the earlier section.

How disability is determined also varies, and triggers for payment are different as well. The concept of disability management is a growing trend in the United States, but it has not yet surfaced in other countries. For example, in the Netherlands, it is very difficult and expensive to lay off or dismiss workers. It is also difficult for older workers to be reemployed. Therefore, it became common practice for employers to declare disability for workers facing redundancy. The company avoided costly termination payments, and the employee saved face and had an income. These abuses have largely been stopped.

Sometimes the disability period is based on different time periods of work loss. When an employee becomes ill, he or she is usually entitled to a number of days of sick pay or what is called "cash sickness benefits." The duration of these payments may be determined by company policy, industry collective, or union agreement. In most countries, there is a minimal government requirement. In some countries, like the United States, employees might be put on short-term disability for a period of time, after which the disability might be deemed long term or permanent.

Payments may be made from different programs. For example, cash sickness payments are usually paid directly through payroll; sometimes, social security picks up a portion of costs after some period of time. Long-term benefits may be from both social security and the company. It is important to be sure that the combined effect is "integrated"—that there is neither a gap in coverage nor a duplication of payments.

Income Benefits

The disabled employee is usually provided with regular installment payments (e.g., monthly or quarterly) for the duration of the disability (i.e., ceasing when the employee is able to return to work or upon the employee's death).

Lump-Sum Payments

A lump-sum payment may be made upon total and permanent disability (TPD). The formula for this payment is usually related to the life insurance lump-sum amount and is provided as a rider to the insurance policy. If the disability is a result of accident or dismemberment, lump-sum benefits may be paid through the accidental death provisions in the life insurance policy.

If there is a defined contribution retirement plan, a decision must be made on whether the lump-sum account balance will be paid out upon total and permanent disability. There may be legal requirements that restrict a company's ability to make an early payout.

Determining the Company-Provided Amount

The same three factors considered for life insurance should be considered in determining the amount of disability insurance to be provided by the company: statutory sources (e.g., social security or workers' compensation), competitive practice, and individual company situation.

Social Security and Other Statutory Sources. Disability benefits from social security may be fairly small or may be rather substantial, depending on the country. In the United States, for example, these payments may be below published poverty levels. By contrast, in the Netherlands, payments can provide up to 70% of a disabled employee's working income. Benefits usually relate to the individual's pay, to the retirement benefit that the disabled wage earner had accrued, or to a projected benefit if the individual would have continued working until normal retirement age.

The requirements of collective agreements may be fairly generous, and companies should review such agreements carefully before deciding to supplement with company-provided disability plans.

Formulas for company-provided benefits may be complicated and need to be integrated with social security. For example, a common company-provided disability benefit in France might be 30% of pay up to the social security wage ceiling and 80% of pay above the ceiling.

Often, local workers' compensation may provide a generous benefit in case of work-related disability. Inclusion of work-related injuries in a company's disability program should be based on a combination of local regulations, common practice, risk management, and business needs.

Competitive Practice. Whether a company defines its competitive market for employment as broad-based or countrywide, or whether it is limited by industry, by a specific geographic area within the country, or by collective agreement, there will be differences in practice.

Disability benefits are usually based on salary and can range from some percentage such as 30% up to 100% of pay. It is important to define what elements of pay are eligible for disability payments. For the most part, eligible pay should be limited to base pay.

Other Circumstances. As with death benefits, companies may provide benefits different from competitive practice because of their own individual circumstances.

Coordination of Retirement and Death Benefits During Disability. There is an issue of whether life insurance coverage and participation in the retirement plan continue during the period of disablement. In the United States, this is often done through "waiver of premium," which means the insurance premium for life insurance is waived when the employee is disabled. In other countries, this is commonly done through a more direct coordination of the disability benefits with the retirement plan and death benefits.

Continuation of the retirement plan is more a matter of company choice, costs, and competitive practice. An insured disability plan could include continued premium payment to the retirement plan, but it need not.

Financing Disability Benefits

Disability is usually unexpected and unanticipated. This means that the cash flow needs are also unpredictable. However, since the benefit is commonly a continuation of salary (perhaps at a reduced rate), there is not the cash flow impact that lump-sum benefits can have.

The choice of whether to self-insure the disability benefits (i.e., to pay the disabled employee directly) or to seek an outside insurance company is a question of risk management. The use of an insurance company means that the company will face budgeted premium payments, while direct payment may mean uneven costs over time.

The same rationale for using a local insurance company that applies to life insurance applies to disability coverage. Namely, benefits from a local insurance company usually receive favorable tax treatment. Benefits from an insurance company that is not licensed in the country could be subject to full taxation; furthermore, there could be tax-related penalties for both the company and the recipient of the benefit. Disability insurance in most countries can be placed within a multinational pooling arrangement, as described in the next section, although not every insurance network will pool disability coverage.

Benefit Pooling: Paying for Benefits

Multinational insurance for benefits is a complex topic that we can only touch on here. In the United States, for example, it is easy for an insurance company to be licensed in many states, so a large U.S. employer can use a single insurance company to cover all its employees, regardless of their state of residence. On the international scene, it is almost impossible for a single insurance company to be licensed in more than one country. The licensing rules of the countries usually do not allow enough flexibility for a company to be licensed in more than one country; for example, a country's insurance regulators may require that a certain portion of assets be invested in the country.

Consequently, it is almost always necessary to use a different insurance company in each country. While it would be convenient to be able to use one insurer and get all coverage put in place around the world, this cannot be done, at present, within the tax and licensing laws, but it can be approximated through the use of multinational insurance pooling.

Admitted/Nonadmitted

Benefit payments receive favorable tax treatment in most countries. However, these must be *admitted* benefits, purchased in the country from a locally licensed insurance company, within any legally imposed limits.

Any benefits purchased out of country through an insurer that is not locally licensed are usually *nonadmitted*. Benefits paid from nonadmitted policies could be subject to a variety of consequences and very likely will be taxable to the beneficiary. This could have the effect of reducing the benefit from 40 to 60%, depending on the country in which it is paid.

An example of such a nonadmitted benefit is a worldwide business-travel accident policy purchased in the United States and covering all employees globally. Although it may be convenient for the company to have one worldwide business-travel accident policy, it is possible that benefits paid to beneficiaries will be taxed, because the worldwide policy may be viewed as nonadmitted by the tax authorities in the country where the beneficiary resides.

Multinational Insurance Pooling

Terminology can be confusing. In the U.S., the term *pooling* means *not* self-experienced. In the international setting, however, pooling means the opposite: a company pools its own risks in different countries, almost as if self-experience rated.

Pooling arrangements can be financially beneficial and should be explored by companies with international locations. Types of coverage that can be pooled successfully include life insurance, disability, and some medical coverage. Typically, pension plans are not pooled. The rationale of benefit pooling is to allow companies with smaller numbers of employees in several countries to take advantage of a "pooled" size. By pooling its own claims experience in each of the countries under one insurer (or network of insurers), the company can receive dividends under an umbrella approach that is managed through the parent corporation.

Pooling can be arranged through a limited number of insurance carriers with affiliates, partnership agreements, and/or wholly owned subsidiaries in many locations. Current insurance arrangements may not necessarily preclude entering into a pooling arrangement. In some countries, there is only one major carrier and all insurers with pooling arrangements use that company (as with Irish Life in Ireland). Insurance coverage is placed with the local entity, under local laws and regulations, but is covered under an umbrella policy held by a company's corporate headquarters. Therefore, this coverage is admitted, receiving favorable tax treatment when benefits are paid, but the company will receive dividends based on its own experience and usage. The operation in each country receives its own dividends, which are paid to the corporate office in a lump sum to be distributed to each location, either in cash or by means of a premium reduction.

Some countries, such as Germany and Japan, are "tariff rated." This means that there is little competition among insurers to provide better rates. Through pooling, it is still possible to implement some cash flow techniques, but prices will vary little. Dividends paid in a tariff-rated country are subject to corporate income tax. As a result, many companies either declare a "premium holiday" (pay required premiums less any outstanding dividend) or leave the dividends out of country where there is a smaller tax implication.

There are about nine major multinational insurance networks, and this list is not meant to be exhaustive. The U.S. representative company for each network is listed for convenience.

- Aetna-Generali—formed by Aetna (large U.S. insurer) and Generali (large Italian insurer with operations throughout Europe)
- AIG/Winterthur ALLIANCE—formed by American International Group (AIG, a large U.S. insurer) and Winterthur (Swiss-based company with operations throughout Europe)
- GAIN—U.S. representative company is Hartford Life Insurance
- IGP—U.S. insurer representative is John Hancock

- MBA or Insurope—one U.S. insurer representative is Prudential
- MAXIS—an alliance, with French-based AXA as one cornerstone; the U.S. representative company is MetLife
- MIA—an alliance, with Principal Financial Group as the U.S. representative
- Swiss Life—a Zurich-headquartered network
- Zurich Life—another Zurich-headquartered network

Effect of EMU on European Benefits

The emergence of the single European currency, the euro, began on January 1, 1999, and will be a three-year process. As of this writing, it is not expected that the formation of the European Economic and Monetary Union (EMU) and the euro will have much immediate effect on the design of benefits in Europe in the foreseeable future. Each of the countries has unique tax laws and social benefit structures, so it is not likely that there will be a common denominator on which to develop company-paid benefit plans. There may be significant issues in compensation, however, especially at regional headquarters, for the "euro-manager."

There have been some strides in the pension area; it is now possible to invest funds in out-of-country investments. Pension reform and less restrictive legislation are being implemented in some European Union countries, allowing for more portability and employee contribution into retirement vehicles. This can be viewed as a positive momentum toward the unification of the European workforce.

Time Off with Pay

No discussion of international benefits is complete without some mention of the policy differences around the world regarding time off with pay. Many of these policies stem from legislation or local culture and tradition. They are often included in industry collectives or union negotiations and are almost always a contractual agreement within the employee work rules (subject to the concept of acquired rights in countries that recognize acquired rights).

Because of the wide variation in customary practices in each country, we will provide some broad-based descriptions and offer a few examples (sometimes our examples are extreme to emphasize the point). Since legislation and collective agreement do change, the examples cited here should be considered illustrative rather than definitive.

Vacation or Annual Holiday

The American term is *vacation;* the British term is *annual holiday*, sometimes simply called *holiday*.

In the United States, the most common practice is to offer employees two weeks of vacation at full pay, increasing to three weeks after completion of five years of employment. Production workers and retail and food service employees often begin with one week's vacation. There is little legislation concerning vacation provision, except that unused accrued vacation must be paid out at termination of employment. Unused vacation need not be carried over to the next year. If the company does allow unused vacation to be carried over, then any accruals must be shown as a liability on the company books.

In Europe, practices are vastly different. Common practice and local legislation begin with four weeks of vacation per year, growing rapidly to six weeks, but there is considerable variation by country. Often, the vacation cannot be taken until after the completion of one full year of service. In Germany, the legal requirement is 24 days of vacation after six months of employment; however, common practice is the provision of 30 days of vacation. Whereas many American technical, professional, and managerial employees may not take their full vacation entitlement, most Europeans do take their annual vacation time in full. Requirements concerning accrual, or carryover, of vacation time are limited, and practice again varies by country.

In Latin America, four weeks of vacation is prevalent. Brazil's regulation of 30 days of vacation is reduced by other absences taken during the year. Asian policies concerning vacation are less liberal and frequently start at two weeks of paid vacation per year.

In many countries, employees are given a "vacation loading" or "vacation premium"—that is, additional pay during vacation time over and above normal pay. In Mexico, for example, employers are required to give employees an additional 25% of compensation during paid time off as a vacation premium; most employers provide more, commonly 80%. In Belgium, the required vacation premium is 85% of one month's pay. Vacation premiums are also required for virtually all unionized employees in Australia (typically, 17.5% of four weeks' pay) and are generally extended to nonunionized staff as well.

The 13th month's pay, so common in many countries, including France, Germany, and the Netherlands, usually began as a holiday premium or vacation allowance, but now it has become a regular part of direct cash compensation.

Exhibit 15-1 provides more details on country practice in a few countries.

Exhibit 15-1. Time Off with Pay

Country	Statutory Vacation	Customary Additional Vacation	Customary Public Holidays
France	2.5 days/month	—	1 day required; 10 additional days customary
Germany	24 workdays	—	9 days plus 4 days in some states
Italy	Set by industry-wide collective agreements; 35 days for executives	—	11 days
Netherlands	4 x number of workdays in a workweek; collective agreement usually requires more; generally, a total of 24 days	—	8 days
United Kingdom	15 days[1]	—	8 days
Australia	4 weeks; award (collective agreement) may require more	Long-service leave of 13 weeks after 15 years of service; varies by state	9 days plus several state holidays
Hong Kong	7 workdays after 1 year, increasing to 14 days after 9 years	—	12 days; many offices give an additional 6 days
India	1 day for every 20 days of work (after 240 days of work in a calendar year)	—	3 national days plus at least 5 state days; typically, total of 10–12 days

Japan	10 workdays after 6 months plus 1 day per year up to 20 days	—	14 days
Singapore	7 days after 12 months of service plus 1 day per year up to 14 days	—	11 days
Brazil	30 calendar days	—	7 federal days; typically, an additional 6 bank holidays
Canada	Varies by province (minimum 2 weeks; maximum 3 weeks in Saskatchewan)	—	Varies by province; general 9 federal holidays
Chile	15 days; after 10 years, 1 additional day every 3 years up to 35 days	—	15 days
Mexico	6 days after 1 year, increasing to 12 days in 9th year, then 2 additional days every 5 years	—	7 days required; typically, an additional 3 provided
United States	None required	2 weeks after 1 year of service	None required; 9 days customary

1. Increasing to 20 days starting November 23, 1999.

Public Holidays

Public holidays also vary around the world, based on legislation and common practice. The term *bank holiday* is used to describe public holidays in the United Kingdom and to distinguish them from "annual holidays." There may be national holidays, state or provincial holidays, or local holidays, and paid time off may be required or may be customary.

For example, in both Germany and Australia, there are nine paid national holidays per year. However, there are a number of additional paid holidays that vary from state to state in each country. In Korea and Japan, national holidays are not specified in labor law, but employers generally provide a minimum of 15 holidays per year. In addition, in Japan, the New Year's holiday is traditionally extended for three to five days.

In Mexico and Brazil, there are normally seven national holidays. However, in Mexico, every six years, when a new president is elected, three to five additional holidays are often granted. In Brazil, Election Day is a holiday every two years, and most companies also provide paid time off for six to seven annual bank holidays.

In the United States, there is little legislation regarding paid holidays. Most companies observe five common national holidays and two to four additional national or state holidays. Additional "personal days" are often permitted, and sometimes flexible or cafeteria plans allow employees to trade other benefits for additional paid time off.

In many countries, there may be statutory provisions or common practice requiring that holidays that fall on weekends or other rest days be observed on working days. Furthermore, collective agreements or labor law may require an overtime premium to be paid to employees who work on a public holiday. Premium amounts vary from country to country and from one collective agreement to another, ranging from 125% to 250% of pay for hours worked on a company-observed holiday.

Special Time Off: Long-Service Leave and Sabbaticals

In many countries, special sabbatical leave may be required or customary. For example, in Australia, employees are entitled to paid sabbatical leave, called "long-service leave," for defined periods of continuous service. The original intent of long-service leave was to allow exiles to return to England to visit family after a period of servitude in Australia when it was a penal colony. As shown in Exhibit 15-1, the benefit is generally 13 weeks' paid leave after 15 years of service, although the requirements differ among the states. In New South Wales, long-service leave is two months after ten years of service. Long-service leave is in addition to the regular annual vacation that each employee normally receives. After the first long-service leave, entitlement accrues after each additional 5, 10, or 15 years (varying by state). Any unused long-service leave is accrued (carried forward) as a liability on the company books and paid at termination or retirement.

In the United States, some high-tech companies have adopted the practice of providing sabbatical leaves, ranging from four to six weeks after several years' employment (typically six or seven years). This practice is also common in academia but rare in other industries. The intent in the United States is to allow professors and technical workers additional time for study and research.

In Belgium, employees are entitled to take three sabbaticals during their working careers, lasting from three months to one year. In Indonesia, labor law requires a paid long-service leave of three months after six years of employment. In many Moslem countries, an extended time off is permitted, once in an employee's career, for making a religious pilgrimage *(hajj)* to Mecca. This is often paid leave.

Sick Leave

Sick-leave provisions can be unregulated and vary greatly by company, as in the United States, or they can be highly regulated through legislation or collective agreements, as in many other countries around the world. In some countries, companies are required to provide sick pay for a period of time; then social security continues payment for some longer period. The company may be reimbursed from the government or social security system for all or part of sick pay. For example, in the United Kingdom, social security pays part of the sick employee's salary and the company provides the balance. In Germany, the company pays full sick pay for six weeks, after which the employee is paid through the social security system.

In Korea, employees are entitled to 60% of their wages if they are sick, paid entirely by the company. In Mexico, sickness benefits are paid through the social security system. In the United States, companies are free to determine their own sick-leave policies. Practices differ based on industry, region, and competitive practice. Common practices include plans that pay no sickness benefits for the first two or three days of an illness. Some companies may allow up to two weeks of sick time per year, whereas others have an accrual of sick days based on years of service and attendance record. Others may have unlimited sick leave.

Maternity Benefits

In the United States, maternity is viewed (legally) as a specialized form of disability; in other countries, maternity may be considered "illness" rather than disability or may be considered as a separate category altogether.

In most European countries, Australasia, and the Americas, maternity benefits are legislated. The length of time covered by maternity benefits varies by country. As with sick pay, the source of payments during maternity leave can be the company or social security or a combination of both. There are some regulations regarding maternity time off that are noteworthy, particularly in Europe. In the Netherlands and in Germany, for example, benefits extend for a two-year and three-year period, respectively, although the time off is without pay. After that time, the employee may return to her own job. In the meantime, a company may hire a "temporary" employee to perform the vacated job, and it must treat that employee as a permanent employee, with full company benefits.

There are some countries, such as the Dominican Republic and Denmark, that extend paid paternity leave as well. Many countries, such as Australia and most provinces of Canada, require that employers provide unpaid paternity leave (or "parental leave"). Some countries, such as Germany, also allow paid time for nursing.

In Asia, there are few benefits for maternity. In many Asian countries, it is still common for women to resign and not return to work after the birth of a child. This practice is changing and should be monitored on a country-by-country basis.

Other Time Off with Pay

There are many practices that are specific to certain countries. Often, there are requirements imposed by labor law, other legislation, or collective agreement. Sometimes, companies provide additional paid time off voluntarily, without statutory requirements, and such practice may be prevalent and competitive. The following list provides an indication of the variety of time-off policies that can be found around the world. A few countries are cited as examples, but such listings are not meant to be comprehensive.

- *Jury duty and other civic responsibilities.* Time off with pay for service on jury duty, for example, is provided in the United States and the United Kingdom; paid time off to vote is given in Costa Rica, Ecuador, and Guatemala; and paid time off for civic duties is provided in Brazil and Hungary.
- *Military leave.* In the Czech Republic, the United States, Taiwan, and Israel (for example), paid time off is provided for military service.
- *Funeral leave (sometimes called compassionate leave or bereavement leave).* Most countries allow paid time off for a death in the immediate

Exhibit 15-2. Statutory Maternity Leave

Country	Duration	Pay During Leave
France	16 weeks[1]	100% of Tranche A pay
Germany	14 weeks	100% of pay[2]
Italy	5 months	80% of pay[3]
Netherlands	16 weeks	100% of pay up to specified ceiling
United Kingdom	18 weeks	90% of pay for first 6 weeks; flat-rate benefit for additional 12 weeks[4]
Australia[5]	6 weeks[6]	Unpaid
Hong Kong	10 weeks	80% of pay[7]
India	Up to 12 weeks	100% of pay
Japan	14 weeks	60% of covered pay[8]
Singapore	8 weeks	100% of pay[9]
Brazil	120 days	100% of pay
Canada	25 weeks	55% of covered pay
Chile	126 days	100% of pay up to specified ceiling
Mexico	12 weeks	100% of pay up to specified ceiling
United States	Up to 12 weeks in any 12-month period	Unpaid

1. Increases to 26 weeks upon birth of third child.
2. Daily allowance paid by sickness fund; employer pays balance.
3. Collective agreements usually require employers to pay the remaining 20% of pay.
4. Partially paid by employer.
5. Provisions are generally determined by "awards" (agreements defining the employment relationship, including pay, leave, etc.). Maternity leave is covered by state law in New South Wales.
6. Can be up to 52 weeks under some awards. Maximum combined leave (both parents) is one year.
7. Leave is unpaid for employees with fewer than 40 weeks of service.
8. Reduced by any pay continued by the employer.
9. Paid by the employer.

family, and some countries offer a cash benefit to the bereaved. Time off varies by country, usually from two to ten days, and may vary by relationship to the deceased. In Australia, five days are required; in Argentina, it is three days for the death of a spouse, child, or parent and one day for the death of a brother or sister. Two days are provided in France, three days in Guatemala, and one day in Hungary.

- *Marriage leave.* Paid time off may be provided for the employee's marriage, varying by country from 3 days to 15 days (for example, in Japan, Brazil, Spain, and Italy). In some countries, such as France, Poland, and Japan, there is also paid time off for the marriage of a child.
- *Care for a sick family member.* There may be a limited time-off policy for caring for a sick child or immediate family member (50 days per year in Germany). In the United States, time off for this purpose is guaranteed through the Family and Medical Leave Act (FMLA), but payment for time off is not required.
- *Menstrual leave.* In Japan and Korea, as well as in many countries with a strong Moslem influence, female employees are entitled to one day off, with pay, each month.
- *Religious time.* In many countries with a sizable Moslem population (such as Indonesia), employees may be entitled to paid time off during the workday for prayer. Office buildings and companies usually provide a prayer room. In some countries, employees may be given a day off for the baptism or circumcision of a child or the ordination of a family member.
- *Blood donation.* Employees in Brazil must be provided with one paid day off to donate blood.
- *Moving.* Employees are given a day off to move their household in Austria, France, India, Spain, and elsewhere.
- *Exams.* Employees in Singapore, Uruguay, and other countries may be given one day off with pay for university or other exams.

In addition to time off with pay, some countries require time off without pay for special circumstances. For example, as was mentioned earlier, extended parental leave may be required to be offered but without pay. The relation of time off to other benefits (e.g., retirement accrual, coverage for death or disability) varies by country and should be reviewed in this connection.

Summary

As stressed in the benefits section, it is important to be aware of the differences in paid time-off policies and to design work rules based on laws and customs within each country. Managers who are used to doing business only domestically may have difficulty understanding other countries' practices. Training and awareness are, as always, vital to the success of any global expansion.

Flexible Benefits

The concept of flexible benefit plans was developed in the United States in the 1970s, and it has since become quite popular. Sometimes called "cafeteria plans," and enabled through Section 125 and other sections of the U.S. Internal Revenue Code, such plans allow individual employees to choose their own mix of benefits. The most common approach is to give the employees an "account" that they may use to purchase those benefits that best suit their needs—if both spouses are working, for example, they may only need one company's medical plan. A single employee may elect a lower level of life insurance than a married employee or a higher medical deductible, and so forth.

The approach is now prevalent in the United States, but it has been less popular around the world, for several reasons:

- When medical coverage is removed from the package—for example, in countries where medical care is provided through the socialized medical system—the impetus behind flexible plans is greatly reduced.
- In many countries, employees are not used to choice and do not expect to have to make decisions about their benefits. They expect the company to make these decisions for them. In the United Kingdom, for instance, most flexible plans have a "default"—the fallback if the employee doesn't choose something else. And the vast majority of employees in flexplans in the United Kingdom elect that "default."
- There is often no enabling legislation. If the plan allows the choice of cash (or other taxable elements), the employee may be subject to tax on the total account.

In most situations, flexible plans are aimed at being more tax effective for the higher paid. The outstanding example is Australia, which instituted a Fringe Benefits Tax, essentially taxing the company (rather than the employee) on "fringe benefits" provided to the employees. That has led to the ultimate in flexibility, at least at executive levels. The company determines an amount that it is willing to pay the employee, inclusive of

Fringe Benefits Tax. The employee then arranges his or her own mix of compensation to suit his or her own needs and tax situation, as long as the total cost to the company is unchanged. A typical package can include a company car, additional contributions to a retirement plan, club memberships, and the like.

Another interesting example of flexible benefits is the managers' insurance frequently offered by Israeli companies to all their employees. The employee is allowed a certain percentage of pay to purchase insured coverage from a number of options, choosing those most suitable for his or her needs. Choices include retirement supplements, medical coverage, life insurance, and other insured products.

Stock Option Plans

Strictly speaking (according to U.S. classifications), stock ownership probably is a compensation issue rather than a benefits issue. However, the rest of the world does not necessarily view the situation as so compartmentalized.

In the United States, stock plans (such as stock option plans, stock purchase plans, and the like) are a popular method of sharing in ownership of the company, encouraging employees to work in a concentrated effort to maximize company growth. This concept is not necessarily understood in all countries around the globe. Language barriers and perceptions of the value of stock may be impediments to simply extending the U.S. plan. There could be procedural issues in implementing the plan as well. Communication is the critical factor.

Stock options for employees in the United States have high perceived value and are taxed either at the time of exercise or at the time of sale, depending on the type of plan. By now, most U.S. corporate parents have extended some sort of stock option program to top-level executives around the world, sometimes with little thought about the specific situation in each country.

As companies now think about extending stock options or stock purchase plans lower in the organization, a number of issues that have an impact on non-U.S. nationals need to be addressed.

Employee Taxation

The impact of local taxes on the exercise of the option and the subsequent sale of securities may be a decisive factor in employee appreciation. Tax treatment varies widely by country. In some high-tax countries, such as the Netherlands and Belgium, options may be taxed at the date of grant. That minimizes the value of the options. In many countries, options will be taxed at the point they become vested, regardless of whether they have been exercised.

Some countries impose no capital gains tax on appreciation, which would make options or a stock purchase plan very attractive. Some countries (e.g., the United Kingdom and France) allow a tax advantage if the option program meets certain requirements. Many countries, particularly in Europe, are reviewing their positions on taxation of stock options. Your international tax consultant is the best resource for current information.

Expatriate stock option grants and exercises will be taxed on local rules and are often included in tax equalization policies. This can be costly to the company, trying to tax equalize a very heavy tax rate on a large payment. Companies experiencing high growth might consider providing incentives to expatriates to delay exercise of stock options until they return to the United States and are no longer subject to host-country tax. Some companies go so far as to exclude stock options from the tax equalization policy.

Registration

Sometimes subsidiaries of U.S. companies fail to register the stock grants, and therefore the recipient of the grant avoids tax payments. In some countries, this practice can lead to heavy fines imposed on the company for noncompliance. It is recommended that companies granting stock options to local nationals be aware of local tax laws and comply with registration rules.

Exchange-Rate Fluctuations

Variations in the currency exchange rates may affect the value of company stock to non-U.S. employees. Both U.S. and foreign participants in a plan are exposed to some element of investment risk, but exchange-rate fluctuations represent an added element of risk for the non-U.S. employee. There are two different aspects to the exchange-rate risk:

- Prior to exercise, there is the risk that the option price, in local currency terms, will increase between the date of grant and the date of exercise. This happens if the U.S. dollar increases in value relative to the local currency, making the exercise price more expensive in local currency terms.

- After exercise, there is the risk that the value of the local currency is appreciating against the dollar, resulting in the U.S. dollar value of the stock increasing but the value in local currency declining.

These exchange-rate fluctuations can result in totally opposite financial results for the non-U.S. employee. For example, the stock price in the United States could be up, so the U.S. executives are quite pleased, but the local currency may have appreciated against the dollar enough to wipe out any gains for the German executives. In another scenario, the stock price could be flat, so the U.S. executives feel unhappy, but the local currency has devalued against the dollar and the Indonesian executives are ecstatic that their stock options have doubled or tripled in value.

Acquired Rights

We defined *acquired rights* earlier as the legal notion in many countries that a repeated condition of employment may become part of the employment contract and may not be reduced later. In a country with acquired rights, it may be difficult to suspend or terminate a stock option plan after three or four years of operation. The plan document may allow the U.S. company to discontinue the plan, but the company may have to continue equivalent arrangements (or make some other concession) in countries with acquired rights.

Due Diligence for Benefits

The due diligence process for employee benefits can be very helpful to an acquiring company in evaluating liabilities, considering human resource approaches for the future, and integrating a newly acquired company. The human resources practitioner cannot take it for granted that the company being acquired has followed accounting standards, tax treatment, or even HR policies that match the acquiring company's home country. Unfortunately, due diligence for human resources is often carried out by finance and treasury, with little regard for the potential importance of the topic. It is important that HR be aware of the complexity of the programs and potential liabilities and assure their involvement early on in the acquisition/merger process.

Benefit design in any country can be relatively complex because of nuances in local custom, tax laws, labor laws, and so forth. Furthermore, the differences between one country and another, even between countries that are contiguous, are rooted in legal requirements and cultural norms that need to be understood prior to design and implementation of any benefit program. Whether you are planning to do business in a country for the first time, expanding current facilities, or participating in an acquisition or merger, it is vital that a thorough due diligence be performed at an early stage in the process.

A thorough due diligence review of human resources practices during an acquisition or merger can uncover hidden liabilities. One example of a not-so-obvious liability is Australian long-service leave, commonly three months' paid leave after 10 years of service and again each five years thereafter. This liability can be accrued on the books until the leave is taken and can be a substantial amount. Without a careful due diligence, the liability can be overlooked, causing an unpleasant surprise when later claimed by employees.

Another example is severance pay. In Chapter 14, it was noted that in many countries, particularly in Asia and Central America, severance pay due an employee upon any termination, regardless of cause, is commonly one month's pay times years of service. Consequently, there can be a substantial liability, which might not be reflected on the books (depending on the accounting standards and requirements of the country). These accumulated severance liabilities can make workforce reduction a very expensive undertaking. The due diligence process should reveal whether any provision has been made for this liability.

If the acquiring company is a U.S. parent, the application of U.S. financial accounting standards to the company being acquired can produce liabilities that were not reflected on the local books under local accounting standards.

If you are already doing business in a country and acquire or merge with another company in the same country, work rules and benefits may need to be merged to provide consistency and economy of scale. Here, a perceived diminution of benefit can be unpleasant, and it may be a violation of a union, industry collective, or works council provision. There may be laws in the country regulating processes for informing, consulting with, or negotiating with employees or their representatives. There may be laws requiring uniform treatment of all employees, necessitating a single set of rules and benefits.

Exhibit 15-3 provides a suggested guideline for how and what pertinent information should be assembled during the due diligence period to assist with this process.

The column headings in the matrix (Exhibit 15-3) are explained below.

Exhibit 15-3. Acquisition and Post-Merger Checklist for Benefits

Benefit Type	Social Benefits	Legally Required Benefits	Company-Sponsored Benefits—Ours	Company-Sponsored Benefits—XYZ	Suggested Changes/ Integration Issues	Notes and Comments
Pension and Retirement						
Medical						
Disability						
Life						
Savings/Profit Sharing						
Severance Termination Pay Dismissal, Layoff, etc.						
Stock Options						
24-Hour Accident						
Business Travel Accident						
Union Works Council Collective Agreement						
Other						

Social Benefits

These are benefits provided by the social security system and similar institutions in the country. A summary of those benefits and their costs is critical in analyzing the expected labor costs of the operation's going forward.

It is important to check that all social security payments (or equivalent) have been made, especially in the acquisition of a family-owned firm. We have seen instances in which management withheld social security contributions from the employees' paychecks but was eight months delinquent in sending that money to the social security system.

Legally Required Benefits

These are benefits that must be provided by the company and can include "hidden" benefits that might create unrecognized liabilities on the company books. The critical factor here is to be sure that any liabilities are reflected appropriately in the company's accounts.

If you are planning workforce reduction after the acquisition, it is especially important to be aware of the cost of layoffs or dismissals. There may also be legal requirements that apply during merger and acquisition, such as the transfer of undertakings directives of the European Union.

Company-Sponsored Benefits—Ours

This column is for a description of current employer-sponsored benefit plans, if the company already has operations in this location. This summary is not critical for the due diligence phase of an acquisition, but it is important later if the company wants to integrate the operations in the country.

Company-Sponsored Benefits—XYZ

This column includes a summary of the terms of benefit plans that are provided by the company being merged or acquired (the "target" company called XYZ in this example). Be sure to review books and plan provisions with local human resources, finance, and management, asking probing questions to be sure that nothing is left unnoticed. Discussions with the local broker, consultant, and insurance provider are important sources for information.

This is the first critical step of the due diligence process for benefits: Determining exactly what benefit programs are in place at the target company and determining their ongoing cost.

Information should be collected on both benefit design and funding. A suggested checklist for benefits might start with the following:

- All current employee booklets and summaries of changes to plans not described in the booklets
- Copies of any executive agreements (golden parachutes, special executive benefits, etc.)
- Current collective bargaining agreements (and those prior to the last round of negotiations)
- Statement or estimate of potential liabilities for severance payments related to past service
- Annual financial statements for retirement plans, including income statements and balance sheet; if plan is not funded, statements of annual expense and cumulative book reserve
- Actuarial reports for defined-benefit plans
- Copies of filings for tax deductions or certificates of deductions for benefit plans for the past few years
- Demographic data on the participants, including birth date, sex, hire date, and current pay rate (alternately, employee counts by gender, pay, age, and service)
- Annual financial statements, claims experience, and dividend statements for any insurance arrangements
- Copies of relevant personnel policies (benefits philosophy and objectives, travel, vacations and holidays, leaves of absence, sick care, medical care, termination, expatriate policies, employee communication, etc.)

Suggested Changes/Integration Issues

This information matrix can be used after the acquisition to help plan how to integrate the benefit programs at the two different companies. There can be significant economies of scale by using the same providers, administrator, and plan-design features, for instance. Strictly speaking, the integration process is not part of due diligence, but it is a critical factor for the success of the acquisition.

Notes and Comments

Comments pertinent for management regarding the benefit or any particular provision should be recorded here. For example, "There are 50 out of 300 employees eligible for long service, for a current accrued liability of AUD xxxx"; "Changing legislation; conforms to new regulations"; or "Must be reviewed and negotiated with works council."

If the acquiring company has corporate guidelines for benefits policies, comments could be directed at how close the existing plan(s) is to global guidelines. Other comments might be addressed at competitiveness of the existing programs.

SECTION FOUR

REGIONAL/COUNTRY CHARACTERISTICS OF LOCAL REMUNERATION PRACTICES

CHAPTER 16

CANADA

JAMES G. DELANEY AND RUTHANNE HUISING

Introduction

Canada is one of the largest countries geographically but has a population of only 30 million people. The population continues to grow by approximately 1% each year. In the past 10 years, approximately 50% of the growth has been the result of immigration. Even with a declining birthrate and an aging population, this number is expected to continue to increase. Approximately 50% of immigrants to Canada are considered "economic immigrants" and are selected because of their special skills, because specific jobs need to be filled, or because they have money to invest. Most are likely to have higher levels of education than their Canadian-born counterparts. This gives Canada an increasingly diverse population in terms of ethnicity, language, and culture.

As a nation, education is a priority. Approximately 8% of the gross domestic product (GDP) is spent on education. For the most part (90%), these are public dollars. There are 77 universities and 216 community colleges, colleges of art and technology, and other specialized institutions. Some 40% of Canadians ages 15 and over have a postsecondary degree, diploma, or certificate.

The two official languages in Canada are English and French. In the province of Quebec, French is the official language of the province and the primary language of the workplace, communications, and business. The most recent census results indicate that Canada's two official languages are the mother tongue of 84% of the population (English, 60%; French, 24%). This means, then, that 16% of Canadians have a first language other than English or French. The top three nonofficial languages have changed markedly since 1971, from Italian, German, and Ukrainian to Chinese, Italian, and Punjabi.

The Labor Force

Unemployment rates, which were 9.7% in 1996, decreased to 7.8% in 1999. Rates vary widely among the provinces. Those provinces in the

Atlantic Canada region have the highest rates, and those in the Prairie region have the lowest.

Seven out of ten workers are employed in the service industry—more specifically, in the categories of business, education, health, and social services.

The prevalence of unions in the Canadian workplace is greater than in the United States but less than in Northern Europe. Approximately 3.6 million, or 30.7%, of Canada workers belong to a union. A decline in strikes and lockouts occurred in the 1990s. The average person-days per year not worked because of union action has declined from 4,521 between 1984 and 1990 to 2,321 between 1991 and 1997.

Economy

The Canadian economy has felt the negative impact of the global economic downturn and, in particular, the fall of commodity prices. The health of the economy continues to be heavily influenced by the economic, monetary, and financial trends in the United States, and the robust U.S. economy has provided a degree of economic protection to Canada.

Recent projections forecast that GDP will grow at a rate of 2.5% in 1999 and 2.4% in 2000. This represents a slight reduction in growth from prior projections and reflects the impact of the financial crisis in Russia and Latin America. This projected growth is considerably lower than the robust 3.7% growth that occurred in 1997.

Trade export volumes should continue to grow as a result of the improved competitiveness that resulted from the 1997 and 1998 currency depreciation and strong price and cost performance relative to Canada's major trading partners.

Inflation, as measured by the Canadian Consumer Price Index, has remained low and stable (1.6% in 1996 and 1997; 1.1% and 1.5% estimated in 1999 and 2000, respectively).

The Components of a Compensation Program

The components of a Canadian compensation program are similar to those in the United States, but tax legislation, public funding of health care, and other less obvious differences in the Canadian context are sufficient to give Canada its own unique compensation programs.

The five most frequently referenced geographic regions are British Columbia, Prairie Provinces, Central Canada, Quebec, and Atlantic Provinces. Each region tends to have different economic and cultural circumstances, and compensation programs vary in prevalence and design across industries, provinces, and regions. As such, it is inaccurate to make reference to a "Canadian compensation program." For the purposes of this discussion, however, we will attempt to give a general flavor of compensation programs in Canada.

Taxes

Income tax is paid at the Canadian federal and provincial level. There are also sales taxes, which vary by province, and a federal goods and services tax (GST) that is applied to the sale price of all goods and services.

The highest federal marginal income tax rate is about 29%, which is in addition to the provincial income taxes. The highest combined federal and provincial tax rates are 45.6% in Alberta, 54.2% in British Columbia, 50.3% in Ontario, and 52.6% in Quebec. Because of a predicted government budget surplus in 1999, federal tax rates are forecast to decrease.

The combined federal and provincial sales tax rate in each of the provinces is about 15%. Alberta does not have a provincial sales tax in addition to the federal GST of 7%.

Taxes, deductions, and exemptions do have significant effects on the design and the types of compensation programs offered, but there are relatively few compensation programs that provide a tax advantage.

Base Pay

The predominant form of cash compensation is a fixed rate of pay that is generally communicated as an annual rate of pay for office, technical, and professional work and as an hourly rate of pay for production or manufacturing jobs. The average annual pay level in Canada is about C$36,900, and the average hourly wage reported for bargaining units in Canada is C$18.08 (1998).

For administration, technical, and professional positions, most Canadian organizations would administer pay using some system of job evaluation in which jobs are grouped into grades or bands and these bands are attached to pay levels that are representative of their particular marketplace.

Large national employers have different salary and wage scales in the different regions of Canada. In general, pay levels are higher in the major city centers and decline somewhat with distance from the city core. Toronto center is usually the highest, followed by Vancouver, Calgary, and Montreal. Lower levels are usually expected in the Atlantic Provinces. This is, of course, not always true, especially when we consider specific jobs or skills (e.g., information technology) that may be in temporary short supply in a particular region.

Most companies adjust base pay levels each year. This is approached through "structure movement" whereby the entire pay system is adjusted upward after referring to overall market trends and their impact on different organizational levels. Structure movement is aligned with, but not entirely attributable to, changes in the Consumer Price Index (CPI).

Average annual change in base pay levels includes this structure movement as well as increases attributable to such things as promotions, progression in career, and performance. Total increases in base pay are usually about 1 to 1.5% higher than structure movement. For example, forecasts made in late 1998 suggest that, in 1999, the private sector will increase pay structure by about 2.3%; in total, base pay will increase by about 3.2%, with CPI increasing by about 1.5%.

Exhibit 16-1 shows a 10-year history of base pay increase relative to the Canadian Consumer Price Index.

Exhibit 16-1. Base Salary Increases Relative to the Consumer Price Index (1990–1999)

	Base Salary	CPI
1990	5.9	5.0
1991	5.0	3.8
1992	3.8	2.1
1993	3.1	1.7
1994	2.6	0.2
1995	2.6	1.7
1996	2.8	1.6
1997	2.9	1.8
1998	3.4	2.2
1999	3.34	1.6

Short-Term Variable Pay

Variable pay programs became more prevalent during the economic stresses of the early 1990s. Organizations wanted to emphasize organizational and individual performance as well as control over payroll expenses. Individuals were concerned with job security in the context of corporate downsizing and reorganizing and were willing to take less in fixed pay, with the possibility of receiving incentives or performance bonuses later.

Exhibit 16-2 shows the pattern of eligibility for variable pay, displayed by base pay level. The amount, as a percentage of base pay, actually paid in these years has increased only modestly, and this increase is easily attributed to overall economic improvement rather than a change in variable pay plan design. Exhibit 16-3 shows the amounts of variable pay actually paid.

Exhibit 16-2. Percentage of Employees Eligible for Variable Pay (by Base Pay Category)

ANNUAL BASE PAY (in Thousands of Canadian Dollars)	1992	1998
$40–$49	26%	58%
$50–$59	36%	63%
$60–$69	46%	68%
$70–$79	56%	72%
$80–$89	66%	75%

Exhibit 16-3. Variable Pay Actually Paid as a Percentage of Base Pay (by Base Pay Category)

ANNUAL BASE PAY (in Thousands of Canadian Dollars)	1992	1998
$40–$49	4.6%	6.4%
$50–$59	7.6%	8.3%
$60–$69	9.7%	10.1%
$70–$79	11.3%	11.9%
$80–$89	12.4%	13.8%

Variable pay, often referred to as "short-term incentives," includes a large category of programs that attempt to focus employee efforts on goals that are beneficial to the organization.

The less precise designs are based on organizational success, usually financial, and are determined annually. These would include profit-sharing plans and annual bonus programs, which are predominantly retrospective in nature. They have very general or high-level targets such as organizational profit level or return on capital.

The more precise designs may consider organizational success as a component but are more prospective and specific in the setting of measures. They tend to be individual- or team-based measures. The definition of *team* could mean a small group, a geographic location, a product line, or some other method of aggregating performance. The performance measures may be sales revenue, customer satisfaction, "new" sales revenue, or other such quantifiable results. These programs often contain measures that are more discretionary, particularly when the desired results cannot be credibly measured in a timely way.

The payment of awards is almost always based on annual performance relative to target. An increasing number of plans, however, pay a portion of the annual award on a quarterly or monthly basis. This is done to move the payment as close to the achievement of the result as possible.

Long-Term Incentive Programs

Short-term incentives attempt to focus employees on annual, or shorter, performance periods. This generates positive energy with regard to these goals but may divert appropriate attention away from issues that are necessary for the long-term success of the organization. For example, a manager whose short-term incentive is based on positive cash flow and expense management may not elect to invest in production facilities or hire needed staff.

A variable pay program based on long-term success measures can offset these negative tendencies. The most common forms of long-term incentive plans in Canada are those based on equity participation, stock options in particular. Vehicles such as long-term cash plans or phantom stock plans are in use but are much less prevalent than stock options.

Capital Accumulation Programs

Registered Pension Plans (Known as "Qualified Plans" in the United States)

It is common for companies to make some provision for the eventual retirement of employees. The Canadian tax laws support employee participation in such programs by allowing deductions or tax credits in the year in which an employee makes his or her contribution. Traditionally, these programs have been in the form of defined-benefit pension plans, but governmental controls and the paper burden associated with defined-benefit plans have influenced companies to use defined-contribution plans instead. Large organizations would still be expected to have a defined-benefit plan, but smaller companies, as well as recent start-up companies, would likely have some form of a defined-contribution plan. Employee contributions to a registered retirement savings plan (described below) are coordinated with membership in, or contributions to, a registered pension plan.

Registered Retirement Savings Plans

In some cases, employers have elected to avoid funding pension plans and have instead turned to the use of registered retirement savings plans (RRSPs). An RRSP allows an employee to make a tax-deductible contribution of up to $13,500 or 18% of current-year employment earnings, whichever is less. This amount, as well as investment income, accumulates to eventually be paid as retirement income to the employee. An employer can make a contribution on the employee's behalf, provided the payment "passes through" the employee's hands for tax purposes. The underlying contract is between the employee and the custodian, and the employer has no further call on the funds.

Savings Plans

Employee savings plans do exist in Canada, but they are different from the U.S. plans, which are often 401(k) plans. In Canada, there are no tax advantages to membership in a savings plan, but the other provisions are similar to a 401(k) plan. There is often an employee contribution, such as 6% of earnings, and an employer match, such as 50% of the employee contribution. The funds are often used to purchase equity shares in the employer, with some other investment options available. Because of the tax treatment, they are usually immediately vested, and the shares are immediately available for sale.

Benefits Plans

Health coverage is nearly universal and is provided through provincial health programs. These programs are funded in part from general government revenue and in part from employer-paid premiums or payroll taxes.

For example, in Ontario, there is a progressive payroll tax of between 0.98% and 1.95% of Ontario payroll. These programs essentially cover all services rendered by a medical practitioner at home, office, or hospital. In some cases, the provincial plans include drug, dental, and vision coverage, although these are usually provided through employer-paid or employer-provided supplementary coverage.

Disability Plans

Short-term disability programs are often provided by employers, but the available benefits and terms of payment vary widely. Typically, employees are 100% covered for six months. Thereafter, long-term disability kicks in. This is usually employer provided, although use of employee contributions is increasing. Employee contributions enable the insurance contractor to pay benefits that are nontaxable. Consequently, the level of coverage can be reduced but still remain adequate.

There is also a disability benefit payable under the Canada/Quebec pension plan, which is usually integrated under any employer-provided long-term disability plan.

Life Insurance

While there are some modest death benefits provided through provincial programs, the primary source of life insurance coverage is through employer-paid or optional employee-paid life insurance.

Vacation

Vacation is usually three weeks of paid leave for employees with more than, say, three years of service. The maximum number of weeks available is usually about five or six. Generally speaking, vacation time cannot be accumulated from year to year. There are certain statutory minimums set at the provincial level.

Holidays

Holidays are single days off with pay. The actual days available follow a provincial convention. Certain core holidays, such as July 1, December 25, and January 1, tend to cross provincial boundaries. There are generally between 9 and 13 such holidays each year, depending on the province.

Statutory Programs

There are fairly complex provisions to each of the statutory programs. The following provides a brief summary of each such program but without reference to specific provincial variations.

Canada/Quebec Pension Plan

This plan is a contributory, earnings-related social insurance program providing universal coverage for employed persons. It requires a combined employee and employer premium of 6.4% of earnings between $3,500 and $36,900 to a maximum of $1,068.80 each in each year, which is tax deductible.

This premium will increase to a combined 9.9% of earnings in 2003. Full benefits are payable at age 65. The maximum monthly retirement benefit in 1998 was $744.79 ($750.69 in Quebec) and will be adjusted annually to reflect cost-of-living increases. All benefits are subject to income tax.

Old-Age Security

Anyone who has resided in Canada for 40 years is covered by old-age security. A full, taxable, monthly pension of $407.15 as of January 1, 1998, is subject to residency requirements as well as to a "clawback" clause. The clawback provides for 15% of income in excess of $53,215 to be repaid to the government. There are also a spouses allowance (up to $722.32 per month) and a guaranteed income supplement (up to $483.86 per month), both of which are subject to income and residency tests. The pension is payable at age 65, and no contributions are required by employees or employers.

Workers' Compensation

Each province provides for income continuance when there is a loss of income as a result of work-related injury. Benefits differ by province. In

British Columbia, for example, the plan pays 75% of gross eligible earnings; in Ontario, the plan pays 85% of net eligible earnings, with some upper limits on benefits. But the benefits are, essentially, not taxed. The system is funded 100% by employers with rating methods varying by province. Contributions are deductible.

Employment Insurance

Benefits for those laid off from employment are provided by the federal government across the provincial boundaries. Benefits are 55% of average insurable earnings of the last 26 weeks of work, to a maximum benefit of $413 per week. Premiums in 1998 were $2.70 for the employee and $3.78 for the employer per $100 of employee insurable earnings, to a maximum annual premium of $1,053 for the employee and $1,474.20 for the employer.

Employment Law and Labor Relations

Employment law and labor relations are within the jurisdiction of the provinces, except for certain specific industries such as telecommunications, railways, banks, and the federal government itself, which are covered within the federal jurisdiction.

This generates some differences in employment law, labor law, benefit plan design, and tax consequences for contributions to and benefits from benefit programs. Differences are also created with regard to government monitoring and compliance requirements.

Canada has an advanced and relatively mature compensation and benefits environment, which is heavily influenced by U.S. practices. Some aspects, however, still carry a European flavor. Protection of employees is highly regarded, and catastrophic protection is expected.

Termination of an employment relationship by an employer tends to carry more severe financial penalties than in the United States, but the previous "employment for life" expectation has diminished significantly over the last few years.

Further Reading

Butteriss, Margaret, ed. *Re-Inventing HR: Changing Roles to Create the High-Performance Organisation.* Toronto: Wiley, 1998.

Canadian Master Labour Guide. North York, Ontario: CCH Canadian Limited, 1998.

Canadian Outlook. Ottawa: Conference Board of Canada, 1998.

Compensation Planning Outlook 1999. Ottawa: Conference Board of Canada, 1998.

Hall, Gordon M., ed. *Mercer Handbook of Canadian Pension and Benefit Plans*. 11th ed. North York, Ontario: CCH Canadian Limited, 1996.

Human Resources Management in Canada. Scarborough, Ontario: Prentice-Hall Canada, 1998.

Kelly, John. *Pay Equity Management.* Toronto: CCH Canadian Limited, 1988.

1999 Compensation Planning Report. Toronto: William M. Mercer Limited, 1998.

Performance Management and Competency-Based Systems. Toronto: William M. Mercer Limited, 1996.

Statistics Canada. *Canada Year Book 1999.* Altona, Manitoba: Friesens Corporation, 1998.

Theriault, Roland. *Mercer Compensation Manual: Theory and Practice*. Boucherville, Quebec: G. Morin, 1992.

CHAPTER 17

LATIN AMERICA

JOHN DE LEON AND
MARGARET COOLBAUGH

Introduction

Latin America is a region of political and economic volatility as well as remarkable cultural diversity. First-time visitors to Latin America often do not immediately recognize the scope of this diversity, but the unique nature of each country—and the challenges to the management of human resources—soon become apparent. To help the reader understand the complexities that exist, we have highlighted the differences (and similarities) among the various countries, and have provided some general guidelines for compensation and benefit design.

The region known as Latin America stretches from the United States–Mexico border to the Tierra del Fuego at the southern tip of Argentina. (The Caribbean Island countries and the West Indies are sometimes grouped within the region, but for our purposes, we have focused on the mainland.) The predominant language in the region is Spanish, with Portuguese-speaking Brazil a significant exception.

Our specific focus will be on those countries usually referred to by international human resource professionals as the "big five": Argentina, Brazil, Colombia, Mexico, and Venezuela. Key infrastructure information for these five countries is shown in Exhibit 17-1. It is anticipated that, by the year 2000, the combined total population of these five countries will be more than 360 million. The size of the economy of each major country, as measured by gross domestic product, varies greatly, but the human resource challenges are quite similar.

The information provided is intended to be a broad overview of issues concerning local employees. Each topic dealing with compensation and benefits planning objectives in a given country should be researched in greater detail before making decisions that commit a company to additional people-related costs.

Exhibit 17-1. Economic and Geographic Overview of the Region

Dimension	Argentina	Brazil	Colombia	Mexico	Venezuela
Total Area (sq. km.)	2,766,890	8,511,965	1,138,910	1,972,550	912,050
Population	36,000,000	170,000,000	39,000,000	102,000,000	23,000,000
Gross Domestic Product[1]	317,419.7	793,042.7	96,292.6	402,316.9	88,434.0
Independence Date	July 9, 1816	Sept. 7, 1822	July 20, 1810	Sept. 16, 1810	July 5, 1811

1. Millions of Current U.S. Dollars for 1997

Source: *Inter-American Development Bank.*

Similarities and Differences

For compensation and benefits professionals first visiting Latin America, recognizing that there are similarities and differences is key to understanding the region. They should also realize that the issues most important to gaining this understanding are regional cultures and regional economic activity.

Cultural Similarities

Language. Spanish and Portuguese are the predominant languages spoken throughout Latin America. Just as there are regional accents in the United States, there is a range of accents among the countries, as well as slight regional differences in vocabulary (especially colloquial speech). In general, however, someone who is fluent in Spanish has no difficulty communicating with Spanish-speaking colleagues anywhere in Latin America and can even converse in Brazil to an extent after learning some basic Portuguese vocabulary.

Role of Relationships. In Latin America, interpersonal relationships play a key role in business transactions. It is customary to begin most business encounters by exchanging nonbusiness information, such as family or perhaps travel experiences. People who display a genuine interest in developing interpersonal ties and who work to build them reap the benefits of increased cooperation and acceptance.

Importance of Family. In most Latin American countries, family plays a critical role in daily life. Not surprisingly, the emphasis on family also influences personal decisions about work matters. For example, family members are routinely included in many company social gatherings. More important from a human resource perspective, people are not generally willing to put work before family. For example, people do not readily cancel or reschedule planned vacations to accommodate work. Latin Americans are reluctant to agree to relocations from one city to another, let alone to another country.

Economic Similarities

Volatile Economies. Latin American countries have historically been subject to periods of economic volatility. Frequent devaluation of currencies followed by very high rates of inflation have challenged compensation planners on how to protect the purchasing power of employees while ensuring the economic stability of the business during economic downturns. In recent years, the growth of democracy, the privatization of state-run businesses, and more competent management of state revenue collections have improved the stability of most economies. Nonetheless, some of the historical challenges still exist.

The most far-reaching consequences of volatile and unpredictable economies include the following, which are of particular importance to the international compensation and benefits professional:

- *Short-Term Focus.* Employees in Latin American countries tend to focus on the value of base pay and current payments such as Christmas bonuses. There are two reasons for this: The average age of Latin American workers is young by world standards, and they realize that the value of money erodes quickly during periods of high rates of inflation. Employees value long-term incentives more for the recognition they bestow than for the possibility of future economic gain.
- *Distribution of Wealth.* The wealthy and the middle class represent a relatively small percentage of Latin American society; most of the population is poor. As a result, blue-collar employees place great

importance on benefits that address practical needs. Blue-collar employees in many countries, for example, place a high value on the quantity of food served in highly subsidized employee cafeterias. For employees who do not have the economic means to purchase and maintain an automobile to commute to work, company-provided transportation is more than merely a perquisite.

Cultural Differences

Ethnic Heritage. One of the keys to understanding the cultural interactions in any country is to comprehend the ethnic heritage and the current sociological makeup of the population. The population of Latin America is a mixture of Spanish, Portuguese, Indian (e.g., Pre-Colombian), and African ancestry. Different regions have somewhat different ancestry; Mexico and Peru have more Indian ties, whereas Brazil and the coastal region of Venezuela have more African ties. Travelers to Latin American countries who demonstrate some knowledge and interest in their regional history will have an advantage when trying to develop strong relationships with local colleagues.

Equal opportunity legislation as we know it in the United States either does not exist or is not enforced. Human resource visitors need to concern themselves with the sound business practice of equal treatment of employees and must work to meet the challenge of managing a business effectively in a defined local culture while ensuring fairness of treatment for their employees.

As a rule, however, acceptance and respect of other ethnic backgrounds tends to be the norm despite (or perhaps because of) the wide array of different groups throughout the region. Consequently, many Latin Americans do not see a need for diversity training.

Compensation and Benefits

The approach to compensation and benefit decisions in Latin America should be focused on the usual goals of maintaining desired external competitiveness while treating people equitably based on job size and performance. Compensation philosophies and principles that serve as business and strategic objectives in the headquarters country should apply in Latin America. What could vary (depending on the country) is the type of pay program or benefit provided to employees.

In the case of Latin America, several specific caveats should be addressed before human resource programs are finalized and implemented. These modifications are best determined in the context of what works best in the headquarters country vis-à-vis the differences encountered in each country (whether stemming from either statutory requirements or customary practice and employees' basic needs).

Statutory Requirements

The focus of labor legislation in Latin America differs significantly from that of the United States. While the compliance focus in the United States appears to be concentrated on equal opportunity and pay matters, Latin American labor law leans more toward addressing direct payments and benefits, vacation and holiday entitlements, and severance payments resulting from unjust termination.

Other workforce management practices must be in compliance with legislation that regulates minimum wage, overtime, definition of *workweek,* and frequency of delivery of pay.

Statutory Pensions. Throughout Latin America, social security pension plans are legislated, but in more and more instances, the defined-benefit approach is giving way to defined contribution. This is often a matter of necessity. Most traditional state-sponsored defined social security plans are either underfunded or nearly bankrupt.

Chile provides the basic approach now being used by many governments in the region as the model for change. In 1981, Chile replaced its defined-benefit pension plan with a defined-contribution plan in which employees contribute 10% of pretax earned income to fund the pension and an additional approximate 3% for disability and survivor benefits. Fund assets are deposited in each employee's account and are managed by private pension-fund investment managers. Retirement age is 65 for men and 60 for women. At retirement, account balances are converted to a retirement annuity, and programmed withdrawals are scheduled. This can be accomplished by leaving the funds with the investment management firm, by transferring the funds to an insurance company, or by a combination of these alternatives. Argentina, Bolivia, Colombia, Costa Rica, Mexico, Peru, and Uruguay have adopted variations of the Chilean model. Venezuela is considering a similar change in approach to legislated retirement funding.

In Chile and elsewhere, it is widely anticipated that retirees in the coming years will have insufficient account balances to provide for a comfortable retirement. This will no doubt result in pressure from older employees for company-sponsored supplemental pensions.

Traditionally, many multinational organizations and major local-national companies have established supplemental pension plans. These plans are most often seen in Argentina, Brazil, and Mexico. Medium-sized and smaller local companies in the region do not customarily institute formal pension plans. As state pension schemes continue to change, existing company-funded pension plans will likely need to be revised. Any review of new retirement plans should always take the termination indemnity requirement into consideration as a possible future benefit to the retiree and a cost to the company.

Employment Termination Indemnities. The United States is one of the few countries that has no mandatory severance payments for involuntary termination. Latin American countries have a mandated requirement for severance pay, at least in the case of a company-initiated termination for which there is no just cause. Exhibit 17-2 provides information on mandated severance-pay requirements for the five key countries in the region.

Exhibit 17-2. Termination Payment Provisions for Employees Dismissed for Reasons Other Than Just Cause

Argentina

Two months' notice (or pay in lieu of notice) plus one month's salary per year of service. Monthly salary calculation capped at three times the minimum wage.

Brazil

Thirty days' notice (or pay in lieu of notice) plus a payment equal to 40% of the employee's FGTS *(Fondo da Garantia por Tempo de Serviço)* account balance accrued during employment with the company (after adjustment for inflation).

Colombia

Calculation is related to years of service. For service of less than one year, 45 days' pay. For service to five years, 45 days' pay plus 15 days' pay for all years after year one. For service to 10 years, 45 days' pay plus 20 days' pay for all years of service after year one. For service in excess of 10 years, 45 days' pay plus 40 days' pay for each year after year one.

Mexico

Severance *(indemnización legal)* is three months' pay plus 20 days' pay for each full year of service. An additional payment called *antigüedad legal* is a required payment when total service is more than 15 years. The *antigüedad* payment is equal to 12 days' pay for each year of service, based on a salary capped at twice the applicable minimum wage in effect on the termination date calculated.

Venezuela

A new labor law signed in June 1997 eliminated the very costly retroactive calculation of pay at time of termination, but the basic formula of two months' pay for each year of service is unchanged. Each month, an amount equal to five days of salary (characterized as a seniority payment or *antigüedad)* is deposited into a trust fund administered by a bank, into a company-administered account, or into a special pension fund to be defined by future legislation. When there is a company-initiated termination of employment for reasons other than just cause, an additional payment is required, equal to the seniority account balance, with appropriate additional deposits for the final months of employment.

Note: In some countries, notice requirements and severance-payment calculations may vary for employment termination with accrued service of less than 12 months. Proportionate calculations are required for partial years of service.

Labor court decisions on the payment of termination indemnities almost always favor the employee. In Latin America, unlike in the United States, the burden of proof is on the company, not the ex-employee, to demonstrate that the dismissal was for cause. Latin American human resource professionals generally subscribe to the practice that a very expensive negotiated termination settlement in exchange for a signed resignation is ultimately preferable to a good fight in labor court. Negotiated resignations in return for a severance payment are common in some countries. For instance, in Mexico, a typical result of such a bargaining process is a payment equivalent to 50% of the legally mandated severance in exchange for a voluntary resignation and a positive response to reference checks from new employers. While some multinational employers believe that mandated severance pay is a costly windfall, others view these payments in the context of unemployment compensation, which is paid as a lump sum.

Structure of Pay Packages

Because of legislation requiring the payment of special bonuses, all countries' pay packages have compensation components in addition to base pay. Thus, the true measure of annual guaranteed pay is the sum of all yearly pay components, not just monthly salary times 12. Exhibit 17-3 shows pay components for 14 countries in the region.

Exhibit 17-3. Latin American Pay Practices: Statutory Compensation Elements

Argentina

13th month payment (half paid in June, the other half at year-end)

Brazil

13th month payment (half paid in November, the other half in December)
Vacation bonus of 30% of one month's pay

Chile

Annual mandated profit-sharing payment is required. This obligation is waived when a company pays its employees a bonus of 25% of pay based on a maximum of 4.75 monthly minimum wages.

Colombia

13th month salary (half paid in June, the other half in December)
Transportation subsidy to lower-paid employees

Dominican Republic

13th month salary in the form of a Christmas bonus

Ecuador

13th month salary in the form of a Christmas bonus

14th month equivalent to two minimum monthly salaries

15th month equivalent to five payments during the year of 10,000 *sucres* each

16th month equal to one-eighth of a monthly salary but never less than one-sixth of the minimum monthly wage, paid monthly

Transportation subsidies and cost-of-living bonuses for lower-paid employees

Profit-sharing payments for all employees

El Salvador

December bonus equal to 10 days' pay for up to three years of service; 15 days' pay for up to 10 years of service; and 18 days' pay in excess of 10 years of service

Guatemala

13th month salary (half paid in December, the other half in January)

An additional one month's salary, called an annual bonus, paid in July

Honduras

13th month salary paid as a Christmas bonus

14th month salary paid in June

Mexico

Christmas bonus equal to 50% of one month's pay

Vacation bonus equal to 25% of one month's pay times days of vacation entitlement

Mandatory profit sharing

Panama

13th month salary paid in three installments (April, August, and December)

Peru

13th month for *fiestas patrias* paid in July

14th month as a Christmas bonus

Puerto Rico

A Christmas bonus equal to 2% of first $10,000 wages (i.e., a maximum $200 bonus)

Venezuela

Utilidades or *aguinaldo,* a minimum of two months' pay and up to four months' base pay

Vacation bonus of 15 to 45 days' pay

Prestaciones sociales of up to 60 days' pay

Note: Market practice in some countries results in enhanced payments. For example, in Mexico, the more customary Christmas bonus is 30 days' pay, and the vacation premium is frequently increased to 50% or 100%.

Unemployment Compensation

This is rare in Latin America, because the termination indemnity is the mechanism to provide for economic relief during periods of unemployment.

Medical, Dental, and Vision Care

Most state social schemes in Latin America provide a reasonable level of medical care. The quality of facilities and the overall level of service and care vary greatly, however. The usual approach is to provide supplementary medical coverage for nonunion personnel. Dental and vision care benefits are not commonly found in most countries.

Compensation and Employment Costs

Legal Framework. Recent important revisions to labor legislation in Argentina, Brazil, and Peru allow employers to pursue a more aggressive temporary employment and fixed-term contract strategy. These changes provide a welcome and much-needed change in a region where fluctuating business conditions make flexible scheduling critical. Before the laws were revised, flexible scheduling was dramatically limited.

Another example of gradual but significant labor reform is the revised Venezuelan labor code of June 1997, which eliminated the "retroactive seniority payment calculation." Mandated severance costs are still equivalent to two months' pay per year of service, but overall employer costs have been substantially reduced.

Minimum Wage. Mandated minimum wages are prevalent throughout Latin America. Most employers pay their lowest-salaried employees at somewhat above the minimum wage requirement. Contrary to the propaganda distributed by some international labor organizations, many companies in the region are concerned about offering decent living wages, but to remain competitive, their pay rates are reviewed in the context of sound market pricing in each country.

Pay Determination: Nonmanagement Personnel. Across Latin America, there are more similarities than differences in the way appropriate and competitive pay rates are determined. At the shop-floor and unskilled levels, collective bargaining agreements (and the available pool of people) generally define market wages. Labor negotiations are usually focused almost exclusively on pay rates rather than work rules, pensions, and union input in management of the business.

Nonunion organizations are aware of collective bargaining rates of pay and benefits. These companies either match or improve prevailing compensation rates to attract skilled people and to avoid unwanted union organization drives.

Management and Clerical Employees. Compensation levels for clerical and management employees are set in accordance with an assessment of organization design and job level, a concern for internal pay equity, and ongoing market-pricing activities. The company generally sets the initial levels of pay. After that, compensation is managed in the usual manner; the company assesses individual performance, its own ability to pay, and market movement. Employees, especially new hires, have a greater tendency to approach pay issues in a negotiating mode.

Annual Cash Compensation. Because there are several elements to the average cash compensation package, straight base pay is not the best indicator of how much an employee earns. Salary surveys usually provide multiple pay comparisons not just base salary practices. It is customary to measure pay in annual terms by multiplying monthly base pay by 12, then adding additional components (e.g., Christmas and vacation bonuses and other non-performance-related elements) that are part of the guaranteed compensation package.

Tax-Effective Remuneration. Because tax legislation has been vague in many countries, with enforcement generally lax, employees often adopt a laissez-faire attitude when dealing with the need to comply with personal income tax obligations. The market has responded to pressure from managers by providing nontaxable remuneration when feasible. For instance, providing a company car for both business and personal use is far more predominant in Latin America than in the United States. Within the region, Mexico is the country with the broadest incidence of auto benefit coverage. The value of the benefit is not taxed even though the cost of providing cars may not be deductible. In some countries, subsidized country club membership for top managers is not uncommon.

Dollar Denominated Pay. It is not unusual to receive requests for pay denominated in hard currency and for disbursement of pay outside the country of employment. Senior-management candidates frequently make these requests during initial job negotiations.

The vast majority of companies doing business in the region denominate pay exclusively in the currency of the country of employment, but there are some notable exceptions. Pay is frequently denominated in U.S. dollars for managing directors of large companies and for senior-management employees of *maquiladoras* (in-bond assembly plants) on the United States–Mexican border. While this is not a "best practice," it is a reality of the marketplace.

The rationale for denominating pay in local currency is based on the need to compete effectively in the local market. When a company competes in the local market, its cost structure should be local-currency driven. Tracking market movement is a much more simple process when focused on the local currency, especially during times of inflation and devaluation. Also, the denomination of pay in nonlocal currency (usually U.S. dollars) provides automatic local-currency pay increases when devaluation occurs. This deprives the company of control of local pay rates when the overall cost of doing business is increasing.

Pay Delivery Venue. Smaller companies frequently report that managers request delivery of pay outside the country of employment. These requests are almost always denied. Companies' codes of ethics address the objective of complying with all host-country laws in spirit and in practice. Payments outside the country of employment serve to facilitate income tax evasion—a practice companies prefer not to encourage.

Salary Planning and Pay Programs

Sophisticated Latin American companies carry out a salary-planning process similar to most other countries of the world. The process of aligning jobs in terms of either relative position value or market alignment is a first and fundamental step. The "broadband" approach is not as prevalent here as it is in the United States. Pay ranges for a given grade have a spread of 30 to 60%, with a norm of 50% from minimum to maximum. When internal salary comparisons do not appear logical and consistent, the customary cause is an attempt to manipulate the range to fit the actual pay practice within a company, not necessarily an inconsistent external market condition.

Salary Planning. Pay range values are adjusted in accordance with market movement. During periods of low inflation, the determination of each individual pay increase is usually based on position in range, personal performance rating, and salary-increase matrix parameters. Since the revised salary structure midpoints have been adjusted based on market movement (which is heavily influenced by inflation), separate cost-of-living increases are not common.

During periods of high inflation, more frequent increases may be granted to offset the effects of rising prices. There is no clear and accepted definition of *high* inflation; historically, however, when it goes beyond the

25 to 35% range, companies will explore the possibility of adjusting pay more frequently than once a year.

Individual Pay Decisions. In some Latin American countries, there is a tendency to hire people below the minimum value of the pay range. Employers may also resist offering immediate promotional pay increases to employees who assume increased responsibilities. The usual rationale for this is that the employer wants to make sure the employee is really capable of performing in the bigger job. But a more important issue is the legal concept of acquired rights. Once an employee has been provided a specific level of employment-related conditions, any change to his or her detriment constitutes a condition of constructive discharge.

Performance Management

Performance management programs and pay-for-performance practices are quite common in Latin America. Because pay and performance are, in theory, closely linked, managers are often reluctant to take any action that could have a negative impact on an employee's salary. There is a strong tendency to overevaluate performance and to avoid negative comments during performance discussions. Because of this subjectivity in performance evaluation, companies may not necessarily be paying for high levels of measurable performance. Instead, they are paying for a loyal staff and a harmonious workplace. Some companies do, of course, set standards of measurement that are more closely tied to the overall business measures of performance and to employees' ability to influence the overall business outcome.

Noncash recognition programs are more favorably received in Latin America than in other regions of the world. For instance, travel, training, and development are highly valued by employees. Rather than offering significant cash rewards, some organizations choose to budget training and education sessions away from the workplace.

Benefits

Pay for Time Off. Latin Americans say that while North Americans live to work, they work to live. (The amount of paid time off in the United States is one of the lowest by worldwide standards.) Understandably, paid time off has a high value in Latin America. As noted, labor law establishes the baseline for vacation day entitlements and mandatory paid holidays. In some countries, market practice improves on the legislated minimums. For example, Mexico has relatively few paid vacation days, but customary practice there expands vacation days for new employees from six days a year to ten or more. It is important to have an exact understanding of how this benefit is measured. For example, vacation entitlements are expressed as calendar days in Brazil and as working days in Mexico.

State Plans. Much like the United States, Latin American countries have social systems funded through the collection of payroll taxes and employee contributions. In Chile, the employee bears a large contribution burden; in other countries, the company pays the majority of state-provided benefit costs. Before adding or improving fringe benefits, it is important to calculate by country the cost borne by the employee and by the company. These calculations will result in a very different approach to providing company-funded benefits, based on the payroll-added cost comparisons from one country to another.

The customary practice in most countries is to provide different levels of benefits depending on the employee's position. For instance, blue-collar direct-labor employees usually rely on state-run medical facilities. Managers and their families, however, receive access to private facilities where medical care is more individualized and treatment options are readily available. Companies may contract a medical plan for clerical and management employees but not for others.

State-funded life insurance is usually paid out as a widow's pension. While there is rarely compensation for nonoccupational disabilities, lump-sum or annuity payments are provided to cover work-related injuries. The value of these benefits is usually insignificant.

Company-Provided Benefits. The composition of a company-provided benefit package in the region typically includes two categories of benefits. The first category usually includes a medical plan, group life insurance, and perhaps a defined-benefit pension plan or savings fund. The second category includes components that are responsive to the special needs of employees in the context of their social and economic environment.

Examples of socioeconomic benefits are highly subsidized employee cafeterias, transportation to and from work, uniforms, equipment for company sports teams, and sports facilities such as a soccer field on company property. By offering these benefits, the company is telling the employees that it understands the local culture and that it knows the value of these basic needs.

Medical Care. There are practically as many approaches to medical care delivery as there are countries in the region. In Argentina, the state-sponsored system is quite popular, but some companies contract with preferred provider organizations on a selective basis. In Brazil, employers typically supplement the national health care delivery system by contracting with a network of clinics and preferred provider organizations. State medical facilities in Colombia are generally considered inferior, and employees' dependents are not covered for all the usual services. As a result, many companies provide additional supplemental coverage. Mexican medical care, provided by its social security system, is comprehensive, but employees prefer to be treated in private care facilities. Companies traditionally provide major medical plans with a deductible and share charges 90%/10% with employees. The Venezuelan social system includes comprehensive medical care facilities in the larger cities, but again, employees prefer private medical care. Most companies offer an indemnity-plan benefit to their employees and dependents.

Although company vision and dental plans are not a common benefit, most seasoned international companies will study local practices and then provide some type of coverage if there is a competitive reason to do so.

Life and Nonoccupational Disability Insurance. Most companies throughout the region provide group life and disability coverage for employees. In some instances, the coverage for unionized employees will be less than that for salaried individuals. A typical life insurance benefit is 24 times monthly salary, with another 24 months paid in the case of accidental death.

Short-term disability payments are coordinated within the provisions of the social security system, which in some countries requires partial payments to a worker who is ill and unable to report for work. Payments usually continue for six months, at which point long-term disability benefits may begin. Long-term disability plans are not as common, however, in part because the cost of insuring this benefit is high.

Pensions and Retirement. Since the movement in the region toward the Chilean defined-contribution approach, benefits designers have been moving cautiously in the implementation of new pension plans. It is expected that no matter how Latin American governments choose to handle state-controlled retirement plans, private-sector employers will have to provide additional supplementation to allow retirees a reasonable level of financial security.

As a general rule, a company just starting up or a company with anticipated high turnover (such as a *maquiladora* in Mexico or the Dominican Republic) is best served by focusing on competitive rates of pay and a well-designed medical plan before adopting a pension plan.

Organizations that should seriously review the possibility of sponsoring and funding pension plans are those with the goal of maintaining low employee turnover and those with an older and more established workforce. New pension schemes should be defined-contribution plans, not defined benefits. By adopting a defined-contribution plan, a company can identify and fund pension costs on a current basis and avoid pressure from current retirees to increase the amount of pension payments during periods of high inflation.

Other Human Resource Differences

Role of Women in the Workplace. Although it is not unusual to see women in middle-management roles in Latin America, it is less common to see them in upper-management positions and rare to see them in top management. This less visible role can be explained, in part, by the fact that many women remain home with their children rather than pursue a career during their childbearing years. For women who do actively pursue a career, the traditional male-oriented focus creates a barrier. That focus is changing, however, just as it has changed in the United States. This is particularly evident in Puerto Rico, Venezuela, and the Dominican Republic, where women tend to play a more active role in management.

Sexual Harassment. The basic problem of sexual harassment exists in Latin America as much as it does anywhere else in the world. There are virtually no enforced penalties for harassment in any country in the region. The Latin American culture does not view with disdain or disapproval many of the nonovert actions that might be considered sexual harassment in the United States (e.g., giving compliments on physical appearance or platonic hugs and kisses on appropriate occasions). Despite the stereotype of Latin machismo, however, unambiguous sexual harassment is not tolerated in professionally managed multinational or local companies.

Costs and Availability of People. Latin American countries have a large pool of blue-collar workers; thus, total employment costs are relatively low. This means that, as the need for technical skills rises, the availability of qualified people begins to diminish. The supply-and-demand equation continues to shift significantly when the staffing needs are at upper- and senior-management levels—and especially when fluency in English is required. As a result, market rates for seasoned and bilingual managers are often comparable to U.S. compensation costs. In Argentina, Mexico, and Brazil, they may sometimes be higher when the local currency is overvalued.

Use of Innovative Human Resource Practices. Latin American managers are familiar with all the major trends in human resources as promoted by prominent figures in management. Many of these principles are put into practice by larger local and international company subsidiaries. Human resource practices and programs followed by many medium-size companies and public-sector organizations are much more traditional. As in the United States, *reengineering* in most companies really means *downsizing*.

Empowerment, self-directed work teams, and similar approaches to increasing productivity and quality are being tested cautiously. The greatest barrier to organizational change is the hierarchical nature of Latin American societies. As organizational layers are removed, people at lower levels are required to make more responsible decisions. Many local cultures present a barrier to the creation of a high level of trust in the workplace and to the willingness of managers to rely on workers to do their job in an environment with minimal supervision.

Organization and Staffing

Latin American companies are well into the process of redesigning and reengineering their organizations. The primary external forces of change are the privatization of public-sector businesses and the gradual disappearance of trade barriers. The business environment is much more competitive, and there are few opportunities to pass on higher costs to customers and consumers without losing market share.

Subsidiaries of multinational companies implement change at the direction of corporate headquarters, but there are a number of characteristic barriers to change in the region. Among these barriers, the most significant are a reluctance to modify traditional roles, lack of trust between managers and their employees, and, in some countries, limited availability of executive talent.

Many Latin American societies, despite undergoing significant changes, are still very hierarchical. Historically, the culture has valued job titles more than job content. In general, there is a stronger emphasis on form than on content. This can be seen in résumés, in which four pages are dedicated to courses attended and one page to accomplishments.

It is not uncommon to still encounter "assistant directors" in large local-national companies. Senior-level directors may still expect to be provided with a private secretary who is available to take and make telephone calls. Voice mail is now a basic communication tool, but individual computer usage by senior executives is not as prevalent as in the United States.

Flatter organizations are generally more efficient—as long as employees are capable of assuming more responsibility and willing to make decisions without fear of reprimand or termination when they make a mistake. Latin American companies that have succeeded in corporate-culture modification have done so by rewarding management and supervisory behavior that encourages risk taking and individual initiative.

In most Latin American countries, there is an insufficient number of high school and college graduates each year to fill available job openings. Recruiters comment that it is difficult to find enough qualified—or qualifiable—candidates for positions with expanded job content. Aggressive starting salaries are needed to attract high-potential college graduates, especially when fluency in English is a job requirement. It is wise to assume that people will compare their levels of compensation, so it is a challenge to hire people with attractive pay packages while maintaining a reasonable level of internal equity and avoiding pay compression difficulties with superiors.

Human resource professionals have the opportunity to support healthy change by taking a leading role in culture modification. Probably the best way to do this is to redirect employees' focus from valuing effort to rewarding results and to motivate superiors to acquire sound people development and delegation skills. The highest rewards should go to people who get results and who encourage their staff members to make decisions and be accountable.

The most successful compensation and benefits professionals in Latin America make a genuine effort to understand the culture and its underlying values. They develop a highly productive and rewarding relationship with local company peers and with vendors by placing greater emphasis on the personal aspects of the relationship than would be typical in the United States. These professionals then develop remuneration strategies by building on the foundation of parent-company values and philosophies, modifying existing programs and practices as necessary in the context of local conditions. The Latin American region is fertile ground for new and innovative compensation and benefits approaches, as long as the best ideas serve to further the business interests of the organization in a cost-effective manner while addressing the diverse needs of employees in each country.

Latin American Region Resources

Of the major geographic areas of the world, Latin America presents some of the most difficult conditions for locating resources, both printed and Internet-based. Networking is the resource most relied on to obtain information and follow new developments. The most helpful sources of information are in-country labor lawyers, multinational insurers, the large accounting firms, and compensation and benefits consulting organizations.

The Society for Human Resource Management's International Institute for Human Resources organization has dramatically upgraded its database on international contacts and issues. The on-line resource address is www.shrmglobal.org.

CHAPTER 18

WESTERN EUROPE

PETE BURGESS

Introduction

In this chapter, "Western Europe" refers to the 15 members of the European Union (EU), the three countries of the European Economic Area (EEA), and Switzerland.[1] We are not concerned here with any of the former Eastern Bloc nations. Since 1994, Western and Northern Europe have been practically synonymous with the EU. Only Switzerland remains outside, but its key role in finance (plus its hosting of important multinational businesses in the food, engineering, and pharmaceutical industries) endows it with a unique importance far outstripping its size and population. Membership in the EU and European Economic Area can have a specific impact on human resource (HR) management through shared legal obligations to comply with EU-level legislation in a number of fields—including collective dismissals ("retrenchments"), acquired rights, and gender equality.

Western Europe embraces hugely diverse economic, industrial, social, and political histories and customs. All share common historical roots in the Christian tradition and as part of a self-perceived "European" cultural tradition. Despite these common roots, however, the cultural and religious differences are marked enough that they can have a profound impact on management styles and employee behavior. After all, the region includes Protestant Swedes, Catholic Italians, and Orthodox Greeks. Religious divides run through many countries; even though organized religion has weakened across Europe, it has left deeply important cultural residues. In addition, there is a substantial Islamic urban minority (as a result of past migration) in parts of Britain, France, and Germany, which creates important subcultures in these countries.

These cultural issues can affect work issues such as recruitment, reward and appraisal systems, management hierarchy, even how meetings are conducted. It is important to remember, however, that whatever similarities Europeans may have, national cultures are not homogeneous.

Given this level of national and cultural diversity, it is advisable to consider a more limited number of concrete examples. For the most part, we concern ourselves here with HR practices in the larger economies within the EU—France, Germany, Italy, and the United Kingdom. Taken together, these four nations account for some 73% of total EU gross domestic product (GDP), and they absorb the bulk of foreign direct investment from the United States. These countries also exemplify some of the typical models that can be found in HR practice and employee relations in the EU. We will refer to other countries when they serve to highlight an important issue; the Netherlands, Spain, and Switzerland all possess important distinctive features that merit attention. The United Kingdom is dealt with in a separate chapter in this book; however, we refer here to some distinct aspects of the "Anglo-Saxon" model that distinguish it from its continental European neighbors.

We do not wish to fall into the trap of stereotyping. Europe's HR cultures are in a state of flux under the combined pressures of economic globalization and the development of the EU, and in particular through the unique process of the European Economic and Monetary Union (EMU).[2] Although important national differences are likely to prevail, and may even intensify as countries mobilize around their comparative advantage to succeed economically, the development of the EU is promoting some areas of convergent practice. The wave of mergers, acquisitions, and business consolidation within Europe—in part triggered by the European Economic and Monetary Union—is also leading to a blurring, but not a disappearance, of distinctive national business cultures. The creation of more pan-European businesses is promoting a distinctively European approach, which differs in a number of respects from what is found in the United States or Asia. This is perhaps best exemplified in the debates concerning the pursuit of shareholder value, executive compensation, and the role of organized labor in employment regulation and corporate life.

Although U.K. companies have begun to take a highly shareholder-value-driven approach, this has been more muted in mainland Europe. In fact, in many cases, those mainland European companies that have been active in shareholder-value-based strategies (breaking up conglomerates, share buybacks, etc.) have often felt compelled to balance this with a "stakeholder value" statement emphasizing their responsibilities to employees, the environment, and the community. Executive compensation in Europe is also lower (as a multiple of average earnings) than in the United States, and in countries such as the United Kingdom and, to some degree, the Netherlands, it is subject to considerable external scrutiny and comment. However, in other countries, such as Switzerland or Italy, pay and executive benefits are issues that remain shrouded in secrecy. Moreover, as we discuss in more detail below, elected employee representatives have legal rights to information, consultation, and, on some issues, even co–decision making in Europe's businesses.

The social constraints (with their balance of advantages and disadvantages) that these issues reflect also serve to highlight some of the distinctive features of HR management in Europe. This needs to be qualified, however, by examining the diversity of practices and the substantial differences that still separate the "Anglo-Saxon" and "Mainland Europe" models.

Use of Innovative HR Approaches

Large companies throughout Europe are highly professional and competent in HR management, with practices tailored to and reflecting their national industrial and business cultures and legal frameworks. How this is embodied within the institutions of corporate governance may vary considerably, however. The Price Waterhouse Cranfield Study[3] found considerable differences in the extent to which HR was represented at main board level in companies and the degree to which HR policies were formally integrated into corporate strategy. Interestingly, while France rated highly on formal integration, Germany and Italy were at the bottom of the ranking. The fact that this ranking manifestly fails to capture the true role of HR in German and Italian companies says something interesting and significant about how HR is perceived in Europe. It is important to realize that HR is more than a set of narrow techniques closely tied to corporate objectives. Rather, as we detail below, it encompasses a broader range of interactions within companies and a greater variety of channels of influence for a number of internal and external "stakeholders" within the corporate process (including elected employee representatives and trade unions). Many crucial exchanges between first-line managers and employees take place in both the formal and informal spaces created by traditional representational structures.

Greater national differences emerge when attention switches to medium-sized and smaller enterprises (SMEs). Companies exposed to foreign trade or stiff domestic competition usually have well-developed HR policies and practices. Small companies or those less exposed to competition may lag in this respect. Attention in the United Kingdom has recently been focused on the "long tail of underperforming companies" behind the corporate heights of world-class performers. In contrast to what is seen in the United States, SMEs in Europe have much higher exposure to international trade. The bulk of this trade remains within Europe, with some notable exceptions. The sophisticated engineering or design-based companies (mostly midsized) in Germany or northern Italy, for example, seek to dominate their own global niche with product and process advances, rooted in institutional and regional training arrangements. Such companies, which are typically subject to statutory or agreed procedures for employee representation and binding labor agreements, often engage in what is dubbed in academic circles *microconcertation* with their employees (i.e., highly cooperative employee relations based on established rights and a recognition of competitive necessities and consultation on key decisions).

Recent Economic Performance

Real living standards in Western Europe are not as high as in the United States; however, GDP per head in parts of Northern Europe approaches U.S. values (and actually exceeds in sheer U.S. dollars per head before adjustment for the higher cost of living in Europe). There are also important regional differences. The former West Germany, with a population of some 65 million, has a per capita income not far short of the United States. Northern Italy, southeastern England, and the region surrounding Paris are also all high-income areas, with GDP per head well above the EU average. In contrast, areas of rural Greece and Portugal, parts of northern England, and areas of several inner cities all exhibit either low incomes or other symptoms of deprivation such as chronically high unemployment or poor housing.

In contrast to the United States over the past 10 years or so, Western Europe's rate of economic growth and job creation has been disappointing. This stems in part from overall slower economic growth. It is also tied to lagging opportunities for women's employment in some countries and a marked trend to early exit from the workforce in others. Exhibit 18-1 provides some salient features of the broader European economy, with U.S. data added as a benchmark.

Recently, the European Commission noted,

> *Twenty years ago, the EU's employment rate was 64 per cent...that of the United States was 62 per cent. By 1997, however, the EU rate had dropped to 60.5 per cent...that of the United States had increased to 74 per cent, a spread of almost 14 percentage points—equivalent to about 34 million jobs.*

Exhibit 18-1. Population and Economic Statistics of the European Union, Switzerland, and the United States

Country	Population (million)	GDP per head (U.S.$)[1]	Economic Growth (%)			Inflation (%)		
			1998	1999	2000	1998	1999	2000
Austria	8.0	23,077	3.3	2.0	2.5	0.9	1.0	1.3
Belgium	10.2	23,242	2.9	1.9	2.2	1.0	1.1	1.4
Denmark	5.2	25,514	2.9	1.3	2.0	1.7	1.9	2.1
Finland	5.1	20,488	5.0	3.1	3.5	1.5	1.5	2.0
France	58.4	21,293	3.1	2.2	2.9	0.7	0.5	1.1
Germany[2]	81.8	22,049	2.8	1.5	2.8	0.9	0.6	1.0
Greece	10.5	13,912	3.7	3.3	3.4	4.8	2.5	2.9
Irish Republic	3.6	20,634	9.0	6.7	6.4	2.4	2.0	2.0
Italy	57.5	21,265	1.4	1.5	2.4	1.8	1.3	1.5
Luxembourg	0.5	33,119	4.1	3.9	4.4	1.6	1.7	1.7
Netherlands	15.5	22,142	3.7	2.3	2.6	2.0	1.6	2.2
Portugal	9.9	14,562	3.9	3.1	3.2	2.8	2.3	2.0
Spain	39.3	15,990	3.8	3.3	3.5	1.8	1.8	2.1
Sweden	8.9	20,439	2.9	2.1	2.8	-0.1	0.2	1.0
United Kingdom	58.8	20,483	2.1	0.7	2.1	2.7	2.7	2.4
Total EU	373.2	20,546	2.8	1.8	2.7	1.5	1.3	1.6
Switzerland	7.1	25,920	2.1	1.2	2.0	0.0	0.8	1.0
United States	265.6	29,326	3.9	3.3	2.2	1.6	2.1	2.4

1. 1997. Adjusted for cost of living (current prices at purchasing power parities).
2. Western Germany, US$24,200; Eastern Germany, US$13,800.

Source: *OECD, International Monetary Fund, World Economic Outlook, April 1999*

Although real living standards are generally high and in most countries incomes are more equally distributed than they are in the United States—with notably excellent public services—there are legitimate fears about the future. Lagging economic growth, a drive for industrial productivity to offset high labor costs, and an environment considered less favorable for creating a service and entrepreneurial culture could be creating large pools of socially excluded people. This could include older workers, very young workers, and ethnic minorities. Here is one noteworthy observation about economic performance between the United States and Europe: Productivity advances in Europe, especially in manufacturing, have allowed the real wages of workers to rise; in the United States, real wages have stagnated or even fallen for some groups, but employment has increased.

Some European regions continue to display intractably high levels of unemployment—although often for quite disparate reasons. Whereas unemployment in the north of England reflects a longtime process of industrial change and difficulties in labor market adjustment, the problems of southern Italy or rural Spain are of a quite different character, reflecting the difficulties of transition from an agrarian peasant society to an industrial and service economy.

The establishment of the EMU was preceded by a phase of austerity in several countries whose governments sought to ensure that their economies would meet the criteria for joining the new currency. (Eligibility required a public-sector deficit of no more than 3% of GDP and price and interest rate performance in line with the best performing nations in the EU.) This suppressed economic growth between 1995 and 1997, but there was moderate improvement toward the end of 1997 and into 1998 on the back of good export performance (aided by the United States as the "importer of last resort"). Most EU countries enjoy substantial trade surpluses. Only the United Kingdom, which was not seeking to join the EMU immediately and which had benefited from a currency depreciation in the early 1990s, was able to buck this trend for a period—pushing its own trade into deficit.

The severe economic problems in Russia and eastern Asia made their mark on export performance in late 1998, holding back growth in export-dependent countries such as Germany. At the same time, domestic consumer expenditure has not yet moved forward strongly enough to take up the slack. In fact, 1999 is expected to see a slackening of growth, with a recovery in 2000 once the shaky economies in other parts of the world begin to regain their bearings.

The European Union: What It Means

European Union is the most recent name for the grouping that grew out of the European Economic Community, established in 1956 when West Germany, France, Italy, Belgium, the Netherlands, and Luxembourg signed the Treaty of Rome. Other countries joined during the 1970s (the United Kingdom, Denmark, the Irish Republic), the 1980s (Greece, Spain, Portugal), and the 1990s (Austria, Sweden, Finland).

The EU is governed by the Treaty on European Union (otherwise known as the "Maastricht Treaty" signed in February 1992), which has been amended several times (most recently by the Treaty of Amsterdam, which became effective on May 1, 1999). The treaty provides for the institutions that govern the European Union, the process by which EU legislation can be implemented and enforced, the rights of European citizens, and the mutual commitments of the member states.

Although much of the legislation passed within the EU deals with trade and agricultural matters, the EU has always had a social dimension, which gained significantly in importance in the early 1990s. This came about in part because of treaty provisions that allowed majority voting (instead of a unanimous vote) on some issues within the EU's legislative organ, the intergovernmental Council of Ministers. The main legislative vehicle for setting social and employment policy is the "directive." This instrument is adopted at the EU level by the Council of Ministers on the recommendation of the EU's executive arm, the European Commission. Once adopted, individual member states must pass national legislation to "transpose" the directive into their own domestic law. The transposition does not have to be literal, but each member state must ensure that its existing laws (or fresh legislation if needed) achieve the result intended by the directive. In one crucial area, gender equality and equal pay, the EU treaty itself grants rights to citizens that apply directly. Under the treaty, all EU citizens enjoy the right to work in another EU member state without the need to apply for a work permit.

In practice, HR managers at the national level in Europe will need to understand EU law as transposed into national legislation. Since it can take several years before a specific directive is adopted, a grasp of EU institutions and procedures is vital to allow forward planning (and possibly lobbying) to take place. Directives also frequently embody legal principles that are not common to all EU member states, given the different but equally venerable traditions of Roman law versus English common law. As a consequence, understanding other countries' approaches can make it easier to follow a directive and understand where its focus comes from. (We illustrate this later in the case of EU provisions on working hours.) Finally, disputes over the interpretation of EU law and individual cases can be heard before the court of final instance on European law, the European Court of Justice (ECJ) in Strasbourg (France). The ECJ's decisions on EU law are not only binding on the jurisdiction from which a case was referred but will have implications for all other member states' jurisdictions as well. Keeping an eye on the proceedings at Strasbourg is therefore another important component of the European HR manager's job.

Important areas in which EU legislation and court rulings are decisive include the following:

- Equality for women in the workplace (including equal pay); through the concept of "indirect sex discrimination," this has also affected areas such as the rights of part-time workers (most of whom are women)
- Maternity rights and parental leave
- Acquired rights on business transfers
- Collective economic dismissals
- Health and safety at work, including the scheduling of working hours
- Information and consultation in large multinational enterprises in Europe ("European Works Councils")
- Rights for part-time workers and workers on fixed-term contracts
- Mutual recognition of professional qualifications between member states
- Proof of an employment relationship, rights of posted workers, data protection

The Employment Context

Exhibit 18-2 sets a number of key labor market parameters for the larger EU economies.

Exhibit 18-2. Selected European Labor Market Statistics

Country	Participation Rate of Women	Part-Time Work	Unemployment (1998)	Union Density
France	53%	16%	11.8%	10%
Germany	54%	17%	9.3%	30%
Italy	37%	7%	12.3%	34%
United Kingdom	63%	25%	6.2%	30%

Pay Determination

Statutory Requirements

The setting of minimum wage rates in Europe is achieved by one of the following:

- A statutory minimum wage
- Binding collective agreements

Both France and the United Kingdom have a statutory minimum wage (the United Kingdom's was just introduced on April 1, 1999). In France, the national statutory minimum wage was introduced in its current form in 1970 and covers some 9% of the workforce. There are prescribed procedures for adjusting for cost-of-living changes, and the government may also intervene to raise minimum rates in line with the overall growth of earnings, especially blue-collar pay. In the United Kingdom, the minimum wage is still an institutional novelty, set at £3.60 per hour, and experience with it is necessarily limited. At the time of writing, it appeared that most companies were complying with the new regulation and did not anticipate major problems such as staff cuts to offset higher costs. In contrast to most other European countries with statutory minimum wages, no mechanism has been specified for raising it. This will remain, for the present, a matter of political and economic judgment.

Other countries with a statutory minimum wage include the Netherlands, Belgium, Spain, Greece, and Portugal. Belgium is also the last country in Europe to operate a formal indexation procedure for automatically raising wages (both minimum and agreed) in line with consumer price inflation.

In both Germany and Italy, minimum wages are set for most employees by a structure of industry-level collective agreements that encompass about 80% of the dependent labor force in Germany and some 90% in Italy. As a result, there are a variety of mandatory minimal requirements, depending on industry and region (or whatever the appropriate scope of the agreement is). In the first instance, these labor agreements apply only to employers that are members of recognized employers' associations.

In addition, mechanisms exist in these countries, and most of those with statutory minimum wages, to "extend" the pay rates set by collective bargaining to employers who are not directly party to agreement and not members of recognized employers' associations. The procedures and impact of such provisions vary widely but can mean that a company will be covered by the terms of a collective agreement in which it has no direct participation as a negotiator or signatory.

Compared with a formal statutory regime, however, some significant sections of those economies in which minimum requirements are set exclusively by collective agreement may well embrace a large number of low-paid workers in sectors where trade union membership has been historically low or wage competition especially severe. Recent cases in Germany have found ultra-low pay rates unlawful on the grounds that they "violate good morals," especially when individual employees (in some cases coming from Eastern Europe to work on German construction projects) have been paid much less than a benchmark collective agreement.

Furthermore, there are legal provisions in some countries (now matched by parallel legislation at the EU level) that require employers to pay the same rates to all employees within a national territory, including any foreign workers assigned to that jurisdiction to perform specified services.

Definition of the Workweek

Compared with the United States and Japan, working hours in Europe are relatively short on a weekly basis, and particularly so on an annual basis. The latter phenomenon is attributable to longer annual leaves (five to six weeks for most employees) and additional public and religious holidays. Provisions in this area are discussed in more detail later.

Hours of work in EU countries are a function of several intersecting sets of legal regulations at both the European and national level, as well as collective agreements. The underlying mandatory provision is the EU Directive on Working Time, which sets a maximum workweek of 48 hours, includes requirements for work breaks, and sets mandatory requirements for health and safety protection for night workers.

One interesting feature of this directive (which reflects mainland European employment traditions) is that deviation from the law is possible, provided this is encapsulated within a collective labor agreement. This embodies the principle that collective agreements are a type of lawmaking within the industrial sphere and the notion that collective agreements can allow more flexibility because they can incorporate a fair balance between the needs of employers and union-organized employees. Typical areas for deviation ("derogation") from the law are rescheduling of breaks and agreement on reference periods for averaging out hours to comply with overall total, but in a way that recognizes both operational requirements and employee choice.

In the United Kingdom, the introduction of the EU directive was the first time that hours of work have been regulated by statute (except for specific groups of employees such as truck drivers). Before this, the workweek was a matter for individual or collective negotiation. In the United Kingdom, there has been a long tradition of granting shorter work hours to white-collar employees, with manual workers often on 38–40 hours and white-collar staff on 35–36 hours. Such differences are being eroded as companies seek to introduce parity of status, simplify personnel administration, and bring in more flexible forms of work time such as annual hours.

Although nominal hours in the United Kingdom are not widely out of line with those in Europe (see Exhibit 18-3), actual hours worked tend to be considerably higher. One reason is the prevalence of an "overtime" culture among some workers—often reflecting low base salaries and the lack of protection through law or agreement against certain employer requests. In France, by contrast, the standard workweek has long been the subject of statutory regulation, and cuts in work hours have been achieved more by statute than by collective agreement. This reflects the organizational weakness and political focus of trade unions in France. Two steps in particular had a strong impact. First, in 1981, the workweek was reduced from 40 to 39 hours. In 1998, controversial legislation was passed requiring companies to introduce a 35-hour week by 2001, with financial incentives for companies that move earlier and tie the hours reductions to job creation measures. Although they have raised concerns about competitiveness, these new regulations have also been viewed by many companies (especially those with more sophisticated HR approaches) as an opportunity to bargain for greater flexibility in the organization of work hours.

In practice, work hours in Germany are set by collective agreement, against a background of statutory regulation that embodies the requirements of the EU Working Time Directive. Although this allows for a maximum normal workweek of 48 hours, with a number of flexibility options to accommodate special projects, actual hours according to collective agreement are much lower. The average in the western part of Germany is 37.4 hours; in the eastern part, it is 39 hours. One notable development in Germany is the conclusion of a standard 35-hour week for a number of industrial branches, including metalworking (engineering, electronics, automotive, aerospace), printing, and steel. These cuts in the workweek were mostly in place by the early 1990s (often they followed

Exhibit 18-3. Hours and Holidays in Manufacturing in Key EU Countries and in the U.S.

Country	Annual Total Nominal Hours	Annual Leave (days)	Public Holidays (days)
France	1,771	25	9
West Germany	1,573	30	11.3[1]
Italy	1,736	27	9
United Kingdom	1,774	25	8
United States	1,904	12–15	11

1. Includes average of national and regional holidays.

Source: *German Confederation of Employers' Associations (BDA)*

serious industrial disputes) and reflected trade union concerns both to raise employees' quality of life and to provide for a form of "work sharing" following the economic slowdown of the early 1980s.

Unions have made a number of important concessions in the interest of reaching agreement on cuts in hours. In Germany, for example, these have included greater flexibility in the organization of work hours (annual hours), exemptions for some key groups (typically managers, specialists, and skilled technicians), and an acceptance that pay growth would be moderated in years in which hours were reduced. Between 1997 and 1999, one important development that could have far-reaching consequences has been a series of agreements at industry and company level on "individual work time accounts." These would allow employees to "deposit" any hours of overtime worked into their "account" (either with cash payment of the higher overtime rate or a larger credit), which they could use for longer holidays, other time off, or even early retirement. For their part, employers can use this flexibility to attune employee hours more closely with operational requirements—with the account ironing out the discrepancies with agreed weekly hours.

Exhibit 18-3 sets out hours and holidays in the manufacturing industry for key EU countries, with the United States as a comparison.

Collective Bargaining: Incidence and Structure

One of the key features of employment in Western Europe is the extensive reach of collective bargaining, often supported by statutory provisions that ensure that collectively agreed terms and conditions can be applied to employers outside the immediate scope of labor agreements. Consider the proportion of the labor force covered by national-, industry-, or company-level agreements in key Western European countries:

- France—about 75%
- Germany—about 85% (c. 65% in the private sector)
- Italy—about 90%
- United Kingdom—about 36% (c. 25% in the private sector)

The environment set by collective bargaining is also of critical importance to employers outside its scope because collective agreements set the benchmark for an entire range of terms and conditions and, in particular, for pay and hours of work.

The incidence and importance of collective bargaining is undergoing a number of changes. First, the workforce covered by collective agreements is declining—slowly in countries such as Germany, where it is deeply established, but much more swiftly in the United Kingdom. For the most part, this has not been the product of deliberate antiunionism by employers (although this did happen in some sectors). Rather, it mirrors the industrial transformation of the past 20 or so years, marked by a shrinkage of the manufacturing labor force (especially in the United Kingdom) and the emergence of new service industries in regions where trade union organizations and traditions have been weaker. The development of more advanced methods of HR management has certainly made it more difficult for unions to gain a toehold in newer industries, but new industries are being brought within the scope of collective bargaining in some countries.

Second, where collective bargaining is strongly institutionalized and legally protected—and where employers are loath to undermine the social role of bargaining—there has been intense pressure from employers to make collective agreements more flexible and responsive to workplace needs. This is especially true in Italy, Germany, and France, where the fundamental framework of collective bargaining is at industry, not company, level. Key areas of negotiation and controversy include the following:

- The proportion of employees' pay set at industry level and the scope for locally determined rewards, in particular pay tied to individual or group performance and corporate profitability
- Flexible work time
- Scope for exemption from key negotiated terms

Third, the pursuit of national macroeconomic and employment policies has led to a revival of "social pacts" in a number of countries—with trade unions, employers, and government cooperating and negotiating in a variety of institutional settings. Although some countries, such as the Netherlands and Belgium, have long had formal institutions for tripartite cooperation, the structure elsewhere (notably in the Irish Republic) has been more ad hoc, though no less enduring. The Irish series of national pay accords has continued since 1987.

The existence of social pacts also serves to confirm the continuing strong institutional role of trade unions and collective bargaining in many European countries, although the United Kingdom represents an important exception in this respect. Collective agreements are seen as complementing laws as a type of distinct agreed jurisdiction. As noted above, they dovetail with formal legal provisions in several respects.

The final point is that the "European level" as such is beginning to figure as a new element in collective bargaining, especially as trade unions seek to develop common approaches to forestall what they fear as a downward spiral of pay competition within the harsher economic environment created by the EMU. Such considerations have also been fostered to some degree by the possibilities of employee contact created by the EU directive requiring large multinational firms in Europe to establish forums for informing and consulting their workforces.

What all this means is that the industry-level agreement—the customary level of collective bargaining for much of Western Europe—is under pressure from workers to become more flexible, while part of its regulatory role is being absorbed in some countries by national pacts that are setting a bargaining framework. In the background lurks the new environment created by the EMU, the long-term impact of which remains impossible to gauge.

Cash Compensation

Base Pay

Base pay for employees (both blue- and white-collar) in countries with high levels of collective bargaining coverage is typically set by an industry or possibly company pay scale. As noted above, this encompasses a substantial proportion of the workforce in mainland Europe and sets the pay levels for a good deal of the nonunionized sector. (Conversely, the nonunionized sector can exert pressure on unionized employees in some situations.)

Industry-level basic minimum wages are usually supplemented by additional payments made at company or workplace level, giving rise to a two-tiered pay structure in many European countries. These supplements may be formally negotiated with workforce representatives or may be awarded by management in response to labor market pressures. In general, the larger the company, the larger the supplement; although for managerial employees, small firms often have to offer a premium to offset reduced career opportunities and uncertain job security.

The divergence between base pay and the actual contracted wage or salary may range from a few percent to as high as 50%. Some industry agreements—for example, in the Netherlands—may include clauses to restrict such "pay drift" between minimum industry requirements and company-level pay to ensure that the agreement meshes with what employees receive, at the same time preventing larger companies from grabbing up all the most skilled employees.

Other Regular Payments

Virtually all employees in mainland European countries receive approximately an extra month's pay each year (the "13th month"), and in some countries (notably Spain), they receive a "14th" or even "15th" month. This is usually provided under the terms of collective agreement; however, employers not covered by a collective agreement will also invariably pay it to other employees. The additional payment usually comes in two portions: a summer vacation bonus and a Christmas bonus. The precise methods of calculation can vary considerably.

In the United Kingdom and Irish Republic, a 13th month payment as such is much more of a rarity—so rare, in fact, that it is virtually unknown. However, the growth of profit-related bonuses in the financial services sector in the United Kingdom (typically paid out early in the year) has begun to create a form of compensation that is coming to resemble a 13th month for some employees.

The existence of a 13th month (combined in some cases with the two-tier bargaining structures outlined above) can add a useful measure of flexibility to total annual compensation. This can be an important cushion during critical periods and allows the creation of a "negotiating mass" in which complex trades and offsets become possible. At Volkswagen, for example, employees agreed to work a basic 28.8-hour week in 1993 to stave off the threat of 30,000 lost jobs. Monthly pay was cut, but the existence of the 13th month meant that this sum could be averaged out over the year instead of being paid out in one lump sum. The result was that monthly incomes could be sustained, at least nominally.

In the past, payment of a full 13th month has been virtually automatic and remains so under most collective agreements. Increasing numbers of companies, however, have been turning toward the creation of a company-level supplement to earmark part of the bonus as an incentive payment. Such an incentive may reflect general corporate performance, but it can also be tied to specific objectives such as reduced absenteeism.

Full pay for annual vacation is the norm, and, as noted above, many employees also receive a vacation bonus.

Incentive and Variable Pay

Performance-based rewards have been slow to catch on in many parts of Europe where salary structures have often been tied to length of service and numerous individual allowances. In recent years, this picture has been changing, especially for managers and specialists. These changes are most likely irreversible. It is important to note, however, that the proportion of pay "at risk" is still typically lower in Europe than in the United States.

In Germany, the economic slowdown of 1993–1994 led to a wave of downsizing and reducing layers and stimulated the search for more effective strategies to promote innovation and entrepreneurship, especially within large industrial groups. Industrial giants such as Daimler-Benz (now Daimler-Chrysler) and Siemens, for example, set about reforming their compensation strategies by introducing a significant element of variable pay, together with stock options for senior management, and fostering a performance culture through individual appraisal and incentive pay for middle managers. This has all entailed major change, sometimes encompassing tens of thousands of employees, and, in the case of middle managers, was often introduced after long negotiations with elected employee representations.

Various types of incentive pay (aside from piecework) are often provided for in collective agreements for shop-floor workers. Hourly workers may receive merit allowances, which are theoretically conditional on supervisor appraisal but are often paid out in equal measure across the board. Bonus payments may also be tied to quality objectives, such as finding more efficient ways to use supplies and raw materials.

Formerly laggards in the area of performance-related payment for manual workers, many mainland European businesses (particularly larger ones) have been intensively developing compensation systems to reward blue-collar employees for performance (including the acquisition of new skills). For example, Europe's specialized engineering businesses have historically been run with fairly low levels of supervision (especially compared with the United States). This has been balanced with the requirement that shop-floor employees maintain a higher level of skill and responsibility. Given Europe's high labor costs, the pursuit of top-quality engineering standards is an economic imperative, and effective performance strategies are seen as a critical means of fostering these sources of comparative advantage. It is interesting to note that one feature of many incentive schemes in mainland Europe has been a focus on group rather than individual reward.

Salary Planning and Pay Programs

Inflation and Salary Increase Trends

The pay environment in most Western European countries continues to be set by collective bargaining, especially in Germany and Italy, which have fairly centralized and coordinated systems. The results of this bargaining, which receive extensive publicity in the media, set benchmarks for other pay-setting processes, including salary reviews. Some settlements figure prominently as "lead settlements," setting a trend that in some countries sets the prevailing standard. The metalworking industry and the public sector are important pacesetters in all countries. Although pay is nationally coordinated in only a few countries, the institutional structure of Western European society is sufficiently cohesive, as the range of settlements tends to be narrow.

Collectively agreed-upon increases, whether at the industry or national level, also offer access to a pay environment that must be gauged by salary surveys in countries whose bargaining practices are more decentralized, such as the United States or, to a lesser extent, the United Kingdom. In fact, the number of salary surveys in the United Kingdom probably equals the total number of surveys in all other EU countries combined. However, the "headline" rate of settlements can be somewhat misleading, since they have to be translated into company reality (where local conditions might necessitate some modifications).

Trade union negotiating objectives are customarily set by a mixture of economic factors, the most important being inflation and productivity developments. Pay objectives may be brought within a wider frame of reference and set against other targets, however—depending on the context. As already noted, in Germany, trade unions have been prepared to offer implicit concessions on pay in return for cuts in work time. More recently, pay concessions in the form of reduced annual bonuses were agreed to in return for maintaining the value of sick pay. This process can lead to more formalized "national pacts" to promote competitiveness and to create or preserve jobs.

Bargaining in most countries takes place annually (this is mirrored by typical annual pay reviews for employees not subject to collective bargaining). The actual duration of collective agreements can vary, with each side often seeking to pick a period that suits its interests. As such, contract duration can become as much a bargaining issue as what the contract says.

Tax Efficiency and Net/Gross Comparisons

The tax efficiency of compensation packages will depend almost entirely on national law, with wide variations on issues such as the tax treatment of pension contributions, share options, and grants, and the tax treatment of families. Not surprisingly, some common trends can be observed. Direct tax rates have been falling for some years, a development prompted by the "Thatcher revolution" in the United Kingdom in the mid-1980s. In addition, there are moves to greater simplicity and transparency of taxation. Traditionally, high tax rates in Germany have been offset by allowances and coverage of allowable employee expenses; these have cut the effective tax rate, while unwittingly generating a major tax avoidance industry. Cuts in direct taxation have gone hand in hand with increases in sales ("value-added") taxes, taxes on fuel (in part reflecting greater environmental awareness), and a range of other charges. Exhibit 18-4 illustrates net/gross comparisons for single persons and families in the mid-1990s.

One further important consideration is that, for most of mainland Europe, key statutory benefits are organized by earmarked funds financed out of employer and employee contributions. Contributions are usually payable above a minimum threshold of earnings and up to a pay ceiling. Rates can be high: 45% of pay as employer contributions in Italy and France and 22% in Germany. In the United Kingdom and Denmark, employer social contributions are much lower—10% and 5%, respectively—with revenue

Exhibit 18-4. Net as a Percentage of Gross Income in the Mid-1990s for Selected Countries

	Single Person	Two-Child Family
France	72.6	86.3
Germany	61.8	76.8
Italy	73.3	82.4
United Kingdom	73.5	82.5
United States	74.1	81.0

raised by general taxation. Efforts are under way in high-contribution countries to tackle what is effectively a tax on employment, either by trimming entitlements or shifting taxation to other objects, such as energy use. However, given the fact that such benefit schemes are part of the social fabric of many countries, change is likely to be steady but not abrupt, and subject to negotiation at all social levels.

Long-Term Incentives and Broad-Based Share Programs

Compared with the United States (and the United Kingdom within Europe), mainland European stock markets remain narrowly based; however, this is changing quickly as flotation and the development of an "equity culture" become more attractive to managers and budding entrepreneurs. In the past, this narrow market base has inhibited the growth of stock option plans for indigenous European companies outside the United Kingdom, but it has created the potential for developing other forms of long-term incentives tied to a range of individual and business objectives.

Changes in legislation on stock options—both for managers and across the board—are taking place in several countries, using a variety of valuation and taxation methods. In the United Kingdom, continental managers have observed the problems and perverse incentives created by the widespread use of stock options with weak performance criteria. New plans—especially in Germany—are being tied to long-term corporate criteria, including share price performance against national or European indexes.

Profit Sharing

Profit-sharing arrangements have a long history in Europe and have increased in number and scope in recent years. In some countries, there are tax incentives for certain types of schemes. One of the most developed sets of schemes is in France. Two types of schemes are in operation (subject to notification to the tax and labor authorities), covering more than 3 million workers. Under deferred profit-sharing arrangements (which must apply to a company's entire workforce), payments into a fund are free of tax or social insurance contributions—provided the funds are held for a specified length of time (usually five years). So-called immediate profit-sharing schemes can exist for selected groups of employees, but they must be set up through an agreement with a trade union. Payments can be made subject to a range of criteria, including corporate performance and HR targets such as absenteeism; the payments are taxable.

Benefits and Perquisites

Time Off

The most important component of time off for employees is the annual vacation, which in many countries is five to six weeks, not including public and religious holidays. The European Working Time Directive, which applies to all EU member states, requires a *minimum* four weeks' annual vacation for all employees. Aside from the United Kingdom, employee status rarely has any impact on length of vacation. Many countries go through a virtual industry shutdown every August. During the Christmas holiday, employees often use their individual days of holiday entitlement plus the three or four public holidays to stretch their overall break out to nearly two weeks.

Public holidays and vacation are usually paid in full, and in many countries, employees receive extra pay (the "13th month" noted earlier) during the summer holiday.

Europe's workforce also enjoys a range of other rights to time off, some mandated by European and national law and some by binding collective agreement. Typical examples include two to three days off for family needs or family events (e.g., weddings, bereavement, care of sick children). (Maternity and sick leave are discussed separately below.) The shortage of skilled workers had compelled many European companies to look at ways of making their operations more "family friendly," with a variety of employee time-off entitlements added to the statutory and agreed foundation. Typical examples include the following:

- Parental leave
- Educational leave
- Time off for training as employee representatives
- Family leave
- Career breaks and sabbaticals

Benefits

Medical and Dental. Medical and dental programs for most of Europe's workforce are paid for by state-administered schemes. The precise mechanics of financing and the institutional structures through which health care services are delivered, however, vary considerably. In some countries, such as the United Kingdom, payments into the system come from general tax funds and are disbursed to hospitals and general practitioners by the government. In much of mainland Europe, statutory social benefits are financed through earmarked funds, typically deducted from the employee's gross income and matched by an equivalent employer contribution. Most schemes involve some user fees, but these rarely cover the full cost of the service. In some countries, employees earning above a certain income threshold can opt to take out private medical insurance, which usually means better facilities, lower premiums, and a greater number of services. Patients often have a right to go straight to a consultant, and medical practitioners will normally indicate which sickness insurance funds they accept. The funds themselves often maintain a specialist service that can issue guidelines on treatments covered by the fund.

Typical contribution levels are as follows:

- Germany—12 to 13% of gross income, paid equally by employer and employee
- France—12.8% of gross income for the employer and about 1% for the employee

In general, the cost of medical benefits to employers in Europe is considerably lower than in the United States, reflecting generally lower administration costs, a narrower range of choice in some countries (such as the United Kingdom), and greater scope for control over treatments and charges.

Private medical insurance, as noted above, is frequently offered as an additional benefit to all or selected groups of employees, with additional benefits typically offered to managers. In countries where the development of health provision still lags (or where waiting lists can be long), this can be an attractive benefit.

The one exception to the rule on state-administered health systems is Switzerland, where all medical benefits are delivered through private insurance plans. However, insurance for most employees is organized through company-based group schemes that have much the same contribution rates as elsewhere.

Maternity and Sick Leave. Maternity leave is required under an EU directive that mandates at least 14 weeks of leave around the period of childbirth, with payment provided either as an allowance or a continuation of wages. In most countries, this was already the accepted level of care before the directive came into force; in fact, those existing national provisions may improve on the directive's mandate. In most countries, women on maternity leave receive a combination of payments from the state and the employer, which generally ensures that income is maintained at least during statutory maternity leave.

Longer periods of "parental leave" (which last up to three years in some countries) are handled differently, often with no salary obligation and a low or means-tested benefit. There is also an EU directive that requires a minimum of three months' leave to men and women workers on the grounds of the birth or adoption of a child up to a maximum age of eight years. This provision is independent of any maternity provisions, and national practice varies considerably. One interesting case is Sweden, where parents have the right to 450 days' paid parental leave. To encourage men to take up the option, one month each of this amount is reserved for the mother and father individually, with the balance freely transferable between them. The right to parental leave may be used until the child is eight years old and may be taken either as a single block or several blocks.

Sick leave is determined by national legislation and collective or individually agreed-upon provisions. In recent years, there have been initiatives in several countries (notably the Netherlands and Sweden) to move from a system of state sick benefits to employer payments for sick time. The aim has been twofold: to cut state spending and to encourage employers to develop ways to create a "healthier" workforce and thus cut down on absenteeism. Typical employer obligations include the following:

- Germany—100% of previous usual earnings for the first six weeks of illness, by law and agreement.
- France—By law, 90% pay for the first 30 days of illness, followed by 66% for the next 30 days, and further staged reductions should the illness progress. This is topped up to full pay for an initial period by a number of collective agreements. A portion of sick pay can be reclaimed from the authorities.

Pensions

Western Europe provides its workers with statutory pension schemes financed on a pay-as-you-go basis from earmarked contributions. These contributions are typically supplemented by general taxation. In most cases, the level of pension is a function of the individual's revalued earnings plus the number of contribution years. Most plans offer a minimum pension guarantee, which may be tied to the level of the statutory minimum wage or the subsistence threshold for welfare payments. The proportion of final salary paid out varies but often hovers around the 50% mark. To what extent other pension vehicles have developed depends strongly on the scale and scope of these state schemes—in particular, on the proportion of earnings covered for contributions assessment. In Italy and France, for example, senior managers will be part of the executive pension schemes within the state system. In the United Kingdom, company-based schemes or private arrangements will provide the bulk of postretirement income for managers. In Denmark and the Netherlands, there is a range of industry-level schemes, agreed with trade unions, that are financed on a funded basis with assets held in mortgage bonds (as in Denmark) or in equity (the Netherlands). Personal pensions, usually based on insurance, can supplement state pensions in all countries.

The United Kingdom offers a flat-rate pension financed from social insurance contributions and general taxation, with some additional amounts available through the state scheme based on lifetime earnings. However, the United Kingdom differs (as does the Netherlands in this regard) from most of Western Europe in the important role played in securing postretirement income by funded pension schemes, the vast bulk of which are organized by individual employers as a benefit.

Statutory pension schemes usually offer a variety of other benefits such as disability benefits, survivors' benefits, and so on. The statutory retirement age is typically 65, but most schemes include provisions for early retirement or retirement after a set number of years of contributions.

There are major concerns that these systems will become progressively more difficult to sustain as demographic changes reduce the number of active employees per pensioner in the coming 30 to 40 years. This will push up contribution rates for those in work and add to the effective taxation of employment, which is already a problem in Europe. These demographic shifts are expected to have the most impact in Italy and Germany. Among the measures being taken to stem the possible difficulties are abolition of early retirement options, reductions in prospective pension payments, and alteration of the formulas for uprating pensions in payment. Not surprisingly, many of these measures have been highly controversial.

The likely reductions in benefits paid by state systems will mean that occupational schemes are likely to take on a larger role, with a number of mechanisms being made to divert cash or other types of benefits into pension or savings vehicles. A number of countries are beginning to develop "top-up" pensions, either at the sector level or on a company/individual basis, and, as in France and Italy, are beginning to explore the use of funded programs, in some cases for the first time.

These problems are markedly less serious in the United Kingdom and the Irish Republic, where the demographic outlook is more favorable. The fact that these two countries also feature a stronger role for funded schemes is often looked on as an escape route from the problems of the "unfunded liabilities" of the large state schemes on the mainland. To the extent that funded schemes can tap sources of revenue outside of the country's national boundaries, this may be true. However, private schemes in the United Kingdom have themselves been the focus of controversy—if not scandal—during the 1980s and 1990s. During that time, thousands of employees were encouraged by private pension providers to leave their employers' schemes and buy inappropriate personal pensions. Pensioners who have not made individual provision, or whose provision turns out to be inadequate, will be forced to rely on state help in their old age—no less an "unfunded liability" than the reasonably accurately predicted outgoings in the state systems.

One further difficulty with the United Kingdom's approach is that there are huge disparities between groups of pensioners, a problem likely to grow as tenures shorten or as people spend more of their working lives in more precarious forms of employment. As a way of addressing this problem, the British government is now seeking to develop a new range of "stakeholder" pensions to encourage lower-paid employees to make provision for their old age.

"Occupational pensions," organized at the company or industry level, can be found in many countries, and their role and relevance are quite dependent on the levels of provision (and contributions) in the statutory pension systems. Many are financed through either private insurance or book reserves, secured against employer insolvency. In many countries, there are limits on the degree of equity finance and concern about the risks involved. As noted above, in the United Kingdom, the company-based occupational scheme, typically offering a proportion of final salary depending on length of service and financed by a pension fund with assets in shares and government securities, is a central mechanism in pension offerings.

In many countries, senior managers with earnings above the social security ceiling often either take out or are awarded supplementary pensions, typically through private insurance schemes.

Organization and Staffing

Selection, Recruitment, and Staffing

Recruitment arrangements in many European countries (especially the Latin ones) were notoriously overregulated into the early 1990s. Vacancies and hirings had to be reported to the authorities, restrictions on hiring temporary workers existed in many countries, and some countries forbade private employment agencies. Although some of the restrictions (or at least their echoes) still remain, much of the rigidity has been swept away throughout the 1990s because of growing pressure to make labor markets function more effectively and to meet employer demand for more flexible employment relationships. In most countries, employers are free to hire whomever they want, with a variety of options for finding applicants in addition to the state employment services. The efficiency of these services varies markedly, although all have suffered from being stereotyped as repositories for the unemployed rather than for more active players in the labor market.

Statute law and collective agreements may provide for employee representatives to be informed on individual hirings, with a right of objection if the representatives feel that the appointment violates accepted law or procedures.

In Spain, for example, workplace employee representatives have a right to scrutinize all employment contracts to ensure that companies are not seeking to misuse fixed-term contracts to avoid taking on permanent employees.

The field of executive recruitment is changing rapidly throughout Europe. Corporate restructuring, mergers, and acquisitions have all served to change the profile and sought-for competencies of the European manager and to reshape employees' own expectations of their careers. In the past, mainland European companies (as well as the United Kingdom, except less so) tended to recruit senior managers internally, with the scope of promotion stretching from shop floor to boardroom. In southern Europe and Austria, word-of-mouth recruitment has played (and continues to play) an important role in filling management posts. But this internally oriented and informal recruitment culture is now beginning to shift.

Executive search and selection has grown rapidly in Europe over the past 20 years, and it is expected to continue to grow as companies respond to a more competitive environment and weaken their commitment to internal recruitment.

In most of mainland Europe, salaries are never indicated in job advertisements, and salary discussion among white-collar employees is taboo (and, not surprisingly, often the focus of intense curiosity). The one exception is the United Kingdom, where pay rates or salary ranges are indicated for a variety of jobs, including those at quite senior levels.

Regional Mobility

Compared with the United States, regional (and international) mobility is fairly low in Europe for most categories of employees, including managers and specialists. Levels of mobility may have been higher in the 1950s and 1960s, as hundreds of thousands of people moved from Southern to Northern Europe and there were large internal shifts of population inside Germany. Europe's citizens exhibit strong regional and urban loyalties, and they are often loath to disrupt support networks of friends and family. In Europe, the people most willing (or obliged) to move between regions or countries are top managers, unskilled workers, and young employees. In the Nordic countries, the high percentage of women in the workforce means a greater number of dual-career couples—and less likelihood that either one would move. As more women in other European countries enter the workforce and attain management positions, the dual-career issue will become more critical.

At the same time, many younger managers recognize that international experience can be important, if not essential, for career advancement. In several countries, those just starting their careers are expected to have competence in English (and often English plus a third European language). Indeed, to some degree, Europe is being integrated socially and economically through the medium of the English language, with many leading mainland European companies adopting English as their "official" language at management level and for many internal communications. This does not mean, however, that Europeans are in any way eager to ditch their cultural and linguistic heritages, and learning the language of one's corporate host and business partners can be richly rewarded.

Employment Law and Labor Relations

Labor Relations Environment

The labor relations environment in Western Europe shares a number of common features that serve to distinguish it from the United States and Japan. These common features, however, are abstractions. In reality, there are important national differences in law, custom, and culture, all of which require a detailed understanding wherever practical management is involved.

Trade Unions. In general, trade unions play a strong role in the institutional makeup and regulatory structure of Western Europe. That said, trade union organization has been declining, with a precipitous fall in the United Kingdom since the late 1970s and more gentle declines elsewhere. (Sometimes, these declines are masked temporarily by an aging membership concentrated in older industries.) Only in the Netherlands and the Irish Republic has membership actually grown over the past decade, and there are some signs that union membership may be stabilizing in the United Kingdom. This generalization does not account for the different levels of union organization—from 80+% in the Nordic countries to 5 to 10% in France. Trade union traditions are also very different, although the marked political differences in countries such as France and Italy are now much less acute than previously. Where trade union membership is low, there are often other mechanisms that support trade union activity or aims. These include procedures for "extending" collective agreements to nonsignatory companies, legal preferment for trade unions in negotiating workplace accords, and the presence of elected union representatives on such bodies as social welfare management institutions and labor tribunals.

The obligation of employers to recognize trade unions for bargaining purposes varies considerably. In most jurisdictions, there is no statutory obligation to recognize trade unions; however, this is qualified to a considerable degree by mandatory employee representation provisions (see below). In France, there is an obligation on employers to negotiate with trade unions at the workplace level at least once annually, but there is no requirement for this to be "in good faith" or to lead to an agreed outcome. In both the United Kingdom and the Irish Republic, moves are under way to provide for procedures for establishing recognition. Neither of these countries has statutory arrangements for workplace representation, and therefore unions provide the sole channel through which employee interests and grievances can be articulated. In the United Kingdom, the Labour government elected in May 1997 has introduced measures to provide for compulsory recognition in which a union can demonstrate majority support through a ballot.

Employee Representation. Employee representation (whether statutory or not) exists at a variety of levels within companies, typically at the company and group level. In the largest companies with transnational operations in Europe, representation exists at the European level. The institutions that provide this representation are typically works councils or works committees. Only the United Kingdom and the Irish Republic currently have no statutory arrangements or agreed-upon equivalent (as found in Denmark and Italy, for example). In these countries, there is "single-channel" representation through trade unions. In some countries, workplace representative bodies must be established by law, often by the employer; in others, this is a matter for the workforce to take up. In practice, most medium-sized and all large businesses can be expected to have developed structures of employee workplace representation. However, regardless of the employer's level of obligation, coverage declines rapidly as workforce numbers fall.

It is important to understand that representatives are the institutional counterpoint to trade unions in systems characterized by predominantly industry-level bargaining; the prime exemplars of this are Germany and Italy, but the Netherlands also provides a comparable picture. In such situations—and in contrast to the primacy of company bargaining in the United Kingdom—trade unions negotiate collective agreements on pay and hours at the industry level. Trade unions have a right to strike, and in some countries, employers have a right to lockout. In contrast, there may be a statutory injunction to maintain industrial peace at the workplace itself and limitations on what employee representatives may negotiate with local management. The role of workplace (or company) representation is to provide a forum for information and consultation on a range of workplace issues. Statute law typically states what sort of information must be disclosed, when it must be disclosed, and how it should be disclosed, and it has regulations on confidentiality. Examples include:

- The state of the business, business plans, and investments; and
- Employment-related matters such as hiring and terminations and types of employment contracts used (part-time, fixed-term, etc.).

In addition, in some cases, statute law may prescribe a range of issues that are subject to employee codetermination. In effect, this means that management may not proceed with an action unless it has secured the prior consent of employee representatives. When agreement cannot be reached, there are usually procedures for arbitration, or the employer may be able to resort to the courts to obtain authorization to proceed. The issues vary between countries, but typical examples include the following:

- Organization of working time and holidays (Germany, the Netherlands)
- Health and safety issues, monitoring of employees (France, Germany)
- Hiring, transfer, and regrading of employees (Germany)

Mandatory consultation requirements mean that, in comparison to the United States, it may take longer to reach and implement decisions. However, once decided on, the agreement of employee representatives may give decisions greater legitimacy and facilitate effective implementation.

Employment Contracts

National differences can be very telling in the field of employment contracts, with important detailed provisions affecting permitted variants in contractual arrangements. If not in law, then in practice, employment contracts are invariably in writing. If employees are not given an employment contract as such, with the existence of the employment relationship implied from the behavior of the parties, an EU-level directive requires employers to provide all employees a written statement of terms and conditions shortly after commencement of employment.

Probationary periods can usually be freely agreed between the parties, although national statute law—and in some cases collective agreements—put limits on how long a probationary period can be. Fixed-term contracts of employment can be subject to more stringent regulation. In Germany, for example, there is a basic presumption that a "material reason" must be cited before a fixed-term contract can be agreed to. When no material reason is applicable, fixed-term contracts may still be agreed on; however, there are limits on their duration and on the circumstances under which they can be renewed.

Termination of Employment

In general, Europe does not embrace a "hire and fire" culture, and dismissal is generally seen as the last resort. Indeed, an employer may be required by law to demonstrate to employee representatives and the labor authorities that every other avenue has been explored and exhausted before proceeding to terminate an employee's contract.

Dismissal for Cause

Dismissal for cause is typically defined in statute law, and provided proper procedures are observed, it does not, for the most part, raise insurmountable problems. Most countries have employment protection legislation that protects employees from unfair, arbitrary, or abusive termination. In some cases, these are attached to seniority criteria or establishment size. In some countries (notably the Netherlands), dismissal on any grounds may involve seeking administrative approval from the authorities. There is also statutory provision for prior consultation with employee representatives in a number of jurisdictions.

Economic Dismissals

Dismissal on economic grounds—especially collective dismissals (see below)—tends to be more closely regulated. Until recently, in Southern

Europe, it was quite difficult to dismiss employees on economic grounds for all but the most narrow range of circumstances. Official approval or notification is still required in Spain.

In Northern Europe, the employer's freedom to make economic dismissals is less constrained in principle but is subject to a range of limitations in practice, primarily connected with mandatory consultation requirements (especially in the Netherlands and Germany) and severance-pay requirements. Although no consultation requirement exists in France, employers must offer employees "retraining contracts" jointly financed by the employer and the state.

Often, employers must present documentation to establish why a dismissal is necessary and have a justification concerning their selection of employees who will lose their posts. Although "last in, first out" is still the norm in most jurisdictions, social criteria (such as age or number of dependents) may take precedence, complicating the process from the management's standpoint.

Collective dismissals are regulated by an EU-level directive requiring official notification, workforce consultation, and steps to mitigate or avoid dismissals above certain threshold values (depending on the size of the establishment).

Notice Periods

Notice periods are determined through a mixture of national law, collective agreement, and individual contract. Practice varies widely between jurisdictions, but there are some common points. Notice periods can be long (up to six months) at all employee levels. This applies especially for those with long seniority and for higher-level managers.

Severance Pay

Provisions for severance compensation are also set at the national level by law, collective agreement, and individual contract. Most jurisdictions provide for statutory payments in the event of economic dismissal, subject to an earnings ceiling. In Italy, no matter what the reason for dismissal (even when the employee is culpable), employees receive a termination payment financed out of payments that the employer must set aside during employment. This practice is designed to compensate for the fact that Italy has only the most minimal form of state financial support for the unemployed; employees in large companies are often put onto a special fund (the *cassa integrazione)* that pays their wages for a period prior to any final termination of contract. In the past, employees could spend several years in such limbo.

In Germany, there is no mandatory severance payment in the event of individual dismissal. Most employers prefer to negotiate a severance package, usually one month's pay per year of service up to a year's wages; this helps avoid dispute and possible court action. At the same time, in the event of multiple dismissals or other significant changes in the workforce, German law requires an employer to negotiate a collective severance package—a "social compensation plan"—with elected employee representatives. Such plans, which are typical in other countries, include severance payments, hardship compensation, and, increasingly, outplacement support.

Conclusion

At first blush, Western Europe seems to be a highly regulated labor market whose range of obligations on companies can slow decision making and inhibit growth. This is one component of a "European" model, however, in which business operations are subject to wider social considerations, including institutionalized employee rights, and which is reflected in a high quality of life and cultural opportunities, good public services and infrastructure, and social consensus. Employee skills are high, and industrial training is state-of-the-art, especially in Northern Europe. Management training, too, is comprehensive, having developed rapidly over the past 20 years with a wide range of MBA opportunities in several countries but a smaller number of top schools. European governments, in consort with the EU, are looking for ways to foster an entrepreneurial spirit and, in so doing, to promote employability and employment while retaining key aspects of this social model.

Notes

1. The European Union consists of 15 "member states": Austria, Belgium, Denmark, Finland, France, Germany, Greece, the Irish Republic, Italy, Luxembourg, the Netherlands, Portugal, Spain, Sweden, and the United Kingdom. Norway, Iceland, and

Liechtenstein are members of the European Economic Area (EEA), which includes a requirement to comply with some EU legal obligations, including in the employment and social field. A separate section below outlines the main aspects and implications of EU/EEA membership.

2. Since January 1, 1999, participating countries—which include all the EU member states with the exception of the United Kingdom, Greece, Sweden, and Denmark—have irrevocably locked together their currencies, which now represent subdivisions of the new European currency, the euro. Monetary policy is determined not by national central banks but by a new institution, the European Central Bank (ECB). Separate currencies will continue to exist in EMU countries until 2002, although the exchange rates between them are now fixed. From 2002, for ordinary transactions, these currencies will be replaced by the euro.
3. Chris Brewster and Ariane Hegewisch, eds., *Policy and Practice in European Human Resource Management* (London and New York: Routledge 1994).

Further Reading

Brewster, Chris, and Hegewisch, Ariane, eds. *Policy and Practice in European Human Resource Management*. London and New York: Routledge 1994

Incomes Data Services/IPD. *European Management Guides*. Vol. 1, *Contracts and Terms and Conditions of Employment;* Vol. 2, *Industrial Relations and Collective Bargaining;* Vol. 3, *Recruitment, Training, and Development.* 1994–1997.

Incomes Data Services. IDS International Documents series.

International Monetary Fund, *World Economic Outlook*, April 1999.

Organization for Economic Cooperation and Development (OECD), *Employment Outlook*, various issues.

CHAPTER 19

SENIOR EXECUTIVE REMUNERATION IN THE UNITED KINGDOM

GILES TULK AND
DAVID ATKINS

U.K. Economic Background

The picture emerging from the United Kingdom's economy over the last 12 months has been a mixed one. Although there has been good news on both unemployment (6.3% as of January 1999) and retail price inflation (2.1% in February), there is nonetheless some concern that the U.K. economy may be on the brink of a recession. Although GDP grew by about 1.3% over the last year, in fact industrial production declined by 0.1%. The service sector appears relatively buoyant in terms of company profitability, but companies in the manufacturing sector have seen profits reduced as a result of the high value of sterling and increased competition.

Yet even with low retail price inflation and weakness in the manufacturing sector, earnings increased over the past year by a relatively high 4.1%. As we will note later, the level of salary increase for senior managers and main board directors is even higher, with median increases ranging from about 5 to 8%.

It appears that there is a relative shortage of suitably skilled and qualified employees at all levels of the workforce and in most business sectors. The result is an upward pressure on base salaries. Even those companies in the manufacturing sector whose profits have been hit in the past year need to ensure that they competitively compensate their managers to avoid losing them. A competitive base salary can be particularly important, especially if an annual bonus payment is unlikely to be paid because of declining company profitability.

The issue of top executive pay continues to attract considerable media attention. The current government has recently indicated that it has concerns over what it views as excessively high compensation packages of some executive directors of publicly traded companies. The

Department of Trade and Industry is considering two approaches to moderating pay packages:

- Persuading the Stock Exchange to alter its listing requirements to require the boards of all quoted companies to obtain annual shareholder consent for directors' pay and continuation in office
- Amending the Companies Act to force through these changes

In an increasingly transatlantic (if not global) pay market for the executive directors of major quoted companies, it seems unlikely that there will be any significant reduction in the level of their compensation packages. In most cases, the total value of the packages offered by major U.K.-quoted companies to executive directors is still significantly lower than similar packages in the United States, especially with respect to annual and long-term incentive arrangements. Some major U.K. companies have addressed this issue by introducing what may be termed a "mid-atlantic" pay package for their senior executives. These packages may provide annual and long-term incentive opportunities that are above U.K. norms but below typical U.S. practice (even with a base salary higher than that paid for a comparable role in a U.S. company).

Looking ahead to the year 2000 it appears that unless the U.K. economy enters a full recession there is no reason to expect a significant tailing off of the level of senior executive pay increases seen over the past year.

Compensation Package Components

A senior executive in the U.K. can typically expect to receive a compensation package that consists of some or all of the following:

- Base salary
- Variable annual bonus
- Some form of long-term incentive arrangement
- Company-provided pension plan
- Company car
- Other noncash benefits such as private medical insurance

The following comments on current market practice vis-à-vis these components are based on data culled from Monks Partnership's April 1999 survey report Remuneration of Directors & Managers, as well as Monks' databank based on analyses of over 1,000 company annual reports.

Base Salary

Despite the increase in annual and long-term incentive plans, a competitive base salary is still considered by most senior executives in the U.K. to be the key offering of the compensation package. Most companies will have a target market position for setting their base salary policy. This may be, for example, the median or upper quartile of a sector-based group of comparable companies. Companies will typically review their market base salary position against the chosen comparison group on an annual basis. As a result, there tends to be a continued upward pressure on salaries, with companies awarding increases merely to maintain their market position before any performance issues are taken into account. This upward pressure on salaries has increased over the past year or so, thanks to the relative shortage of experienced senior executives with a proven track record of success in managing major businesses. The lack of suitable candidates at home has recently led a number of major U.K. companies to look to the United States when recruiting a new chief executive. The type of package being offered to these recruits puts additional upward pressure on senior executive pay.

The upward pressure on base salaries is illustrated by the base salary increases between April 1998 and April 1999 for both directors and senior managers of parent and subsidiary companies participating in Monks' U.K. survey databank. (See Exhibit 19-1.)

Exhibit 19-1. Base Salary Increases

		Parent Companies	Subsidiary Companies
		(%)	(%)
Directors	Lower Quartile	4.9	3.5
	Median	8.0	5.1
	Upper Quartile	14.3	7.9
Senior Managers	Lower Quartile	4.0	3.5
	Median	5.7	4.5
	Upper Quartile	10.0	7.2

Source: *RDM U.K. April 1999*

The median base salary increase for an executive director of a parent company during this period was around 8%; for a senior manager, 5.7%. This compares with the 2.1% retail price inflation mentioned earlier. There has been a considerable amount of media comment about the issue of so-called "fat-cat" salaries in the U.K. This will likely continue in light of the present level of salary increase-as will the government's consideration of possible legislation.

Analysis of Monks' U.K. survey database indicates that base salary increases accelerate with the size of U.K.-base salary (see Exhibit 19-2). The effect of this is a widening of the salary differential between top executives and more junior managers.

Exhibit 19-2. Median Base Salary Increases by Salary Band—All Senior Managers

Salary Band	Median Base Salary Increase (%)
£30,000 – £50,000	4.9
£50,000 – £80,000	5.6
£80,000 – £150,000	6.5
£150,000 plus	7.6

Source: *RDM U.K. April 1999*

As shown in Exhibit 19-3, industry sector also has some impact on the level of base salary increase. Among the sectors with the smallest base salary increase are utilities and building materials and construction (traditionally low-paying sectors in the U.K.). Even these sectors, however, have seen increases at twice the current level of retail price inflation. It is no surprise to see that the sector comprising oil, chemicals, and pharmaceuticals has the largest base salary increases, as companies in this sector are increasingly competing with U.S. companies for top executives.

Exhibit 19-3. Median Base Salary Increases

	Median Base Salary Increase (%)
Oil, Chemicals, and Pharmaceuticals	6.8
Retail and Distribution	6.1
Engineering	5.7
Electronics and Computers	5.6
Business Services	5.6

Food, Drink, and Tobacco	5.2
Consumer Goods	5.0
Financial and Property	4.7
Building Materials and Construction	4.6
Utilities	4.5
Leisure and Publishing	4.2

Source: *RDM U.K. April 1999*

Variable Annual Bonus

An annual bonus plan is a standard compensation package feature for most senior executives and managers in parent companies in the U.K. (see Exhibit 19-4).

Exhibit 19-4. Eligibility for Annual Bonus—All Parent Companies

	% of Positions
Main Board Director	91
Senior Head of Function	96
Senior Manager	85

Source: *RDM U.K. April 1999*

Although more than 80% of senior and top managers are entitled to participate in an annual bonus plan, the maximum award under the plans does vary significantly by status. The executive director of a larger parent company (over £500m in revenues) might typically have a maximum bonus payment of 50% of salary. A senior vice president could see a maximum of 40% of salary, while a senior manager could expect a maximum bonus of about 25% of salary.

Bonus payments for on-target performance are usually set at about half the maximum bonus level; in other words, an annual bonus plan with a maximum bonus of 50% of salary might have an on-target payment of about 25% of salary.

Our research indicates that most annual bonus plans will include a financial measure such as group (or divisional) profit or earnings per share as the key performance indicator for determining bonus payments. Around a fifth of companies, however, also take into account personal job-related measures when determining bonus payments; a minority of companies also have some discretionary component for determining award level.

A financial performance measure that has been attracting some interest in respect to annual bonus plans is economic value added (EVA).

Exhibit 19-5 displays the typical bonus payments made (as a percentage of salary) during the last fiscal year in larger parent companies. The figures include zero bonus payments. Between 20 and 25% of positions eligible for a bonus in the last financial year did not receive a bonus payment.

Exhibit 19-5. Actual Annual Bonus Payments

	% of Annual Salary		
	Main Board Director	**Senior Function Head**	**Senior Manager**
Lower Quartile	8	0	3
Median	26	17	12
Upper Quartile	41	30	19

Source: *RDM U.K. April 1999*

An increasing number of companies in the U.K. have introduced some form of deferred element to their annual bonus arrangements. As of January 1999 about 39% of Financial Times Stock Exchange (FT-SE) 100 companies (the companies listed on the London Stock Exchange with the 100 highest market capitalizations) had a deferred annual bonus arrangement in place for their executive directors. Deferred annual bonus arrangements can typically take one of three forms (sometimes these exist in combination):

1. An individual may voluntarily use all or part of his or her annual bonus to purchase shares in the company, which usually must be held for three years. The company may then award matching shares, which may be restricted for an additional three years. The award of matching shares under a voluntarily deferred bonus plan is not normally subject to performance targets, but depends on the whether executive is still with the company when the matching shares vest.
2. There may be a compulsory requirement that a proportion of annual bonus be taken in the form of restricted/deferred shares. The company may then award matching shares on an appropriate basis but typically no more than one-for-one. The vesting of the deferred and matching shares will again depend on the executive's employment status at the end of the deferral period.

3. There may be both a voluntary and compulsory deferred annual bonus plan. For example, a company may require that part of the bonus be invested in company shares with the option to voluntarily invest part or all of the balance in company shares. Matching shares may then be awarded for both the compulsory and voluntarily deferred elements or just the voluntary element.

Deferred annual bonus arrangements are becoming more popular as a means to encourage senior executives to invest part of their earnings in company shares and to provide a medium- to long-term incentive arrangement.

Long-Term Incentive Arrangements

Long-term incentive practices among major U.K. companies are becoming more diverse, as evidenced by the summary of long-term incentives for the executive directors of FT-SE 100 companies shown in Exhibit 19-6.

For many years share options (typically called stock options in the United States) were the only long-term incentive offered by U.K. companies. Since

Exhibit 19-6. Long-Term Incentive Arrangements—Executive Directors in FT-SE 100 Companies

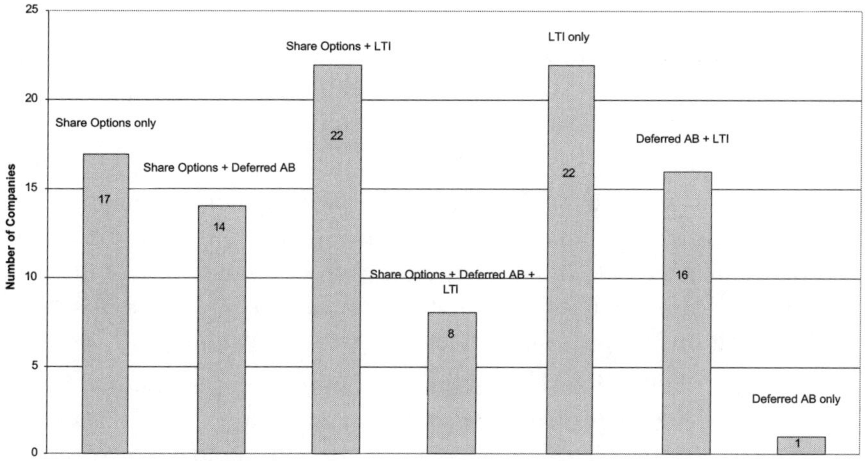

Legend: AB = Annual Bonus
LTI = Long-term Incentive

the early 1990s a growing number of companies have introduced alternative long-term arrangements. Today, only 17% of the FT-SE 100 companies make share options their sole long-term offering; 68% have introduced some form of alternative long-term incentive plan, either as the sole long-term incentive or in combination with other forms of long-term incentive. Because of the complexity of some of these arrangements, however, a number of companies, after reviewing possible alternatives, have recently reverted to their executive share option plan as their sole long-term arrangement.

Summarized below are the main features of the different types of long-term incentive arrangements in the U.K.

Executive Share Option Plan

In an executive share option plan, the company grants an option to an executive to purchase a given number of shares at a future date at the market price of the shares on the date the option was granted. The potential gain from share options is the increase in share price between the date of grant and the date of exercise, less the tax paid. The exercise of options will usually depend on how well the company has achieved its performance targets. In the U.K., options from this sort of plan are not normally exercisable until a minimum of three years from the date of grant.

Most executive share option plans in the U.K. will have both approved and unapproved sections:

- The approved (by the Inland Revenue) covers share options worth up to a maximum value of £30,000. Any gain in the value of the options once exercised and sold is subject to capital gains tax.
- The unapproved (by the Inland Revenue) covers options granted in excess of a value of £30,000. The tax treatment of unapproved options is less favorable, since they are subject to income tax (at the participant's marginal tax rate) once exercised rather than at the time of the ultimate sale of the shares. There are also National Insurance implications for the company on unapproved options.
- To limit the dilution of shareholder equity, U.K. institutional investors have issued guidelines limiting the number of shares that can be issued to employee share plans. However, few companies exceed the current normal limit on individual executive share option holdings of four times earnings.

- Executive Director—options worth 4 times salary
- Senior Function Head—options worth 3 times salary
- Function Head—options worth 2 times salary
- Senior Professional—options worth 1½–2 times salary

In most companies executive share options are granted on an annual or phased basis, with annual grants of about one times salary per year for executive directors and about one half of salary per year at the function head level.

Most share option plans have performance conditions attached to how and when options are exercised. Recently introduced plans (which will normally have required shareholder approval) typically have a performance hurdle related to earnings per share that must exceed retail price inflation by 3% per year or 9% over a three-year period before an option can be exercised. Existing plans may have a lower hurdle of 2% per annum over a three-year period.

Super Options

A small number of major companies have introduced "super-option" plans. These companies include the high street retailer Marks & Spencer, the entertainment group Granada, and the engineering and defense company GEC. Super-option plans permit the granting of share options valued at an additional four times annual salary. Exercising these options is subject to stringent performance conditions and is only allowed after five years.

Performance Share Plan (or Restricted Share Plan with Performance Targets)

Under this type of plan, participants are typically awarded shares at a specified value with vesting conditional on the achievement of pre-defined long-term performance targets. Although the potential payment is often expressed as a percentage of salary, the ultimate benefit to the participant will depend on the share price at the end of the performance period. Such plans are mainly operated on a "rolling" basis with awards made annually. Usually there is a threshold target below which no part of the award can be exercised, and a maximum level of achievement at which the full award can be exercised and all shares vest. The typical maximum incentive payment for executive directors of FT-SE 100 companies that use this type of plan in lieu of executive share options is about 100% of salary.

Long-Term Cash Plan

Long-term cash plans tend to operate in much the same way as performance share plans, but the potential payout will be expressed as a percentage of salary. Performance may be measured relative to comparable companies, against the plan, or against absolute performance improvements. The main difference between this type of plan and a restricted share plan is that there is no link between the final award and the change in share price over the performance period. The maximum payment under these plans is similar to performance share plans, but with no additional benefit from any increase in share price over the period.

Share Appreciation Rights (Phantom Share Options)

With this type of plan an executive is granted an "option" over an agreed number of phantom or "notional" shares. When the option is exercised, the executive receives a cash payment equal to the increase in share price between the date of grant and the date of exercise. This type of plan is often employed by companies that are unable to grant further share options to their senior executives because of constraints on share dilution.

Total Maximum Incentive Opportunity

In the FT-SE 100 industrial and service companies that have ceased to grant executive share options, the typical maximum incentive opportunity (from both annual and long-term incentive plans) is about 140% of salary. In FT-SE 100 companies that still use executive share options in addition to a long-term performance share plan or a deferred annual bonus plan, the maximum incentive opportunity is about 105% of salary excluding any gain from executive share options.

Pensions

About 90% of all companies participating in the 1999 Remuneration of Directors & Managers survey operate a company pension plan for their senior managers and directors. As Exhibit 19-7 indicates, in larger companies the pension plan is usually a defined benefit plan, while in smaller companies the defined contribution plan is more common. [Note: The RDM Survey defines smaller companies as those with annual revenues up to £50m, medium companies as having £51 to £500m in revenues, and larger companies as those with more than £500m in revenues. These size categories are used throughout this chapter.]

Exhibit 19-7. Type of Pension Plan—Parent Companies

		% of Positions	
	Smaller Companies	Medium Companies	Larger Companies
Defined Benefit Plan	41	66	97
Defined Contribution Plan	59	34	3

Source: *RDM U.K. April 1999*

Defined contribution plans are more common in smaller and medium-size companies partly because of concerns about the future costs of financing defined benefit arrangements. Under a defined contribution pension plan employer and employee contributions will be put in an investment fund. When the employee retires, the accumulated individual's fund can be used to purchase an annuity to provide an income stream in retirement.

Exhibit 19-8 lists the typical retirement age in companies that offer a defined benefit plan. At the main board director level about half the positions have a normal retirement age of 60 years; at the function head level only about one quarter of positions have a retirement age of 60, with the majority having a normal retirement age of 65 years.

Exhibit 19-8. Retirement Age—Parent Companies

		% of Positions	
	Main Board Director	Senior Function Head	Function Head
60 or under	50	42	26
61–64	19	26	22
65	31	32	52

Source: *RDM U.K. April 1999*

The majority of company pension plans require an employee contribution, as shown in Exhibit 19-9. This is usually somewhere between 5 and 6% of salary.

Exhibit 19-9. Requirement for Employee Contribution to Pension Plan

	% of Parent Companies		
	Smaller Companies	**Medium Companies**	**Larger Companies**
Contributory	74	84	77
Noncontributory	26	16	23

Source: *RDM U.K. April 1999*

Under defined benefit pension plan the accrual rate is one of the three key factors (along with years of service and final salary) in determining the size of any pension paid at retirement age. Exhibit 19-10 displays the typical number of years of service required at director or senior management level to achieve the maximum pension permitted by the Inland Revenue of two thirds of final pensionable earnings.

Regardless of company size, 20 years of service is the most common requirement from a top-level pension plan for collecting a maximum pension of two thirds of pensionable earnings. This indicates an accrual rate of 1/30th; in other words, a pension of 1/30th of final pensionable earnings will be provided for each year of pensionable service. For the majority of the management and professional population the typical accrual rate will be about 1/60th-requiring 40 years of service to achieve the maximum pension of two thirds of final salary.

Exhibit 19-10. Number of Years' Service for Maximum Pension—Defined Benefit Plans

	% of Positions at Director/Sr. Management Level		
Years of Service	**Smaller Companies**	**Medium Companies**	**Larger Companies**
20	62	64	74
21–30	19	21	13
31–39	0	4	0
40	19	11	13

Source: *Monks' Top Level Pension Practice Survey*

Earnings Cap

The earnings cap is the limitation introduced by the Finance Act 1989 on the amount of remuneration on which tax-efficient pension benefits may be accrued. The earnings cap is set at £90,600 for the tax year 1999/2000. The limitation applies to new members joining schemes after June 1989.

For example, a typical FT-SE 100 finance director with 20 years of service and a final salary of £250,000 could look forward to a maximum pension of around £165,000 from the company's final-salary pension plan. On the other hand, a capped finance director at the same salary who joined after June 1989 would be limited to a maximum pension from the company plan of two thirds of the current pensions earnings cap, or £60,400. This could be achieved after just five years of service.

Our research suggests that companies have introduced a variety of approaches to provide benefits above the earnings cap. One of the earliest approaches was for companies to provide an unfunded promise to capped executives regarding the provision of an income in retirement. Such arrangements have become known as Unfunded Unapproved Retirement Benefit Schemes (UURBS).

An increasing number of companies are moving away from an unfunded approach to a funded approach or a Funded Unapproved Retirement Benefit Scheme (FURBS). An alternative approach is for the company to provide a supplement to salary as compensation for future retirement benefits that will not be provided by the company for earnings above the cap.

Exhibit 19-11 summarizes the approaches companies have adopted both now and in the past. (The percentages in the table total more than 100% because companies may adopt more than one approach.)

Exhibit 19-11. Approaches to the Earnings Cap

	% of Companies	
	Existing Executives	**New Recruits**
Approved Plan Only	9	11
Unfunded Unapproved Retirement Benefit Scheme (UURBS)	52	48
Funded Unapproved Retirement Benefit Scheme (FURBS)	44	35
Salary Supplement	17	9
No Policy	4	7

Source: *Monks' Top Level Pension Practice Survey*

Although the table shows that UURBS are the most common approach for dealing with the earnings cap for both existing executives and new recruits, our discussions with companies indicate to us that more companies are considering funded arrangements or salary supplements.

Company Cars

Next to the provision of a company pension plan, the most valued component of the senior executive benefits package in the U.K. is the company car. The government's 1999 budget continued the trend of making the company car a less attractive benefit to employees. Proposed measures were announced that after April 2002 would:

- Remove any incentive to drive more business miles as a way to reduce the tax charge on company cars.
- Provide an incentive to both the employee and employer to choose fuel-efficient cars.
- Encourage manufacturers to produce cars with lower carbon dioxide emissions.
- Base the tax charge on the car's price and emission levels.

The government has invited comments on the proposed changes, but it seems likely that the company-car driver will face an increasing tax charge for driving the same level of car in the future.

In the meantime the taxation of company cars would be based on the list price of cars and annual business mileage, as shown in Exhibit 19-12, for cars that are less than four years old. Individuals are assessed at their highest marginal tax rate on the resultant tax charge shown in Exhibit 19-12.

Exhibit 19-12. Price of Cars and Annual Business Mileage

Business Miles	Tax Charge
Under 2,500	35% of list price of car
2,500 – 17,999	25% of list price of car
18,000 or more	15% of list price or car

In addition, for those who receive the benefit of company-provided fuel for private motoring, the tax charge on this benefit was increased by 20%.

This tax charge is scheduled to increase by a minimum of 20% per annum until 2002.

Nonetheless, as shown in Exhibit 19-13, a company car remains the norm for senior executives in companies of all sizes.

Exhibit 19-13. Company Provided Car—Parent Companies

	% of Positions		
	Smaller Companies	**Medium Companies**	**Larger Companies**
Main Board Director	85	91	85
Senior Head of Function	84	76	91
Head of Function	51	73	85

Source: *RDM U.K. 1999*

The benefit of a company car is further enhanced for most senior executives by the provision of company-subsidized fuel for private motoring, as shown in Exhibit 19-14. It is only in smaller companies that this is not a standard benefit at the level of senior head of function or function head.

Exhibit 19-14. Company Provided Fuel for Private Motoring—All Companies

	% of Positions		
	Smaller Companies	**Medium Companies**	**Larger Companies**
Main Board Director	84	90	89
Senior Head of Function	41	90	83
Head of Function	41	74	72

Source: *RDM U.K. 1999*

Cash Allowances

About 72% of companies now offer a choice of a car or cash allowance in lieu of a company car. As shown in Exhibit 19-15, the availability of cash allowances increased rapidly in the years 1992 to 1995.

Exhibit 19-15. Cash Allowances in Lieu of a Company Car

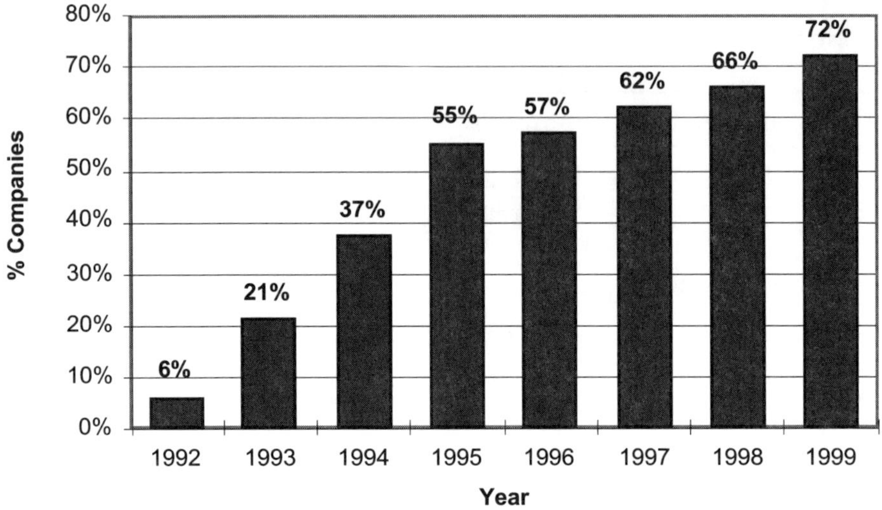

Our research indicates that although about 72% of companies now offer a cash allowance in lieu of a company car, the number of executives taking up the offer is not large, in most instances less than 20% of those eligible (see Exhibit 19-16).

Exhibit 19-16. Cash Allowance Take-Up Rates—All Companies

Take-up Rate (% of Individuals)	% of Positions Directors	Senior Managers	Middle Manager
Nil	44	30	7
1–10	14	30	45
11–20	13	12	18
21–30	9	9	10
31+	20	19	20

Source: *Monks' Company Car Policy*

Other Elements of the Benefits Package

Notice Periods

Exhibit 19-17 summarizes notice periods for main board directors, senior heads of function, and senior managers in parent companies of all sizes.

Exhibit 19-17. Notice Periods—Parent Companies

	% of Positions		
Notice Period	**Main Board Director**	**Senior Head of Function**	**Senior Manager**
3 months or less	3	13	34
3–11 months	12	29	50
12 months	37	44	15
13–23 months	3	4	1
24 months	43	10	-
25–35 months	-	-	-
36 months	2	-	-

Source: *RDM U.K. April 1999*

At the main board level in the majority of larger companies, notice periods remain at 24 months, despite the following recommendations of the Combined Code on Corporate Governance, which forms an annex to the Listing Rules of The London Stock Exchange:

There is a strong case for setting notice or contract periods at, or reducing them to, one year or less. Boards should set this as an objective, but they should recognize that it may not be possible to achieve it immediately (paragraph B.1.7).

At the level of senior function head in larger companies the typical notice period is 12 months, with a notice period of about six months at the senior management level.

Vacation Entitlement

Vacation entitlement for the majority of senior executives in the U.K. remains at 25 days per year. However, about a quarter of main board directors in larger companies have an annual entitlement of 30 days per year.

Private Medical Insurance

Despite increasing premium costs, the majority of companies appear to be continuing to offer private medical insurance coverage to their senior executives, which in most cases covers the employee and dependent family members.

Life Insurance

Life insurance provided by the company is a standard part of most senior executive remuneration packages. The level of coverage is typically four times salary.

Permanent Health Insurance

The majority of senior executives are provided with permanent health insurance. In most cases this will provide a benefit of 50 to 75% of salary or prospective pension.

The Future

Despite the government's increasing uneasiness about the rising level of executive compensation, for some companies it is the most effective way to remain competitive in a tight job market. Some U.K. companies are seeking to recruit talent from outside the U.K.—frequently from the United States. To attract and retain executives from overseas, the compensation will almost inevitably have to match or exceed that available in the job seeker's home country.

The effects in the U.K. are already being felt. From our analyses we have observed that the typical maximum annual bonus potential in FT-SE 100 companies for main board directors has increased from around 40% of base salary in the early part of the decade to around 50% today.

We have observed a similar increase in the potential maximum rewards from long-term incentive arrangements. It should be noted, however, that because of the performance criteria that apply to many plans, only those in the most successful companies are likely to receive the maximum awards. As more executives are locked into long-term performance plans in which conditional share holdings are forfeited if he or she leaves the company before the end of the performance period, the premium required for an executive to move may well increase. Consequently, "golden hellos"—which compensate for the loss of not only an annual bonus but also shareholdings in long-term incentive plans—may well become more common.

In the past, most executives sold the shares they purchased through the exercise of a share option; the same practice frequently applies to shares acquired through a performance share plan. Currently only a handful of U.K. companies have target share holdings for their most senior executives—an increasingly common requirement in the United States. From our consulting experience we are aware of a number of U.K. companies that are considering a target share holding whereby continued participation in a long-term plan is dependent on a certain percentage of shares being retained after shares in long-term plan vest.

A further issue for many companies and executives is pension provision. The pensions earnings cap usually rises each year in line with the Retail Price Index, yet salaries are known to be running at a higher rate. As a result, the number of employees who will be affected by the cap will increase.

Clearly, international compensation practices and U.K. pension legislation are likely to have a significant impact on senior executive remuneration in the U.K. as we enter the 21st century. The one event that could alter this picture would be a major upheaval in the world economy; the resulting recession could have a strong effect on compensation in the U.K. and abroad.

CHAPTER 20

AUSTRALIA AND NEW ZEALAND

GRAHAM O'NEILL,
KIM NEUHOLD, AND
ANDREW MACKMURDIE

Australia and New Zealand share many common social and political factors relevant to the determination and administration of exempt and nonexempt pay and benefits. For example, up till the late 1980s, each country had a strongly centralized tripartite process for nonexempt pay determination, providing for employer, government, and trade union representation. Under these arrangements, it is not surprising that, until recently, the emphasis in pay and benefit determination in each country focused on relative work value and universality of benefits as primary issues of the day. Similarly, both nations have had periods in which the top marginal rates of personal income tax encouraged the delivery of benefits to exempt employees—particularly management and executives—in lieu of direct compensation. During the 1980s, this led to the prominent usage of company-provided pensions (superannuation) and motor vehicles as major benefits to senior professional and management employees.

The issue of high marginal tax rates explains why Australia and New Zealand—as distinct from other Western economies—have generally adopted a compensation packaging approach to exempt compensation. In both countries, this is generally referred to as total employment cost, or, more simply, TEC. The areas in which Australia and New Zealand are individually unique are in those practices directly affected by government policy and legislation. This includes pay and benefits issues subject to industrial relations resolution, pensions, and the general taxation impact on benefits and perquisites.

Compensation management between local and multinational companies does not differ substantially, except for issues relating to the location of policy decision making. However, U.S. and European companies need to be aware of the prevalence of compensation packaging, as well as the widespread inclusion of motor vehicles (particularly in Australia) commencing at senior professional and middle-management positions.

Exhibit 20-1. Economic Indicators: Australia and New Zealand

	Australia 1997	Australia 1998	New Zealand 1997	New Zealand 1998
Gross Domestic Product	2.8%	4.0%	4.2%	3.6%
Inflation (Consumer Price Index)	0.3%	0.7%	1.8%	1.3%
Unemployment Rate	9.0%	8.6%	6.5%	7.1%

Regional Economic Indicators

Exhibit 20-1 shows the key economic indicators for Australia and New Zealand for the last two financial years. Both are significant traders within Asia, and the current economic crisis was a major factor for both countries in 1997 and 1998. Low commodity prices have particularly affected Australian resource companies, and both currencies have deteriorated in value against the U.S. dollar and major European currencies. While economic growth has generally slowed, New Zealand has technically been in recession since June 1998. Local stock market fluctuations are similar to general global trends and are particularly influenced by New York and Tokyo.

There are three factors common to Australia and New Zealand that have influenced compensation and benefits planning over the past decade and a half:

1. Introduction of fringe benefit taxation
2. Changes to the previously centralized systems of pay determination for nonexempt employees
3. Substantial deregulation of the respective economies

In each case, the original initiatives were taken in New Zealand and subsequently adopted by Australia. Despite the significant overlap, the differences between the two countries make it necessary to discuss each within in its own social and legislative context.

Australia

Pay Determination

The dramatic changes in the legislative framework of Australian wages determination originated in the substantial deregulation of the economy during the mid- to late 1980s. Under the previous protectionist regime, wages were determined on a national or an industry-wide basis through formal advocacy by the government and employer and the union representatives to the federal Conciliation and Arbitration Commission. The union case was often supported by militant action.

The current Workplace Relations Act legitimizes negotiations at the enterprise level to agreements on terms and conditions jointly beneficial to employer and employee. The inclusion of unions in this process is no longer mandatory, and employees are able to enter into individual contracts (known as Australian workplace agreements). Importantly, the legislation allows for negotiation of virtually all practices and policies affecting the employment contract. This has led to the introduction of fundamental human resource initiatives to establish desired work culture, communication, performance management, and reward systems. The consequent collapse of traditional work demarcation has further facilitated the introduction of employee multiskilling, and more progressive enterprise agreements have sought to roll base pay rates and allowances (particularly those related to overtime and shift work) into an annualized salary. As a result, the incidence of individual, team, and enterprise performance rewards is increasing.

Components of Pay

Base pay remains the foundation for most employees; however, more than 50% of organizations now use a TEC concept at the management level. This is widespread in large private-sector corporations, particularly within the financial services sector. Nevertheless, the public sector and smaller firms are increasing flexibility in compensation delivery to exempt employees.

The TEC approach involves determining a total compensation "budget," with employee choice determining the delivery. On average, some 70% is taken as base pay; the remainder is used to fund motor vehicles (usually leased), pension contributions, and other benefits such as medical insurance or low-interest loans. The compensation budget includes fringe benefit taxation (FBT) costs associated with the provision of benefits to ensure a cost-neutral outcome to the employer.

Apart from performance-based pay programs, additional payments to the TEC are uncommon. The declining number of firms using a traditional "pay plus benefits" approach often provide other benefits, usually dependent on employee level and industry. However, under the Australian FBT

Exhibit 20-2. Australia: Common Employee Benefits

Payment	Description	Prevalence
Annual Leave Loading	17.5% (or occasionally more) of base salary paid for the four weeks of annual leave (vacation) each year. Some organizations have a ceiling based on the highest salary level of an industrial award. Over recent years, many organizations have absorbed this payment into base salary.	59% of organizations provide as a separate payment
Allowances	Tend to be industry, site, or work specific. Can include cash allowances for dirty or dangerous working conditions, for working at remote sites, or for using various types of equipment. In some industries, medical insurance or loan interest subsidies are provided in place of cash allowances.	Varies depending on industry
Overtime	For office and factory workers, practice varies considerably, with the following alternatives all prevalent: • not paid (provision included in base pay) • time off in lieu • payment for some or all hours worked—typically time-and-a-half or double time Overtime is not usually paid above line supervisor or staff equivalent level.	40% of office workers; 50–60% of factory workers
Shift Allowances/ Differentials	Paid for afternoon and night shifts based on shift loading (typically 15% for afternoon and 20–30% for night shift) and the roster across weekends and public holidays.	Varies depending on industry

legislation, superannuation and company-provided automobiles are the only tax-effective benefits. Common benefits provided by "pay plus benefits" employers are detailed in Exhibit 20-2.

Exhibit 20-3. Australia: Annual Increases—Base Salary and Total Employment Cost

Employee Level	Base Salary	TEC
Staff and Professional Levels	3.8%	3.8%
Middle Management	4.1%	4.3%
Senior Management	8.0%	6.4%
Chief Executives	10.9%	8.8%

Source: *Hay Remuneration Comparison Quarterly Report, May 1998.*

Exhibit 20-4. Australia: Consumer Price Index and Base Salary Increases 1994–1998

Year	Consumer Price Index (year to June 30)	Average Base Salary Increase (year to May 31)
1994	1.8%	3.0%
1995	3.2%	3.6%
1996	4.2%	4.9%
1997	0.3%	5.5%
1998	0.7%	4.0%

Source: *Australian Bureau of Statistics and Hay Remuneration Comparison Quarterly Report, May 1998.*

Salary Planning and Pay Programs

The majority of medium to large firms use traditional grading or banding structure for salary administration purposes. Broadbanding, skill-based pay, and other "new generation" approaches are in use but not widespread.

Compensation reviews (using either base salary or TEC) are typically annual, with January, July, and October the most common review months. Some organizations undertake interim reviews to address any "hot spots" or market premiums for specific job functions. A single percentage figure covering cost-of-living and merit increases is generally used for review planning. Compensation increases from the Hay Group's 1998 remuneration surveys are shown in Exhibit 20-3.

Exhibit 20-4 compares inflation rates for Australia (as measured by the Consumer Price Index) with annual base salary increases over the last five years.

Exhibit 20-5 shows current income tax rates for Australian residents. Increases in the tax-free threshold ($5,400) apply to taxpayers with dependent children. In addition to the rates shown, a 1.5% Medicare levy applies

Exhibit 20-5. Australia: Income Tax Rates

Taxable Income (Column 1) A$	Tax on Column 1	% on Excess (Marginal Rate)
5,400	Nil	20
20,700	3,060	34
38,000	8,942	43
50,000	14,102	47

on incomes above approximately $14,000. This increases to 2.5% for high-income earners without private hospital insurance. In October 1998, the liberal/national coalition government was returned to office on a platform of tax reform, including introduction of a goods and services tax. These changes are due for implementation in July 2000, but a hostile Senate may force amendments to the proposed legislation.

Performance Management

The issue of performance management is a "hot button" for line and human resource executives in the private and public sectors. In this respect, Australian practices mirror those in the United States, the United Kingdom, and other Western economies. In particular, there is a growing interest in implementing a balanced performance management process focusing on end results and requisite behaviors to achieve more sustainable business outcomes. The application of competencies in assessing job performance and as a basis for other human resource processes is growing in Australian organizations. (See O'Neill and Doig, 1997, for a comprehensive review of the use of competencies in Australian human resource management.)

Performance management systems play an increasing role in pay decisions for fixed-pay and short-term incentive plans. More recent incentive plans indicate a shift away from the sole dependence on financial measures, and they typically incorporate a combination of performance measures that include quantitative (e.g., organization and business unit financial performance) and qualitative outcomes (e.g., behavioral ratings and organizational climate measures).

Broad-based long-term incentive plans for all employees are less common in Australia than short-term incentives are. Recent legislation provides a $1,000 tax exemption available for broad-based employee stock plans; this has prompted wide interest (and application) by large corporations. Plan designs usually allow for interest-free loans for employees to purchase company stock or restricted stock award plans in which shares are purchased and held in a trust for the employee's future benefit.

Share option plans are common at the senior executive level in large companies; approximately 50% of organizations provide such plans to their executives. Because of the appointment of several high-profile U.S. executives to CEO positions in Australia, the number of options issued has escalated rapidly over the last five years. Non-equity-based long-term incentive plans are less common and offered by less than 20% of organizations, according to available survey data.

Benefits and Perquisites

As discussed previously, for many employees, the majority of benefits and perquisites are provided and costed within the employee's compensation package. For organizations using "pay plus benefits," the benefits are in addition to fixed pay and are provided at employer expense, including any fringe benefit taxation.

Superannuation. Superannuation is the most prevalent benefit and has been compulsory under government legislation since 1992. The Superannuation Guarantee Scheme (SGC) requires all employers to contribute a prescribed minimum level of superannuation support for employees. The SGC is currently set at 7% of the employee's average earnings, but it rises to 8% in 2000 and to 9% in 2002.

Employers can contribute to any complying superannuation fund; employee choice of funds will be compulsory from July 1, 2000. Benefits from superannuation funds must be preserved within the superannuation system until retirement, at which time they can be taken as a lump-sum payment or converted into a pension stream. Taxation on withdrawal from the superannuation system depends on factors such as the individual's age, pay level, period of contribution, and method of withdrawal (lump sum or pension).

The superannuation fund deducts a concessional rate of tax from contributions (15% for most employees, 30% for high-income earners). About half of the organizations using a TEC approach include superannuation in their compensation packages; the remainder provide superannuation at employer cost.

In practice, the majority of large employers run their own superannuation funds—either defined-contribution (accumulation) or defined-benefit plans. The SGC legislation has seen a decline in the prevalence of defined-benefit plans (although existing members can usually remain in these plans), with most new employees joining a defined-contribution plan. Other defined-contribution funds are run by the union movement for specific industries (to allow for portability of employee entitlements) and by commercial fund managers.

Life insurance and permanent disability insurance are typically offered within the superannuation fund. These are paid for by the employer or have the cost of the premium deducted from the account balance. Australia's superannuation law is quite complex and has significant taxation implications for employers and employees. For these reasons, specialist advice is critical.

Leave Entitlements. Annual leave (vacation) entitlement is four weeks fully paid per annum for all employees regardless of length of service. A minority of organizations provide an additional week to their most senior executives or to employees who have had a long period of service (e.g., 25 years). An extra one to two weeks may accrue for shift workers or those working at remote sites. The value of accrued but unused annual leave is paid out upon termination of employment. It is important to note that the pay rate for annual leave is the rate at which the leave is taken, not when it was accumulated.

Sick leave entitlements vary but are typically between 8 and 12 fully paid days per annum, with unused days accumulating. Accrued but unused sick leave is not typically paid out upon termination.

Long-service leave is an additional period of paid leave awarded to employees with a long period of service with one company. Legislated requirements vary between the Australian states, and some organizations provide more generous provisions. The most common entitlement is three months' leave after 15 years of service. A pro rata amount is payable if the employee leaves the company after a minimum 10 years' service.

Unpaid maternity leave of 12 months is a legislative requirement, and the employee has the right to return to the same or equivalent position. A minority of public-sector organizations and large corporations provide a period of paid leave (typically six weeks) within the 12-month period. Some organizations allow the father to take up to 12 months' unpaid leave, provided that he is the primary caregiver.

Health/Medical Insurance. Australia has a universal health care scheme (Medicare) that provides free public hospital and medical treatment to all Australian residents. It is funded through the taxation system, primarily by the Medicare levy. Private health insurance is available for treatment in private hospitals and for ancillary services such as dental, optical, and physiotherapy. Approximately 25% of organizations provide a private health insurance benefit to at least some employees; however, only about 12% of the employee population is covered.

Company Cars. Company-provided motor vehicles are extremely common in Australia (at and above senior professional level), whether included as part of a remuneration package or in addition to base salary. Although the tax advantage for providing a vehicle instead of salary is less than it was previously, there is still some tax benefit in an employer-provided vehicle. Past practices have led to an established expectation that a vehicle will be provided for senior management and executive positions in organizations.

Vehicles are either purchased by the company for the employee's use, leased by the company, or leased by the employee (in which case, the lease is assigned to the company through a "novated lease agreement"). The novated lease option allows employees to choose any type of vehicle, but they retain responsibility for disposing of the vehicle at the end of the lease.

Other Benefits. Perquisites other than company cars are now uncommon because of the FBT. Some organizations provide "status"-type items, such as club memberships, to senior employees when there is a perceived business benefit to the organization. Others provide benefits related to their industry (e.g., discounts on company products).

Employment Law

Formal employment contracts are prevalent for senior executives and increasingly so for lower-level nonexempt employees. Contracts for senior executives are typically designed to protect both parties in regard to issues of role clarity, tenure, and stability of the senior management team and to impose a restrictive covenant on an executive's postemployment activities. Individual contracts for lower-level staff are a result of the federal government's policy to move away from centralized national or industry awards. The majority of employees between these two levels are not covered by a formal legal contract. Typical practice is to write a letter of offer setting out terms and conditions for employment.

Unless specified in a contract or an industrial award, notice periods for employee-initiated termination of employment relate to the pay period (i.e., one week's notice is required for weekly paid employees, one month for monthly paid). The situation is more complex for employer-initiated termination. Unfair dismissal legislation requires employers to have legally defensible reasons for termination. For example, dismissal for poor performance requires the employer to document performance counseling and to allow the employee appropriate time for performance improvement.

Redundancy termination (i.e., abolition of the position) attracts additional termination payments. The amount varies depending on the industry and any industrial award or company practice. A typical amount is four weeks' pay in lieu of notice, plus two additional weeks for each year of service.

Employees' rights are protected under federal industrial relations legislation and under varying provisions in the states. Minimum wages in most industries are set by enterprise agreements and awards; the federal government legislates a "safety net" minimum wage for employees not covered by an award or enterprise agreement.

Foreign nationals wishing to work in Australia must have either a resident visa or a temporary visa, which includes the right to work.

New Zealand

Pay Determination

Historically, the individual employment relationship in New Zealand was based on common law, with pay determination largely driven by national settlements in key collective bargained documents. As mentioned previously, New Zealand led the trans-Tasman move away from centralized pay determination when its national legislature adopted the Employment Contracts Act (ECA) in 1991. The employment relationship is now defined by enterprise-based contracts, with collective bargaining focused on the needs of local business units as individual enterprises.

Coupled with the introduction of the ECA was New Zealand's earlier introduction of a fringe benefit tax and its own tax equalization legislation. As with Australia, this means that the provision of benefits (e.g., cars, low-interest loans, and subsidized meals) now has no tax advantage; this has resulted in a steady move toward "cashing up" compensation packages to a TEC approach and to annualized salaries in traditional blue-collar areas.

Components of Pay

It is difficult to define components of pay in the New Zealand setting at this time because of the steady transition of compensation policies. As with

Australia—although at a somewhat slower pace—the move is toward a TEC figure, with some degree of employee choice between cash and benefits. New Zealand's finance sector is now almost totally TEC driven, and smaller professional and service-related organizations have increasingly been following the trend. The manufacturing sector is slowly removing its large range of work-related benefits in its traditional hourly paid and salaried workforces.

Again, as with Australia, the two benefits that linger are employer-provided motor vehicles and superannuation. The motor vehicle has long been an entrenched status symbol; however, with the growing opportunity for cashing this benefit out, status is slowly giving way to cash.

The superannuation debate is causing more difficulty. Organizations have found it difficult to move away from a traditional (if not paternal) cradle-to-grave employment approach. However, this attitude is declining as more flexible superannuation options are introduced by insurance companies. Many firms are considering whether to retain their superannuation plans, traditionally offered only to salaried employees, and some have ceased offering superannuation to new employees. In this environment, employees are generally accepting the fact that they have more personal responsibility for their own postemployment financial security.

Apart from variable pay programs, additional payments consist almost solely of work-related practices such as shift work loadings. These continue to attract additional compensation and benefits (e.g., additional vacation leave).

Salary Planning and Pay Programs

The majority of large organizations use pay grades for compensation administration, but some companies experiment with broadbanded pay structures. Because of the small size of most New Zealand firms, traditional work value methods such as job evaluation remain prevalent. Some larger firms are moving toward broadbanded pay structures. New approaches to pay (e.g., skill-based pay) are experimented with, but it is too early to gauge their success.

New Zealand's move to enterprise- and individual-based remuneration practices has resulted in market pressures, company performance, and individual contribution as the main determinants of pay. Cost-of-living adjustments now play a minor role, except in collective bargaining situations with external bargaining agents (typically trade unions). The majority of firms

**Exhibit 20-6. New Zealand: Annual Increases—
Base Salary and Total Employment**

Employee Level	Base Salary	Fixed Package
Staff	4.5	2.0
Professional	4.0	3.4
Middle Management	3.7	4.0
Executive/Senior Management	—	5.1

conduct annual pay reviews, with January, April, July, and October being the most common months.

Exhibit 20-6 shows compensation movements in terms of base salary and fixed-package (TEC) increases for the year ended September 1998. Exhibit 20-7 compares movements in the Consumer Price Index with base salary and fixed-package movements for the period 1994 through 1998. Current income tax rates are shown in Exhibit 20-8. It should be noted that 1999 is an election year and these rates may change if a Labor-led coalition wins office.

Performance Management

Issues in performance management for New Zealand organizations are largely identical to Australia. There is a growing realization that properly constructed and communicated performance management systems can affect change in behavior and performance. Although variable, performance-based pay schemes

**Exhibit 20-7. New Zealand: Consumer Price Index
and Remuneration Increases**

Year	Consumer Price Index	Base Salary Movement	Fixed-Package Movement
1994	1.3%	1.0%	1.4%
1995	4.0%	3.5%	4.0%
1996	2.2%	4.3%	4.5%
1997	1.8%	4.9%	5.1%
1998	1.3%	4.0%	3.4%

Exhibit 20-8. New Zealand: Income Tax Rates

Taxable Income ($)	Tax Rate (%)
0–34,200	20.0
34,201–38,000	22.875
Over 38,000	33.0

have previously been largely restricted to executive and management employees—with participation by sales and some production staff in some firms—there is a growth in target-based, short-term incentives, gain-sharing schemes, and long-term incentive plans.

Benefits and Perquisites

The move to cashing out benefits has seen their slow disappearance from the New Zealand compensation landscape. When employer-provided benefits are provided, they are typically restricted to motor vehicles, superannuation, medical insurance, and additional vacation.

Superannuation. New Zealand provides a universal taxation-funded superannuation scheme. In addition, many firms have traditionally provided their own staff superannuation plans (either defined contribution or defined benefit). Most company-provided schemes apply only to exempt employees, and the union movement has not been active in providing nonexempt schemes, primarily because of the scattered nature and size of the New Zealand workforce and the view that the government-funded scheme is adequate. The majority of plans provide for some form of death and disability insurance.

Leave Entitlements. Statutory minimum annual paid leave entitlement is 15 days. Many companies provide an additional five days per annum based on status, service, and industry market practice. Middle-management roles and above usually receive 20 days' annual leave automatically, and it is common practice for the statutory minimum to apply to other employees. Many organizations with a history of collective bargaining (e.g., manufacturing, public sector) still provide long-service leave. Entitlements vary and range from an additional, one-off 15 days at 10 years to 30 days at 25 years.

Sick leave entitlements vary and depend on the negotiation skills of the bargaining agent or individual. The statutory minimum is five days per annum, but some employers provide more and may allow nonused leave to be accumulated.

A continuous period of 14 weeks' unpaid maternity leave is provided by legislation under the Parental and Employment Protection Act. This may be extended to a maximum of 52 weeks under certain conditions. Parental leave may be taken by either partner. Paid parental leave is at the employer's discretion, but it is rare.

Medical Insurance. New Zealand has a universal taxpayer-funded health system; nevertheless, many companies still provide some form of medical benefit. When firms operate a TEC approach, employees may "buy" back a medical insurance cover and take the benefit of employer discounts. Private health insurance is a major benefit in New Zealand.

Company Cars. Company-provided vehicles are no longer an issue for firms with TEC compensation. For firms operating the traditional "pay plus benefits" system, the provision of a vehicle remains an entrenched benefit for middle and senior management. In general, the cash equivalent is replacing the vehicle. It is envisaged that, under the current taxation regime, this benefit will disappear in the next two to five years.

Employment Law

The New Zealand labor relations climate has undergone significant change since the implementation of the ECA. The employment relationship is far more contractual and provides greater protection for exempt employees than it previously did. Legislation governing strike actions has also led to a less disruptive work climate. However, this has been countered by a period of dramatic change in the private and public sectors, culminating in increasing levels of insecurity and uncertainty.

The courts have provided significant precedence in stating that only the matters mentioned in the contract or in statute are enforceable. For example, if the contractual document omits mention of redundancy, then redundancy payments are not required. Similarly, probationary periods may be enforceable if provided in the employment contract. The more popular approach is to accept new hires on a six-month contract, with an undertaking for confirmation of employment depending on performance.

Employment termination processes have also been clarified by requiring specification in the employment contract. Typical notice periods vary from one week at the hourly paid level to one month for salaried staff and two to six months for senior executives. When termination is involuntary, the minimum acceptable procedure is set out in the ECA and takes precedence regardless of the merits of the termination. The right to any form of severance pay is dictated by the employment contract, with no guidance established in the legislation. Redundancy arrangements are wide ranging, but average payments are four weeks' pay for the first year of service and two weeks' pay for every year thereafter, to a maximum, plus payout of unused sick leave. This is in addition to unused holidays, superannuation, and normal notice periods.

The New Zealand government has established minimum wage legislation based on a percentage of the average wage and subject to annual review.

Other than Australians, most foreign nationals require a work permit before entering paid employment. These are generally easy to obtain when international transfers occur or when the employer can show that there are no New Zealand nationals with sufficient skills prepared to undertake the work offered.

In recent years, New Zealand has introduced or strengthened a number of statutes related to human resource management issues. These include health and safety, privacy, human rights, and accident compensation.

Regional Organization Issues Affecting Australia and New Zealand

Organization structures in the region differ considerably depending on ownership and industry, but they do not differ markedly from overseas practices. There has been a flattening of organizational structures in recent years, particularly affecting middle-management layers. Major differences between local and foreign-owned companies center on board structures (local companies typically have a majority of nonexecutive directors) and reporting relationships (foreign companies often have local managers reporting to an overseas division rather than to a local CEO).

Recruitment might be expected to be relatively easy, given the high unemployment rates in both countries. However, the bulk of the long-term unemployment is unskilled and semiskilled labor. Consequently, recruitment of skilled and professional employees remains competitive. Skill shortages tend to be cyclical, with information technology professionals currently being in shortest supply.

Australian and New Zealand employees are typically less mobile than their U.S. counterparts. This is primarily because the major business centers in each country are the two largest cities—Melbourne and Sydney in Australia and Auckland and Wellington in New Zealand. Nevertheless, senior professionals and managers expect to move within the respective country or offshore for career development. Both countries consist largely of a respective national labor market at the professional and management levels, with little constant variation between cities.

Standard workweeks for office-based staff are typically between 35 and 40 hours, Monday to Friday. Operational staff in manufacturing, mining, and primary industry organizations work different hours, and rotating shifts (including 12-hour shifts) are common. Flexitime (the ability to work flexible hours at the employee's discretion) and rostered days off (one day off per month or per fortnight) are less common now than they were in the 1980s, but they still exist in some public-sector organizations. Management and professional staff typically work longer hours than the standard week indicates, with 50-hour weeks not uncommon.

Vacations are based around the December/January summer period and school holiday periods. The majority of businesses in the region shut down over the Christmas and New Year period. Australia has seven national public holidays plus an additional two or three that vary among the states; New Zealand has 11 statutory holidays.

International human resources trends are followed closely within the region, and practitioners generally have a strong willingness to adapt and customize overseas practices. This is particularly so with executive compensation trends. Several leading Australia corporations now have CEOs and senior executives from the United States, and this has led to strong interest and adoption of equity-based long-term incentive programs.

Further Reading

Australian Economic Indicators. Canberra: Australian Bureau of Statistics, published monthly.

Australian Master Tax Guide 1998. Sydney: CCH Australia, 1998.

Compensation Reports 1998. Auckland, New Zealand: Hay Group, 1998.

Executive Reward Service Report 1998. Melbourne: Hay Group, 1998.

New Zealand Inland Revenue Tax Guides.

O'Neill, G., and Doig, D. "Definition and Use of Competencies by Australian Organizations: A Survey of HR Practitioners," *American Compensation Association Journal 6*, no. 4 (1997): 45-56.

O'Neill, G., and Kramar, R., eds. *Australian Human Resource Management: Current Trends in Management Practice.* Vol. 1. Melbourne: Woodslane, 1995.

O'Neill, G., and Kramar, R., eds. *Australian Human Resource Management: Current Trends in Management Practice.* Vol. 2. Melbourne: Woodslane, 1998.

Performance Recognition Report 1997. Auckland, New Zealand: Hay Group, 1997.

Remuneration Comparison Quarterly Report May 1998. Melbourne: Hay Group, 1998.

Short Term Incentives Report 1998/99. Melbourne: Hay Group, 1998.

Year Book Australia 1998. Canberra: Australian Bureau of Statistics, 1998.

Australia & New Zealand Remuneration Practices.

CHAPTER 21

ASIA

HEATHER BOWKER

Introduction

This chapter covers eight countries in the Asian region: Korea, Taiwan, Hong Kong, the Philippines, Thailand, Malaysia, Singapore, and Indonesia. India will also be mentioned briefly. (China and Japan are discussed in separate chapters.)

It is a challenge to drive common themes across Asia given its diverse mix of social, political, and economic environments. Some simple demographics underscore the differences. The 1997 gross national product (GNP) per capita (excluding India) ranged from just over US$1,000 in Indonesia and the Philippines to over US$24,000 in Hong Kong and US$30,000 in Singapore (see Exhibit 21-1). Singapore has a population of only 3 million people; Hong Kong has 6 million; and the other six countries range from 20 million to 200 million (in Indonesia, the fourth

Exhibit 21-1. Comparison of Gross National Product (GNP) per Capita

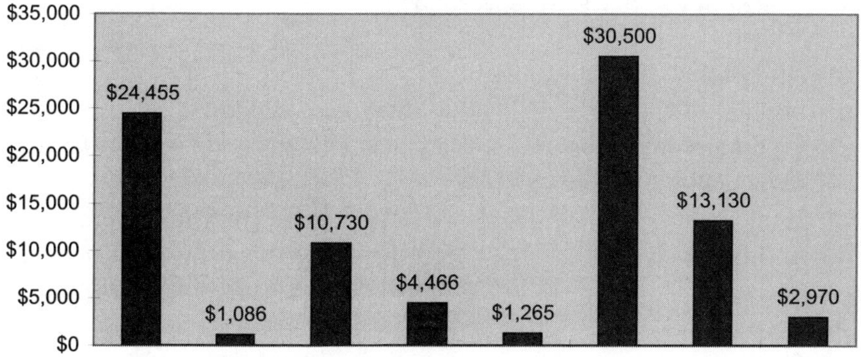

Source: *Asiaweek*

largest population in the world after China, India, and the United States). The West tends to forget that "Asia" is a region embracing myriad cultures, languages, and religions.

For those of us who have tracked the success and growth of the Asian region during the last few decades, the 1998 economic crisis (which actually began in 1997 in Thailand) represents a turning point in the region's history. The implications of this crisis are far reaching, possibly permanent, since the downturn involves fundamental restructuring of business operations in most countries. The manufacturing sector, in particular, will ultimately be reduced to a fraction of its former size.

Before the 1998 economic recession that took so much of the world by surprise, Asia was for nearly two decades the jewel in the crown of many multinationals' global expansion strategies. The region offered the following distinct advantages:

- Untapped markets and high consumer demand
- Reasonable labor costs, with flexibility in employment practices
- A young, vibrant, generally well educated workforce displaying a strong work ethic, eagerness to learn, high ambition, and capacity for change
- Technological advancement that has surpassed that of many other regions
- Widespread use of the English language (taught in schools, spoken broadly on the street, and adopted as the business language in many countries)

The biggest challenges facing multinationals doing business in Asia during most of the 1990s were as follows:

- Building employee loyalty (at a time when "job-hopping" was commonplace, especially in the multinational community)
- Finding scarce talent and specialized skills in certain sectors (e.g., in the technology industry)
- Implementing more "progressive" Westernized human resources programs and pay practices (e.g., pay-for-performance in terms of merit-based salary reviews, individualized incentives, and performance management)
- Dealing with the accelerating pace of political, economic, and social change

As this is being written, the economic crisis in Asia has captured the attention of the business community and media worldwide. It is beyond the scope of this book to analyze in any detail the economic factors leading up to the crisis. We can point out, however, that among the most notable factors leading to this deflationary spiral was excess capacity, which arose from a focus on aggressive growth and market share expansion rather than profitability. This focus on growth at the expense of profitability has resulted in a steadily falling return on capital investments during the last 20 years.

The impact of the economic crisis is most evident in the once overheated economies of Thailand, Korea, and Indonesia; it is less evident (so far) in countries such as Taiwan and Singapore, where companies have generally been more interested in managing the bottom line (profits) rather than the top line (revenues). Lack of fiscal discipline in corporate borrowing, the laissez-faire approach of many governments, and the region's inexperience with global financial markets have further exacerbated the problems.

Hong Kong has had an additional challenge: Since 1983, the Hong Kong dollar has been pegged to the U.S. dollar (the exchange rate has been fixed at HK$7.8 to US$1). While this pegging was intended to protect Hong Kong's currency by tying it to a stronger one, one negative consequence has been that Hong Kong has become less competitive in the Asian region (on which it depends for much of its trade). In particular, the construction, manufacturing, retail, and tourist industries have been badly hit. Hong Kong exports are viewed as overpriced in relation to comparable products from other parts of the world.

Reports from the International Labour Organization (ILO) indicate that 1998 levels of unemployment across Southeast Asia are two to three times their comparable rates in 1996, with the exception of Singapore and Taiwan-the only countries with rates below 5%. Based on approximations from the ILO, the highest unemployment rates are in Indonesia (15%), the Philippines (13%), and Thailand (9%).

Responses to the crisis have varied. Malaysia recently introduced exchange controls in an attempt to insulate itself from the region's woes. Hong Kong has attempted government intervention in the local stock market. Meanwhile, the hardest-hit countries—Korea, Indonesia, and Thailand-are attempting to comply with the International Monetary Fund's (IMF) recovery strategy. There is some skepticism about whether these IMF strategies will make a difference; however, some initial signs of economic recovery are evident in Korea and Thailand. Indonesia's political upheavals, unfortunately, will further delay its economic recovery.

The impact of the economic crisis, although playing out somewhat differently in each country, has some common themes from an employment perspective:

- Organizational change has been dramatic and sweeping; major institutions are either closing down, undergoing acquisition, or massively restructuring and "rightsizing."
- Unemployment is accelerating: Companies are resorting to both voluntary and involuntary terminations; laws are being reworked to help keep businesses afloat (e.g., terminations are now permitted in Korea, and social security contribution increases in Thailand have been delayed). Few workers are seeking new jobs, let alone job-hopping.
- Western international assignees are being repatriated, perceived as too costly a burden on a region that is already under severe financial pressure. (We will, however, see an increase in transfers within the Asian region, as a redeployment of experienced talent to shore up the countries facing the keenest difficulties or as a strategy for retaining key talent within the company.)
- Salary increases are down. For the first time in recent history, annual salary increases are not keeping pace with inflation, and they have fallen significantly from levels seen in past years.
- Time-honored pay practices are under scrutiny: Traditional compensation approaches such as seniority-linked salary structures, additional months' pay in the form of "seasonal bonuses," and standard allowances unrelated to job performance are increasingly ripe for redesign.

In the midst of all the doom and gloom as compensation practices are being revamped, one bright aspect appears. Companies now have a key opportunity to redesign their compensation programs to drive pay according to job worth, contribution, and performance (whether at the company, business unit, and/or individual level). Bonus amounts will be tied much more closely to results rather than paid across the board as an entitlement.

Pay Determination

Although unionization is strong in some Asian countries (e.g., Indonesia, Korea, the Philippines, and Taiwan), unions play a less central role in collective bargaining in some of the more developed countries such as Hong Kong, Singapore, and Malaysia. Depending on the industry, pay is more often determined by supply and demand. Individual, not collective, negotiation is the norm. Although there is no specified minimum wage in these three countries, other countries have set minimum wages, either nationally, by industry, or by region.

The typical workweek throughout the region varies from 40 to 48 hours, with Saturday hours common in the manufacturing sector and often in the office as well. Typically, minimum premium rates for overtime work are mandated by either the applicable employment laws or industry agreements. Overtime premiums vary by country but tend to fall in the range of 25 to 50% of standard rates for weekday and Saturday working and 100% of standard rates for Sundays and public holidays.

Cash Compensation

Exhibit 21-2 summarizes some of the key elements of compensation in each country by amount, projected raises, hours, and paid time off.

Base pay is typically defined on an hourly or weekly basis for workers and on a monthly basis for salaried employees. The preference for defining

Exhibit 21-2. Asia—Key Human Resources Practices

Program	Hong Kong	Indonesia	Korea	Malaysia	Philippines	Singapore	Taiwan	Thailand
Currency	Hong Kong Dollar	Rupiah	Korean Won	Ringgit	Philippine Peso	Singapore Dollar	New Taiwan Dollar	Baht
Typical Number of Months Regularly Paid	13	13	16–18	13	13	13	14	13–14
Projected 1998 Salary Increase	5.5%	16.3%	5.5%	8.5%	12.2%	4.8%	7.6%	6.0%
Standard Working Hours per Week	40–44 hours	40 hours	44–48 hours	40–48 hours	Maximum 48 hours	40–44 hours	48 hours; Saturdays are workdays	Maximum 54 hours
Paid Time Off:								
Mandated Public Holidays	Minimum of 11 days	13 days	18 days	10 days	12 days	11 days	18 days	Minimum of 13 days
Typical Vacation Days	12–20 days based on service	12–24 days based on service	10–20 days based on service	15–23 days based on service	15–22 days based on service	12–21 days based on service	10–30 days based on service	10–15 days based on service

***Source:** Watson Wyatt*

monthly rather than annual pay relates to the prevalent practice of paying additional months' pay over and above 12 months. The custom of providing a 13th and sometimes a 14th month at Chinese New Year (typically late January or early February) or another religious event (in Indonesia) is well established across the region.

Hong Kong, Indonesia, Malaysia, and Singapore customarily pay 13 months' pay; Thailand pays 13 to 14 months; and Taiwan pays 14 months. Companies in Korea typically provide up to six additional months in the form of a seasonal bonus paid twice a year (similar to the Japanese practice). Unlike Europe and Latin America, the provision of additional months or partial months of pay designated as vacation or "holiday" bonuses is generally neither customary nor mandated in Asia.

Employees consider the additional months paid as deferred income and an entitlement, even though in most countries such bonuses are not mandated. To maintain local competitiveness, U.S. multinationals that have opted to maintain a 12-month pay schedule, regardless of local practice, need to ensure that they compare the total number of months regularly paid in other companies when establishing pay ranges. Even though a 12-month schedule will result in a relatively higher monthly base pay, clear communications are essential to assure employees that they have not "lost out" when they do not receive additional pay at Chinese New Year.

During times of prosperity or tight labor markets, there can be a significant upside provided in the form of additional "bonus" months being paid (as was seen, for example, in Taiwan's high-tech sector during the second half of the 1990s). Recent economic pressures are causing many employers to withhold the additional months of pay during the lean times as an effective cost-cutting strategy.

Cash allowances and fringe benefits or perquisites tend to vary by country and by industry. In the manufacturing sector, traditional allowances for lunches, transportation, uniforms, and so on are still seen. Korea offers an elaborate range of allowances relating to both job level (e.g., managers' allowance) and personal situation (e.g., family, housing).

In most Asian countries, executive-level perquisites are offered for reasons of tax efficiency, prestige, and increased quality of life. Typical examples are housing allowances, company cars (often chauffeur-driven for the top executive), social and sports club memberships, and business or first-class travel. Visiting representatives of U.S. multinationals, drilled in nondiscriminatory practices, can sometimes be surprised by such a conspicuous display of perquisites, but in Asia, these accoutrements are viewed as badges of success—lifestyle enhancements for the busy executive.

Tax rates vary across the region. Apart from the famously low 15% flat-rate tax in Hong Kong, most marginal tax rates on personal income fall in the 30 to 40% range. Although some compensation elements (e.g., housing, transportation, and education allowances) may receive favorable tax treatment in some countries, the tax savings have not been significant enough for employers to focus much attention on tax-effective compensation. (This is not the case in India, however; high tax rates in the past have led to a total compensation design in which base pay represents less than 50% of regular income. An intricate set of allowances for housing, leaves, conveyance, medical reimbursement, and so on are provided as part of regular pay.)

Though incentive pay linked to company, business unit, and/or individual performance has been surprisingly slow to take off in the region, the recent economic woes will surely accelerate its acceptance. Sales commission and bonus plans are now more commonplace for sales employees, although the mix of base to variable tends to be much less leveraged than in the United States. Similarly, executive-level bonuses are slowly gaining momentum, typically in the range of 20 to 40% of base pay. Broad-based profit-sharing plans are most often seen when a corporate plan in the United States has been extended to all employees worldwide.

Stock plans are gaining in popularity in the region, despite sometimes arduous registration procedures (such as in India), a lack of any special tax concessions in most countries, and unpredictable exchange-rate fluctuations. Interestingly, the recent weakening of many of the Asian currencies against the U.S. dollar actually provides a compelling case for stock plans. Employees see an advantage in receiving at least one element of their compensation in a more robust currency.

Broad-based stock purchase plans are becoming more prevalent, since the recent trend among U.S. multinationals is to offer these plans worldwide, wherever it is legally possible to do so. Clear and comprehensive communication is essential when implementing this type of program. Employees must understand both the potential gains and adverse consequences of stock price movement, exchange-rate fluctuations, and tax treatment.

In Asia, even in those companies typically providing more broad-based ownership, stock options are typically offered only to more senior employees. Some companies have defined eligibility for stock options by salary level rather than grade or job level. (This approach can cause problems as exchange rates fluctuate and should be avoided if possible.) Companies are now considering extending stock options to other key employees they wish to retain, even in the midst of salary freezes or slashed bonuses.

Salary Planning and Pay Programs

Inflation rates vary dramatically across the region, from as low as 1.5% in Singapore to more than 10% in the Philippines and Thailand in 1998. Indonesia's inflation rate is "off the chart" at 65%. Salary increases have traditionally outpaced inflation trends, but with the recent economic crisis, this pattern has been reversed—most noticeably in Korea, Indonesia, and Thailand, where inflation is far outpacing salary increases.

A comparison of salary increase trends from 1997 to 1998 shows that, in Hong Kong, Korea, Singapore, and Thailand, salary increase rates have fallen by as much as 30 to 50%. In contrast, Indonesia, the Philippines, and Taiwan have, for the most part, matched 1997 rates. Exhibit 21-3 contrasts 1997 and 1998 salary increase rates, alongside 1998 projected inflation levels.

Salary increases tend to be given out at least annually and sometimes twice a year in the higher trend countries such as India and, now, Indonesia. Multinationals operating in the region often align their local salary review date with that of their parent company, but just as many have set different dates from their parent—according to calendar year, fiscal year, date of inception in the country, or local practice. Anniversary date reviews are also fairly common.

The challenge for companies in the coming years will be to anticipate market trends in light of the economic crisis so that they do not overshoot

Exhibit 21-3. 1997 and 1998 Salary Increases Compared with 1998 Inflation

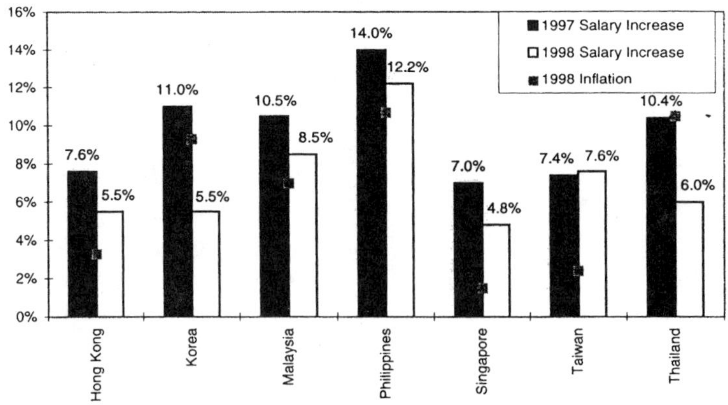

Source: *Watson Wyatt*

the market. The typical published compensation survey is not too helpful for this, since a nearly three-month time frame is needed to gather the data, then analyze it, and finally print up the results. On-line and real-time access to constantly updated compensation databases will become a critical tool for compensation managers to track market movements on a month-by-month basis.

In the end, each company's own financial situation will have to be the primary driver for setting salary review budgets during the next few years. In the short term, many companies have resorted to pay freezes and other cutbacks in compensation. Companies struggle to strike a balance between what they can afford to spend today and what they need to spend to retain the key talent that could pull them through the crisis and ensure future success in the region.

Salary management practices in Asia tend to lag behind those of other countries, with the norm still being the 1980s model of job evaluation and narrow, tightly managed salary ranges. Although HR managers may be eagerly discussing newer techniques such as skill-based pay, competency modeling, and broadbanding, these are not being broadly implemented at this time.

Performance Management

Companies still struggle with some of the Asian cultural barriers encumbering effective performance management. Managers, for example, need to be extremely careful about how they give performance input to their employees; they need to provide a clear message while ensuring that the employee "saves face" and is not humiliated. Not surprisingly, it is also quite difficult to encourage employees to provide upward input to their managers; even when sanctioned, this is construed as insubordination and lack of respect. Any recognition program that singles out individuals from the rest of the work group may not align well with the ingrained collectivist values that mark much of Asian culture.

Because of these cultural challenges, companies often award pay increases and bonuses across the board, with little or no differentiation between the exceptional and the marginal performer. To do otherwise would invite a discussion that many Asian managers are not comfortable starting. Major investment in management education and coaching will be needed to change this mind-set, especially in light of employers' need to retain and motivate key talent during the next few years.

Exhibit 21-4. Asia—Employee Benefits

Program	Hong Kong	Indonesia	Korea	Malaysia	Philippines	Singapore	Taiwan	Thailand
Medical	Insured or preferred provider	Self-insured	Medical Insurance Society	Self-funded outpatient; insured inpatient	Insured	Insured	Insured	Insured
Death and Disability	2–4 x salary	1–3 x salary	1–2 x salary	3 x salary	2 x salary	2–3 x salary	2 x salary	1–3 x salary
Sickness Leave/Pay	Employer provides 80% of salary up to 120 days; accrual of 2 days/month for 1st year, 4 days/month after 1st year	Employer provides 100% of salary for 1–3 months; 75% for 4–6 mos.; 50% for 7–9 mos.; and 25% for 10–12 mos.	Employer provides 70% of salary after 3 days for up to 2 years	Employer provides 14–22 paid days/year based on service; if hospitalized, 60 paid days/year	Social security provides 90% of covered pay after 3 days for up to 120 days	Employers provide 14 paid days/year; if hospitalized, 60 paid days/year	Employers provide 30 days/year at 50% pay; if hospitalized, entitled to 1-year leave without pay	Employers provide 30 days/year
Maternity Leave	10 weeks at 80% pay; employer paid	3 months at full pay; employer paid	60 days at full pay; employer paid	60 days at full pay; employer paid	60 days paid by social security	8 weeks at full pay; employer paid	8 weeks at full pay; employer paid	90 days; 50/50 paid by employer/ social security
Termination	Long service 2/3 salary x years of service	1 month per year of service minimum	1 month per year of service minimum	10–20 days based on service	½–1 month per year of service minimum	2–4 weeks per year of service	1 month per year of service minimum	30–180 days based on service
Retirement	Defined contribution (some defined benefit)	Defined benefit	Defined benefit	Defined contribution	Defined benefit	Defined contribution (supplemental plans not typical)	Defined benefit	Defined contribution
Social Security Contribution:[1]								
Employer	0%	10–14.5%	3.0%	13.75%	5.07%	20.0%	7.0–10%	1.0%
Employee	0%	2.0%	3.0%	11.5%	3.33%	20.0%	2.6%	1.0%

1. Approximate levels only.

Source: *Watson Wyatt*

Paid Time Off and Benefits

Public holidays range from 10 days in Malaysia to 18 days in Taiwan. Public holidays falling on a Saturday do not typically result in a compensatory day off; Saturday is viewed as a workday in this context.

Vacation practices vary significantly but tend to fall in a range of 10 to 15 days after the first year, increasing with years of service to a ceiling of 20 to 30 days. Minimum vacation standards are often legislated, but companies' policies often exceed the minimum requirement.

Exhibit 21-4 summarizes typical benefits programs provided in each country. To a large extent, company-sponsored benefits programs are a function of the degree to which social security and other statutory programs are lacking or nonexistent.

Korea offers a government-sponsored medical program under its Medical Insurance Society, so company-sponsored plans are obviously not common there. In the other Asian countries reviewed here, however, government services and facilities are considered inadequate. Company-sponsored medical plans provide access to better accommodation and faster service for noncritical care. Doctors and/or nurses may be in attendance in the bigger manufacturing operations. Companies provide health care for inpatient, outpatient, and dental services primarily through insured indemnity-type plans, with possible outpatient self-funding by the bigger companies. Dependent coverage is offered, although often the employee pays half the premium costs. Often, health plan provisions discriminate by job level.

While the cost of health care is still low relative to the United States, clearly the recent economic challenges in the region will fuel the growing problem of medical cost inflation. As a result, there will be more of a move toward employee cost sharing—not only for dependents but possibly for employees themselves. A full system of managed care, including preferred providers and health maintenance organizations (HMOs), is not in place at present but will certainly become an important option as costs increase. Such plans are already on the increase in Hong Kong, the Philippines, and Malaysia.

Death and total permanent disability plans are universally provided, predominantly in the form of a lump-sum insured benefit, ranging from one to three times annual salary depending on the country. Benefits are often doubled in the event of an accident. Salary continuance plans to replace income during illness are usually not insured arrangements. Sick leave provisions are generally mandated and vary widely by country. In most cases, the employer is required to pay a specified number of weeks on full or partial pay (see Exhibit 21-4 for details). Maternity leave tends to range from 60 to 90 days, and, in most cases, the employer is required to provide leave on a fully paid basis.

Termination indemnities (in a range of two weeks' to two months' final pay per year of service) are often mandated and tend to be payable upon severance, death, total permanent disability, and retirement. Where such termination liabilities exist (Indonesia, Korea, the Philippines, and Taiwan), companies have often established company-sponsored retirement plans to fund termination liabilities on a tax-qualified basis. By definition, such plans tend to take the form of a defined-benefit plan, to align with the final salary benefit definition of the termination indemnity.

In addition to covering termination liabilities, company-sponsored arrangements are also seen where the social security benefit is minimal or nonexistent. For example, social security contributions are currently zero in Hong Kong and approximately 1% in Thailand, reflecting the minimal statutory benefits available. In these two countries, the government has made company-sponsored plans mandatory in an attempt to pass the burden on to employers. Employers, in turn, have encouraged or mandated employee participation as a means of defraying costs.

Defined-contribution plans tend to be popular in Asian countries, particularly those with a younger workforce. These plans typically require both employer and employee contributions, usually in a range of a 1:1 or even 2:1 ratio (the reverse of typical U.S. 401(k) practice, where the company's total contribution tends to represent 50% or less of the employee's contribution).

The highest contributions to state-run plans in the region can be found in Singapore, where 20% of salary is paid by both employer and employee into the Central Provident Fund (CPF). The CPF, established on the basis of individually allocated funds, is a comprehensive and well-run system designed to enforce savings for retirement and other lifetime needs such as home purchase, children's education, and medical care. Because the CPF serves employees so well, company-sponsored retirement plans are rare in Singapore.

Organization and Staffing

Asian companies are similar to American companies of two decades ago in that they include many layers of middle management, with fewer layers of top management. The downsizing cycle in the United States during the last decade has most often hit middle management, and no doubt the same phenomenon will now manifest itself in the Asian countries as nonessential jobs are eliminated.

The human resources function has evolved steadily during the last 20 years, and it is gradually being considered an integral contributor to business success. Since scarcity of talent has been a major issue in many industries over the last decade, many HR professionals have focused on recruiting and retaining top-notch employees. Employers have looked for creative ways to attract talent in light of fierce competition. Companies have placed increased emphasis on training and education, career planning (often with opportunities for an international assignment), and immigration sponsorship as ways to differentiate themselves from the competition.

In some markets, it has been difficult to attract new recruits to U.S. companies. Candidates question the degree to which the company is committed to the region in general as well as to the specific country. Does the company have the depth of management talent in place to ensure successful penetration of the market? Does it respect the culture and employee expectations of that country?

It is clear that the focus for HR professionals during the next decade will be somewhat different. They will spend their efforts on restructuring organizations and pay practices to restore company success. In the future, there will be zero tolerance for retaining and rewarding mediocre performance.

In an effort to repatriate Western international assignees, more companies are actively working toward "fast-tracking" local managers. More local managers are being sent on assignment to the United States or to another country within the Asian region to provide them with more international business experience and to broaden their perspective. Companies are also looking at cost-effective ways of structuring intraregional assignment policies to encourage mobility while avoiding some of the more costly elements. For example, a policy incorporating localized compensation practices, short-term allowances to assist with the move, and home- or international-based benefits may be a useful approach for reducing overall costs while facilitating the move.

Employment Law and Labor Relations

As noted earlier, the labor relations environment varies tremendously by country. Unionization is strongest in Indonesia, Korea, the Philippines, and Taiwan and less so in Hong Kong and Singapore, where the forces of supply and demand tend to determine compensation levels. Even in countries in which the employer-employee relationship has been rocky, the most recent economic events have encouraged representatives on both sides to work more collaboratively together, with the hope of finding the right short-term and long-term solutions.

Minimum standards for terms and conditions of employment are typically stipulated under local legislation: the Employment Ordinance (Hong Kong), the Labor Codes (Indonesia and the Philippines), the Labor Standards Act (Korea), the Employment Acts (Malaysia and Singapore), the Labor Standards Law (Taiwan), and the Labor Protection Law (Thailand). These labor codes typically define regulations around working hours and time off, overtime arrangements, employment contracts and probationary periods, notice periods, and severance payments in the event of termination. Immigration regulations vary by country but can be tightly enforced (such as in Malaysia, which has severe restrictions on the nationals eligible to work there).

Asia is a fascinating and vibrant region in which to do business, provided companies take the time to understand the subtlety of the employment relationship in each country, which is a function of each nation's political history, cultural values, and future aspirations. Multinational companies have reaped significant returns on investment from their Asian operations in the last few decades; the next decade will demonstrate the extent to which these same companies remain committed to the region over the longer term.

Further Reading

Watson Wyatt. Benefits Report: Asia/Pacific. 1998/1999.

Watson Wyatt. Employment Terms and Conditions: Asia/Pacific. 1998/1999.

CHAPTER 22

PEOPLE'S REPUBLIC OF CHINA

WILLIS SHEN

Introduction

China's most noteworthy economic asset is a potential market 1.2 billion people strong. The pace of economic reform continues to capture the imagination of businesspeople around the world. When Zhu Rongji became premier in March 1998, he announced a series of nationwide initiatives: reform of China's financial and banking systems, restructuring of central government institutions, reform of state-owned enterprises within a three-year timetable, and transformation of housing from a welfare benefit to a market commodity. These changes are viewed as vital as the People's Republic of China (PRC) moves further from central planning to a socialist market economy.

This transition has not been an easy one. Many state-owned enterprises have been shut down, leading to steadily growing unemployment. By the end of the third quarter of 1998, gross domestic product (GDP) growth had fallen short of the 8% target rate—considered a critical number for creating new jobs and staving off social unrest. The Asian economic crisis has reduced both export growth and the rate of foreign investment in China, and there is continuing pressure to devalue the yuan.

To counteract these problems, the government is aiming to stimulate domestic growth through the investment of hundreds of billions of dollars in rural area projects, as well as public works and housing construction. Beijing has ordered a loosening up on credit and has injected new funds, allowing banks to shed bad loans and provide much-needed capital to developers and homeowners.

The Unique PRC Market

The Western-style approach to managing human resources is a new frontier for China. Under the old state system, workers benefited from the "iron rice bowl" of guaranteed lifetime employment and cradle-to-grave benefits. The objective was to make sure everyone had a job—often at the expense of efficiency. As a result, pay was quite low, and advancement was determined on the basis of seniority rather than performance. With the increasing presence of foreign investment in China, worker mobility has increased. A phenomenon known as "one family, two systems" has emerged: One spouse works for a cash-rich foreign company for a high salary, while the other spouse works for a state-owned company to enjoy a benefits-rich package that includes housing and medical coverage. Pay for performance is the likely future for employees at all levels. As China shifts from central planning to a market economy, human resources concerns will focus on issues pertaining to staff development, training, retention, and performance management.

To deal with human resources issues in China, it is essential to understand or at least be aware of the different types of foreign investment in China; each type has its own unique human resources issues to consider. Companies establishing a presence in China typically set up one of the following entities: a representative office, a wholly foreign-owned enterprise (WFOE), or a joint venture.

Companies entering the Chinese market without any partnership or investment with a local Chinese company initially establish a representative office. By law, representative offices are restricted to marketing and liaison activities and are not permitted to generate business revenue or conduct business transactions. In practice, however, many representative offices do conduct business and simply arrange for invoices to go through regional or corporate head offices.

A representative office cannot directly hire its own local staff. Instead, all of its Chinese workers are employed by a local employment service company such as FESCO or CIIC. The arrangement is intended to protect local workers in the event that a representative office suddenly closes down and leaves China.

Subject to governmental approval, a representative office can apply to the State Administration Bureau for a WFOE license, which allows the company to conduct business legally in China. These licenses are under tight government control and are usually difficult to obtain. Companies that succeed in getting a license have full control over management and can recruit and hire their own local employees.

A major issue surrounding direct employment in China is whether WFOEs must direct-hire their local employees or whether they can continue using FESCO as the labor provider. According to the regulations, WFOEs are entitled, not required, to direct-hire their local employees. Eventually, however, the local labor bureau would expect a WFOE to directly employ the workers under a company employment contract. At issue is FESCO's practice of capping employees' wages to help pay company social insurance contributions (which do not always comply with local social insurance regulations). By using FESCO, firms (especially in Shanghai) can realize significant cost savings with regard to company social insurance contributions. The presumption by some companies is that if they continue using FESCO as the labor provider and benefits administrator, FESCO, not the company, will be responsible for underfunding of company social insurance, should underfunding occur. This is not the case, however, and companies should not look to exploit FESCO as a means of paying less-than-full social insurance contributions.

Direct investment through joint ventures is another option. Foreign companies will often provide the technology and management expertise while local partners commonly provide the staffing, local distribution networks, and facilities. In establishing human resources policies, a foreign company must also consult with its Chinese partner. Historically, the Chinese partner has been responsible for dealing with human resources; this trend is changing, however, as foreign companies look to establish human resources policies that are aligned with the direction and goals of the business. Ultimately, these policies should encourage high-performing employees who contribute positively to the company's financial performance.

Pay Determination

The labor law states that all workers must be paid at least the local minimum wage standard in each city. By way of reference, the 1998 minimum city salary for Beijing was 310 yuan (around US$38) per month. Statutory requirements dictate that employees of foreign enterprises receive at minimum between 120 and 150% of the real wages paid to workers in similar positions in state-owned enterprises in the same industry and locality. Real wages are set yearly by local regional labor bureaus and include wages, benefits, subsidies, and allowances paid to employees in the relevant state-owned enterprise. Foreign companies commonly apply only the amount of base wages to determine the state-owned enterprise wage level. Many foreign companies in China, however, offer wages in excess of the minimum wage to attract and retain talented employees.

The board of directors or top management of foreign companies is authorized to determine wage increases based on production levels of the particular enterprise; they are not mandated to synchronize wage hikes with those of state-owned enterprises. The labor law implies that wages should reflect the actual economic development within the local city. Labor bureaus provide price indexes and local average city wage guidelines for companies to take into account when determining wage increases.

State-owned enterprises tend to base annual salary increases on local economic conditions and government pressures. Foreign companies have a different concern; they face the challenge of finding enough highly skilled labor in China. Remuneration by foreign companies is driven by several factors. One is type of industry. High-tech companies, followed by pharmaceutical and consumer product firms, pay in the upper range; manufacturing tends to pay on the lower end. The type of business entity also influences the salary level. Because of their association with local Chinese partners, joint ventures commonly pay less than WFOEs and representative offices. Representative offices pay slightly more than WFOEs because of the management fee incurred under FESCO. In addition, because representative offices are the first initial presence for foreign companies setting up in a local market, a higher salary may be required to attract properly skilled candidates. Major cities such as Guangzhou, Beijing, and Shanghai—with a higher cost of living and a concentration of foreign companies—pay the highest salaries. Supply and demand comes into play for certain positions. Experienced managers are in short supply, with the greatest need in human resources, finance, sales and marketing, and legal professions.

One area of contention for foreign companies operating as joint ventures is the labor law pertaining to salary levels for senior local managers. The law states that local Chinese senior managers should be paid on the same pay scale as their expatriate counterparts—equal pay for equal work. The Chinese senior managers, however, are not permitted to keep the full amount of their salaries. The salary is broken down into actual and nominal salary components, of which the manager can keep only a small portion; most of the salary is paid into a fund for social welfare benefits for workers. Foreign companies often negotiate with their local Chinese partners; the wages as paid according to law may be applied to fund and offset social insurance company obligations.

Within the last few years, the Ministry of Labor has established regulations on collective bargaining in an effort to increase the bargaining power of Chinese employees. There is concern that there will be increasing conflict between foreign companies and their workers over compensation and benefits levels. Foreign companies doing business in China are required to enter into collective wage bargaining if either the relevant trade union or half the employees request it and if the company has the basic information needed to bargain (e.g., financial performance data). While setting up a labor union is a legal requirement, as a rule, multinational companies prefer to avoid dealing with unions and collective bargaining. Instead, they often choose to enter into individual employment contracts (as covered below in the section on employment law).

Components of Pay

Pay structures in China are still based heavily on guaranteed payment, although variable pay schemes are gaining in popularity. Discretionary company bonus plans tend to be based on individual performance rather than departmental or company performance. This is especially true among those companies that are still in an investment phase and thus do not project a profit for a few years.

Discretionary bonus and sales incentive schemes are more prevalent in the northern and eastern regions of China, which have a higher concentration of senior management and sales staff. Southern and central cities in China center more heavily on production and manufacturing and rely more on fixed pay packages than variable pay incentive schemes.

Payment of allowances still exists to some extent—a remnant of the old state-owned enterprise system in which base salaries were extremely low but allowances for everything from housing to haircuts ultimately covered expenses. The most common types of allowances offered by foreign companies are for meals, transportation, and housing. Only about one in four companies offer these allowances, however. In general, pay packages in foreign companies include a higher base salary to make up for the reduced allowances. Moreover, allowances are taxed at the same income tax rate as normal cash income; therefore, there is no tax advantage for employers to offer them to their employees.

Companies are required to provide overtime pay when an employee works extra hours or works on a rest day. When an employee works more than 40 hours per week or more than eight hours per day, overtime pay must not be less than 150% of the normal wage rate. If an employee works on a rest day, the rate is 200% of the normal wage rate; on a public holiday, the minimum rate is 300%.

Salary Planning and Pay Programs

China maintains a uniform salary structure for all state-owned enterprises. Different cities, however, have varying allowance levels depending on cost of living, industrial base, and companies' financial conditions. When foreign companies entered China, they found that the supply of skilled workers fell short of demand. To attract skilled and talented workers, they paid many times above the statutory minimum salary levels.

The salary-planning approaches of foreign companies are, not surprisingly, also different from those of state-owned enterprises. Foreign companies rely on survey and market salary data to decide on salary levels for each job rather than apply a uniform salary structure. Given the competition for skilled labor, there is a considerable variance between salary levels in foreign companies and state-owned companies.

Because of the wide salary ranges and fast-changing salary levels resulting from the shortage of qualified employees in certain jobs, traditional salary structures cannot efficiently keep pace with market movements. As a result, companies are exploring broadbanding and skill-based pay as more flexible approaches that are easier to handle. Once the labor market in China becomes more mature and stable, more foreign companies will adopt a larger-scale, traditional salary management system and pay program that is efficient to administer and that effectively rewards their employees.

Gross-to-Net Pay

There are nine tax rates for individual income tax based on income bracket levels. Different cities in China also have different deduction bases. Exhibit 22-1 shows the tax rates and levels on monthly gross income for Shanghai.

Exhibit 22-1. Shanghai: Income Tax Rates

Example	Gross Income	Taxable Income	Tax Rate	Quick Deduction	Tax Amount	Net Income
1	1,400	400	5% (for 0–500)	—	20	1,380
2	2,500	1,500	10% (for 501–2,000)	25	125	2,375
3	5,000	4,000	15% (for 2,001–5,000)	125	475	4,525
4	15,000	14,000	20% (for 5,001–20,000)	375	2,425	12,575
5	35,000	34,000	25% (for 20,001–40,000)	1,375	7,125	27,875
6	55,000	54,000	30% (for 40,001–60,000)	3,375	12,825	42,175
7	75,000	74,000	35% (for 60,001–80,000)	6,375	19,525	55,475
8	95,000	94,000	40% (for 80,001–100,000)	10,375	27,225	67,775
9	110,000	109,000	45% (for above 100,000)	15,375	33,675	76,325

The demand for skilled local labor in China continues to outpace supply. Exhibit 22-2 shows salary increases compared against inflation since 1995.

Performance Management

Concepts of "performance management" differ in state-owned companies and foreign-owned companies. State-owned companies still tend to value length of service, connections, and Communist Party affiliation over actual job performance. In the past, state-owned enterprises followed a system of punishment and reprimand for poor performance—without parallel recognition for outstanding efforts. As an example, state-owned employees who reported to work late or broke company rules received a small deduction in their weekly pay. Foreign-owned companies, on the other hand, view performance management systems as a way to motivate and reward their key employees.

Exhibit 22-2. Salary Increases, GDP, and Inflation Rate in China over the Past Four Years

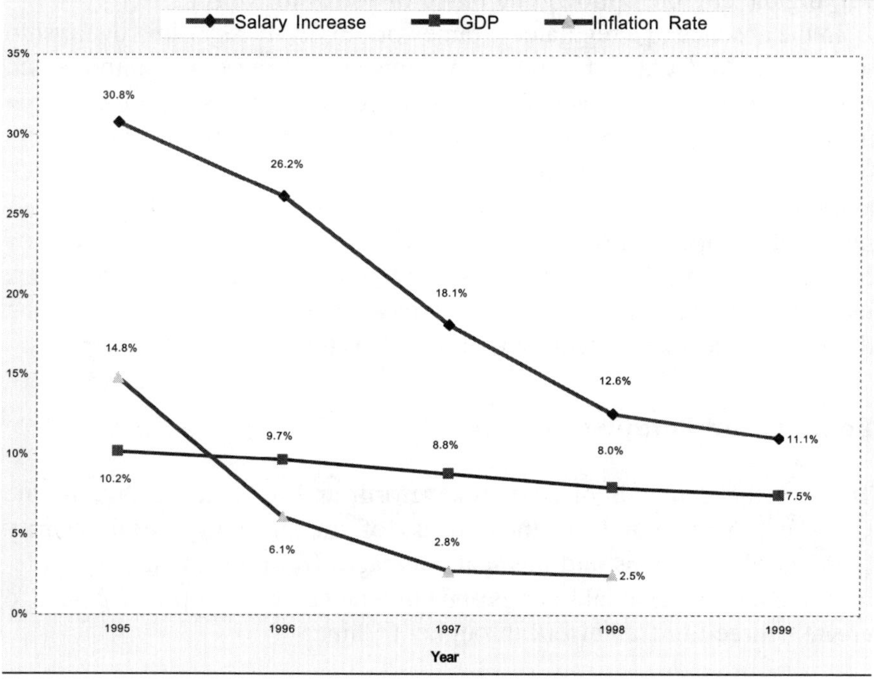

Although primarily applied to management and sales staff, performance management systems in foreign companies are slowly being extended to all staff levels. Performance is a key component, along with competencies and experience, in determining individual pay levels. Similar to performance measurement systems in other countries, these performance management systems involve goal setting, performance input and updates, and review and summary at the end of the performance period. Performance management systems are often linked to each department's business objectives and thus may vary between different business units or departments within the company.

Companies are also designing performance management approaches to help define the necessary skills that employees need to develop. Training programs are sometimes tied to such performance measurements.

A number of foreign companies, particularly consumer products and high-tech companies, are examining ways to implement stock option programs as long-term incentives that support employee retention. Some companies view stock plans as an element of executive compensation programs for select local senior management. Other companies have taken a more egalitarian approach and offer stock options to all levels of staff, varying the eligible option grant based on job grade or seniority.

In the absence of a regulatory framework in China regarding ownership of foreign stock plans, foreign companies are rolling out phantom stock option devices to avoid actual foreign share transactions. These phantom plans are effectively bonus arrangements paying out the difference between the exercise price and the purchase price, less tax. Despite such ambiguity on the securities regulatory side, in early 1998, the State Administration of Taxation issued a circular on the taxation of stocks as a form of compensation. The ruling states that stock options and other stock incentives are taxable when the employee acquires the stock. The ruling does not address any auxiliary issues such as the taxation of expatriates.

Benefits and Perquisites

To meet the demands of economic reform and a market economy, the Chinese government is in the process of transforming social security (particularly pensions and medical coverage) from a program of entitlements to one of personal savings and company sponsorship. The goal is to create a three-tier framework throughout China:

Tier 1: The government will provide a basic level of benefits.

Tier 2: Companies should offer supplemental plans above state benefits.

Tier 3: Employees must contribute to individual personal accounts to fund additional benefits.

Consistent with this three-tier framework, the State Council announced a unified pension plan in 1997 that all cities in China should adopt by the year 2000. Exhibit 22-3 illustrates specific provisions under the unified pension model.

Shanghai moved closer to the concept of this model in April 1998 by revising the company contribution percentage allocated to individual employee accounts. Beijing announced new pension changes for 1998 to align with the unified pension model.

It should be noted that the Shanghai social insurance system is unique to that city. In this system, companies are required to make social insurance retirement contributions based on total payroll (rather than imposing a ceiling as detailed under the unified model). The portion of the company

Exhibit 22-3. Provisions under the Unified Pension Model

Provision	Unified System	Provision	Unified System
Retirement Age **Eligible Employees**	Normal retirement age: Male – 60 Female – 50 (if cadre – 55) All employees (excluding expatriates)	**Employer's Contribution Rate**	20% of employee's last year monthly wage Maximum calculation base: 300% of city's last year average monthly wage.
Employer's Contribution Allocated to Personal Account	From total employer's total contribution, 6% of employee's last year average monthly wage decrease by 1% every 2 years until 3%.	**Employee's Contribution Rate**	5% of employee's last year average monthly wage, plus 1% every 2 years until 8%. Minimum calculation base: city's last year average monthly wage. Maximum calculation base: 300% of city's last year average monthly wage.

payroll exceeding three times the previous year's city average wage is refunded to a company account at the Shanghai Pudong Development Bank. Companies can then set up a supplemental retirement plan to make use of this refunded money. Currently, the Shanghai pension bureau tightly controls the management of this money to prevent companies from using the funds for other benefits such as insurance and housing.

The general sentiment among foreign companies is that social insurance benefit costs in China are extremely high. Common complaints are that a large percentage of the money paid into the social security system will not be available when employees are entitled to it and that foreign companies are subsidizing benefits for state-owned enterprise employees whose companies have not paid into the system. As a result, some companies refuse to pay their entire social insurance contributions or pay only partial obligations.

Local city governments are trying to address this "compliance and collection" dilemma, but it has not been easy. In Shanghai, for example, roughly 1,000 pension bureau employees are assigned to handle more than 40,000 state-owned and foreign companies. There are simply not enough resources to check every company for full compliance. At present, tax collection is a higher government priority—considered the most promising means of collecting back revenues. There have been signs in recent months from officials in Beijing that enforcement of company contributions to the social security system will be the government's next priority. A circular addressing this issue, "The Temporary Provision of Collecting Social Insurance Contribution," was approved in January 1999 by the State Council. Although pension issues are one of the key areas mentioned, this document has broader implications for all social insurance contributions, notably unemployment and medical contributions. Exhibit 22-4 shows company social insurance costs in three cities.

Although high social insurance costs are affecting some companies' willingness to offer additional benefits, the need to attract and retain good employees is an issue and cost that companies cannot ignore. As a result, companies are interested in long-term incentive programs aimed at retaining key staff. Common programs are deferred cash, housing, and retirement programs. In addition, companies may offer supplementary insurance policies providing medical and life insurance coverage.

Housing is a unique benefit offered in China based on the remnants of the old system. To help jump-start the domestic economy, Premier Zhu announced in March 1998 that nationwide housing reform would take effect starting July 1. Under housing reform, housing would shift from a government welfare benefit to a consumer market commodity. There have been estimates that housing reform would add anywhere from 0.5 to 1% to 1998's 8% GDP target, but these estimates were likely overly optimistic. To encourage the new policy:

- Rent subsidies are being phased out, except for those in need. In Shanghai, the government is seeking to increase rents from 3% of household income to 15% to create an incentive for people to buy their own homes rather than rent.
- Loan restrictions have been relaxed.
- Access to housing loan capital through Chinese commercial banks has increased. Before housing reform, only a few select Chinese commercial banks could provide loans for housing. Following housing reform, all Chinese commercial banks, as ordered by the People's Bank of China, must provide up to 15% of their loan pool for residential housing loans.
- Preferential tax policies toward home ownership have been introduced. In Shanghai, for citizens purchasing a home after June 1998, the cost of the home can be deducted from the individual's taxable income base over the next five years.

Exhibit 22-4. Major Cities: Company Social Insurance Costs as Percentages of Wages

Benefits	Shanghai	Beijing	Guangzhou
Retirement	25.5%	19%[1]	23%[2]
Medical	5.5%	2.5%[3]	N/A
Housing	15%–20%	10%	5%–7% [4]
Worker's Compensation	~ 1% [5]	N/A	0.5%–1.5% [5]
Unemployment	1%	1%	0.7%
Maternity	N/A	N/A	0.7%
Total	48%–53%	32.5%	26.9%–32.9%

1 Up to 300% prior year's city average wage
2 Up to 200% prior year's city average wage
3 Apply city average wage base
4 Depending on employee's wage
5 Depending on type of business /industry

Despite all of these measures, nationwide housing reform is behind schedule. Given China's unemployment problem, which is leading to fears of social unrest and resistance to public rental increases, the State Council decided in June 1998 to delay the privatization of housing for six months. Beijing adhered to this schedule; Shanghai, meanwhile, has clearly been one of the pioneer cities by moving forward with the housing reform agenda.

Watson Wyatt undertook a study in September 1998 to gauge the effects of housing reform on company-sponsored housing programs in China. In particular, the study examined whether companies would review their existing company housing policies as a result of housing reform and, if so, what changes were being considered. As it turns out, 43% of participating companies were considering changing their company housing policy. Specific suggestions included the following:

- Move away from ad hoc policies to a more defined formal company policy.
- Increase the level of benefit and scope of coverage to all staff rather than simply targeting senior management employees.
- Shift the burden of housing obligation from the company to the employee.

Companies that do not yet have a housing program in place are exploring the possibility of implementing a company housing plan in the near future.

In dealing with China's unemployment situation, many cities in China have increased the overall social insurance contribution rate for companies from 1 to 2% of total payroll. (Employees are also required to contribute 1% of their pay toward the unemployment fund.)

Organization, Staffing, and Other HR Issues

Applicable labor regulations specifically permit foreign companies to recruit and select local Chinese candidates on the basis of merit. A foreign company looking to hire a local national within China will typically pursue several different options to locate appropriate staff, including selecting qualified workers supplied by its Chinese joint venture partner, directly recruiting qualified candidates from the open labor market, and hiring university and college graduates from China's universities.

The PRC labor authorities prefer that foreign companies recruit employees from their Chinese joint venture partner (if applicable), then from the locality, and then from outside the locality if the locality has insufficient qualified personnel. Labor mobility in China is complicated by the fact that people must, in general, find work in the city where their hukou (residency permit) is registered. This policy is designed to prevent mass migrations from the interior or rural sections of China to the coastal or major cities where jobs are more plentiful. Workers must receive approval from the local public security bureau to shift their hukou to another city.

In addition, recruitment restrictions exist in China. A provision of China's labor law prohibits enterprises from interfering with existing employment relations, requiring the payment of economic damages when such interference occurs. This restriction was likely intended to prevent foreign companies from poaching the most skilled workers in the state-owned enterprises, but in fact the reverse is common today. State-owned companies and government ministries have been actively recruiting the employees of foreign companies in an effort to become more skilled and efficient.

After the 1998 Asian economic downturn, expatriate positions in the region and in China were hard hit as companies looked to cut costs. Many expatriates are now being repatriated, and companies are reviewing expatriate premiums such as "rest and relaxation" allowances, hardship allowances, and per diem allowances. There is a profound trend in China for companies to localize positions wherever possible as a means of saving money. There have been many debates about the extent and speed with which localization can occur given Chinese locals' lack of experience in and exposure to management responsibility. The general feeling is that companies can slowly localize positions; however, expatriates will continue to fill a need, providing management expertise and helping to train their local successors.

A special group of local employees are "returnees"—Chinese citizens who have either worked or studied overseas. Depending on their experience level and type of position, returnees are offered salary and benefit packages somewhere between those of a local hire and an expatriate. For example, returnees may be offered a base pay package in U.S. dollars, housing, and even children's education. With the trend toward localization, coupled with an increase in the supply of local skilled labor, returnee packages will likely be scaled down—to what extent will depend on the employee skill or management level.

The labor law requires that all employers establish a job-training system and carry out vocational training. While foreign companies will be required to satisfy training obligations, the new labor law does not elaborate on precisely what those training obligations are. Nonetheless, training remains a critical area for companies in China that want to develop their local staff and attract and retain key employees. Some companies design their training programs as a retention program for key employees. Other training programs are designed to offer overseas training in other locations outside of China or at corporate headquarters. (This is especially common among the foreign banks in Shanghai.) The length of such training ranges from one month to one year. In return for the experience and opportunity, employees may be required to sign an agreement with the company that they will not leave the company for a period of typically up to two years. If the agreement is breached, the employee must repay part of the training costs, including travel and lodging expenses. In theory, this may deter employees from leaving the company following training; in practice, however, rival companies often assume the cost of this training on behalf of the recruited employee.

Chinese law sets a 40-hour workweek (maximum eight hours per day). Employees working more than the standard workweek are entitled to overtime pay. Overtime is restricted, and workers are not permitted to exceed three overtime hours per day or 36 hours per month.

Companies are required to observe four holidays: Chinese Lunar New Year or Spring Festival, International Labor Day, National Day, and New Year's Day. These statutory holidays are paid days off. For annual leave or vacation, the median market practice ranges from 10 to 12 days off.

Joint ventures and WFOEs are required to set up a company trade union. Representative offices generally do not require a company trade union because the labor agency (such as FESCO or CIIC) that provides the workers already has its own trade union committee in place to represent workers.

Because of the sheer number of unions and the system's organizational structure, trade unions in China do not hold the kind of power or spheres of influence that their counterparts do in the United States. The basic goals of company trade unions in China are to provide a voice for employees in company matters and to foster an environment of goodwill between employees and the company.

Resolution of labor disputes is set forth in the PRC Handling of Enterprises Labor Disputes Regulations, which became effective in August 1993 and express the will that all labor disputes be resolved through consultation, mediation, arbitration, or court proceedings. Labor contracts also commonly call for labor disputes to be resolved through amicable consultation between the parties. In individual cases in which employees believe they have been wrongly punished or terminated, they may appeal the decision to their trade union. The trade union will in turn meet with the management of the company to resolve the dispute through clarification or conciliation. If an agreement cannot be reached, either party may seek arbitration, and if either party disagrees with the outcome of arbitration, a lawsuit in the relevant court is the final action that can be taken.

Employment Law

Under the labor law, all workers in foreign companies must be employed according to written contracts negotiated on the basis of "equality, voluntariness, and unanimity" in compliance with the policies of the Chinese government and local regulations. A written labor contract may be collective or individual in coverage. Many local labor bureaus have developed "template" employment contracts that they recommend companies use; often, however, local labor bureaus are flexible about the forms they will accept.

A collective labor contract may be negotiated between the management of a foreign company and its trade union on behalf of the workers of the enterprise. Such a contract must include the following provisions: pay, working hours, rest and vacation, safety and health, insurance, and welfare. A draft of the contract must be submitted to the staff for discussion and approval before it can be finalized and carried out.

Foreign companies have the option of entering into individual employment contracts with their employees. In general, foreign companies prefer individual contracts to collective ones because individual contracts offer more flexibility in dealing with special circumstances or arrangements. Also, individual contracts are a way for these companies to avoid having to go through collective bargaining with trade unions.

Collective labor contracts for foreign companies must be submitted to the local labor department for certification within one month of execution, and they are not considered valid until after this certification is obtained. The labor law does not mandate approval of individual labor contracts.

In accordance with the labor law, employment contracts must address the following issues:

- Job requirement details, including the tasks of production and other work
- Terms of employment and duration of probation period

- Matters pertaining to labor discipline, dismissal, and resignation of employees
- Production and working conditions
- Remuneration, including wages, bonuses, and employee allowances
- Labor protection
- Liabilities for violating the labor contract
- Conditions for terminating the labor contract
- Any other terms deemed necessary by the parties

Contracts may also include provisions addressing working hours, holidays, vacations, labor insurance and social benefits, confidentiality obligations, noncompete requirements, special training, and arbitration of labor disputes. Including these additional provisions is a matter of negotiation between the contracting parties, although the practical enforceability of some of these provisions, such as noncompete agreements, has not been entirely established under PRC law.

Foreign company labor contracts often provide a three- to six-month probation period for new workers. China's labor law stipulates six months as the maximum length of a probation period. Under the labor law, an employee who fails to meet the employment requirements during probation may be dismissed.

As China reforms its state-owned enterprise sector, termination of employees is a sensitive issue, especially in light of rising unemployment. There are laws that stipulate the proper conditions under which Chinese employees may be dismissed and a list of procedural requirements. A company may face great difficulty shedding a large number of local employees in the wake of a merger or an acquisition. Terminating employees on an individual basis, however, is permissible under the following (not all-inclusive) conditions:

- Employee is no longer needed (redundancy)
- Employee commits a serious offense or does not comply with the company rules and regulations
- Employee is not competent even after repeated training or having been assigned other positions within the company
- Company faces grave financial difficulty and is undergoing reorganization

If a company decides to dismiss an employee, in general, it must provide at least one month's notice to both the employee and his or her trade union. In addition, the company is expected to file a dismissal report with the local labor authorities. Companies dismissing an employee for disciplinary reasons are not required to provide advance notice, provided that the trade union is notified and the employee is given an opportunity to defend the actions that led to the dismissal.

Companies are required to provide severance payments to employees who are dismissed or whose employment contracts are not renewed after the initial terms. Exceptions are when the employee has been dismissed during probation for failure to meet the company's standards, when the employee is dismissed for disciplinary reasons, or when the employee voluntarily resigns or elects not to renew contract terms. Severance payments are based on the length of a worker's employment with the company; employees are entitled to a onetime payment of one month's salary for each year of service. In addition to cash payment, the company is required to provide a payment for certain medical benefits to employees who are dismissed because of non-work-related medical reasons. Employees with five or fewer years of service are entitled to payment of three months' actual wages as a medical benefit, while those with more than five years of service are entitled to six months of their actual wages as a medical benefit.

The legal right for local employees to work is not all that different from that which pertains in other parts of the world. Laborers have the right to be employed on an equal basis and cannot be discriminated against on the basis of ethnicity, race, gender, or religious belief. Except under special circumstances, companies cannot recruit workers under the age of 16. The difference in employment requirements, which was touched on earlier, is that citizens in China are entitled to work only in the city in which their residence permit (hukou) is registered. Exceptions to this can be made if a company sponsors an employee outside the local area who has a special skill or knowledge. These approvals are reviewed and granted by the local labor and human resources bureau on a case-by-case basis.

The Ministry of Labor has adopted strict rules on the employment of foreigners in China. These rules limit the hiring of expatriates working in China, except when the expatriate's skills cannot be provided locally. To employ a nonlocal, the company must obtain the permission of the labor administrative authorities, and the foreign employee must secure an employment permit and a residency certificate before starting employment.

Foreign companies are required to store permanent files for each employee. A typical employee file might include the following information:

- Employee's name
- Employee's identification card number
- Employee's date of hire
- Employee's job title
- Employee's wage
- Accrued annual leave
- Accrued sick leave
- Maternity leave
- Holidays
- Amount of employee's bonus
- Notice period for termination
- Date of termination of employment

Foreign companies are also required to keep an employee handbook and a social insurance handbook, which should be submitted to the local labor bureau for approval. These handbooks set forth company policies and outline the benefits to which employees are entitled. Work rules and disciplinary procedures should also be included in the handbooks.

CHAPTER 23

JAPAN

TOSHIO NIREI AND
JUNKO KUDO

Once viewed as virtually unstoppable, the Japanese business environment of late has been plagued by a series of setbacks. The combined effects of a sluggish economy, intensified global competition, and significant demographic shifts have led to a slowdown of business growth. While these economic and social pressures represent a turning point, they are not insurmountable. To survive the current recession and regain their competitive edge, Japanese companies have had to reexamine their management practices—in particular, the long-held traditions and policies of lifetime employment and seniority-based rewards.

This chapter discusses a number of the issues facing Japanese companies, the actions they have taken to streamline and reinvigorate their organizations, and the near- and possible long-term implications for HR policies and practices. Although many of these changes may seem commonplace to U.S. and European employers that have already been forced to confront these issues and make similar changes, in Japan, these changes are nothing short of a dramatic upheaval in the relationship between Japanese workers and their employers.

Environmental Change

Economic Conditions

According to several indicators, the Japanese economy is currently at its weakest level since the end of World War II. Six of the last seven years have seen very slow or negligible growth in Japan's gross domestic product (see Exhibit 23-1).

Japan's Economic Planning Agency has warned that the nation's economy could conceivably suffer through a growing deflationary spiral. This has prompted companies to seek ways to improve profitability—stimulating demand for goods by reducing prices, for example, or adding

Exhibit 23-1. Changes in the Japanese Gross Domestic Product

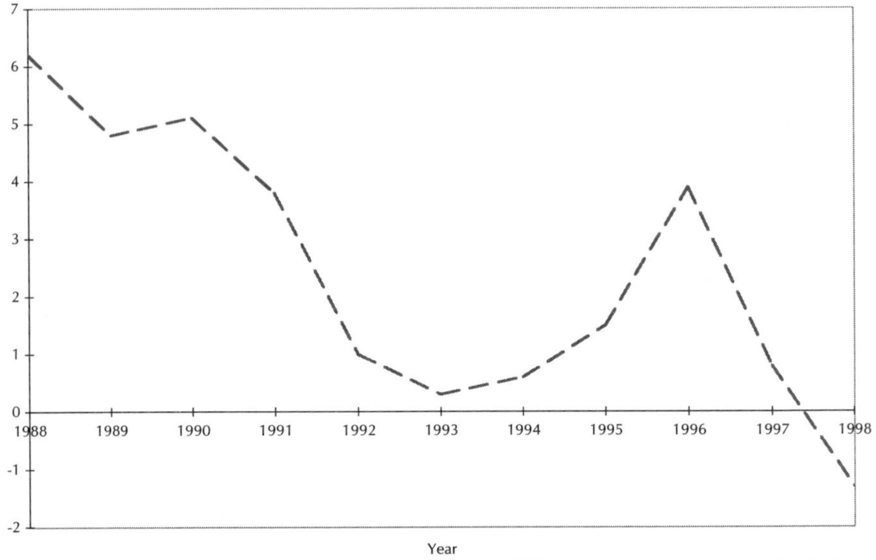

Source: *Ministry of Labor, "White Paper on Labor," 1998*

value within their existing markets. This presents a challenge because the markets for Japanese goods, both domestic and international, have developed more diverse needs. To meet those needs, companies are facing the necessity of adopting strategies that encourage greater productivity and more flexibility and innovation in the workforce. This has implications for the way employees are recruited, trained, retained, and rewarded.

Globalization and Deregulation

As part of the Plaza Accord of 1985, in which France, Germany, Japan, the United Kingdom, and the United States agreed to take measures that would ensure sustained growth for the global economy, Japan pledged to encourage the vitality of its private sector and to further open the domestic market to foreign goods and services. As a result, the Japanese economy has experienced significant changes. Japanese companies have increasingly sought foreign markets for their products, which, in many cases, has been an effective strategy for finding new life overseas for products that have reached marketing maturity in Japan. High labor costs at home, coupled with wide fluctuations in the value of the yen, have made foreign labor an appealing option, and other countries (primarily in Asia) are now viewed as sources of relatively cheap labor. The volume of local production of Japanese products in foreign countries has nearly tripled since the Plaza Accord. During the same period, the amount of direct foreign investment in Japan has quadrupled.

On the domestic front, radical financial reforms much like the 1986 "Big Bang" in Britain were introduced last year in the securities, banking, and insurance industries to remove barriers to outside competition in money and capital markets. These have resulted in, among other things, an increase in the amount of imports flowing into Japan. Consequently, the Japanese are forced to compete harder to maintain their share in the domestic market—often with mature products. In confronting this dilemma, Japanese companies are at last beginning to see the need for major improvements in their business practices.

Demographic Changes

Japan has experienced many of the significant demographic shifts that are evident in the United States and Europe. Naturally, these have implications for the workforce and pose a serious challenge to traditional human resources management practices.

Aging. The number of people age 60 and over in the Japanese workforce rose from 4.9 million in 1975 to 9.1 million in 1997—a growth of roughly 86%.[1] The combined effects of greater longevity for the elderly and a declining birthrate mean that, by 2010, there will likely be fewer young people (ages 15 to 29) in Japan than people over 60. Meanwhile, the median age of the population is rising. As Exhibit 23-2 shows, the largest segment of the labor force in 1975 was between 25 and 29 years of age; by 2020, it is expected to be between 45 and 49 years of age.

Women. One of the most significant changes in the Japanese workforce is the increased participation of women. The percentage of women in the workforce rose from 45.7% in 1975 to 50.4% in 1997. As shown in Exhibit 23-3, noticeable increases in the number of working women occurred among nearly all age groups during this period.

Furthermore, the average age of working women has risen from between 24 and 29 years to between 30 and 34 years.

This reflects two demographic shifts: Japanese women are marrying later, and they are staying at their jobs after marriage and even after the birth of their children.

Higher Education. Since the 1970s, the percentage of people enrolling in colleges and universities has been steadily rising, with fully 34.9% of high school graduates going on to higher education in 1997. The percentage of workers holding bachelor degrees rose from 12.7% in 1975 to 22.5% in 1997.

These demographic changes have forced Japanese companies to reexamine their traditional HR practices: lifetime employment with "no layoff" policies, seniority-based compensation practices, and a male-oriented work culture. There is a growing recognition that employers will need to institute new policies that reflect a more diverse workforce, such as equal opportunity, day care benefits, and flexible work schedules, to name a few.

Legal and Regulatory Changes

Two important changes in labor law and regulations have recently been adopted by the diet. The first is a revision of the equal employment

Exhibit 23-2. Distribution of Workforce by Age

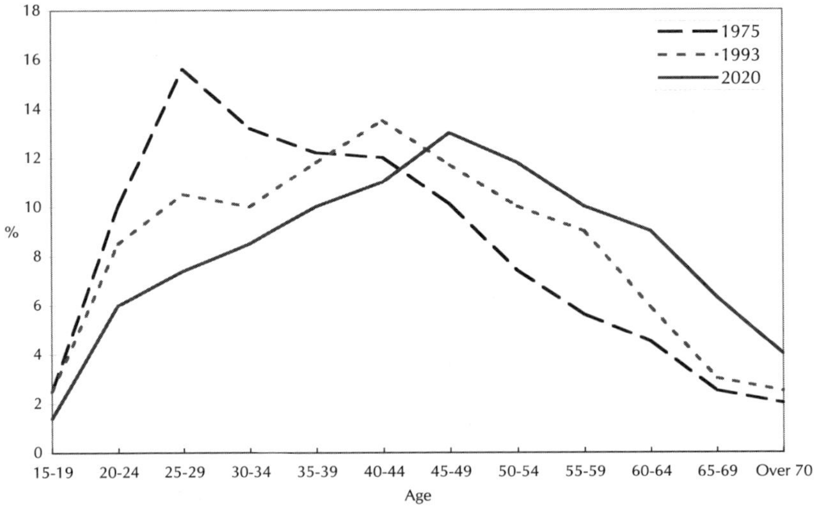

Source: *Naohiro Yashiro, "Economics of Japanese-Style Management," Nikkeishinbunsha, 1998*

opportunity law (EEOL) and the Labor Standard Law, which was passed in 1997 and became effective in April 1998. The highlight of this revision is the abolition of the law's protective provision that restricted women from working overtime, late at night, or on holidays. This gives women an opportunity to take jobs that by design were open almost solely to men. It also compels companies to ensure that their HR policies on such issues as day care, leave, and flextime are current and equitable.

The second important change is an expanded application of the "discretionary working hours" rule. Before this change, any nonmanagerial employee (even in a white-collar job) was restricted from working extra hours (because nonmanagerial employees are required to receive overtime pay). There were some positions that allowed "discretionary" overtime (reporters and editors, lawyers, and television producers, for example), but this additional application covers many more jobs. Essentially, it allows employees greater flexibility in how they do their work—which ostensibly has the added benefit of making them more motivated. Companies will need to revise their HR policies to make sure that they recognize and reward those employees who make the most effective use of their work time. (The establishment of appraisal systems based on concepts like management by objectives and 360-degree evaluation is a step in this direction.)

Exhibit 23-3. Percentage of Working Women by Age Group

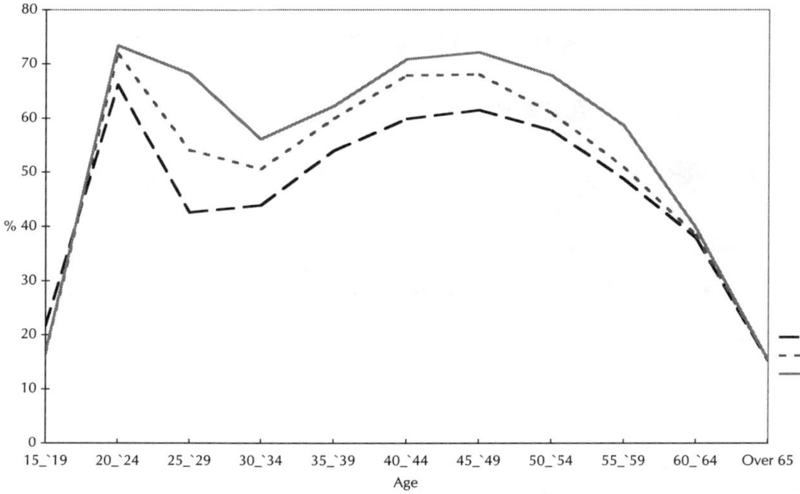

Source: *Ministry of Labor, "White Paper on Labor," 1998*

Labor Market Conditions

In addition to the social and demographic changes, recent changes within the Japanese labor market are also causing companies to modify their HR policies and practices.

Transition to Service Industries

The past few decades have seen a gradual but steady decline in industries such as agriculture, forestry, and fishing and an increase in so-called service-industry jobs. Manufacturing, whose growth continued after the oil crisis of 1973 (albeit more slowly), is also declining, the result of jobs being shifted to countries with lower labor costs. By 1995, service-industry jobs accounted for nearly 60% of the Japanese labor force (see Exhibit 23-4).

Exhibit 23-4. Workforce Distribution by Industry

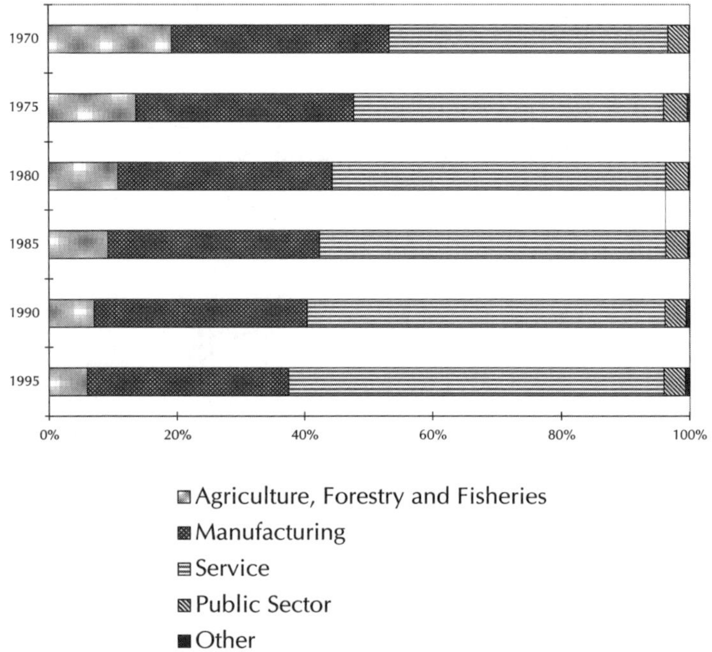

Source: *Ministry of Labor, "White Paper on Labor," 1998*

Transition to White-Collar Jobs

Along with the increase in service-industry jobs, the number of white-collar jobs (e.g., administrative, managerial, sales and marketing, and engineering) has risen as well. The percentage of white-collar workers increased from 41.9% in 1975 to 50.3% in 1995, marking another important shift in the makeup of the workforce.

Diversification of Work Patterns

A particularly noteworthy change in employment patterns has been the growing number of temporary workers in the workforce. As Exhibit 23-5 illustrates, the percentage of full-time workers with full benefits has been steadily decreasing, while the number of part-time workers has been significantly increasing.

From a supply perspective, this can be attributed to the growing number of middle-aged women entering the part-time labor market. From a demand perspective, companies are coming to the realization that a more flexible part-time workforce is cheaper than a full-time, full-benefits staff.

Exhibit 23-5. Full-Time Workers versus Part-Time Workers

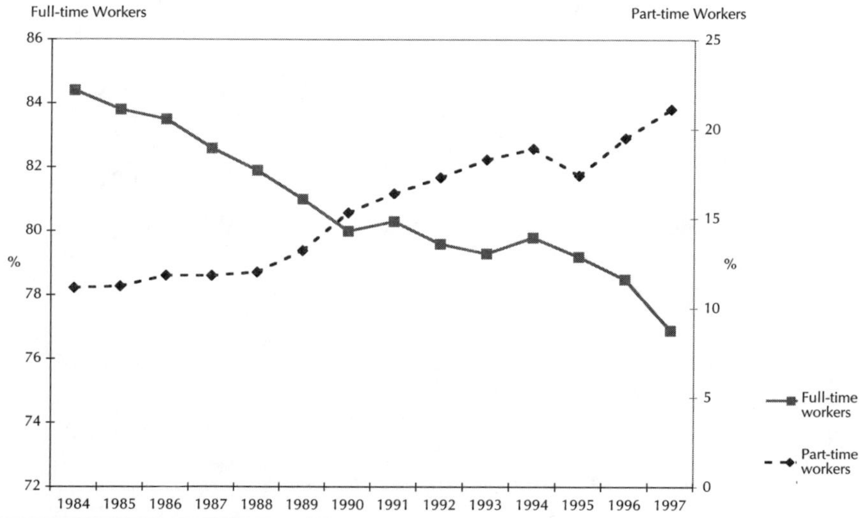

Source: *Ministry of Labor, "White Paper on Labor," 1998*

Turnover Rate

Since 1995, the turnover rate has been steadily rising. Turnover is most frequent among younger workers and women. This is not surprising, since both groups make up much of the growing part-time and temporary sector (in which turnover is traditionally high).

Unemployment

The labor shortage of the 1980s gave way in the mid-1990s when the economic boom began to fade. Companies began looking for ways to reduce their fixed costs-including labor. By May 1998, the unemployment rate had risen to 4.3% (see Exhibit 23-6). While still low by many standards, this was the highest level of unemployment in Japan since just after World War II.

Exhibit 23-6. Rate of Unemployment and Job Openings per Applicant

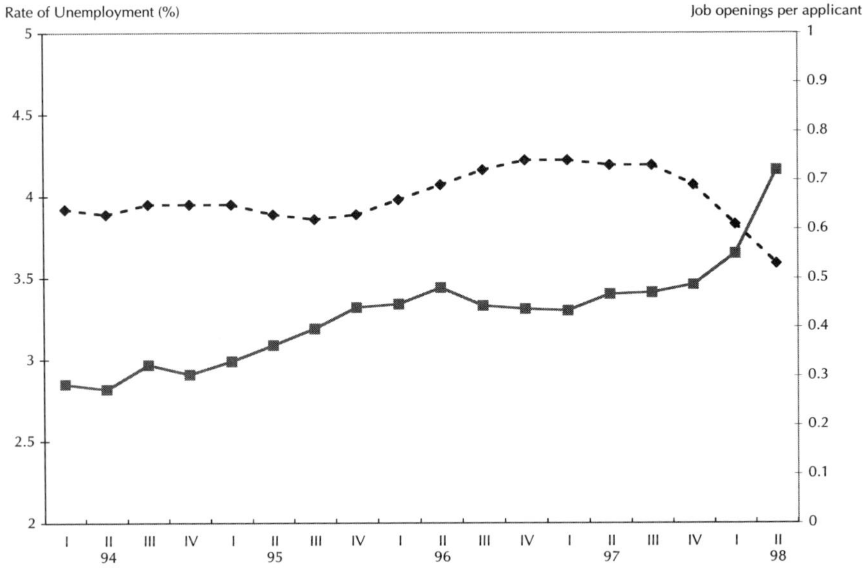

Source: *Ministry of Labor, "White Paper on Labor," 1998*

This has been harder on more experienced workers than on younger ones. Younger workers have seen reductions in recruitment, which has made it more difficult for them to enter the workforce. At the same time, it is younger workers who are most likely to leave a company voluntarily, usually to seek a more lucrative or fulfilling job. Middle-aged workers, whose opportunities to find new employment are limited (in part by their relatively high salaries), are increasingly facing the prospect of having to leave their jobs involuntarily. Their number has grown considerably since 1996. Thus, unemployment is not only a hardship but also a polarizing force for those who are affected.

Job Opening per Applicant

As efforts to reduce labor costs continue, companies are beginning to fill formerly full-time positions (e.g., clerical jobs) with part-timers or temporary workers. The result is fewer full-time jobs, which has led to a decline in the number of job openings per applicant (see Exhibit 23-6). This is especially problematic for middle-aged workers, who are most likely to seek full-time work. Despite this trend, scarcity of skilled labor in certain fields such as engineering is a critical problem for many Japanese companies.

Traditional Japanese HR Practices

Lifetime Employment

For many years, the norm in Japanese human resources management has been the seniority system, in which salary and advancement are based on age and length of service. This system is closely linked to lifetime employment, which has long been one of the fundamentals of Japanese management, particularly in midsized and large firms. A worker typically stays with the same company throughout his or her career, until reaching the mandatory retirement age. (Japanese companies are allowed to enforce mandatory retirement age, which is now at 60.) Employees are rewarded for their entire tenure, not just for specific achievements as they occur. Unlike most U.S. companies (and, to a lesser extent, those in Europe), Japanese companies exercise a "no layoff" policy and rarely dismiss employees.

Traditionally, Japanese companies recruit and hire new college graduates every April. Through such practices as internal rotations, these new employees acquire a broad range of skills and continue to move up, for which they are rewarded regularly. Employees are assumed to grow professionally throughout their career, constantly gaining from their experience and enhancing their skills and expertise.

Salary growth continues as the employee gets older, which makes it easier to cope with the outlays needed for marriage, children, home ownership, and other major life events. The seniority system guarantees that income will continue to rise regardless of the employee's position; however, it does not necessarily reward all performers the same. Age and length of service being equal, a poor performer will not progress at the same rate as a good performer, who will typically be promoted to higher positions.

Compensation

The typical compensation plan offered by Japanese companies includes the following:

- Base salary (an amount based on rank and qualification plus an additional monthly allowance for housing, commuting, etc.)
- Seasonal bonus (up to six months' salary)
- Statutory benefits (health insurance, employment insurance, public pension insurance, etc.)
- Nonstatutory benefits (company housing, corporate pension plan, corporate recreation facilities, etc.)

In addition, when an employee leaves the company, whether at or before the mandatory retirement age, a retirement allowance is provided. This allowance (paid either in a lump sum or as a pension supplement) is considered a kind of deferred compensation and offers partial postretirement support; the longer the employee's tenure, the higher the amount.

Innovations in Human Resources Management in Japan

The chief advantage of the lifetime employment and seniority system, the Japanese have long held, is that the stability of steady employment and income creates a feeling of company loyalty among the workers. That said, it has also created a workplace devoid of flexibility and fluidity—a workplace in which individuals never get a chance to engage in self-development. In fact, the "no layoff" policy promises a lifelong increase in salary (and labor costs) regardless of employees' productivity. Faced with mounting costs, an aging employee population, and a weakened economy, Japanese companies are now painfully aware that their chief hope of becoming more competitive is to develop HR practices that cut labor costs while increasing productivity. In response, many are beginning to shift the focus of their employment policy away from the seniority system and toward merit and performance (see Exhibit 23-7).

Selection and Staffing

This shift in focus is very evident in recruitment and staffing practices. The rapid changes in the Japanese corporate climate have compelled companies to explore more efficient means of filling jobs. Many companies are taking the once unheard-of steps of shrinking the core workforce and filling positions with experienced workers whose capabilities match the company's needs. For some jobs requiring highly specific skills, companies are hiring experienced midcareer people from the external labor pool instead of training their own employees to do the work. This is in part replacing the traditional April recruitment of new college graduates. Hiring now takes place throughout the year and focuses on a more diverse applicant pool. According to one recent survey, almost 75% of companies are now hiring more experienced midcareer employees, with 45.5% actually hiring fewer

Exhibit 23-7. Trends in Promotion and Compensation Policies

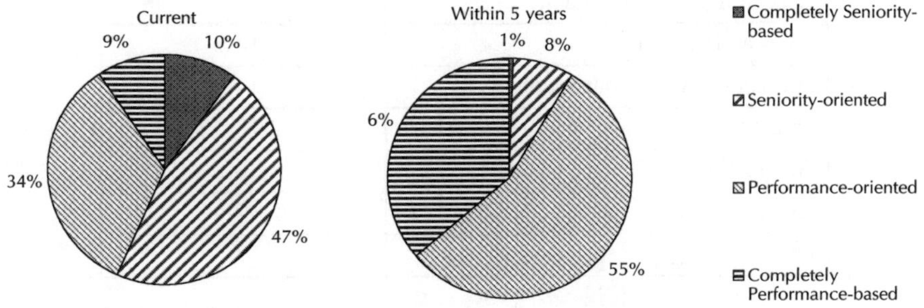

***Source:** Economic Planning Agency, "Reconsidering the Japanese-Style Management System," 1998*

new college graduates. Fully one-third of companies surveyed said they were pleased with the introduction of year-round recruitment.

To fill support positions, companies are beginning to turn to part-time and temporary workers as a means of keeping labor costs down. Outsourcing has also been introduced as a viable option (see Exhibit 23-8). Japanese HR managers have been reluctant to make use of outsourcing services because of the need to disclose information (e.g., salary information) that has traditionally been considered confidential. But the potential increases in efficiency and productivity, along with the increased flexibility, have helped to lessen this reluctance.

Dealing with the relatively high labor costs of a mature workforce presents another challenge. Larger companies have begun shifting workers around to make optimal use of their skills—through temporary transfers (shukko) or permanent reassignment (tenseki) to affiliated companies or

Exhibit 23-8. Status of Outsourcing

Types of Jobs Outsourced	Percent of Companies[1]
Information technology	59.4
Security	55.3
Logistics	50.2
Production/Engineering	43.8
Corporate benefits	40.9
Maintenance	34.8
Training and development	25.3
Advertising	24.6
Research and development	22.5
Sales and marketing	15.8
Human resources management	14.3
Other clerical jobs	13.1
Accounting	8.2
Client service	7.6
Other	7.2

1. Responses from companies with more than 1,000 employees.

Source: *Japanese Ministry of Labor, "White Paper on Labor," 1998* subsidiaries. Outplacement is another option—one that some companies are offering as a part of early retirement packages. These packages offer simple cash incentives or provide tuition for seminars and courses as well as outplacement counseling. The goal is not merely to provide employees with an incentive to leave before the mandatory retirement age but to encourage them to develop a second career. Fully 56% of companies were offering some sort of early retirement package by 1997. Even the programs that offer only cash benefits can be quite generous. For example, employees who retire early from the Kansai Electric Power Co., Ltd., receive a year of paid leave. At Matsushita Electric, employees who leave at age 50 receive three months of paid leave and a cash bonus equal to 2.5 times their annual salary.

Compensation

The traditional seniority-based system pays inadequate attention to younger workers who show promise and ambition. Faced with the prospect of spending long years moving slowly up the corporate ladder, they will have little motivation to stay put; if they do, their performance may never equal their abilities. Meanwhile, senior employees receive their guaranteed pay increases regardless of whether they excel at their work. Companies are finally beginning to view the reward system as an essential tool for retaining good employees and motivating good performance. As Exhibit 23-9 illustrates, many companies have begun to restructure their compensation systems to allow for rewards based on merit, regardless of length of service, which is probably one of the most critical changes to occur in the Japanese corporate environment.

Base Salary. According to Japan's Ministry of Labor, the traditional average cash compensation mix is as follows:

- Base salary—71%
- Seasonal bonus—23%
- Overtime—6%

Base pay, which is increased annually, is a fixed cost that has no ties to corporate performance. During years of economic sluggishness, this fixed cost becomes a huge burden. By switching at least in part from a seniority-based to a merit-based compensation system, companies can reduce or hold the line on fixed costs and replace them in part with variable costs.

According to one survey, Japanese companies are exploring three options (for use individually or in combination):

- A revised job-qualification/grading system
- Merit-based or performance-based annual salary review system
- A "pay for job" system

Revised job-qualification/grading systems are typically applied to nonmanagerial employees. They entail a very strict review of qualifications required to do the job competently.

Merit pay or pay-for-performance systems are already in place or ready for implementation in 40% of large companies, such as Sony, Fujisawa Pharmaceutical, Honda Motors, and Fujitsu. Most companies initially adopt this second option for managerial employees, adding nonmanagerial employees later. Because this represents a significant departure from the traditional system, most companies adopt this approach gradually. The portion of salary linked to performance is typically limited to between 10% and 30% of the total salary, with the merit increase limited to between 10% and 15% of this performance portion of salary.

Exhibit 23-9. Changes in Compensation Systems

Type of Change		**Percent of Companies**	
		1985	**1998**
Base Pay[1]	Increase portion of pay for qualifications	71.9	56.2
	Increase portion of pay for job	—	16.3
	Increase portion of pay for seniority	2.1	0.5
Promotion	Based on merit	83.9	84.4
	Based on seniority	0.6	0.3
Increase portion of seasonal bonus in annual salary		8.3	9.7
Increase portion of individual performance in seasonal bonus		—	56.6
Introduce stock options		—	1.6
Introduce annual salary system		—	24.0

1. Base monthly salary typically consists of payment for three elements—qualifications, rank, and seniority—plus some kinds of allowances.

Source: *Japanese Ministry of Labor, "White Paper on Labor," 1998*

The third option, the "pay for job" system, is not quite as popular as annual salary review, but many HR managers find it intriguing because it is highly subjective and it can be applied to all employees, even those overseas. Companies can define a portion of salary to be administered under the "pay for job" system. Performance pay can be given as a merit increase or even combined with an incentive for the best performers, enabling the company to reward individual performance while still controlling the overall corporate budget. Top-performing employees are more motivated because their raises and promotions are not tied to seniority. One obstacle to a "pay for job" system is that it requires ongoing job evaluation and performance measurement, which are not common practices for Japanese companies. Many firms are now exploring this system to determine if it is suitable for their long-term needs.

Incentive Plans. Perhaps the most important development in employee incentives in Japan has been the adoption of stock option plans. Only recently, it was illegal for employees to own stock in their employer's companies, but a June 1997 revision of the commercial law governing stock purchases eliminated this ban. Sony, Toyota, Orix Corp., and Daiwa Securities Co., Ltd., are among the companies that have already introduced stock option plans; others are expected to follow suit, although many are moving cautiously. Despite the obvious benefits of stock option plans (e.g., linking pay increases to the company's performance), several

Exhibit 23-10. Issues with New Performance Evaluation Systems

Issue	Percent of Companies
Variance among evaluators	65.5
Difficulty in evaluating different types of jobs with the same tool	60.0
Difficulty in making clear performance distinctions among employees	35.4
Tendency to evaluate progress rather than results/achievements	27.3
Lack of evaluator training	23.6
Difficulty in reasonably distributing the budget	18.2
Other	7.3

Source: *Japan Productivity Center of Socio-Economic Development, "Current Status and Challenges of Japanese-Style Management," 1998*

factors unique to Japan must be considered in deciding whether to adopt stock option plans:

- Nearly 75% of existing stock in Japanese companies is held by either affiliated companies or major banks, with a relatively small portion held by institutional investors. Thus, stock market performance is influenced more by these loyal shareholders than by corporate performance.
- Because the Japanese stock market is so weak at present, potential payouts linked to its performance are not likely to be viewed by employees as an effective incentive.
- Tax issues related to stock options are still unclear.

As of this writing, it is not certain whether stock option plans will become as prevalent and popular in Japan as they are in the United States.

Performance Appraisal

The shift toward some form of performance-based compensation has required Japanese businesses to reexamine the manner in which they measure performance. Under the traditional system, performance evaluations were often relegated to the figurative "black box," with managers

Exhibit 23-11. Average Monthly Benefits Costs per Employee

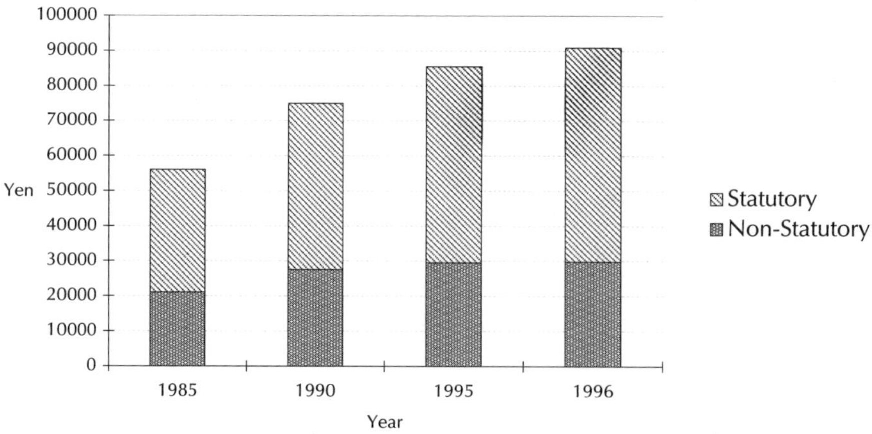

Source: *Asahi Shimbun. 1998/7/4*

rarely disclosing the results with employees. Employees are now becoming concerned with the content of their appraisals, since the results have some impact on their pay, and they wish to take an active role in the appraisal process to ensure that their performance is being measured accurately and fairly. Companies are learning that a merit-based system simply will not work without the company's willingness to be open with its employees.

The need for better two-way communication has increased with other changes as well. The use of processes such as management by objectives (MBO) is becoming more prevalent, and some companies have introduced the 360-degree assessment, which provides for multiple input to performance appraisals. Ultimately, these tools will enable employees to set goals, evaluate their own performance, and communicate their concerns openly with their supervisors. Recent research, however, shows that both companies and employees still have a way to go to make these new processes work as intended (see Exhibit 23-10).

For example, a vital element of MBO is goal setting, but the goals that are set can be too vague, too difficult, or too counterintuitive to motivate employees. In addition, some MBO programs introduce performance standards and performance assessments that are not linked to the organization's overall purpose. The appraisers themselves are often inadequately trained to communicate effectively with employees, which makes the process less than rewarding. Japanese companies will need to work hard to overcome these obstacles. That said, it is also clear that, once the challenges are met, communication will improve and a true merit-based culture will be able to develop.

Benefits

Trends in Corporate Benefits. As seen in Exhibit 23-11, the costs associated with corporate benefits have been steadily increasing over the past several years. Statutory benefits costs have risen dramatically; this is a particularly burdensome development because they are fixed costs. Some companies, such as Kao Corporation and Mitsui Mining and Smelting Co., Ltd., have decided to abolish some nonstatutory benefits by selling off corporate housing and resort facilities. This has reduced costs and brought in a onetime income from the sales. A new policy at another company, Matsushita Electric, gives employees additional salary to replace nonstatutory benefits.

The need to broaden benefits options to reflect the demographic changes in the labor force has likewise saddled companies with high costs. Companies are now compelled to offer a menu of benefits from which employees with diverse needs can choose. The cafeteria plan approach has been adopted by companies such as Seiyu, Ltd., and Benesse Corporation. In this approach, employees are given additional benefits choices, which they can purchase at different levels with benefit "credits." This enables the company to maintain control over the benefits budget while giving employees more say in the benefits they receive. But maintaining the benefits menu can be expensive. Moreover, there is still the issue of whether a cafeteria plan is fair to an employee who chooses no benefits—what should the company do for them? With so many different offerings, some employees are now voicing their annoyance at the perceived unfairness of who gets which benefits. As a result, it has remained a relatively unpopular approach. Toyota's announcement last October that it would introduce a cafeteria plan by 2000, however, may give this option greater viability.

Corporate Pension Plans. Corporate pension plans in Japan are now facing a dilemma: The aging population, coupled with the decline in the number of younger employees, raises questions about who will fund the plans for today's middle-aged employees. The low interest rate, resulting from the collapse of Japan's "bubble economy," has resulted in pension funds earning less than projected. As a result, some corporate pension plan foundations have either reduced benefits or liquidated their assets.

Companies are now looking to supplement defined-benefit plans with defined-contribution plans, which provide employees with some options. Japan's Ministry of Health and Welfare, in fact, has recommended that defined-contribution plans be used to supplement the basic benefits of employee pension plans. The Ministry of Labor proposes to change regulations to create tax-advantaged portable pension plans, similar to 401(k) plans in the United States. Although no decision has yet been reached by the government, the prospect of introducing this kind of plan holds considerable promise for companies and employees.

Retirement Allowance. The growing number of retirees also raises the prospect that companies will be unable to afford the burgeoning costs of retirement allowances. As a result, some companies have changed the formula they use to calculate the allowance. Under this new system, each employer provides "points" for retirement allowance based on position or qualifications (regardless of seniority); the accumulated points are then multiplied by a unit amount per point to determine the size of the allowance.

In May 1997, Matsushita announced that it would implement a multitier pay structure in which new employees would have the choice of three different pay systems:

1. The traditional package of cash remuneration, retirement benefits, and other benefits
2. Higher cash remuneration and some benefits but no retirement benefits
3. Solely cash remuneration with no benefits at all

Some 44% of Matsushita's employees chose the cash remuneration option, gaining between 240,000 and 360,000 yen in addition to their annual salary. However, the new system cannot take advantage of taxation rates on retirement allowance; thus, other employers are now examining the issue quite carefully before implementing such an approach.

Expatriate Compensation

As Japanese companies continue to seek foreign markets, the number of Japanese who live and work in foreign countries has been increasing. According to a survey by the Ministry of Foreign Affairs, the number of Japanese expatriates employed by private industry was 300,000 in 1996—nearly 1.8 times higher than the number in the late 1980s.

Japanese companies doing business abroad have been faced with a number of challenges as a result of using the "budget approach," which extended their traditional policies to expatriate compensation. Under the budget approach, salary is determined by a two-part formula: the foreign currency portion, based on the costs that the expatriate typically incurs in the assignment location (annually revised according to consumer price indexes, etc.), and the home-currency portion, based on the expatriate's normal domestic monthly salary. In addition to this monthly salary, the expatriates could receive seasonal bonuses comparable to those of peers back in Japan. However, as the standard of living of Japanese rose, and as the yen became stronger, the amount of compensation for expatriates became huge. Upon examination, companies realized that this approach to expatriate compensation had several problems, including the following:

- Inequities among expatriates assigned to different locations
- The inability to account for exchange-rate fluctuations
- Lack of applicability to foreigners living in Japan
- Feelings of resentment among employees who were local nationals (and whose salaries did not match those of the expatriates)

Furthermore, the high costs incurred put Japanese companies at a distinct economic disadvantage relative to other global competitors.

As a result, more companies are now relying on data provided by independent organizations specializing in these issues. In 1989, Yokogawa Electric Co. introduced its "balance sheet approach." At the time, this approach was a radical departure from the traditional compensation system, but it is now the way in which nearly two-thirds of all Japanese expatriates are paid.

Unions

Decline in Union Membership. As Exhibit 23-12 shows, the number of union members has remained virtually unchanged since 1970, even though the total number of employees in 1997 had risen to nearly 1.7 times the 1970 figure. Consequently, the rate of union representation has declined from 35% in 1970 to 22.6% in 1997.

This situation is partly the result of a shift from manufacturing to service-industry jobs (in which many employees are not unionized). The rise in the number of part-time jobs (also not typically unionized) has further contributed to a decline in union representation rates.

Diversified Role for Unions. Since 1955, industrial and trade unions have engaged in shunto, or collective bargaining, every spring. The industrial unions put forth their unified demands around March, and the trade unions begin their bargaining soon afterward. Not surprisingly, the demands of trade unions, especially within the same industry, were always coordinated and unified. The principle behind collective bargaining had been that union members should be guaranteed the same level of living no matter where they work (and no matter how well the company performs).

During the spring bargaining in 1996, many observers were surprised by the divergence in wage settlements among companies in the same economic sector, as well as among different sectors. In 1997, steelworkers received the lowest increase, 1.56%, up from 1.54% in 1996; electrical

Exhibit 23-12. Union Representation

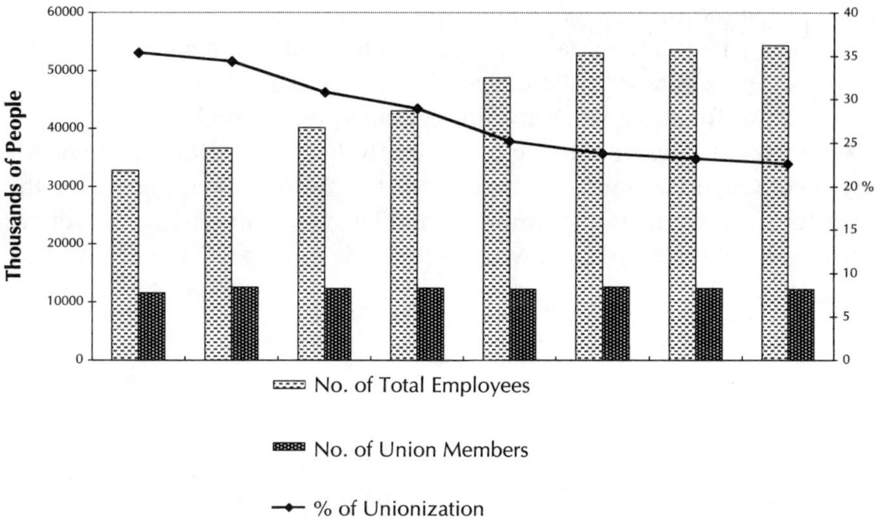

Source: *Ministry of Labor, "White Paper on Labor," 1998*

machinery workers received 3.17%, up from 3.14%; and autoworkers received 2.96%, compared with between 2.65 and 3.11% in 1996. This seems to suggest a growing diversity in employee interests that can no longer be met by a single bargaining agenda. Thus, labor unions have begun to explore what alternative roles they can play. Recently, labor unions expressed their willingness to work with management by offering new business policies and HR practices. For example, the Japanese Electrical Electronic and Information Union (Denkirengo) attracted attention by introducing new policies that would radically change the conventional seniority—based compensation system in 1997. The increasing diversification of agreements may spell the end of the traditional unified annual wage bargaining—and a change in the role of the unions.

Conclusion

Japanese companies have come to recognize that their ability to compete on the world stage may depend in part on whether they can restructure their conventional seniority-based employment and compensation system. Their challenge at present is to develop the most suitable HR strategies for their workers, strategies based on performance and merit, without losing all the advantages of the traditional practices. Since this refocus is still new, it is far too early to judge precisely how well these new strategies will be implemented among Japanese companies and accepted by their employees. There is always the danger that such changes will have negative implications for some workers—in particular, older employees who have spent their entire careers being rewarded for longevity. Despite the possibly severe repercussions that may result for these workers, however, the long-term effects of transforming an outdated system will be a stronger corporate environment and a workforce that is more productive and better motivated.

Note

1. Unless otherwise noted, the statistics quoted throughout this chapter are from the Japanese Ministry of Labor, "White Paper on Labor," 1998.

CHAPTER 24

EMERGING ECONOMIES IN AFRICA, THE MIDDLE EAST, AND EASTERN/CENTRAL EUROPE

Z. SAMUEL BERNSTEIN

This chapter is devoted to handling human resources in the emerging economies or developing nations, focusing on Africa, the Middle East, and Eastern/Central Europe. (China is covered in a separate chapter, and India is partly covered in the chapter on Asia.) At the outset, there is a problem with terminology. Unfortunately, there are no standard definitions, and each attempt at regulating definitions is problematic. Classifications are notoriously inconsistent.

The Encyclopaedia Britannica identified the "developed countries" as Canada, the United States, the countries in Western Europe and most of Eastern Europe, the former Soviet Union, Japan, South Africa, Australia, and New Zealand. All the other countries, often former colonies with low living standards, were called "undeveloped." As living standards in most poor countries began to rise following the end of the colonial era, they were renamed "developing." Thus, Eastern Europe would be considered "developed" by this definition.

The World Bank bases its classifications on per capita income levels. With this system, a country like Kuwait is not considered "developing" because of its high per capita income (from the vast oil wealth in the hands of a tiny portion of the population).

The term third world is no longer applicable since the "second world" (the Communist countries and centrally planned economies) has vanished as a useful classification.

The term developing nation is being replaced with emerging economy, which is seen as being more sensitive to people's feelings. No one wants to hear that his or her nation is "undeveloped."

So we are left with either two classifications (developed and emerging) or three (developed, developing/emerging, and undeveloped). I consider the two-classification system to be inadequate; frankly, any categorization that classifies Poland and the Congo as the same is too broad to be useful.

For practical purposes and to avoid getting tangled in definitions, I shall be loose in my use of the terms. There is a scale (however fuzzy and subjective) based primarily on the degree of infrastructure that allows us to call some nations developing or emerging and other nations greatly underdeveloped. The terms emerging economies and developing nations will be used synonymously, reflecting common usage in the literature, and I ask the forgiveness of any who feels either term is offensive.

In general, we can think of three levels of development. There are enormous differences among the countries in all aspects of life, society, and business based on these three levels.

In Africa, for instance, South Africa is much further developed than Nigeria or Kenya, which in turn are further developed than Rwanda, Angola, or Namibia. In the Middle East, Israel and Turkey are far more developed than Jordan and Egypt, which in turn are further developed than Afghanistan, Iraq, or Bangladesh. One hesitates whether to classify countries like South Africa or Israel as "emerging." Among the former Communist bloc, those that share a common border with Western European countries (e.g., Poland, Hungary, Slovenia, and the Czech Republic) stand out as very hopeful for Western business prospects; a less inspiring picture would be painted of those further away from Western influence (e.g., Belarus and Ukraine); and a much less hopeful view would be given for the countries far removed from Western influence (e.g., Uzbekistan and Kazakhstan).

It is important to recognize that, although there are some similarities, the problems and issues in each country are significantly different. A solution for a particular problem in Afghanistan will probably not work in Kenya, and a significant issue in Egypt may be irrelevant in nearby Saudi Arabia. In that vein, let us start with some of the reasons for these differences and then see what helpful generalizations might apply in many developing nations.

For ease of communication, I will use the term *Central* or *Eastern Europe* to refer to the former Communist bloc, recognizing that many of these countries are clearly in Asia. Similarly, I will use the term *Western* to mean "Western Europe and North America," recognizing the political incorrectness and geographic absurdity of such a term.

Cultural Differences

Different national cultures differ in basic attitudes toward life, employment, family, teamwork, and risk. It is important to stress that there is no "right" or "wrong" attitude; these values and beliefs have (perhaps subconsciously) molded each society over generations, and they will not be easily changed. Certainly, they will not be changed for anything as temporary as an employer's whim or mere monetary compensation.

It should also be noted that we are describing societal norms. Individuals within any society may be at the extreme ends of the bell curve. Thinking that all individuals in a country or group have the same attitudes or behaviors would be stereotyping.

It is perhaps best to understand that these traits are not opposites but are gradations along a continuum. For example, relationships—with friends, with family, with coworkers—are important to every human being. What differs from country to country, or society to society, is the emphasis placed on friendships and relationships compared with profession and business.

A few examples may be helpful in understanding some of the differences between developed and developing nations. These are largely taken from the writings of Fons Trompenaars, a Dutch sociologist who has dealt extensively with cultural norms.

Relationships

In developing countries, relationships are extremely important, far more so than in Western countries. In most Western countries, for example, employment has to do with a position and a job. In much of Africa, Central Europe, and the Middle East, employment has to do with friendships and loyalties. If a supervisor in Pakistan or India leaves the company, it is likely that many of the employees he supervised, with whom he has a personal relationship, will go with him. Loyalty is not to the profession but to the individual—and, by extension, to one's social friendship group.

In many developing nations, this concept is taken to an extreme, with rampant nepotism. The families of important political figures may have jobs solely for the sake of the family and relationship.

Another example is that often the written, contractual document is unimportant in comparison with the relationship. When American firms began creating deals in China, their focus was on the written contract. The Chinese did not generally care much about the written contract; they wanted to build the relationships. For instance, the written contract says I should have produced X amount of material this year, but I was unable to do so for reasons outside my control (poor economy, changing market, etc.). The contract says I should be penalized, but the long-term relationship says we should be flexible and accepting and restate the goals.

Communication: High Context versus Low Context

Most English-speaking countries are "low context": You say what you mean. The words (for example, in the legal contract) are crucial to mutual understanding. Much of Asia, Africa, and South America are "high context": Meaning comes from the surrounding context and not just the words themselves. The written contract is meaningless; the relationship is what is important. A famous example of this is the Japanese method of saying "no" without ever actually saying "no." The negative is conveyed by tone, body language, context, and form of the message—all clues to which a Westerner (listening only to the words) is often oblivious. Edward T. Hall has written extensively about this topic, and there is much material available.

Sense of Time: Long-Term versus Short-Term Focus

The difference in focus among cultures is illustrated by this common example: An American businessman, exasperated at the slow pace of negotiations, says to his Chinese counterpart, "Don't you understand that time is money?" The Chinese gentleman, with a puzzled look, replies, "Don't you understand that time is eternity?" The haste and speed of Western business are not compatible with that slower-paced environment. The speed with which a business meeting gets to the point may vary considerably, from almost immediately in the United States to following a slow (perhaps painfully slow) social etiquette in much of the Middle East.

Sense of Time: Linear versus Synchronic

Americans and Northern Europeans tend to view time as linear: A person can do only one task at a time. In Southern Europe, Africa, Asia, and Latin America, time is often viewed as synchronic: Time is elastic; time is flexible; people can "multitask"; they can carry on two conversations at once. Americans may perceive people who are late as lazy, but in fact they may have simply been busy with other things, and time is flexible enough that tardiness doesn't matter.

Concept of Business

Central and Eastern Europe were under Communist rule for 50 years or more, and the repressive Communist regime bred poor business habits (largely incompatible with Western ideas) and a differing notion of "property" and "ownership." Entrepreneurial behaviors, sales techniques, and financial accountability were discouraged. The skills that were rewarded were flexibility and adaptability to change, but not strategic thinking or people management. The gap in business acumen in these countries is intense and is now being bridged only slowly.

Religious Differences

Many of the developing countries of Africa, Asia, and the Middle East are predominantly influenced by Islam. This results in attitudes toward life and employment that are different from those in predominantly Christian nations, and it also results in practical differences in human resource practices. In Moslem countries, employers commonly provide daily time off for prayers. Religious Moslems fast during the day for the entire month of Ramadan; this often causes a fairly relaxed workday by Western standards and may lead to altered work hours (such as evening hours for work). The human resource manager unfamiliar with the Moslem religion may inadvertently cause dissension or arouse ill will by expecting Western behaviors.

Degree of Control over the Environment

In many developing countries, there is a prevalent belief that outcomes are largely influenced by external forces (e.g., fate or by God) and not by human beings. This is very different from an American perspective, for example, of "can do" or self-determination. Clearly, reality for every human being is a mix of both; there are some things that are under a person's control and some things that are not. The difference is one of emphasis.

The attitude that external forces constrain activity may be rooted in religion and is common in Moslem countries, but there are non-Moslem countries as well where the belief in fate is very strong.

An illustration is the Arabic term *inshallah*, loosely translated as "God willing." Can I make my budget targets? Inshallah. Will the company pay me benefits when I retire? Inshallah. Will I be at work tomorrow morning? Inshallah. If people from certain cultural backgrounds believe that outcomes are dependent on God or fate rather than on the individual, their attitudes toward responsibility, performance, and security will be very different from what most Americans or Europeans would feel—and the impact on human resources is critical.

This belief may be so strict in some Moslem countries that it makes insurance difficult to obtain. An insurer, by promising to deliver a benefit, may be perceived as showing arrogance or hubris—such a promise can only be made inshallah. An additional difficulty is that strict Islamic law prohibits interest charges. Obtaining insurance coverage in such locations may require intricate verbal and legal technical maneuvering to avoid the sin of trying to thwart God's will.

By the way, the term *inshallah* is most commonly used to mean "I will try, but I can only succeed with God's help." However, it is sometimes used as a joke, meaning "I'm not going to try; the only way this will be done is if God does it."

These cultural differences can produce distrust between local nationals and corporate or regional headquarters. There is also the risk of friction between the expatriate brought in to manage the operation and the local nationals who must make the operation work. Understanding the cultural differences is critical to successful management of global human resources; using the differences to build multicultural strength is the mark of the successful global company.

Political Differences

One of the difficulties in dealing with developing nations is the degree of political stability. While some developing countries have reasonably stable democracies, favorable to welcoming foreign business, others may be in turmoil. "Stability," of course, may be in the eye of the beholder. Some emerging markets may appear to be quite stable: The ruling party (or individual) retains all power, and the opposition is enfeebled or suppressed. However, such stability may be only superficial, and when the dictator dies or is displaced, the underlying fragility of the system may be evident.

Military dictatorships dominate Africa and some of the Middle East. Many of the other countries in the Middle East are monarchies, with all power held by the king. There is serious tension between those who want a liberal market economy and those who want a planned economy. Such tension can lead to serious political unrest.

Tribal clashes persist in much of Africa, where colonial powers drew national boundaries without regard for local custom, language, or historic rivalries. At best, these conflicts are expressed and resolved through a democratic process, but there may be strong potential for social unrest and violence. Within the company, a manager from one tribe may find that he or she has little respect or cooperation from direct reports from a rival tribe. Thus, topics such as career paths, training, and management may require extra efforts for success.

Central Europe is struggling to develop a capitalist democracy, but many countries are fighting against organized black-market crime syndicates. This instability often means that employees are focused on very short-term needs (e.g., cash compensation) rather than longer-term needs (e.g., retirement benefits). Curbing corruption and crime is one of the paramount objectives of many governments in Central Europe. Again, there is a great difference between the fledgling democracies such as Poland and Hungary and the mafia-like syndicates in Belarus, Russia, and Ukraine. In many countries of Central/Eastern Europe, the legal frameworks are still developing. This makes for a somewhat chaotic political situation.

A harsh attitude among local nationals may be expressed toward a foreign firm. The foreign-owned firm may be viewed as "deep pockets" in any legal or political situation and thus could be the target of "legal extortion."

Economic Differences

One of the most obvious differences between developed and developing countries is per capita income. Salary levels may seem appallingly low to Western HR practitioners, but they may be in line with the competitive environment in the developing country. Although low compensation levels may seem attractive, recognize the likelihood of low productivity as well.

The infrastructure in developing countries may be severely limited or may be lacking altogether. Transportation, communication, banking, and finance, for example, cannot be taken for granted. When I was in Lagos, Nigeria, I found that the hotel telephones could not connect international calls. Trying to reach offices in Romania or Ukraine by phone can take hours or even days. Brownouts and loss of electric power are still quite common in the Philippines. And the postal service in most undeveloped countries is corrupt or unreliable. In such environments, the idea of employee investment choices in a savings plan is still very far away.

It should be stressed that there are always exceptions. Poland, for instance, has made incredible progress in the last decade or so. The wide range within the broad category of developing countries cannot be emphasized enough.

Although the world is now firmly entrenched in capitalism, the concept is viewed differently in different countries. In Asia, for example, the extended family clans that dominate business and the flow of capital form a sort of "family capitalism." It can be difficult in these environments to create modern corporate organizations. For the 40 or 70 years before the collapse of the Soviet Union, people in Central Europe lived with a different concept of property and ownership. Thus, in Russia and much of Central Europe, "frontier capitalism" is in its infancy: The government is pursuing for-profit business activities, criminal activities are rampant, and an entrepreneurial class is sprouting.

Currencies of most developing nations are "soft"—that is, they are not easily converted into "hard" currencies such as the U.S. dollar or British pound sterling. Soft currencies can be very volatile, leading to dramatic fluctuations in value. Executives in such environments may look into the use of split payroll, in which a portion of salary is paid in hard currency outside the country. This subject should be considered carefully, and the following issues should be raised.

- Is it legal for the executive to hold money outside the country? Currency exchange restrictions should be reviewed; in fact, they are often more severely enforced than tax regulations. Furthermore, exchange restrictions may be changed rather suddenly. Countries facing high inflation sometimes feel that restricting the flow of money away from the country will somehow help reduce the inflation; however, neither economics theory nor past examples favor this.
- Does a split payroll provide a tax advantage to the executive? In some situations, there may be a legitimate tax advantage in having some income offshore. More often, the only tax advantage is that the employee could (illegally) not report the income and the chances of the tax authorities discovering the evasion might be small. Companies do not want to be accused of "aiding" or "conspiring" to evade taxes and should take precautions to protect themselves (e.g., by notifying the employee in writing whether the offshore payments are taxable income and should be reported).
- Currencies may devaluate faster than inflation. Consider an employee in Indonesia whose salary was denominated in U.S. dollars. On September 1, 1997, a salary of US$50,000 was converted to IDR 147,000,000. On December 1, 1997, that same salary was converted to IDR 185,500,000, yet inflation was modest during that period. The

employee whose pay was denoted in U.S. dollars rather than in Indonesian rupiahs essentially received a 26% salary increase during those three months. But the reverse situation can happen as well: The inflation is high but the government freezes the currency exchange rates, which happened in Brazil a few years ago. In this case, the local employees can suffer a loss of purchasing power because of their dollar-denominated pay.

Exhibit 24-1. Annual Inflation Rate

	1997	1998
Czech Republic	8.4%	10.7%
Egypt	4.6%	3.3%
Hungary	18.3%	14.4%
India	7.2%	15.4%
Israel	9.0%	5.4%
Kenya	12.0%	5.8%
Nigeria	8.5%	11.1%
Pakistan	11.4%	6.2%
Poland	15.9%	11.7%
Russia	14.6%	27.8%
Slovenia	9.1%	8.6%
South Africa	8.6%	6.9%

Coupled with soft currency may be a high rate of inflation. Coping with 30 or 50% rates of inflation—or even higher rates—is a challenge for any compensation or benefit program. Official inflation rates may be manipulated by the government and may not reflect true price inflation.

At the moment, inflation is fairly low around the world. There are a few exceptions, such as Angola (over 90% estimated for 1998), but note that even the 10 to 15% rates in the table are quite high compared with the United States or United Kingdom.

Some HR issues to consider in high-inflation economies include the following:

- Frequent salary adjustments may be necessary. When inflation exceeds 100% a year, for example, there will usually be legislation or collective bargaining requiring more frequent salary increases (e.g., quarterly, semiannually, or based on inflation exceeding a certain percentage).

- Timing of payments is critical. Consider a bonus program for calendar year 1998, paid in March 1999, providing 25% of salary based on January 1, 1998, base pay. At 50% annual inflation, the bonus is worth perhaps 10% of purchasing power at the time it is paid. So what the company views as a high bonus to reward outstanding performance may be perceived by the employee as a lukewarm bonus (at best).
- Merit increases may need to be carefully considered. If inflation is 500% a year, what is the value of a 2% merit increase? For most employees, such small merit increases may not be perceived as doing much more than keeping pace with inflation.
- Postretirement payments, such as monthly annuities, must be indexed on a regular basis or the loss of purchasing power will leave retirees destitute very quickly. British parent companies are used to automatic indexation, but American parent companies tend to resist automatic pension increases. The mind-set must be adjusted to recognize the difficulties of a high-inflation environment.

Tax Rules

In countries where political stability cannot be taken for granted, the law (as a tool of the state) may be viewed with suspicion; it may provide guidelines but not a strict code. In many emerging economies, the letter of the law may not be very important compared with the spirit of the law. HR professionals used to a legal system based on the written law may find difficulty accepting the attitude that the intent behind the law is more important than what the law says.

In the design of compensation and benefits programs, and especially when it comes to perquisites and similar noncash payments, "gray areas" of tax law may be more heavily exploited than they would be in Western countries. What to a Westerner may appear to be "cheating on income tax" may be viewed locally as common, indeed prevalent, "stretching an ambiguity in the tax law."

In many countries, tax is collected (or the tax filings are reviewed) by local inspectors, with little coordination at a national level. These inspectors may vary in their sophistication, knowledge, and attitudes. If stock options are extremely rare in a country, for example, and not directly addressed by the tax law, then different local inspectors may make different rulings on the appropriate tax treatment. This leads to a gray area in which the rules are nonexistent or ambiguous, and practice may vary.

In addition to income tax, there are often very high social charges (e.g., social security contributions). Forms of compensation that avoid or reduce such charges enable the company to be more efficient.

Throughout Central and Eastern Europe, the legal structures (and tax laws) are still emerging. The only certainty is change, frequent and dynamic. Unfortunately, it may be very difficult to obtain accurate, up-to-date information. In Russia, for instance, change in the tax laws has been so rapid that most of the administrative staff in government services cannot keep up; when asked for information, they will only provide it in exchange for a cash payment.

In addition to gray areas and legal tax avoidance, one may encounter illegal tax evasion. Local firms may pay "under the table" or "payment in envelopes" (cash payments that are not reported for tax purposes). Such practice is very rare at the local operations of Western multinational companies but is sometimes found in local family-owned companies that may be acquired. A careful due diligence process should uncover such practices.

It therefore becomes very difficult for the employer to tread what may be a delicate balance. On the one hand, the competitive market (local companies) may provide employees with forms of remuneration that are tax effective—either through legal avoidance, through illegal evasion, or through a gray area between the two. On the other hand, foreign-owned firms may provide a total compensation package that strictly adheres to the law, since they may be subject to closer scrutiny than local firms are. The HR issue is how to be competitive and yet not run afoul of the law.

Government Requirements and Employment Laws

Government structures around human resources and employment laws (social security systems, income tax collection systems, labor laws, a strong judiciary, etc.) may be taken for granted in developed nations. These may be lacking in developing nations. The taxes collected by social security may be being used currently to build roads or for similar government uses but not to provide for retirement income. In the worst-case scenario, sadly true in much of central Africa, social security contributions and taxes may be lining the pockets of corrupt politicians and not even being used to build an infrastructure.

At the other end of the spectrum, nations such as Poland, Hungary, and South Africa have reasonably developed infrastructures. Social security is undergoing revision and evolution in these countries to reflect a defined-contribution, free-choice model (see the description of the Chilean model under "Statutory Pensions" in Chapter 17), but a basically sound social security system is in place. Such reform is also being considered in the Czech Republic, Croatia, Slovenia, and Romania.

In other countries, the social security system may be close to collapse, and employees cannot count on benefits ever being received.

Labor laws may be changing, but they can be reasonably relied on to reflect the reality of the environment. The rate of change can be quite rapid.

Coming to grips with government requirements (or lack of requirements) regarding employment is the first step on the road to developing a compensation and benefits program for the developing nation.

Safety Issues

Companies in emerging markets may have need to protect their employees, especially in countries more likely to experience political or social upheaval. American firms in the Middle East, for example, may be targeted by the government or mobs (or government-promoted mobs) expressing their dislike of American policies. Other multinational parents may face similar problems. In late 1998, Italy refused to extradite the leader of the Kurdistan Worker's Party, causing a boycott of Italian goods in Turkey; firms identified as Italian were targets for violence.

Executive perquisites may therefore include elements of physical protection such as bodyguards and home security or even stronger measures. Company-provided chauffeurs may not be a perquisite of convenience but a necessary security precaution. Many Austrian companies, for example, do not allow their employees to use private cars for business trips into Eastern Europe because the theft rates are so high there.

In remote areas or hardship locations away from major cities, companies may build compounds to house employees, protecting them from a hazardous environment.

In a few developing countries, outsiders might be caught in the crossfire of violent opposition to the government from terrorist groups or militant minorities. Companies doing business in such countries would do well to think of heightened security and emergency evacuation plans—arguably, elements of "wellness."

Employment

There are several topics relating to employment that are relevant: unemployment rates, protective labor codes, past practices, and human rights issues.

Unemployment rates may be very high. Official rates may be distorted, sometimes including underemployment and sometimes manipulated for political purposes.

Exhibit 24-2. Official Rates of Unemployment (1999 Estimates)

Czech Republic	5%
Egypt	12%
Hungary	9%
India	22%
Israel	9%
Lithuania	7%
Nigeria	28%
Poland	12%
Russia	11%
Slovenia	8%
South Africa	25%
Ukraine	3%

High unemployment can create an environment in which employees do not willingly leave the company. Labor laws and courts may rule unfavorably for employers that are considering workforce reductions.

Labor codes in most developing nations tend to favor the employees. In fact, it may be very difficult to dismiss employees, even for severe underperformance. Stories are told of employees who are defrauding the company but cannot be fired. Severance payments upon dismissal may be very high, such as a lump sum from one to two months' pay times years of service. Russian labor law is particularly strict in this regard, and almost any dispute is resolved in favor of the employee.

In many developing countries, companies have been "overstaffed" in the past. This was especially true in the former Communist countries, such as China and Slovenia. Positions may have been broken down into the smallest possible task components, so several employees would do a job that could be done far more productively and efficiently by only one employee.

Human rights may not be a high priority in developing nations. That may come as a shock to the human resource specialist, and it may be an issue on which the company chooses to confront the local culture by taking a firm position for its employees.

The issue of child labor is a difficult one. Western firms frown on child labor as a human rights encroachment, and I certainly do not want to be seen as supporting the exploitation of children. However, for a starving family in cramped living conditions, if the children can work at minimum-wage jobs, the money is desperately needed.

Availability of Talent in the Market

Hiring and retaining talent is likely the highest-priority item for human resources. The supply of skilled employees may be scarce. One of the greatest difficulties for a Western company trying to do business in a developing country is to identify local talent. In much of the former Communist bloc, for instance, there are many individuals who think they are entrepreneurs, but very few individuals truly have an entrepreneurial spirit. Candidates may be deficient in communication skills, lack commitment, be indecisive, or have knowledge gaps in accounting, marketing, and finance.

Companies tend to want to hire younger employees, believing (often correctly) that the older employees have the older mind-set of the Communist regime.

One of the obvious traps to avoid is don't assume that employees have the right skills or outlooks just because they speak English well. Contrariwise, in Central Europe, for example, at various points during the Communist regime, English was discouraged, so qualified key managers may not speak English well or at all.

This is not to say that local talent is unavailable. For example, there are qualified people in Poland and the Czech Republic, but locating them requires patience and a much more diligent search than in Western countries.

People with skills in finance and marketing are in high demand and short supply; such skills were not needed during the Communist regimes. The scarcity of talent has led to bidding wars, job-hopping, and luring talent from competitors—perhaps by doubling the salary. As a result, in much of Eastern and Central Europe, even the best salary survey data may be unreliable. Survey data can only measure what happens at a point in time and not the trend or the volatility.

In regions where retention of talent is a major issue, companies would do well to invest in training and development and in building relationships with the key employees. There is no sure way to stop a competitor from hiring away your trained personnel at double their salaries, of course, but building a strong relationship with the individual key employee helps, so the employee views the company as "family" rather than simply the provider of a paycheck.

Despite job-hopping, employees may not be very geographically mobile. Career advancement and pay increases may not be sufficient incentive to uproot families and lives. In much of Eastern and Central Europe, for example, there is often unwillingness to move from the metropolitan area to the smaller towns. Recruitment in the Czech Republic is difficult because young people cannot afford housing. One approach is to tie an acceptance bonus to housing costs.

In much of Africa, employees may come into the city from the tribal areas looking for work, but movement from one tribal area to another is rare and difficult.

Also affecting mobility are contractual agreements between employer and employee. Employment contracts are often required, spelling out the duties and responsibilities of each side. In Russia, for example, employment contracts may mention the area where the employee is to work. It may then be difficult for the company to move the employee, without a breach of contract (and payment of potentially large termination indemnities).

"Returnees"

Of growing interest to U.S. companies is hiring local nationals from universities in the United States. An Indian student, for example, who has just received an MBA from a prestigious American university is presumably trained in Western thought and yet understands the language, environment, tradition, and opportunities in India. Hiring such students with the intention of having them return to their home country is almost an obsession at many firms.

But the competitive market for compensation and benefits for such an employee is the United States, not India. Rare indeed would be the Indian student with an MBA from an American university who was willing to return home on a salary one-tenth or one-quarter of what he or she could get by staying in the United States. Such "returnees" can be less expensive than expatriates because allowances can be reduced or removed. Returnees can be very effective hires. But the notion of hiring them on purely local terms is largely illusory. Only a dedicated few will return home at local salaries when the competitive market for their talents is global and will pay far more than they would get at home.

Often, these returnees have difficulty when they return home because they have acquired Western business thought and so "speak a different language" from their home-country colleagues.

Management

The very definition of "good" management is heavily culture-bound. The "proper" relationship between employee and manager may be very different from country to country, even among developed countries.

In much of Eastern and Central Europe, there are few people with management skills. Finding an employee in Poland with 10 or 15 years of management experience would be almost impossible. Because there is no history of people management in the country prior to the fall of communism, seven or eight years of experience would be the best one could hope for. In contrast to Western countries, managers in Eastern Europe tend to wait for orders rather than make decisions, and decisions may be based more on emotion than on rational success models.

Managers in Eastern and Central Europe may not see themselves as managers but more as "family" owners. They may think of the company's resources (assets, people, cars, etc.) as being available for their own private use. This is not the notion of "ownership" that most Western companies want to instill. As mentioned before, the idea of "property" and "ownership" in the former Communist bloc is not aligned with Western thought.

In some countries, corruption, nepotism, and mismanagement may be prevalent. Nigeria is probably the world leader in this highly competitive field, but it is not alone. Trying to overcome past mismanagement may be a fearsome task for the HR manager.

Total Compensation Package

It is especially important in emerging markets to be focused on the total compensation package rather than on any individual element. Otherwise, the wide mix of compensation elements can lead the unwary HR manager to erroneous decisions. One company may put more emphasis on base salary, while another focuses on nontaxed allowances, and yet another emphasizes benefit programs. The focus should be on the total package—the cost to the company and the economic value received by the employees.

Base Pay

Direct compensation in many developing countries is more fragmented than in Western countries. Generally, Western cash compensation would be classified as base pay and a short-term (annual) incentive bonus. In many developing nations, this is far too simple.

To begin with, of course, monthly base pay may be paid more than 12 times each year. The 13th or 14th month's pay is fairly common and sometimes required under labor law. In addition, there may be other regular payments tied to base pay. Vacation premiums (an additional percentage of base pay for vacation days) are quite common.

Salary structures are often in place for the local operation of a Western parent but may not be used by purely local firms. The salary structures may be somewhat looser than the Western HR manager might expect or somewhat tighter. I saw a salary structure in Nigeria that had more than 100 grades below manager level.

Pay levels in emerging markets are usually very low by Western standards. A local manager in Romania might earn less than US$150 per month. The lower levels of pay are balanced by lower costs of living in these countries, of course, but the gulf between pay in developed versus undeveloped countries is extreme. The presence of high-paid expatriates in a country can cause tensions; I know of a CEO in Uganda whose total expatriate package was more than the salaries of all the government ministers put together.

Often, pay rates are significantly higher in the major cities than in the provinces. The differential in Hungary or Russia can be as high as 100%.

As already discussed, some employees wish to be paid in hard currency, outside the country. This practice can be illegal and is often a source of serious inequities. A manager in Bulgaria who is paid in deutsche marks has already had effective salary increases exceeding the 40% inflation rate last year just from the currency devaluation. Every month, he exchanges his fixed DM amount for more and more local currency.

Allowances and Regular Payments

Allowances may be (but need not be) tied to base pay. Especially in undeveloped nations, the list of allowances can be quite extensive, commonly including allowances for meals, transportation, or clothing. In India, the typical package might also include special allowances for cost of living (called "dearness"), conveyance (fuel reimbursement), house rent, house maintenance, vacation travel, education for children, clothing/uniforms, soft furniture, hard furniture, business entertainment (without the need for receipts), domestic help, utilities, and professional development. In Nigeria, allowances might cover housing, furniture, utilities, domestic help, transportation, education, clothes, club membership, business entertainment, reimbursable business expenditures (without the need for receipts), and a variety of others. Such allowances may be provided to all employees or may be limited to special categories such as upper-level positions, lower-level positions, sales positions, and so on.

These allowances are often provided at tax-favored rates (or even not taxed at all). Because of the favorable tax treatment, a company providing the same total cash amount but not using these allowances would be at a competitive disadvantage. Even though the costs to the company are the same for providing total cash or providing allowances, the value received by the employees can be quite different.

There may be other regular payments. The 13th or 14th month's pay may be considered part of base pay. Special payments at vacation time or similar regular add-on payments may also be found. Practice will vary by country, of course.

Incentive Bonus

Annual "incentive" bonuses, despite the plan description, may be fixed (e.g., as a percentage of pay or expressed as a multiple of monthly pay). The employees then view the "bonus" as an expected, regular pay element regardless of performance.

The notion of pay for performance may not be well understood. In the former Communist countries, for example, several generations have been brought up with the notion that pay is distinctly not related to performance. The process of teaching new ways may be an uphill struggle. The idea is commonly expressed as "I worked very hard, I did my best, it wasn't my fault that we didn't make our targets, so I should get my bonus anyway."

This attitude is not unique to developing countries but may be expressed most strongly there.

In some countries in Eastern Europe, there is a practice of employees taking "commissions." An unforgiving Westerner might call these "bribes."

As discussed earlier, currencies of most developing nations are "soft," and executives may want to be paid in a "hard" currency such as U.S. dollars or British pounds. These issues have already been addressed, and, as suggested, it is usually prudent not to pay in outside currencies.

Benefits

Provision of retirement benefits in developing countries is somewhat problematic. In an environment where neither government nor banks are particularly stable, does the company truly want to put money aside in some long-term pension vehicle? Does a reasonable long-term investment facility exist?

Lump sums at retirement (or earlier termination) are usually preferred over annuities. Often, this is for tax reasons, but in many cases, it may be for convenience. In many African nations, the employee leaves the city upon retirement and goes back to his or her native village to live with extended family. The mail cannot be trusted, certainly not for delivery of a personal check. The trip into the city to collect the check in person is too time-consuming and expensive, so the monthly annuity check may go unclaimed. In this situation, a company that insists on monthly installment payments is doing the employee a serious disservice.

The issue of medical benefits can be very difficult. This is not merely the question of who pays for medical care but often the deeper question of how to get treatment. In many developing countries, government-sponsored medical facilities are severely oversubscribed and undersupplied. Such basics as sterile equipment, simple vaccines, or antibiotics may not be available. Private hospitals may not be much better off. The oil companies, for example, often set up their own medical clinics for their employees, not trusting the local services. Medical evacuation may be part of the benefit package for key employees. Each country's situation is somewhat different, so generalizations are awkward; the operation in each country must be considered carefully.

A few examples of the differences that one can find include the following:

- Special problems affect some regions. For example, the widespread AIDS epidemic in Africa poses severe health care problems for employers, as well as increasing premiums for death benefits.

- Termination indemnities or redundancy payments ("golden handshakes") are sometimes found in Central and Eastern Europe. Managers in state-owned (or former state-owned) operations may have arrangements with the company for payment of huge sums of money in case of their termination of employment.
- In countries where polygamy is practiced, the company may want to provide some forms of coverage only to the principal wife (e.g., joint-and-survivor coverage under a retirement plan).
- The definition of family may include parents, grandparents, brothers and sisters, and other relatives not normally considered in Western medical plans.
- Western medical plans often exclude traditional medicines or treatments such as witch doctors, acupuncture, or similar methods. Such exclusions may destroy the usefulness of the plan if the traditional (but excluded) treatment is popular. For example, in Indonesia, the witch doctor often serves the role of general practitioner. The patient goes to the witch doctor first before going to a medical specialist.

Perquisites

Whereas most U.S. companies shy away from discrimination, companies in developing countries usually have no such bias. Special allowances or fringe benefits typically are provided to higher-level employees. Club memberships and company cars are quite common. Security may be necessary, through the form of personal bodyguards or drivers for executives (as company employees), as was discussed earlier. Other company staff may work at the executive's home as gardeners, maids, babysitters, drivers, or similar personal servants. Perquisites are usually tax driven, but there may be a strong element of status involved as well.

Tax rules in emerging markets are often ambiguous and perhaps loosely enforced. As noted earlier, there can be differences in tax treatment based on the ruling of the local tax inspector. The company must take care not to be caught at tax fraud, but practices that may seem dubious to the Western corporate executive may be commonly accepted in a developing country.

Since practices may seem unusual to the Western mind, it is important to understand local tax rules and competitive practice. In Nigeria, for example, the government allows companies to provide "assets" to employees in an effort to increase home ownership. Only 5% of the value of such assets is taxed. Many companies therefore interpret "assets" somewhat loosely, providing the employees with washing machines, television sets, and even clothes—all under the category of assets receiving favorable tax treatment.

Employees in Central Europe, for example, are often focused on immediate cash payments. They need cash to pay for housing, to buy goods that are newly available, to educate their children, or to take a vacation in the West. Long-term benefits such as stock options or retirement plans are only beginning to be of interest. Under the prior Communist regime, the company took care of employees from "cradle to grave." Social funds provided housing, sports facilities, preschool, consumer goods, meals, vacation, recreation, and so forth. Companies acquiring an older business in Central Europe must come to grips with some of the perquisites provided by the old social funds.

Availability of Information

Western companies are used to having, and demanding, statistics and detailed information. Such information may be lacking entirely in emerging markets, may be unreliable, or may be difficult to obtain.

It has been mentioned that the tax laws may be ambiguous or incomplete. It has also been mentioned that the legal frameworks may still be developing, and in an environment of constant change, yesterday's information is worthless today.

Accurate statistics on inflation or unemployment may be hard to find and, once uncovered, may be unreliable. These are areas of vital concern to the government.

Data on competitive practice for compensation or benefits may be difficult to obtain. Information is often shared informally by human resource professionals, without formal surveys. In Nigeria, for instance, we found some resistance to conducting a formal survey, primarily from companies who feared that the government would obtain a copy. We have also seen instances in which only a handful of companies in a country have a retirement plan but the survey produced by local management includes all those companies, giving a distorted picture of the market. Of course, the use of a biased sample for a survey is by no means limited to developing countries.

The main message here is to not be too demanding of outside survey evidence or statistical verification and to entertain a somewhat healthy skepticism of any such data you do receive.

Conclusion

Human resource specialists now face issues in the emerging markets in general that are quite different from those in developed countries. Moreover, the issues differ from one developing country to the next. In many countries, such as Poland, Hungary, Israel, and South Africa, there is reason to be optimistic about the present and the future. In many other countries, frankly the outlook is bleak.

The key to managing human resources in these countries is flexibility-and the old adage "Act globally, think locally." Converting the business strategy into human resource policies and practices in the emerging markets is perhaps the major challenge posed to the corporate (or regional) human resources professionals today.

SECTION FIVE

OTHER GLOBAL STRATEGY ISSUES

CHAPTER 25

INTERNATIONAL SALES COMPENSATION PLAN DESIGN

WILLIAM O'CONNELL

As many readers can attest, getting a sales compensation plan designed and implemented can be one of the most interesting and aggravating assignments of a career. So multiplying the emotion, hard tradeoffs, and impossible-to-please constituencies of a domestic situation across the cultural, language, and situational differences that would confront someone responsible for international sales compensation could be a fool's errand for all but the calmest souls.

This chapter provides some hard-won advice for those who would tread in these waters. This will be done by answering the most perplexing questions that faced individuals responsible for sales compensation design and administration at Pepsi Cola; AT&T; Baxter Healthcare; Unisys; Thomas Cook, Ltd.; NCR; and Colgate Palmolive.

What's Changing?

Well, first of all, the number of businesses that have international outposts and the number of countries in which they are likely to have sales organizations have increased.

Fifteen years ago, it was common to hear international executives contend that certain cultures were naturally biased for or against selling or that selling in certain countries was based only on "old boy," "school," or class relationships. Today, international managers probably have modulated their "stereotypes" of the past to match the growing success American firms have had overseas and to match the growing contributions to their firm that professionals from other nations have made.

What's more, as multinational customers have increasingly single-sourced the best multinational solutions available, the cross-country coordination demands made on selling organizations have increased proportionally. Correspondingly, many firms have created global-account executive positions and organizations to coordinate and further penetrate their firm's efforts with the highest potential global customers.

One other major thing of interest to sales compensation designers has also changed: the greater availability of data about pay levels for salespeople in the most populous and attractive countries where business is conducted.

Finally, the omnipresence of e-mail, the Internet, fax machines, cell phones, and so on has made communications between headquarters and the field operations of any country easier and more frequent.

Despite the fact that it is easier to reach common ground between the various cultures and perspectives of a multinational firm, the answers to many of the questions that must be considered before sales compensation design can be completed will be different from country to country.

What Is Most Likely to Be Different?

As you can see from Exhibits 25-1 and 25-2, several important questions need to be answered before the degree of incentive pay versus base salary is determined for salespeople in each country. In general, the

Exhibit 25-1. Factors Determining Sales Representative Personal Prominence in Gaining Sales Results

Salespersons' Efforts are not as Prominent in Gaining Revenue Results as a Percent of Overall Firm Efforts	0 ← 1 — 2 — 3 → 4	Salespersons' Efforts are a Highly Prominent Part of Overall Firm Success
High	Market Share	Low
Finite	Market Size	Infinite
High	Customer Acceptance of Product	Low
Repetitive and Predictable	Buying Pattern	Few/One-of-a-Kind
High	Sales Support	Low
Frequent	Team Selling	Never
Farmers	Job Definition	Hunters
High	Close Rate	Low
Low Prominence of Incentive Pay as a Percent of Total Cash Compensation		Higher Prominence of Incentive Pay as a Percent of Total Cash Compensation

newer the product, the broader the customer base, and the more dispersed the channels of distribution are, the greater the role of a salesperson in creating results.

Exhibit 25-2. Balancing Incentives and Salary

More Weight (70% or More) on Salary When:	More Weight (30% or More) on Incentives When:
Selling is more of a team effort	Job requires high level of drive
Heavy use of advertising and promotion	Company is not well-known
Product or service requires little sales effort	Short sales cycle
Job includes many non-sales duties	Competition is strong
Typical sales cycle is one year or more	Low advancement opportunities with company

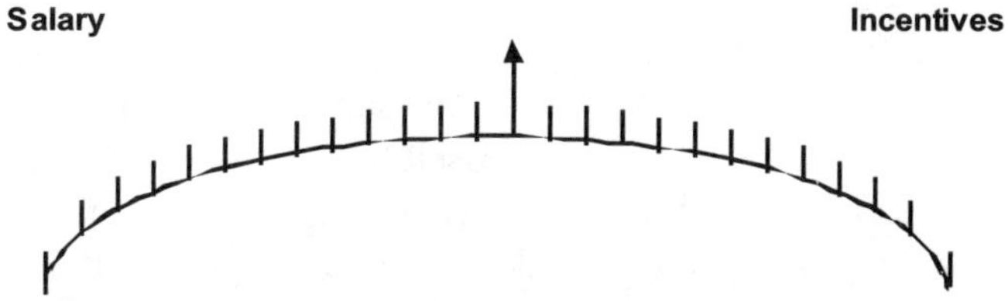

Factors Determining Sales Representative Personal Prominence in Gaining Sales Results

Balancing Incentives and Salary

One of the biggest mistakes that firms make when they enter a new country is to assume that their success, even brand strength, at home is going to be carried forward to a new market. Even if the product is the best product on the market and, therefore, should "sell itself," the firm's support from its supporting channels of distribution might be much weaker than in the United States (which enjoys the stability that powerful channel players like Wal-Mart bring to a market). Thus, a salesperson is required to work much harder per sales dollar.

When market conditions make the salesperson's role more difficult, there is no doubt that the incentive rewards should be higher than they are in the same role in an easier market. However, deciding to increase the mix of incentive pay might not be the right choice. If the market conditions are likely to increase the length of the sales cycle by adding steps to what it takes to get an order, the right answer might be to increase the percentage of base salary as a percentage of expected total cash compensation, to protect the salesperson from the harshness of doing without incentive pay (personal cash flow), but increase the amount of incentives for overtarget sales performance. This is especially true if success in the new market is more unpredictable than in the home market, thereby making accurate target-setting problematic and the use of a commission rate for above-target performance a more reasonable feature of plan design.

What Is Most Likely to Be the Same?

Regardless of varying market conditions, the performance expectation, products, services, and strategies of the firm are likely to be the same. As a result, the selection of performance measures for plan design that align with the firm's business strategies is likely to be the same from country to country.

There is one caveat. It's entirely possible that the information systems that capture orders, shipments, and payroll data are different from market to market. If that is true, a plan designer has a tough choice to make. Should the plan designer keep the same measures everywhere and therefore manually calculate (administer) the plan payouts or vary the plan design to accommodate the inherent capabilities of local market information systems? Answering this question is a lot easier if the firm has a set of corporate-wide guiding principles for plan design.

What Role Should Corporate Headquarters Play?

Best practices around this question appear to be emerging from the experiences of several global firms.

First and foremost, best-practice firms do not ask their headquarters personnel to get overinvolved in the plan design debates of their local market organizations. Rather, they provide everyone in the organization with a set of guiding principles around which the questions that arise in the field can be answered. Then they audit the performance results of salespeople in the field and the related incentive plan payout levels.

For example, Exhibit 25-3 illustrates the guiding principles one financial services company adopted for its multiple location divisions in the field.

Exhibit 25-3. Corporate International Sales Compensation Plan Design

Category	Illustrative Guiding Principles
Eligibility for rewards	Only sales jobs that call on and directly represent the firm in face-to-face dealings with customers will be eligible for "sales" incentives. The efforts and results of all other positions that support the customer coverage process (e.g., customer service, industry specialists, etc.) will be recognized through other types of incentives such as team rewards based on overall business-unit performance.
Comparative framework	Comparator companies will include competitors for people, which will often include business competitors.
Pay positioning	• Base salary will be positioned at the median of comparator companies. • For expected performance, incentive pay will also be positioned at the median of comparator companies for most positions. However, new business developers will be allowed to make up to 75th percentile incentive pay for expected performance if they are highly prominent in influencing the customer's decision to buy. • There will not be caps on payouts to individuals. However, caps will be placed on incentive payouts for "deals" in which multiple people and management are involved in the sales and credit process. • New business leads will be given 100% "credit." Internal referrals will be given 25 to 75% "credit" toward incentive plan payouts.

Performance measurement and goal setting	Sales incentive plans will only include measures that will: • Represent "hard" results • Be controllable and understandable by participants • Differentiate excellent from average performance In no case will a measure represent less than 10% of total cash compensation. Performance thresholds will be set at at least 85% of expected performance. Goals will be set to: • Require an improvement over the prior year's performance • Over the long term, allow approximately two-thirds of participants to reach expected performance levels
Pay mix	Pay mix will become increasingly variable based on the degree of cold-calling and persuasion necessary to convince a customer to buy or expand his or her relationship with the firm. • Up to 50% fixed and 50% variable for positions that spend 50% of their time prospecting and qualifying leads and 50% of their time closing the sale • 100% fixed to 75–90% fixed and 10–25% variable for positions that spend 100% of their time analyzing, maintaining, and supporting client relationships
Pay variability	• For most sales positions, incentive pay will be moderately leveraged. However, for new business developers who have significant influence over the customer's decision to buy,

incentive pay will be highly leveraged and even more highly leveraged for overtarget performance.

- For sales support and credit positions, incentive pay will be moderately leveraged.

Pay-for-performance relationship

The size of overall business-unit incentive payouts and overall business-unit performance should vary directly each year.

Notice that the guiding principles are written to allow each division to make the detailed decisions appropriate to its local market conditions, yet they maintain a common approach and similar pay-for-performance philosophies around the globe.

It's a common practice for corporate headquarters to also play a role in auditing the efficacy and efficiency of the field plan designs and reporting their findings to senior management.

Rather than audit pay levels and market prices per sales job, the most important items to check during an international sales compensation audit are as follows:

- The percentage of salespeople who make target performance levels. In general, more than 75% of all salespeople should make at least target levels of performance. If they do not, then payout levels will be too low to retain people at competitive market pay levels. It is not at all unusual for it to be difficult to set stretch but achievable targets in new markets; unfortunately, the consequence is unfair for salespeople paid for target pay at target performance or perhaps on too low a commission rate.
- The total of all compensation pay for all sales jobs (the compensation cost of sales) in a market should be roughly similar for all similar market conditions. In general, total pay as a percentage of total sales in markets in which the firm is established should be low and relatively higher in emerging markets.
- The relationship between the total pay of each performer in a market and their total sales performance should graphically be an upward trend line, as in Exhibit 25-4.

Exhibit 25-4. Illustrative Pay-for-Performance Audit Analysis

Illustrative Pay-for-Performance Audit Analysis

If it is not an upward trend line, then once again the target-setting process is flawed or accounts vary in size so much that they significantly distort pay results (in which case, you may need to create a new sales job with a higher base salary and a lower incentive rate for those who handle the largest accounts).

Summary

The keys to being a successful sales compensation plan designer in an international setting are the following:

- Assess the local market by local market (country is local enough) differences in the prominence of the salesperson's role in creating sales results, and vary either the mix of base salary and incentive pay for target performance or the richness of the incentive pay rate for above-target performance.
- Provide a framework of guiding principles for local plan designers rather than dictate or approve every little plan detail. Allow local cultural sensitivities to influence plan design within the framework of the guiding principles.

- Allow plenty of preparation time before local markets start the plan "live," because many countries have legal guidelines about informing people before these pay plans are changed significantly.
- Periodically audit the plan payout results, the target-setting process, and the cost of sales compensation relative to sales results.

CHAPTER 26

REWARD AND RECOGNITION FOR GLOBAL R&D ORGANIZATIONS

JERROLD R. BRATKOVICH AND
RONALD F. SCHAEFFER

Globalizing R&D

In the 1960s, Marshall McLuhan coined the term global village to describe what he saw as an increasingly interdependent world, spurred on by technological advances. As his insights have accurately played out, we have seen numerous changes; many of these have in fact contributed to the growth of business globalization. Since the mid-1980s, global-based competition in many industries has been intensifying—resulting in increased pressure on profitability and, in some cases, company viability. As we approach the 21st century, most organizations will continue to search for new and better ways to compete in this steadily globalizing economy.

Up until the 1980s, a relatively small circle of highly industrialized nations, mainly in North America and Europe, dominated world markets—primarily by implementing new technologies and reaping the benefits of the resulting high productivity. The balance has shifted over the last 20 years, notably with the emergence of Pacific Rim–based organizations that offer high-quality manufactured products and much improved productivity.[1] The deregulation (and globalization) of financial markets has steadily progressed, and the emergence of new technologies, particularly in telecommunications, has both enabled and compelled the global growth of many industrial markets.

The rapid diffusion of technologies across borders has made countries more similar in terms of infrastructure, distribution channels, and marketing strategies. In addition, the new and stronger players in the emerging world have actually attempted to leapfrog over competitors by exploiting the technological changes and setting higher standards for competitive success.[2]

The rapid pace of technological change has reduced both product life cycles and costs. As a result, the timely contribution of research and development (R&D) has become increasingly important, as has the ongoing introduction of new technology as a competitive advantage on a broader global basis. The international diffusion of technology has influenced the pace and the location of innovation as well as the mission and operating approach of R&D.

In general, the R&D function has taken longer to embrace the globalization trend. Recently, however, the need for companies to tightly align technology strategy with overall business strategy has given renewed priority to R&D (although a few companies, such as 3M, have been at this for more than 30 years). Product and process innovations have been key drivers in the globalization push of the last two decades, not only in high tech but also in the more traditional heavy industries such as oil and automobiles. Gaining access to global sources of new technology and exploiting products and advanced process technology across different markets and regions have become a proven way to improve competitiveness. In many firms, R&D networks are now playing a key role in the globalization of product and process development. Studies of R&D investment in Sweden, Japan, Germany, and North America have confirmed the increase since the early 1980s of multinational firms' R&D investment outside the home country.[3]

Another important implication for the R&D function is the growing specialization of scientific and engineering knowledge-the skills and technical capabilities necessary to create and manage technology-based innovation. This specialization tends to spring up near universities and research complexes, further necessitating the development of interactive global networks to manage a well-focused R&D effort.[4] It also increases the demands on individual scientists and engineers to collaborate across disciplines and cultures, which is not something that most technical people have been encouraged, much less trained, to do in many companies until recently. Whether in planning products, processes, or market development, cross-discipline and interorganizational teams have become much more common in R&D as it becomes a more integral component of business strategy.

One more important mission for R&D is to give real-time technical support to other operational areas such as marketing and production. The globalization of this element of R&D follows naturally from the globalization of marketing and production operations, particularly when the technology is sophisticated or changes rapidly (e.g., electronics and telecommunications). This component of R&D may not require highly focused central coordination, but it is vital to cost and quality competitiveness. In addition, it provides an ideal venue for the development and early training of new technical staff, placing the demands of mobility and cultural adaptiveness on relatively young and less experienced employees.

In broad terms, the implications of recognizing the R&D function as a component of globalization strategy are twofold. At the strategic level, R&D must be organized to manage the company's technical-based innovation in the most effective way. At the human resources level, key competencies must be identified, and R&D professionals must be motivated to meet competitive challenges with innovation and creativity.

Firms have approached this growing globalization pressure on R&D in a number of ways. There is clearly no single answer; the approach depends substantially on the business and market context for the individual company. A 1996 IRI/MIT study, which combined written questionnaire and interview input, identified six possible modes of global R&D management:

1. Home base: New technology development concentrated in the home country and transferred to offshore markets through alliances and foreign-based technical support units
2. Multiple home bases: A single R&D center for each business, usually co-located with the business unit's headquarters, which could be outside the home country
3. Worldwide lead center: One lead center in a dispersed network responsible for developing specific new technology
4. Regional bases: One R&D unit in each major region, with coordination of new technology developments with other regional R&D units
5. Regional technology headquarters: One regional center designated as the lead for the region, managing a dispersed network within the region and coordinating with the other regional R&D headquarters
6. Flexible network: The leader role assigned by project to one of many dispersed centers

Each of the six modes, of course, has its own strengths and weaknesses.[5] The factors to consider include cost, critical mass, control of technology, the mix between basic and developmental research work, customer access (to identify emerging needs and to respond to problems), project management capability, sustaining technical competencies, attracting and keeping talent, and infrastructure support. The right answer for any one company requires analysis and weighting of all these factors, as well as recognition of the current and potential future markets.

A 1997 article in Industry Week provided several examples. Tokyo-based Sony has four R&D centers in the United States to leverage home-grown technology by transferring it (along with some key technical staff) to sites outside Japan. Hoffmann-La Roche is doing essentially the same thing with five R&D sites around the world. General Electric, on the other hand, requires its diverse businesses to be responsible for their own R&D. As a result, the Schenectady center accounts for only 10% of GE's total research today, with the rest spread throughout a dozen countries. Microsoft is following a similar strategy by setting up an R&D center in Cambridge, England, to gain access to the engineering resources associated with the university and the area's famed science park.[6]

An excellent example of how globalization and R&D can mesh over a long period of time is 3M, which has located nearly one-third of its technical staff (2,500 employees) in labs outside the United States. Two important factors driving this approach are the emphasis on technical service and the high priority placed on early identification of new product opportunities worldwide. 3M began its R&D globalization in 1963 when it established a research laboratory in Harlow, England. The company currently has more than 35 labs worldwide, always keeping a firm commitment to innovating for the customer. Geoffrey Nicholson, 3M's vice president for international technical operations, notes that "If we are to be focused on what customers really need, then our laboratories must have the flexibility and responsibility around the world to develop new products and new businesses. We have a responsibility to develop technologies and then to effectively share them around our 3M technical community." 3M may be one of the best business case examples of maintaining solid long-term linkage between corporate and R&D strategies, using detailed plans and measurements to evaluate progress and to upgrade targets as markets develop, expand, and mature.[7]

Strategically Driven R&D

One of the classic struggles in R&D is establishing precisely how much latitude and freedom there should be to explore potential new areas of opportunity. As companies become more global, a dual mind-set typically emerges. On one hand is the need to broaden the perspective but on the other is a need to maintain focus on the company's central vision.

The best strategies combine an understanding of the market opportunities with a realistic assessment of the company's capabilities. Business plans that ignore one or the other of these considerations end up either offering products and services that the market does not want or attempting to go after markets that the company is incapable of serving.

To optimize its contribution, the R&D function must also operate within the framework of market opportunities and corporate capabilities. Within those boundaries, however, R&D needs wide latitude to explore, investigate, create, and innovate. The ability to function within this paradox of clear direction and high flexibility is characteristic of high-performance companies.[8] Orchestrating this mind-set and behavior at the global level adds complexity and requires additional diligence in the form of communications and key performance indexes.

Sometimes there will be developments that have significant potential but do not fit corporate strategy. If companies are too rigid about which ideas to pursue, they may incur a double loss: the lost opportunity to participate in an emerging business and the loss of talent when key people leave in frustration over not being able to pursue a promising technology. A solution to this problem is to structure alternative mechanisms for these types of developments that could include one or more of the following: internal venture units, external ventures with seed funding by the corporation, licensing agreements, or joint ventures with a strategic partner.

The first test of any compensation program for R&D should be an assessment of how it will help to reinforce the right level of focus regarding the R&D initiatives without hindering the creative process.

The Globalization-Compensation Intersection: Complexity

It has long been acknowledged that one of the most difficult (and, hence, often the last) issues to be formally addressed in globalization is the people issue. The globalization of product development, manufacturing capacity, supply chains, and even information systems is widely viewed as less difficult than the globalization of the workforce itself. If, however, the people responsible for the new systems, methods, and resource configurations are not capable of operating with a global mind-set and acting accordingly, the other elements of the company's global strategy will be, at minimum, suboptimized and likely ineffective in achieving the intended benefits.

This is at least as true for the R&D organization as it is for other components of the business. Since the globalization of the R&D function is almost exclusively dependent on the interactive, integrative, iterative, and interdependent exchange of ideas, the organizational and human resources considerations are particularly significant and can determine the success of the R&D globalization strategy.

The issues of managing a global workforce are obvious, but they are worth a summary citing. They include variances and differences in culture, language, communications, interaction styles, time zones, geographic priorities, regional vested interests, and motivational factors.

Compensation, of course, is a key issue. Any move toward globalization must address technical issues such as tax considerations, currency exchange factors, and different levels of comfort and perspective pertaining to risk orientation (i.e., how much of the compensation opportunity should be contingent on performance/results and/or future outcomes such as stock price movement).

The complexity of dealing with compensation increases when attempting to globalize R&D. Within any organization, compensation is of keen interest and quite often controversial. When addressing the issue of how to compensate R&D professionals effectively, the arguments and opinions multiply. There are numerous points of view at either end of the spectrum; Exhibit 26-1 gives a small sampling.

Exhibit 26-1. R&D Compensation Perspectives

R&D professionals are motivated by the intrinsic value of the work itself.	R&D professionals want their value recognized through extrinsic rewards.
Directive compensation hinders the creative process.	Directive compensation channels the creative energies.
Tying compensation to outcomes takes the fun out of R&D and makes it work.	Not tying compensation to outcomes prevents the R&D professionals from participating in the value they create.
Compensation is not a motivator for R&D professionals.	The organization cannot attract and retain the quality of R&D staff it needs without an aggressive compensation program.

Added to these philosophical debates are growing concerns and, in some cases, increasing litigation concerning intellectual property (IP) rights, particularly when R&D is concerned. There are also other issues pertaining to the equality of treatment of technical professionals, including R&D staff, in comparison with other employees, particularly those on the management track. Even companies widely recognized as well-run, well-managed enterprises (such as 3M) have not been able to avoid controversy over whether technical professionals have the same opportunities as others for career advancement, compensation, equity participation, and influence.[9]

Typically, the company might ask an R&D professional questions such as the following: "Given the length of time over which development may occur, how do you accurately determine who made what level of contribution-and at which point in the development process?" "Is the development itself of greater value, or is the commercialization of the development of most value?" "How do we reward individuals versus teams, and how do we make sure that the compensation system does not inhibit collaboration and teamwork?"

Combining the issues of managing a global workforce with the special issues of recognizing and rewarding R&D professionals magnifies the complexity of developing an effective compensation system, raising perhaps the most challenging question: "How in the world—literally and figuratively—are we going to figure out this compensation conundrum?"

The remainder of this chapter is not intended as a blueprint for finding the answers. Rather, it provides a framework of considerations, a tool kit of specific elements and techniques, and guidelines for the development and application of compensation approaches for R&D that meet the needs of companies that want to be truly global in all aspects of their business.

Risk Management

The question "Why bother?" may seem legitimate at this juncture. "Why not pay competitive salaries," the reasoning goes, "throw in a few nonmonetary recognition awards, and take our chances?" In fact, that may actually be the right approach in certain cases. That said, how much a company's continued growth and success depend on new developments that cater to an increasingly large and diverse customer base determines whether the compensation program warrants special attention. If this is the case, then the compensation program should be viewed as part of a risk management strategy designed to protect a critical element of the enterprise's knowledge base.

As knowledge becomes an increasingly significant component of the value proposition, the R&D function typically increases in importance. Thus, the use of compensation—specifically, the expenditure of compensation dollars to protect against the loss of critical talent that embody that knowledge—is a wise and prudent investment.

Certainly, compensation is not the only factor affecting the loss of critical R&D talent. In a study done for a major corporation, the following reasons were identified as contributing to the turnover among highly valued technical staff in R&D centers:[10]

- *Unwillingness to fund ideas:* Rigid guidelines regarding funding, which frequently frustrated people who had developed promising technologies, many of which were often later successfully introduced by other companies
- *Inability to follow the technology:* Strong barriers or "one-way gates" restricting an individual from moving with the new technologies through operational and commercialization phases and then returning to R&D
- *Intellectual competition from supervisors:* Unwillingness of technical supervisors and managers to acknowledge, recognize, and encourage superior technical expertise and achievement, particularly in disciplines in which they were once considered a company's leading expert
- *Inequities:* Reluctance to provide scientists and engineers a fair share of monetary rewards reaped by their inventions (in some cases, for example, a salesperson earned considerably more from selling a technology than the technologist(s) who developed it did)
- *Lack of investment in professional development:* Insufficient investment in the professional growth of R&D employees in the forms of continuing education, specialized training, time for intellectual pursuits, up-to-date equipment, and so on
- *Limited career advancement:* Perceived lack of a clear path for professional and personal development
- *Capped responsibility:* Limited opportunity to take on greater responsibility
- *No ownership stake:* Inability to achieve an ownership position and to enjoy the influence and rewards commensurate with ownership

It is clear that the retention and application of a company's intellectual assets, as embodied by R&D professionals, requires a comprehensive approach involving a number of organizational management interventions. One critical element is a carefully designed reward and recognition system—one that takes into consideration both the value system of the R&D workforce and the interests of the corporation.

Compensation Architecture

Assumptions

There is no shortage of articles on how to compensate R&D professionals effectively. Virtually every one of them raises the issue of intrinsic versus extrinsic rewards. There is also almost always a discussion of monetary versus nonmonetary reward and recognition. Presumptions about the unique motivational characteristics of the R&D workforce are typically stated or implied—sometimes supported by opinion survey data or other evidence. The following assumptions are offered as a starting point for developing a compensation architecture that supports the achievement of a global R&D strategy:

- *R&D professionals are different.* At the very least, they are distinctive in terms of their motivations and expectations regarding the work environment.
- *Extrinsic and intrinsic rewards must be addressed.* R&D professionals do work for money, but not only for money.
- *Multifaceted approaches are essential.* No single program will address the range of attraction, retention, motivation, recognition, and reward objectives.
- *Individuals and teams should be rewarded.* The compensation plan should encourage individual initiative and contribution and reinforce team collaboration and collective ownership of results.
- *Compensation programs should be bold.* Minimal or token efforts to recognize achievements by R&D professionals are, at best, ineffective and not worth the effort and, at worst, insulting.
- *Cultural variances need to be considered.* Differences in how people from different cultures will respond to being recognized and rewarded need to be factored into the design of the compensation elements.

- *Compensation plans go stale.* Recognition and reward programs need to be assessed for their efficacy and revitalized every two to three years.
- *There are no perfect compensation plans.* Every reward system ever developed has potential downsides to it (e.g., a special recognition program can build resentment among either those who do not receive the award or those who are ineligible to participate in the program). The critical question each organization must ask itself is, "Does doing nothing have greater risks than doing something?"

Components

The following list is a sampling of reward and recognition programs and techniques that can be part of the compensation portfolio for R&D professionals:

- Monetary awards (cash, stock, other vehicles having monetary value)
  - — Key contributor plans (e.g., restricted stock or cash grants with vesting provisions for the retention of critical talent)
  - — Stock option participation
  - — Team awards (e.g., product development awards, project incentives, milestone acceleration incentives)
  - — Royalties and licensing-fee participation/sharing
  - — Patent awards (filing and award bonuses)
  - — Superior achievement awards
  - — Trips and gifts (with special significance to the individual's or team's accomplishments and interests)

- Nonmonetary recognition
  - — Election to internal scientific society
  - — Fellow status
  - — Product development award
  - — Technical excellence award
  - — Team-of-the-year award
  - — Inventors club
  - — Entrepreneurial award for commercialization insights
  - — Peer awards

- Work-life considerations
  - Professional development investments
  - Greater influence and involvement in decisions
  - Funding for special projects
  - International assignments and rotational opportunities
  - Multiple career track and advancement options
  - "Play" time for pursuing new ideas
  - Exposure to and direct involvement with customers

Additional Options

Other types of programs, such as those cited below, can have a powerful impact on the achievement of an organization's R&D objectives when applied in the right situations:

- *Executive tie-in.* Link a portion of management incentives to the results of the R&D initiatives to reinforce managers' supportive behavior; create a special award to recognize those senior managers who contribute in special ways to the success of the R&D initiatives.
- *Extension awards.* Provide recognition and, in some cases, partial participation in monetary awards for those individuals or units outside R&D that support the R&D efforts in special ways.
- *Import-export awards.* Provide special recognition for those who share R&D ideas, resources, and developments with other parts of the global operations and for those who adopt ideas and input from others.
- *Venture plans.* Create an equity simulator (e.g., phantom stock plan) for special development teams to create a stronger "ownership" stake in the endeavor and to emulate an early-stage start-up venture.
- *Worldwide R&D performance share pool.* Create a pool that is funded on the basis of a key measure(s) of R&D success (e.g., percent of revenue generated from products three years old or less) and distributed globally to the R&D staff in a manner similar to a profit-sharing plan.
- *Customer linkage.* Explore ways in which to tie an element of recognition, and possibly a portion of compensation, to the level

of internal/external customer satisfaction in areas relevant to R&D efforts.

Case Examples

The following case examples of IBM and 3M, both recognized worldwide for their expertise in global business and R&D, illustrate how both companies have used compensation and other rewards to support their global research organizations.

IBM

About 80% of IBM's worldwide research staff is located at two sites in the United States, and the remaining 20% is distributed among two sites in Europe and one site each in the Middle East, China, India, and Japan. Since IBM is a multinational organization, the research labs are part of the local organization. Thus, there is a matrix management approach between the corporate research management in the United States and the local management teams, similar to how other functional IBM groups operate.

Phil Summers, program director of quality and reengineering at IBM Research, cites the dispersion of the labs across several time zones and the diversity of cultures encompassed by the staff as factors that make collaboration and communication especially difficult to manage. Language differences further complicate the situation. Although the research organization exploits information technology to help manage and communicate, this is not enough to surmount the geographic and cultural challenges facing a global research organization. The key, according to Summers, is to establish a truly global work culture that encourages and facilitates collaboration to solve technical problems and develop new product opportunities.

IBM achieves this through cross-lab teaming to bring together the necessary technical and managerial expertise for projects, task forces, and study groups. Teams meet face-to-face early in the process to get acquainted and to formulate a plan and schedule to work together over the long term. Compensation, recognition, and rewards play a major role in making these arrangements succeed. Nationality and region are factored out of the model, although cash awards may need to be adjusted for exchange rates. Global teams and individuals are honored for global or local research accomplishments and contributions at the annual corporate IBM recognition event, at which IBM fellows are also announced and significant awards from other organizations presented.

IBM research continues to develop as a global organization. For example, Summers noted the recent designation of the top position at IBM's Zurich laboratory as a division vice president, which extends strategic responsibility for research outside the United States.

3M Corporation

According to Geoffrey Nicholson, staff vice president for international technical operations at 3M Corporation,

> *Technology belongs to the entire company. A key goal is to make the company's technologies available to everyone throughout the organization. Along with this is our goal of encouraging every employee to be innovative. Finally, an important goal from Corporate is to have 30% of product revenue coming from products introduced within the last three years. This puts significant pressure on the R&D Labs to help lead the development of new products.*

In pursuit of these goals, 3M has developed a network of 35 R&D sites, only two of which are in the United States.

3M uses recognition programs extensively to reinforce innovation throughout the global research organization. In addition, R&D employees are given up to 15% of their time to pursue their own research interests. Scientific breakthroughs, new business start-ups, and technical excellence are publicly recognized through special honors. 3M also gives a team award for new business efforts outside the United States. The company believes that consideration of the impact of recognition and incentive programs on overseas staff is critical.

Nicholson indicates that the diversity of 3M's far-flung R&D organization brings several benefits, including a cultural sensitivity about how 3M products developed elsewhere might do in local markets. This diversity often leads to innovative solutions to R&D challenges. Patience with cultural and language differences is important; these differences, in fact, are viewed as opportunities to expand the ways problems and opportunities are examined.

The Checklist

In determining whether to implement recognition and reward programs for global R&D staff, the following questions are essential to consider:

- Do such programs reinforce the globalization strategy and help to focus and channel R&D efforts accordingly?
- Do they meet the values and expectations of the recipients?
- Are they linked to customer needs and market opportunities?
- Are they tied, directly or indirectly, to business outcomes?
- Are the economics of the plans sound (i.e., do the results justify the payouts and administrative costs)?
- Are they culturally sensitive?
- Do they reinforce desired behaviors (e.g., cross-fertilization of ideas among geographies)?
- Do they create any barriers to the effective assignment and use of resources?
- Do they create an equitable sharing of value between the R&D employees and the company?
- Are the awards significant enough to make a real impact?
- Do they encourage a sense of commitment among the R&D staff?

Expatriate Assignments for R&D Staff

As companies globalize their R&D functions, scientists and engineers will increasingly be asked to accept expatriate assignments. Dr. Matthias H. Schaublin,[11] who has spent a major part of his career managing international assignments and supporting R&D teams in the pharmaceutical industry, shared with us his experience and insights on issues concerning the mobility of R&D staff.

Dr. Schaublin believes that "the mobility of scientists is a key point to be recognized up-front when hiring, and it has become even more important in today's world as R&D has become a truly global endeavor. Mobility can mean numerous short-term assignments: 12 to 18 months is typical to start up a project, with shorter assignments more typical for highly specialized scientists. Longer-term assignments—two to four years—can become more common as a scientist moves into a project leadership role, and eventually into a scientific management capacity. In all cases, however, the expatriate's family members are affected even if they do not move, and their needs must be addressed as well as those of the employee-the family as well as the individual employee must be motivated to make the assignment successful.

Expatriate compensation packages for these diverse kinds of assignments typically include base pay plus incentives, including premiums tied to the achievement of goals. Dr. Schaublin points out that

> *Base pay is, of course, standard and competitively structured. Bonuses are generally a large component of the package. You can compare this model to that of a financial specialist. The difference is that the scientist tends to be interested in the scientific work and the project first. Second—although not unimportant—is the compensation package, including those things related to the family's needs.*

Although many companies have expatriate policies, such policies may not adequately address the needs of scientists and engineers in the fast-moving global arena. "This is a difficult concept for many large companies, but it is readily accepted by smaller start-ups and entrepreneurial entities," says Dr. Schaublin. There may be need for a special bonus policy for mobile scientists-one for reaching his/her scientific objectives on a project or a bonus for a successful new product. There are always tax consequences, which must be considered when deciding how to pay these bonuses out.

There are noncash benefits or perquisites that are also important to scientists on assignment. Dr. Schaublin cites the need to provide support for attendance at conferences, publication of scientists' work, laboratory equipment or resources, or even a commitment around a future assignment for a very special project or additional research. All of these can be equally important incentives in inducing an R&D staff member to accept—and remain committed to—an international assignment.

Closing Thoughts

The development of reward systems for R&D professionals in a global environment is not for the faint of heart. We can point to numerous examples of what psychologists call approach-avoidance behavior, as companies contemplate and then back away from creating special compensation and recognition programs for R&D staff. The increasingly competitive world market, however, demands that companies find innovative and creative approaches to properly recognize and reward their most innovative and creative employees. Standard or "one-size-fits-all" approaches will become less and less sufficient to attract, retain, and motivate the high-quality R&D experts that companies must have if they want to compete successfully in the global marketplace.

Notes

1. *OECD, Technology and the Economy* (Paris: Organization for Economic Cooperation and Development, 1992), 209.
2. M. E. Porter, ed., *Competition in Global Industries* (Boston: Harvard Business School Press, 1986), 2-3.
3. A. DeMeyer, "Management of an International Network of Industrial R&D Laboratories," *R&D Management 23*, no. 2 (April 1993), 99, 109–110.
4. Vittorio Chiesa, "Strategies for Global R&D," *Research Technology Management 39*, no. 5 (October 1996): 20–21.
5. Eleanor Westney, "IRI/MIT Investigate Global R&D Management," *Research Technology Management 39*, no. 6 (November/December 1996): 5.
6. E. M. Mervosh, "The Next Walkman," *Industry Week* (October 1997): 85–86.
7. G. C. Nicholson, "How 3M Manages Its Global Laboratory Network," *Research Technology Management 37*, no. 4 (July/August 1994): 21–24.
8. J. R. Bratkovich, "Understanding Paradoxes Is Essential to High Performance," *HR News* (February 1997).
9. "3M Accused of Inequity in Pay System Covering Managers and Technical Employees," *Daily Labor Report, Bureau of National Affairs*, no. 92, May 13, 1998, p. A8.
10. R. F. Schaeffer, "The Special Challenges of Managing HR in R&D Organizations," *Organizations & People,* (New York: Organization Resources Counselors, Inc., Summer 1997).
11. Matthias H. Schaublin is currently senior manager and international human resources consultant at ATAG Ernst & Young. He has

held numerous HR management positions, including both head of relocation, compensation, and benefits and project leader to revise the relocation policy for Hoffmann-La Roche. He also led the reengineering of the International Mobility Practice for the Zurich Insurance Group, was head of human resources at the University Hospital in Basel, and is an expert to the Swiss Federal Examination in HR Management.

CHAPTER 27

GLOBAL HUMAN RESOURCES INFORMATION TECHNOLOGY

GARY L. PARKER

The globalization of business is having a profound impact on the human resources function. The effective utilization of the human element in any enterprise will be the most important challenge to the future of business. In this dynamic, ever-changing business environment, it is critical to have accurate information on employees worldwide. Data must be arrayed in logical and relational ways for administration and planning. One would not expect to introduce a new business process or begin a new core activity without having information on all employees involved. Most organizations do not have the ability to obtain a total personnel complement count or to report on the total human resources expense on a worldwide basis in real time.

From Personnel to Human Resources

Traditionally, HR has been treated as an administrative support function to the organization, extending back to its personnel department roots. HR was responsible for the care and feeding of employees, with the bulk of activities devoted to administrative record keeping and reporting. Human resources systems have evolved from payroll systems to electronic filing cabinets for transactions that contain little planning and modeling capability. As transaction types changed and the statutory requirements of equal employment opportunity were introduced, systems were modified to satisfy these critical demands. Perhaps the most significant impact on HR systems in the last 15 years has been the complexity of employee benefit changes from the statutory record-keeping and income tests requirements to the myriad plans and provisions offered today. Legacy systems were stretched to the maximum to fulfill these demands, and a plethora of add-on subsystems were created both internally by companies' information technology (IT) departments and externally by software vendors that were seeking to fill the functionality gap.

The expatriate administration requirement was first satisfied by payroll software. The driving force of technology here was again the necessity of pay delivery and tax reporting. The construction of the expatriate package, traditionally the balance sheet, could not be satisfied by most payroll systems; in rushed the tax accounting firms and a few allowance data providers to develop software to calculate the packages. Most of these were stand-alone systems. Unfortunately, the accounting firms designed their systems in a way that was not user friendly, and the functionality was focused on supporting their tax practices.

Most foreign assignments require local tax accounting and filing; in the case of a U.S. national, these requirements must be completed in both the United States and the assignment location's tax jurisdiction. Unfortunately, there is no current system that will calculate the tax and pro rata allowance requirements in multiple assignment locations or satisfy the reporting requirements for those countries that tax worldwide income (e.g., the United States). Even the local tax software of most tax accounting firms is not integrated with their expatriate administration systems. The reconciliation and tax return preparation are completed outside of the systems they have, with a great deal of expensive manual intervention. Those expatriate administration systems, which have some key identifier and indicative data capability, must be operated as stand-alone packages. Often, these packages are not designed with the technology to even upload or download data to another system.

The Enterprise System Approach

The domestic human resources systems developed in the 1970s and 1980s have given way to those developed by vendors such as Oracle, PeopleSoft, SAP, and others of lesser note. Although these offer fourth-generation technology, they fall short of providing all of the functionality required by organizations to fully manage the human element. Some organizations' legacy HR systems contain more functionality than these so-called advanced systems. Functionality shortfall continues to be addressed by a myriad of add-ons. These add-ons are subsystems to effect and support the processes of employee benefits, international assignees, employee relations tracking, and training, all of which require varying degrees of modification and patching into an organization's main HR system.

Processes that are central to every company, such as benefit enrollment, expense reporting, travel authorization, salary planning, hiring, and the purchase of office supplies, are still bogged down in paper. This slow-moving administrative environment is in sharp contrast to the fast-paced business world, and it becomes further complicated as companies globalize their operations.

In the past decade, corporations have invested billions of dollars in reengineering enterprise back offices and in enhancing their ability to adapt to change. Because of the widespread implementation of client/server systems from PeopleSoft, SAP, Oracle, and others, HR information processing is now automated at most companies, but data and functionality continue to be disjointed.

Unfortunately, these new systems are designed for administrators, not for strategic planners and casual users. This is because an enterprise human resources information system (HRIS) concentrates on the final step of an HR transaction, which is to enter a change of information into the system. For example, an HR administrator can easily enter a salary change, but what about the steps the manager took to arrive at the salary decision?

Mainframes dominated the initial rise of "personnel systems." Large organizations installed equally large hardware and software systems in their cold rooms, usually requiring several years before project completion. Individual departments, frustrated by implementation time frames and the rigidity required to implement even minimal functionality, often implemented microcomputers and LAN-based personnel systems.

Then in the late 1980s, the graphical user interface, coupled with the emerging technology of client/server computing, began a second wave of HRIS technology ascension. The original big-iron-era HRIS is showing its age; migration to client/server has increased over the last few years as companies attempt to dodge problems like the Y2K bullet. We have made significant strides in the mechanization of record keeping but have not changed the basic nature of HRIS itself.

We have also repeated the development of commodity functionality during each cycle. Even though expenditures on more current HR and payroll systems have been at an all-time high, purchasers and current system users have been looking to the next wave of information management for human resources: the World Wide Web. To date, the Web has been used for the publishing of static information and communication. However, publishing static information does not fully exploit the Web's dynamism. During 1999 to 2005, the next phase of the HR front-office automation movement will focus on transaction-based systems, predicted to provide a significant return on investment in the areas directly related to planning and streamlining the contact with all people-constituencies, employees, and clients.

Perhaps one of the most important impacts on the future development of HR systems will be the fear that sensitive personal information will either be compromised or, even worse, used by the employer to impede or deny employee progression (in terms of pay or advancement). The right of a multinational employer to have qualitative and perhaps quantitative data on its employees around the world will give rise to a clash of immense proportions involving the tripartite keepers of the rights of workers (business, government, and labor).

Global Challenges

Although the "global village" is not yet a reality, things that happen in one part of the world often stimulate trends and initiate business approaches in other parts of the globe. The Canadian data privacy directive has been the model for the European Union's data privacy regulation, and both are now stimulating significant data privacy initiatives in the Asia Pacific area. An HR system that provides a centralized repository for core data, the ability to adapt standard functions to local business needs, and worldwide employee and manager access are now common requirements of most global organizations.

The basic nature of the Internet has propelled these and other business requirements into the forefront of our planning. North America has a mature HRIS market, which regularly sees new trends in HR information management, technology management, and HRIS organizational development. Companies are seeking more than just cost reduction. They want more advanced HR functionality, including employee and manager self-service, strategic competency management, workforce planning, and decision-support/data-warehousing functions to enhance the HR function's role as strategic partner in the organization.

European companies are also looking for more advanced functionality, particularly in the areas of employment planning, salary planning, HR management, and new auxiliary access methods such as the Internet/intranet. Europe often looks to North America as a source of innovation and for new ways of doing business. The European business environment can be increasingly characterized by intensifying competition, growing uncertainty in some industry sectors, and widespread restructuring and consolidation, with accompanying cost-cutting measures. As a result, companies are looking to their HR systems to help them meet these challenges and to provide solutions that will help them do more with less.

One major challenge for HR in Europe has to do with the labor markets. Europe's labor markets are the most rigid and highly regulated in the world. The challenge for Europe is to strike a balance between measures protecting the worker who already has a job and initiatives to promote employment. The challenge for HR systems in Europe is to provide the flexibility to deal with a diverse set of workforce requirements and the ability to support changing labor regulations.

Information safety has not kept pace with technology. For example, Australia may have been on a collision course with disaster during 1998 when the European Union (EU) data privacy conditions came into force and Australia relied too much on U.S. HRIS solutions, which may lack the logic or flexibility to support new privacy legislation.

If it were not for the Internet, the spotlight would not have fallen so quickly on the technology that stores and uses information about people. There is no doubt that the real driving force behind the rush to introduce privacy legislation is the commercial influence brought about by the EU directive to trading partners on data privacy adherence.

All the countries in the Asia Pacific region are at different stages of introducing regulation; some are more advanced than others.

On an international level, a working group was set up by the International Standards Organization (ISO) to see if an international standard should be established. The feature that must be delivered includes a good security module that allows logical programming and data structuring along the company's hierarchical lines, represents supervisory accountability, and specifies the need for employee record access.

Whether an organization is completely replacing its current software or attempting to keep up with the pace of technology, planning for that future implementation or upgrade is essential to realizing success. Technology is driving change so rapidly that each new release of an HRIS system may require an effort exceeding that of actual implementation.

Another challenge, a technological one, is related to our rarely challenged legacy patterns of software production. The major enterprise human resource management system (HRMS) implements business logic with procedural code like "C" and COBOL; programmers who write business logic with discrete syntax create this procedural code. The specialist model further requires someone to translate business requirements from the language of real people to a less ambiguous, more exacting form. This person has traditionally been the systems analyst. The artifacts or persistent, near-physical entities generated by legacy development have been volumes of procedural code, tons of requirements, documents more tedious than any Victorian novel, and business processes to support these antecedent artifacts.

Subscribers to recent industry analyst news should have noted that, in general, client/server implementations have a relatively high failure rate (35% canceled before completion, at a cost of more than US$40 billion). Of these completed, more than 50% come in 150% or more over budget, accounting for an additional US$30 billion.

One related issue is the current complexity of vendor solutions. Inherently, large-scale systems cannot be commercial-off-the-shelf (COTS). Instead, vendors and clients may rely on teams of implementers (analysts, developers, and project managers) to modify the delivered code and meet client requirements. The systems should instead be driven by business needs and processes and quickly translated and implemented into an executable form. The complexity of our current monolithic systems exacerbates the already difficult tasks of project estimation and management.

We need a better way to deliver systems and applications to the enterprise. The expectation that information systems will lower administrative costs will continue, but managers and executives want more than just cost reduction. Strategic competency management, workforce planning, and decision support/warehousing are at the core of value-added services. Their integration with business will be central to the future development of technology and to the growth of HRIS's value to the institutions we serve. Over the past year, we have seen more changes in the world of HRMS than we have seen in any other period in the history of automated personnel systems. Client/server not only promised to be cheaper and faster but also was designed to replace mainframe applications and to move the processing where it was needed.

Some implementations of new HR systems developed by client/server software vendors have had only limited success, as many have found that one size does not fit all. Most of these systems are developed in an attempt at a plain vanilla system that fits no particular company's business process but is close enough to give it a head start. Many new client/server systems that have been installed are not yet being used to their full potential by end users. Quite often, this is simply because of the complexities of HR applications.

It's All Relational

People and their competencies are "the last competitive advantage" in most modern organizations, where technology is readily available, mass production advantages no longer apply, quality depends on customer satisfaction, and innovation is more important than reputation or size. The "naturally related" HR functions to be conceptually integrated in enterprise-wide systems include the following:

- The assessment process
- Human resource development
- Enterprise-wide staffing
- Performance management
- Competency-based pay
- International assignment management

The development of a comprehensive global human resources system, which is fully integrated and relational, will most probably find a functional basis in many existing subsystems. The ability to use future systems as planning tools will be largely dependent on the strategic, not the tactical, human resources thinkers. This topic could be the subject of several manuscripts and is currently the major debate among the major HRMS developers; to a large degree, it is also a significant concern of those smaller developers who wish to ensure their place in the future of system or subsystem sales.

International Assignment Management

Since the subject of this chapter is related to international assignment management, the "naturally related" HR function, which is to be examined, would logically be this one. Although I have a holistic view of system solution for HR, each function would require detailed evaluation prior to institutionalizing that discrete functionality in an enterprise HRMS.

The first phase of developing any subsystem of an integrated enterprise system would find its beginnings in an extensive review of all of the requirements and constituencies of that functionality. The examination would also include a detailed look at current subsystems in the marketplace. It is this phase that is appropriate for this chapter.

The international assignment management function is currently a transaction-based activity, either centralized or decentralized (or outsourced). All of the traditional activities-personal, payroll, tax, employee benefits, manpower planning and development, and relocation-would be required. The significant difference between domestic and international is that the latter is multidimensional in nature and scope. This is because of the structure of the remuneration package, the possibility of dual tax jurisdictions, the duplication and coordination of employee benefits, and linking the package to the home country with all price and exchange-rate parity recalculation implied.

The users of international assignment information and systems are the international human resources (IHR) department, payroll, tax (to include outside tax preparation), and most of the strategic (or planning) functions at headquarters. In the event that a greater functional or planning capability was available, the user list would expand by, at least, management and the field locations, domestic and internationally. Perhaps the most interested user of this information is the financial function.

Over the years, a number of different software products in evolving technologies have been targeted at those responsible for managing international assignments. In the majority of cases, the design of these systems strongly indicates that the key factor behind their development has been the need to manage the complex tax issues associated with such assignments.

When it comes to moving employees around the globe, there is no escaping the fact that taxation is one of the largest elements in a cost equation, which can increase the cost by a power of four. With a cost premium like that, it is little wonder that the expatriate policies adopted by international employers are subject to regular scrutiny concerning cost reduction, with particular attention on the tax piece. For many years, the big five have sought to impress international assignment managers with their expertise in this area. Over the last decade, advances in computer technology have helped create a new playing field on which they can try and prove their superior strength. The adrenaline rush has been matched by the scale of investment. The systems have been designed to benefit the tax firms, and they are often so complicated that a company's international assignment function is not capable of using the software. Often, this is outsourced to the tax firm. Perhaps this is by design.

Several of these big five international assignment management systems allow some minor level of integration with larger enterprise systems. But those companies that acquire them rarely, if ever, use some of the functionality in these systems. For example, the general ledger interface of one big five system, although purchased by all companies using this software, has never been used. As one would imagine, the duplication of data elements, functionality, and technology to create a stand-alone subsystem is simply a waste.

Although the emphasis on powerful tax-planning capabilities suits the tax professionals within the accounting/tax firms, the tactical and strategic aspects of tax are the least of an international company's concern. A 1995 survey of international assignment managers found that, from a list of 19 possible features of expatriate software, "comprehensive tax planning" was rated as the least important. The feature of "basic tax-planning hints" fared little better.

Responding to the apparent indifference to international tax-planning features in expatriate software, more recent software offerings have a much stronger focus on international assignment management. In some quarters, this focus is so severe that products are even appearing on the market with virtually no international tax coverage. Such systems purport to be international human resources management systems in their own right. One cannot help but question if tax professionals are as well qualified to develop such applications as are such long-established players like PeopleSoft. The new direction evident in expatriate software also misses the point that tax is important. International assignment managers require tax calculations with a coverage that matches the diversity of their expatriate population. Indeed, as more and more international employers implement global human resource management systems, the need for an additional expatriate database will diminish, but the demand for tax calculations will remain. How else can an international assignment manager project the total cost of an assignment? In this context, however, the sophistication required of the tax calculation is not high. Spurious accuracy will be exchanged without a second thought for a less sophisticated calculation that uses this year's, rather than last year's, rates.

The opportunity for tax cost reduction in international assignments needs to be seen in the context of the overall business process of which it is a part. The complex, powerful tax-planning capabilities that have been the cornerstone of most expatriate software over the past decade are immensely important-to the tax professionals who have designed them. The burgeoning expatriate databases are immensely important-to the steadily diminishing band of those who do not yet have a global human resource management system. Yet having a place to store the data is only the start. Just imagine what needs to be done with them in terms of financial reporting and strategic planning.

International Assignment Management Systems Evaluation

The Expatriate Technology Forum (ETF) has conducted an in-depth review of expatriate software. ETF has reviewed all of the major software packages that purport to handle international assignment management. ETF is an independent association of leading companies. Its purpose is to explore information technology solutions to the key issues in international assignment management. It offers major organizations the opportunity to join forces in meeting these common challenges in a cost-effective manner.

The study drilled down to the number of keystrokes required to complete each expatriate transaction. All of the big five accounting/tax firms' software was part of the study, including several of the better-known enterprise-level HRMS software. All vendors were requested to make their software available on their preferred equipment at the ETF site for examination and testing for a period of four to eight weeks. Although most vendors complied, two vendors were only prepared to allow them to examine the software at their own location. The completed survey revealed some very interesting results.

As anticipated at the outset, the market for international assignment software is still rather immature. Despite major investment programs from a number of competing vendors, the functionality designed into projections is limited. When a database has been incorporated, its capabilities are severely limited. For example, the available products reflect a lack of detailed analysis of the requirements of those managing international assignments. Much of the investment to date has been in highly detailed and complex tax calculations. Most users place powerful and easy-to-use reporting capabilities high on their list of requirements, yet many vendors are content to rely on off-the-shelf report writers to meet the needs of their users.

In light of the above, it is perhaps not too surprising to observe a lack of attention on the international assignments process in all of the systems reviewed. One or two are starting to introduce process concepts in their systems, but these are at a very shallow level, typically involving a list of sequential tasks to be completed. Several of the large HRMS enterprise systems offer customization tools, which allow users to introduce process concepts into their version, but again there has been no attempt to analyze common requirements and offer any features to support standard processes.

Besides the two niche applications that are still DOS applications, many of the other systems reviewed clearly reflected their DOS origins. The impression given was that all the investment in time and energy had been spent in porting the applications to the new platform, leaving little to spend on taking advantage of the new opportunities offered by the Windows environment. Even a newly combined accounting/tax firm's system-which has been written in a powerful modern development environment-suffers from a need to satisfy the base of existing users, the DOS HR database application around which it is being designed. The immaturity of the market is well illustrated by the fact that this vendor has two competing products on the market-one in the United States and one in Europe.

When it comes to large-scale HRMS software, the vendor that currently has the largest global sales has established clear credentials. Yet it is not an international assignments database system but, rather, a general human resource database with some elements that touch on this specialist area. The new system from Deloitte Touche Tomatsu (DTT) has the most adventurous aims-it is the only system that seeks to automate just about everything. Unfortunately, while this may offer an outsourcing solution to its clients, the lack of modularization in this system makes it unsuitable for those with more modest requirements. For those whose organizations have an information management strategy built around Lotus Notes, the Coopers Lybrand (C-L) system clearly has some attraction. It is unfortunate that the implementation of the system is so awkward and cumbersome.

In essence, the full review revealed that none of these products is likely to satisfy even those core requirements that a company with the need for international assignment management software would have.

A Guide to the Future

To service the requirements of these HR information markets, one needs to bring a set of technologies that includes, but is not limited to, the following:

- Systems hardware platforms
- Communications technology
- Relational architecture and software
- Applications software
- Packaged software

Client/server (C/S) technology is continuing to penetrate the market, but not everyone has adopted it. Less than 50% of the respondents in a survey of large multinationals had C/S core systems, HR payroll, and benefits. Another 25% planned to add them in the next two years. C/S systems have penetrated least into payroll. However, C/S systems are being used to support subsystems that operate independently of the core systems. Most people reported their systems as only somewhat integrated, with widespread use of add-on systems.

Many companies mobilize groups of people in organizations to provide systems and technology to support HR services. These support organizations may be structured as part of an HR department or as part of IT, or they may be split between the two.

Formal data modeling and life cycle methodologies are generally in use, but they are not being rigorously applied. This may indicate that organizations are able to get along without strict adherence to formal methodology, or it may indicate a substantial risk of trouble in the future with less system functionality, poor system performance, and limited ability to provide needed services.

Integrated HR transaction environments are an important complement to back-office systems, dramatically speeding the execution of routine transactions. By shifting the technology focus to the desktop, these new systems automate the full range of activities and interactions that must occur before a simple information change is made in the HRIS. Sophisticated client/server HRIS systems consolidate human resources information and offer improved accessibility through advanced reporting functions. New solutions must be developed to establish a dynamic framework for communication and collaboration while providing a link to back-office systems.

The period 1994–1997 can be characterized as Phase 1 of the Web's rise in popularity, as companies implemented publishing applications to help automate front-office activities. In 1997, an estimated 59% of U.S. corporations had implemented corporate intranets, as had 38% of European corporations. In 1998, intranet penetration is expected to rise to 77% in the United States and 75% in Europe.

Integrated HR systems must also address a number of key technology issues. A Web-based approach offers additional benefits through its ability to address these issues in a cost-effective, technically elegant fashion. Technology issues and their Web-centric solutions include the following:

- *Security.* The confidentiality of information must be maintained as it travels throughout the organization. In Web-based systems, the use of role-based security mechanisms and dynamically generated HTML panels rather than hard-coded panels ensures that users receive information on a onetime, as requested basis only, as retrieved from the corporate HRIS and other sources.

- *Workflow*. Documents must be dynamically routed to appropriate parties for approval and action on a local global basis. This functionality can be built into the system's application framework to automatically manage a variety of business processes and events.
- *Scalability*. Systems supporting integrated HR transactions must be able to grow easily and rapidly to support widespread deployment and new users. A native Web implementation helps ensure that the collaborative transaction system can quickly expand to serve large global user bases.
- *Connectivity to databases*. This capability is extremely important in allowing the new desktop-oriented systems to fully integrate with back-office HR information systems.
- *Availability*. The system must be accessible around the clock. Using the Web as an operating platform allows it to be continuously available on a global basis.
- *Ease of deployment*. For maximum utility, the integrated transaction system must be a "minimum administration" addition to the enterprise HRIS, centrally deployed and managed. Unlike PC-based applications that require individually administered upgrades and maintenance, browser-based access does not increase administrative overhead.
- *"Assistant," not "gatekeeper."* For the new system to be embraced by users, it must provide appropriate functionality accessed through a user-friendly, intuitive interface that anticipates user's needs. Innovative use of native-Web technologies and Web metaphor can create interactive, intelligent user interface that expedites business processes.

These new kinds of applications offer distinctive benefits, including the following:

- Improved employee service and participation as HR transactions are dynamically routed through the organization and participants are prompted to deliver their contribution
- Enhanced communication through e-mail and triggers and workflow automation

- Improved productivity as employees and managers spend less time pushing HR transactions through the organization
- Lower administrative costs as less time is spent on unproductive, manual-transaction management

The general IT industry has proposed object orientation as a long-term solution to both quality and maintenance issues. Object modeling addresses a certain portion of the engineering problem space; data modeling addresses another.

The focus of competitive advantage today is the human element of the organization. Effective strategies for maximizing human talent are a necessity for every organization. HR leaders must be able to create new business strategies that leverage the workforce to create this competitive advantage.

Key organizational strategy leaders, especially the CEO, have previously focused on traditional business improvements in the areas of production, financial management, and supply and inventory management. The focus is now shifting to the attraction, development, and utilization of the organization's workers to create, produce, and deliver better products and services. High-caliber talent matched to business objectives will yield an organization better equipped to compete and win.

HR must think and act strategically at the upper echelons of the organization. Understanding strategic policy and procedures will be a necessity to effectively integrate and perform to CEO expectations and, ultimately, shareholders' satisfaction. Today, HR must create value for the organization and deliver quantifiable results.

HR must alter its course and dramatically change its mission. One of the high-level objectives in many organizations is to provide mechanisms for business to perform its own HR-related activities as an integrated component, not a separate functional silo. HR must become an active part of each business unit, production line, and work group instead of an external support function. HR leaders must drive this change. Change to offload transaction-oriented administration and refocus staff and activities toward strategic, value-added initiatives does not come easily.

Some of the strategic initiatives that human resources must now focus on include the following:

- Creating mechanisms for attracting and retaining the highest level of talent for the organization. (Quality talent is becoming more difficult to locate and even more difficult to retain.) The inability to bring quality people into the organization can be a big inhibitor to market growth.

- Developing new compensation programs that adequately recognize and reward employees for their contributions. Legacy pay scales no longer provide the incentive or reward that is necessary to drive a business. As business strategy hinges more and more on the contributions of employees, HR will be required to map appropriate plans and procedures to link pay with performance and to integrate it with organizational business goals.
- Implementing information systems that provide sophisticated and timely data analysis functions to support real-time HR decision analysis for the purpose of business strategy formulation and execution. HR must make information available to the right person, at the right time, and at the right place across the enterprise.
- Developing and promoting communications channels to constantly improve service and add value to HR customers, including employees, managers, executives, retirees, applicants, and external partners/vendors.
- Initiatives to improve and shared-service models for one-stop service. The combination yields a comprehensive solution to maximize service to the customer and minimize organizational cost.

As HR leaders migrate from an administrative-support position to a strategy-driver position, they must recognize the importance of understanding strategy. Many people fail to recognize that strategy is much more than doing something new and different. Describing a new process or function as "strategic" seems to be the trend. It is important not to confuse strategy with management. There is a distinction between "doing the right things" and "doing things right." With many HR leaders still entrenched in their traditional administrative state, it will probably be very difficult for them to adapt to becoming effective strategic business partners.

Strategy is dependent on market pressures, economic indicators, competitors, and buyers and suppliers, as described by the early pioneers at the Harvard Business School in the 1960s. Strategy is a cross-functional activity that takes a holistic view of the organization and the upper-management level of hierarchical structures traditionally performed.

One of the key actions HR must take is to develop a closer relationship with the CEO and executive management team surrounding the CEO. Few HR leaders have been admitted to this exclusive club until recently. Many initiatives that HR leadership is driving are facilitated through the applications of technology to create a business solution. Information is the lifeblood of organizations. Putting information in the right hands at the right time yields faster and better decisions that benefit the organization and put it ahead of the competition.

HR can provide multilevel applications targeted at various user groups, including the following:

- Generic communication to all employees
- Employee-specific data inquiry and transactions
- Compensation, staffing models, and transactions geared toward easy use by managers
- Data interaction with external HR customers and suppliers (e.g., insurers, banks, funds managers, or doctors)
- Recruitment automation
- Retiree communication and tractions
- Summary-analysis data for executive decision making

Competitive advantage and market dominance will increasingly depend on well-formed and properly executed strategies that maximize talent and on the inherent intellectual capital of the entire organization. Human resources leaders must prepare for the new challenges that present themselves when the highest level of the organization asks them to contribute to organizational strategy.

HRIS is moving beyond the days of processing single transactions (e.g., hire employee, change salary, send on international assignment). Today's HRIS needs to take a more holistic view of the HR process and look at the total environment for the "larger transaction," involving decision making, progress tracking, approval routing, and status checking. Human resources practitioners need to seize the giant strides in technology to gain their rightful place in the management hierarchy.

CHAPTER 28

THE FUTURE OF GLOBAL COMPENSATION AND BENEFITS

CALVIN REYNOLDS

Four major forces are molding the future of global compensation and benefits:

1. Strategy—tradition versus innovation
2. Human resources' emerging role as a "business partner" and its interaction with line management
3. Globalization and its impact on organization structures and people
4. Outsourcing significant HR activities traditionally handled "in-house"

The objective of this chapter is to assess the impact and importance of these forces on compensation and benefits and attempt to project the future of the field during the early years of the 21st century.

Strategy: Tradition and Innovation

In the 1960s, Professor Howard Perlmutter of Wharton introduced the concept of the *geocentric corporation,*[1] the multinational corporation that successfully integrates the best ideas and practices from all its operations worldwide into a cohesive strategy and modus operandi. The geocentric company contrasts sharply with the *ethnocentric* company, in which the dominant belief is that all wisdom emanates from headquarters, and with the *polycentric* company that encourages foreign subsidiaries to do their own thing with a minimum of headquarters interference. For some today, "globalization" is geocentrism in real time. For others, it is ethnocentrism or polycentrism in real time. But despite the passage of time, Perlmutter's characterizations remain as valid today as they were 30 years ago. There are still companies that fall into each of the three categories. And the most successful ones still opt for, or at least work toward, geocentrism, even if we now call it *globalization.*

The major differences, compared with 30 years ago, relate to speed of execution, thanks largely to technology, not to concepts.

The concept of geocentrism is particularly important in relation to compensation and benefits. Some excellent ideas and practices can be found throughout the world. Those companies that capture the best that they have within their worldwide networks and benchmark globally with others will be the organizations that have the most effective strategies and practices. Some companies are much better at this than others. To illustrate, Tom Friedman, the *New York Times* columnist, in his recent best-seller *The Lexus and the Olive Tree,* reported on the excellence of Chevron as a "learning company." He also remarked on the weakness of Siemens, the major German manufacturing company, in this regard when he quoted the insight of an observer: "If Siemens only knew what Siemens knows, it would be a rich company." Those organizations that do not learn from their own global networks will fall behind. Those that remain in or fall into ethnocentrism or polycentrism will also lag behind.

Compensation and benefits, like many other corporate activities, struggles constantly between tradition and innovation: "We've always done it that way" versus "Wow, what a great new idea!" As Samuel Bernstein points out in Chapter 24 on compensation practices in emerging economies, the United States has had a long tradition of paying people for the jobs they hold or for what they produce, not for what they know, their experience, or their family situations. Indeed, many North Americans have been scornful of the Japanese, and to some extent continental Europeans, for considering such factors as age and company service as determinants of pay. And the recent adoption by many Japanese and continental European companies of such "typically American" practices as pay for performance and even stock options reinforces the American conviction that "We know best." Is this ethnocentrism? You bet it is.

Despite the influence of tradition, North Americans have had a long fascination with innovation, new approaches, and, not infrequently, the latest passing fads. Perhaps broad-based stock options are not a fad, but consider that they have only gained popularity since PepsiCo introduced Share Power a decade ago. Granted, change is happening at lightning speed, but it is a bit of a stretch to think of a 10-year-old practice as a tradition.

Practitioners are constantly looking for great new ideas, and that is commendable. The search for innovation is particularly intense when a popular compensation or benefits approach does not fit the criteria that professionals perceive as "in our tradition." A striking example of this is the frequent attacks on the balance sheet approach to expatriate compensation. The balance sheet approach includes elements of compensation based on family size, the age and educational requirements of expatriates' children, and a variety of other factors that have little to do with performance. Although the balance sheet approach has been the expatriate compensation standard for half a century, and there is currently no indication that its popularity is waning, it will continue to be attacked because of its "entitlement" characteristics. Virtually every alternative that has been proposed takes aim at this countertraditional aspect of the methodology.

The search will go on. Innovations will gradually erode "traditional" practices, replace them, and become traditions themselves, only to be replaced by more innovation—the process Joseph Schumpeter labeled "creative destruction." The companies that lead the way will be those that are organized to tap ideas worldwide and strike an effective balance between time-tested practices and viable innovation. The remainder of this chapter looks at organizational options, particularly in regard to human resources and remuneration, which will enable some companies to lead the way and gain competitive advantage.

Human Resources as a Business Partner

Priorities for Competitive Advantage,[2] a landmark IBM human resources study prepared by Towers Perrin in the early 1990s, found that "Human resources is being transformed from a specialized, stand-alone function to a broad corporate competency in which HR and line managers build partnerships to gain competitive advantage and achieve overall business goals." While this "finding" is put in terms of a transition taking place, it was, and I believe still is, more accurately described as a high priority on the wish lists of both line executives and senior human resources professionals. There has been some movement in this direction, but in this period of real-time mutation, progress has been at a glacial pace.

In the international arena, most of the progress to date has been realized by eliminating specialist positions in headquarters staff departments and by creating HR generalist positions in operating units. In U.S.-based companies, most of these new positions have been in business divisions located in the United States, not in other countries. Many of the transactional and routine types of activities formerly handled by the headquarters staffs are progressively being outsourced. These moves are positive in that they place HR practitioners closer to the line and make them part of operating management teams. They focus attention on core competencies.

To the extent, however, that these transitions weaken the headquarters HR function and eliminate what little global expertise that existed, they may be counterproductive.

To have an effective partnership between line management and human resources practitioners, HR generalists and specialists must bring to the management table skills and services that are perceived by line management as essential to the growth and profitability of the organization. Technical excellence is not enough. Globally, exporting human resources programs that have worked well in the headquarters country will not suffice. The HR business partner must be familiar with the best HR practices that can be identified anywhere in the world, innovate on the foundation of that knowledge, and demonstrate, as part of the management team, how that knowledge and innovation can be used for competitive advantage. This is particularly true in the field of compensation and benefits.

One of the major constraints limiting HR's participation with line management as a business partner, particularly on a global basis, has been the specialized skill sets and limited career paths of most HR managers. Very few HR professionals have had relevant experience in other functions.[3] Even fewer have had assignments abroad.[4] The Conference Board reports that "only 7 percent of respondents indicate that HR professionals are often transferred internationally; in more than a third of companies, there are no such transfers."[5]

This lack of shared experience with most line executives has made it difficult for many HR executives to be accepted as global business partners. Some companies have tried to address these weaknesses by rotating internationally experienced line executives through one or more of the top human resources positions. Although this approach addresses HR's narrow skill set and experience limitations, it creates problems of its own:

- Senior line executives are unlikely to have sufficiently broad knowledge of HR practices to be effective HR business partners. And many of them find the function a less-than-exciting diversion from their real interest of line management.
- If the top HR positions are filled by executives who have little or no HR experience, it will be difficult to hire, retain, and develop first-class HR careerists. They sense that their upward mobility is too limited.

Here's a case in point. A major global financial institution that for many years successfully rotated several senior line executives, some with overseas experience, through the top HR executive position has given up the practice. The CEO made some bad senior-staffing decisions that he rightly or wrongly attributed to the HR executive's lack of solid HR skills and experience. Several of the company's most able human resources practitioners resigned. A seasoned HR executive recruited from another company filled the position.

There are several approaches that companies can take (and some have taken) to develop senior human resources executives as acceptable and qualified business partners:

- As already identified above, *assign high-potential human resources practitioners to worldwide operating divisions and global management teams* to provide experience implementing policy and working closely with line management.
- *Assign some human resources generalists and specialists to regional and country operating companies abroad.* Many companies avoid these assignments, reserving expatriation for line management, marketing, finance, and various technical specialty positions for which qualified staff cannot be found locally. But a recent study of 18 of North America's most successful global companies, conducted for a leading pharmaceutical company, revealed that, on average, 2.5% of their expatriates, 2.7% of their assignees to headquarters, and 2.3% of their third-country nationals were in human resources. Indeed, in three of the companies, more than 7% of their international assignees were human resources professionals. These averages compare with 1.0% of employees in human resources for U.S. companies overall and 0.6% for large companies comparable to the survey participants.[6] This and other broader-based studies have indicated that the primary activities of these overseas HR professionals are management development and compensation and benefits.
- *Assign some young, relatively inexperienced employees to human resources positions overseas.* This will give them operating experience early in their careers and get their international cards punched before professional and family obligations constrain their mobility. While most U.S.-based multinationals have resisted these types of assignments, several major European companies, such as the Union Bank of Switzerland,[7] and a majority of global Japanese companies have followed this approach successfully. Note here that one of the major impediments to assigning inexperienced employees overseas has been the perception that they must receive overly generous standard expatriate compensation packages. As discussed in Chapter 5 on expatriate strategies, there are other more viable options.

- *Provide high-potential line executives at least one assignment in human resources before they reach senior management and provide up-and-coming human resources professionals assignments in other functions* to broaden their experience and develop their management skills. Historically, human resources, in general, and compensation and benefits, in particular, have been functional silos. While specialists who want to remain within the function will always be needed, generalists who broaden their skills and experience will have greater opportunities to advance to senior management positions and become effective business partners.

This list of options describes what companies can do to develop human resources professionals and others to become credible business partners representing human resources. Equally, it describes the types of experience that human resources practitioners should strive to acquire if they aspire to become HR business partners themselves. Clearly, it is essential not only to hone specialized compensation and benefits skills but to gain other HR and non-HR experience as well.

Globalization

Chapter 1 reported that, historically and through the early 1990s, the primary focus and activity of corporate international human resources functions was expatriate compensation. A majority of the corporate practitioners were expatriate compensation specialists who also served as conduits through which expatriates could communicate with line management about their human resources grievances. Most never worked abroad but a fortunate few did have ample opportunity to travel to other countries to interact with expatriates, and this has been a major attraction of the field. One important but unfortunate characteristic of the function is that the highly specialized and extremely complex skills involved in expatriate compensation have very little application in other functions, and thus there has been very little upward mobility for practitioners. Most have found their challenges interacting with their peers in other companies and exchanging information on a multitude of arcane issues. Surveys have always been, and still are, an important preoccupation and tool of the function.

To overcome the skill and experience limitations of many expatriate compensation administrators, some companies have assigned returning expatriates experienced in other functions to international HR. When solid candidates have been chosen to strengthen the function, broaden their experience to include HR, and provide stepping-stones to higher management, these assignments generally have worked well. This has been particularly true when key international HR managers have been recognized and become active participants on the international management team.

Often, however, returning assignees whose performance abroad has been marginal and whom the company has found difficult to place in domestic operations have been assigned to international HR. This not only further downgrades the function but also forecloses advancement possibilities for capable professionals looking for promotion opportunities within international HR.

Some companies have given domestically experienced compensation and benefits specialists international responsibilities. Certainly, domestic experience is a valuable asset, but too often those assigned have been given specialized headquarters staff positions in which it has been difficult to translate experience into implementation. Some of the most successful domestically experienced professionals have been those assigned to overseas regional management organizations where they can interact on a daily basis with line management and local compensation and benefits administrators. In these positions, they can learn as well as teach and become essential links between corporate and local operating management.

Throughout this guide, several contributors have discussed the valuable skills and contributions of practitioners worldwide. In Chapter 2, for example, Alan Ritchie and Steven Seltz of Lucent Technologies stressed the value of incorporating into the corporate compensation and benefits staff professionals from foreign operations. There are many possibilities for transferring foreign nationals to headquarters for both short-term and permanent assignments.

In summary, some of the possibilities for strengthening the international HR and compensation and benefits functions include several of the same approaches discussed above for enabling human resources professionals to become business partners:

- One or more international assignments for HR professionals, preferably in regional headquarters
- One or more assignments in another function
- Participation on international management teams and task forces
- Temporary assignment of other professionals, possibly from the line or finance, into international HR
- Integration of compensation and benefits professionals from other countries into corporate staff and domestic operations.

Outsourcing

In a 1993 *Harvard Business Review* interview,[8] Peter Drucker predicted that "ten years from now a company will outsource all work that does not have a career ladder up to senior management." As discussed in earlier chapters, global compensation and benefits functions have already been seriously affected by this trend, and there is every indication that the trend will continue. Many activities, particularly in the benefits and expatriate compensation specialties, have been standardized and converted into commodities sold off the shelf by the major benefits and accounting firms. Other providers, such as Prudential Resources and Cendant, offer bundled services that are particularly attractive to companies entering the international arena for the first time. And even globally mature companies that have experienced international compensation and benefits staffs are examining the possibilities of outsourcing some administrative functions they have traditionally handled internally.

It is important to recognize the difference between outsourcing and obtaining outside consulting advice. The companies that have been most successful with outsourcing have maintained solid control of policy within their organizations. Often, they get consulting help in designing their policies, but it is very clear to their employees that the policies are theirs and not delegated to an outside firm. What they outsource is administration within clearly defined corporate parameters.

A primary obstacle to further outsourcing by major global corporations is the shortage of third-party providers that are fully qualified to offer the full range of compensation and benefits options and services that these corporations require. Many mature multinationals have honed their international remuneration systems over decades and believe that no one else can duplicate their unique approach or approaches. To the extent that these systems represent strategic interaction among management, HR, and employees, they are largely correct. But there remains a very significant amount of routine compensation and benefits administration that can be standardized and handled more cost effectively. These are the types of activities that can and ultimately will be outsourced when specialist firms develop the skills and products to provide them.

The most important challenge for both global companies and third-party providers that will enable both to grow and concentrate on their unique core competencies is staffing in the broadest sense. How can global corporations find and develop effective global HR executives who are strategic thinkers, competent functional professionals, and effective business partners? And how can third-party providers develop the compensation and benefits products and services (and by extension the qualified staff to deliver them) that will fully satisfy the perceived needs of the global companies?

Implicit in this analysis is the prediction that most international compensation and benefits administration now handled internally by corporations will be outsourced. To the extent that this prediction is correct, how will corporations develop competent staff to fulfill the strategic HR requirements that will remain? Since international remuneration administration will largely disappear from these companies, administrative departments will no longer be feeders to more responsible corporate compensation and benefits positions. Many of the answers to this dilemma were suggested in the earlier discussions about the development of HR business partners and the effects of globalization on organizations. In addition, however, there will be some movement of staff back and forth between corporations and third-party providers. To date, most movement has been from corporations to service providers, but, as experience is gained, this will change. Corporations will need some technical expertise that will be difficult to develop internally, and such expertise will become the essential strength of specialist firms. The relationship between global corporations and providers of compensation and benefits services will more closely resemble the relationships of corporate legal departments and law firms. Some skills will be common to both, but strategy, policy, and the related communication with employees will be the domain of the global corporations; administration of that policy will be outsourced to specialized providers.

To date, the major accounting firms have been the dominant providers of international compensation and benefits services, particularly those related to expatriate compensation. Some HR professionals have observed, however, that the accounting orientation of these firms shows a demonstrable lack of understanding of human resource processes and has discouraged some corporations from using their HR services. It is reasonable to expect that either the accounting firms will develop the HR sensitivity necessary to change these perceptions or others will fill the void. A primary challenge for the accounting firms will be to attract first-class talent for their HR outsourcing functions. These positions are unlikely to provide upward mobility within the accounting organizations. HR administration is not a core competency in the world of accounting.

The specialist compensation and benefits providers have a serious staffing challenge. To date, most of the firms have satisfied their staffing requirements by recruiting experienced compensation and benefits professionals from major corporations. Indeed, many corporations have been pleased to turn over their experienced staff to these firms with the understanding that their former employees will continue to provide them with services. This approach provides continuity and reduces corporate head count. It may or may not reduce costs and improve service, and in this regard, experience has been mixed. Others have assumed that administering international compensation and benefits is just like administering any other function that deals with numbers. Some with this perspective have understandably had limited success.

But despite growing pains that several of the specialist providers have experienced, there is every reason to believe that, ultimately, they will prevail and deliver most international compensation and benefits administrative services. Part of their success, however, will depend on how well the global corporations learn to use their services. Many of the problems to date have resulted from companies' expecting the providers to take over strategy as well as administration. This makes little sense from the perspective of either the corporations or the service providers. Progressively, the two types of organizations will learn to work more effectively with each other.

Our analysis of international compensation and benefits tends to support Peter Drucker's prediction, quoted above, that "all work that does not have a career ladder up to senior management" will be outsourced. In provider firms, specialized international compensation and benefits skills and management capability will provide some opportunities for career advancement. In global corporations, broader skills and experience will be required to make it to the top.

Technology

Our discussion up till this point in this final chapter has focused on strategy and organizational issues: tradition and strategic innovation, the changing roles of HR and international compensation and benefits professionals, the impact of globalization, and the evolving balance between do-it-yourself and outsourcing. Technology could have a significant impact on these issues and, in some companies, completely change the dynamics.

As Gary Parker observed in Chapter 27 on technology, most currently available computer software programs handle international compensation and benefits issues off-line and do not integrate them into a holistic corporate system. The fact that they are not integral components of a primary corporate system makes international compensation and benefits a prime candidate for outsourcing. Since they are currently handled on a stand-alone basis, why not have the process handled by an outside provider?

But if new technology were developed that integrates international compensation and benefits more effectively into a holistic corporate system, the arguments favoring outsourcing would be weaker. Improved internal efficiency would effectively compete with the attractions of outsourcing. There is no doubt that the systems used by the specialist providers can and will be improved. But if past experience has any value as a predictor, it is likely that the service providers will make every effort to improve their internal integration and efficiency at the expense of external integration. However, there is a significant potential for someone to develop an effective integrated corporate management system that includes all aspects of global compensation and benefits. The person who does will have an important impact on the trend toward outsourcing.

In addition to the technology issues associated with integrated corporate compensation and benefits systems, it is important to consider technology and its advantages in communicating with employees worldwide. The Internet provides a wealth of information, accessible instantly, that has been available in past years only from consultants for a fee. The present generation of human resource practitioners has a clear advantage since the information-gathering process has become much quicker and, in many cases, more affordable.

Another significant improvement in the ability to increase productivity at a lower operating cost is the increasing use of electronic mail and intranet capabilities. The intranet enhances communications with employees around the world and helps to sustain positive employee relations. E-mail will virtually replace phone calls as a communications medium and obviates the need to be concerned about calling only, or at least primarily, during business hours.

Conclusions

Compensation and benefits strategies have, and will continue to have, an important impact on the competitiveness and profitability of global corporations. The companies that most effectively mine the best thinking and methodologies from their operations worldwide, and successfully implement them, will capitalize on the potential of compensation and benefits for competitive advantage.

While there will be many opportunities for compensation and benefits specialists to enjoy interesting careers, the emerging dynamics suggest that the best opportunities will be in consulting and specialist provider firms. Those who prefer the corporate world will have to expand their skill bases in other HR and non-HR functions if they expect to advance within their organizations.

Technology is a wild card in the near-term future. Will the software designers be more successful in developing holistic corporate systems that include all aspects of global remuneration, or will the emphasis continue to be on refining off-line systems? The answer to this question will seriously influence how corporations divide their compensation and benefits activities between internal systems and outside specialist firms and thus will affect the future of the profession.

Notes

1. Howard V. Perlmutter, "The Tortuous Evolution of the Multinational Company," *Columbia Journal of World Business* (January/February 1969).
2. Towers Perrin, *Priorities for Competitive Advantage* (1992).
3. Ibid.
4. Ibid.
5. The Conference Board, *The Changing Global Role of the Human Resource Function,* Report No. 1062-94-RR (1994).
6. SHRM-BNA, *Survey of Human Resource Activities, Budgets, and Staffs,* Survey No. 63 (1998).
7. The Conference Board, op. cit.
8. George T. Harris, "The Post-Capitalist Executive: An Interview with Peter Drucker," *Harvard Business Review* (May/June 1993).

ABOUT THE CONTRIBUTORS

Calvin Reynolds is a senior counselor of Organization Resources Counselors, Inc. (ORC), and an adviser to global organizations on international human resources strategies and issues. He is on the faculty of the American Compensation Association (ACA) and teaches courses in global total remuneration and expatriate compensation. He is on the editorial review board and is a contributing author of AlignMark's *Compensation Guide.*

Mr. Reynolds was a senior vice president of ORC, responsible for its international consulting, data services, publications, and meeting groups. He has managed and participated in consulting projects for the United Nations; the governments of Canada, France, and Australia; and global organizations in Europe, the Americas, Africa, the Middle East, and several countries on the Pacific Rim. He was on the board and was chairman of the International Council of the American Compensation Association. Mr. Reynolds was also an adjunct associate professor of international management at New York University's Graduate School of Business Administration and a senior fellow at Wharton, and he has lectured at various other universities. In addition, he spent several years as an expatriate executive for a Fortune 100 multinational, where his latest role was as director of European operating services in Geneva, Switzerland.

Mr. Reynolds has written dozens of articles on international human resources and compensation that have been published in several publications, including *Journal of World Business, Human Resource Planning, ACA Journal, California Management Review, Business Horizons,* and *Benefits and Compensation International.* He wrote chapters on international compensation for McGraw-Hill's *Handbook of Human Resources Administration* (2nd ed.) and *The Executive Handbook of Compensation* published by the Free Press (forthcoming). He is also the author of two booklets on international compensation for the ACA's Building Block Series. Mr. Reynolds was the creator and first publisher of *Innovations in International Compensation*, now ORC's *Innovations in International Human Resources.*

He has bachelor's and master's degrees in business from Columbia University.

David Atkins joined Monks Partnership in 1993. Besides working with companies on board and senior management remuneration reviews, he assists organizations with issues relating to company cars.

Z. Samuel Bernstein is an owner at Hewitt Associates, where he consults with U.S. multinational parent companies on international compensation and benefits for local nationals and international transferees. He focuses on total compensation for key executives, including stock-based programs and tax-effective delivery of remuneration. Mr. Bernstein analyzes the financing of international employee benefit plans, with special focus on U.S. accounting and tax requirements, and assists in their design and implementation.

Prior to joining Hewitt Associates in 1976, he served as assistant professor and instructor in the mathematics and actuarial sciences departments at several major universities. Mr. Bernstein is an associate in the Society of Actuaries and an enrolled actuary (retired status) in the American Academy of Actuaries. He received his BS in mathematics from the University of Chicago in 1969 and his PhD in mathematics from Northwestern University in Evanston, IL, in 1971.

Heather Bowker is the president and managing consultant of Bowker Consulting, Inc., in Mill Valley, California, a company specializing in global human resources strategy and organization effectiveness. Recent clients include Adobe, Advanced Micro Devices, Applied Materials, Bank America, Charles Schwab, Cisco Systems, KLA-Tencor, and Levi-Strauss & Co.

Prior to establishing her own firm, Ms. Bowker worked with Watson Wyatt Worldwide for 17 years, most recently as vice president and director of account management in the San Francisco office. Ms. Bowker joined Watson Wyatt in London in 1979, where she specialized in compensation, then transferred to Hong Kong in 1981 to establish the company's compensation consulting and survey practice in the Asia Pacific region. In 1983, she returned to Europe to manage Watson Wyatt's Brussels office.

Ms. Bowker earned a BA from the University of Warwick and has completed her coursework for a master's degree in organization development at the University of San Francisco.

Jerrold R. Bratkovich is the chief operating officer of the Columbus Group, which provides management consulting, public affairs, and venture-related services. His clients throughout his career have ranged from small entrepreneurial organizations to Fortune 100 corporations covering several industries.

As CEO of the U.S. group, he managed the U.S. business operations of Opinion Research Corporation, a business-to-business market research and consulting firm. His previous positions include partner/managing director for Hay Management Consultants, president and COO of Organization Resources Counselors, Inc., a founding principal in Management Assets Group, and managing partner for ARK Enterprises.

Mr. Bratkovich has a BA degree in psychology from Wheaton College.

Pete Burgess, a member of the International Department of Incomes Data Services (IDS) since 1986, edits IDS's international reference documents and is the general editor of the series "European Management Guides." He is also the joint author of studies on international human resources due diligence and ethical sourcing. Mr. Burgess studied politics, philosophy, and economics at Oxford, followed by research and teaching in sociology and industrial relations at the Universities of Essex (United Kingdom) and Frankfurt-am-Main (Germany).

Neil K. Coleman is vice president of Organization Resources Counselors, Inc., and is responsible for ORC's international pay practice. His specialty is local-national compensation on a global basis, and he coordinates the work of ORC's regional offices in this function.

Mr. Coleman began his career at the Standard Oil Company (NJ), now Exxon, where he worked in executive compensation and international human resources. He subsequently held senior compensation positions at National Starch and Chemical Corporation, W. R. Grace & Company, Continental Group, and NL Industries. Most recently, he was the senior human resources vice president at the European American Bank.

Mr. Coleman received BA and MA degrees from Brigham Young University and a PhD in organization behavior from New York University.

Margaret M. Coolbaugh is an international human resources consultant who assists local-national and multinational organizations in Latin America and elsewhere in the world. She specializes in the design and delivery of innovative solutions to support change initiatives and organization effectiveness objectives.

Ms. Coolbaugh initiated her consulting career in Mexico with the Hay Group, where she assisted Mexican, U.S., and European clients with the development and implementation of remuneration and performance management programs. She also served as the managing director of the Hay

Group in Argentina and as human resources planning and development director for Hay in Mexico. In this role, she was a key contributor to the implementation of human resources and planning processes for local-national employees in Latin America.

Ms. Coolbaugh earned her undergraduate and master's degrees in psychology from the University of the Americas in Mexico.

John de Leon is director of consulting services at Organization Resources Counselors, Inc., in Los Angeles. His 30 years' experience in international human resources management includes helping major U.S. companies address organization issues associated with entrance to Latin America and other international markets. He specializes in helping clients develop international transfer policies, organization effectiveness processes, and compensation and benefits programs for both international assignees and local-national employees.

Prior to joining ORC, he was managing director of the Hay Group in Mexico, where he oversaw the provision of HR consulting services to clients in Mexico and elsewhere in the region. Before that, he was regional director of Deloitte Touche Tohmatsu, serving the HR needs of U.S. and other multinational companies. He has also held international HR and operations management positions with FMC Corporation and Sears Roebuck in Latin America and Europe.

Mr. De Leon is a graduate of the University of San Francisco and the American Graduate School of International Management.

James G. Delaney is a principal with William M. Mercer Limited in Toronto and has been with the company since 1972, with six of those years in Washington D.C. In 1990, he was appointed a managing director of William M. Mercer Companies, Inc. His main area of consulting activity is the compensation of employees and executives.

Emily F. Giffin is an associate in Winston & Strawn's New York office, practicing in the areas of litigation and employment relations. Ms. Giffin graduated summa cum laude from Wake Forest University in 1994 and in 1997 received a JD from the University of Virginia School of Law, where she was a member of the Virginia Journal of International Law.

Ruthanne Huising is a consultant with William M. Mercer Limited in Toronto and works with organizations in the design of base and incentive pay programs. Huising has a bachelor of arts degree from the University of

Alberta and a graduate diploma from the London School of Economics. She joined Mercer in 1997.

Carol Y. Kaplan, CCP, has had a 21-year career in compensation and benefits in a variety of industries. She has worked for county government, United Airlines, Apple Computer, Applied Materials, and Applied Power and currently works for Donnelly Corporation as global director of compensation, benefits, wellness, and HRIS.

Since 1982, much of Ms. Kaplan's work has been devoted to the development and implementation of global programs, including expatriate compensation and local-national compensation, benefits, and HRIS. She is experienced in managing acquisitions, joint ventures, new start-ups, and existing operations, both domestic and international.

Ms. Kaplan has her undergraduate degree from Roosevelt University in Chicago and has done graduate work at Northern Illinois University.

Junko Kudo, a Yokogawa ORC consultant in Japan, specializes in international compensation. She works with Japanese companies, as well as multinational businesses in Japan, in helping them design their expatriate and global compensation policies and systems. Ms. Kudo conducts research and surveys and speaks on expatriate policies at seminars.

Before joining ORC, Ms. Kudo worked with Sumitomo Corporation, one of Japan's largest trading companies. While there, she was a member of a special project team that successfully acquired exclusive representative agreements with major U.S. manufacturers.

Ms. Kudo earned a BA degree in international and cultural studies from Tsuda College in Japan and an MILR from the Graduate School of Industrial and Labor Relations, Cornell University.

Andrew Mackmurdie joined the Auckland office of Hay Management Consultants (NZ) Ltd. in 1986 as a senior consultant and has been involved in a wide variety of private and public-sector organizations in both New Zealand and Fiji. This work has involved organization audit and design, organizational change, job analysis and design, work measurement, strategic remuneration, performance management, and advice on a wide range of human resource and industrial relations issues. In 1999, Mr. Mackmurdie was appointed manager of operations for the Auckland-based consulting activities.

Mr. Mackmurdie has extensive corporate experience in New Zealand and England. He graduated from the University of Canterbury with a bachelor of law (LLB), has a diploma of management, and is a member of the New Zealand Institute of Personnel Management.

Eric P. Marquardt is a senior consultant in the executive compensation practice of Towers Perrin's Chicago office. Before joining Towers Perrin, he managed a regional executive compensation consulting practice and served as director of executive compensation and management programs for Merck & Co.

During Mr. Marquardt's tenure at Merck & Co., he advised senior management, the chairman's staff, and the compensation committee of the board on strategy and issues related to executive compensation and, specifically, human resource issues related to mergers, acquisitions, divestitures, and joint ventures. Prior to Merck & Co., Mr. Marquardt was with the Wyatt Company, where he led the integrated human resources consulting practice on the West Coast. He was also responsible for setting up and staffing a satellite consulting office in the Silicon Valley and for providing executive compensation consulting to major San Francisco Bay Area clients.

Previously, Mr. Marquardt was a manager at KPMG Peat Marwick, served as the manager of corporate compensation for PepsiCo, Inc., and was a human resources specialist for Texas Instruments.

Mr. Marquardt has been published in a number of industry periodicals, including the *Journal of Compensation & Benefits, Washington CEO,* and the *ACA Journal.* He has also authored a chapter in *Compensation Guide* (a book published by Warren, Gorham, and Lamont). Mr. Marquardt is a frequent speaker on executive compensation issues and has been interviewed and quoted by *Business Week, Chicago Tribune,* and the *New York Times*. He is also a faculty member of the American Compensation Association.

Mr. Marquardt is a graduate of the University of Michigan and received a master's of labor and industrial relations from Michigan State University.

John S. Maxwell, PhD, CCP, GRP, FAHRI, is president and CEO of Sidstar, a global human resources consulting firm in Scottsdale, Arizona. He has a professional career spanning over 25 years in a number of industries, including manufacturing, engineering, retail, construction, and finance. He also has considerable international human resource consulting experience.

Mr. Maxwell is a past president of the World Federation of Personnel Management Associations (WFPMA), which represents some 60 national associations and more than 300,000 professional members worldwide. He served on that body's executive committee from 1984 to 1996, as secretary-general from 1984 to 1988 and as president from 1988 to 1992. He was also on the executive committee of the Asian Pacific Human Resource Association from 1982 to 1988 as secretary-general.

In Australia, he has served the Australian Human Resource Institute (AHRI) in a number of executive positions, including that of national president in 1984. He was chairman of AHRI's International Relations Committee from 1983 to 1988. Mr. Maxwell was made a fellow of the AHRI in 1982 and an honorary fellow of the Institute of Southern Africa in 1989 for his services to the institutes on the African continent.

In 1996, he was awarded the George Petitpas Memorial Award by the WFPMA for his ongoing contribution to international human resources. He was only the sixth such recipient of this most prestigious award.

Mr. Maxwell has lectured in human resource management at both undergraduate and graduate levels at several major universities. He has also been the keynote speaker at conferences in Europe, North America, South America, Asia Pacific, Africa, and India.

In 1995, he was asked by the American Compensation Association to accept the "missionary" role of director general of the Global Remuneration Organisation (GRO), of which ACA became the founding member. During the past three years, he has developed the GRP designation, which is rapidly becoming the worldwide mark of professional excellence in reward management and has firmly established the organization on a sound financial footing. Its seven-person board now has members from five countries.

A graduate from the University of New South Wales, Australia, Mr. Maxwell also possesses postgraduate qualifications in personnel and industrial relations from the University of Technology, Sydney, and he completed his PhD at La Salle.

Betsy Stelle Morgan, counsel with Baker & McKenzie in Chicago, is a member of the firm's International Executive Transfer Practice Group and runs the Chicago practice. She graduated from the John Marshall Law School in Chicago and is admitted to the Illinois Bar. Her practice concentrates on the visa and immigration issues related to the international transfer of executives, primarily into the United States. Ms. Morgan manages a team of more than 10 attorneys and paralegals in the Chicago office who are dedicated to the international executive transfer/corporate immigration practice. She counsels multinational corporations in managing their expatriate portfolios and the related immigration policy concerns. Ms. Morgan advises on U.S. employment visas, green card issues, and I-9 employment verification requirements. She also works with Baker & McKenzie's offices worldwide in transferring employees of U.S. companies to foreign operations.

Ms. Morgan is the editor of Baker & McKenzie's *International Executive Transfer Update,* which focuses on immigration, tax, and benefits issues relating to corporate expatriate planning and is published on a quarterly basis. She is a member of both the American Bar Association and the American Immigration Lawyers Association and speaks frequently on immigration issues affecting executive transfers.

Kim Neuhold has seven years of consulting experience with the Hay Group (Australia), specializing in reward and related issues. Her experience has been gained across a wide range of industry sectors, including financial services manufacturing, resources, and the public sector.

In addition to her consulting experience, Ms. Neuhold has some 10 years' experience in the Australian financial sector, working with the ANZ Bank, Elders Finance Group, and Macquarie Bank. Roles held have included both line and human resources roles, the latter including both generalist HR and remuneration and benefits management positions.

Ms. Neuhold has a BS majoring in psychology from Monash University and a graduate diploma in applied psychology. She is a registered psychologist in the state of Victoria and a member of the Australian Human Resources Institute.

Toshio Nirei is president of Yokogawa Organization Resources Counselors, Inc., Tokyo, a joint venture company formed in 1990 between Yokogawa Electric Corporation and Organization Resources Counselors, Inc. Prior to his current duties, Mr. Nirei served in a variety of positions with Yokogawa Electric Corporation. After joining Yokogawa in 1973, he was posted to the corporate marketing staff and then moved on to corporate finance. From there, between 1981 and 1985, Mr. Nirei was assigned to Yokogawa Corporation of America in Georgia, where he served as chief financial officer and manager of finance and administration, management information systems, and production control. Upon his return to Japan, he joined Yokogawa's corporate human resource group as manager of international personnel operations and later assumed the position of manager of personnel strategy planning.

Mr. Nirei is a graduate of Meiji University in Tokyo. He also completed an international business course at the Georgia Institute of Technology and a management development course at Keio Business School. Mr. Nirei is the first member of the Tokyo International Personnel Manager's Association, started in 1986, and one of the founders of the Japan Society for Business Ethics Study, formed in 1993.

William A. O'Connell is a principal and national practice leader of sales and marketing effectiveness for Sibson & Company in Princeton, New Jersey. Mr. O'Connell assists organizations in forming and executing their going-to-market strategies by focusing on market dynamics, decision processes, information flows, learning interventions, channels of distribution, and performance management, measures, and rewards that must mesh to achieve business results.

Before joining Sibson, Mr. O'Connell served as chief operating officer of GTN Industries' multiple divisions in television production, engineering and design services, radio, real estate, and specialty fabrication. He has an MBA from New York University and a bachelor's degree from St. John's University.

Graham O'Neill is the director of business development for the Melbourne office of the Hay Group and leads the marketing function and Reward and Recognition Knowledge Center for Hay Pacific. Mr. O'Neill has some 20 years' experience consulting in areas related to organization structure, work design, performance management and assessment, and reward planning.

Mr. O'Neill rejoined Hay in 1996 from the ANZ Banking Group, where he was responsible for planning and design of remuneration and performance management for the group's worldwide operations. Apart from his consulting career, Mr. O'Neill has also held corporate management roles as group manager of personnel and employee relations for the Australian operations of Daimler-Benz and as an organization development consultant with General Motors. He commenced his working career undertaking teaching and research in psychology at various Australian institutions.

Mr. O'Neill has a first-class BA (Hons) degree in psychology and a postgraduate diploma in applied psychology. He was elected a fellow of the Australian Human Resource Institute in 1988 and is a member of the American Compensation Association.

He has published three books, *Corporate Remuneration in the 90s: Strategies for Decision Makers* and, with Dr. Robin Kramar of Macquarie University, the two-volume work titled *Australian Human Resource Management: Trends in Management Practice*. He is the author of some 30 papers that have appeared in magazines, professional journals, and books in Australia and overseas. Mr. O'Neill is a past editor of the AHRI journal *Human Resource Management* (now *Asia Pacific Journal of Human Resources)* and remains on the editorial board of that journal; he is also on the editorial board of the bimonthly *Reward Management Bulletin* published by John Libby & Company.

Dan Orchant is a partner with KPMG's IES practice. Mr. Orchant is based in New York and has more than 15 years of experience assisting companies meet the tax and compensation challenges of competing globally. Mr. Orchant has served in Tokyo and Hong Kong and has written for numerous publications geared toward international human resources professionals.

Gary L. Parker is a senior vice president and chair of Aon Compensation Consulting Group's international practice. During the past 30 years, Mr. Parker has held senior executive positions at the Coca-Cola Company, Chase Manhattan Bank, Dresdner Bank, Travelers Insurance Companies, and Goodyear Tire & Rubber Company in the field of international human resources. He has lived and worked extensively in Asia and Western Europe.

Prior to joining Aon, Mr. Parker was the chief operating officer of a joint venture between ECA, Ltd., a London-based research and advisory services firm, and Windham International, a consulting and tactical outsourcing firm. ECA Windham, LLC, specializes in all aspects of the international relocation of employees and provides data on global living along with human resources consulting.

Mr. Parker has comprehensive experience in the design and implementation of global compensation methods and systems such as statutory and nonstatutory benefit plans and executive pay plans. He has many years of experience in international labor relations and has advised many Fortune 500 companies in the areas of manpower planning and organizational development. He is a regular on the professional speaking circuit and has written and provided counsel extensively on most functional aspects of international human resources.

A Fulbright scholar, Mr. Parker holds a JD from the Cumberland School of Law and received an MBA from INSEAD. He is fluent in Farsi, French, German, and Italian.

Julian Pollard worked as a consultant in the New York office of Organization Resources Counselors, Inc., where he specialized in international employee relations and expatriate compensation. He was involved in a wide variety of expatriate policy development projects for clients. He managed ORC's international assignment policies and practices surveys and several other research areas. Before joining ORC, Mr. Pollard was an associate with Price Waterhouse in London and New York, where he was involved in tax consulting and compliance for U.S. expatriates and foreign nationals in the United States.

Born in the United Kingdom, Mr. Pollard has a law degree from the University of London and is admitted to the bar of the State of New York. He left ORC in 1998 to pursue a master's of business administration at New York University.

Ronald N. Reynolds is a principal in the Chicago office of Compensation Resource Group, Inc. He has more than 13 years of compensation experience in the financial, consumer products, and manufacturing industries. Mr. Reynolds has practiced all aspects of compensation design, including sales and productivity incentives, board compensation, executive compensation, international and expatriate compensation, and nonqualified benefit programs.

Mr. Reynolds's strengths are the strategic and technical aspects of executive, international, and expatriate compensation. However, he also possesses an in-depth understanding of the nonqualified benefits discipline. Mr. Reynolds has assisted various clients with, among other projects, the design of executive short-term cash plans, global broad-based stock option plans, executive compensation strategies for IPOs and spin-offs, and expatriate programs. He has written several articles on executive and international compensation topics and has been quoted several times in prominent newspapers on various executive compensation issues.

Prior to joining CRG, Mr. Reynolds was the global compensation director for an $8 billion consumer products company. Before that, he held various compensation leadership roles in several financial institutions.

Mr. Reynolds graduated from Radford University with an MS in industrial/organizational psychology and a BS in education. He has additional coursework in finance and accounting.

Alan J. Ritchie is vice president of compensation, employee benefits, and health services for Lucent Technologies. Mr. Ritchie joined Lucent in September 1996 from General Mills, Inc., in Minneapolis. During his 22 years at General Mills, he held several increasingly responsible positions in corporate human resources, most recently serving as vice president of compensation and benefits.

Mr. Ritchie holds a BS degree in insurance and finance from the University of Connecticut and an MBA from American University in Washington, D.C. He served as chairman of the board of the 21,000-member American Compensation Association in 1996 and is currently chairman of the board of the Global Remuneration Organisation, which markets compensation and benefits training programs worldwide. In addition, Mr. Ritchie is a member of the board of the Washington Business Group on Health and the 170,000-member Experimental Aircraft Association.

Samuel M. Russo is a partner with KPMG's international executive services (IES) practice. Mr. Russo is based in New York and has more than 25 years of experience assisting global companies with tax planning and payroll services. He also serves as national director for KPMG's expatriate cost minimization practice, which implements tax-planning strategies for global companies.

Ronald F. Schaeffer, an ORC consultant, specializes in applying human resources programs to improve strategic and operational effectiveness. He has a background in assessing HR's contribution to strategic business goals, designing measurement and planning processes, and organizing HR functions to deliver services and guidance to management.

Mr. Schaeffer worked for 29 years at Exxon as an HR manager in its chemical and refining operations, at headquarters, and in R&D organizations. He served 10 years as compensation manager for Exxon Research and Engineering.

Mr. Schaeffer has a BS degree in chemical engineering from the University of Pennsylvania and an MBA from Stanford University.

Susan Schenkel-Savitt, a partner in the law firm of Winston & Strawn, practices employment law, advice and counsel, and litigation on behalf of management from the firm's New York office, representing both domestic and multinational companies and public-sector employers. Ms. Schenkel-Savitt graduated with distinction from the Pennsylvania State University (BA, magna cum laude, 1964), where she was a member of Phi Beta Kappa. After attending a graduate program at the Bryn Mawr School of Social Work and Social Research on a National Institute of Mental Health Scholarship grant, Ms. Schenkel-Savitt entered the Columbia University School of Law, where she was awarded a JD degree in 1968.

Prior to joining Winston & Strawn, Ms. Schenkel-Savitt was a senior partner and litigator in private practice in a major New York law firm. Ms. Schenkel-Savitt has served as chief counsel for public-sector and multinational corporations before administrative agencies and state and federal courts in major Title VII, ADA, ADEA, OWBPA, ERISA, MPPAA, sexual harassment, and FLSA class action and single-plaintiff litigation, as well as wage and hour issues. She is a frequent lecturer and author on international and domestic employment law issues and litigation.

Steven P. Seltz is the international compensation and benefits vice president for Lucent Technologies. He has more than 17 years of compensation and benefits experience, including corporate and consulting assignments in the United States and abroad.

At Lucent, Mr. Seltz is responsible for compensation and benefits activities in the 60-plus countries in which the company operates outside the United States. He is a long-standing faculty member of the American Compensation Association and the Global Remuneration Organisation, and he teaches courses and lectures on various compensation issues for private corporations and associations internationally and domestically.

Mr. Seltz holds an MBA from the Wharton School at the University of Pennsylvania, a certificate in foreign studies from Kansai University in Japan, and a BA from Vassar College. He has taught at Johns Hopkins University; has held senior human resources and compensation management positions for Mobil Oil, Brown-Forman, and Arinc, Inc.; and has consulted for William M. Mercer.

Willis Shen is the consultant in charge of the Shanghai office of Watson Wyatt. He has been with Watson Wyatt for over five years, first working in the actuarial practice of the Washington, D.C., office for two years before transferring to the San Francisco office to work on the international team as a benefits consultant. In 1997, Mr. Shen was selected as a Michael H. Davis fellow to spend two to three years on an international assignment outside his home country.

As a Davis fellow, Mr. Shen has been focusing on developing the benefits market in China. He has worked with multinational companies on the design and development of various long-term incentive programs, including retirement and housing programs, and advises clients on the impact of social security reform on company-sponsored benefit programs. He is a frequent speaker on human resources issues in China.

Mr. Shen graduated from Brown University in Providence, Rhode Island, with a degree in applied mathematics.

Giles Tulk is a senior consultant with Monks Partnership in Great Britain specializing in all aspects of senior executive remuneration and job evaluation. His clients include companies across all business sectors in the FT-SE 100 and FT-SE 250, together with privately owned groups. He is also responsible for Monks' European pay surveys.

Jonathan M. Zamet is the assistant vice president of compensation at AXA Client Solutions, LLC, a subsidiary of AXA Financial, Inc. He is responsible for all aspects of domestic and expatriate compensation programs. Prior to joining Equitable Life (now a member of the Global AXA Group), from 1982 to 1986, he was a consultant for Organization Resources Counselors, Inc., specializing in expatriate compensation and human resources management.

Mr. Zamet has BA and MA degrees from Oxford University and an MA from Columbia University. He is a certified compensation professional and serves on the faculty of the American Compensation Association.

GLOBAL COMPENSATION, BENEFITS, AND EXPATRIATE MANAGEMENT: RESOURCE DIRECTORY

GLOBAL COMPENSATION AND BENEFITS CONSULTANTS: THE AMERICAS

Aon Corporate Consulting Group—International

Mr. Gary Parker*
Senior Vice President
2 World Trade Center, 101st Floor
New York, NY 10048
Tel: (212) 441-2430
Fax: (212) 441-2049
Gparker@aoncons.com

Bowker Consulting, Inc.

Ms. Heather Bowker*
President
950 Smith Road
Mill Valley, CA 94941
Tel: (415) 389-4950
Fax: (415) 389-0186
heather@bowkerconsulting.com

The Columbus Group

Mr. Jerrold R. Bratkovich*, COO
2111 Wilson Boulevard,
Suite 1200, Arlington, VA 22201
Tel: (703) 351-6620

Hewitt Associates, LLC

Mr. Z. Samuel Bernstein*
100 Half Day Road
Lincolnshire, IL 60069
Tel: (847) 295-5000
Fax: (847) 913-6986
Zsbernst@hewitt.com

William M. Mercer

Mr. Giles Archibald
Senior Vice President
1166 Avenue of the Americas
New York, NY 10036
Tel: (212) 345-7010
Fax: (212) 345-7296

William M. Mercer, Limited

Mr. James G. Delaney,* Principal
Ms. Ruthanne Huising,* Consultant
BCE Place,
161 Bay Street,
PO Box 501
Toronto, Canada M5J 2S5
Tel: (416) 868-2563
Fax: (416) 868-9634
Jim_DelaneyMERCER-TOR@mercer.ca
Ruthanne_Huising@mercer.ca

Organization Resources Counselors, Inc.

Mr. Neil K. Coleman,* Vice President
Mr. Ronald F. Schaeffer*
1211 Avenue of the Americas
New York, NY 10036
Tel: (212) 719-3400
Fax: (212) 398-1358

Organization Resources Counselors, Inc.

Mr. John de Leon*
Director of Consulting Services
12400 Wilshire Boulevard
Los Angeles, CA 90025-1025
Tel: (310) 820-3800
Fax: (310) 207-8174
John.deLeon@orcinc.com

Organization Resources Counselors, Inc.

Mr. Calvin Reynolds*
Senior Counselor
52 Underhill Road
Ossining, NY 10562
Tel: (914) 941-1324
Fax: (914) 923-9152
reynolds@bestweb.net

Sibson & Company

Mr. William A. O'Connell*
Practice Leader, Sales and Marketing Effectiveness
504 Carnegie Crescent
Princeton, NJ 08543
Tel: (609) 520-2704
Fax: (609) 520-0369

Sidstar, Inc.

Mr. John S. Maxwell,* President
7127 E. Becker Ln., Suite 110
Scottsdale, AZ 85254
Tel: (480) 369-9369
Fax: (480) 595-8470
Jmaxwell@sidstar.com

Towers Perrin

Mr. Eric P. Marquard,
Senior Consultant
200 W. Madison, Suite 3100
Chicago, IL 60606
Tel: (312) 609-9541
Fax: (312) 609-9406
marquae@towers.com

GLOBAL COMPENSATION AND BENEFITS: EUROPE

Incomes Data Services

Mr. Pete Burgess*
77 Bastwick Street
London EC1V 3TT
England
Tel: (44) 171 250 3434
peteb@incomesdata.co.uk

Monks Partnership Limited

Mr. Giles Tulk,* Senior Consultant
Mr. David Atkins*

The Mill House
Wendens Ambo
Saffron Walden
Essex CB11 4JX
England
Tel: (44) 1799 542222

Fax: (44) 1799 541805
info@monkspartnership.co.uk

Organization Resources Counselors, Inc.

Ms. Siobhan Cummins
Managing Director
Liscartan House
127/131 Sloane Street
London SW1X 9BA
England
Tel: (44) 171 591 5600
Fax: (44) 171 591 5905
Siobhan.cummins@orc-lon.co.uk

GLOBAL COMPENSATION AND BENEFITS: ASIA/ PACIFIC

The Hay Group Pty., Ltd.

Mr. Graham O'Neill,* Director, Business Development
Ms. Kim Neuhold,* Consultant (Melbourne)
Mr. Andrew Mackmurdie* (Auckland)
Lvl. 11-1
Spring Street
Melbourne, Victoria 3000
Australia
Tel: (61) 3 9667 2666
Fax: (61) 3 9667 2699
Graham_O'Neill@haygroup.com

Watson Wyatt

Mr. Willis Shen*
Consultant in Charge
21/F, E2,
Shanghai Industrial Investment Building No. 18,
Cao Xi
Shanghai 200030 P.R. China
Tel: (8621) 6427 1891/2/3/4
Fax: (8621) 6427 1889
Willis_shen@watsonwyatt.com

Yokogawa Organization Resources Counselors Corporation

Mr. Toshio Nirei,* President
Ms. Junko Kudo,* Consultant
Mitaka Takagi Building, 2F
1-15-5 Nakacho,
Musashino-shi,
Tokyo 180, Japan
Tel: (81) 422 37 6701
Fax: (81) 422 37 6705
tn-nirei@y-orc.co.jp
junko-k@y-orc.co.jp

EXPATRIATE COMPENSATION CONSULTANTS

Aon Corporate Consulting Group—International

Mr. Gary Parker*
Senior Vice President
2 World Trade Center,
101st Floor
New York, NY 10048
Tel: (212) 441-2430
Fax: (212) 441-2049
Gparker@aoncons.com

Associates for International Research (AIRINC)

Mr. Jim Reid, Vice President
1100 Massachusetts Avenue
Cambridge, MA 02138
Tel: (617) 354-2133
Fax: (617) 547-1535

ECA-Windham

Paul Bailey,
Director of Compensation
55 Fifth Avenue
New York, NY 10003
Tel: (212) 647-0555
Fax: (212) 647-0494

Organization Resources Counselors, Inc.

Mr. Geoffrey W. Latta
Executive Vice President
1211 Avenue of the Americas,
15th Floor
New York, NY 10036-8701
Tel: (212) 719-3400
Fax: (212) 719-5625

Mr. Roger Herod,Vice President
Triangle Plaza,
Suite 520
8750 West Bryn Mawr Avenue
Chicago, IL 60631-3508
Tel: (773) 380-4530
Fax: (773) 380-4535

Organization Resources Counselors, Inc.

Mr. Calvin Reynolds*
Senior Counselor
52 Underhill Road
Ossining, NY 10562
Tel: (914) 941-1324
Fax: (914) 923-9152
reynolds@bestweb.net

Runzheimer International

Ms. Denise R. A. Oemig
Director of International Services
Runzheimer Park
Rochester, WI 53167-0009
Tel: (414) 767-2402;
(800) 558-1702
Fax: (414) 767-2388

Towers Perrin

Mr. Thomas S. Tilghman
Global Human Resources Group
335 Madison Avenue
New York, NY 10017-4605
Tel: (212) 309-3684
Fax: (212) 309-3730

Watson Wyatt Worldwide

Ms. Marcia Marsh, Practice Leader,
Int'l Consulting for the Americas
461 Fifth Avenue
New York, NY 10017
Tel: (212) 725-7550
Fax: (212) 779-4019

EMPLOYMENT LAW

Winston & Strawn

Susan Schenkel-Savitt, Esq.,*
Partner

Emily F. Giffin, Esq.,*
Associate
200 Park Avenue
New York, NY 10166-4193
Tel: (212) 294-4772
Fax: (212) 294-4700
Ssavitt@winston.com

VISA/IMMIGRATION

Baker & McKenzie

Betsy Stelle Morgan, Esq.*
Counsel
One Prudential Plaza
130 E. Randolph,
Suite 3900
Chicago, IL 60601
Tel: (312) 861-8944
Fax: (312) 861-2898
Betsy.Morgan@bakernet.com

Fragomen, Del Rey & Bernsen

Austin Fragomen, Esq.
Managing Partner
515 Madison Avenue
New York, NY 10022
Tel: (212) 891-7536
Fax: (212) 758-7215

Munro, Nelson & Pearl

Ms. Julie Pearl
Managing Partner
525 Market Street,
Suite 3400
San Francisco, CA 94105-2742
Tel: (415) 771-7500
Fax: (415) 771-5009

CROSS-CULTURAL TRAINING

Berlitz Cross-Cultural

Mr. Dean Foster
Director, Cross-Cultural Services
257 Park Avenue South
New York, NY 10010
Tel: (212) 598-2556

Cendant Intercultural, The Bennett Group

Ms. Rita Bennett
Managing Partner
1 N. Franklin, Suite 750
Chicago, IL 60606
Tel: (312) 251-9000
Fax: (312) 251-9015

CIAO! International

Ms. Lorelei Carobolante
President
245-M Mount Hermon Road,
Suite C
Scotts Valley, CA 95066
Tel: (408) 461-8090, ext. 114
Fax: (408) 461-8099

International Orientation Resources (IOR)

Ms. Noel Kreicker
President
500 Skokie Boulevard,
Suite 600
Northbrook, IL 60062
Tel: (847) 205-0066
Fax: (847) 205-0085

Prudential Relocation Intercultural Services

Dr. Noel Minor, Vice President
2555 55th Street
Boulder, CO 80301
Tel: (303) 546-1013
Fax: (303) 449-1064
or
Mr. Thomas R. Jago
Vice President, Marketing
Prudential Resources Management
200 Summit Lake Drive
Valhalla, NY 10595
Tel: (914) 749-4160
Fax: (914) 749-4149

Windham International

Ms. Ilene Dolins, Vice President
55 Fifth Avenue
New York, NY 10003
Tel: (212) 647-0555
Fax: (212) 647-0494

TAX/ACCOUNTING

Global Practice Leader

Arthur Andersen
Mr. Gardiner Hempel
1345 Avenue of the Americas
New York, NY 10105
Tel: (212) 708-4056
Fax: (212) 245-2753

Deloitte & Touche

Ms. Tracey K. Edwards, Partner
60 South Market Street,
Suite 800
San Jose, CA 95113-2303
Tel: (408) 920-2403
Fax: (408) 998-3083

Ernst & Young

Ms. Linda Watson
National Director,
Expatriate Services
787 Seventh Avenue
New York, NY 10019
Tel: (212) 407-2595

KPMG Peat Marwick, LLP

Mr. William J. Hibbitt,
Partner-National Director
International Executive Services
Mr. Dan Orchant,*
Partner
Mr. Sam Russo,*
Partner
345 Park Avenue
New York, NY 10154
Tel: (212) 872-3340
Fax: (212) 872-3311
dorchant@kpmg.com
srusso@kpmg.com

PricewaterhouseCoopers, LLP

Mr. Michael Budnick
Global Leader, International
Assignment Solutions
11 Madison Avenue,
17th Floor
New York, NY 10010
Tel: (212) 591-5360
Fax: (212) 596-8940

RELOCATION

AmeriCorp Relocation Management

Mr. Stuart Bergon
Executive Vice President
17304 Preston Road,
Suite 400
Dallas, TX 75252
Tel: (972) 931-1776
Fax: (972) 447-3224

The Associates

Mr. Don R. Watson
President
250 E. Carpenter Freeway #5D
Irving, TX 75062
Tel: (972) 657-6310
Fax: (972) 657-6312

Cendant International Assignment Services

Mr. John B. Arcario
Senior Vice President and
General Manager
40 Apple Ridge Road
Danbury, CT 06810
Tel: (203) 796-1772
Fax: (203) 796-3102

CIAO! International Relocation Management

Ms. Lorelei Carobolante
President
245-M Mount Hermon Road,
Suite C
Scotts Valley, CA 95066
Tel: (408) 461-8090, ext. 14 (ext?)
Fax: (408) 461-8099

MML Relocation Management

Mr. Mark R. Roussy
President
10707 Corporate Drive,
Suite 138
Stafford, TX 77477
Tel: (281) 634-0530
Fax: (281) 240-2224

Prudential Resources Management

Mr. Thomas R. Jago
Vice President, Marketing
200 Summit Lake Drive
Valhalla, NY 10595
Tel: (914) 749-4160
Fax: (914) 749-4149

Relocation Resources International

Mr. Stephen Branch
International Operations Director
120 Longwater Drive
Norwell, MA 02061
Tel: (781) 659-5268
Fax: (781) 659-5270

MOVERS

Crown Pacific

Ms. Debbi-Lee Irwin
Corporate Services Manager
5252 Argosy Drive

Huntington Beach, CA 92649
Tel: (714) 898-0955
Fax: (714) 898-5640

Graebel Movers International

Mr. Mario Amato
President
401 S. Airport Boulevard
Aurora, CO 80017-2122
Tel: (303) 338-6683
Fax: (303) 338-6997

Movers International

Mr. Donald M. Rankin
Executive Vice President
Eastern Region
1051 Commerce Court
Buffalo Grove, IL 60093
Tel: (847) 541-1051
Fax: (847) 541-1094

Ryder Move Management

Mr. John Libretto
Int'l Business Development Manager
3607 Parkway Lane, Suite 300
Norcross, GA 30092
Tel: (800) 287-6011, ext. 5446
Fax: (770) 449-3482

INTERNATIONAL SPOUSAL CAREER

Resource Careers

Ms. Marjorie B. Shorrock
President
1422 Euclid Avenue, Suite 1604
Cleveland, OH 44115
Tel: (216) 579-1414
Fax: (216) 579-1453

EDUCATION SERVICES

Bennett Educational Resources

Ms. Georgia C. Bennett
President
310 N. High Street
West Chester, PA 19380
Tel: (610) 692-9096
Fax: (610) 692-9132

International Schools Services

Ms. Mary Rabbitt
Vice President
15 Roszel Road
Princeton, NJ 08543
Tel: (609) 452-0990
Fax: (609) 452-2690

MEDICAL ASSISTANCE

International SOS Assistance

Mr. William Bradley
Regional Sales Director
10800 Alpharetta Highway, Suite 546
Roswell, GA 30076
Tel: (770) 521-8831
Fax: (770) 521-8832

Tel: (703) 893-0083
Fax: (703) 893-8611

Kroll-O'Gara

Mr. Wilfred T. O'Gara
President and
Chief Operating Officer
900 Third Avenue
New York, NY 10022
Tel: (212) 593-1000
Fax: (212) 593-2631

Vance International

Mr. Charles F. Vance, President
10467 White Granite Drive
Oakton, VA 22124-2700
Tel: (703) 385-6754
Fax: (703) 359-8456

HOUSEHOLD FURNISHINGS

Appliances Overseas

Mr. Allen Sausen
President
276 Fifth Avenue, Suite 407
New York, NY 10001-4509
Tel: (212) 545-8001
Fax: (212) 545-8005

Home Essentials

Mr. Christopher Exline
President
1700 Pacific Avenue, Suite 4425
Dallas, TX 75201
Tel: (214) 741-7000
Fax: (214) 741-3700

GLOBAL SECURITY

The Ackerman Group

Mr. E. C. Ackerman
Managing Director
1666 Kennedy Causeway,
Suite 700
Miami Beach, FL 33141
Tel: (305) 865-0072
Fax: (305) 865-0218

Control Risks Group

Mr. Edward Grubb
Managing Director
1749 Old Meadow Road,
Suite 120
McLean, VA 22102

RISK INSURANCE

UNIRISC, Inc.

Mr. Ken McClinton
Senior Vice President
205 Robin Road, Suite 230
Paramus, NJ 07862
Tel: (201) 967-7810
Fax: (201) 967-7110

INTERNATIONAL BANKING SERVICES

Chase Manhattan Bank

Mr. Dan Bostwick
Vice President

55 Water Street,
Room 300
New York, NY 10041-0199
Tel: (212) 638-0286
Fax: (212) 638-0271

Citibank

Mr. W. Dwight Raiford
Vice President, PBOE
666 Fifth Avenue,
7th Floor
New York, NY 10103
Tel: (212) 307-8205
Fax: (212) 757-3179

SETTLING-IN SERVICES

American International Group

Mr. David Murphy
Vice President, Global Marketing
AIG International Services
80 Pine Street, 11th Floor
New York, NY 10005
Tel: (212) 770-8417
Fax: (212) 269-8786

COUNTRY PUBLICATIONS

Craighead Publications, Inc.

Mr. Scott B. Craighead
President
PO Box 1253
Darien, CT 06820-1253
Tel: (203) 655-1007
Fax: (203) 655-0018

NEWSLETTER

Expatriate Management Update

Mr. Llyn Clague*, Publisher
100 Euclid Avenue
Hastings-on-Hudson, NY 10706
Tel: (914) 478-4616
Fax: (914) 478-4509

ASSOCIATIONS

American Compensation Association

Mr. Wallace J. Nichols
Executive Director
14040 N. Northsight Boulevard
Scottsdale, AZ 85260-3601
Tel: (480) 951-9191
Fax: (480) 483-8352
http://www.acaonline.org

Employee Relocation Council

Ms. Sylvia Lamb
Director, Membership
1720 N Street NW
Washington, DC 20036-2900
Tel: (202) 857-0857
Fax: (202) 467-4012

Institute for International Human Resources Society for Human Resource Management

1800 Duke Street
Alexandria, VA 22314
Tel: (800) 283-SHRM;

(703) 548-3440
Fax: (703) 836-0367
Shrm@shrm.org
http://www.shrm.org

National Foreign Trade Council

Mr. Bill Sheridan
Director, International Compensation
1270 Avenue of the Americas
New York, NY 10020
Tel: (212) 399-7128
Fax: (212) 399-7144

OUTSOURCING

Arthur Andersen

Cendant International Assignment Services

Deloitte & Touche

Ernst & Young

Hewitt Associates

KPMG Peat Marwick

PricewaterhouseCoopers

Prudential Relocation

Compiled by Llyn Clague, Publisher, Expatriate Management Update and Others

*Contributor to this guide

PERIODICALS, BOOKS, AND WEB SITES

PERIODICALS

AMERICAN COMPENSATION ASSOCIATION

14040 North Northsight Blvd.
Scottsdale, AZ 85260
Tel: (480) 951-9191
Fax: (480) 483-8352
acajournal@acaonline.org

ACA Journal
Chris Burawa, Editor

ACA News
Rodney K. Platt, Editor

Global Remuneration Organisation GROing CONNEXIONS
Jeremy Handel, Editor
Tel: (480) 922-2081
Fax: (480) 951-1195

AMERICAN MANAGEMENT ASSOCIATION

1601 Broadway
New York, NY 10019-7420
Tel: (212) 903-8069
Fax: (212) 903-8083

Compensation & Benefits Review
Linda Bennett, Managing Editor
lbennett@amanet.org

HR Focus
Genevieve Capowski, Editor
Tel: (212) 903-8066
Fax: (212) 903-8083
gcapowski@amanet.org

BENEFITS & COMPENSATION INTERNATIONAL

Pension Publications Limited
East Wing, 4th Floor
Hope House, 45 Great Peter Street
London, England SW1P 3LT
Tel: 011 44 171 222 0288
Fax: 011 44 171 799 2163
irena@benecompintl.com

BENEFITS & COMPENSATION SOLUTIONS

2001 West Main Street, Suite 225
Stamford, CT 06902
Tel: (203) 358-0101
Fax: (203) 961-9624

CORPORATE RELOCATION NEWS

Edwin B. Cohen,
Publisher and Editor
7910 Ivanhoe Avenue, Suite 432
La Jolla, CA 92037
Tel: (619) 456-7020;
(800) 872-6863
Fax: (619) 456-1603
bound4@boundinternational.com

COST OF LIVING NEWS

Cost Comparison Counselors Inc.
PO Box 77192
Washington, DC 20013
Tel: (703) 893-5355

EXPATRIATE MANAGEMENT UPDATE

Clague Enterprises, Inc.
Mr. Llyn Clague
100 Euclid Avenue
Hastings, NY 10706
Tel: (914) 478-4616
Fax: (914) 478-4509

EXPORT TODAY

Trade Communications, Inc.
Rolf Rykken
733 15th Street NW
Washington, DC 20005
Tel: (202) 737-3138
Fax: (202) 783-5966
rolf202@earthlink.net

GLOBAL WORKFORCE

Valerie Frazee,
Editor
245 Fischer Avenue, Suite B-2
Costa Mesa, CA 92626
Tel: (714) 751-1883, ext. 237
Fax: (714) 751-4106
frazeev@globalworkforce.com

HR REPORT

Bureau of National Affairs
Susan Hobbs, Editor
1231 25th Street NW
Washington, DC 20037
Tel: (202) 452-4035
Fax: (202) 728-3340
Shobbs@bna.com

HR WORLD

Martin Leach Publishing
Godfrey Golzen, Editor-in-Chief
2-6 Northburgh Street
London EC1V OAY UK
Tel: 011 44 171 608 8000
Fax: 011 44 171 608 8001
general@martin-leach-group.co.uk

INTERNATIONAL HERALD TRIBUNE

Judith Rehack (freelance writer)
45 East 89th Street
New York, NY 10128
Tel: (212) 410-9142

INTERNATIONAL HR JOURNAL

Linda Mark, Editor
395 Hudson Street
New York, NY 10014
Tel: (212) 367-6399
Fax: (212) 367-6305

JOURNAL OF BUSINESS STRATEGY

Faulkner & Gray, Inc.
Pamela Goett,
Editor and Publisher
11 Penn Plaza
New York, NY 10001
Tel: (212) 967-7000
Fax: (212) 629-7885
pam_goett@faulknergray.com

MOBILITY

Employee Relocation Council
Ms. Chris Wilson, Editor
1720 N Street NW
Washington, DC 20036
Tel: (202) 857-0857
Fax: (202) 659-8631
cwilson@erc.org

MULTINATIONAL EMPLOYER

Multinational Publishing
Sally Simon Beatrice Falzone, Editor
PO Box 149
Farnham, Surrey GU9 8YH
UK
Tel: 44 1252 726416
Fax: 44 1252 713730

ORGANIZATION RESOURCES COUNSELORS, INC.

Virginia G. McMorrow
1211 Avenue of the Americas
New York, NY 10036
Tel: (212) 719-3400
Fax: (212) 719-5625
Virginia.McMorrow@orcinc.com

Innovations in International HR

Expatriate Observer

ORC Taxline

RELOCATION BUSINESS NEWS

Liam St. John Murphy, Editor
117 Gutzon Borglum Road
Stamford, CT 06903-4726
Tel: (203) 322-4666
Fax: (203) 968-6569
liammurphy@aol.com

RELOCATION COMPASS

Greg Brewer,
President and Publisher
600 West Jackson Boulevard,
Suite 580
Chicago, IL 60661
Tel: (312) 559-9900
Fax: (312) 559-9902
gbrewer@dotsero.com

RELOCATION JOURNAL

Jen Reichenbacher
124 High Street
PO Box 242
Newburyport, MA 01950
Tel: (508) 462-9011
Fax: (978) 465-1479

SHRM PUBLICATIONS

Bob Thompson,
Managing Editor
Tel: (703) 548-3440
Fax: (703) 836-0367

Brian Glade, Vice President
International Program
Institute for International HR
bglade@shrm.org

HR Magazine/HR News

Leon Rubis, Editor
Tel: (703) 548-3440
Fax: (703) 836-0367
hrmag@shrm.org

International HR Update

Michelle Martinez,
Editor-in-Chief
7819 Bold Lion Lane
Alexandria, VA 22315
Tel: (703) 550-9882
Fax: (703) 550-9637
martinezmn@aol.com

WORKFORCE JOURNAL

Allan Halcrow, Editor-in-Chief/
Special Projects Editor
245 Fischer Avenue, Suite B-2
Costa Mesa, CA 92626
Tel: (714) 751-1883
Fax: (714) 751-4106
halcrowa@workforcemag.com

BOOKS

Bartlett, Christopher A., and Ghoshal, Sumantra. *Managing Across Borders.* Cambridge, MA: Harvard Business School Press, 1991.

Black, J. Stewart, Gregersen, Hal B., and Mendenhall, Mark E. *Global Assignments.* San Francisco: Jossey-Bass, 1992.

Carter, Nancy. *Conducting an Audit of the International Assignment Process.* Scottsdale, AZ: American Compensation Association, 1999.

Craggs, Andrew. *Entering Global Markets: An Approach to Designing HR Programs and Policies.* Scottsdale, AZ: American Compensation Association, 1997.

Cyr, Dianne J. *The Human Resource Challenge of International Joint Ventures.* Westport, CT: Quorum Books, 1995.

Dowling, Peter J., Welch, Denice E., and Schuler, Randall S. *International Human Resource Management. 3rd ed.* Cincinnati, OH: South-Western College Publishing, 1999.

Doz, Yves L., and Hamel, Gary. *Alliance Advantage.* Cambridge, MA: Harvard Business School Press, 1998.

Hampden-Turner, Charles, and Trompenaars, Fons. *The Seven Cultures of Capitalism.* Garden City, NY: Doubleday, 1993.

Harvard Business Review. *Global Strategies.* Boston, MA: Harvard Business School Press, 1994.

Harzing, Anne-Wil, and Van Ruysseveldt, Joris. *International Human Resource Management.* Thousand Oaks, CA: Sage, 1995.

Hofstede, Geert. *Cultures and Organizations.* Maidenhead, Berkshire, England: McGraw-Hill Book Company Europe, 1991.

Odenwald, Sylvia, and Matheny, William G. *Global Impact.* Chicago, IL: Irwin, 1996.

Ohmae, Kenichi. *The Evolving Global Economy*. Cambridge, MA: Harvard Business School Press, 1995.

Pucik, Vladimir, Tichy, Noel M., and Barnett, Carole K. *Globalizing Management*. New York: Wiley, 1992.

Reynolds, Calvin. *Compensating Globally Mobile Employees*. Scottsdale, AZ: American Compensation Association, 1995.

Reynolds, Calvin. *Compensation Basics for North American Expatriates*. Scottsdale, AZ: American Compensation Association, 1998.

Rhinesmith, Stephen H. *A Manager's Guide to Globalization*. Homewood, IL: Business One/Irwin, ASTD, 1993.

Schell, Michael S., and Solomon, Charlene Marmer. *Capitalizing on the Global Workforce*. Chicago, IL: Irwin Professional Publishing, 1997.

Selmer, Jan. *Expatriate Management*. Westport, CT: Quorum Books, 1995.

Trompenaars, Fons. *Riding the Waves of Culture*. Burr Ridge, IL: Irwin, 1994.

WEB SITES

American Compensation Association: *http://www.acaonline.org*

Employee Relocation Council: *http://www.erc.org/*

Human Resource Management Professionals Worldwide: *http://www.the-hrnet.com/*

Institute of Personnel and Development (UK): *http://www.ipd.co.uk*

Society for Human Resource Management (SHRM): *http://www.shrm.org*

Compiled principally by Virginia McMorrow, Organization Resources Counselors, Inc.

INDEX

A

B

C

D

E

F

M

N

Q

R

S

HARCOURT SOFTWARE LICENSE AGREEMENT

READ THE TERMS AND CONDITIONS OF THIS LICENSE AGREEMENT CAREFULLY BEFORE INSTALLING THE SOFTWARE (THE "PROGRAM") TO ACCOMPANY *Guide to Global Compensation and Benefits*. THE PROGRAM IS COPYRIGHTED AND LICENSED (NOT SOLD). BY INSTALLING THE PROGRAM, YOU ARE ACCEPTING AND AGREEING TO THE TERMS OF THIS LICENSE AGREEMENT. IF YOU ARE NOT WILLING TO BE BOUND BY THE TERMS OF THIS LICENSE AGREEMENT, YOU SHOULD PROMPTLY RETURN THE PACKAGE IN RESALABLE CONDITION AND YOU WILL RECEIVE A REFUND OF YOUR MONEY. THIS LICENSE AGREEMENT REPRESENTS THE ENTIRE AGREEMENT CONCERNING THE PROGRAM BETWEEN YOU AND HARCOURT, INC. (REFERRED TO AS "LICENSOR"), AND IT SUPERSEDES ANY PRIOR PROPOSAL, REPRESENTATION, OR UNDERSTANDING BETWEEN THE PARTIES.

1. License Grant. Licensor hereby grants to you, and you accept, a nonexclusive license to use the Program CD-ROM and the computer programs contained therein in machine-readable, object code form only (collectively referred to as the "Software"), and the accompanying User Documentation, only as authorized in this License Agreement. The Software may be used only on a single computer owned, leased, or otherwise controlled by you; or in the event of the inoperability of that computer, on a backup computer selected by you. Neither concurrent use on two or more computers nor use in a local area network or other network is permitted without separate authorization and the possible payment of other license fees. You agree that you will not assign, sublease, transfer, pledge, lease, rent, or share your rights under the License Agreement. You agree that you may not reverse engineer, decompile dissemble, or otherwise adapt, modify, or translate the Software.

Upon loading the Software into your computer, you may retain the Program CD-ROM for backup purposes. In addition, you may make one copy of the Software on a set of diskettes (or other storage medium) for the purpose of backup in the event the Program CD-ROM is damaged or destroyed. You may make one copy of any additional User Documentation (such as the README.TXT file or the "About the Electronic Workpapers" section of the Book) for backup purposes. Any such copies of the Software or the User Documentation shall include Licensor's copyright and other proprietary notices. Except as authorized under this paragraph, no copies of the program or any portions thereof may be made by you or any person under your authority or control.

2. Licensor's Rights. You acknowledge and agree that the Software and the User Documentation are proprietary products of Licensor protected under U.S. copyright law. You further acknowledge and agree that all right, title, and interest in and to the Program, including associated intellectual property rights, are and shall remain with Licensor. This License Agreement does not convey to you an interest in or to the Program, including associated intellectual property rights, are and shall remain with Licensor. This License Agreement does not convey to you an interest in or to the Program, but only a limited right of use revocable in accordance with the terms of the License Agreement.
3. License Fees. The license fees paid by you are paid in consideration of the licenses granted under this License Agreement.
4. Term. This License Agreement is effective upon your installing this software and shall continue until terminated. You may terminate this License Agreement at any time by returning the Program and all copies thereof and extracts therefrom to Licensor. Licensor may terminate this License Agreement upon the breach by you of any term hereof. Upon such termination by Licensor, you agree to return to Licensor the Program and all copies and portions thereof.
5. Limited Warranty. Licensor warrants, for our benefit alone, for a period of 90 days from the date of commencement of this License Agreement (referred to as the "Warranty Period") that the Program CD-ROM in which the Software is contained is free from defects in material and workmanship. If during the Warranty Period, a defect appears in the Program CD-ROM, you may return the Program to Licensor for either replacement or, at Licensor's option, refund of amounts paid by you under this License Agreement. You agree that the foregoing constitutes your sole and exclusive remedy for breach by Licensor of any warranties made under this Agreement. EXCEPT FOR THE WARRANTIES SET FORTH ABOVE, THE PROGRAM, AND THE SOFTWARE CONTAINED THEREIN, ARE LICENSED "AS IS," AND LICENSOR DISCLAIMS ANY AND ALL OTHER WARRANTIES, WHETHER EXPRESS OR IMPLIED, INCLUDING, WITHOUT LIMITATION, ANY IMPLIED WARRANTIES OF MERCHANTABILITY OR FITNESS FOR A PARTICULAR PURPOSE.
6. Limitation of Liability. Licensor's cumulative liability to you or any other party for any loss or damages resulting from any claims, demands, or actions arising out of or relating to this Agreement shall not exceed the license free paid to Licensor for the use of the Program. IN NO EVENT SHALL LICENSOR BE LIABLE FOR ANY INDIRECT, INCIDENTAL, CONSEQUENTIAL, SPECIAL, OR EXEMPLARY DAMAGES (INCLUDING, BUT NOT LIMITED TO, LOSS OF DATA, BUSINESS INTERRUPTION, OR LOST PROFITS) EVEN IF LICENSOR HAS BEEN ADVISED OF THE POSSIBILITY OF SUCH DAMAGES.
7. Miscellaneous. This License Agreement shall be construed and governed in accordance with the laws of the State of California. Should any term of this License Agreement be declared void or unenforceable by any court of competent jurisdiction, such declaration shall have no effect on the remaining terms hereof. The failure of either party to enforce any rights granted hereunder or to take action against the other party in the event of any breach hereunder shall not be deemed a waiver by that party as to subsequent enforcement of rights or subsequent actions in the event of future breaches.